W9-BBD-597

ROOTS OF RADICALISM

Roots of Radicalism

JEWS, CHRISTIANS, AND THE NEW LEFT

Stanley Rothman
S. Robert Lichter

New York   Oxford
OXFORD UNIVERSITY PRESS
1982

To my sons,
David and Michael Rothman,
both of whom were affected by the 1960s
in more ways than they know

To my parents,
Carl and Elaine Lichter

Copyright © 1982 by Stanley Rothman and S. Robert Lichter

Library of Congress Cataloging in Publication Data

Rothman, Stanley, 1927–
   Roots of radicalism.

   Bibliography: p.
   Includes index.
   1. Students—Political activity. 2. Radicalism—
United States. 3. Radicalism—Germany (West) 4. College
students, Jewish—Political activity. I. Lichter,
S. Robert. II. Title.
LB3610.R67   322.4'4'0973   81-22564
ISBN 0-19-503125-3   AACR2

Grateful acknowledgment is given for permission to reprint material from the following:

Howl & Other Poems, by Allen Ginsberg. Copyright © 1956, 1959 by Allen Ginsberg.
   Reprinted by permission of City Lights Books.
Portnoy's Complaint, by Philip Roth. Copyright © 1967, 1968, 1969 by Philip Roth.
   Reprinted by permission of Random House, Inc.

Printing (last digit): 9 8 7 6 5 4 3 2 1

Printed in the United States of America

Acknowledgments

A large and diverse group of people contributed to the researching and writing of this book. Anne Bedlington and Lawrence Rosen assisted in the early stages of data analysis. Dr. Phillip Isenberg and Robert Schnitzer helped with the clinical interviewing and interpreting the clinical Thematic Apperception Tests and Rorschachs. Professor David Gutmann provided an alternate interpretation of Rorschach scores, and Dr. Jennifer Cole scored the survey Thematic Apperception Tests for narcissistic pathology. She independently developed a number of ideas that have been incorporated into our argument. Dr. Isenberg also contributed importantly to Rothman's understanding of clinical psychoanalysis. None of these persons would necessarily agree with our overall interpretation.

Our grasp of psychoanalytic theory was greatly enriched by our personal and professional interaction with other members of the psychiatric community. We are particularly grateful to Dr. Donald Thompson, M.D., Dr. Renatus Hartogs, M.D., and the late Dr. Donald Fearn, M.D., of Beth Israel Hospital in Boston.

We also wish to thank the Boston and New York Psychoanalytic Societies for permitting us to attend seminars and meetings. In addition, McLean and Beth Israel Hospitals permitted Rothman to attend seminars and intake conferences and to conduct psychotherapy sessions under the supervision of senior staff.

Among our social scientific colleagues who offered valuable insights and suggestions are Stanley Elkins of Smith College and Guenter Lewy and Gerald Platt of the University of Massachusetts. All three read various versions of the manuscript. We especially wish to acknowledge Platt's valuable suggestions, which he made despite important intellectual disagreements with our perspective.

We are also indebted to the social psychologists who introduced Rothman to survey applications of TATs and even found trained scorers to analyze the results. They include David McClelland of Harvard University, David Winter of Wesleyan, Abigail Stewart of Boston University, and Dan P. McAdams of Loyola University in Chicago.

The West German segment of the study was made possible through the assistance of Ernst Bargel and Bernhard Cloetta of Zentrum I Bildungsforschung and Bernhard Badura of the University of Konstanz. Guido Goldman and Stanley Hoffman added their encouragement and the support of Harvard University's Center for European Studies. S. M. Lipset and Sidney Verba of Harvard and Thomas Childers of the University of Pennsylvania also contributed valuable suggestions on this part of the project.

It is impossible to name all the others who contributed to our research, from those who administered or completed interviews to those who scored TAT protocols. We thank them all.

Finally, Rothman wishes to acknowledge a special debt of thanks to his wife. Her contribution to the successful completion of this project cannot be overstated. Despite her own professional work, she managed to find the time (continuing a very old tradition) to remove stones from his path, and even to help him up when he (not infrequently) fell.

Funds for the study were provided by grants from the National Institute of Mental Health, the National Science Foundation, the Ford Foundation, and the Harry Frank Guggenheim Foundation.

The study was sponsored by the Research Institute on International Change at Columbia University. Both the Institute and Smith College were extraordinarily generous in providing support services.

Northampton, Mass.   S. R.
Washington, D.C.   S. R. L.
May 1982

Contents

Part IV: CONCLUSION

Preface

In writing this book, we set for ourselves a number of goals. Overall, we have tried to better understand the causes, nature, and consequences of the student movement of the 1960s. Specifically, we explain why, in the American student movement, young people of Jewish background played so large a role. We also examine the role played by Protestants and Catholics who joined with Jews in the American student movement and dominated the "New Left" in western Europe.[1] In addition, we throw new light on the relationship between personality and political behavior by testing psychoanalytic hypotheses about the motivation of radicals.

The core of the book consists of these studies of student radicals and their supporters, which we conducted in the United States and West Germany. The two American studies were undertaken to test hypotheses that Rothman had developed about the role of Jews in the New Left and the differences in the motivational patterns of Jews and non-Jews in the movement. The third was carried out independently by Lichter in West Germany, using a slightly modified version of the questionnaire developed by Rothman. We decided to collaborate primarily because we discovered that our findings for non-Jewish students in both countries were almost exactly the same. In the course of our work, we were led to modify our perspectives slightly but not in fundamental ways. In all important respects, the results confirmed the initial predictions.

1. Rather than rely on the rather cumbersome phrase, "students of Jewish (or Christian) background," we will in the book generally speak of Jewish and non-Jewish students. We did not feel that we could simply call radical non-Jewish students Christians because so many of them no longer considered themselves Christians, although the overwhelming majority were from Catholic or Protestant backgrounds. The same pattern was characteristic, to an even larger degree, of radical students of Jewish background. However, we consider American Jews to be both a religious and an ethnic group and thus feel we can refer to such students as Jews.

The book begins with an historical overview of the rise and decline of the student movement. The second chapter critiques the major studies of the student movement. We argue that most of these studies are seriously flawed and provide a quite erroneous picture of the student movement, its causes, and its consequences. Indeed, these studies tell us more about the nature of the American and European intellectual community than about the student movement.

In Chapters 3 and 4 we develop our own theory. At the outset, we argue that the origins of the student movement lay in certain basic crises in American society, which were compounded by the civil rights revolution and the Vietnam War. We then suggest that the idealism of those who led the movement had a darker side that we call "inverse authoritarianism." We also differentiate between "authoritarian" types among Jewish and non-Jewish radicals.

Americans of Jewish background dominated the New Left in its early years. Indeed, in important ways, they were largely responsible for the emergence of the New Left. Jews have long been drawn to such movements because their social marginality in Christian societies has led them to take a radical stance when the opportunity presents itself. The crises of the 1960s provided such an opportunity. Further, we argue that Jewish marginality has produced personality tendencies among some Jews which, in the 1960s, encouraged identification with selected revolutionary movements perceived as symbolic sources of power and virility. Unconsciously, many Jewish radicals joined the New Left to gain strength against an evil and powerful establishment, which they saw as punitive and destructive.

Some non-Jewish radicals, on the other hand, desired to destroy an establishment they perceived as evil but *weak*, and to find a moral justification for their hostile feelings. Their ultimate, albeit unconscious, goal was less to eliminate existing inequalities than to establish a new, more powerful and "righteous" authority structure that they could lead or join. The personalities of these young radicals, often the children of very politically conservative parents, resembled the traditional authoritarian personality described by Adorno and others.

The evolution of the student movement toward violence and terrorism was partly a function of the ideology and psychopolitical style created by these types of individuals. Of course, other factors were important, including the lack of an adequate social base for a radical movement. In Chapters 3 and 4, we provide evidence for our argument by drawing upon a wide range of historical and psychological materials. In Chapters 5 through 9, we present the results of the empirical studies we conducted to test our theory.

Chapter 5 provides a brief overview of our hypotheses and the research strategies we employed to test them. Chapter 6 describes a large-scale study of

American college students, conducted during 1971 and 1972, which relied heavily upon projective psychological tests. Such tests are designed to plumb aspects of the personality in ways that circumvent the tendency of relatively articulate individuals (especially intellectuals) to present an "ideal" image of themselves to interviewers. We used the Thematic Apperception Test (TAT), a set of ambiguous pictures about which subjects are asked to create stories, as well as other instruments with a similar approach. These tests were scored by people who knew nothing about either the purposes of the study or the characteristics of our subjects.

Chapter 7 describes an intensive study of a small subsample of these students. Trained clinicians conducted indepth interviews with this group, which was divided according to both ideology and ethnicity. The interviews lasted several hours and included the administration of Rorschach (inkblot) tests and clinical TATs. Again, whenever possible, the tests were interpreted by professionals who knew little or nothing about the nature or purposes of the study.

In Chapter 8, we describe a study of prominent leaders and supporters of the student movement during the early and middle 1960s. Many of these early radicals achieved national reputations during that period, and some retain them today. We sought them out in order to determine whether our findings about early 1970s student radicals held true for the movement's founders, as well as its later converts.

In Chapter 9, we present the findings of the independent study conducted in West Germany, where students of Jewish background played almost no role in the student Left. The German findings replicated our results for non-Jewish American students.

We have tried to provide enough information about our results to allow readers to form their own judgments in crucial areas. We have also deposited our questionnaires with the Roper Public Opinion Center at the University of Connecticut at Storrs in order to enable other scholars to check our results and, perhaps, to draw additional findings from our data. We have by no means exhausted this very rich data set.

Our concluding chapter summarizes our argument and places our findings in a broader perspective. We stress here, as we do throughout the book, that neither our hypotheses nor our findings attempt to explain the student movement in terms of the psychological characteristics of its members. Rather, we suggest that social and political crises tend to elevate certain personality types into positions of leadership, while encouraging large numbers of ordinary people to act out unconscious wishes in the political arena. We are not arguing that 1960s radicals were more pathological, or even more likely to be acting on the basis of unconscious impulses, than were conservatives or liberals. And we certainly do not maintain that our findings discredit the student movement or the ideas developed by its leadership. An evaluation of those ideas requires a very different mode of analysis from the type we have employed. Our empirical findings might be interpreted in terms of a variety of theoretical perspectives. For reasons we discuss in the text, however, a psychoanalytic model explains our data better than alternate models.

Our work represents an effort to integrate a psychodynamic understanding of human motivation with an analysis of social and cultural forces. We have modified our original perspective somewhat because our data pointed to the necessity of enriching a classical psychoanalytic view with contributions from ego psychology and the analysis of "object relations."

Psychohistory and the psychoanalytic study of politics have become quite popular in recent years. Unfortunately, most studies derived from classical psychoanalysis tend to reduce social and political life to individual neuroses. At the other end of the spectrum, social psychological theorists like Erich Fromm tend to replace psychoanalytic insights with cultural and social variables. We believe that the social and psychological represent two distinct levels of analysis. The task of the scholar is to integrate them into a coherent whole, rather than to reduce one level to the other.

We believe that our analysis retains the cutting edge of mainstream psychoanalysis, but also places its insights within a broader social and historical context. We would not reduce the student movement to the psychological characteristics of its participants. Yet, that movement cannot be fully understood without an examination of these characteristics.

Our efforts have been greatly influenced by the work of Fred Weinstein and Gerald Platt, whose book, *The Wish To Be Free*, has yet to receive the attention it deserves. We agree with them that relationship between unconscious drives and fantasies and conscious thought processes is profoundly influenced by social and cultural variables. For example, while authoritarian traits may be considered the result of a particular pattern of parenting, the incidence of such traits in any society is also affected by "social reality." The psychological balance of individuals is just that: a balance of competing forces that is never completely frozen. Cultural conflict or political crisis in the society can upset that balance. Individuals will be affected differently according to age, genetic endowment, or childhood experiences. Thus, understanding the changing behavior of large groups of individuals requires the analysis of both social and psychological factors. These points are developed in the course of the book.

Our study differs from most that have appeared in recent years in two additional ways. First, many popular studies draw promiscuously from various schools of psychoanalytic thought (some of which are mutually incompatible) and apply competing insights to their material in an *ad hoc* fashion. Second, most are not very rigorous. One often gets the impression that the authors are using psychoanalysis as a weapon to reinforce prejudices rather than as a source of ideas that have to be tested.

We have attempted to overcome both these weaknesses by working within an explicitly defined theoretical framework and by testing our hypotheses empirically. In this sense, our model has been the pioneer work in this field, *The Authoritarian Personality*. Critical as we are of that work, it still stands head and shoulders above most of the studies that have followed it.

We wanted to write a book that could be read without specialized knowledge or technical training. Therefore, we have included relatively few statistical tables in the text and relegated a few more to appendices. We have also kept the use of psychoanalytic terminology to a minimum.

For those interested in the scholarly debates surrounding the many controversial topics touched upon in the text, we list our more technical articles.

Gutmann, David, Stanley Rothman, and S. Robert Lichter, "Two Kinds of Radicals: A Discriminant Analysis of a Projective Test," *The Journal of Personality Assessment* 47, no. 1 (1979):12–22.

Isenberg, Phillip, Robert Schnitzer, and Stanley Rothman, "Psychological Variables in Student Activism: The Radical Triad and Some Religious Differences," *Journal of Youth and Adolescence* 6 (Mar. 1977):11–24.

Lichter, S. Robert, "Young Rebels: A Psychological Study of West German Male Radical Students," *Comparative Politics* 12, no. 1 (Oct. 1979):27–48.

Lichter, S. Robert, and Stanley Rothman, "Radical Jews, Radical Christians: A Comparative Analysis of the Psychological Correlates to Political Behavior," presented at the Annual Meeting of the American Political Science Association, Washington, D.C., 1979.

Lichter, S. Robert, and Stanley Rothman, "Jewish Ethnicity and Radical Culture," *Political Psychology* 3, nos. 1–2 (Spring/Summer 1981–82):116–57.

Lichter, S. Robert, and Stanley Rothman, "Jews on The Left: The Student Movement Reconsidered," *Polity* 14, no. 2 (Winter 1982):347–66.

McAdams, Dan P., Stanley Rothman, and S. Robert Lichter, "Motivational Profits of Former Political Radicals and Politically Moderate Adults," *Personal and Social Psychology Bulletin,* in press.

Rothman, Stanley, and S. Robert Lichter, "The Case of the Student Left," *Social Research* 45, no. 3 (Autumn 1978):535–609.

Rothman, Stanley, and S. Robert Lichter, "Personality Development and Political Dissent: A Reassessment of the New Left," *Journal of Political and Military Sociology* 8, no. 2 (Fall 1980):191–204.

Schnitzer, Robert, Phillip Isenberg, and Stanley Rothman, "Faces in the Crowd: Portraits of Radical (and Non-Radical) Youth," in Sherman C. Feinstein, M.D., ed., *Adolescent Psychiatry,* vol. VII (Chicago: University of Chicago Press, 1978), pp. 195–223.

Chapter 2 of our book is a shorter, less technical discussion of material developed in Rothman and Lichter, "The Case of the Student Left." Portions of that article are reprinted by permission of *Social Research.* Chapter 8 combines in less technical form material from three articles: Phillip Isenberg, Robert Schnitzer, and Stanley Rothman, "Psychological Variables in Student Activism"; David Gutmann, Stanley Rothman, and S. Robert Lichter, "Two Kinds of Radicals"; and Robert Schnitzer, Phillip Isenberg, and Stanley Rothman, "Faces in the Crowd."

Our study took a long time to complete. In addition to the usual illnesses and confusions that cause delays, the computer proved an ambivalent ally. The study could not have been undertaken without its aid, but it did treat our efforts with a certain malevolence that belies the optimism of those who think of it as an unmixed blessing.

May 1982   S.R.
                                                                                                        S.R.L.

Part I

INTRODUCTION

1 The Rise and Fall of the New Left

YOUNG PEOPLE, especially the brightest and best educated, have long been in the forefront of movements for social change. Their political identity is typically charged with idealism, moralism, and emotionalism. Their elders, just as typically, praise their boldness and integrity or condemn their immaturity, depending on the particular cause in which youth's considerable energies are enlisted. More generally, those who prize moderation and restraint are likely to fear the excesses produced by youthful fervor. Aristotle complained that the young "have exalted notions because they have not yet been humbled by life or learned its necessary limitations. . . . They would always rather do noble deeds than useful ones: their lives are regulated more by moral feeling than by reasoning. . . . They love too much, hate too much, and the same with everything else. They think they know everything, [which] is why they overdo everything."[1]

On the other hand, reformers and radicals have historically depended upon youthful exuberance and idealism as sources of social and cultural renewal. The young have often responded with a spirit of selfless idealism that has served many ideological masters—among them democracy, socialism, communism, fascism, and any number of religious ideologies. Students and educated youth have been in the forefront of self-conscious revolutionary movements at least since the appearance of the first German student movement in the early nineteenth century. Young intellectuals thereafter played major roles in revolutionary movements in France, Italy, Russia, and Japan. In the current era, third world revolutions are almost invariably triggered, at least in part, by dissatisfied elements of the newly educated young.

Nor has the United States been immune to youth movements and student unrest. Student protest was common in colonial America, and Samuel Eliot Morison described the typical late nineteenth-century student as an "atheist in religion, an experimentalist in morals, a rebel against authority."[2] Although most of the protest of this period was aimed at university reform, student sentiments were occasionally engaged by larger social issues. The abolitionist movement, for example, elicited strong support on Northern campuses, and the bohemian youth culture of the 1920s was essentially a rebellion against conventional manners and morals. Students at the elite institutions of higher learning have regularly criticized the content of their college educations as being both impersonal and irrelevant to contemporary life.

The spontaneous decisions of American youth to involve themselves periodically in popular causes or to rebel against parental or school authority differed considerably from the sustained efforts by political parties in continental Europe or Latin America to bring youth into organized political action at an early age. By the late nineteenth century, student movements in Europe were beginning to take on sustained ideological positions, and both radical and conservative political parties were organizing youth affiliates. After World War I the more extremist parties (communist or fascist) generally attracted the largest number of students.

In America the pattern was quite different. In England and elsewhere in Europe, liberal capitalism developed in the midst of societies emerging out of feudalism. The entrepreneurs who brought capitalism into being in these countries, as well as those intellectuals who supported them, were engaged from the first in a conflict with traditional feudal culture and class structure. As a consequence, the entrepreneurs saw themselves as a new class, in competition with the older aristocratic elites. Their class consciousness was reinforced when, soon thereafter, a class-conscious working class emerged, supported by new intellectuals, to challenge them as they had challenged the aristocracies.

The United States, as Louis Hartz and many others have pointed out, was a European fragment culture.[3] It was settled initially by English Protestants, who stamped their imprint upon the nation. It was from a secularized version of Calvinism that liberal capitalist ideology emerged in England and, by imitation, in the United States. Whereas liberal capitalism was one part of a complex whole in Europe, in America it was everything. As America lacked a peasantry, so it lacked a genuine aristocracy, a class-conscious middle class, and later a class-conscious working class.

Ideologically, at least, America became the quintessential bourgeois capitalist nation. Liberal capitalism constituted America's "civic religion" or "civic myth."[4] Little wonder, then, that creative intellectuals played so small a role. In a society lacking fundamental ideological conflict, potentially critical intellectuals lacked a favorable environment, including an adequate class base. In Europe, the first critical intellectuals had been part of a leisured aristocracy that had absorbed some intellectual values. In America, only the remnants of such a class existed. By the 1830s the business of America was business, and the god of America was hard, practical work.[5]

Given the lack of ideological ferment, and of ideologically oriented political parties that could institutionalize such ferment, most students could not conceive of mass political action against "the system." The relative few who did could not create an enduring organizational structure. Students might rebel against particular educational or social evils, but these *ad hoc* rebellions did not call into question the system's legitimacy.

There were also cultural constraints on the boundaries of protest. American culture emphasized the importance of education as a means of acquiring technical knowledge and personal advancement. In contrast to many European countries, the university system (at least by the late nineteenth century) was not comprised of elite institutions for the few. Myriad institutions of higher learning were available to students of varied backgrounds and financial status. At the more elite institutions, the fraternity system and institutionalized athletics provided the basis of a youth culture that encouraged the sowing of wild oats in nonpolitical ways. Even when student movements did emerge in such institutions, their impact was marginal outside the east and a few sophisticated areas in the rest of the country. Students in the land-grant colleges and state universities rarely heard of such activities or, if they did, ignored them. The great majority were busy developing those skills that might facilitate social mobility.

The rapid democratization of American family life also reduced the possibility of the kind of rebellion characteristic of bourgeois youth in Europe or Latin America. When rebellion did occur, it took a highly personal form. Perhaps the most poignant breaks occurred between immigrant parents and their children. These generally involved youthful rejection of traditional "old country" attitudes and acceptance of the broadly liberal Protestant values of American society.

During the 1930s, it briefly seemed as if the United States was beginning to conform to the European pattern. Economic hardship and the desire to avoid involvement in European conflicts drew thousands to a new student movement. The organizational force was provided by the American Student Union and the American Youth Conference, both strongly influenced by the Communist party. As Murray Kempton later recalled:

The communists set the tone for the student movement of the thirties . . . because they had the advantage of numbers, because they offered the weak the impression of strength, and because they had a church which no one else could match. . . . The communists were a tiny fragment of the whole, but they were a majority of the committed.[6]

The Communist party was aided for a time by the Comintern's popular-front "line," which decreed support for F.D.R. and the New Deal and for popular-front electoral politics. By the same token, the Communist party's influence was dealt a severe blow when Russia and Germany signed the 1939 Soviet-Nazi pact, leaving Hitler secure on his Eastern Front so that he could make his aggressive move to the west.

That, of course, was not the only reason for the collapse of the student movement in the late 1930s and its failure to revive in the postwar period. The movement was basically a casualty of Pearl Harbor, the end of the depression, and, equally important, Hitler's decision in 1941 to break the pact and attack Russia, thereby silencing the former calls for pacifism by Communist and Socialist organizers. These developments transformed the issues that had brought most students into the movement. Genuine political radicalism was largely confined to students of Jewish background, primarily in New York, and to upper-middle-class Protestant students at a few elite universities.[7] Once the onset of war eroded their constituency, there was little left for them to rebuild.

Those who continued to hold radical views during the cold war were deterred from espousing them by the political atmosphere of the McCarthy period and its aftermath. In a 1957 issue of *The Nation*, Stanley Kunitz complained that his students had accepted conformity as the price of security:

"Why should we go out on a limb about anything?" one of them remarked in class. "We know what happened to those who did." Another expressed a measure of gratitude towards Senator McCarthy for having taught his generation a valuable lesson: "to keep its mouth shut."[8]

Nonetheless, the disappearance of radicalism cannot be explained entirely by the domestic climate of oppression. Central to the new political quiescence was the international situation in general, and the Soviet Union's behavior in particular. The Left's earlier disillusionment with communism was intensified by the Czechoslovakian coup, the Berlin blockade, the Korean War, and increased awareness of the horrors of Stalinism. As a result, the Soviet Union lost its claim to leadership among Western leftist intellectuals. Indeed, it all but replaced Nazi Germany as the devil figure of international politics. Faced with the moral poverty of international communism, many radicals simply kept silent, while retaining their hostility against American institutions and values. Others became converted to support of the "Free World." In practice, this usually meant defense of the status quo, coupled with mild reformist prescriptions. The single overriding moral and political issue was that of freedom vs. totalitarianism. Concern over internal inequalities of wealth and power virtually disappeared from the public ideological agenda.

It is clear in retrospect that new currents were emerging underneath the public consensus. Paradoxically, they began to develop in the late 1950s, during a period of unprecedented affluence. A small but significant segment of the population was becoming increasingly skeptical of the American civic myth. Some felt that private affluence was associated with public squalor. Others began to argue that American foreign policy was preventing genuine social reform in third world countries. Still others argued that liberal capitalism encouraged conformity at the same time that it destroyed community, producing a collection of one-dimensional automatons. Finally, a small group rejected America simply because they hated what they considered its obsessive concern with material goods per se.[9]

Why the American social myth was eroding has been the subject of much debate. We will examine some of the issues in more detail after we have presented the results of our studies. For the moment, we note that the rejection was most pronounced among professional people in the service sector of society, which was rapidly growing. The new critics were concentrated in areas associated with the creation and dissemination of knowledge, especially the universities and the media.[10] The influence of this segment of the population was growing even as its members became more liberal and cosmopolitan.[11] For one thing, more and more Americans were enrolled in colleges and universities. (Over twelve million Americans had completed four years of college by the early 1960s.)[12] For another, with the advent of television and rapid technological advances in transportation, America and the rest of the world were becoming ever smaller. Indeed, the events and cultural styles of New York and Washington spread to "backwater" small communities with a rapidity which would have been inconceivable even twenty-five years earlier.[13]

Europe shared many of the same developments, and changes in American culture were having a profound influence upon Europeans, especially European youth. Because of America's power and dynamism during the 1950s, the United States seemed to represent the wave of the future. Young Europeans self-consciously absorbed what came to them from America, much of it through the television programs and movies that blanketed Europe during the period.[14] When the student movement began in the U.S., it spread rapidly to Europe in an almost unprecedented reversal of roles. Since the mid-nineteenth century, new ideologies had always begun in Europe and then traveled to the United States. Soon it was to be the other way around.

For the moment, opposition to the dominant culture in America took apolitical forms. The best-known example from this period was the beat generation. Faced with a society that proclaimed its moral superiority but (in their eyes) offered no clear moral vision, yet lacking any alternative vision, the beats opted out. They created an anti-Establishment subculture dedicated to the rejection of American Puritanism and materialism. In a widely read poem, Allen Ginsberg portrayed America as "Moloch": "Moloch whose love is endless oil and stone! Moloch whose soul is electricity and banks! . . . Moloch who frightened me out of my natural ecstasy! Moloch whom I abandon!"[15]

In both their revulsion against American society and their personal life style, the beats prefigured many themes of both the New Left and the counter-culture. The radical journalist Jack Newfield has noted that

> the beats' mysticism, anarchy, anti-intellectualism, sexual and drug experimentation, hostility to middle-class values, and idealization of the Negro and of voluntary poverty all have clear parallels in the New Left. Moreover, there is a broad area of overlap between the beats' creative expressions and the cultural taste of the New Left.[16]

One longtime activist put the case more directly: "The beatniks were—and are—just the Movement without altruism and energy. They are alienated by exactly the same things we are, but they just can't act on their discontent in an effective political way."[17]

By the late 1950s a growing number of students and others were becoming hostile to, or at least skeptical of, American institutions and culture. At the time, however, they lacked a public outlet, a cause or mission that could channel these concerns into political action. The students also lacked a broad campus constituency. As one student expressed her quandary:

> What we all lack who are under 30 is some guiding passion, some moral vision if you will. We are unable to wind the loose threads of our experience into some larger pattern, and we know it. We write to please this authority or that professor while the universe skids about under our feet. We profess to disbelieve everything partially because, at heart, we do not yet believe in ourselves . . . if our revolt seems mild, it is because we have not found anything to promote. . . .[18]

In the coming decade, young rebels would once again find both a cause and a constituency.

S. M. Lipset has argued that the unrest of the 1960s fits into a long-term cycle of recurrent student rebellion in America.[19] From this perspective, the quiescence of the 1950s was atypical. As our brief historical overview indicates, we do not agree.

This was the first time that a substantial number of young Americans adopted a stance involving total rejection of American institutions. Abolitionist youth had demanded that America live up to its promises, and the radical ferment of the 1930s was limited to a relatively small number of students at a few select colleges and universities. By the late 1960s, however, a massive shift in attitudes and orientations toward traditional American values and support for the system had taken place on many American campuses, even if most young people did not perceive of themselves as revolutionaries or even radicals.[20]

The civil rights movement and the Vietnam War precipitated the unraveling of the American consensus and the massive disaffection of large numbers of American youth from their society. The effects of both sets of events were quite complex. To liberal cosmopolitans who were already partly disaffected from American culture, the war and the race issue constituted additional evidence of the essential correctness of their positions. For large numbers of other Americans, the events of the 1960s brought into question previously unquestioned loyalties. But the erosion of their faith in the system was certainly accelerated by the images that the fast-growing knowledge strata conveyed to the public at large.

The civil rights movement came first. The American black had long been, in Ralph Ellison's memorable phrase, an invisible man. The nation had been relatively successful in integrating large numbers of white Europeans. It had congratulated itself on this success as proof of the American Dream's vitality. Many middle-class Americans assumed that the integration of blacks into the system would follow a similar course. Blacks would gradually take their place as individuals alongside other Americans. Very few really faced up to the complexity and difficulty of the black experience or to the entrenchment of both subtle and blatant discrimination.

As the nature of that experience and the real problems of integration forced themselves upon the attention of young people, their benign image of American society was bound to suffer. They could no longer assume that America had the right to educate other peoples, much less to impose its will by force.

Their disillusionment was soon compounded by the prospect of fighting (and perhaps dying) in an ambiguous war whose horrors they watched daily on television. The Vietnam War and the draft, far more than any other factors, created a mass movement of student protest and provided the New Left with a national forum. If America's faith in itself had not already been weakened by the civil rights revolution, however, the Left would not have had so great an impact during the early sixties. In this sense the civil rights movement was the crucible of fire for what was to become "the Movement."

The spark that would flare into a decade of tumult and protest was struck by four black college freshmen in Greensboro, North Carolina. On February 1, 1960, they sat down at a lunch counter of a local Woolworth's and requested coffee. The waitress told them what they already knew—the counter was reserved for whites only. They refused to leave until they were served, to the consternation of both the white management and embarrassed black kitchen workers. Unlike legal and congressional battles in faraway Washington, D.C., this was a direct and immediate threat to racial segregation.

That first sit-in ended in a stalemate. The four students were not served, but they remained at the counter until closing time. The next day there were twenty black students at the lunch counter. The following day an integrated group of fifty local undergraduates crowded into the store. Within two weeks the spontaneous sit-in movement had spread across North Carolina, South Carolina, and Virginia. In March, police in Orangeburg, South Carolina, scattered peaceful demonstrators with tear gas and high-pressure fire hoses. The Orangeburg jails overflowed with protesters, and 350 had to be imprisoned in an eight-foot-high chicken coop. Within a year, over 3,000 demonstrators were jailed, 150 Woolworth branches were desegregated, and the nation's conscience was pricked.

The sit-ins owed much of their initial success to the personal traits and orientations of the participants. In outlook and appearance, they were avowedly respectable and "straight," in striking contrast to the hip, anti-bourgeois spirit that would soon characterize radical style. The call for "freedom now" seemed reasonable and just, coming from such well-mannered young people, particularlly when the freedom they demanded was no more than access to the American Dream. Conservative in their personal manner, liberal in their aims, radical but disciplined and nonviolent in their actions, they created a moral impetus that attracted black leaders and white students to their cause.

In April the Southern Christian Leadership Conference (SCLC) sponsored a gathering of student civil rights activists in Raleigh, North Carolina. The goal of this conference was to help coordinate the many local sit-in movements that had sprung up in the preceding months. Hundreds of students from all over the south came, and many northern colleges sent observers. After resisting pressures to affiliate with the SCLC or other established civil rights organizations, the conference established an umbrella organization they called the Student

Nonviolent Coordinating Committee (SNCC). In October this group adopted a statement of purpose that reflects the intense idealism of the Movement's first months:

> We affirm the philosophical or religious ideal of non-violence as the foundation of our purpose, the presupposition of our belief, and the manner of our action. . . .
>
> Through non-violence, courage displaces fear. Love transcends hate. Acceptance dissipates prejudice; hope ends despair. Faith reconciles doubt. Peace dominates war. Mutual regards cancel enmity. Justice for all overthrows injustice. The redemptive community supersedes immoral social systems.[21]

During the next few years, SNCC's faith in nonviolence, in reformism, and in America itself would quickly wane, as its members attempted to translate their ideals into concrete political and economic gains for southern blacks. By 1965 the goal of integration was superseded by that of black power. Marxist formulas filled the intellectual void left by earlier rejections of "ideology." Religiously rooted nonviolence was discarded for military rhetoric, and staff members armed themselves in "self-defense." How did such a rapid and radical transformation come about?

In the early years, before the first wave of moral fervor had crested, SNCC seemed destined to lead a movement that transcended differences of party, ideology, race, and class. In the spring of 1961 SNCC's members were joined by integrated buses of freedom riders, drawn largely from northern university campuses. That summer SNCC began voter registration drives in Mississippi and Georgia. But the quick triumphs of the sit-ins gave way to months of tedium, punctuated by moments of danger, in rural Mississippi. Voter registration efforts were thwarted by violence and the threat of violence. SNCC was all but forgotten by the northern public, while the focus of civil rights agitation shifted to other fronts. James Meredith gained entry to the University of Mississippi; peaceful demonstrations in Birmingham, Alabama, gave way to rioting despite the efforts of Martin Luther King, Jr.; half a million New York City students boycotted schools to protest de facto segregation. Meanwhile, SNCC workers in the Mississippi delta struggled and suffered, and grew tired and bitter.

Only with a new influx of white northern students into Mississippi in summer 1964 did national attention shift back to SNCC's ongoing efforts to register voters. These volunteers were drawn from a growing constituency that had developed in the interim on major college campuses.

The sit-ins and SNCC helped create a radical student movement, but the early civil rights activists were cast in the mold of founding father rather than typical participant. They were predominantly black, southern, and lower-middle or middle class. The second generation of activists was drawn mainly from a white, affluent, upper-middle-class Jewish and liberal Protestant constituency. They were often the bright children of liberal or Old Left parents, now studying sociology, political science, or philosophy at elite universities, and searching for a personal and political identity.

To many self-consciously alienated young people, the political arena had offered only the equally unpleasant options of irrelevance or accommodation with the status quo. Suddenly social action could be a source of drama, heroism, personal commitment, and fulfillment. In addition, it offered a way to throw off the yoke of privilege, to identify with the wretched of the earth in their struggle against privation and oppression.

Southern black student activists thought of freedom primarily in terms of the American Dream—the freedom to pursue happiness like everyone else. For many of the white volunteer workers, though, the moving force was psychological freedom—freedom from guilt over one's own privilege. Their empathy for the oppressed poor stemmed from concerns very different from the wants of the poor themselves. Instead of desiring to integrate society's outcasts and outsiders into the American system, many white SNCC workers identified with their "freedom" from bourgeois concerns and life styles. One 1964 summer volunteer wrote, "One sees a freedom here that is so much more than just the ironical fact that the enslaved people are, at least relatively, the liberated ones. Some 'white' people sit at their feet wondering at this sorrow freed and made beautiful, sensing dimly in themselves a similar pain. . . ." Another expressed "strong ambivalence" over his work, because "I sometimes fear that I am only helping to integrate some beautiful people into modern white society with all its depersonalization. . . ."[22]

Thus many who extolled the virtues of "participatory democracy" and "letting the people decide" did not themselves share the hopes and dreams of those they sought to help. SNCC volunteer Bruce Payne observed that "SNCC and the rest of the new left faces the problem that the values which they denounce are likely to be those that will be pursued by anyone liberated from poverty, indeed, that they may *already* be the values which the poor aspire to."[23] In short, the poor and oppressed were idealized for not being bourgeois, and for offering middle-class students a haven from the psychic prison of privilege. A founder of SNCC put it succinctly: "Segregation, in a very real sense, freed the Negro from a society which enslaves the self."[24]

So the forces that motivated many New Leftists were more complex than simple "idealism" or empathy with the underdog. They empathized with the poor as outsiders, as a potential community in opposition to the dominant society. SDS President Todd Gitlin wrote in 1964, "The battlefields we have chosen as organizers, and organizers of organizers, are the communities of the under-America: cities and towns and rural areas where people live materially deprived, politically alienated and used and victimized. . . . This is entirely as it should be, . . . since people strongly afflicted with the rottenness of our society are best capable of exorcising that rot."[25]

The New Left was implicitly revolutionary from the beginning, despite an initial reliance on liberal rhetoric. Their patronage of the oppressed stemmed from a strong hostility toward American society, and particularly toward the middle-class world they sought to escape. Another SNCC volunteer worker expressed this antipathy in terms that recall the beats and presage the counterculture: "We crap on the clean, antiseptic, acceptable, decent middle class 'image'. It is that decency that we want to change, to 'overcome.' "[26]

Freedom meant the destruction of a decadent, rotten society, rather than access to its rewards. And "now" meant showing adults that there would be no wait for change, that no delay would be tolerated, that gratification must be immediate. Compromise was not tolerated, for it meant being co-opted, yanked out of the Movement community and into the mainstream of "corporate liberalism." Thus a keynote speech at a 1962 SDS convention praised the freedom riders, not for furthering civil rights but rather for their "radicalizing" potential, their "clear-cut demonstration of the sterility of legalism." The speaker continued:

> It is not by . . . "learning the rules of the legislative game" that we will succeed in creating the kind of militant alliances that our struggle requires. We shall succeed through force—through the exertion of such pressure as will force our reluctant allies to accommodate to us, in their own interest.[27]

In 1963 and 1964, the Freedom Summer projects brought hundreds of northern students to Mississippi, where they ran "freedom schools," registered black voters, and helped organize the Mississippi Freedom Democratic party (MFDP). They encountered harassment and brutality from the police, unrelieved hostility from local whites, and suspicion from their black co-workers. The worst of these, perhaps, was the cool reaction of local black staffers. Many of them resented the notion of providing a summer vacation for wealthy white collegians anxious to enrich their own lives by "helping the Negro." Paul Jacobs and Saul Landau have discussed these racial tensions within SNCC:

The enormous racial sensitivity the Movement has produced makes interracial cooperation difficult, since each innuendo, every poorly chosen word or facial expression is the subject for criticism and discussion, on the spot or at staff meetings. Either the Northern volunteer "makes it," learns with them and tries to overcome them, or he must go home.[28]

The desire for acceptance intensified the whites' guilt feelings and whetted their thirst for moral purity. Newfield quoted a white SNCC worker who told him, "The Movement is really a search for the moral equivalent of blackness." Newfield found it necessary to remind readers that "there is no inherent virtue in being black."[29]

In 1964, the murder of three white SNCC workers, and the failure to convict their killers, intensified feelings of moral outrage, isolation, and disillusionment with the System. The developing schism between the young Movement people and their liberal allies came to a head late that summer in Atlantic City. At the Democratic convention, the SNCC-sponsored MFDP challenged the all-white regular Mississippi delegation, arguing that they represented the state's 850,000 unregistered blacks. Torn between the conflicting demands of convenience and pragmatism, the party offered a compromise: the MFDP would receive two at-large seats and a guarantee that all delegations in future conventions would be racially integrated. The compromise was supported by white liberals and by black civil rights leaders like Martin Luther King, Roy Wilkins, and Bayard Rustin. It was rejected outright by the MFDP delegation.

This was the first public indication of the truly radical spirit that permeated the Movement. The MFDP delegates had been handpicked by SNCC workers more concerned with "the creation of popular left opposition" than with the kind of incremental change represented by the Democrats' offer.[30] Sympathetic commentators stressed that resistance to compromise stemmed from the frustrating and disillusioning experience of trying to realize the American Dream in rural Mississippi. In this interpretation, the Movement's radicalism can be attributed to America's failure to live up to its own ideals. As a young white SNCC worker put it, "I curse this country every day of my life because it made me hate it, and I never wanted to."[31]

But this explanation is incomplete. For one thing, the frustrations and suffering of SNCC radicals paled before the experience of the black "Toms" they derided, King among them. For another, the civil rights movement, including SNCC's own efforts, had achieved considerable success by the mid-1960s. In November 1963, some 80,000 Mississippi blacks voted for a SNCC-sponsored integrated "freedom ticket" in opposition to the all-white Democratic gubernatorial slate. Between 1962 and 1965, black voter registration in the state more than doubled. SNCC's 1964 Summer Project had attracted 800 volunteers, most of them college students from the north. Moreover, the Movement had acquired respectability in liberal circles. For example, the 1964 Freedom Summer project was co-sponsored by the National Council of Churches.

On the national level, more moderate civil rights leaders were successfully making use of direct action tactics. The most important was, of course, Martin Luther King. In 1963, at the first of many marches on Washington, a gathering of over 200,000 listened raptly to his "I have a dream" oration. In 1965 he led thousands of blacks and whites on a march from Selma to Montgomery, Alabama. Later that year, largely in response to such moral and political pressures, Congress passed the Voting Rights Act. Within SNCC, though, King was bitterly denounced for making a deal with President Johnson to limit the Selma demonstration, rather than letting "the people" decide.[32]

The reason for SNCC's rejection of compromise and reformism is, quite simply, that it was becoming a self-consciously revolutionary organization. Certainly it lacked any coherent ideology or program, and "elitist" notions of revolutionary organization and leadership were anathema to participants. What they shared—indeed, what held them together—was a revolutionary *spirit*, a desire to transform existing society totally, and a rejection of all halfway reform measures that would perpetuate the existing sociopolitical structure. Jacobs and Landau's sympathetic portrayal of the early SNCC indicates its distance from the mainstream of the civil rights movement:

> SNCC was formed to make a revolution in the South—what kind of revolution they did not know, and they only *felt* how they would do it: they would go out to meet people, talk with them, share their needs . . . the bread-and-butter objectives of King, Farmer, and Wilkins, their view that integration was possible within the existing society and that Negroes could share in American affluence, clashed continuously with the SNCC notion that no matter how much welfare was provided, the society was rotten because men could not achieve dignity. . . .
>
> Instead of dignity from a vote and an anti-poverty program they control, the people are more humiliated, further removed from basic decisions, more indebted and debilitated by welfare capitalism. . . .
>
> Democracy, according to SNCC, cannot be diluted. Either the people decide, with real choices and the resources to make those choices, or democracy is a fraud.[33]

In this context the term "revolution" is quite ambiguous. In effect it simply means that SNCC was radical in its goals and tactics, aiming at a "true" democracy by actively involving the citizenry in the political decisons that shape their lives. The important point is that SNCC's radicalism existed from the beginning, if only in diffuse and even incoherent form. The frustrations of Movement organizing and outrage at the System's intransigence did not produce this radical spirit. Rather, they were intensified by it.

In addition, SNCC's undeveloped but strongly felt radical vision already contained the tensions and contradictions that would bedevil the Movement throughout its brief existence. Already we find a reliance on "the people" and a claim to speak on their behalf, combined with an uneasy awareness that the people's values may be quite different from those of their young patrons. This dilemma was temporarily resolved by recourse to an argument that would become increasingly popular on the Left in the latter '60s: The "people" had been repressed for so long that they did not know what their "true" needs were. Under a truly democratic system, they would throw off the false values imposed by a decadent and repressive Establishment and act in their own best interest. This argument, systematized and given a philosophical patina by Herbert Marcuse, was a staple of New Left thinking by the end of the decade. From the beginning, though, hopes for "participatory democracy" were predicated on some form of this argument. This is clear from Bruce Payne's 1965 in-house critique of what he called the "Mississippi SNCC ideology":

> To the objection that various groups in a city or state, operating according to the terms of participatory democracy, might come to conflicting, and even evil conclusions, SNCC workers . . . [usually reply] that, when freed from the false ideas imposed on them by the middle class and given a chance to work things out for themselves, "the people" can make the right decisions. The charitable view of human nature which the formulation seems to imply is not extended to white liberals, members of the establishment, or people in the Mississippi power structure, although it applies equally to the white and black poor.[34]

Even during the Movement's earliest phase, then, terms like "the people" and their "true needs" had become rhetorical conceits that masked elitist tendencies within its avowed populism. This underlying tension was only one facet of the central dilemma confronting many SNCC workers. They were trying to satisfy revolutionary instincts with reformist activity.

In retrospect, it appears that the radical young were less willing to "learn from the poor" than they realized. They sought to universalize their own desire for autonomy and community, assuming that these values would eventually be shared by the oppressed and dispossessed, who sought only material goods and civil liberties. The problem for the Movement was to help the poor and oppressed get what they wanted, "bourgeois" freedom, without introducing them to middle-class life styles and values.

Within the civil rights struggle, this problem eventually led SNCC away from its religious and pacifistic roots and toward the concept of black power. Long-time radicals like SDS founder Bob Haber had argued since the first sit-ins that "Negroes . . . must take the leadership in this struggle."[35] By the mid-'60s most young white radicals were willing to concede that blacks could learn the value of personal autonomy only by experiencing power. The old mistrust of leaders did not hinder support for a new breed of black leader, who stood for independence, pride, and power rather than love, faith, and nonviolence.

In 1966 SNCC's leadership passed to Stokeley Carmichael. Shortly thereafter, whites were excluded from the organization. Many white civil rights workers and sympathizers were dismayed by SNCC's apparently radical shift in direction. But the SDS National Committee declared its support: "We must not simply *tolerate* this 'black consciousness,' we should *encourage* it [emphasis in original]."[36] By that time it was becoming clear that many white radicals supported "black power" as a surrogate expression of their own hostility against the Establishment. The black underclass was finally fulfilling the role in which it had long been cast—as the vanguard of a revolt *against* the American Dream.

If the Movement began as an adjunct to the struggle for civil rights in the south, it was soon to take center stage, as it made its presence known on campus after campus across the nation. The first stage on which it appeared was the University of California at Berkeley.

Berkeley had been for a long time a center of both bohemianism and political radicalism. A "youth culture" of nonstudents and occasional students had grown up around the university campus, magnifying the potential for generationally linked social conflict. Moreover, many Berkeley students had been quite active in the civil rights movement. The campus provided a fertile recruiting ground for the Freedom Summers as well as for protests in the San Francisco area. In 1963 Berkeley students participated in demonstrations to force the hiring of more blacks at restaurants, auto agencies, and the Sheraton-Palace Hotel. During the course of these efforts more than a thousand students were arrested, including 767 who blocked the Sheraton-Palace's lobby in a massive sit-in. But the campus itself remained relatively quiet.

Then, in September 1964, the university administration banned political activity on a sidewalk that had become a sort of Hyde Park for activists of varying stripes. This action was apparently taken in response to criticism from

the conservative Oakland *Tribune*. Not coincidentally, this "free speech" area
had served as a recruitment point for civil rights groups that had organized
pickets against the *Tribune*. On September 30, five students were summoned
to the dean's office for refusing to leave the tables they were manning. At the
appointed time, over five hundred students arrived at the dean's office, led by
a veteran of the civil rights movement named Mario Savio, who had been
arrested at the Sheraton-Palace sit-in, spent the preceding summer in Mississippi, and was currently head of Campus Friends of SNCC. He was convinced
that this seemingly minor conflict was part of "the same struggle" he had
waged in Mississippi, indeed "a struggle against the same enemy":

> In Mississippi an autocratic and powerful minority rules, through orga-
> nized violence, to suppress the vast, virtually powerless, majority. In
> California, the privileged minority manipulates the University bureau-
> cracy to suppress the students' political expression. That "respectable"
> bureaucracy masks the financial plutocrats; that impersonal bureaucracy
> is the efficient enemy in a "Brave New World."[37]

Thus the Free Speech Movement (FSM) emerged out of the civil rights
movement. The Berkeley activists transferred the Movement's direct action tactics and political vision from southern lunch counters to northern college campuses.

Of course Berkeley was not just any campus. The protests there attracted
enormous public attention, not only because this was the first campus rebellion
of the era but because it occurred at the country's finest public university. Its
president, Clark Kerr, was a leading educational theorist. He viewed the university as the center of a growing knowledge industry, whose function was to
produce highly educated specialists for a technocratic society. Kerr's "multiversity" was intended to serve as gatekeeper to the very "chrome plated con-
sumer's paradise" that Savio and his like-minded peers found so repugnant. It
is not surprising that these unalterably opposed visions eventually came into
direct conflict. It was less predictable, though, that the activists would win
widespread support among the student body and, eventually, the faculty.

Throughout the fall term a scenario was played out that would become quite
familiar over the next few years. Challenged by a few dissenters, the university
responded with a variety of carrot-and-stick techniques which many believed
violated good-faith bargaining and its own regulations. Every step of the way,
the FSM gained more supporters from the ranks of the uncommitted students.
The administration seemed willing to play out the role in which the FSM had
cast it—that of repressive autocrats lurking behind a benign mask of liberalism.

The Berkeley protests showed that campus rebellions were sustained not only by the initiatives of activist students but also by the blunders of university administrators. The greatest of these blunders was to call upon the police for support. No other slogan had the capacity to mobilize a student body more rapidly than did "police brutality."

These were lessons that administrators from Berkeley to Columbia learned the hard way. As a result, the nation would witness endless repetitions of the themes of student protest pioneered by the FSM. Idealistic resolutions combined with direct action tactics would provoke administration blunders, with resultant arrests, resignations, nonstop committee meetings, and gradual politicization and polarization of a heretofore apathetic student body.

The events of this period at Berkeley have been recounted too often to require detailed description here.[38] The ensuing negotiations and protests culminated in a climactic sit-in and police "bust," in which six hundred police arrested over eight hundred protesters in none-too-gentle fashion. This precipitated a tumultuous faculty meeting that produced a no-confidence vote against the administration, in the form of a refusal to discipline the offending students. In January 1965 the administration rescinded its restrictions against political organizing and soliciting (i.e., "free speech") on the disputed sidewalk.

So the FSM emerged victorious on what was ostensibly the main point of contention. But there is widespread agreement that "free speech" was not what the struggle was really all about. Jack Weinberg, a civil rights activist who became a leader of the FSM, quotes a co-worker as saying, "I really don't give a damn about free speech. I'm just tired of being shat upon." To Weinberg, these sentiments were indicative of a broad and deep disaffection with the university, which the free speech issue seemed to trigger:

> The Free Speech Movement has become an outlet for the feelings of hostility and alienation which so many students have toward the university. . . . The free speech issue has been so readily accepted because it has become a vehicle enabling students to express their dissatisfaction with so much of university life, and with so many of the university's institutions.[39]

Weinberg, Savio, and many other FSM leaders suggested that the real issue was the impersonality and bureaucratization of the university. This is closer to the truth, but not in the sense that the revolt stemmed from dissatisfaction with the educational process. The evidence is overwhelmingly against such an interpretation. In response to a survey taken at the height of the crisis, the vast majority of students pronounced themselves satisfied with the educational process and expressed support for Kerr's efforts in this regard. In fact, almost 90 percent of the FSM supporters surveyed agreed that the president and chancellor were "trying very hard to provide top-quality educational experience for students here."[40]

Dissatisfaction with the university certainly existed, but it was a dissatisfaction too amorphous and inchoate to be assuaged with proposals for educational reform. The hostility and alienation so many students felt was not directed against bad teachers or even arbitrary administrators per se. Instead they felt alienated from the larger social order of which the multiversity claimed to be an integral part, and whose failures of moral leadership it seemed to reflect. This is why Kerr was so overwhelmed by the intensity of student dissent. He didn't realize that the university was beginning to serve as a lightning rod for perceived societal inequities. Weinberg captured the new mood quite well:

> The University of California is a microcosm in which all of the problems of our society are reflected. . . . Throughout the society, the individual has lost more and more control over his environment. . . . He finds it increasingly more difficult to find meaning in his job or in his life . . . in increasing numbers [students] do not desire to become a part of the society. From their peripheral social position they are able to maintain human values, values they know will be distorted or destroyed when they enter the compromising, practical, "adult" world.[41]

Insofar as the university existed to filter skilled technicians into an increasingly technological and bureaucratized society, it was found guilty of complicity in creating the "brave new world" denounced by the young activists. The multiversity could provide skills. It could not make life meaningful or impart a sense of personal autonomy. So when the administration acted in what was perceived as an arbitrary fashion to repress student political activity, it merely confirmed the students' suspicion that universities were no better than any other social institution.

Of course it is a considerable oversimplification to ascribe these sentiments to "the students," or even to the protesters. Fortunately data collected that November by Berkeley sociologist Robert Somers provide a more precise image of students who supported the FSM's direct action tactics as well as their goals.[42] Somers found that almost two thirds of the students sampled favored the goals of the demonstrators, but only one third voiced support for their tactics. He calls those who supported both goals and tactics the "militants"; those who opposed both goals and tactics are labelled the "conservatives." Two thirds of the militants called themselves liberal Democrats or political independents, while three fifths of the conservatives were Republicans or independents. The militants were drawn primarily from the social sciences and humanities, while the conservatives tended to major in business, engineering, architecture, or agriculture. The militants were drawn disproportionately from Jewish families and, to some degree, from "professional" upper-middle-class households, although there was no relation between family income and FSM support. They tended to agree with their parents on intellectual issues, future goals, and religion, although the small number of students who strongly disagreed with their parents on these topics were drawn to the pro-FSM group.

This demographic profile replicates the picture we have of white civil rights activists. As we shall see, it recurs among the early circle of SDS activists as well. New Left supporters on the campuses, on the picket lines, and in protests tended to come from a fairly well-defined social milieu. They were disproportionately the children of liberal, well-educated, Jewish and Protestant professionals, students of the social sciences or humanities at elite universities. Their own political sympathies were liberal or leftist, and they yearned above all to act on their own ideals. When they did so, they often became radicalized by ensuing confrontations with the Establishment.

For campus rebels, as for SNCC workers, radicalization involved the perception that not just Negroes but they themselves were being "oppressed" by a society that denied the individual a meaningful and self-directing existence. Savio echoed the analysis we have heard from others in SNCC:

> What oppresses the American Negro community is merely an exaggerated, grotesque version of what oppresses the rest of the country—and this is eminently true of the middle class, despite its affluence. . . . The Berkeley students now demand what hopefully the rest of an oppressed white middle class will some day demand: freedom for all Americans, not just for Negroes![43]

There can be little doubt that "freedom" does not mean access to the American Dream but rather its rejection. The privileged children of the bourgeoisie were beginning to reject their heritage and their inheritance.

The Students for a Democratic Society national office wired their moral support to the FSM. They lacked the resources to send anything more substantial. As late as 1965, SDS was a small, undernourished organization that claimed only 2,500 members (only about half of them dues-paying) on forty campuses. What it did have was a reputation as the leading national New Left organization, the brains and heart of the student movement, as SNCC moved toward its black power phase and radical white students began to look beyond civil rights.

If SNCC helped launch the student movement, SDS soon came to personify it. From its formation in 1960 until its disintegration almost precisely a decade later, SDS seemed to anticipate and then embody every major trend and tendency of '60s radicalism. It helped build student support for the civil rights sit-ins, then pioneered the use of the teach-in. It helped mobilize the antiwar and the antidraft campaigns, and in the process pushed many participants from single-issue protest to militant "anti-imperialism." It led the Movement's tactical progression from protest to confrontation, then to violence and terror, and its ideological progression from moral witness to Marxist factionalism. In the words of its biographer, Kirkpatrick Sale, "SDS stood as the catalyst, vanguard, and personification of [a] decade of defiance."[44]

At its birth, SDS was neither defiant nor particularly distinguishable from other left-liberal campus youth groups. It began as the student wing of the social democratic League for Industrial Democracy, an educational organization whose political commitments were constrained by its tax-free status. The initial identification of SDS with a "new" Left was largely fortuitous. The organization sponsored a 1960 conference on human rights that happened to coincide with the first flowering of the civil rights movement. Civil rights leaders from CORE and SNCC met with white middle-class students at the University of Michigan, and alliances began to take shape. Soon thereafter, a grant from the United Auto Workers allowed SDS to become a clearinghouse for campus civil rights activity, with an emphasis on direct action. In 1961 the organization contained only a few hundred members on a handful of campuses, but its civil rights newsletter had a circulation of over 10,000. In addition, many individual SDSers became active in the direct action wing of the civil rights movement. Most notable was Tom Hayden, whose dispatches from Mississippi were carried by political publications on northern campuses.

SDS made its first real impact on the nascent movement in 1962 with its *Port Huron Statement,* a radical manifesto written primarily by Hayden. Most of this document criticized American political and social institutions and suggested familiar left-liberal solutions to current issues—disarmament, increased public spending, and the like. As Sale points out, though, this critique was given a radical tinge through its emphasis on the interconnections between social ills like militarism, racism, and poverty, American capitalism, and the need for a comprehensive solution. More important, the paper spelled out a vision of the good society, based on humanism and participatory democracy. Finally, it called for creation of "a new left," based in the universities, that would "transform modern complexity into issues that can be understood and felt close-up by every human being . . . so that people may see the political, social, and economic sources of their private troubles and organize to change society."[45]

The *Port Huron Statement* established SDS as a leading representative of emerging radicalism. It combined an idealistic tone ("Men have unrealized potential for self-cultivation, self-direction, self-understanding, and creativity") with unsparing rejection of a society that failed to live up to those ideals ("America is without community impulse, without the inner momentum necessary for an age . . . when democracy must be viable because of the quality of life, not the quantity of rockets").[46] This conjunction of idealism and disaffection captured the mood of a generation of alienated youth, united by their generational dissatisfaction with the status quo. Within two years, over 20,000 mimeographed copies had been distributed by the SDS national office. Although rarely able to keep up with the demand, SDS eventually printed over 60,000 copies.

As its very popularity might lead one to suspect, the *Port Huron Statement* was not particularly original. It was heavily influenced by social democratic intellectuals like Erich Fromm, Michael Harrington, and especially C. Wright Mills. Its prescriptions for reform echoed respectable older radicals like Norman Thomas and Paul Goodman. But it provided a comprehensive expression of the growing unease and vague longings of the middle-class white liberal students who were its natural audience—"people of this generation, bred in at least modest comfort, housed in universities, looking uncomfortably to the world we inherit."

These expressions of moral concern, political idealism, and intellectual seriousness created a strong impression on many in the democratic Left. Here, it seemed, was a positive force for social change, unfettered by the dogmas and factionalism of the past. One result was a tendency to wax rhapsodic over the personal qualities of early SDSers. Andrew Kopkind described SDS ghetto organizers as "a kind of lay-brotherhood, or worker priests, except that they have no dogma to sell."[47] To Sale, early SDS contained "a remarkable group of people . . . committed, energetic, perceptive . . . human, friendly, warm . . . personable, charismatic, articulate, and [many] good-looking. . . ."[48] Jack Newfield, while less effusive, was just as positive in his assessment: "The finest political people I have ever seen—and that includes those around Bobby Kennedy and anyone else—were those in the early days of the SDS."[49]

However difficult it may be to evaluate this litany of praise, one thing is clear. The founders of SDS resembled, in many ways, the observers on whom they made such a favorable impression. They were predominantly upper middle class, of eastern urban backgrounds, often the children of politically leftist parents. They were also disproportionately Jewish. Sale estimates that "perhaps a third" were of Jewish descent. Our own research, discussed in Chapters 3, 6, and 8, suggests that this group actually constituted a solid majority. Finally, they were intellectually oriented and came mostly from elite universities. In short, the early SDS drew on the kind of sophisticated, cosmopolitan groups that have been fertile breeding grounds of radical intellectuals in twentieth-century America.

Rather ironically, in view of its later widely acknowledged anti-intellectualism, SDS's early influence on the New Left was restricted to the intellectual sphere. The unexpected impact of the *Port Huron Statement* was balanced by the utter failure of SDS's first venture into political activism, the community-action project known as ERAP (Economic Research and Action Project). Prior to its antiwar activities, which began in 1965, SDS activism was centered upon an effort to build an interracial movement of the poor. This entailed moving into working-class and ghetto neighborhoods and organizing "the people" against landlords, police, and city government bureaucrats. Perhaps 500 students spent their summers in Newark, Chicago, Oakland, and a dozen other cities, attempting to serve as "catalysts of protests . . . around such issues as jobs, housing and schools."[50] They were quickly confronted by the same problem that had stymied their spiritual predecessors, the Russian Narodniks. The poor did not wish to be organized by middle-class students with alien backgrounds, values, and habits of speech and dress. Despite Hayden's assertion that "students and poor people make each other feel real,"[51] the collegians' cult of the ghetto was not shared by the ghetto's inhabitants.

The students were nonplussed by the failure of the poor to embrace their would-be liberators. As Michael Harrington wrote, they "expected the poor to act out the moral values of the middle-class radical who has come to the slum."[52] But ERAP organizers found an existential silver lining in their debacle. Although the project did not mobilize the poor, it radicalized many of the students. They blamed the system for the unwillingness of the poor to take control of their own lives. Chicago organizer Richie Rothstein wrote in 1965:

> Those of us involved in ERAP . . . are now enemies of welfare-state capitalism, with little faith or desire that the liberal-labor forces within this system be strengthened vis-a-vis their corporatist and reactionary allies. We view those forces—and the social "reforms" they espouse— as . . . no more than a manipulative fraud perpetuated upon the dignity and humanity of the American people. We owe these conclusions in large measure to four years of ERAP experience.[53]

These conclusions presaged a pattern of analysis that would soon become common within the student Left. The frustration of efforts to organize nonstudents revealed the power and malevolence of the system. To some degree, the students recognized that the inadequacies of their own tactics and analyses played a role as well. But their main conclusion was that the system could not be made to work.

As a kind of corollary to this unyielding faith in their own vision, most ERAPers felt that their activity was valuable in itself, despite all the setbacks. As Sale put it, they decided to "just continue what they were doing for its own sake, unencumbered by theory or explanation or questioning."[54] And in a way it was valuable, for now they were able to savor "victory in defeat," as their very failure to change society helped cement their movement for radical social change. Later on, the New Left would encounter the problem of "defeat in victory." Having successfully prodded the system into reforms, they reduced their ability to broaden their own radical base.

By 1965 the Movement was a vanguard in search of a mass following. More precisely, the search was for issues of such transcendent significance that they could generate a broad-based nationwide social movement. The civil rights struggle was turning away from the patronage of white students, as more radical blacks developed the notion of black power. ERAP's community organizing efforts had proved a failure. The battle of Berkeley had been won, but no one was certain how the spirit of student rebellion could be transferred to other, more typical campuses. All the issues that had impelled and sustained the Movement—civil rights, poverty, the impersonal multiversity—seemed incapable of broadening it.

In February 1965 Lyndon Johnson dramatically escalated American participation in the Vietnam conflict, directing the first bombing of North Vietnam and rapidly increasing the number of American support troops. Equally important, the new manpower requirements were to be met by enlarged draft calls. The campus response was immediate, if somewhat muted in comparison with what was to come. Demonstrations involving hundreds of students broke out at most of the elite schools that were bastions of anti-Establishment feeling, and several hundred students picketed the White House. Then, on March 24, the first teach-in was held at the University of Michigan. Several hundred participants were expected. Perhaps 3000 took part in the all-night session of speeches, songs, and a torchlight parade. The event elicited widespread press coverage, and during the spring term over a hundred campuses followed Michigan's example. In late May over 30,000 people attended a thirty-six-hour teach-in, held, appropriately, at Berkeley.

Local SDSers at Michigan were instrumental in developing the teach-in concept and making it a valuable political tool, but national SDS, which had become cynical by now about how much could be accomplished by "speaking truth to power," did not endorse the teach-ins. That organization's aim was not education but radicalization. This might be produced, its leaders felt, through confrontations generated by mass marches and demonstrations. Accordingly, SDS sponsored the first major antiwar march on Washington.

On April 17, 1965, some 20,000 marchers descended on the Washington Monument.[55] They heard songs by Joan Baez and Judy Collins, mild speeches by sympathizers like radical journalist I. F. Stone and Alaska's Senator Ernest Gruening, and radical critiques by SDS President Paul Potter and historian Staughton Lynd, editor of *Liberation* magazine. After the speeches ended, the crowd moved toward the Capitol, singing "We Shall Overcome," until antiwar chants drowned out the song. The plan was for the march to end at the Capitol, while representatives presented a petition to legislators. But then the chant went up, "Let's *all* go." Lynd expressed the fervor that seized part of the crowd:

> It seemed that the great mass of people would simply flow on through and over the marble buildings, that our forward movement was irresistibly strong, that even had some been shot or arrested nothing could have stopped that crowd from taking possession of its government. Perhaps next time we should keep going, occupying for a time the rooms from which orders are issued and sending to the people of Vietnam and the Dominican Republic the profound apologies which are due; or quietly wait on the Capitol steps until those who make policy for us, and who, like ourselves, are trapped by fear and pride, consent to enter into a dialogue with us and with mankind.[56]

This group proved to be a minority, and the crowd dispersed as planned, after the petition had been presented. But the incident suggested the shape of things to come. A correspondent for the radical journal *Guardian* described the mixed emotions generated by the march's end: "Clearly a frustration for many was the dispersion of the march at the end of a long day without some form of massive civil disobedience, for which many of the participants were ready."[57]

From this moment, the antiwar effort entered a period of rapid and vast expansion. In October antidraft demonstrations attracted perhaps 80,000 protesters in 90 cities. The following month brought another Washington march of 40,000 demonstrators. The highlight was new SDS President Carl Oglesby's fiery speech denouncing the war as the product of "corporate liberalism." SDS, ironically, was still perceived as the leading antiwar organization, a misperception that the media did little to correct.

In any event, this was the time of media breakthrough for the New Left. Many liberal journalists either initially shared the sentiments of the antiwar demonstrators or had been converted by their arguments. But between the reformist sentiments of the antiwar protesters and the increasingly militant New Left elements a widening gulf was forming. The press coverage of the period seemed not at all to distinguish between the two. In this first period of "united front" antiwar activity, favorable articles on SDS and the Movement appeared in radical journals like *The Nation*, liberal magazines like *The New Republic*, and even major mainstream media outlets like the New York *Times* and *Newsweek*. At the same time, Movement celebrities began to appear on national television programs. This development culminated in controversial appearances by radicals like Hayden and Carmichael on *The Dick Cavett Show*, and a few years later by SDS president Mike Klonsky on *Face the Nation*, at the very height of SDS's "revolutionary" phase. Of course, there was already a good deal of angry editorializing about the New Left's increasingly militant tactics. But insofar as any publicity is good publicity, the Movement benefited from the sudden media attention, and its ranks and influence swelled.

An even greater spur to the Movement's growth was provided in 1966 by the Selective Service System. Henceforth, students with low class ranks would be subject to the draft. A year later, the other shoe dropped. Deferments for graduate students were to end altogether. The reaction on campus was powerful and immediate. Harvard undergraduate Steve Kelman described the changes the decision brought to his university: "A peaceful campus, only marginally concerned with Vietnam, suddenly . . . became desperate. . . . Burning frenzy suddenly enveloped Harvard. . . . It was not our oft-praised idealism and sensitivity . . . which led us into mass action against the war. It was something close to self-interest." [58]

Shock and anger were quickly transformed into action, as campus protests escalated with each new troop shipment. An Educational Testing Service survey showed that from academic year 1964–65 to 1967–68 the number of institutions reporting protests skyrocketed. Campuses reporting protests against the war almost doubled, to 327. In addition, hundreds of other schools cited protests against the draft and armed forces recruitment. Only slightly fewer reported protests against CIA or Dow Chemical recruitment. Another survey of 78 prominent universities found that 430 protests occurred during academic year 1966–67. [59]

During this period the Resistance, a west coast draft resistance group, became a nationwide network. In spring 1967 the first mass draft-card burning took place in New York City. That fall a group led by the Reverend Philip Berrigan poured blood on draft records at a Baltimore selective service office. In April over 300,000 people came to antiwar marches in San Francisco and New York.

The expansion of protest was accompanied by increasingly militant behavior and rhetoric. Thus the Movement began to traverse the tortuous route from the peace movement of 1965 to what Oglesby called the "anti-peace" movement favoring continued armed struggle in 1969.[60] Few outside SDS or the Old Left splinter groups carried the logic of anti-imperialism to this conclusion. But the period from 1965 to 1967 saw an increasing tendency to view America as global villain, and to justify those who opposed her "by any means necessary."

Symptomatic of the new militancy was "Stop the Draft Week," a series of demonstrations carried out in October 1967 by a coalition of Berkeley radical groups. The declared aim was to disrupt the Selective Service machinery in Oakland. Traditional tactics proved fruitless, however, as the police easily contained picketers, marchers, and sit-in participants. Then, on October 20, some 10,000 people marched on the draft induction center, armed with helmets and shields. What followed was the first systematic "trashing" and planned armed conflict with police. One participant jubilantly described the action in *New Left Notes:*

> Trash cans and newspaper racks were pulled into the streets. Writing appeared on walls, on sidewalks: "Free Oakland," "Che Lives," "Resist," "Shut It Down." Soon, unlocked cars were pushed into the intersections, along with potted trees and movable benches. . . .
>
> The real change came about when one line of demonstrators, instead of simply backing up before a line of police, dispersed to the sidewalks—then quickly, instinctively, converged on the streets behind the line of cops. The cops suddenly, uncomfortably, found themselves surrounded. . . .
>
> Word spread among the various bands of demonstrators who were now beginning to feel and even act somewhat like urban guerrillas. . . .
>
> Today we had tasted something different—we had taken and held downtown Oakland for the past four hours, we had seen the cops back away from us. . . . Not only the sanctity of property, and the sanctity [invulnerability] of cops had been destroyed that day; we had begun to establish new goals, new criterion [*sic*] for success in what were clearly the early battles of a long, long war.[61]

Another of the activists focused on the long-term significance of this first "day of rage":

> Stop the Draft Week changed the movement. . . . We said to America that at this moment in history we do not recognize the legitimacy of

American political authority. Our little anarchist party was meant to convey the most political of messages: we consider ourselves political outlaws.[62]

The changing tenor of antiwar protest culminated the next day in a famous march on the Pentagon, an event immortalized by Norman Mailer in his best-selling *Armies of the Night*. Mailer's account celebrated the primacy of "symbolic politics," epitomized by a mock-attempt to "exorcise" the Pentagon led by the Yippies. This melding of the New Left with the counter-culture was in fact a significant phenomenon, but it was only part of the story. Of equal importance was the role the event played in crystallizing what some participants conceived of as revolutionary consciousness.

Events like the Pentagon march and Stop the Draft Week signaled a change in outlook and tactics for the Movement. Or perhaps it was only that certain subterranean tendencies now came to the fore. These were hardly "victories" in any pragmatic sense. Such activities changed no policies, stimulated government repression, and alienated both middle-class liberals and working-class "hard hat" social conservatives. The latter group was potentially a significant antiwar force. Their sons, after all, were far less likely to escape the draft than were middle-class collegians. But in the face of the New Left's highly publicized anti-American posture, potential allies of the peace movement became its bitter enemies.

The victories won by the radical left were mainly symbolic, and the significance of this period lies in the increasing focus of the Movement on purely symbolic victories. The draft might go on, the war might go on, but radical youth experienced the thrill of openly baiting the Establishment's armed agents, waving NLF flags at the Secretary of Defense, urinating on the Pentagon. It proved far easier to provoke shock and outrage than to produce lasting and fundamental social change. In a very short time, these "political outlaws" and "urban guerrillas" traded the frustrations of radical organizing for the instant satisfaction of *épater la bourgeoisie*.

Of course, the moderate peace groups disavowed these tactics of the radical fringe, and the mass of antiwar protesters were more repelled than attracted by their "street theater" tactics. On the other hand, more than a few liberals were titillated by the imagery of a self-proclaimed revolutionary army doing battle with the repressive forces of the state—particularly since many of the "revolutionaries" did not take themselves all that seriously. Since protests and marches were having little effect on the American war machine, who could argue against levitating the Pentagon? It certainly provided comic relief, and perhaps a bit of wish-fulfillment. The solemn, self-righteous response of the authorities (along with that sure-fire agent of polarization, "police brutality") reinforced the political and cultural divide between those who identified with its enemies. As Christopher Lasch remarked, the New Left's "chief contribution to American politics" was its ability to push "many liberals several steps leftward."[63]

In the late 1960s and early 1970s, counter-culture fringe groups were less in evidence in "mainstream" antiwar marches. The reasons for this are somewhat ironic. In part, the New Left withdrew by choice, having determined that these marches were no longer where the action was. After Johnson's withdrawal from the 1968 presidential race and the start of peace negotiations, Vietnam and the draft naturally faded as burning issues, except for a brief flare-up after the 1970 Cambodia invasion and Kent State shootings.

The most radical elements had always been leery of single-issue struggles. Now they turned their energies toward building revolutionary cadres, organizing in high schools, and establishing links to black power organizations like the Black Panthers. They also strengthened their ties with radical regimes and movements abroad. For example, several hundred members of the Venceremos brigade aided in harvesting the Cuban sugar crops in the early seventies. Friendly meetings between New Left and Vietcong representatives took place regularly by the late sixties. Groups like the Resistance, which could not escape the issue that brought them into existence, began to suffer from inevitable and ultimately fatal attrition as the war wound down.

Finally, the angriest and most radical turned away from organized protest altogether and vented their frustration in individual acts of violence. In 1968 there were over fifty bombings on campuses, directed mostly against ROTC buildings. Sale writes that this "marked the first concerted use of such tactics of violence by the student left in this generation—indeed, the first use by students in the history of the country."[64] The violence escalated rapidly thereafter, and the targets soon included government buildings used for draft-related purposes and offices of corporations connected with "American imperialism."

If the antiwar movement divested itself of New Left elements largely by default, this did not mean that leadership devolved to groups sharing the liberal politics of the rank-and-file demonstrators. On the contrary, the various antiwar coordinating committees were quickly infiltrated by Old Left groups. The most successful was the Socialist Workers party and its youth group, the Young Socialist Alliance. Although these groups contained only a few thousand active members, they were, in Klaus Mehnert's words, "masters in the tactics of unobtrusive infiltration and indirect rule."[65] By using familiar techniques like stacking "nonpartisan" coalitions with their own sympathizers, they proved influential beyond their numbers from the time of the 1965 Washington march. By late 1967 they controlled the Student Mobilization Committee, which later gave way to the National Peace Action Coalition and then the New Mobilization Committee. (The continual creation of new organizations, staffed by many of the same people, was one tactic of retaining power while expanding the mass base.) By 1970 and 1971 these YSA-dominated groups had sponsored the largest demonstrations in the antiwar movement's history, although as Nigel Young, a sympathetic British commentator, notes, "probably hardly any of the million participants in America had any affinity with, or even idea of, the Trotskyite ideals of the organizers." [66]

In 1964 SDS consisted of a few hundred radical intellectuals and successful ghetto organizers. Within a year, it was awash with new recruits; it had become the spearhead of the antiwar movement and a lightning rod for the New Left. By 1968 it claimed some 80,000 to 100,000 recruits, located primarily on several hundred college campuses. In the eyes of both the general public and the dissident Left, it had become the acknowledged leader and spawning ground of a movement that seemed ready to overturn American society. Its members and graduates staffed all aspects of the Movement—the underground press, community organizing groups, radical intellectual caucuses, the major college uprisings of the late sixties.

The growth of the movement was accompanied by grumblings from the old guard, who saw their own role diminish even as the organization's influence soared. Almost overnight, SDS grew from a group of friends, a typical faction of Left intelligentsia, into an umbrella organization of radical youth. As early as 1963, the intellectual founders of SDS were already being supplanted by young, action-oriented, apolitical ERAPers, whose concerns and life styles pointed toward the New Left's future. At that time, SDS consisted of only 600 paying members on 19 campuses. By 1965 the "SNCC spirit" was making its presence felt at the national meeting. It was this group that would come to dominate SDS in its peak years. The accoutrements of militant radical style were already much in evidence—denim and work boots, long hair and Fu Manchu mustaches, marijuana and the phrase "right on." The moralistic, anarchistic, self-expressive ideas of the founders were simply adopted by the new breed and incorporated into their operating styles. The 1966 national convention resolved that members would "act on their own authority, raise their own funds, send out their own travelers, organize as they see fit. . . ." The old I.W.W. (Industrial Workers of the World) idea of "every man a leader" was updated by SDS President Carl Oglesby as "every member a radical organizer." [67]

Along with these stylistic changes came a demographic shift. Although a majority of the new breed would still be demographically similar to the old guard, more of the new members had been raised in politically conservative, non-Jewish, nonintellectual families. Although there were still few representatives of the working class, there were strong contingents from the midwest and southwest; their influence was recognized within SDS as "prairie power." Such backgrounds contributed to a strong radical commitment and an equally strong sense of alienation from the world they left behind. Texan Jeff Shero, elected vice president in 1965, told an interviewer:

> We were by instinct much more radical, much more willing to take risks, in a way because to become part of something like SDS meant a tremendous number of breaks. . . . If you were from Texas, in SDS . . . you couldn't go home for Christmas. Your mother didn't say, "Oh, isn't that nice, you're involved. We supported the republicans in the Spanish Civil War, and now you're in SDS and I'm glad to see you socially concerned." In most of those places it meant, "You *Goddamn communist.*" There was absolutely no reinforcing sympathy. . . . So we were strong, the commitment in those regions was stronger than it was in the East.[68]

Some sympathetic commentators have stressed the differences between the early, articulate, idealistic old guard of SDS and the less reflective, more militant newcomers who now began to set the tone for the group. The evidence is mixed, however. Richard Flacks, himself a member of the old guard, characterized the New Left as a "liberated generation" on the basis of data he gathered during a 1966 protest at the University of Chicago. The protesters he examined were trying to prevent the university from sending class rank information to the Selective Service. One of many such protests organized and led by local SDS chapters at the time, it represented an early example of the introduction of disruptive tactics into the antiwar and antidraft effort. Four hundred protesters took over the administration building and held it for four days. The spirit among participants was similar to that of the Berkeley sit-ins. Personal and political alienation was temporarily resolved by the communal experience of shared protest: "It was exciting and fun to get to know each other . . . and feel close in the unity of the moment. The sit-in was a communal act, a deeply personal experience for those students involved."[69] (This solidarity never extended to the student body as a whole. University authorities refused to call in the police, and the protesters eventually left.)

It is interesting, though, that this militancy was initiated by those new SDS members with backgrounds quite similar to those of the SDS old guard, as well as white SNCC workers and Free Speech Movement supporters. Their fathers were mostly wealthy, well-educated, upper-middle-class professionals, such as college faculty, doctors, and lawyers. Their parents were politically liberal and also shared the socially liberal values of intellectualism, estheticism, secularism, and self-expression. Finally, almost half the protesters reported that they were of Jewish background. As Flacks summarized these findings, "At major Northern colleges, students involved in protest activity are characteristically from families which are urban, highly educated, Jewish or irreligious, professional and affluent."[70]

It seems that the new militancy, though introduced by the newer members, also appealed to older SDSers and other New Left radicals. The rapid escalation of militant tactics and rhetoric did not simply reflect a transition from a liberated vanguard to "left authoritarian" shock troops. It may have had more to do with the difference between formulating abstract ideals and putting these ideals into action. Certainly many of the founding generation—Hayden, Lynd, and Rennie Davis are among the best known—proved receptive to the emotional militancy that gripped the New Left by the mid-sixties.

By 1966 the SDS leadership (and, to varying degrees, the campus following) was moving toward a policy of resistance and away from the spirit of Port Huron. The American system was widely viewed as irredeemable. Along with this perception went a new intolerance toward opponents. Defenders of the war were harassed, heckled, and shouted down. In one publicized instance, a large crowd of Harvard students, led by SDS members, surrounded a police car carrying Robert McNamara to a campus speaking engagement. *New Left Notes* recounted the ensuing events:

While a dozen SDSers sat down around the car, others passed the signal over the walkie-talkies around the block, and the thousand began running towards McNamara. Within moments, he was surrounded by what must have looked to him like a mob of howling beatniks; they were actually normal Harvard people, including faculty . . . delighted to have trapped the Secretary. . . . The audience loved it. Mac was blowing his cool—unable to handle himself, quite possibly scared. . . . The next question asked for the number of civilian casualties in the South. "We don't know," Mac said. "Why not? Don't you care?" came the shouts. "The number of casualties . . ." Mac began, but was drowned out by the cries of *"Civilian! Civilian!* Napalm victims!" A few PL-types in front were jumping up and down screaming "Murderer! Fascist!" Mac tried to regain his composure and said, "Look fellas, we had an agreement. . . ." A girl shrieked, "What about your agreement to hold elections in 1956?"

Things seemed to be breaking up. The police moved in and whisked McNamara into Leverett House; an SDS leader, fearing violence in the streets, took the microphone and ordered all SDS people to clear the area. The disciplined shock troops of the revolution turned and dispersed quickly, McNamara was hustled out through steam tunnels, and everyone went home to watch themselves on TV.[71]

As the radical Left began to perceive itself as irrevocably anti-American, it began to grope toward a proto-revolutionary posture. In 1967 the New York *Times* quoted SDS National Secretary Greg Calvert as saying, "We are working to build a guerrilla force in an urban environment."[72] Calvert responded in *New Left Notes* that he'd been misquoted: "I felt that young Americans who worked for the radical transformation of this society were similar in many respects to guerrilla organizers in the Third World."[73]

Not quite ready to take on the role of domestic revolutionaries (that would come soon enough), they sought to identify with other revolutionary forces, foreign and domestic. SDS had long since proclaimed solidarity with the National Liberation Front (NLF) in Vietnam. Hayden and Lynd's "fact-finding" trip to Vietnam in 1965 was the first of many fraternal contacts. The centralized, bureaucratized, and hierarchical structures of the NLF and the North Vietnamese government were portrayed as umbrellas for spontaneous "peoples' uprisings." Even the proliferation of Vietcong flags in the late '60s was preceded by a 1965 *National Vietnam Newsletter* containing a map of Vietnam with U.S. and South Vietnamese–controlled territory marked "enemy-occupied areas." Then, in 1967, a "Revolutionary Contingent" enlisted New York radicals to aid Latin American guerrillas. It was the forerunner of the more successful Venceremos brigade, a group that established contacts with the Castro regime in Cuba.

On the home front, SDS found a revolutionary vanguard in the Black Panther party. The politics of guilt that had existed since the early SNCC experiences once again came to the fore. The SDS national convention overwhelmingly adopted a resolution reading, in part:

> We have a special responsibility to fight racism among our own white population. . . . We recognize that racism insinuates itself into both our personal and political attitudes. We are determined to fight it in our personal lives as we fight all the aspects of a racist culture that the system attempts to inject into us.[74]

Meanwhile, a seemingly successful strategy of unlimited radicalization evolved out of the antiwar and antidraft protests between 1966 and 1968. The strategy was one of provocation and confrontation. Its dynamics were simple, its results predictable. A vanguard of campus radicals would engage in activity so obstructive that the administration was goaded to call in the police, thereby escalating the conflict and polarizing the campus. A favored tactic, drawing on the Berkeley experience, was to imprison unpopular recruiters (e.g., recruiters for the military, the CIA, or Dow Chemical Company) in a sea of bodies. Alternatively, some recruiters were physically ejected from the campus. Sale reports that in 1967 personal violence took place in forty-eight separate anti-recruiter demonstrations. On at least twenty occasions, police were called in, and "the inevitable result was simply to escalate the confrontation, create violence, and usually muster broad student support."[75]

This strategy came to fruition in 1968 at Columbia University. The conflagration that engulfed Columbia bore some resemblance to the dynamics of protest at Berkeley four years earlier. Again, the setting was an elite school containing a core of experienced activists. The activists again mobilized around issues of concern to a broader constituency, in this case the allegedly racist displacement of Harlem residents to build a gymnasium, and complicity with the war through involvement with the university's Institute for Defense Analysis. The campus was polarized and radicalized largely by the decisons of the administration, culminating in a police bust. Finally, political commitments were consolidated by the important communal experience of direct action.

Behind the surface resemblance, however, lurk differences of style and content that show how the Movement had developed in the intervening years. Most importantly, the ostensible issues were never taken seriously by the SDS leadership. According to Columbia SDS president Mark Rudd:

> We manufactured the issues. The Institute for Defense Analysis is nothing at Columbia. And the gym issue is bull. It doesn't mean anything to anybody. I had never been to the gym site before the demonstration began. I didn't even know how to get there.[76]

Even Berkeley had a slogan that "the issue is not the issue," meaning that the real issue was not free speech on campus but thoroughgoing social change. Even then, the activists treated the university as a surrogate for the larger society. By the late sixties, this strategy had reached the point of *reductio ad absurdum*. As Mike Goldfield described the process in *New Left Notes*:

> You have to realize that the issue didn't matter. The issues were never the issues. You could have been involved with the Panthers, the Weatherpeople, SLATE, SNCC, SDS. It didn't really matter what. It was the revolution that was everything. The only thing that mattered was what you were doing for the revolution. That's why dope was good. Any-

thing that undermined the system contributed to the revolution and was therefore good. Free Erika. Destroy Amerika.[77]

So the "real" issues at Columbia were the means by which the revolution was to be furthered. And one of these means was the communal experience of life in the occupied or "liberated" buildings which exposed students to a "revolutionary" life style.

Columbia inaugurated a new wave of campus militancy. The National Student Association reported that over 200 major demonstrations took place on over 100 campuses during the spring of 1968. Sale emphasizes the intensity and militancy of post-Columbia protests, estimating that a third involved "sit-ins, strikes, hostages, and takeovers," mostly led by New Left groups.[78] Wherever the familiar scenario of confrontation and polarization was played out, new recruits were won for the Movement. And the recruiting now extended beyond major institutions on the coasts and in the midwest to small, church-affiliated schools in geographic backwaters. Among the new SDS chapters reorganized by the 1968 national conference were Albright College, Bowling Green State, Chico State, Elmhurst College, Wichita State, Danville Junior College, and the appropriately named Defiance College chapter. The New Left was at last reaching the children of middle America.

In fall term 1968, SDS membership peaked at about 100,000. One out of eight Princeton freshmen applied for membership during orientation week. The national office reported that it virtually could not keep up with new chapter applications, but at least a hundred were processed that fall. A Yankelovich survey found that over a million young people identified with the New or Old Left, including 27 percent of collegiate opinion-makers and 8 percent of other college students.[79] Several other polls taken during the late sixties confirm that 10 to 12 percent of college students were "radical dissidents" or out-and-out revolutionaries who believed that the American social system was beyond repair and that violence was a justifiable means of changing it.[80] Hardly a majority, of course, but twice the proportion of students who identified with "communism" in 1936, and a massive upswing in the few short years since Greensboro and Port Huron.

Radicals now constituted an important "critical mass" capable of sparking conflagrations on campuses all across the country. Moreover, networks of radical organizations and publications now existed to assist or co-ordinate local actions and help build "revolutionary consciousness." Much of the underground press was staffed by graduates of SDS, including the nationally distributed *Guardian* and *Radical America,* and locally influential Movement papers like *Old Mole* in Cambridge and *RAT* in New York. In the universities, SDS graduates stimulated the growth of a new breed of radical professors, who organized groups like the Union of Radical Political Economists and the New University Conference. Besides working to radicalize their disciplines (the most publicized success coming within the Modern Language Association), such groups created an invaluable source of organized faculty support for student protesters. So it remained to be seen whether this small but rapidly growing minority of radicals would prove to be a "prophetic minority."

Yet even as the New Left gained in breadth and influence, it suffered less tangible losses. The first casualty of the new militancy was the integrity that had seemed the bedrock of the Movement. Utopian ideals increasingly gave way to quasi-revolutionary ideology, just as the tactics of moral witness were superseded by planned disruption.

To some degree these changes were responses to governmental surveillance and repression, which accelerated after 1968. But this harassment paled in significance before the methods of truly authoritarian regimes. On many well-publicized occasions, Movement lawyers fought the government to a standstill, and the young radicals enjoyed considerable sympathy (for their goals if not their tactics) from the liberal press. In the wake of the Columbia riots, even *Life* and *Look* published surprisingly sympathetic accounts of SDS.[81] The general tenor of such articles was that we should understand and listen to the radicals, without condoning their activity.

More to the point, many New Leftists welcomed and consciously provoked repression in order to prove their revolutionary credentials and speed up the process of polarization that would usher in the revolution. Indeed this was the crux of the confrontationist strategy. In Mark Rudd's words, "confrontation politics puts the enemy up against the wall and forces him to define himself."[82]

By 1968 national SDS was self-consciously revolutionary, ridden with factionalism, shrill and dogmatic in its espousal of proto-Marxist "lines." There was general agreement among leaders of all factions that SDS should become a disciplined vanguard party devoted to a genuine social and political revolution. There was no longer a need, it seemed, for a loosely organized, anti-ideological student-based organization impelled by needs for personal fulfillment and moral witness.[83]

It is not hard to understand why an Old Left faction, the Maoist Progressive Labor party, suddenly gained influence within SDS at the time. For those young radicals who wanted to become serious revolutionaries, PL offered a much better model than did the old SDS. Moreover, the PL faction came armed with the ideological weapons of Marxism-Leninism and the debating and organizational advantages of any disciplined and well-versed group of true believers.

Their program of a worker-student alliance seemed a genuine alternative to radicals in search of a long-range strategy that went beyond putting your body on the line.

Old-line SDSers responded to PL's challenge with panic. They *felt* themselves to be revolutionary, but they had no systematic ideology to match their rivals' glib blend of Marx, Lenin, and Mao. The New Left's new vision of "serious" radicalism proved more amenable to PL's authoritarian Marxism than to its own libertarian and anarchistic roots. Having thus redefined the terms of their radicalism, SDS regulars found themselves consistently outdebated and outorganized by a minority faction with more experience in Old Left formulas and strategies.

Their response was to form their own faction, the Revolutionary Youth Movement (RYM). This became the rallying force of SDS's confrontationist element or "action faction." RYM was the inheritor of many New Left trends in the late '60s—the glorification of black and third world revolutionary groups, the Manichean outlook that split the political world into "the people" and the "pigs," the machismo of violent confrontation, the merger of radical politics with bohemian life styles. RYM members differed from many radicals with similar viewpoints in the extreme to which they carried these tendencies, the shrill and dogmatic rhetoric they used to voice these sentiments, and their willingness to back up their rhetoric with action.

They also differed in certain fundamental ways from most of their radical peers. In order to fight PL, they had accepted the virtues of discipline, hierarchy, and the need for revolutionary cadres rather than a broad-based movement:

> In order for SDS to succeed at this task it will take tremendous self-consciousness and discipline from the membership. . . . Through collective political experience and study, cadre can be developed who can bring these things to SDS. . . . We . . . [must build] the material strength of the white movement to be a conscious, organized, mobilized fighting force. . . .[84]

At the 1968 SDS convention the debate over who represented the right revolutionary path, the Vietnamese (RYM choice) or the Chinese (PL choice), wound up as a contest between rival chants of "Ho Ho Ho Chi Minh" and "Mao Mao Mao Tze-Tung."

The conflict came to a head at the 1969 convention, with PL winning control of the national organization and RYM walking out to form a rump caucus. With that split, SDS effectively ceased to exist as a national force, although many local chapters continued to function by simply ignoring the national office.

With the schism into Maoist and anarcho-terrorist elements, SDS had completed its journey from the New to the Old Left. In its death throes, the onetime harbinger of a New Left recapitulated the split between anarchic and "scientific" socialism that had divided the Left since the First International.

Mike James was one of the first SDSers to undertake ghetto organizing, with a Chicago ERAP project called JOIN (Jobs or Income Now). He served on the SDS national council for three consecutive years, from 1966 through 1968. He wrote regularly for the radical journal *Movement*. So he spoke with the authority of a New Left veteran when he exhorted a Chicago audience in 1969:

> The time will come when we'll have to use guns. Don't let it hang you up. Some of you say violence isn't human. Well, taking oppression isn't human; it's stupid. You only live one time, so you'd better make it good and make it liberating. . . . Violence, when directed at the oppressor, is human as well as necessary. Struggle sometimes means violence, but struggle is necessary, because it is through collective struggle that liberation comes. And life is nothing if it is not about liberation.[85]

The widespread political violence that broke out at the end of the sixties, including the much publicized terrorism of the Weathermen, was one legacy of the New Left. It was carried out and justified by long-time Movement figures as well as by new recruits whose anti-Establishment destructiveness was only superficially political.[86]

For years the New Left had justified violence by blacks, Vietnamese guerrillas, and other agents of liberation. Now the idea began to take hold that radical youth had a part ot play in the revolution. They themselves could engage in justifiably violent resistance against the oppressor.

These sentiments found organized expression in the Weathermen. The RYM faction of SDS took this new name from a Bob Dylan line that goes, "You don't need a weatherman to know which way the wind blows." This was meant as a somewhat esoteric slap at PL's position that you did need a "weatherman," an approved body of theory or correct revolutionary line.

From the Chicago "Days of Rage" in 1969 to the failed Brinks armored car robbery in 1981, the Weathermen were known for their acts, not their ideas. But their willingness to undertake revolutionary violence and terror indicates the depth of their commitment to a revolutionary program that almost no one else took seriously. Yet they were not ideological robots who unquestioningly carried out party policies with no thought of themselves. It was quite the opposite. Their commitment stemmed from the intensely personal quality of their politics. Each revolutionary act was intended as an exercise in self-transformation. However distant the revolution may have seemed, revolutionaries could be created here and now in the crucible of confrontation. Susan Stern wrote of her experience in the "Weather underground":

> Our aim was to make ourselves equal, men and women, practically interchangeable. We had no guidelines, no scruples; we simply started . . . no amount of anguish was intolerable when one considered the end result: a revolutionary warrior, worthy to fight in the world-wide struggle for liberation. . . . [We] were committed to the notion of transforming ourselves into Americong.[87]

The first tool of self-transformation was the "action project." In the summer of 1969, hundreds of young middle-class whites grouped themselves into small "political collectives" in working-class neighborhoods of eastern and midwestern cities. It was the return of ERAP, or perhaps a caricature of ERAP's ghetto organizing. In any case, the results were similar. The middle-class revolutionaries tried to recruit working-class youth by impressing them with militant rhetoric and activity. Sale relates how a Columbus, Ohio, collective attempted to win support by frequenting youth hangouts, spray-painting revolutionary slogans on the local high school, and inviting potential recruits to view their arsenal, which consisted of three guns. These demonstrations of radical machismo impressed the collective far more than they did the local residents, who one night chased the militants out of the neighborhood for good. Like their predecessors in ERAP, the failed organizers embraced the notion of victory in defeat. They were unable to find new recruits, but the very frustration increased their own commitment to the revolution.

The process of self-transformation soon began to transcend the product of societal transformation. Their all-consuming task was to destroy the vestiges of bourgeois society within their own psyches. Their freedom from middle-class hang-ups would serve as a revolutionary example to others. Accordingly they experimented with various aspects of bohemian or counter-cultural life styles— health food, communal sex, drug use (or abstinence from all drugs), abolition of personal property. All this was accompanied by endless sessions of group criticism. Stern recalled that "the process of criticism, self-criticism, transformation was the tool by which we would forge ourselves into new human beings."[88]

This process of cutting the group off from the larger society while binding each individual closer to the group is a familiar phenomenon in the annals of terrorism. Those who have qualms or weaknesses drop out, while the survivors emerge with renewed dedication and fervor. Above all else, they demonstrated to themselves (and, they thought, to others) their toughness, their ability to draw strength from struggle and adversity. This was of paramount importance, because many Weathermen deeply feared their own sense of inner weakness. This problem was widely recognized within the group. One participant wrote, "All of us, both men and women, came off our campuses timid, physically afraid of moving in the streets, but more importantly psychologically afraid of people."[89] Similarly, Stern described a comrade who had once been "a terribly shy, extremely nervous" social work student involved in civil rights activity:

> Lonely, neurotic, and in terrible need of love and understanding, she threw herself into Weatherman totally. With a tremendous effort she repressed her fears and timidity, and became a study of the tough, masculine woman that characterized so many Weatherwomen. Wearing heavy men's boots, jeans, and an army jacket, her hair uncombed, no makeup, chain-smoking with trembling hands and drinking either tea or wine constantly, she learned the Weatherman line and stuck to it. By sheer force of will she managed to function under the tremendous pressure of the collective.[90]

One way of dealing with this pressure, and of proving one's revolutionary credentials beyond doubt, was to engage the enemy in violent confrontation. Weathermen collectives engaged in sporadic physical fights with the police and, occasionally, other leftist groups. They also "liberated" high school classrooms and harangued the students about American imperialism.

The violence for which they are most widely remembered, though, was the Chicago National Action of October 1969, better known as the "Days of Rage." Perhaps 600 radicals gathered for street-fighting that would "bring the war home." Most wore helmets and were armed with weapons more appropriate to youth gangs than to revolutionaries—cudgels, chains, makeshift brass knuckles, and the like. They were young, most in their late teens or early twenties. Most were one-time campus activists and SDS members, with fewer than half currently enrolled in school.[91] And they were not entirely isolated. No less a Movement luminary than Tom Hayden came to convey his support.

Four days of street fighting, trashing, and pitched battles with riot police followed. The new urban guerrillas managed to injure a few dozen policemen and caused $35,000 of property damage. In addition, a city official was seriously injured when he joined in the fray. On the other side, around 200 demonstrators were arrested and an unknown number were beaten by the police. None of those sentenced served more than four months in jail, and most paid fines or went free on probation.

The Weathermen initially claimed a victory. Stern jubilantly claimed, "We had done hundreds of thousands worth of damage. We had injured hundreds of pigs. Greatest of all, one of [Chicago mayor] Richard Daley's chief counsels . . . was paralyzed from the waist down. I had a right to walk with my head high."[92] Both the callousness and the inflated totals in this assessment tell us more about the Weatherman mentality than the actual events. In fact they had failed to stir either working-class youth or the Left. They had inflicted minor damage at best, and they had given the Right a stick with which to beat the New Left. It was clearly a defeat on political grounds. The "victory" lay in the personal transformation achieved through violence. They were no longer armchair radicals but genuine (i.e., blood-stained) revolutionaries. The process had replaced the product in their minds. The action itself was more important than the results.

One observer has suggested that the Weathermen actually hoped the Chicago action would fail, since it left them with "no alternative but to escalate the struggle."[93] In any case they decided soon thereafter to go underground, completing their political isolation. In 1970 they embarked on a program of bombings against government buildings and other symbolic targets, like a monument honoring the police in Haymarket Square, Chicago. By 1972 they had succeeded in setting off bombs in the Capitol building, the Pentagon, and several major courthouses. These were the bombings they took credit for publicly. The full extent of their terrorist activities remains unknown. They also provided continual embarrassment for the FBI, by eluding its grasp while leaders like Bernardine Dohrn and Mark Rudd remained on its Ten Most Wanted list. And they managed to retain a certain sympathy within the Left, despite outrageous pronouncements such as Dohrn's graphic and widely reported endorsement of the Manson gang's murders. ("Dig it: First they killed those pigs, then they ate dinner in the same room with them, then they even shoved a fork into the victim's stomach. Wild!")[94]

Although no more than a few thousand Weathermen activists went underground, their sympathizers numbered in the tens of thousands.[95] Among their supporters were Jerry Rubin, whose book *We Are Everywhere* was dedicated to the group, and Eldridge Cleaver, who pronounced them "part of humanity's solution.'' (Cleaver had attracted considerable publicity with his Manichean dichotomy, ''If you're not part of the solution, you're part of the problem.'') Even Hayden's eventual disavowal of the Weathermen showed the distance the New Left had traveled from the *Port Huron Statement:* ''To us revolution was like birth: blood is inevitable, but the purpose of the act is to create life, not to glorify blood. Yet to the Weathermen bloodshed as such was 'great.' Their violence was structured and artificial. . . .''[96]

Although some of its members were involved in sporadic outbreaks of violence as late as 1981, the Weathermen had all but faded from view almost a decade earlier. During the early 1970s, though, their mythos of the white revolutionary outlaw exerted a powerful attraction on the Left:

> The fact that they . . . continued to defy the authority of the State, and continued to run free, living underground, confounding the most massive police force in the world, gave them a certain stature . . . even if few wanted to join up, many responded to their reverberations. Many political groups would measure themselves against the Weathermen in terms of politics, courage, commitment.[97]

Disillusionment with the System and with peaceful protest reached its peak in the first years of the 1970s. Violent dissent on campus culminated in the uprising against the Cambodia invasion and the Kent State shootings of May 1970. Thirty ROTC buildings were bombed in the first week of May, and that month witnessed the greatest number of bombings since the government began keeping records.[98]

Violence and terror on the Left did not end with the decline of campus protest. According to the International Association of Chiefs of Police, more bombings took place in the United States in 1971 than in any previous year in its history.[99] Stuart Daniels, a writer sympathetic to the New Left, estimates that the American Left was responsible for over a thousand separate bombing incidents that year.[100] A number of terrorist organizations had sprung up in addition to the Weathermen, from Seattle's Quarter Moon Tribe to Houston's John Brown Revolutionary League to Boston's Proud Eagle Tribe. According to a self-proclaimed underground guerrilla quoted in *Newsweek,* upwards of twenty such groups were operating around the country.[101]

Some of these groups attained a certain local notoriety. Others disintegrated before they could make their presence felt. But one cell of underground guerrillas surpassed even the Weathermen in public obloquy—the so-called Symbionese Liberation Army (SLA). The SLA's core consisted of relatively privileged, white, one-time college students. But their parents were not upper-middle-class professionals. Instead they were conservative businessmen, engineers, a Naval officer, even a Lutheran pastor. These young radicals came from socially and politically conservative backgrounds. Many were in open rebellion against their parents. Their hatred of their origins was intertwined with hatred of themselves. Only a revolution offered an opportunity for self-transformation:

> White men themselves have only one avenue to freedom and that is to join in fighting to the death those who are and those who aspire to be the slave masters of the world. . . . We have a long way to go to purify our minds of many bourgeois poisons, but . . . this isn't done through ego tripping and bullshitting—it is done by . . . stalking the pig, seizing him by the tusks, and riding his pig ass into his grave.[102]

The SLA grew out of contacts in 1972–73 between a commune of radical whites and black prisoners in the Oakland, California, area. A decade earlier, neighboring Berkeley had been the first major campus to serve as a center for direct action civil rights activity. Now these white radicals started teaching Maoist and other quasi-Marxist ideas to blacks at Vacaville prison. In return they received a leader—Donald DeFreeze, a petty hood who had escaped prison in March 1973 and began to direct the SLA's activities. In what seemed a caricature of SDS's and the Weathermen's dependence on the Black Panthers, DeFreeze became the SLA's "prophet" and "Field Marshall."

In November 1973 members of the group murdered Marcus Foster, a popular black educator. For all the rhetorical endorsement of revolution and terror that came to permeate the American New Left, this was the first premeditated murder committed in the name of the revolution. Various explanations of this act have been put forth. Foster may have been killed simply because he was a prominent black who worked within the system. Vin McLellan and Paul Avery, who studied the SLA, suggest that the killers never thought in such pragmatic terms:

> There is little in the SLA history, theory, or practice that suggested reasoning so subtle, little hint that the Foster murder was anything more than . . . a spur-of-the-moment decision. It was the act of murder, the declaration that they were willing to go all the way, that was important. The man was just incidental.[103]

Soon thereafter the SLA hit on the idea of kidnapping Patty Hearst, daughter of the head of the Hearst communications empire. This act, on February 4, 1974, started a chain of events that would occupy the nation's attention for over two years. The story was like a tabloid fantasy: the victim is converted to her captors' cause and follows them underground. The core of the group is trapped and killed by police, but Patty escapes and eludes a nationwide dragnet for over a year. She is finally caught and convicted of armed robbery. Before her imprisonment she falls in love with her security guard. She is pardoned in 1979, in time for a Valentine's Day marriage ceremony.

This is a story that mixes tragedy and pathos, as if the yellow journalism pioneered by Hearst writers had collided with the black humor of Thomas Pynchon or Jerzy Kosinski. But what does it tell us about the New Left and its residue?

For one thing, even the political psychopathy of the SLA induced only pragmatic condemnation among some elements of the radical Left. It showed that murder did not "work" as a political tool, not that ideology must be tempered by compromise or even respect for all human beings. As Klaus Mehnert notes, "Some young radicals applauded the words and deeds of the SLA because their people had challenged the authorities and made a laughingstock of the police for a time."[104]

The SLA resembled the New Left, even the later New Left, only as a distorted image in a fun-house mirror. But the resemblance never entirely disappeared, for it reflected the righteousness and militant idealism of many who were shocked by the SLA's moral and political bankruptcy. A romantic vision of revolutionary transformation had motivated the young idealists of SNCC and Port Huron no less than the terrorists of the Weathermen and the SLA. Dotson Rader nostalgically recalled the appeal that revolutionary violence once held for him:

> I was honestly moved by concern for the world, for the suffering of people. Revolution was a word filled with remedy, potent and erect and bringing to my mind pictures of revolutionaries storming the White House. How easy it was. Without the drama of revolution I could envision no future to match the excitement of my youth.[105]

For most young radicals, the drama of revolution faded with the end of the sixties. Some found excitement in the drama of inner revolution promised by eastern and western religions. Others turned to electoral politics and began what the German New Left called "the long march through the institutions." A very few played the drama out until it became their only reality and engulfed them like the flaming house that became the SLA's funeral pyre.

Part II

PROBING THE RADICAL PSYCHE

2 Intellectuals and the Student Movement

THE THEORIES EXPOUNDED by both natural and social scientists are often closely tied to ideologically derived hopes and fears. However, the kind of precision (and consequently public checks) that characterizes theories in the natural sciences, as well as their relatively clear and practical consequences, eventually enables scientists to reach some sort of consensus in most cases. For example, despite strong reservations, the Soviet leadership was eventually forced to accept both the theory of relativity and Mendelian genetics.

In the social sciences the situation is quite different. Assumptions can be based on the loosest of arguments and may lack the support of clear evidence. The conceptual battle is often won on grounds other than those of logic or evidence, and the victors often determine what is to be researched, how it is to be studied, and the kinds of conclusions to be drawn. In short, social scientists tend to operate within the framework of assumptions based on ideological commitments, assumptions that can have a very profound effect on their interpretations of social reality.

In this chapter we examine the interplay of ideology and empirical research in studies of the student movement of the 1960s. A particular view of what constitutes psychological reality profoundly influenced the studies conducted during that period. In consequence, many of these studies were so designed that their conclusions were largely determined by the assumptions brought to them.

We do not suggest that all writing in the social sciences or humanities expresses nothing more than personal ideological commitment. While it is impossible to achieve results comparable to the natural sciences in our field, we can chip away at "reality." Indeed, the difficulties we emphasize imply that those studying society are obligated to examine their own prejudgments as honestly as possible in an effort to transcend them.

Most of the writers we criticize conducted public empirical studies, thus subjecting themselves to a kind of criticism more speculative analyses can avoid. The instruments they used can be examined, their statistics can be recalculated, and their studies can be replicated. In short, almost all of the writers we criticize have contributed to our understanding simply because they have attempted to study the student movement in a manner which permits rational argument about their conclusions.

From its onset, the student movement was subjected to intensive study and comment by social scientists and the mass media. By 1972, a bibliographical survey could list several thousand books and articles in English alone on the events of the 1960s.[1] Since then the flood of publications has continued at an only slightly diminished rate. The great majority of the academic studies were undertaken by Americans. This was especially true of studies that attempted to understand the "psychology" of the young radicals. European scholars tended to use American results to understand their own student radicals. In conducting studies they often relied heavily on instruments devised by American social scientists. For example, the writings of Jürgen Habermas and Erwin Scheuch about German students drew upon analyses developed by American sociologists such as Richard Flacks and psychologists such as Kenneth Keniston.[2] In their empirical studies, European researchers drew upon such instruments as the American-created Omnibus Personality Inventory (OPI).[3]

In the United States and to a lesser extent Europe, most general commentaries and "scientific" studies of the student movement agreed that the radical young represented the best in their societies. They were often portrayed as a new breed, the vanguard of the emerging "postindustrial society."

As Keniston put it:

The emergence of postindustrial societies . . . means that growing numbers of the young are brought up in family environments where abundance, relative economic security, political freedom, and affluence are simply facts of life, not goals to be striven for. To such people the psychological imperatives, social institutions and cultural values of the industrial ethic seem largely outdated and irrelevant to their own lives.[4]

The new revolution also involves a continuing struggle against psychological or institutional closure or rigidity in any form, even the rigidity of a definite adult role. Positively, it extols the virtues of openness, motion, and continuing human development. What Robert J. Lifton has termed the "protean style" is clearly in evidence. There is emerging a concept of a lifetime of personal change, of an adulthood of continuing self-transformation. . . .[5]

Keniston's remarks were paradigmatic. However much they differed over details and causes, the most influential commentators shared his perception of the essential goodness of radical youth. Herbert Marcuse looked to them as possible harbingers of a new "sensual" society that would transcend the excessive rationality and "surplus repression" of contemporary capitalist society.[6] Charles Reich hailed them for embodying a new level of consciousness, which he described enthusiastically:

> Consciousness III starts with self. In contrast to Consciousness II, which accepts society, the public interest, and institutions as the primary reality, III declares that the individual self is the only true reality. Thus it returns to the earlier America: "Myself I sing."[7]
>
> The Consciousness III idea of community is another basic aspect of the new culture. It rests on two integrated concepts: respect for the individual, and the idea expressed by the word "together." . . . "Together" expresses the relationship among people who feel themselves to be members of the same species, who are related to each other and to all of nature by the underlying order of being.[8]

These writers were extraordinarily influential. Keniston's work was widely read, his articles appearing in the New York *Times* and elsewhere. For some time, Marcuse was treated as a guru of the American and European New Left. Reich's *The Greening of America* became a best seller, described by the 1972 Democratic presidential candidate as "one of the most gripping, penetrating, and revealing analyses of American society I have yet seen."[9]

The work of these writers could of course be faulted. Keniston based his analysis on interviews with only fourteen young people and admitted that his sympathies lay with their goals. Although Keniston felt that he had disciplined himself sufficiently so as to take possible biases into account, Joseph Adelson argued that Keniston's portrait of young radicals ignored his subjects' "warts." Others (including some radicals) concluded that the students he interviewed had manipulated him.[10] If Keniston drew upon limited and perhaps suspect data, neither Marcuse nor Reich relied on any empirical data whatsoever.

What gave plausibility to their speculations was the support these authors received from virtually hundreds of studies that seemed to prove that radical students were democratic rather than authoritarian, humanitarian and humanistic rather than pragmatic and self-interested, and generally psychologically healthy and morally advanced. Most of these studies used traditional survey techniques, and some administered psychological tests to large samples of young people. These studies seemed to provide a firm empirical base for the arguments being advanced.[11]

To be sure, there were dissenters. Herman Kahn and his colleagues at the Hudson Institute viewed both the counter-culture and the New Left as representing the cutting edge of decay, a decay whose sources lay in both affluence and the general permissiveness of the culture.[12] David Gutmann (relying upon interviews with students who had come to see him for therapy) saw the youth movement and the intellectuals supporting it as encouraging a new narcissism in which the consumption of life styles was replacing the consumption of goods.[13] Edward Shils criticized student radicals as romantics who asserted their "right" to experience new sensations and gratifications and to realize new sensibilities. He pictured American and European dissident youth as bound together by a common egotism, a shared "ethos of the expansive ego, free from constraint and from sanctions."[14] Lewis Feuer argued that many young radicals were engaging in a self-destructive generational rebellion, which he traced around the world and throughout modern history.[15] Finally, both Irving Howe and Paul Goodman worried about tendencies toward elitist manipulation among elements of the student movement. They never really doubted, however, that the students as a whole represented the best in America and Europe.[16]

All these critical studies were either impressionistic or based on small samples. Among the more scientifically oriented studies, Oscar Glantz's found radical students to be more punitive than nonradicals;[17] Henry Alker's found "quasiparanoid" elements in the manner in which they dealt with reality;[18] and Lawrence Kerpelman's concluded that, on the whole, radical and nonradical activists differed little in major personality attributes.[19] He found that the major differences occurred between activists and nonactivists, with the former scoring higher on "positive" personality traits, regardless of their political persuasion.

Studies such as these, however, represented a small minority of those completed during the 1960s. David Westby's 1976 summary of the literature on the student movement is quite accurate. Responding to the charge that the radical students looked "so good" only because social scientists were biased in their favor, he commented:

> In connection with all such evidence having to do with the qualities of the activists, a potentially powerful criticism has been raised. It has been argued that these "positive" characterizations reflect the bias of

the investigators—social scientists who are mostly liberal investigators holding precisely these values. If so, it is a thoroughgoing indictment of contemporary social science, ironically emanating from the pole politically opposite the usual sources of criticisms of liberal social science—the far Left. While there is little doubt that many social scientists have taken up such studies out of a sense of identification with activist youth, who seem to embody their own values, it does not thereby follow that their research is systematically biased. In fact, the mass of data, in its considerable consistency, suggests that it is not. Until some evidence supporting this line of criticism is advanced, we have only a choice between an interesting hypothesis and a substantial aggregate of data.[20]

In the remainder of this chapter, we attempt to produce the evidence of "bias" that Westby quite correctly insists upon. In our view, however, it is far less a matter of conscious distortion than of adherence to a shared sociopolitical paradigm that has influenced both research on radical students and the reception accorded research findings. The instruments and research methods that produced the mass of data were "contaminated" by the sociopolitical perspective of liberal social science. Moreover, findings were often accepted somewhat uncritically, because they conformed to expectations generated by this same perspective.[21]

We begin with an overview of the weaknesses of instruments used in studies of the student Left. This will be followed by more detailed analysis of some major approaches to the study of student radicalism. The studies tended to replicate each other, repeating—as we shall argue—many of the same errors. As Keniston characterized the literature on the student Left:

I had expected that reviewing this research would show a "progressive" trend from primitive hypotheses, tested in elementary ways, to ever more sophisticated, theoretically based studies. This expectation turned out to be unfounded. Activism research has not in general built upon previous work; most researchers have started more or less from scratch; the comparability of any two studies is usually very tenuous. In much of the research, the level of methodological and theoretical sophistication is not very high. . . . The traditional image of scientific research is of a ladder, with each study building on, amplifying, qualifying or clarifying earlier research. With regard to student activism research, a better image would be that of a widening puddle.[22]

Many social scientists attributed certain "positive" personality attributes or political views to the New Left largely because their questionnaires were either constructed in such a manner as to ascribe such attributes to radical students almost by definition, or because these students, many of whom came from upper-middle-class liberal Protestant, Jewish, or secular backgrounds,[23] knew how to respond "appropriately" to the questions posed.

We are not suggesting that students consciously deceived interviewers. Rather, they had developed a particular view of their own motivations that necessarily influenced their responses to surveys and interviews. This should come as no surprise. The students who initiated the student movement were very often the children (ideologically, if not biologically) of those studying it. In a 1968 study on the academic profession, Everett Ladd and Seymour Martin Lipset asked academics who had children of college age if their children had participated in campus demonstrations. Approximately 50 percent of the social and clinical psychologists responded affirmatively.[24]

It is perhaps for this reason that many researchers failed to perceive the biases or inadequacies built into their instruments. Both issues can be illustrated by examining some fairly typical studies.

Researchers concluded early on that radical students were dedicated to free speech and the rights of minorities. In many cases they came to this conclusion simply by asking students whether they believed in free speech or ranked free speech and political participation higher than certain other values. Ronald Inglehart used responses to this type of question to argue that increasing numbers of young people were part of a "postmaterialist" generation. He discovered that dedication to postmaterialist values correlated with radical politics, and that the greatest shift from materialist to postmaterialist values was found among West German and Italian youth.[25]

Political scientists have long known that the general public's abstract commitment to values such as free speech is not necessarily a good predictor of behavior or even of attitudes in concrete situations. Is there any reason to believe that radical students were so different in this regard? Even members of the Baader-Meinhof gang would probably have chosen the "postmaterialist" values, since the only other alternatives listed on Inglehart's survey were "fighting rising prices" and "maintaining order."

Where the questions dealt with specific issues, the results remain suspect. For the most part, belief in civil liberties was tested by asking about the rights of atheists, communists, homosexuals, and other groups whose rights the American Left has long supported on ideological grounds.[26] Indeed, some instruments measuring support for civil liberties included support for trade unions as a mark of the civil libertarian.[27] Nor has the pattern differed in European research, where, for example, support for strikes and student demonstrations has been equated with support for civil liberties in general.[28]

To be sure, many of the standard attitude scales are not without merit. After all, support for the freedom of such deviant groups is a measure of support for the civil liberties of some. Unfortunately, students were rarely asked whether they extended the same rights to "fascists," "racists," "sexists," or other individuals and groups they might find morally or ideologically repugnant.[29]

Even when they were asked such questions, it is not clear that positive responses represented deep-seated commitments or were predictive of behavior. In the early 1960s, at least, the youth who comprised the New Left's leadership were quite aware that belief in civil liberties was a good thing and probably felt that their libertarianism was genuine. But this did not hinder many of them from interfering with the speech of people they disagreed with, or from disrupting the classes of professors whose opinions they disliked.

The rationalizations offered for such behavior were often disingenuous. At Harvard in 1971, a group of students attempted to organize a pro-Administration Vietnam policy teach-in. They were shouted down by a large group of students, some of whom later argued that they indeed believed in free speech, but that such freedom involved the right to shout people down.[30] Others suggested that the Nixon Administration's position had received more publicity than the antiwar position, so that there was little need to allow it still further publicity. Still a third group held that the teach-in was a government plot designed to create the impression that Harvard students supported Administration policy. Hence it was undeserving of free-speech guarantees.[31]

The social psychological literature is no less exempt from such ambiguities. Some of the best-known studies concentrated on the family backgrounds of radical students and purported to demonstrate that they came from "democratic" homes in which they fully participated in family decisions. Their parents were said to emphasize "humanistic" values and independence rather than traditional discipline.

How did investigators arrive at these conclusions? Too often, they simply asked students (and sometimes their parents) how they had been raised. For example, an influential American study by Haan, Block, and Smith tabulated agreement with such statements as: "My mother respected my opinions and encouraged me to express them." Similar statements were put to the parents of such students, and it was assumed that the responses given reflected actual patterns of child-rearing.[32] Similarly, an influential German study relied on the question, "Who made the decisions in your family?" The favored response among radicals was that each family member made his own decisions.[33] It is questionable whether such responses reflect anything but radical students' rationalizations about their upbringing (or their parents' rationalizations with regard to their own behavior).

Block, Haan, and Smith also purport to demonstrate that at least some radicals (their "constructive activists") were raised by families who were "preparing their young to lead responsible, autonomous lives, but in accordance with inner-directed goals and values rather than externally defined roles. . . ."[34] Their evidence involves agreement with such statements as "When I got into trouble, I was expected to handle the problem mostly by myself" or "My mother taught me that I was responsible for what happened to me." But agreement here may reflect the relative indifference of career-oriented parents rather than genuine involvement and concern. Other evidence indicates that patterns of child-rearing that might yield such responses reduce rather than enhance a capacity to deal with the world effectively and to establish close relations with other people. Herbert Hendin, in a dynamically oriented study of Columbia University students from upper-middle-class backgrounds, emphasizes the pathological results of such parental noninvolvement derived, in part, from their own search for "self-realization."[35]

We suspect that the image of a "democratic" family derived from such studies is largely a myth. The self-reports that created this image seem to have come primarily from thhe upper-middle-class Jewish students (the children of highly career-oriented professionals) who played so large a role in the New Left's early years. This possibility was raised by S. M. Lipset and denied by Block and her colleagues.[36] However, James Wood, using Block's "Child Rearing Practices Report" on a sample of Berkeley students, discovered that differences between radicals and nonradicals did tend to wash out when religion was controlled. For his sample, the "democratic" family seems to be essentially the liberal upper-middle-class professional Jewish family.[37]

If the most influential studies of child-rearing practices are not without flaws, those of the psychological characteristics of the young radicals are even less convincing. For example, a study by Flacks and others[38] characterized radical activists as "humanitarian," defining this attribute as "a concern with the plight of others in society; a desire to help others—value on compassion and sympathy—desire to alleviate suffering." The definition, at least as Flacks uses it, seems to refer to a personality trait or motive. When we look at the questions designed to tap this trait, however, we find that students were asked to agree or disagree with the following type of statement: "I intend to dedicate myself to doing something about eliminating poverty and inequality." The reasons for their agreement or disagreement were then probed. Students who responded with an affirmation of their desire to help the "poor" and the "weak" were scored for "humanitarianism."[39]

Under these circumstances, is it surprising that radicals invariably scored rather higher than conservatives? The scale was so constructed that radicals would emerge as "humanitarians" by definition, given their overt ideological leanings. Items such as these essentially attribute "positive" psychological characteristics to adherents of liberal or leftist political ideology. The results provide an apparently scientific underpinning for the equation of personal goodness with "progressive" politics. But responses to such items give us no information as to the personality correlates of a radical world-view.

"Autonomy" scales are subject to much the same difficulty. A very popular one incorporated into the OPI, and used fairly widely during the 1960s, tended to score respondents as autonomous if they responded positively to statements criticizing the existing social order. Of course, leftist students responding in this fashion might merely be conforming to the values of their parents or peers, thereby demonstrating no more autonomy than do students who are less critical of social institutions.

For example, would agreement with the following statements (drawn from the OPI) really measure the psychological autonomy of a radical child of liberal parents attending Berkeley or Harvard in the mid-1960s?

It is not the duty of a citizen to support his country right or wrong.
Divorce is often justified.
Disobedience to the government is sometimes justified.[40]

Relying on the OPI "Impulse Expression" subscale, or other scales like it, researchers often described radicals as "spontaneous" or expressive, while sometimes admitting that they might lack self-control. The general tone was quite positive, contrasting such students with "up-tight" conservative youth of mainstream America.[41] Here again, conclusions were derived at least partially by definition. The following statements, on which agreement yields a score for "spontaneity," illustrate the point.

Politically, I am probably something of a radical.
Many of my friends would probably be considered unconventional by other people.

The same is true for statements on which disagreement is scored for spontaneity:

I would be uncomfortable in anything other than fairly conventional dress.
I do not like to see people carelessly dressed.

Still other statements are of the kind to which the appropriately socialized children of sophisticated upper-middle-class parents might naturally respond in a "healthy" manner:

Many of my dreams are about sex.
I like worldiness in people.
I dislike women who disregard the usual social or moral conventions.
   [Disagreement scores a plus for impulse expression.]

Finally, the interpretation given to a number of items is clearly the result of a category shift. In classical psychoanalysis, spontaneity is one attribute of the reasonably healthy individual. On the other hand, "acting out" is a primitive defense mechanism that may reflect extreme rigidity.[42] For example, individuals who have not dealt adequately with the anal stage of development may behave in either a rigidly self-controlled or compulsively sloppy manner.

While it is difficult to draw the line in such cases, it is not at all clear that individuals responding positively to the following statements should be characterized as healthily "spontaneous":

At times I have a strong urge to do something harmful or shocking.
Although I seldom admit it, my secret ambition is to become a great person.
It is alright to get around the law if you don't actually break it.
I have the wanderlust and am happiest when I am roaming or traveling around.
Something exciting will almost always pull me out of it when I am feeling low.

The scoring of these OPI items seems based on assumptions introduced by neo-Freudian humanistic psychologists like Abraham Maslow and carried to their ultimate implications by Norman O. Brown and Herbert Marcuse.[43] These assumptions predicate the healthiness of acting on one's impulses. From another perspective, however, positive responses to such items (assuming they are not merely conventional) can be taken as a sign of pathology. Indeed, some of them are used as indicators of paranoia on the Minnesota Multiphasic Personality Inventory, from which they are taken.

Criticisms of OPI scales have not been lacking, but they inhibited neither its widespread usage in studying student activism nor the drawing of inappropriate conclusions about the results.[44] For example, many researchers divided the 400 to 600 items in the OPI into twelve or sixteen scales, and found that seven of these consistently differentiated student radicals from other groups: Autonomy, Religious Liberalism, Complexity, Theoretical Orientation, Thinking Introversion, Estheticism, and Impulse Expression. When a longer form was used, three more differentiating scales were added: Nonauthoritarianism, Social Maturity, and Developmental Status. When statistically significant differences occurred on one of these scales, radicals invariably scored higher than other students. Therefore investigators concluded that radicals had manifested superior psychological traits on a wide variety of measures of psychological health.[45]

As scholars have pointed out, however, most of these scales are really measuring the same two traits, an "intellectual" factor and a much less important "autonomy" factor.[46] We have already discussed some problems of the autonomy dimension, which is largely an indirect measure of social and political ideology. It should come as no surprise that radical students also scored high on "intellectualism." Many of these students came from professional families who stressed intellectuality, a trait that should not be confused with intelligence. Properly speaking, intellectuality is not a "deep" personality variable but rather a value orientation. There is little reason to suppose that a predisposition in this direction is necessarily a sign of mental health or maturity. Indeed, there is some evidence for the opposite conclusion.[47]

One widely reported finding about the psychology of student activism was that radical students were less "authoritarian" than nonradicals. This led many social scientists to assert that the student Left embodied the "democratic personality," the human basis of participatory democracy.

These scholars relied upon questionnaires derived rom the "F (facism) scale," which first appeared in *The Authoritarian Personality*.[48] We discuss the concept of authoritarianism in detail in Chapter 4. Some brief comments are warranted here, because both the concept and the instruments derived from it have significantly influenced the study of politics and personality in this country. Indeed, the extent of this influence tells us a good deal about the paradigms American academics have employed in recent decades.

The concept of an authoritarian personality was developed in this country by a group of emigré German-Jewish scholars, mostly from the "Frankfurt School," in collaboration with American social scientists. One member of the Frankfurt School, Erich Fromm, had been working on the idea for some time as part of an effort to explain the rise of National Socialism in Germany and to synthesize Marxism and psychoanalysis. Originally these scholars held that the obverse of authoritarian personality was not a "democratic" but rather a "revolutionary" personality. It was partly in deference to American sensibilities that this polarity was revised.[49]

Considering the background and ideology of this group, it is not surprising that the F scale and its derivatives tend to equate authoritarianism with conservatism. Indeed, the massive study they described in *The Authoritarian Per-*

sonality was never intended to test their theories about the relationship between personality and ideology. Their data were meant only to concretize a theory whose validity they never questioned. As Adorno wrote:

> We never regarded the theory simply as a set of hypotheses but in some sense as standing on its own two feet, and therefore did not intend to prove or disprove the theory through our findings, but only to derive from it concrete questions for investigation, which must then be judged on their own merit and to demonstrate certain prevalent sociopsychological structures.[50]

This assumption created some built-in weaknesses for the study, and it was vigorously criticized almost from the moment it appeared. In 1954 Hyman and Sheatsley uncovered an array of defects in the research, ranging from inadequate sampling techniques and dubious coding procedures to failure to control for subjects' response sets or to consider nonpsychodynamic alternatives in interpreting findings. Their understated conclusion was that "the authors' theory has not been proved by the data they cite. . . ."[51] In a companion essay, Edward Shils launched an equally powerful attack against the theory of authoritarianism as designed to uncover only right-wing authoritarianism.[52]

The criticisms have continued to this day. They center upon the F scale, the test designed to measure authoritarianism, which many critics consider seriously flawed. As Kirscht and Dillehay pointed out, reviewing the research on authoritarianism a decade ago, the test purports to tap deep personality trends, while measuring nothing deeper than social attitudes.[53]

None of the many revisions of the F scale have eliminated its tendency to equate conservative political beliefs with authoritarian personality traits. This equation can be seen clearly by comparing some typical F-scale items with items appearing on Herbert McCloskey's well-known scale of conservatism, as well as a more recent conservatism scale developed in Germany by Cloetta:

F-Scale Items

The businessman and the manufacturer are much more important to society than the artist and the professor.

Science has its place, but there are many important things that can never possibly be understood by the human mind.

Human nature being what it is, there will always be war and conflict.

People can be divided into two distinct classes: the weak and the strong.[54]

Conservatism Items (McCloskey)

I prefer the practical man anytime to the man of ideas.

No matter how we like to talk about it, political authority comes not from us but from some higher power.

It's not really undemocratic to recognize that the world is divided into superior and inferior people.

The heart is as good a guide as the head.[55]

Conservatism Items (Cloetta)

Every man needs something he can fully and completely believe in.

There will always be wars, just because of the way men are.

Men need an overarching order to provide firm support for their beliefs and actions.

It is only natural for men to need someone to look up to.[56]

What would be more natural than to find that psychological authoritarianism, measured in this fashion, is negatively correlated with education and positively correlated with conservatism? It would be surprising if it were not.

Most efforts to overcome the F scale's biases have failed for some of the same reasons that the F scale itself has failed. For example, Rokeach's attempt to identify authoritarianism with "closed-mindedness" represents an effort to construct a content-free measure.[57] However, his Dogmatism scale taps only the conscious self-conceptions of respondents. And there is reason to believe that the self-conceptions of radical students (except those at the very fringes of the Movement) involved the beliefs that issues are complex, that one should listen to a variety of perspectives, and so forth. As we indicated earlier, however, such perspectives may be rationalizations that guide neither attitudes nor behavior in specific instances.

Despite the weaknesses of scales designed to measure authoritarianism, they are still extraordinarily popular and were used widely during the 1960s (especially the modified F scale used in the OPI) to compare radical and nonradical students. The results might have been predicted. A belief in the democratic (nonauthoritarian) New Left became part of the conventional wisdom.

Perhaps the two most widely quoted authorities on the student movement during the 1960s were Kenneth Keniston and Richard Flacks. Keniston wrote two popular books and numerous articles which drew upon both his own limited sampling of alienated and radical students and the findings of other researchers.

Flacks's prominence was based on a widely cited article reporting preliminary findings from research at the University of Chicago. A thoroughgoing and comprehensive analysis of his data has never been published.

The key to Flacks's influence was his development of a sweeping socio-historical framework, within which the rise of a psychically liberated New Left in contemporary America seemed to make sense. Flacks argued that the student movement was the outcome of an historically conditioned psycho-social process. It began with the efforts of progressive intellectuals during the first decades of this century to restructure American family life and educational practices. Their ideas, which enlisted the work of Dewey and Freud, allegedly influenced the family life of the rapidly expanding sector of professional people and profoundly affected their children's personality development. Specifically, young people who become radical activists were predisposed toward values and motivations likely to bring them into eventual conflict with the dominant values and institutions of their society.

As Flacks put it:

> . . . it now seems that an important defining characteristic of the col-
> lege-educated mother is her willingness to adopt child-centered tech-
> niques of rearing, and of the college-educated couple that they create a
> family which is democratic and egalitarian in style. In this way, the
> values that an earlier generation espoused in an abstract way have be-
> come embodied as *personality traits* in the new generation. The root-
> edness of the bohemian and quasi-bohemian subcultures, and the spread
> of their ideas with the rapid increase in the number of college graduates,
> suggests that there will be a steadily increasing number of families rais-
> ing their children with considerable ambivalence about dominant values,
> incentives, and expectations in the society. In this sense, the students
> who engage in protest or who participated in "alienated" styles of life
> are often not "converts" to a "deviant" adaptation, but people who
> have been socialized into a developing cultural tradition. Rising levels
> of affluence and education . . . [are] creating new sources of alienation
> and idealism, and new constituencies for radicalism.[58]

The impact of Flacks's paper lay not only in this intriguing theoretical account of the roots of student protest but in his effort to validate the theory with evidence collected in the mid-1960s. Unfortunately, the argument far outstrips the data.

The difficulties begin with Flacks's sample. He seems to generalize his results to all New Left activists, at times qualifying his inferences to include only protesters at "major northern colleges" or "in a city like Chicago." But his results are based on a confusing amalgam of two studies, which renders any generalization problematic.

In the first study, fifty students were selected from "mailing lists of various peace, civil rights, and student movement organizations," and an additional fifty from student directories of Chicago-area colleges. The two groups were originally matched with respect to some demographic characteristics, but all one hundred subjects were later reassigned to "activist" or "nonactivist" groups on the basis of interview responses. These groups, then, are not representative of any larger populations.

In the second study, random samples were taken of three groups of University of Chicago students: 65 participants in a sit-in, 35 students who signed a petition opposing the sit-in, and 60 residents of two randomly selected dormitory floors. Of these 160 subjects, 117 filled out questionnaires. The questionnaire items were similar to those used in the first study.

In reporting his findings, Flacks draws selectively from the two studies, citing demographic data from the second and attitudinal data from the first. Thus we do not learn whether the two studies produced similar results. The most important and influential findings concerning the socialization and "personality traits" of activists are drawn only from the first study, despite its ill-defined sampling procedures. Moreover, these data are subjected to no statistical analysis beyond simple tabulation of responses. By limiting his analysis to visual comparisons of the data, Flacks is sometimes led to conclusions that his evidence cannot support.

One is struck first, however, by the paucity of data analysis, considering the breadth and complexity of Flacks's theoretical framework. His published data are contained in only five tables, three of which deal with parent-child relations and two with sociopolitical values and attitudes. We have already criticized Flacks's tendency to treat values such as "humanitarianism" as "nonpolitical" life goals and personality traits, without sufficient regard for their ideological content. The following discussion is confined to his data on child-rearing techniques.

In an interesting measure of parental permissiveness, students were asked to rate their parents to indicate "how my mother (father) treated me as a child." Ten scales were used, and results of four are published: "lenient-severe," "warm-cold," "stern-mild," and "hard-soft." The results are presented in percentage form. We find, for example, that 48 percent of "high-activist" males rated their fathers as "mild," compared with only 33 percent of low-activist males. Summarizing the results, Flacks concluded that "activist sons and daughters tend to rate their parents as 'milder,' more 'lenient,' and 'less severe' than do nonactivists."[59]

This conclusion turns out to be somewhat misleading, because of the small number of subjects involved. In the example mentioned above, the finding that "15 percent more activist than nonactivist males rated their fathers 'mild' " sounds less impressive if we substitute the raw numbers: "three more activists than nonactivists rated their fathers 'mild,' out of a total of 47." Indeed our reanalysis of Flacks' data indicates that many of the differences he cites are not even statistically significant. That is, in the majority of cases they could well have occurred by chance.

Purely statistical problems aside, it is unclear whether the items actually measure the parental trait they purport to measure. The four polarities Flacks does use—mild-stern, soft-hard, lenient-severe, and warm-cold—are alleged to reflect aspects of perceived parental permissiveness, yet no evidence is presented to show that they are related to any external measure, or even to one another. Indeed, the literature on the Semantic Differential test suggests that a soft-hard polarity represents a measure of perceived power or potency rather than permissiveness.[60]

Flacks also uses a measure of permissiveness based on parental self-reports. Parents were asked a series of "hypothetical questions" concerning likely responses to their child's actions. The responses were coded according to the degree of intervention expressed. Flacks presents data for two such hypothetical situations: (1) The child decides to drop out of school without clear plans for the future; (2) The child is living with a member of the opposite sex. Flacks concludes that activists' fathers are much less interventionist than the fathers of nonactivists. Once again, however, more precise analysis reveals that the correlations are very low and statistically insignificant.[61] Thus Flacks's conclusion is not justified by his data.

We would also raise broader issues of the kind we noted earlier. First, at least one of the questions is less a question of permissiveness than of social ideology. Liberal parents, after all, should be less concerned about such issues as young people living together than conservative parents would be. A better test of the permissiveness of liberal fathers might be their response to a child's coming under the influence of an "authoritarian" religious sect. Beyond this, we have no way of knowing the extent to which noninterventionist responses might reflect a liberal father's conception of how a "progressive" parent ought to respond.

Finally, even if it were true that more liberal parents were less likely to intervene, questions remain as to the underlying emotional meaning of nonintervention for both parent and child. Flacks seems to argue that such "permissiveness" reflects deep concern for the child's self-development. It could merely reflect a self-centered concern with professional success that yields low involvement with children. Bronfenbrenner made this point, on the basis of a good deal of data, in comparing Soviet and American children. Now that the student movement has died in the United States and students are once again concentrating on vigorous competition for grades and jobs, some radicals turn Flacks's argument around to account for the emergence of what they see as a narcissistic "sick" generation. Thus, Christopher Lasch, drawing on Hendin's work, suggests that just this pattern of parental noninvolvement is responsible for much of the alienation felt by Americans.[62]

All this does not prove Flacks wrong. It does suggest, however, that the willingness with which intellectuals accepted his findings owed less to compelling data than to the intuitive appeal of an argument that made sense to those sharing his sociopolitical outlook.

Kenneth Keniston first attained national prominence in 1965, with the publication of *The Uncommitted*.[63] He seemed to argue that the great majority of American students resembled the "automaton conformists" whom Fromm regarded as inevitable products of dehumanizing capitalist society. The study itself, however, dealt with a small group of rebels against society, students who had rejected "materialistic," achievement-oriented values for esthetic ones. Although Keniston explained their rebellion partly in terms of the "System," he emphasized the role of a dominating mother who created psychological tensions that inhibited adjustment to social institutions.

In *The Uncommitted*, Keniston was rather pessimistic about the future. Neither the conformists nor the alienated students seemed particularly attractive, and he did not hold out much hope that either group would change the system that had produced them. By the late 1960s, however, his outlook had changed. In his book *Young Radicals: Notes on Committed Youth* and a series of articles, he painted a quite different picture of American youth and its ability to shape the future.[64] In fact, Keniston rapidly became the researcher most popularly associated with the notion that a democratic family culture was producing a generation of psychologically liberated dissenting activists who would grow in number and influence.

In activist-producing families, the mother had a dominant psychological influence on her son's development, but the family ethos was unusually egalitarian, permissive, democratic, and "highly individuated." On the other hand the mother-son relationship in the alienated family was one of control and intrusiveness.[65]

To an even greater degree than Flacks, Keniston saw activists as unusually healthy persons with strong intellectual interests and high capacities for group involvement, self-realization, "empathy," and "nurturant identification with the underdog."

We have already discussed the problem of ascribing psychological health to intellectually oriented young people. The psychological significance of "capacity for group involvement" is equally obscure. The only evidence Keniston offers of this "healthy" capacity is the very fact that the young people he studied were involved in a political group. However, we don't know that these youths are capable of enduring group involvement. All we know is that they were capable of reasonably active involvement in an organization to whose goals they were ideologically committed. But active Nazis or Stalinists would meet this standard of mental health equally well.

It is possible that these young people were and are capable of involving themselves in meaningful and humane ways with all sorts of people, building warm relationships with friends, spouses, children, and neighbors. It is also possible that their organizational commitments reflect a lack of ability to relate to peers in everyday nonideological circumstances. Compare, for example, what we know of the appeal of veterans' organizations. They allow former soldiers who fought together to reexperience the exhilaration of a group activity in which personal difficulties were temporarily cast aside in the interest of a mutually shared "noble" cause. Whether such involvement is healthy or regressive and compensatory involves judgments transcending the mere fact of involvement. Indeed, some of the evidence which Keniston himself offers could support a hypothesis of compensatory participation. The young people he describes did, by and large, have difficulty relating to their peers while they were growing up. Keniston explains this difficulty in terms of their superior sensitivities, but his explanation may reflect no more than a preference for certain life styles and ideological commitments.

As we saw in Chapter 1, a number of young people in the Movement admitted that this involvement provided ways of overcoming inabilities to relate to others or to act effectively. We take up this issue in detail in Chapters 3 and 4. In *The Paranoid Process,* psychiatrist W. W. Meissner describes a patient who was a very effective Movement leader while clearly clinically paranoid.[66] Brent Rutherford conducted a more systematic study of "political" activity in a mental hospital that encouraged patient participation in self-governance. He discovered that patients who had been diagnosed as paranoid schizophrenics were by far the most politically active.[67] We would hardly infer from such evidence that political involvement is pathological. But it is no more evident that such activism is necessarily a sign of health.

The three other "healthy" qualities are of the same type. We shall discuss self-realization when we analyze the work of Inglehart. The only evidence offered regarding activists' "empathy" and "nurturant identification with the underdog" is a restatement of Flacks's position. In essence, an ideological stance is defined as nurturant. These students may indeed possess a generalized capacity for empathy, but neither Keniston nor other commentators on the student movement have demonstrated this.

The danger of confounding idealistic political pronouncements with personality traits can be illustrated by the case of Felix Dzerzhinski, the notorious first head of the Soviet secret police (Cheka). As a young man in prison he wrote:

> What is the way out of present day life, in which the jungle law of exploitation, oppression and force holds sway? The way out is a life based on harmony, a full life embracing the whole of society and humanity; the way out lies in the idea of socialism, the solidarity of the workers.
> Here we have felt and realized how essential man is to man, what man means to man. I think that relations between people are complex. . . . And if we may long here for flowers, it remains a fact that we have learned here to love people as we love flowers.[68]

Dzerzhinski's expressed sentiments did not prevent him from presiding over the imprisonment and killing of large numbers of people who did not share his vision of harmony and self-realization under socialism. His expressed empathy did not extend to political opponents. So, too, many youths who joined the Nazi movement sounded as if they wanted to nurture the underdog. Consider the reminiscence of Melita Maschmann, once a member of the Hitler Youth:

> No catch word has ever fascinated me quite as much as that of the "National Community" (*Volksgemeinschaft*). I heard it first from the lips of this crippled and careworn dressmaker and . . . it acquired a magical glow. I felt it could only be brought into being by declaring war on the class prejudices of the social stratum from which I came and that it must, above all, give protection and justice to the weak. What held my allegiance to this idealistic fantasy was the hope that a state of affairs would be created in which people of all classes could live together like brothers and sisters.[69]

We are by no means suggesting that the young people Keniston interviewed were potential Dzerzhinskis or Nazis. The point is that people in general, and adolescents in particular, are capable of being caught up in such movements for all sorts of reasons. To assume that such ideological commitments necessarily reflect healthy psychological characteristics is to ignore the differences between ideology and personality.

We have already referred to the fact that Keniston's work was based on interviews with fourteen young people who were not necessarily representative of anyone but themselves. Although the author cautions against drawing broad inferences from his sample, he himself engages in such extrapolation quite freely. Despite the weak evidential base, his conclusions were widely accepted because they seemed to "make sense." That is, they resonated with the beliefs of the audience for which he wrote.

Keniston's belief that the portrait he developed from his interviews was basically accurate (due largely to the openness and psychological self-awareness of his respondents) is also questionable. Psychoanalysts are all too aware of how difficult it is for very verbal individuals actively seeking help to face themselves honestly. Indeed, supposedly greater self-awareness may merely reflect a more complex and subtle set of defenses. It is possible that such mechanisms were operative in this study, both in the subjects' accounts and in the investigator's "countertransference."

Despite Keniston's assertion that his subjects were unusually self-aware, his own liberal commitments and relationship with his respondents may well have prevented him from raising any serious questions about the actual extent to which they really understood their own motivations. It is quite clear from his own account that he accepted their self-analyses at face value and did not probe very deeply.

There is also some question whether the published material supports Keniston's claim about these young people's developmental background and its consequences. Three themes emerged from his interview material regarding parent-(male) child relations: (1) "A very close relationship with an achievement-demanding mother"; (2) an "intense and highly ambivalent involvement" with a father perceived as idealistic, sympathetic, honest, highly principled, warm, and admirable, but on the other hand as dominated, humiliated, ineffectual, or unwilling to act on his perceptions of the world; (3) strong parental concern for "the moral dimension of life" as expressed in an ethical orientation toward personal principles and "psychological methods" of discipline (reasoning, explaining, holding up high standards). The general characterization is of a "family atmosphere most often characterized by parental warmth, closeness and idealism."

Yet what are we to make of the following examples, taken from some of the interviews:

[Parodying parents] "Can we *help* you with your math? Be *glad* to go over it with you." That sort of thing. And then when I got a little older, I had a conflict about my not spending enough time at home.[70]

The problem is that my mother is very dominant, very strong, very quick-tempered, quick to criticize. . . . There was a time when I was so uncomfortable in that house, when I was seeing the way she would get irritated and pick on [my father] for little things. Now, I guess, I must learn to accept that.[71]

The quotations might be indicative of normal tensions experienced by close-knit families. Some others, however, raise more fundamental doubts:

My parents never told me what they were thinking about. . . . (They never spent very much time making me happy or being concerned with me. . . .) I mean they talked with me, but it wasn't in any significant kind of way to say what I should be doing and what I shouldn't be doing. I always used to play alone.[72]

She [my mother] was the more ambitious of the two, and that was a bone of contention. He didn't give a shit as long as he was pulling in the scratch . . . but she wanted him to become the world's greatest lawyer.[73]

Themes of parental selfishness and status concerns in fact prove surprisingly recurrent:

For [my father], life was a game that rewarded him with good things— power, prestige, money, comfort, good food, servants.[74]

. . . They said, "Well, if *he* can go to a private school you can go to a private school." She calls up on the phone these private schools and said, "My son wants to go. . . ." I didn't feel any personal desire to go to [a private] school.[75]

Of course the quotations cited above are balanced in the text by more positive recollections of familial warmth, closeness, and "egalitarianism." As Dr. Jennifer Cole has noted, however, even some memories and behavior patterns for which Keniston offers positive evaluations (or at least does not regard as potentially pathological) are subject to quite different interpretations.[76]

In sum, the evidence seems ambiguous. Several of Keniston's subjects sound very much like Hendin's respondents in *The Age of Sensation*. As noted earlier, Hendin draws a very negative portrait of such families, including the impact of family life on the children.

One of the themes implicit in Flacks's analysis, and explicit in Keniston's, is that of "self-realization." A mark of the young activists' liberation was their pursuit of the goal of becoming what one "truly" was or, at one's best, could be. Though not new in social thought, this theme became quite popular during the 1960s. The approach was earlier associated with the psychotherapist Abraham Maslow, who used the term "self-actualization."[77]

Maslow argued that human needs could be arranged hierarchically. As more basic needs are satisfied, individuals increasingly seek to satisfy "higher level" needs. At the top of the hierarchy comes the need for "self-actualization": the need to be oneself, to realize one's unique potential.

This highest goal was adopted by the early SDS in the *Port Huron Statement:*

> The goal of man and society should be human independence: a concern not with the image of popularity but with finding a meaning in life that is personally authentic.[78]

Keniston discovered that this was exactly what his young radicals were seeking. More "scientific" studies seemed to support his conclusion. Perhaps the most influential of these was carried out by Ronald Inglehart, based on material from a large-scale survey in several European countries.

Inglehart's first major article on the subject appeared in 1971.[79] In this study, he analyzed responses to the following question:

> If you had to choose among the following things, which are the *two* that seem most important to you:
> Maintaining order in the nation.
> Giving the people more say in important
>   political decisions.
> Fighting rising prices.
> Protecting freedom of speech.[80]

In general, those who placed greater emphasis on participation and free speech also tended to support European integration, student demonstrations, and various proposals for radical social change. People who shared these views, Inglehart argued, were choosing a "postbourgeois" life style instead of the more traditional emphasis on "acquisitive" values. (In his later book, he calls the distinction that of "material" vs. "postmaterial" values.)[81] These postbourgeois types tended to come from middle-class professional backgrounds.

Drawing upon the theoretical work of Maslow, Marcuse, Reich, Keniston, and Flacks, Inglehart concluded that a new type of person was emerging in Europe and America, a person who resembled Keniston's and Flacks's liberated individual or Maslow's self-actualizing man. In fact, he suggested that West European universities had become repositories of Reich's Consciousness III.[82]

We have no quarrel with the notion that some West European youth, especially university students, have currently adopted a different perspective from that of their elders. But we do question the evaluation of that perspective as a "higher"—that is, more democratic and participatory—state of consciousness. For example, the predominance of "postbourgeois" youth in the universities (Inglehart singles out West Germany) hindered neither the undemocratic tactics of '60s political activists nor the rapid return of political apathy and careerism to many West European campuses.

More fundamentally, we question whether such verbal commitments throw any light on personality dynamics. It is quite reasonable to expect young people reared in relative comfort to place little emphasis on economic issues, unless and until they are forced to face hard economic choices. Although an expressed preference for "postmaterial" values may offer some clues to the direction of their choices in certain areas and at certain times, it is difficult to accept this as evidence of a newly emerging personality type.[83]

Indeed, the concept of "self-realization" or "self-actualization" is rather empty, unless one assumes that each individual is genetically programmed in certain ways which will become manifest only when certain basic needs are fulfilled. Since Maslow, Fromm, and Keniston tend to assume that personality is molded by family and environment, what is there to be actualized or realized? What is the authentic personality? This question was the basis of Marcuse's sharp critique of Fromm and other neo-Freudians, and it applies to all of the above-mentioned writers.[84]

Social theorists who use this or similar terms tend to ascribe "self-actualization" or "authenticity" to those individuals who accept *values* which the theorists regard as good, thus translating an ideological stance into an assertion about psychological functioning. Unfortunately, they often disagree rather sharply as to the real nature of "liberation" or "self-realization." For example, Maccoby, a student of Fromm, regards Maslow's ideal of self-actualization as "curiously asocial and exclusively concerned with limitless individual expressiveness."[85] On the other hand, Marcuse maintains that Fromm's vision is essentially Protestant and petty bourgeois.[86] Certainly Reich's vision of Consciousness III, with its implicit sanctification of the drug culture of the late 1960s, looks very different from the liberated students pictured by Flacks or Keniston. In fact, Keniston takes pains to distinguish his young radicals from the merely alienated, who more closely resemble Reich's ideal type.

There is little reason to interpret Inglehart's data as evidence for the emergence of any of the above types. In fact, now that the student movement has died and campus pressures for radical change have ended, the academic community is beginning to develop a new image of emerging American youth. Protean man has been replaced by narcissistic man.[87] We are almost back where we began in the 1950s, when the prevailing image was that of a silent conformist generation of students. But whereas 1950s students were castigated for their zealous pursuit of the *means* of acquiring happiness (money and status), today's youth are reproved for their concern with immediate gratification. These changing evaluations leave the impression that estimates of the psychological health of young people are often inversely proportional to their participation in approved forms of political activism.[88]

The joint work of Haan, Block, and Smith has been cited widely as providing the most systematic and sophisticated support for the notion of a liberated generation. Its influence derived primarily from the use of a scale of moral development created by Lawrence Kohlberg. As Fishkin, Keniston, and MacKinnon noted, when they attempted to replicate the work of Haan and her co-workers:

> In the more than 300 empirical studies of student activists, no single result is more impressive than the finding of Haan, Smith and Block . . . that level of moral reasoning was intimately related to participation in the Free Speech Movement sit-in in Berkeley in 1964. . . . Nowhere in the literature can so striking a relationship be found between a single personality measure and observed student activism.[89]

Such a finding would indeed be impressive. If there is a clear relationship between radicalism and moral development, radicals may well represent a different—and perhaps superior—breed. Before examining this evidence, however, we shall discuss Kohlberg's test of moral reasoning, for the interest in such empirical research presupposes this instrument's validity.[90]

Kohlberg's test consists of a series of stories posing moral dilemmas, followed by questions designed to elicit the subject's resolution of each dilemma and, more importantly, the reasons on which the resolution is based. A typical story involves a man who steals a drug he cannot afford to prevent his wife's dying of cancer. Follow-up questions concern the drug owner's rights, obligations to relatives vs. nonrelatives, and judgments about the "rightness" of the husband's decision and the appropriate punishment for his theft. The test tries to measure the form or "calculus" rather than the substance of moral reasoning. In this respect it is intended to be content-free.

Kohlberg classifies responses into categories that he conceives of as developmental stages associated, though imperfectly, with increasing age. The two lowest stages are termed "premoral" or "preconventional." Only the second of these is found among college students. It is characterized by egocentric instrumental thinking of the type, "You scratch my back, I'll scratch yours."

Stages 3 and 4 are those of "conventional" moral reasoning. In Stage 3 judgments, the emphasis is on obedience to rules because one wants to be thought of as a "good" girl or a "good" boy according to the conventional norms of the society. Stage 4 judgments are oriented toward obeying communal authority and maintaining social order. It is aptly termed the "law and order" stage.

Kohlberg's first four stages are relatively unexceptional. His fifth and sixth stages, however, have created greater controversy. Both involve reference to "higher universal principles" that may conflict with societal conventions. In this sense they are "postconventional." A Stage 5 person sees rules as necessary for maintaining the "social contract" and derives their worth from utility, in the sense of promoting individual well-being. The emphasis is on the obligation to respect individual autonomy insofar as possible. Stage 6, the highest stage, is that of "individual principles," an orientation toward "abstract concepts of equity, universality and justice. . . . The unifying character of Stage 6 moral reasoning is its universalism, its insistence on the inclusiveness of all moral formulations. . . ."

Despite the widespread popularity of Kohlberg's scheme (and his program of formal education in moral reasoning) his approach has a number of methodological problems. Not the least of these is a relative lack of studies enabling one to test the validity of Stages 5 and 6 by comparing them with behavioral measures. Part of the problem stems from the scoring system's complexity and occasional lack of clarity. In fact, it has been changed many times, and one must apply to Kohlberg directly to obtain copies. Most validation studies seem to have been completed by Kohlberg himself, his students, or individuals who sympathize quite strongly with his approach.

Even these limited studies raise important questions. One finds very few Stage 5 or 6 types, and with some exceptions the two highest stages contribute little to the test's ability to predict behavior.[91] In general, the best predictions in nonpolitical situations have come when the scale was simply divided into low and high scorers (i.e., Stages 1 and 2 as against all those above).

A far more significant criticism can be leveled against this approach. His test is intended to examine the form or "calculus" of moral reasoning rather than the substance of particular moral judgments. Supposedly, it gives researchers access to an important personality dimension that is independent of sociopolitical ideology. Haan and her co-workers strongly imply that there is no political content in the Kohlberg scoring system. Fishkin and his associates expand upon this point:

> The high correlations observed between moral reasoning and radicalism . . . are the more striking because of the disparity between the two kinds of data. Kohlberg's dilemmas pose hypothetical situations that are political only in the broadest sense of probing the kind of core ethical structures . . . that are seen as determining the social-moral order. Moral reasoning scores are derived not from the substance of the individual's conclusions but from the structure of his moral argumentation. . . . High correlations with political ideology indicate a high correspondence between two distinct indices of each subject's functioning.[92]

This assertion is ultimately unconvincing, because its rationale begs an important point. Although the problems and scoring may not be political in a narrow sense, they have a definite political slope. That is, individuals applying general philosophic attitudes (which include a political component) to the solution of given moral problems would, by definition, score at different levels of moral development. For instance, a Burkean conservative is relatively likely to manifest a strong orientation toward "showing respect for authority and maintaining social order for its own sake," thus scoring at Stage 4. Liberals who hold a Lockean view of society would be likely to manifest a "contractual" legalistic orientation that would place them at the "social contract" stage of moral development. On the other hand, radical students socialized by upper-middle-class Protestant or Jewish parents into a world-view derived from Ethical Culture or even "Marxist humanism" would certainly be more likely to score at the stage of "individual principles," which are "logically universal and consistent," when confronted with such a paper-and-pencil problem. In short, Kohlberg has essentially transformed broad ideological stances into psychological categories.[93]

There is yet another issue to be considered. We have argued that such paper-and-pencil tests may measure how people think they should act rather than how they actually behave. Moreover, when such discrepancies occur, sophisticated individuals can rationalize behavior so that it seems to square with professed principles.[94]

Having raised some basic questions about Kohlberg's work, we can return to Haan, Block, and Smith's study of the relationship between moral reasoning and radical politics. These researchers began with an overall sample of over a thousand young people, compiled from random samples of the student bodies at California-Berkeley and San Francisco State College and contact samples of campus political activists (including Free Speech Movement arrestees) and California-based Peace Corps trainees. Their data were collected over the three-year period 1965–67. Response rates varied widely, falling as low as 20 percent for San Francisco State College activists.[95]

From this heterogeneous group, Haan and her co-workers selected 510 subjects who could be assigned to "pure" moral types on the basis of their responses to Kohlberg's test. Of this subsample, 5 percent scored at a "premoral" level of moral judgment, three quarters scored at "conventional" levels, and the remaining 22 percent at "principled" levels. The data analysis focuses upon the differential representation of protesters at the highest and lowest levels of moral reasoning. The authors' principal conclusion was that these data "show strong associations between political protest, social action, and principled reasoning—qualified by the finding that premoral men also protest—and that young people of conventional moral reasoning are inactive."[96]

Keniston regards this "curvilinear relationship" between level of moral reasoning and protest as "probably the most striking single finding in the entire activism literature."[97] The concentration of protesters at Stages 5 and 6 is not especially interesting, we have argued, given the test's conflation of moral judgment with political ideology. In fact, Haan and her co-workers report that the "principled morality" groups are differentially agnostic or atheistic and politically radical, and come from nonreligious, politically liberal homes. The "conventional morality" groups are more politically conservative and religious, and come from strongly Protestant or Catholic, politically conservative, less-educated families. Is it really surprising that the latter groups are more likely to judge moral dilemmas in terms of socially approved roles or maintaining law and order?

The clustering of protesters at the "premoral stage," on the other hand, seems more intriguing. Yet Haan and her co-workers go to some length to minimize the importance of this finding. They speculate that "political-social protest and premoral reasoning are probably not consistently linked across many samples," although they do not similarly question the linkage between principled reasoning and protest. They suggest that Stage 2 protesters may have "regressed" morally as a result of the "stress and moral conflict" produced by their protests. Finally, they assert that this "regression" is itself evidence of an openness to experience and change, implying that even premoral protesters are more open to "growth" than are "conventional" subjects who "protect themselves from disharmonies."[98]

Beyond this, it is not clear that the authors' conclusions accurately reflect their data. They imply that many more radical activists are Stage 6 types than are Stage 3 types. Yet even a cursory analysis reveals that the group contained about the same proportion of "premoral" and "principled" respondents.

Of course, their entire data analysis is rather rudimentary. Few students scored at either the lowest or highest stage, and the causal issues involved cannot be addressed without a more complex statistical analysis. But this does not affect our criticism that the authors accentuate those trends in their data which reflect favorably on the student Left.[99]

Finally, a 1970 study by Fishkin, Keniston, and MacKinnon provides an interesting counterpoint to the contention that protest might be more consistently linked to principled than to premoral reasoning.[100] In an effort to replicate the California findings, Fishkin and his co-workers administered the Kohlberg test and political ideology scales to seventy-five undergraduates at eight major American universities (no attempt at randomization was made). They found that radicalism was positively related to *premoral* reasoning, negatively related to conventional reasoning, and unrelated to principled reasoning. In other words, the association of radicalism with *principled* reasoning disappeared. Fishkin and his associates also differentiated between "violent" and "peaceful" radical attitudes. They found that violent radicalism was positively related to premoral reasoning, but neither measure of radicalism was significantly related to principled reasoning.[101] As expected, conventional "law and order" reasoning was negatively related to both measures of radicalism.

Yet these researchers were no more eager than Haan's group to draw negative conclusions about '60s activists. They offer two explanations for the poor showing of radicals on the Kohlberg test: First, by 1970, the New Left's turn toward violence had changed the Movement's recruitment base, with premoral students joining as the earlier principled radicals dropped out. Second, in their efforts to escape the confines of conventional morality, some radicals regress to the "angry, 'anything goes' orientation characteristic of early childhood." Both explanations minimize the incompatibility of these data with earlier research portraying radicals as psychologically liberated. Unfortunately, neither is supported by empirical evidence.

The notion of a changing recruitment base seems plausible. It echoes Mankoff's and Flacks's[102] assertion that an expanding social movement had attracted more diverse psychological elements, diluting the influence of the liberated vanguard. Mankoff and Flacks, however, presented no psychological data in support of this assertion.

In any case, this argument is ill-suited to the data of Fishkin and his co-workers, since they measured political attitudes rather than behavior. Even if principled students had dropped out of the Movement in response to increasing violence, this should not affect the relationship between moral reasoning and radical *attitudes*. Yet even adherence to peaceful radicalism was virtually unrelated to prir.·ipled moral reasoning. Indeed, peaceful radicalism was more strongly correlated with the lowest states of moral development (premoral and role-conformity reasoning) than with the highest stages (social contract and individual principles), although neither relationship was statistically significant. Moreover, violent radical attitudes were more strongly correlated with principled reasoning than were peaceful radical attitudes. So the "changing recruitment base" explanation appears inconsistent with the results of the Fishkin study.

The apparent slight shift from principled to premoral responses by radicals in the later study may in fact stem from changes in the New Left's social composition. But one might attribute less profound psychological significance to changing recruitment patterns than do Flacks and Keniston. By 1970 large segments of many campuses had been radicalized, and the upper-middle-class Protestants and Jews who had dominated the American Movement during the early 1960s had been swamped by middle- and lower-middle-class types who had not been trained by their parents to offer the "appropriate" humanitarian solutions to the problems posed.

The explanation of "regression" suffers from a similar lack of evidence. Both the Haan and Fishkin research groups raise the possibility that radicals are more likely than others to regress (perhaps temporarily) in their moral reasoning. Neither present any evidence on this point, though. This unsupported hypothesis seems intended to cast a more favorable light on the association between radicalism and premoral reasoning. Thus Haan, Block, and Smith argue that "the stress and moral conflict of the FSM crisis and other Bay Area protests" differentially affected those young people "most open to experience" and hence, "more vulnerable to temporary or permanent regressions."[103] And Fishkin and his co-workers treat this hypothesis as an unqualified certainty.

The only evidence that late adolescents may undergo temporary regression of this sort appears in a seriously flawed study conducted over several years by Kohlberg and Kramer.[104] The number of initial subjects studied was very small, and some of them dropped out of the study. Further, the inference of a general phenomenon of temporary "moral" regression has not been supported by later research. In a review of the Kohlberg scale literature, Hoffman concluded that

there appears to be no evidence as yet for Kohlberg and Kramer's view of temporary regression. . . . Furthermore, there appears to be no evidence that cognitive structural or stage concepts are needed to explain the findings. It may simply be true that if an individual is confronted by evidence for relativism and the fact that his prior moral values do not fit the real world, his prior values will be undermined, thus creating a void of meaning. To fill this void he may search for new values, which, for some individuals, entails selecting from an array of available ideologies.[105]

In sum, the researchers seem to want it both ways. If radical students score at the postconventional level of moral reasoning, it is because they adhere to higher standards than nonactivists. If, on the other hand, their scores are preconventional, it is because they have temporarily regressed. We cannot help but wonder what conclusion would have been drawn had right-wing activists scored predominantly at level two. We suspect it would have been seen as a sign of arrested moral development.

Thus the key studies of student radicals completed during the 1960s and early 1970s tended to be contaminated by ideological bias. This bias derived largely from the fact that radical students and those who studied them shared common assumptions about the relationships among child-rearing patterns, personality, and political action.

This tendency toward "contamination" is not limited to social and political contexts. The recent work of Nisbett and Wilson indicates that it is a more general problem. Reviewing a wide range of experimental studies, they conclude that, in general, individuals are unable to recognize or accurately describe the mental processes that motivate their own behavior. Indeed, "the accuracy of subjective reports is so poor as to suggest that any introspective access that may exist is not sufficient to produce generally correct or reliable results. . . . when people attempt to report on their cognitive processes, . . . they do not do so on the basis of any true introspection."[106]

We believe that those who studied the New Left deceived themselves in this fashion. Such self-deception is not new. In the 1920s white Anglo-Saxon Protestant psychologists were still administering "objective" tests that "demonstrated" that various minority groups were less healthy than white Anglo-Saxon Protestants.[107]

We are more sophisticated now, but perhaps not that much more. We have already pointed out that many in the New Left were the ideological or even biological children of those who created the tests to study them. Indeed, some of those who studied the movement were themselves part of it. The best-known example is Richard Flacks, a founding member of SDS who at one point worked out of an office in Tom Hayden's basement.[108]

It is not impossible to rise above prejudgments even if one is so involved. Many of those who studied the student movement, however, could not make the transition from interested participant to disinterested observer. As Richard Blum pointed out at the time,

> When [social scientists] and clinicians undertake to evaluate today's . . . students, they are often looking at people very much like themselves. . . . [Their] "liking" reactions probably reflect preferences for people . . . acting more as . . . they thought people ought to act.[109]

3   Radical Jews:
The Dilemmas of Marginality

MOST COMMENTATORS on the student movement of the 1960s thought it represented something quite new. Indeed, many argued that it had been brought into existence by the emergence of a "post-industrial society," of which the student Left was the cutting edge. Some of the same observers stressed generational differences.

These young people were seen as the children of liberal upper-middle-class parents who had created a home environment characterized by both affection and democracy. As a result they refused to accept both the authoritarian features of American society and its racism. Rather, they were fighting to democratize America: to synchronize its values with its own aspirations and the requirements of a new epoch.[1]

In retrospect it seems clear that the New Left did represent the cutting edge of some very important shifts in American and European society, although not with quite the predicted consequences. To stress the newness of the Movement, however, is to miss some key elements in the backgrounds and motivations of its participants.

To begin with, Americans of Jewish background were disproportionately represented among the leadership and cadres of the Movement until the mid-1960s. At the time they constituted under 3 percent of the population of the United States, and about 10 percent of the students at colleges and universities. Yet, they provided a majority of its most active members and perhaps even a larger proportion of its top leadership. They also provided a very significant proportion of the intellectual community's most vocal supporters of the student movement.

Many of these young people came from liberal or radical families. Some of their parents had been quite active on the Left during the 1930s but later toned down their political activities while retaining their basic value orientations. As early as the 1962 Washington peace demonstration, students of Jewish background constituted over 40 percent of those participants whose religious background could be identified.[2] Perhaps more significantly, the early SDS was heavily Jewish both in its leadership and its activist cadres. Key SDS leaders included Richard Flacks, who played an important role in its formation and growth, as well as Al Haber, Robb Ross, Steve Max, Mike Spiegal, Mike Klonsky, Todd Gitlin, Mark Rudd, and others. Indeed, during its first few years, SDS was largely funded by the League for Industrial Democracy, a heavily Jewish socialist (but anti-communist) organization.[3]

SDS's early successes were at elite universities containing substantial numbers of Jewish students and sympathetic Jewish faculty, including the University of Wisconsin at Madison, Brandeis, Oberlin, and the University of California at Berkeley. SDS leaders were not unaware of their roots. As Robb Ross put it, describing the situation at the University of Wisconsin in the early 1960s,

. . . my impression is that the left at Madison is not a new left, but a revival of the old . . . with all the problems that entails. I am struck by the lack of Wisconsin born people [in the left] and the massive preponderance of New York Jews. The situation at the University of Minnesota is similar.[4]

Fellow SDSer C. Clark Kissinger confirmed Ross's observations in his reply: "As you perceived, the Madison left is built on New York Jews."[5]

The same was true elsewhere. When the Free Speech Movement erupted at Berkeley, a majority of the FSM steering committee was Jewish, as was half the membership. During the pivotal sit-in at the Berkeley Administration building, a Chanukah service was conducted, and the Hatikvah was sung.[6] Sixty-three percent of the Chicago radicals studied by Flacks and his associates were of Jewish background.[7] Similarly, in Richard Braungart's 1966 survey of leading SDS activists, 60 percent of those whose religious background could be identified were Jewish.[8] In Joseph Adelson's early 1960s research into politics and personality at the University of Michigan, fully 90 percent of the radical subjects had Jewish backgrounds.[9]

At many schools, Jewish predominance continued into the late 1960s. In a national survey sponsored by the American Council of Education in 1966–67, the best single predictor of campus protest was the presence of a substantial number of students from Jewish families.[10] Schweitzer and Elden reported that approximately 50 percent of California's mid-1960s Peace and Freedom party was Jewish;[11] Berns and his associates found that 83 percent of a small radical activist sample studied at the University of California in the early 1970s was of Jewish background; and Thomas Piazza discovered that, as late as 1971, only 25 percent of non-Jewish freshmen at Berkeley considered themselves to be on the left, compared with 58 percent of Jewish freshmen.[12] Nationwide, a 1970 Harris survey reported that 23 percent of all Jewish college students termed themselves "far left," compared to only 4 percent of Protestant students and 2 percent of Catholics.[13]

Until very recently, the role of Jewish students in the upheavals of the 1960s was generally underestimated. This seems to have resulted partly from either reticence or simple oversight by those who studied the Movement. For example, Flacks reported that 40 percent of his radical respondents were Jewish, after his original sample had been "adjusted" to obtain better balance.[14] Braungart reported that 40 percent of his sample was of Jewish background, but this figure did not include participants who described both themselves and their parents as atheists. We discovered that a very large proportion of such young people came from Eastern European or German backgrounds. Further analysis revealed that the overwhelming majority of radical students from these countries whose religion or religious background could be ascertained were Jewish.[15]

Jewish influence on the emergence and growth of the student movement extended far beyond its youthful cadres. Especially in its early days, the presence of some liberal supportive faculty members was crucial to the relative success of the movement at a given school.[16] As Ladd and Lipset have shown, Jewish faculty were far more likely to offer that support than were their non-Jewish colleagues.[17] Jews played a similar role in creating some sympathy for student activists among the broader public, owing to their key role in the American cultural establishment during the 1960s.

By the late 1960s, the demographic composition of the student Left had undergone significant changes, as it spread to non-Jewish segments of the population. This marked the beginning of the real generation gap. Radical Jewish students tended to come from liberal if not radical homes. While their parents might express some opposition, often on tactical grounds, they were generally quite supportive. Indeed, many Jewish parents spoke with pride of their "revolutionary" children. During the 1968 Columbia upheavals, Mark Rudd's mother commented: "My revolutionary helped me plant these tulips last November, my rebel." Rudd, in turn, according to the same New York *Times* story,

> speaks of his parents with respect and affection, and they maintain that they are "100 percent behind him," even though they don't agree with all his views. On Mother's Day (during the riotous period at Columbia) his parents went to the Columbia campus and bought a veal parmigiana dinner, which the family ate in their parked car on Amsterdam Avenue.[18]

Among non-Jewish radicals the pattern was rather different. Many came from quite conservative families, against whom they were in sharp rebellion.[19] Further, the SDS grew more receptive to organized political violence as its non-Jewish contingent grew in size and influence. Although Jewish students might engage in some "street violence," they were unlikely to go beyond using their fists, rocks, or clubs. As Sale points out, many non-Jewish members were a rather different breed:

> These were people generally raised outside of the East, many from the Midwest and Southwest . . . more violent, more individualistic, more bare-knuckled . . . than that of the early SDSers. They were non-Jewish, nonintellectual, nonurban, from a nonprofessional class and often without any family tradition of political involvement, much less radicalism.[20]

Some of them, like Dotson Rader, were openly fascinated by violence, though even Rader grew disturbed by their talk of blowing up members of the "liberal" Establishment. He reports that, in the final days of the Movement, some cadres were not above "ripping off" money ostensibly raised for the cause.[21] And in a few cases, the result was murder barely masquerading as social purpose. Annie Gottleib described one young man who killed a police officer for being a "pig":

> But . . . Charlie Simpson is never quite more than just one of those disturbed kids who latched on the ideas of the movement as expressions of their own inarticulate troubles and seized its occasions and excuses for cathartic violence.[22]

Thus the student movement in the United States changed somewhat as it spread from its initially Jewish base to a wider constituency. The spread of radicalism (and this particular type of radicalism) to non-Jewish students in the United States certainly did mark a watershed in the American historical experience. However, the radicalism of those young Americans of Jewish background, who were so instrumental in creating the Movement and providing an initial critical mass, was not new. Rather, whatever the ideological differences between them and a previous generation of Jewish radicals, they were part of a tradition that began much earlier.

Since the middle of the nineteenth century, Jews have acted as a powerful radical leaven in both Western and Eastern Europe, as well as in countries of

European settlement, including the United States. With their release from European ghettos under the aegis of the Enlightenment, they joined in various bourgeois revolutions (usually on the Left) in numbers far out of proportion to their percentage of the population. Later, they became active among the cadres, leadership, and intellectual supporters of socialist and/or communist parties. During the revolutionary upheavals of 1848, Jews played a very prominent role among those calling for a democratic (or even socialist) republic in Germany. In France during roughly the same period, they all but dominated those groups responsible for disseminating and propagating the work of Saint-Simon. And they played important roles in the beginnings of the Socialist International.[23]

Marx, of course, was of Jewish background, though his parents converted to Christianity. So was Ferdinand Lassalle, a key figure in the founding of the German Social Democratic party. By the late nineteenth century the role of Jews in such movements had become sufficiently significant to warrant comment by scholars as well as anti-Semites. As Robert Michels pointed out in his classic *Political Parties,* Jews at that time were playing a key role in socialist parties in almost every European country in which they had settled in any numbers.[24] While Jews also played a minimal (if noticeable) role in conservative movements, their natural position was on the Left, in Germany and elsewhere.[25]

The Jewish role in the German Left reached a high point in the aftermath of World War I. The Spartacist movement had a heavy Jewish component that included Rosa Luxemburg and Paul Levi. Kurt Eisner briefly led a left-wing revolutionary government in Bavaria.[26]

Jews were also prominent in the radical wing of the Socialist party and in the formation of the German Communist party, although the advent of Bolshevization and "proletarianization" drove them from the latter. Nevertheless, they continued to play a major role in the Social Democratic party. Eduard Bernstein contended that 10 percent of the delegates to party conferences in the early 1920s were Jews. Of the 153 Socialists elected to the Reichstag in 1928, at least 17 (11 percent) were of Jewish background, although Jews constituted less than 1 percent of the German population.[27]

Even more substantial, though, was the role played by Germans of Jewish background in the "nonattached" radical group of journalists, intellectuals, and producers of culture in the Weimar Republic. The most famous of these groups was the circle of intellectuals associated with *Die Weltbühne,* a radical journal whose satirical critiques of German social and political life were quite influential among a much larger segment of Germans during the 1920s. Istvan Deak has calculated that of the sixty writers for *Weltbühne* whose religious background could be ascertained, forty-two were of Jewish descent, two were half Jews, and only twenty-four were non-Jews. Of the latter, three were married to Jewish women.[28]

The great majority of German Jews were moderate or liberal in their politics, and some were quite conservative. Thus, in dealing with the role of Jewish intellectuals, we are concerned with a relatively small proportion of the Jewish community. Furthermore, most Jews on the Left were "deracinated," in that they no longer considered themselves to be part of the Jewish community. Nevertheless, this relatively small group exercised considerable cultural influence during the Weimar period and was very much in the public eye.

As Deak points out, Jews played highly significant roles in those aspects of literary and artistic movements critical of traditional German society.

> Apart from orthodox Communist literature where there were a majority of non-Jews, Jews were responsible for a great part of leftist literature in Germany. *Die Weltbühne* was in this respect not unique; Jews published, edited, and to a great part wrote the other left-wing intellectual magazines. Jews played a decisive role in the pacifist and feminist movements, and in the campaigns for sexual enlightenment.
>
> The left-wing intellectuals did not simply "happen to be mostly Jews" as some pious historiography would have us believe, *but Jews created the left-wing intellectual movement in Germany* [emphasis added].[29]

The predominantly Jewish writers associated with *Weltbühne* despaired of the timidity of the Social Democrats, even as they attacked the rigidity of the Communists. In the later years of the Republic, they tended to stress the need for unity between the two for a revolutionary policy. Most importantly, however, they violently attacked everything about German society. They despised the military, the judiciary, and the middle class in general.

Perhaps the best-known writer of the *Weltbühne* circle was Kurt Tucholsky, whose biting satire made him a hero of the more cosmopolitan segments of the German middle class. The son of a successful Jewish businessman-lawyer, Tucholsky flayed Germans and German values mercilessly. By the late 1920s, he had decided that Germany was hopeless and that most middle-class Germans were either idiots or positively evil.[30]

Germans of Jewish background dominated another important group of intellectuals during the Weimar period, the Frankfurt-based *Institut für Sozialforschung,* whose leading members became collectively known as the "Frankfurt School." This roster included some extraordinarily distinguished and influential figures, including T. W. Adorno, Max Horkheimer, Erich Fromm, Herbert

Marcuse, and Walter Benjamin. With the exception of Karl Wittfogel, who left the Institute rather early to become an anti-Marxist conservative, all the initial members were of Jewish background. (Adorno was half-Jewish.)[31] Paradoxically, perhaps the most important and creative work of Institute members was completed during their exile in the United States. Their greatest direct influence in both Germany and the United States occurred during the 1960s, when the writings of Adorno, Horkheimer, and Marcuse became widely known. Indeed, Marcuse became something of a guru for the New Left in both America and Germany.

Most members of the Frankfurt School were the sons of successful businessmen. The founding spirit of the Institute, Felix J. Weil, was the only son of a German-born merchant who had migrated to Argentina and amassed a sizable fortune in the grain business. It was Weil's father who provided the initial endowment for the Institute. In most cases, the families of Institute members had little sense of identification with the Jewish community. In fact, with the exception of Erich Fromm, most did not think of themselves as Jews.

From the beginning, Institute members exhibited considerable diversity in their political and philosophic views. All were strongly influenced by Marx, however, and were initially quite sympathetic toward the Soviet Union. By the late 1920s, their commitment to orthodox Marxism had eroded somewhat, as a result of both developments in the Soviet Union and the failure of the German working class to exhibit revolutionary consciousness.

Especially after the Nazi conquest of power, which led to their exile, members of the Institute engaged in an effort to revise Marxism to take into account its failure to deal adequately with contemporary developments in Germany and the Soviet Union. In so doing they attempted to combine elements of Marxism and psychoanalysis, and thereby to give more credit to both volition and culture in explaining social change. By and large, they retained their hostility to capitalism, predicting its inevitable collapse or degeneration into totalitarianism while hoping for the emergence of a socialist society that would permit the fuller development of human potential. Their experiences in the United States eventually led to further diversification of their views. Some ultimately adapted to American culture and society and developed non-Marxist reformist orientations. Others, however, remained quite critical, although from rather different stances. Both Horkheimer and Adorno returned to Germany after the war, having become quite pessimistic about any amelioration of the human situation. Before they died, both broke with the New Left and, in turn, were rejected by its adherents. Marcuse, on the other hand, remained in the United States, alternating between optimistic and pessimistic appraisals of the possibility of transforming society in a humanistic socialist direction.

All contributed in very important ways to making American social science more cosmopolitan, as did other German Jewish scholars. As we have already noted, *The Authoritarian Personality,* overseen by Horkheimer and Adorno, had major impact on American social science by identifying some traditional American social values with an authoritarian personality structure. And a whole generation of college-educated Americans was deeply influenced by Erich Fromm's argument, in *Escape from Freedom,*[32] that National Socialism was the natural outcome of the interplay between a Protestant sensibility and the contradictions inherent in capitalism. In a number of widely read books published during the 1940s and 1950s, Fromm continued to stress the irrational and alienating features of capitalism, even as he suggested that the advent of "humanistic" socialism would allow human beings to establish the loving relations of which they were inherently capable.[33]

The influence of the Frankfurt School in the United States did not stem merely from the quality of these scholars' work. Their orientation harmonized with certain developing themes in American culture. Just as importantly, the work of Fromm and others was introduced at a time when Americans of Jewish background were beginning to play key roles in an academic and communications network whose influence was steadily growing.

The role of Jews as a radical leaven in German social and political life was paralleled by their role in the pre–World War I Austro-Hungarian empire, and then in postwar Austria and Hungary. In perhaps no other part of Europe did Jews play so striking a role in the cultural, economic, and radical political life of the society. This was especially true around the turn of the century among the relatively large Jewish communities of Vienna and Budapest, but it was also true of other communities with Jewish populations.[34]

The Viennese Jewish community was both prosperous and extraordinarily influential in the sphere of high culture.[35] It also provided a good portion of the intellectual leadership for both cultural and political radicalism. Thus, while the bulk of Jewish voters probably supported liberal parties, Jewish intellectuals played a key role in the Austrian labor movement and in the Austrian Socialist party.[36]

Most of these intellectuals were deracinated Jews who had more or less broken with their religious heritage. Most also came from middle-class backgrounds. What Francois Fejtö has said of Jewish radicals in Hungary applies equally to socialist Jews in Austria: "the grandfathers were capitalists, the sons liberals, and the grandchildren professed socialist ideas."[37] The Austrian Social Democratic party was founded by Victor Adler, a deracinated Jew from a well-known Prague Jewish family, and the party paper was edited by Friedrich Austerlitz, a Moravian Jew. Other prominent Jews in the party leadership included Wilhelm Ellenbogen, Otto Bauer, Robert Dannenberg, and Max Adler.

In many respects, the background and orientation of these intellectual and political radicals are typified by Adler. Brought up in a nonreligious atmosphere in an upper-class home, he embraced the idea of assimilation to German culture very early in life. He became a Protestant in 1878, although he remained quite sensitive about his Jewish background throughout his life. During his leadership of the Austrian Socialist party, Adler remained an assimilationist, rejecting Zionism out of hand and refusing to become especially concerned with Jewish questions per se. Indeed, Adler sometimes refused to criticize anti-Semitic outbreaks, for fear of right-wing charges that the party was dominated by Jews.[38]

In the truncated Austria that emerged after World War I, the Social Democrats were a major force, and Vienna was their greatest stronghold. During this period Otto Bauer, another Jew of middle-class background, played a key role in the leadership of the party. While the great majority of Jews were not actively political, they continued to play an important role among Socialist party cadres and voted for its candidates in larger numbers than did other segments of the population.[39]

The Socialist party's decline and the emergence of a conservative clerical regime led to a gradual worsening of the position of the Jews in Austria. After the 1938 *Anschluss,* those who had not fled were subject to ever-increasing harassment and, eventually, to genocide.

If Austria had allowed for the emergence of a large well-to-do Jewish middle class, the situation of Jews in pre–World War I Hungary had been even more favorable. Situated in a multi-ethnic kingdom, Jews were beneficiaries of a general tolerance toward the various ethnic constituencies. Indeed the Magyar government, which represented a minority of the country's population, sought Jewish help in their relations with other ethnic groups long before the "compromise" of 1867. In 1848, the Magyar Diet abolished most residential restrictions on Jews, and full emancipation came after 1867. By the turn of the century Jews had achieved considerable success in both the commercial and cultural life of Budapest.

Nor were Jews barred from political office. At least twelve Jews held the rank of State Secretary in the government prior to the Revolution of 1918. And Jews who converted to Christianity found the path to the highest political offices open.[40]

As in Austria, however, the Left attracted the bulk of political activists of Jewish background. Béla Kun, the leader of the short-lived Hungarian Soviet Republic of March–August 1919, was Jewish, as were thirty of the forty-eight People's Commissars in his revolutionary government. Most managers of the new state farms were also Jewish, as were the bureau chiefs of the Central Administration and the leading police officers. Overall, of 202 high officials in the Kun government, 161 were Jewish. Jews remained active in the Communist party during the Horthy regime of 1920–44, dominating its leadership. Again, most were from established, middle-class (or, at worst, lower-middle-class) backgrounds. Hardly any were proletarians or peasants.[41]

Most of the Hungarian Jewish community was massacred during World War II. By the end of the war only about 140,000 remained alive of a community that had numbered 725,000. Nonetheless, the leading cadres of the Communist party in the postwar period were Jews, who completely dominated the regime until 1952–53. Then a series of purges, stemming in part from Stalin's anti-Semitism, eliminated many of them. Jews were also active in other parties, including the Social Democrats, before such parties were crushed by the Communist regime. Their role was most significant, however, within the Communist party. The top membership of the new Communist regime, including the secret police, during its first years was almost entirely Jewish. The wags of Budapest explained the presence of a lone gentile in the party leadership on the grounds that a "goy" was needed to turn on the lights on Saturday.[42]

Once again, these were largely deracinated Jews who had little or no sense of their Jewish background and little or no sympathy for their Jewish compatriots. Indeed, the remnants of the Hungarian Jewish middle class suffered considerably during their reign, as did Jews in other political parties. Most of the Jews in the party leadership were Stalinists by temperament as well as conviction. As Richard Burks notes, ". . . they did not let mercy or other humanitarian considerations stand in their way when it came to dealing with the class enemy."[43] Their rule was Draconian, dominated by terror and characterized by the extensive use of the secret police.

Jews were on both sides of the 1956 Hungarian revolution. Many old-line Stalinists feared the possibility of retribution should a noncommunist or more liberal communist regime come to power. On the other hand, many Jewish writers and intellectuals were in the forefront of the reform movement.[44]

The Jewish role in the Communist parties of most other Eastern European countries has been comparable to that of Hungary. In Poland, limited statistical evidence indicates that Jews voted for the Communist party in numbers far larger than would be expected, given their proportion of the population. The Communist party of Greece received over 15 percent of the Jewish vote in both

1928 and 1933. By contrast, non-Jewish residents of Salonika, where most Jews were concentrated, gave only 1.3 percent of their vote to the Communist party in 1928. In 1933, the figure rose to 7.2 percent, still less than half the proportion among Jews.[45]

It was among the cadres of Communist parties, however, that Jews had the greatest influence. Official party sources place the Jewish proportion of Polish party cadres at 25 to 30 percent during the prewar years. Some observers, however, estimate the actual proportions as high as 50 percent. (Jews constituted approximately 10 percent of the population of Poland.)[46] It should be added that, since party membership at the time was no more than about 5000, the sheer number of Jews involved was quite small. In Lithuania about 54 percent of the party cadres were Jewish.[47] Salonika Jewry played a major role in the foundation of the Greek Communist party and remained prominent until the early 1940s. Similar patterns prevailed in Rumania and Czechoslovakia.

Jews played quite prominent roles in the top and second echelon leadership of the communist regimes in all of these countries in the immediate postwar period. They were often associated with Stalinist policies and were strongly represented in the secret police. In Poland, for example, three of the five members of the original Politburo were Jewish and a fourth, Wladyslaw Gomulka, was married to a woman of Jewish background. In both Rumania and Czechoslovakia, at least two of the four key figures in the Communist party were of Jewish background.[48]

By the 1960s Jewish influence in East European Communist parties and state apparatuses had become minimal, although the pattern varied somewhat from country to country. The fate of the surviving Jewish community also varied. In Poland, Czechoslovakia, and Rumania a substantial portion of the remaining Jewish community had emigrated by the 1970s. In Poland and Czechoslovakia, its departure was hastened by the regimes' willingness to tolerate anti-Semitism under the guise of anti-Zionism.

We lack the data to document the role of Jews in the political Left of other European countries and countries settled by Europeans. The Polish Jews of London's East End did provide a base for Jewish radicalism at the turn of the century. But there exists little systematic information about their role since then (although a 1960s study of British teachers indicates that Jews are farther to the left than any other religious group in the teaching population).[49] We also lack systematic information from France, although Jewish students played an important role in the leadership of the 1968 student revolt.[50] They also voted in disproportionate numbers for radical parties in pre–World War II Holland.[51] Jews of Polish background played an important role in the founding of the Cuban Communist party, and there are scattered indications of their significance in left-wing parties and groups in other Latin American countries.[52] Jews were also prominent in the formation of Communist parties in various North African countries.[53]

Finally, Jews have played a key role in the American Left since the turn of the century. Indeed, Arthur Liebman has argued that, until recently, Jews effectively *were* the American Left.[54] Before we turn to the American pattern, however, we shall briefly describe the role of Jews in Russia and the Soviet Union. We do so in part because of the intrinsic importance of this phenomenon, but also because the American Jewish community consists largely of immigrants from the old Russian empire.

By the 1870s, about five million Jews resided in Russia, constituting 4 percent of the population. The great bulk of the Jewish population was confined to the so-called Pale of settlement, an area consisting of ten Polish and fifteen adjoining Russian provinces.[55] Unlike Jews in the West, most were still deeply immersed in a traditional diaspora culture. They also lived at the very margin of subsistance. Their dire economic condition was the result of Russia's relative backwardness, their own traditional orientations, and, not least, discrimination by the Czarist regime. They suffered not only from poverty but also from physical terror. They were repeatedly subjected to both spontaneous and officially encouraged pogroms in which thousands died.

The position of Jews improved somewhat during the reign of Alexander II. After Alexander's assassination in 1881, however, many of his policies were reversed, and a new period of oppression began. There is also evidence that the economic situation of most Jews deteriorated at this time. One response to renewed persecution and economic hardship was mass migration to the United States.

Within the Russian Pale of settlement, Jews were rapidly becoming an urban people. During the late nineteenth century, they migrated in increasing numbers to larger cities. Unlike many transplanted peasants, however, most did not find work in the large factories that characterized Russian industrialization. Rather, they remained primarily artisans and small tradesmen. Those who did engage in factory work tended to move into small factories run by Jews in marginal sectors of the economy such as the clothing industry. Urbanization did, however, weaken the hold of traditional communal religious authorities, and Jews increasingly came into contact with the major secular currents of Russian and European ideas.

The initial impact of these ideas was greatest among economically successful Jews and their children, around whom a new intelligentsia began to coalesce. As in other European countries, a substantial segment of the emerging Jewish intelligentsia rejected their ethnic backgrounds as they came to identify with radical ideas and movements. They left the Jewish community and thought of themselves as cosmopolitan reformers or radicals dedicated to universalistic social change. Indeed, many held the Jewish masses in contempt for their traditional and reactionary ways. Their hope was to join with non-Jewish intellectuals to overthrow a repressive social order. Others, retaining their Jewish identity, hoped to modernize Judaism, drawing upon the ideas of the German Reform movement. Many of these, too, had absorbed very negative attitudes toward poor, less educated Jews. They despised the Jewish community for its "petty" materialistic concerns and its "parasite" status.[56]

It is hard to document the precise extent of Jewish participation in the Russian revolutionary movements of the late nineteenth century. Most authorities, however, feel that arrest figures for "subversive" activity provide at least a rough measure. According to the official reports, 13 percent of those who stood trial on such charges between 1884 and 1890 were of Jewish background. Between 1901 and 1903 the proportion of Jews rose to 29 percent.[57]

We do know that Jewish individuals were prominent in almost every radical movement that emerged, from the Socialist Revolutionaries to the Bolsheviks. The creation of Land and Liberty, one of the first socialist groups founded in Russia, owed much to M. A. Natanson. Pavel Axelrod was instrumental (along with Plekhanov) in organizing the Group for the Liberation of Labor. Gregory Zinoviev and Lev Kamenev worked closely with Lenin from the formation of the Bolshevik faction. Before 1917, however, Jewish participation was highest among the Mensheviks. At the 1907 Menshevik Party Congress, for example, one hundred delegates, about one third of those present (if one includes delegates from the Jewish Bund), were of Jewish background.[58] Many of these were intellectuals from middle-class or artisan backgrounds who had broken sharply with their cultural traditions.[59] When Trotsky was asked whether he considered himself a Russian or a Jew, his reply was paradigmatic: "No, you are mistaken! I am a social democrat and that's all."[60] Even socialists like Martov, who recognized that Jews in Russia were faced with particular problems, nonetheless regarded themselves as assimilationists.[61] In the long run, they believed, the "Jewish question" would be dissolved by socialism. Lieberman, the most nationalistic of the early Jewish socialists, who proudly affirmed his own Jewishness even as he set out to spread socialism among the Jews, still believed that the only solution lay in a secular socialist society that would end the differences between Christians and Jews.[62]

On the other hand, many Jewish intellectuals whose ultimate goal was assimilation nonetheless felt that Russian Jews faced special disabilities which necessitated a special defense of their interests. Partly for this reason, a number of labor and socialist organizations gathered in 1897 to form the "Bund" and to dedicate themselves to working among the Jewish masses, relying heavily upon Yiddish, the language of the Russian Jewish people. Their decision was based on pragmatic grounds as well. They had attempted to work among the non-Jewish masses, usually with little success:

> Very often someone would send along a bottle of *monopolke* [whiskey]. They would pour it into tea glasses and drink it down like a glass of water. I had to drink along with them, otherwise I would have not been a "good brother." I hoped that I would be able to make them class conscious. In the end neither of us achieved anything. They could not make me a drunkard and I could not make them class conscious.[63]

The Bund became perhaps the most powerful organization among Russian Jews, although not among Jewish intellectuals. At its peak it reached a membership of 40,000, and its organizational efforts among workers and youth groups affected a far larger number of Jews. With the emergence of Zionism, it found itself emphasizing Jewish rights perhaps more than its founders had intended, although eventual assimilation probably remained the ultimate goal for most of the leaders.[64]

Both the Mensheviks and Bolsheviks opposed the Bundist program, although both eventually compromised with it to some extent. Lenin was especially adamant about what he considered the more nationalistic aspects of the program. The Jews were not a nation, he argued, and the emphasis on Jewish culture could only serve reactionary purposes. At the same time, he was sympathetic to the historical plight of the Jews. He also recognized their revolutionary potential.[65] Lenin confided to his sister that, while the Russians were too easy-going and tired too easily of the revolutionary struggle, the stubbornness and fanaticism of Jews made them excellent revolutionaries. This was perhaps one reason, as Adam Ulam suggests, that Lenin refused to entertain seriously the desire of some Jews for a federated party. He was unwilling to abandon direct control over Jewish revolutionaries to a semi-independent organization.[66]

With the success of the Revolution, Jewish intellectuals (including ex-Bundists and ex-Mensheviks) flocked to the Bolshevik party, where many quickly rose to positions of leadership. At the Party Congresses of 1917 and 1922, some 15 to 20 percent of the delegates were Jewish. Of twenty-one Central Committee members in August, 1917, six were of Jewish origin.[67] One of these was Leon Trotsky, who ranked far above all party members save Lenin himself in prestige. Jews also flocked to other government posts, including the secret police, the Cheka, and its successors, the GPU, the OGPU, and the NKVD. As late as 1937, well after many of the early Bolsheviks (including Trotsky's supporters) had been read out of the party, 11 percent of 407 Cheka officials decorated by the party had recognizably Jewish names.[68]

Of course, most Jews were not politically active. Many were seriously injured by the Revolution, and many others fled the country. Among those who had been dispossessed was Trotsky's father, who came to Moscow in the vain hope of obtaining aid from his son. As the Chief Rabbi of Moscow was supposed to have said in 1920: "The Trotskys make the revolution. The Bronsteins pay the bills." (Bronstein was Trotsky's real name. Like many other Bolsheviks, he had taken on a non-Jewish pseudonym.)[69]

During the 1920s Jews formed about 5 percent of the Communist party's membership, roughly two-and-one-half times their proportion of the population in the diminished Russian state. They were far more heavily represented in the administration, especially in non-Great Russian areas. In the Ukraine, for example, in 1927, Great Russians and Jews each held roughly one fifth of the official posts. Lazar Kaganovich, a Jew and a close collaborator of Stalin, was given the assignment of pacifying (by force) the often rebellious Ukrainians.[70]

By the late 1930s the role of Jews in the party had been considerably reduced. Many Jewish party members sided with Trotsky against Stalin and found themselves in labor camps or in front of firing squads. There is little evidence to indicate that Stalin relied on overt anti-Semitism to defeat Trotsky. But party members were aware that Trotsky and many of his supporters were Jewish, and many preferred one of their own kind, even if he was a Georgian.

The proportion of party cadres who were of Jewish background continued to drop in the 1940s and 1950s. By 1970 there were only five Jewish deputies in the Supreme Soviet and only one on the Central Committee. In part this reflected the feelings of Soviet leadership that underlying anti-Semitism in the populace made it unwise for Jews to play a dominant role in leadership cadres.[71]

Stalin seemed to share some of the anti-Semitic prejudices of the second generation of Communist party leadership, even though a number of those very close to him were of Jewish background (including a sister-in-law, a daughter-in-law, and, for three years, a son-in-law). These feelings seem to have become more pronounced as he grew older.

The great mass of Soviet Jews remained relatively nonpolitical during the Stalinist period. For them, life in the Soviet Union has been a very mixed experience. Since the late 1940s, the Soviet Union has been increasingly anti-Zionist and distrustful of Soviet Jews who express sympathy for Israel. The regime has been especially harsh toward Jews who wish to emigrate, and on occasion its anti-Zionism has come perilously close to anti-Semitism. Partly as a result, one assumes, Jews have recently constituted a significant portion of the Soviet Union's dissenting intellectuals.

Jewish immigration into the United States first reached significant proportions in the 1850s, with most of the immigrants drawn from Germany. The migrants increased throughout the 1840s and 1850s and included many middle-class Jews who had been disappointed by the failures of continental liberalism. Although halted temporarily by the Civil War, the German Jewish migration did not drop off until the 1880s. The Jewish population of the United States was estimated at 15,000 in 1840, 50,000 in 1850, 150,000 in 1860, and 250,000 in 1880.[72]

By the late nineteenth century, German Jews had achieved considerable success in the New World, at least relative to other migrant groups. While most Irishmen were still day laborers in the 1880s, only one in eight German Jews was a manual worker. Half were in business, 20 percent were clerks or accountants, 10 percent were salesmen, and 7 percent were either white-collar workers or professionals. Of course, classification as businessmen was not necessarily a sign of economic success, for the category includes small shopkeepers and peddlers operating on the margins of the economy. However, the fact that 40 percent of German Jewish families had at least one servant indicates that many were "making it."[73]

Many German Jews at the time voted Republican. On the other hand, some joined the small Socialist Labor party, founded in 1877, most of whose 2,000 members were of German background. The head of the S.L.P. in the 1880s and 1890s was Daniel deLeon, a Sephardic Jew originally from the West Indies. DeLeon attempted to conceal his Jewish background, pretending that he was descended from an aristocratic family of Catholic background.[74]

By the turn of the century, a mass migration of Jews from Russia and Eastern Europe to America was well under way. Between 1880 and 1925, when new restrictive laws went into effect, about three-and-one-half million Jews entered the United States, mostly from these areas.

Eastern European Jews possessed far fewer skills than the Germans who had migrated earlier. Many were illiterate, and most with urban backgrounds had been employed in marginal occupations. Thus the image of intellectually oriented, educated Jews who could easily transform their skills into an American success story is something of an exaggeration. What Jews did possess was a passion for learning and a desire that their children learn. Max Gordon, the Broadway producer, has described his family thus:

> Of culture in my house there was none. No one in my home had any impelling drive toward serious music, or art or reading. Aside from the daily Yiddish newspaper that my father read after dinner, aside from the prayer books read by my father and mother, there was no other reading in the home. *That seemed to have been left to me.* As the baby of the family, with none of the responsibility for helping to support the household, I was the one whose schooling was important. . . . By my tenth year I had become an omnivorous if indiscriminate reader, a regular visitor to the library on Grand Street and the happy discoverer of the Educational Alliance.[75]

Initially their prospects seemed bleak. Crowded into tenements in the northeastern ports where they had landed and settled, speaking a foreign tongue, and skilled primarily in highly competitive and marginal industries (such as the garment industry), they found their very existence to be precarious. In these circumstances, the rapidity with which Jews achieved economic success, both in absolute terms and relative to other religious or ethnic groups, is little short of astonishing. Part of their success stemmed from the rapid rise of wages in the clothing industry. More importantly, however, many immigrants succeeded in creating successful businesses of their own. Their children enlarged these or moved into the professions. By 1931 only 10 percent of second generation Jews were laborers, compared to 31 percent of second generation Italians. By 1937 7 percent of gainfully employed foreign Jews and 19 percent of native-born Jews were employed in the professions. By 1953, some 66 percent of New York Jews were in nonmanual occupations, and by the late 1950s Americans of Jewish background boasted the highest per capita income of any religious group in the United States.[76]

The period after World War II, especially, was a time of advance. Before then Jews had moved into the entertainment field, dominating Hollywood, and had begun to move into medicine, the sciences, academia, journalism, and cultural life in general. By the 1960s, they were disproportionately represented in most professions having to do with the creation or dissemination of culture. Describing New York City in 1960, Sam Welles pointed out:

> . . . perhaps a third of the City's art galleries are Jewish owned or managed. In the theatre, Jews are prominent as owners, directors, playwrights and actors. They have been leaders in radio and television from

the earliest days of these media. In music they have enriched the city with special abundance.[77]

As Jews spread out from New York in the postwar period, they began to play the same role elsewhere. As Alvin Toffler noted:

> . . . although there is no statistical data that even attempts to ana-lyze the racial or religious background of the arts public, conversations with gallery directors, orchestra managers, and other art administrators in many cities lead one to conclude that the culture public contains a higher than proportionate number of Jewish people. Jews, of course, have always been prominent as artists. . . . The extension director of a University of California, in discussing the rising level of cultural ac-tivity in Los Angeles, cites the growth of the Jewish population as the causative agent. A museum director in San Antonio says: ''The vast majority of collectors here are Jewish.'' In Dallas, the arts attract con-siderable support from the Jewish community.[78]

Their role was especially pronounced in the mass media and the academic professions. Although Jews today constitute less than 3 percent of the Ameri-can population, a 1976 study found that 25 percent of the Washington press corps were of Jewish background.[79] Earlier studies estimated that 58 percent of television news producers and editors at ABC television were of Jewish descent.[80] In a study completed in the 1960s, Muriel Cantor found that almost half of the Hollywood producers of prime time television shows were of Jewish background.[81] In addition, a study of media critics of film, literature, television, and radio revealed that, while Jews were only 10 percent of the total population of critics, they constituted 32 percent of the ''influential'' critics, i.e., those with major national reputations.[82] Finally, a 1979 study found that 27 percent of those working for the most influential media outlets (the New York *Times,* the Washington *Post,* the *Wall Street Journal, U.S. News and World Report, Time, Newsweek,* the three television networks, and PBS) were of Jewish back-ground.[83]

Jews became equally prominent in academia, especially in the social sci-ences. A 1968 study found that Jews accounted for 9 percent of all college and university teachers and more than twice that proportion (20 percent) at ''elite'' schools. Moreover, they comprised 25 percent of all social scientists at elite colleges and universities and 30 percent of those who published heavily.[84] Thus Jews were not only disproportionately represented in the academy; they were most heavily represented in its most prestigious and socially influential sectors.

In the legal profession, a similar profile emerges. By the mid-1960s one in five lawyers in the United States was of Jewish ancestry. Jews also constituted 12 percent of the faculty of law schools in the United States and, more importantly, about 38 percent of the faculty at elite law schools.[85]

Jews still tended to be underrepresented (given their education and qualifications) in the top ranks of heavy industry and in Wall Street law firms, although this too was changing. Part of this lack of representation was undoubtedly a function of continued anti-Semitism. However, as Dennis Wrong has noted, some of it was a matter of cultural style:

> More or less accurately, non-Jews in these circles (academic, professional and intellectual) are apt to attribute to Jews such traits as intellectuality, political liberalism, intense parental solicitude with close bonds between mothers and sons, strong attachments to the extended family, a liking for food and physical comforts in general, volubility and emotional expressiveness, fear of violence and ironic humor.[86]

Perhaps more importantly, as Nathan Glazer suggests, Jews are still less likely than non-Jews to seek careers in large bureaucratized business organizations. They prefer to be their own bosses in business or to seek out intellectual or social service jobs. When they go into law practice, many today seek positions in "reformist" public interest law firms or in government agencies rather than in firms catering to large corporations.[87]

In sum, Americans of Jewish background have become an elite group in American society, with a cultural and intellectual influence far beyond their numbers. Writing about the "Eastern Establishment," Thomas Dye lists a number of symbolic figures to which this establishment looks. Four of seven listed are of Jewish background.[88] Whether or not one accepts Dye's classification, it is clear that the culture of diaspora East European and German Jewry has had a powerful impact upon the United States.

It is equally clear that Americans of East European Jewish background have played a key role in the American Left throughout this century. For long periods of time they dominated American Socialist and, later, Communist parties; they kept alive the remnants of a radical tradition during the 1950s; and they provided a "critical mass" for the New Left until the mid-1960s, when its social base began to broaden. Today they remain more liberal on most issues than the population as a whole, despite the fact that their economic status and social position would seem to dictate otherwise.

The first hard evidence of Jewish involvement with the American Left is the endorsement of Henry George by the Jewish Worker's Verein in 1886. There is some evidence that their support contributed substantially to his electoral strength. In any event, by the 1890s the Socialist Labor party was receiving from 5 to 18 percent of the vote in New York's heavily Jewish districts, while its vote in the rest of the city rarely rose above 2 percent of the electorate. Similar patterns prevailed in other cities. Thus by the turn of the century East European Jews played a substantial role in both the rank and file and the leadership of the organization.

The same pattern characterized the Socialist Party of America. Until 1918 the SPA drew its greatest relative strength from non-Jewish areas of the country. Nonetheless, Jews already dominated the party's organization, aside from the very top leadership (i.e., Eugene Debs and his immediate followers). By 1920 Jews constituted the main prop of both the party leadership and cadres, a position they maintained through the 1960s. They tended to avoid the very top leadership positions, however, lest attempts to develop a broader base be weakened. Their role in the American Communist party would soon follow the same pattern.

As in most European countries, the Communist party in the United States arose out of the schism that followed the Russian Revolution and the creation of the Comintern. From its inception, Americans of Jewish background played a key role in the Communist party. During the 1920s they constituted about 25 percent of rank-and-file members, competing for numerical dominance with Finnish immigrants. (At that time, the party also drew heavily from other immigrant groups and from certain marginal segments of the working class, such as loggers in the northwest.) Jews were even more heavily represented among the leadership cadres. Key figures such as Benjamin Gitlow, Jay Lovestone, Alexander Bittleman, and many others were of Jewish background.

By the 1930s the Jewish role in the party had increased dramatically. Jews now constituted fully half the party's membership, according to estimates by Melech Epstein and others.[89] Their predominance continued as party membership declined during the 1940s and 1950s. Indeed, when the Department of Justice completed a study of the ethnic origins of 5,000 known communists in the 1940s, the report noted that 56.5 percent had at least one parent who had been born in Russia or a country adjacent to Russia.[90]

As the role of Jews in the party increased, its working-class base shrank. This was partly the result of the loss of non-Jewish working-class support. It also reflected the fact that many Jewish unions, such as the International Ladies Garment Workers, had become militantly anti-communist.[91] Moreover, an ever larger segment of the Jewish population was becoming middle class. And the college-educated children of immigrants were more likely to remain radicals than were working-class Jews. The reasons are not difficult to ascertain. By and large, working-class Jews were more likely to retain some Jewish identification and to become Zionists (and, later, supporters of Israel). A much larger proportion of middle-class Jews were anxious to break with their ethnic heritage. As Irving Howe put it, writing about an earlier generation of radicals:

> Rebelling against the parochialism of traditional Jewish life, the Jewish radicals improvised a parochialism of their own—but with this difference: they called it "universalism." In one leap they hoped to move from yeshivas to modern culture, from shtetl to urban sophistication, from blessing the Sabbath wine to declaring the strategy of international revolution. They yearned to bleach away their past and become men without, or above, a country.[92]

Indeed, when instructed to change their names for party purposes, most American Jewish Communists chose non-Jewish pseudonyms.

From the 1930s through the 1950s, Jews were quite active in the party leadership. Almost half the Communist leaders tried for violation of the Smith Act in 1947 were Jewish. In the 1940s, the editor of the *Daily Worker*, the managing editor, and the labor editor were all of Jewish background. The publicly visible top leadership, however, was non-Jewish.[93] It seems clear that this represented self-conscious decisions by party cadres to broaden the party's appeal and, conversely, to reduce the likelihood of an anti-Semitic backlash, by concealing the extent of Jewish predominance.

Beyond this, Allen Weinstein's study, *Perjury*, seems to indicate that Jews constituted a substantial majority of known members of the Soviet underground apparatus in the United States during the 1930s. Soviet agents whose backgrounds were probably Jewish include J. Peters, Lee Pressman, Harry Dexter White, Marian Bachrach, Hedda Gompertz, and many others.[94]

Many studies demonstrate the large role played by Jews in providing voting support for the Communist party. They also indicate that Jews were the mainstay of the American Labor party, which for a time was a major Communist party electoral vehicle. Americans of Jewish background also provided one third of the votes for Henry Wallace's Progressive party in 1948.[95]

To be sure, many Jews who voted for Wallace were "progressives" rather than communists, and the great majority of American Jews had no connection with the Communist party. Even among noncommunist Jews, however, sympathy for various radical ideas was far greater than among other segments of the population. In 1946, some 32 percent of Jewish respondents, as against 13 percent of non-Jews, expressed "warm" feelings toward the Soviet Union; 15 percent of non-Jews described their feelings as "frigid," compared to only 3 percent of Jewish respondents.[96]

Jews also tended to be far more supportive of the civil liberties of radicals than did other groups. In Samuel Stouffer's well-known study of civil liberties (which actually studied attitudes toward the civil liberties of leftists and other opponents of nativism), Jews were about twice as likely as non-Jews to permit an anti-religious speaker to speak, or a socialist teacher to hold his job.[97]

Within the intellectual and artistic communities, Jews were also far to the left of their non-Jewish colleagues in the 1930s and 1950s, and far more active in supporting communist or "progressive" causes. As Jews moved into the professions, government service, the media, and academia, they served as a radical leaven for these groups and for the ever larger number of Americans coming into contact with them. By the 1930s Jews were beginning to replace Protestants as the writers for radical or liberal publications. Intellectuals such as Mike Gold and Joseph Freeman, both the sons of immigrant Jewish workers, helped introduce many non-Jewish writers to Marxism.[98] In the academic community, they served the same role for their students. A 1956 study of academic voting found that approximately 30 percent of Jewish academics had voted for the Progressive party in 1948. The comparable figures for Protestant and Catholic academics were 3 and 5 percent, respectively.[99]

Jewish students played a similar role. The American Student Union, the most prominent radical student group during the 1930s, was heavily concentrated in New York colleges and universities with large Jewish enrollments. And on other campuses, such as the University of Illinois, substantial portions of its limited membership were students of Jewish background from New York City.[100]

Jewish commitment to the Communist party and other left-wing causes stemmed partly from the depression and partly from concern over anti-Semitism and fascism. After all, the radical parties (especially the Communists) were, until 1939, the most effective fighters against both these pernicious doctrines. In that year, the nonaggression pact between Germany and Russia disillusioned many Jewish radicals. Others had become disillusioned far earlier. During the 1930s, Stalinists, Trotskyites, and other revolutionary socialist groups fought each other perhaps more violently than they fought the capitalist system. The combat resembled a civil war, partly because the combatants shared a common ideological background, but also because so many came from the same ethnic background.

Right-wing groups here and abroad actively publicized the role of Jewish radicals during the 1930s. But most Americans who were aware of the facts played the issue down, lest it contribute to anti-Semitism. The unwillingness to deal with Jewish radicalism (except by Jews) continued through the 1960s. To mention the role of Jews in left-wing movements seemed to many, in light of the Holocaust, to open the doors to a renewal of fascism. It was only in the mid-1970s, after traditional anti-Semitism had greatly receded in the United States, that the subject of Jewish radicalism began to be discussed with some openness.

The 1950s were difficult times for both Jewish and non-Jewish radicals. The cold war, the Korean War, the increasingly anti-Israeli stance of the Soviet Union, and the purges of Jewish Communist party leadership in Eastern Europe all took their toll. These were followed by Khrushchev's revelations of the "crimes" of Stalin, the Hungarian rebellion, and the Soviet invasion of Hungary. Many who had in the past admitted weaknesses in the Soviet regime had also pointed to what they considered its unique humane accomplishments. Now these seemed of little account, compared to the regime's record of ruthlessness. Domestic prosperity during the decade and increased opportunities for social mobility for Jews and other Americans also weakened the Left, as did the anti-Communist nativism of Joe McCarthy.

Their comparative public silence did not mean that all Jewish radicals and progressives had changed their minds. While they concentrated on careers, they made sure that their children received a "progressive" education. Politics was widely discussed at home. And where possible, young people were sent to certain select private schools and particular universities. Even the children of the less affluent found support for their ideas among the liberal and radical Jewish teachers in the New York public high schools. These schools were certainly not dominated by Jewish radicals or even cosmopolitan liberals. Nonetheless, there were sufficiently large numbers to ensure that young people hostile to the Establishment would not feel completely isolated.[101]

In a sense, many Jewish radicals and progressives used the period of silence to regroup and reexamine their views of the world. The loss of the Soviet model and the continued prosperity of capitalist America seemed to indicate that classical Marxism, as conventionally interpreted, was no longer adequate. New approaches had to be developed. They came to fruition in the 1960s, as new problems emerged in the American scene. Marx could be reinterpreted in ways that emphasized his earlier "humanist" writings, and the work of the Frankfurt School could be used to establish the new socialist humanism.

Thus the loss of the Soviet ideal was both devastating and liberating. Their new freedom from the bonds of Soviet policy allowed Jewish radicals to direct their barbs against evils of "Amerika" without having to defend the practices of any particular socialist regime. Further, accusations by conservatives that they were in the service of Moscow lost much of their effectiveness.

Some Jewish radicals and progressives employed in teaching, television, and the motion picture industry lost their jobs or were blacklisted during the 1950s. Most were not so seriously affected, although they were inhibited from expressing their political views in public. By the early 1960s, however, McCarthyism was dead, and Jews were even more heavily represented in the knowledge professions than they had been a decade earlier. They clearly dominated the political culture of New York, where their style and views had been adopted by relatively large numbers of non-Jewish intellectuals. They also became increasingly influential in other cosmopolitan centers such as Chicago, San Francisco, Los Angeles, and Berkeley. In all these cities, they played an important role in educating non-Jews to a more cosmopolitan perspective.

Nevertheless, until the late 1960s Jewish academics were still considerably more liberal than their non-Jewish colleagues. In 1968, for example, Jews constituted 9 percent of the faculty at American colleges and universities. According to Ladd and Lipset's study of the academic community, however, they constituted 20 percent of the most "liberal" faculty, and 35 percent of those liberals who published most heavily (20 or more articles). Among social scientists, ethnic Jews constituted 12 percent of all faculty members and 35 percent of liberals who published heavily. On the other hand, Jews constituted only 1.7 percent of heavily published conservative social scientists.[102]

The pattern was even more pronounced at elite colleges and universities. At these schools, ethnic Jews comprised 20 percent of all faculty members, 30 percent of the most liberal, and 40 percent of the liberal faculty who published heavily (compared to less than 10 percent of the heavily published conservatives). Here, too, their influence was strongest in the social sciences. Jews constituted 25 percent of the social science faculty at elite schools, and over 40 percent of liberal faculty who published heavily, but only 8 percent of conservatives who published heavily.[103] A somewhat similar pattern was found in the nation's law schools, where Jewish academics defined themselves as being on the left twice as frequently as their non-Jewish colleagues.[104]

Striking as these figures are, Ladd and Lipset's data probably understate the influence of Jews on American intellectual life. Because they used college or university endowment as a key variable, a number of engineering schools, at which Jewish representation was much smaller, were included in their elite sample, along with Harvard, Columbia, Berkeley, etc.

Many of these Jewish faculty passed their values on to their children, who helped provide the critical mass for the student movement of the 1960s. For example, in the 1968 Lipset-Ladd study some 56 percent of Jewish academics with college-age children reported that their offspring had taken part in protest demonstrations, as compared to 22 percent of their non-Jewish peers.[105] In our own research, described in Chapter 6, we found the children of Jewish academics to be by far the most radical group studied, much more so than the children of non-Jewish academics.

Jewish academics also played an important role in persuading a much larger public of the merits of 1960s student activists. A very significant proportion of the key studies of the student movement were conducted by scholars of Jewish background, using instruments developed by scholars of Jewish background. We have already pointed out the weaknesses of some of these studies. We suspect that many of the "truths" established in other areas of the social sciences during this period suffer from similar weaknesses. Their widespread acceptance (many are now part of the "conventional wisdom") may have had as much to do with the changing ethnic and ideological characteristics of those who dominated the social science community as they did with any real advance in knowledge.

We noted earlier the curious inversion that occurred in American politics during the 1960s. Before then, people with college educations tended to be somewhat more conservative than those who had not attended college. Today, in key areas involving the new liberal cosmopolitan orientation, the reverse is true. In light of the other data we have presented, it seems plausible that the influence of liberal cosmopolitan Jews in academia during the period from 1940 to 1960 played a significant role in this shift.

Within academia, Jewish faculty sparked revolts against the "establishment" in their professions, struggling to turn them in the direction of direct radical political action. In the American Political Science Association, for example, the membership of the Caucus for a New Politics, a radical activist group, was initially overwhelmingly Jewish.[106] (Jews were also heavily represented on the "liberal" opposition *Ad Hoc* Committee, but here they constituted no more than about half of a highly fluctuating and informal membership.)[107]

The same pattern emerged in the Modern Language Association, where the radical caucus was led by Louis Kampf and Paul Lauter, both of Jewish background. The Union of Radical Political Economists also initially contained a disproportionate number of individuals of Jewish background.[108] While William Appleman Williams, the dean of the group, was not Jewish, a majority of the leading cold war revisionists among historians were (Alperowitz, Kolko, Horowitz, etc.).[109] The largest number of those radical educators and writers on education who argued that American education was linked to capitalism's need to keep the lower classes (including blacks) in their place were also of Jewish background (e.g., Herbert Gintis, Donald and Beatrice Gross, Jonathan Kozol, Edgar Z. Friedenberg, Herbert Kohl, Charles Weingartner, Gerald

Weinstein).[110] The same was true in sociology, where, in the middle 1960s, the leading radical sociological journal, *Transaction,* was edited by Irving Louis Horowitz and Alvin Gouldner.[111]

Of course, the role of Jews was not confined to academia. Radical and progressive Jews were also prominent among a wider group of intellectuals whose influence was rapidly increasing. Jews figured prominently in the leading liberal and radical journals of opinion, sometimes as editors or publishers, more often among the contributors to magazines like *The Nation, The New Republic, Ramparts,* and *The Progressive.* Perhaps the most important of these was the *New York Review of Books,* which turned decisively to the left in the mid-1960s. Since that time, the *New York Review of Books* was edited by Robert Silvers and Barbara Epstein, and the bulk of its political contributions (especially articles on American politics) in the mid-1960s was written by Jews.[112] By and large, then, as Tom Wolfe has pointed out, "radical chic" in New York was a heavily Jewish phenomenon, and the influence of such people spread well beyond their own circle.[113]

To be sure, the major opposition to the New Left, both inside and outside the academic community, also came from intellectuals of Jewish background. During the late 1950s, the new editor of *Commentary,* Norman Podhoretz, took the lead in reintroducing a radical sensibility into American politics. For example, he published sections of Paul Goodman's *Growing Up Absurd,* after it had been rejected by a number of publishers. By the mid-1960s, however, Podhoretz and *Commentary* had become part of a new intellectual movement which was later to be labeled "neo-conservative," although not all its members would accept that appellation. Podhoretz was joined in his battles with the New Left and the "new liberalism" by such prominent Jewish intellectuals as S. M. Lipset, Nathan Glazer, Irving Kristol, and Daniel Bell, who became associated with *The Public Interest,* initially edited jointly by Kristol and Bell.[114]

For Podhoretz and other New York intellectuals who joined him, the shift involved the breaking of old friendships and a bitter internecine ideological struggle. In New York and on many campuses, then, the most violent ideological clashes occurred between radical Jews and their Jewish neo-conservative opponents. Like the radicals, the neo-conservatives had read Marx, Freud, Max Weber, and Herbert Marcuse. Thus among Jews on college campuses this conflict took on all the bitterness of a civil war, as more traditional non-Jewish conservatives sat back in horror or bemused (and often confused) wonderment.

In part this ideological schism was linked to differences in Jewish identity. Many of the neo-conservatives identified themselves as Jews in terms of both ethnic ties and strong support for Israel. As the New Left moved toward identification with the third world, including the Arab cause, many Jewish radicals found themselves gradually taking a somewhat less radical stance. For example, Martin Peretz, who helped bankroll SDS, *Ramparts,* and other radical causes, had modified his position somewhat by the late 1960s. Nevertheless, for most of the decade, the tilt of Jewish intellectuals was clearly to the left, including some intellectuals of the Old Left who had once again captured the vision of the "pure revolution."

The disputes among Jewish intellectuals would have been relatively unimportant (as indeed they were during the 1940s) except for the now widespread influence of the national media, especially television, and higher education. In the 1960s the issues first broached in intellectual journals increasingly reverberated through the mass media, through university campuses, and, finally, through the decisions made by bureaucrats, judges, and legislators, even when such people were unaware of their original sources.[115]

The greater impact of ideas during this decade was partly a function of the increased social influence of intellectuals per se as educators of a far wider segment of the middle class. The impact of progressive Jews extended even further. By the 1960s, for example, they held many key posts in book publishing. Publishing houses with Jewish editors or owners were usually more open to progressive ideas than were their non-Jewish competitors. Indeed, this had long been the case, as Charles Madison has noted:

> [Jewish publishers and editors] have definitely stimulated the emergence of book publishing from its parochial and genteel smugness at the end of the nineteenth century and brought it into the sophisticated mainstream of world publishing. The Jewish publishers were predominant in encouraging American authors who had broken away from the restraints of Victorian conventions and were expressing themselves freely and creatively. . . .
>
> While the long established conventional publishers limited their lists to the works of traditional American and British authors . . . the Jewish publishers did not hesitate to bring out the writings of men and women considered radical or immoral or esoteric by their conservative competitors.[116]

In the early 1960s, firms like Random House, Alfred A. Knopf, Simon and Schuster, George Braziller, Grove Press (and, somewhat later, Atheneum and Academic Press) were more sympathetic to publishing progressive or radical authors than were most non-Jewish firms.[117] Of course, by the end of the decade the Jewish role had become less important, as an increasingly large non-Jewish middle-class audience was drawn to such books.

In addition, ethnic Jews played key roles in the national mass media.[118] In this profession as well, they were well to the left of their non-Jewish colleagues. The study of American elites conducted by Sidney Verba in the early 1970s found that Jews in the media (and especially television) were still more "progressive" than media personnel of other religious backgrounds, although by that point the differences were probably smaller than they had once been.[119] Data from an earlier study by Johnstone et al. indicate that 40 percent of the Jews employed by the national media rated themselves as "left" or "far left," more than four times the proportion among non-Jews.[120] Johnstone found that 10 percent of the staffs of radical 1960s "underground" periodicals were Jewish. However, at the leading exemplars of this genre, such as the *East Village Other*, the Los Angeles *Free Press*, the Berkeley *Barb*, and Detroit's the *Fifth Estate*, as well as "alternative" papers like the *Village Voice*, the key personnel were invariably of Jewish background.[121]

The role of Americans of Jewish background in television drama was equally pronounced. Michael Robinson and Ben Stein have pointed to the negative portrayals of businessmen, the military, and other "establishment" groups that characterized dramatic series and soap operas during the 1960s, as well as the counter-cultural themes that were openly introduced in such dramas.[122] Although Stein does not make the point directly, his interviews with television writers and producers suggest the importance of Jews in formulating the social imagery of television entertainment.

Describing the attitudes of drama writers and producers toward businessmen, Stein notes that they

> spoke of businessmen from AT&T or IBM in terms that contrasted their Gentile, Ivy League backgrounds with the more ethnic, "school-of-hard-knocks" backgrounds of the TV writers.

> There was a distinct feeling that, despite the high pay and the access to powerful media that TV writers and producers enjoy, they are still part of a despised underclass, oppressed psychologically and (potentially) physically by an Aryan ruling class of businessmen and others. This feeling was by no means confined to Jews.

> The belief in a ruling class of white, East Coast Protestants meeting occasionally in corporate board rooms to give its orders to whoever happens to be elected to office is so strong that no amount of argument to the contrary makes a dent. And hostility to that real or imagined class is just as strong.

The same pattern seems to prevail with respect to the military:

There is also at least a hint of ethnic animosity in the feelings of TV writers toward the military . . . the writers clearly thought of military men as clean-shaven, blond, and of completely WASP background. In the minds of a few of the people I interviewed, these blond officers were always a hair's breadth away from becoming National Socialists. They were thought of as part of an Aryan ruling class that actually or potentially repressed those of different ethnic backgrounds. But this was an opinion not widely held. . . .[123]

In their study of the opinions of Americans during the 1960s and 1970s, Lipset and Schneider point to a curious fact. While the views of the general public toward businessmen in general grew increasingly negative during this period, most Americans continued to report favorably on their *personal* contacts with business enterprises with which they dealt. The authors suggest that the media's emphasis on controversy explains the growth of distrust. They are certainly partly right.[124] As a recent study demonstrates, however, it is also clear that the hostility of prime time television writers toward business was reflected in these programs.[125]

Americans of Jewish background developed a direct and important influence on adolescents and even pre-adolescents in other ways. Starting in the 1950s, *Mad Magazine* developed wide popularity among this group, and, as Marie Winn had pointed out, it played a significant role in "the move toward free expression among children; its relentless exposure of parental dishonesty caused shock waves and reaction among its young readers."[126] From the beginning *Mad*'s editors have been Jewish and, as they themselves would agree, hostile to the American civic myth. To be sure, they were not completely supportive of the New Left, and, during the 1960s they satirized aspects of student protest. Nevertheless, as their admirers point out, they helped create the climate in which student protest flourished.[127]

Finally, during the 1960s ethnic Jews were key figures in the development of an "adversary" culture. They were prominently represented among the new breed of "radical" judges, in various Ralph Nader pro-consumer groups, and in progressive think tanks such as the Institute for Policy Studies.[128] Many of these progressive or radical groups were heavily bankrolled, at least initially, by a few small but influential foundations, such as the Stern Family Fund, the Rabinowitz Fund, and the Rubin Foundation.[129]

With the disappearance of the New Left in the 1970s, the United States seemed to have entered a period of relative social peace and political conservatism. But this did not produce a return to the political culture of the 1950s. Many important changes had taken root. For example, the faith of Americans in most of their institutions had seriously declined; most Americans accepted and supported far more active government intervention in the economy than they ever had before; and attitudes on sexual morality, the family, and drug use had changed dramatically. The greatest change occurred in the attitudes of the educated strata of society, who now were far more progressive (especially on social and cultural issues) than were their less well-educated compatriots.

On most social issues that divided Americans in the 1970s, such as the legalization of marijuana, abortion, prisoners' rights, expenditures for defense as opposed to social welfare programs, and so on, Jews remained considerably more progressive than non-Jews at every income level. As Everett Ladd points out, the gap remained almost as great as it had been prior to the turmoil of the 1960s. Thus the country as a whole has become more "liberal-cosmopolitan" and less supportive of traditional institutions, but Jewish Americans have retained their lead in most issue areas. We may legitimately regard them as the advance guard of the liberal-cosmopolitan sensibility, which dominates (rhetorically, at least) American culture on both the east and west coasts and has begun to penetrate America's heartland.[130]

During the 1970s, then, Jews continued to play active (if no longer decisive) roles in various movements associated with attacks on the traditional establishment. Thus Jeremy Rifkin headed the People's Bicentennial (or anti-Bicentennial), before turning to attacks on DNA research.[131] Several leading members of "Science for the People," which led the attack on both DNA research and sociobiology, are also of Jewish background.[132] Newspaper accounts of the activities of the Clamshell Alliance and gay power groups suggest that Jews continued to be disproportionately represented in a wide variety of counter-cultural or anti-Establishment organizations.[133] The same is true for the early days of the woman's liberation movement, judging from its spokespersons and publicists.[134] Some systematic data are also available on this issue. Carolyn Stoloff conducted a study of the backgrounds of those active in the woman's liberation movement among graduate students at the University of Michigan. She discovered that, of those whose religious background could be ascertained, almost 58 percent were Jewish. Among a comparison group, matched for year of graduate study and field of concentration, the proportion of ethnic Jews was under 10 percent.[135]

We would argue, then, that Pete Hamill's remarks concerning Jewish writing in America may be equally appropriate to a much broader context than literature:

the makers of Jewish American literature of the past 30 years, by celebrating the marginal man . . . have made irony the linchpin of the

American style, and a people that is ironic about itself can no longer kill strangers . . . rally to patriotic jingles or otherwise place its faith in princes.[136]

There is probably more truth than caricature in Glazer and Moynihan's description of the New Left "adversary culture" as a victory of a New York Jewish style over an older tradition.[137]

For most of the diaspora, Jews suffered from extraordinarily harsh persecution in European Christian society. By the nineteenth century their situation had begun to change. Although they continued to face serious disabilities in some countries, in others they had achieved considerable economic, cultural, and even political success. Whatever their situation, however, in almost every country about which we have information, a segment of the Jewish community played a very vital role in movements designed to undermine the existing order. This was true even in the United States, where Jews had achieved unparalleled economic, cultural, and social success.

By and large, those in the Jewish community most drawn to radical movements were deracinated Jews, from middle- or upper-middle-class families. How does one explain these facts?

On the eve of World War I, Robert Michels, attempting to understand the prominence of "bourgeois" Jews in European socialist parties, suggested that their personal experience of injustice had led them to a general opposition to injustice everywhere:

> The origin of this predominant position . . . is to be found, as far at least as concerns Germany and the countries of eastern Europe, in the peculiar position which the Jews have occupied and in many respects still occupy. The legal emancipation of the Jews has not there been followed by their social and moral emancipation. In large sections of the German people a hatred of the Jews and the spirit of the Jew-baiter still prevail, and contempt for the Jews is a permanent feeling. The Jew's chances in public life are injuriously affected; he is practically excluded from the judicial profession, from a military career, and from official employment. Yet everywhere in the Jewish race there continues to prevail an ancient and justified spirit of rebellion against the wrongs from which it suffers, and this sentiment, idealist in its origin, animating the members of an impassioned race, becomes in them more easily than in those of Germanic blood transformed into a disinterested abhorrence of injustice in general and elevated into a revolutionary impulse towards a gradually conceived world-amelioration.

Even when they are rich, the Jews constitute, at least in Eastern Europe, a category of persons who are excluded from the social advantages which the prevailing political, economic, and intellectual system ensures for the corresponding portion of the Gentile population. Society, in the narrower sense of the term, is distrustful of them, and public opinion is unfavorable to them. Besides the sentiment which is naturally aroused in their minds by this injustice, they are often affected by that cosmopolitan tendency which has been highly developed in the Jews by the historical experiences of the race, and these combine to push them into the arms of the working-class party. It is owing to these tendencies that the Jews, guided in part by reason and in part by sentimental considerations, so readily disregard the barriers which the bourgeoisie endeavors to erect against the rising flood of the revolution by the accusation that its advocates are *des sans patrie.* [138]

Other writers have appropriated the theme that Jews have been a marginal people in Christian society. Their marginality gives Jews a clearer perception of the evils of their society, produces an identification with other sufferers (the underdogs), and enables them to perceive new humanistic and universalistic alternatives to traditional parochial attachments. As three very different Jewish radicals have expressed this sentiment:

The vision of universal peace and harmony between all nations touched me deeply when I was twelve and thirteen years old. Probably the immediate reason for this absorption by the idea of peace and internationalism is to be found in the situation in which I found myself: a Jewish boy in a Christian environment, experiencing small episodes of anti-Semitism but, more importantly, a feeling of strangeness and of clannishness on both sides. I disliked clannishness, maybe all the more so because I had an overwhelming wish to transcend the emotional isolation of a lonely, pampered boy; what could be more exciting and beautiful to me than the prophetic vision of universal brotherhood and peace? [Erich Fromm] [139]

They lived in the margins or in the nooks and crannies of their respective nations. Each of them was in society and yet not in it, of it and yet not of it. It was this that enabled them to rise in thought above their nations, above their times and generations, and to strike out mentally into wide new horizons and far into the future. [Isaac Deutscher] [140]

It is the Jew who should always be on the side of the poor, the oppressed, the underdog, the wretched of the earth, because of the Jewish experience. And thousands of young ex-Amerikan ex-Jews are. Three of the kids killed at Kent State were Jews. An unusually high proportion of hippies and revolutionaries are Jews. Amerikan Jews are losing their kids at a faster rate than any other religious or social group 'cause young Jews are becoming hippies and yippies. [Jerry Rubin] [141]

Others have suggested that the nature of Judaism itself has contributed to Jewish liberalism or radicalism. Lawrence Fuchs argues that the Jewish Torah inculcates the values of learning, charity, and life's pleasures (nonasceticism). Thus, Jews tend to be drawn to intellectual endeavors, to be concerned with the poor and needy, and to emphasize the here and now, i.e., to be more receptive ". . . to plans for a better life, for reconstructing society . . . for socialism. . . ." [142]

Both these explanations seem rather self-serving. Jews appear as either victims or heroes, but in both cases the portrait is the obverse of that of the anti-Semite. Jews lack warts. Their motives are pure, their idealism genuine. In short, they seem to lack the unconscious aggressive drives one would expect to find among any group of individuals, particularly among those subjected to many centuries of oppression.

The explanations are unsatisfactory on other grounds as well. Charles Liebman has effectively undermined Fuch's argument. As he points out, traditional Judaism was communal rather than universalistic and ambivalent, at best, regarding "intellectuality." It contained important anti-philosophic elements, and the pattern of Talmudic exegesis is not to be confused with the system-building of modern "rationalistic" radicals or even of medieval Catholicism. Contemporary Jewish intellectuality is a post-ghetto phenomenon. Further, there is little evidence that the humane concerns of traditional Judaism were more pronounced than those of many other traditional religious creeds. Indeed, the more religiously conservative a Jew is today, the less likely he or she is to identify with universalistic ideologies or with the non-Jewish "poor and downtrodden." [143]

The marginality hypothesis, in the form developed by Deutscher and others, is not much more plausible. Marginality can broaden one's perspective, and intellectuals of Jewish background (as well as those from other marginal groups) have often contributed significantly to the understanding of their host cultures. They have done so by questioning cultural assumptions that those more deeply embedded in the society often accept as givens. On the other hand, marginality can also serve to narrow one's vision. The oppressed may see only the worst side of a culture or social system. Indeed, it is rational for them to do so. Excessive suspicion about the potential hostility of the dominant group, and behavior based on that suspicion, provides a better margin of safety than does a more generous perspective. Thus marginal or oppressed groups are as likely to exaggerate the negative features of a society as privileged groups are to exaggerate its good points.

Nor is there solid evidence that marginality increases humaneness. Freud felt that, on the contrary, Jewish history had produced some negative psychological results. In his essay, "Some Character Types Met with in Psychoanalytic Work," he discusses the "exception": the person who justifies his rebelliousness and claims to special favor to himself by some injury he has suffered and of which he considers himself blameless. Such people, Freud notes, often feel quite justified in injuring others. He refers to Shakespeare's Richard III as a prime example of the type.

In the midst of this discussion Freud notes:

> For reasons which will be easily understood I cannot communicate very much about these and other case histories. Nor do I propose to go into the obvious analogy between deformities of character resulting from protracted sickness in childhood, and the behavior of whole nations, whose past history has been full of suffering.[144]

As Theodore Reik points out, the reference is obviously to Jews.[145]

Marxists have rarely attempted to explore the sources of Jewish radicalism. However, Arthur Liebman (no relation to Charles) has recently developed a neo-Marxist interpretation of the tradition that calls for a somewhat more extended discussion.[146]

Liebman dismisses the theories described above on the grounds we have cited, and for other reasons as well. He stresses the fact that none of them can explain the behavior of all Jews. Why did some Jews not become radicals; why did others become Zionists? He maintains that any theory which cannot account for the behavior of all (or at least most) Jews is unsatisfactory.[147]

Liebman argues that the origins of Jewish radicalism in the United States must be understood in terms of the Jewish experience in Russia. After all, most American Jews emigrated from the old Russian empire, and Jews of German background in the United States were not noted for their radicalism.

The key to the Russian Jewish experience was the manner in which capitalism came to Russia and affected its Jewish population. Because Jews were confined to the Pale of settlement, and their choice of occupations was limited, they were especially hard hit by the new factories. Industrialization reduced their ability to compete as petty traders and artisans. It was their increasing poverty, then, that led Russian Jews to socialism.

The pattern continued in the United States, where Jews again found themselves an impoverished group operating on the margins of capitalism. In the

United States as in Russia, however, their sense of ethnic solidarity and ethnic oppression was an additional factor. This solidarity enabled them to create a set of self-sufficient community institutions that protected them from the outside world. Thus the Jewish community, unlike other communities of immigrants, was able to maintain a socialist institutional and cultural tradition.

Unfortunately, Liebman adds, a tension developed between ethnic identification and commitments to universalistic socialism or radicalism. When universalistic policies conflicted with ethnic imperatives, as in the case of radical critiques of Israel, Jews were torn in opposite directions, and their attachment to radicalism was weakened. Beyond this, the later economic and social success of Jews in the United States led them gradually to give up their radicalism and become absorbed by the mainstream of American life.

Liebman does not regard the New Left as a genuinely radical movement. Rather, he feels it emphasized cosmopolitan humanistic themes that could appeal to bourgeois middle-class liberals. In Liebman's view, then, the Jews' continued attachment to middle-class progressive liberalism stems from their concentration in the intellectual professions. He argues that Jews have not been engaged in exploitative relations with others, and hence lack a self-interested attachment to capitalist institutions. In the late 1960s the conservatism of middle-class Jews was indicated by their failure to support a liberal candidate like John Lindsay in New York when he campaigned for reelection.

Liebman is aware that his analysis of Jewish radicalism does not explain the political behavior of *all* Jews.

> Capitalism, it is important to point out, set the stage for Jews to move toward socialism, it did not *determine* this political direction for them. Jews *chose* to be socialists or pro-socialists. This choice was, of course, very much influenced by the nature of their socio-economic conditions but it was still a choice. Not all Jews, not all Jewish workers, and not all impoverished Jewish laborers made this choice. Some opted for nationalism or Zionism while others remained loyal to traditional Judaism or remained politically apathetic. The selection of political radicalism as one alternative out of several was typically made by only a minority. . . . [emphasis in original]

> It was this dedicated and gifted minority that constructed a Jewish left subculture and Jewish socialist organizations and parties.[148]

But this statement illuminates the weakness of his argument. After criticizing other theorists for failing to explain why some Jews became socialists and others did not, Liebman offers no explanation himself, beyond suggesting that Jews who became socialists were dedicated and gifted. In fact this criticism of other theories seems misplaced. No theory can hope to explain *all* the facts. We pick from among competing theories that which, among other things, explains the most facts with the fewest *ad hoc* generalizations. Thus our criticism of Liebman will not be complete until we have offered our own model of Jewish radicalism and presented evidence for it. Nevertheless, Liebman's attempt to relate the emergence of a radical Jewish tradition in Russia and the United States to the unique hardship of Jews under capitalism breaks down within his own study, and he is forced to reintroduce the marginality hypothesis he earlier rejected.

Industrialization was clearly a precondition for the breakdown of traditional religious controls. It is far from clear, though, that capitalist industrialization was the key factor. Indeed, as Liebman points out, the state played a major role in the industrialization process in Russia. There is every reason to believe that the same shift would have occurred regardless of the aegis under which industrialization occurred. In fact, the processes of industrialization in socialist countries have been associated with even more rapid deterioration of traditional communities than occurs under capitalism.

More importantly, as Liebman recognizes, it was the anti-Semitism of both Russian officialdom and the general population, rather than capitalism itself, that prevented Jews from entering the modern sector of the economy. Most Jews were artisans or journeymen who worked in very small factories, where differences between social strata were relatively minor and unstable. Marxists have traditionally argued that this pattern is the least conducive to the development of class consciousness among workers, who come to socialism as the result of employment in larger, more impersonal factory situations. As Liebman notes, the findings of most contemporary sociologists confirm this.

For this very reason, Russian Jewish socialists were initially hesitant to propagandize among Jewish artisans. Jews, they felt, were too petty bourgeois, too interested in individual success:

As Ber Borochov (quoted by Liebman) observed:

This desire to achieve "success" is a deeply ingrained characteristic of the Jewish laboring masses. Tailors, shoemakers, and cigarmakers eagerly await the opportunity to rid themselves of their tools, and to climb into the higher strata of insurance, dentistry, medicine, law, or into an independent business. This continuous exodus of thousands from the ranks of Jewish labor, and the necessary influx of thousands to replace them, furnishes the explanation of the Jewish laboring masses.[149]

Thus Russian Jewish Marxists looked upon Jews as very poor material for conversion to socialism. They also regarded them with the same kind of contempt that Jewish radicals have always directed against Jews who wished to prosper within the system rather than overthrow it. Indeed, the same theme can be found in Weimar Germany and 1960s America. As one Marxist Jew quoted by Liebman noted:

> We looked upon artisans almost as exploiters. Because the majority of the Jewish toilers were artisans and had to occupy themselves with small trade, we were ready to classify them as business people. To conduct any propaganda among them and yet in jargon [Yiddish] appeared to us, if not harmful, at least a waste of time and energy.[150]

As a consequence, many Russian Jewish intellectuals preferred to work among the Russian masses. They turned to Jews only after it became evident that they would have little or no success with the "goyim."

Since neither Marxist theory nor the empirical evidence suggests that the experience of Jews under capitalism per se should have led to the development of socialism among Jewish artisans, Liebman has difficulty explaining how "factors that should have inhibited the development of militancy appeared to be contributing to it."[151] He answers that Jewish artisans turned to socialism because of their worsening economic situation. But the hostility of the Christian state and their Christian neighbors was the problem, not capitalism per se. It was against these groups that their hostility should have been directed. Indeed, many Jews seem to have been aware of the real sources of their difficulties. Liebman correctly points out that Jewish migration to the United States, the capitalist nation par excellence, rose and fell with the intensity of anti-Semitic policies.

In fact, Jewish artisans did not come to socialism by themselves. They were steered to it by bourgeois intellectuals. These were intellectuals who had become socialists, as Liebman (quoting Deutscher) notes, because they were marginal. In a careful analysis of the Jewish intelligentsia before the Revolution, Robert Brym demonstrates that the major differences between Marxists and Bundists lay not in social-economic status but in the fact that the Bundists' backgrounds involved closer ties with the Jewish community. In short, in Russia as elsewhere, the strongest support for socialist universalism came from semi-assimilated bourgeois Jews whose economic prospects were fairly good.[152]

What of the Jewish artisans themselves? Was it their economic experience that led them to socialism? In his text, as against his theoretical chapters, Liebman is forced to admit that the appeal of Marxism to Jewish artisans and intellectuals was strongly related to their status as a minority. As he summarizes the point himself:

> Their own despised minority status was also obviously a factor in their propensity to look leftward. As educated Jews they were acutely aware of the disabilities of being Jewish under a "liberal" regime.

> All of these intellectual and social forces combined to make these Jewish students of the last decade of the nineteenth century seekers of movements that would offer them a new world of equality and acceptance. In the 1870's many thought that they had found the solution in populism.[153]

> Marxism was to prove a more compatible variant of socialism for these Jewish radicals than populism. . . . It was a cosmopolitan ideology not bound by national or particularistic forms and themes. Equality would follow from class membership which was devoid of a national or ethnic context.[154]

Liebman's analysis of the American scene is even weaker than his discussion of Russian Jews. It is extremely difficult to argue that American Jews were more seriously disadvantaged by capitalism than were other ethnic groups. The reverse is more nearly true. More generally, the attraction of socialism for American Jews cannot be traced simply to their Russian background. Deracinated Jewish middle-class intellectuals have been drawn to radicalism in *every* European country. Liebman dismisses the role of middle-class intellectuals, arguing that they represented only a small segment of the Jewish community. Granting this, one must still explain why they acted against what Marxists would perceive as their class interests to a much greater degree than did their Christian counterparts.

Liebman attempts to demonstrate that economic variables have led to a decline in radicalism among American Jews. The evidence suggests otherwise. The New Left of the 1960s was not merely reformist but radical and anticapitalist. The initial failure of Jewish New Leftists to adopt a classical socialist position did not reflect their middle-class status. Rather, their choice was largely tactical. If Liebman were correct, middle-class Jews should have been less radical than working-class Jews. Our own study indicates that the reverse was true.[155] And, *pace* Liebman, it was working-class and lower-middle-class Jews who turned against Mayor Lindsay. Middle-class Jews continued to support him.[156]

The suggestion that the professional position of Jews led them to a "humanist" radicalism is no more persuasive. First, one must still explain why

Jews chose intellectual professions when other opportunities were present. Moreover, even *within* intellectual professions, Jews remain to the left of their non-Jewish counterparts.[157]

Liebman attempts to place Jewish radicalism in a broader perspective, but his analysis retains the exceptionalism that typifies most studies of Jewish radicalism written by Jews. When an economic explanation falters, differential radicalism among Jews is attributed to the free choice of a gifted minority. More importantly, there is no attempt to compare Jews with other minority groups that chose radical alternatives, such as the Magyars in Hungary or the Chinese in Malaysia after World War II. The economic position of the Chinese was, of course, quite good.

Liebman's volume contains a considerable amount of useful historical data, and it is often quite insightful. For example, he describes in detail the role of Jewish community institutions in the United States in perpetuating a radical subculture. Nevertheless one must ultimately look elsewhere for an explanation of the historical roots of Jewish radicalism. Liebman's own evidence suggests that the historical marginality of Jews in Christian society is probably the single most important explanatory factor.

We have criticized the marginality hypothesis because it has been used in a self-serving manner. Nevertheless we believe that historical marginality is the most significant single variable in explaining the differential role of Jews in radical movements in Europe and the United States. Marginality has had a direct cognitive impact upon the manner in which Jews have perceived both Christians and themselves. It has also had a more indirect (though no less powerful) impact by influencing the development of a particular set of family dynamics, with significant consequences for personality patterns among Jews. Finally, Jewish radicalism, once established, has been perpetuated by straightforward parental political socialization of children. We will argue, too, that such radicalism is most likely to emerge during social crisis in the host society.[158]

The most suggestive discussion of Jewish marginality and its political consequences is found in the work of Charles Liebman. He suggests that Jewish attachment to liberal or radical universalistic ideas, many of which tend to undermine existing cultural norms, is basically a mechanism for ending felt marginality by subverting the cultural categories that have defined Jews as subordinate and different.[159] Liebman's argument can be generalized. Groups can attempt to end their marginality in one of three possible ways: they can assimilate to the culture; they can attach themselves to a more universalistic ideology or movement that subverts the cultural categories that define them as marginal;

or they can develop ideologies or institutions that legitimize their own social and political equality or dominance.

For Jews the first path has involved conversion or, at least, Reform Judaism. Radical secular rationalism, of which Marxism is the prime example, is a second path. Finally, Zionism is prototypical of the third path. Of course, many Zionists have attempted to combine elements of the second and third paths by uniting a universalistic creed (socialism) with their nationalism.

By adopting variants of Marxist ideology, Jews deny the reality of cultural or religious differences between Jews and Christians. These differences become "epiphenomenal," compared to the more fundamental opposition of workers and capitalists. Thus Jews and non-Jews are really brothers under the skin. Even when not adopting a Marxist position, many Jews have tended toward radical environmentalist perspectives, which serve a similar function. As Ralph Partai points out, the desire to deny that groups might differ in fundamental ways led some Jewish scholars to support the Lamarckian view that acquired characteristics can be inherited. The value of this notion was so important to one Jewish intellectual, Paul Kammerer, that he committed suicide after his "proof" of the Lamarckian argument was invalidated.[160]

Of course, Jews have not been alone in adopting these means of ending perceived marginality. As Robert Haddad has pointed out, the role played by Syrian Christians in secular nationalist movements in the Middle East can be explained in the same terms.[161] The replacement of Islamic consciousness by secular Arab states would, it was thought, eliminate the distinction between Muslim and Christian Arabs, and hence end the subordination of the latter, because all would become predominantly Syrians or Iraquis, etc. Secular nationalism, however, could never be *the* universalistic solution for Central and East European Jews. In Eastern Europe, ethnicity and religion were too closely tied to the national question for this purpose. Thus Austrians wishing to break from the Austro-Hungarian Empire and unite with Germany were interested not in a secular national state but in a German state. By the same token, Poles wanted a state that would serve the interests of a people who were at once Polish and Catholic. Jews espousing "pan-Germanism" or other nationalist movements invariably found that such movements, by their very nature, eventually became even more exclusivist than the old order.

Other groups, too, have found themselves in a position where the universalist position seemed the wisest course, after attempts to create a secular nationalist movement had failed. Thus the Magyar minority in prewar Czechoslovakia disproportionately supported the Communist party.[162] Similarly, the Ibos of Nigeria found themselves caught in a tragic bind. As Himmelstrand notes, they were initially the strongest supporters of a nationalist state that would transcend tribalism. However, their very success during the early years of Nigerian independence produced a violent backlash by numerically dominant groups, precipitating their abortive attempt at an Ibo nationalist solution.[163]

The marginality hypothesis can also be applied to American blacks. In their case, conformity to middle-class white norms represented attempts at assimilation; radical Marxist movements of the 1930s and 1960s represented the universalist solution; and the various nationalist groups that emerged during the 1920s and the late 1960s were the functional equivalent of Zionism.

The key point is that, for all these groups, the underlying attack of those choosing the "universalist" alternative is upon the institutions of the society which, in their perception, defines them as marginal. Thus Herbert Marcuse and others in the Frankfurt School, in shifting from a more purely Marxist critique of western capitalism to a critique of the "excessive" rationalization produced by western (Christian) culture in general, were developing an analysis closer to their underlying purposes. During this period, of course, they continued to deny that their Jewish background had anything to do with their own thinking, as they had earlier denied that anti-Semitism in Germany was anything more than epiphenomenal.[164]

Political radicalism, then, is but one form of the attack leveled by the marginal person upon the larger society. The basic thrust is to undermine all aspects of the *culture* which contribute to his or her marginality. Thus Jews in the United States and Europe have been in the forefront of not only political radicalism but also various forms of cultural "subversion." The Weltbühne circle played this role in the Weimar Republic. In America, there was a tradition of literary criticism. Nevertheless, in the 1960s deracinated Jewish authors such as E. L. Doctorow, Joseph Heller, and Norman Mailer were disproportionately represented among those whose critical efforts, even when not overtly political, were designed to demonstrate the "sickness" of the society. These writers were joined by producers such as Frederick Wiseman and Norman Lear in the visual media.

Often such subversion involves an attack upon genuine inequities or irrationalities. Since all societies abound in both, there is never an absence of targets. However, the attack is generally not directed at the particular inequity or irrationality per se. Rather, such inequities or irrationalities are used as a means for achieving a larger purpose: the general weakening of the social order itself. Thus many Jewish radicals have shifted their arguments about the evils and inevitable collapse of American society from decade to decade, often taking contradictory stances. Others have idealized one revolutionary regime after another (e.g., Russia, China, Cuba, North Vietnam), in the hope, as Paul Hollander suggests, of finding an ideal in terms of which they can judge their own society lacking.[165] There is some truth in Harold Cruse's argument, in *The*

Crisis of the Negro Intellectual, that a few Jewish radicals were less interested in helping blacks than in using them for their own ends.[166]

Marxism and other forms of radicalism have served one other function for many Jews. After being nurtured by a culture that saw itself as superior by virtue of a special relationship to God, many Jews must have experienced their contact with modern Europe as traumatic. It was difficult to continue to think Jewish life superior to the achievements of European civilization once the protective mantle of the shtetl was no longer present. What better way to reestablish claims to superiority than by adopting the most "advanced" social position of the larger society and viewing this adoption as a reflection of the Jewish heritage? Thus many radical Jewish intellectuals were able to continue to assert Jewish superiority, even as they denied their Jewishness.[167]

As one Jewish political scientist has put it:

> Does there remain any way—any really important way—in which the Jew can know and feel and do things that others cannot know and feel and do? The older answer was that fundamentally you have to be Jewish to be a good guy. We didn't parade that answer in public, but that is what most of us believed. Not, of course, that there weren't any decent non-Jews; but if there were, they were decent by accident, we by design.[168]

Phillip Roth concretizes many of these points in *Portnoy's Complaint*. Portnoy's tirade to his analyst reveals that his professed love for suffering humanity is far less important than his envy and hatred of WASPs and his desire to literally "screw" the "goyim." As he puts it:

> I was on the staff of the House subcommittee investigating the television quiz scandals. Perfect for the closet socialist like myself; commercial deceit on a national scale, exploitation of the innocent public, elaborate corporate chicanery—in short, good, old capitalist greed. And then of course that extra bonus, Charles Van Doren. Such character, such brains, such breeding, that candor and schoolboyish charm—that WASP, wouldn't you say? And turns out he's a fake. Well, what do you know about that, Gentile America? Supergoy, a "gonif"! Steals money—Goodness, gracious me, almost as bad as Jews—you sanctimonious WASPs!
>
> Yes, I was one happy yiddle down there in Washington, a little Stern gang of my own, busily exploring Charlie's honor and integrity, while simultaneously becoming lover to the aristocratic Yankee beauty whose forebears arrived on these shores in the seventeenth century.[169]

The situation, however, is not quite so simple. Portnoy also wants to become one of those strong, blond "goyim" who own America and whose brothers are "the engaging, good-natured, confident, clean, swift and powerful halfbacks for the college football teams."[170] His unconscious hope is that he can somehow become a goy by sleeping with the "shikses."[171] In addition, he has hopes that some of his emotional problems will be solved if he goes to Israel, although he fails here too.

Although Portnoy is a caricature, one can find the same aggressive themes discussed (and given similar interpretations) in Theodore Reik's analysis, *Jewish Wit*. Reik explains Jewish wit as a safety valve that transforms perceived hostility toward non-Jews in a manner designed to reduce the danger of retaliation. Sometimes, however, Jewish jokes (told, of course, among Jews only) reveal the anger quite directly:

> Little Moritz sees an historical film showing the early persecutions of the Christians. During a Roman circus scene in which many Christians are thrown to the lions, Moritz breaks out in sobs and says to his mother: "Look at that poor little lion there, it has not got any Goy to eat!" Under the disguise of duty for the neglected beast is an old hatred and repressed cruelty toward Gentiles. It breaks through here, surprisingly, and reaches the emotional surface.[172]

In *The Ordeal of Civility*, John Murray Cuddihy has gathered a number of quotations by Jews who recognize the depths of their hostility. In reviewing this work, Irving Louis Horowitz, the editor of *Society* (formerly *Transaction*), essentially agrees that Cuddihy is correct in pointing out the anger which Jews do feel, although he disagrees with Cuddihy's argument:

> By denying the anti-semitic factor . . . Cuddihy liquidates the culture of revolution, which is very much what the Jewish tradition is all about. Jews can be quite civil without suffering it as an ordeal, given a modicum of equity in their treatment, as the Dutch Jews and Italian Jews demonstrate.[173]

Other radicals have been even more direct. Jerry Rubin ascribes his own radicalism to being Jewish, and finds that Cohn-Bendit shares the same feelings. It is clear, too, that his primary hostility is toward Christianity. He tells "Pat Boone that Christianity has murdered more people than any other ism in the history of the world."[174] Roger Kahn, writing about the Columbia conflict, keeps remembering how badly Jews are treated by the WASP establishment,[175] and Paul Cowan is convinced from his experiences at Choate that the WASPs are all anti-Semitic racists.[176]

For all the hostility and rhetoric, though, the desire to assimilate continually reappears: Bob Dylan changes his name from Zimmerman and for years conceals his Jewishness;[177] Vivian Gornick, in *The Romance of American Communism,* exults upon finding one old member of the party who was a "native American";[178] Phil Ochs identifies with John Wayne;[179] and some liberal or radical parents do their best to get their children into the best WASP prep schools and universities,[180] especially those with reputations for being rather liberal.

Indeed, as is the case with the fictional Portnoy, hostility toward the dominant Christian community sometimes combines with self-hatred, manifested in attacks upon Jews and Judaism per se. Such attacks often serve a double purpose. First, they enable some deracinated Jews to disassociate themselves from negative images of Jews which, they feel, the dominant community accepts. Secondly, given the peculiar relationship between Judaism and Christianity, an attack on the former can be a surrogate for an attack on the latter. If Judaism is false or "evil," then that which springs from it is also false or evil. Marx's argument in his famous essay on the "Jewish question" follows just this strategy.[181] It was also followed by the Nazis, who attempted to discredit traditional Christianity for a new "positive" Christianity in Germany.[182]

The combination of self-hatred and the use of Jews as a surrogate for Christian culture seems obvious in Marx's early essay on the "Jewish question," but his general hatred of Jews as Jews (and blacks) emerges repeatedly in his writings. He constantly described Jews whom he did not like in terms that emphasized the negative qualities of Jews per se.[183]

What Marx did not say about himself is just as interesting. His father had reluctantly converted to Protestantism for social reasons shortly before Marx's birth, although there is no evidence that he ever attended church. His mother, on the other hand, did not convert until Marx was about six years old. Marx knew that many of his enemies were aware of his Jewish background. Indeed, some made a point of mentioning it. Yet never did Marx discuss this background, even to note why he rejected it.[184]

Ferdinand Lassalle himself was not without self-hatred of this kind. At one point he wrote:

> I do not like Jews at all. I even detest them in general. I see in them nothing but the degenerate sons of a great but long past epoch. As a result of centuries of servitude these people have taken on the characteristics of slaves, and for this reason I am so hostile to them.[185]

And when Victor Adler, the founder of Austrian socialism, was asked by a friend what he thought of anti-Semitism, he replied: "My dear comrade, one

must have Jews, only not too many." He argued strongly that "The last anti-
Semite will disappear with the last Jew."[186]

Such self-hatred is, of course, common to many marginal groups. Its existence has been well documented among many Jewish radicals, and Theodore
Reik analyzes its expression in some detail in *Jewish Wit*.[187]

Interestingly, the themes have remained more or less the same since Marx
enunciated them. Radical deracinated Jews and right-wing Jews who have converted to Christianity, as well as right-wing non-Jews, all see Jews as representing the worst of bourgeois culture, including the attribute of "degenerate"
cowardice. Thus Marx could attack Jews as representing the quintessence of
capitalism. Some Russian Jewish radicals felt and argued the same way. And
in Germany during the 1920s, Kurt Tucholsky created a character called Herr
Wendriner as the prototype of the Jewish German businessman.[188] Wendriner
was interested only in money. He was egocentric, petty, cruel, and stupid. As
Harold Poor, Tucholsky's biographer, notes, these sketches were extremely
popular in Germany during the Weimar period. Later, after the Nazis had come
to power and Tucholsky had fled to France, he vehemently denounced Jews as
a group for their cowardice:

> Jewry has suffered defeat, a defeat which it deserves. It is not true that
> it has fought for thousands of years. It does not fight.
>
> And now they [Jews] crawl out, sad, beaten, up to their ears in shit,
> broke, robbed of their money—and without honor. . . .
>
> Heroism would have been the better business here. Why did they
> not choose that way? Because they are not able to be heroic; because
> they have no idea what it is.[189]

In the 1960s, similar themes were repeated by Jerry Rubin and others:

> Judaism no longer means much to us because the Judeo-Christian
> tradition has died of hypocrisy. Jews have become landlords, business-
> men, judges and prosecutors in Amerika. I do not believe in "freedom"
> for Jews at the expense of Arabs and black people. . . .
>
> If Moses were alive today, he'd be an Arab guerrilla.[190]

On the other side, Otto Weininger, a Jew who converted to Protestantism
and became a proto-fascist, violently attacked both women and Jews, to whom
he attributed all the "female" vices. To him Jews were shameless material-
ists.[191]

Some of the same motivations, although without the self-hatred, can be found in the work of Sigmund Freud. Though it is sometimes forgotten today, Freud's work was profoundly subversive of the cultural underpinnings of European Christian society, a subversiveness of which he was not unaware. There is evidence that some of the impetus for the creation of psychoanalysis lay in his hostility to Christianity.[192] It is not without reason that Isaac Deutscher places Freud among those "non-Jewish" Jews who so profoundly influenced the intellectual climate of Europe:

> It is very obvious why Freud belongs to the same intellectual line [as Spinoza and Marx]. . . . The man whom he analyzes is not a German or an Englishmen, a Russian or a Jew—he is the universal man in whom the subconscious and the unconscious struggle . . . the man whose desires and cravings, scruples and predicaments are essentially the same no matter to what race, religion or nation he belongs. From their viewpoint, the Nazis were right when they coupled Freud's name with that of Marx and burnt the books of both.[193]

In sum, the aim of the Jewish radical is to estrange the Christian from society, as he feels estranged from it. The fact that the United States is no longer "Christian" in any real sense, or that Jews have moved to positions of considerable power and influence, is of little import. Its Christian base is still unconsciously identified as the decisive oppressive element. Nor should this come as a surprise. We know that sociopolitical stances adopted in the wake of traumatic experiences tend to be self-perpetuating. In France, the radicalism of the Midi can be traced back to the Albigensian Crusades, and the radicalism of certain northern regions to Jansenism. Areas that voted "left" in 1848 were still voting "left" in the 1960s.[194] Thus many radical Jews, even when they do not identify with Judaism, unconsciously retain a generalized hostility to Christian culture. Again, Portnoy is a good example. Only on the analyst's couch is he willing to admit the hostility that he feels.

For many Jews, social marginality has had psychological consequences of a type first outlined by Nietzsche and explicated by psychoanalytic perspectives.[195] Faced by persecutors too powerful to resist physically, Jewish families of the diaspora gradually came to place tremendous emphasis upon inhibiting the direct expression of physical aggression, particularly by male children. Nor was it enough merely to counsel prudence, for prudence might be tossed aside in the face of extreme provocation. Rather, as Rudolph Lowenstein pointed out in *Christians and Jews,* survival called for the creation of controls that became an integral part of character structure. He describes the results for Jews in the United States in the 1930s:

> Some interesting facts on the maternal attitude of Jewish women are contained in a comparative study made on three groups of fifty families each, selected from among the Jewish, Polish and Negro population of one of the poorer districts in Chicago. The Jewish mother was found to be overanxious, obsessed with the idea that her infant was not getting enough to eat, forcing him by all sorts of means to take nourishment, and weaning him much later than mothers in the other two groups.
>
> Another manifestation of this overanxious behavior is the tendency of Jewish mothers to make their children overfearful in the face of physical danger. This maternal attitude discourages the childhood desire to seek parental approval through a show of physical strength and prowess.[196]

The stereotype of the "emasculating" Jewish mother may have its roots here. The material Lowenstein reports is taken from studies conducted during the 1930s. We shall argue that this pattern continued in modified form until well into the 1960s, and extended back to earlier child-rearing patterns in Eastern and Western Europe.

Good studies of "Jewish personality traits" are few in number for a variety of reasons, including a tendency by scholars to avoid the subject. Nevertheless, there is evidence to support these notions. Zborowski and Tursky and Sternbach found that Jewish subjects seemed to have lower pain thresholds than Protestants.[197] Argyle, Lowenstein, Goldberg, and others have noted the low rate of crimes of violence among Jews in both Europe and the United States.[198] Bieri, Lobeck, and Plotnick have associated high rates of social mobility among some Jews with avoidance of occupations that call for directly aggressive behavior. These Jews seek professions in which the expression of aggression is more indirect (i.e., verbal). Such professions usually require higher levels of educational attainment.[199]

The low rate of alcoholism among Jews has frequently been noted. Most commentators, however, have avoided dealing seriously with Kant's suggestion that Jews do not drink to excess for fear of acting in unseemly ways in the context of a Christian community.[200] However, David McClelland and others have argued that people characterized by strong power drives and *strong needs to inhibit these drives* are also characterized by low to moderate drinking patterns. On the other hand, individuals with high power drives and little need to inhibit these drives were found to drink more heavily.[201] Indeed, Lowenstein, agreeing with Hartman, explains the Jewish propensity for intellectuality in just these terms, i.e., the need to inhibit aggressive (power) drives.[202]

What kinds of upbringing and early experience might account for such tendencies? It is at least plausible to suggest that the European diaspora and the ghetto experience encouraged among Jews the emergence of a particular family pattern: a pattern characterized by mothers who were protective and controlling, especially with their male children.

The institutionalization of this pattern was to have profound effects upon both Jewish males and females. It had already developed in the shtetl and in other traditional European communities. There, however, the male's religious role enabled him to remain an important symbol of authority. Ritual and learning were honorific male occupations. The husband studied sacred literature and promoted the book-learning tradition of Israel. In the synagogue and in religious ceremonies in the home, his position was clearly that of a superior. In practical matters, however, the woman took charge:

> The father too becomes like a child to her [the mother] in the home, except when he is studying or performing ritual acts; only outside the home, in the synagogue or in business, does he enter upon a fully adult role. Mother is frequently described as "a loving despot," always busy, always nagging, "the last and highest court of appeal."[203]

In the new secular world, the religious prop to the father's authority was destroyed:

> The same father who would not be judged "weak" in an all-Jewish East European community, may be judged "weak" if his American son uses older generations of Jewish or non-Jewish American families as his reference group.[204]

Thus in the new secular world of America, as well as Eastern and Western Europe, the Jewish family became a kind of matriarchy. Within the family, as Greta Bibring writes, the husband was perceived by the children as more fearful, less capable, and weaker than the wife who cared for and somewhat dominated him in crucial areas, whatever his professional and/or business achievements.[205]

At the same time, the pattern of extremely close bonding between mother and son continued. In the shtetl, as Landes and Zborowski point out:

The woman in the home personifies emotionality—the mother most of all. A young son often sleeps with her, unlike the husband, who is prohibited by sacred law from remaining in her bed. In one memoir a boy slept with his mother until he was 13, that is, ritually a man. Although displays of endearment between husband and wife are frowned upon, regarded as vulgar whether in speech or gesture, a great deal of demonstrative behavior is allowed between mother and son, which mothers encourage.

It seems to us that, though the marital obligations are fulfilled with the husband, the romance exists with the son.[206]

For Jewish males, then, the early years of life were in some ways like a "Garden of Eden," to be looked back upon with considerable longing, as a time of great joy. The joy derived from the sensation that seemingly all one's wishes would be gratified.

Unconsciously, of course, these years were also associated with considerable anxiety. As we shall argue, the son senses that the mother's attachment to him is motivated partly by narcissistic needs. Further, his pre-Oedipal attachments were so powerful that they inhibited an effective resolution of Oedipal issues and placed great inhibitions upon the development of normal sexuality. Finally, as the male matured, he would always be struggling with the much-feared, unconscious wish to merge with the mother once again, which could only bring the loss of his individuality.[207]

The problem may not have been terribly serious in a shtetl culture which provided a host of institutional supports. It was to become more complex and difficult in cultures which emphasized individual autonomy and achievement such as those of western Europe and the United States. To be sure, such child-rearing practices could produce considerable strengths for cultures of that type. The inhibition of both sexuality and the direct physical expression of aggression could be transformed into intellectual and other forms of creative mastery of the environment. Nevertheless, such patterns could also lead to difficulties which, if not effectively managed, would yield serious problems during adolescence and adulthood.

Bibring suggests that the Oedipal phase and its resolution in such families will take on quite different characteristics than in patriarchal families. Since the father is considered inadequate, castration fears may seem lower among Jewish males. On the other hand, with the mother continually perceived as a devouring pre-Oedipal figure (and the father as a fellow sufferer), males may doubt their masculine potency. As a result, they may attempt to identify with powerful males or movements which enable them to perceive themselves as powerful.

On the other hand, they may give up the battle and seek to resolve their problems by denying the reality of sexual differences and adopting a homosexual stance.

The situation is actually somewhat more complicated, and we can understand it only by examining the rather different case of the Jewish woman. In European society, the female's desire for power could traditionally be satisfied by identification with a husband or lover, or by the birth of a male child. For the Jewish female the first course was not open, and her deprecation of her husband was only exacerbated by his failure to provide such gratification. In one sense the intensity of bonding with her male child was quite narcissistic. She hoped the son would serve functions that the husband could not. Given the ambivalence of her treatment of her sons, however, such narcissistic goals could never be realized. As choices broadened, some Jewish women actively sought careers which, in their fantasies, enabled them to create their own power. They also joined radical political movements and the feminist movement in large numbers. Martha Wolfenstein, in her classic article, "Two Types of Jewish Mother," argues that the younger generation of Jewish women broke the pattern associated with an older tradition. Her description of the young, well-educated Jewish mother, however, indicates that many elements of the older pattern were retained, despite cultural shifts.[208]

Thus the narcissistic deficits of the Jewish mother were passed on to her children, although the results were rather different for males and females.[209] For Jewish males, the key element was probably the mother's use of the child as a narcissistic extension of herself. For females, on the other hand, the mother's relative coldness and the father's failure to provide the desired "power" yielded similar results.

The identification of some Jewish males and females with the Russian proletariat during the Soviet revolution, with Irish and Italian workers during the 1930s, and with the black underclass or third world nations during the 1960s may have reflected motives beyond mere sympathy with the underdog. Kazin and Himmelfarb have suggested that in both the 1930s and the 1960s many Jewish radicals were projecting their own needs and desires upon those groups.[210]

The needs of male and female radicals were somewhat different, though. Both were driven by the desire to fill narcissistic deficits. Males could identify with a powerful cause to quiet doubts about their masculinity. Jewish women, on the other hand, could satisfy those power needs that other women achieved by identifying with their husbands and lovers. Both sought a sense of power but for slightly different reasons: the male to convince himself he was a male, the woman to satisfy that part of her psyche that shared male identifications.

For the male child, at least, there is another side to the equation. On one level the father might be perceived as weak or effectively absent. On a deeper level, however, childhood fantasies of his potential power persist. As Christopher Lasch put it: "Precisely because the father's absence allows early fantasies to persist unmodified the child fears the terrible vengeance that his father can inflict even while he scorns the everyday father who never inflicts it."[211] Lasch was speaking of 1960s youth in general. We are not persuaded that his characterization is accurate for all youth during that period. It does, however, seem to fit radical youth of Jewish background, both then and earlier.

Under such circumstances, the early nonrational linkage of fantasied gratification (the desired mother) with deferred retribution leads to a lasting ambivalence toward authority. In reality the youth encounters relatively few paternal hindrances to his efforts at self-assertion and self-aggrandizement. But he lives in what Lasch calls "a state of chronic uneasiness"—the gnawing fear that his transgressions will one day be uncovered and punished. The pleasures of his fantasies are mitigated by guilt, fear of punishment, and resentment at an authority that seems contemptible but ever-dangerous.

To be fully satisfying, impulse gratification must be cloaked in a sense of purpose; it requires a moral patina. Otherwise even a childhood of relatively unrestrained self-assertion and self-expression may go hand in hand with a debilitating image of oneself as both outlaw and victim. For life to be meaningful as well as pleasant, apparently weak authority must be shorn of its remaining power to threaten and to inhibit. To be deposed, it must first be exposed as fraudulent and illegitimate. A moral consensus in opposition is thereby established.

But the controlling desire is to expose and shame authority, not to overthrow it. One gains a sense of self-worth by demonstrating superiority over powerful figures who are "unmasked" as weak and corruptible. And a sense of personal autonomy is sustained by opposition and revolt against those in power, not by taking power for oneself. The latter course would activate repressed conflicts over submission and dependency. The desire for victory over authority, even authority perceived as illegitimate, is always leavened by a simultaneous desire for defeat. For defeat and consequent punishment free the young rebel from debilitating fantasies of future punishment, which would only be strengthened by outright victory. Not revolution but reassurance is wanted— reassurance that the apparent autonomy experienced in childhood will not suddenly be denied and punished. This requires repeated demonstrations of moral superiority, which presuppose the continued existence of nominally superior but morally weak authority figures.

For some Jewish youth in the 1930s, membership in the Communist party provided a solution for the various binds created by the family relationship, although the solution varied, depending upon their earlier attempts to deal with the tensions involved. The various ways in which such people actually coped are illustrated in Herbert Krugman's study of fifty American communists and ex-communists, almost all of them Jewish. All had been in therapy and analysis, and Krugman's data are based on interviews with their analysts. His evidence, therefore, is indirect. Nevertheless, many of his findings were replicated in our own study of 1960s and early 1970s radicals.[212]

The analysts' reports indicate that the mother was often the dominant figure in the family:

> We do not know how common in American society is the mother-dominated family. What does seem unusual in our cases . . . however is the amount of belittling of the father.

> The consequences are quite important for the children. The early inability to accept the love of the father, and in the case of boys to want to "be like him when I grow up" or with girls "to marry a man like Daddy when I grow up" reinforces underlying confusions in self image . . . in that later deep conflicts involved very commonly the problem of homosexuality.[213]

In many cases, Krugman notes, joining the Communist party allowed both male and female members to express hostility against nonparty authority figures without feeling guilty. Thus it enabled the male members, who tended to emphasize toughness and hardness, to convince themselves that they were "real" men. The women, who were unable to identify with their fathers as successful male figures, instead used the party to try to "become" men.

Other party members found a different solution to the problem of gender confusion. Several adopted a passive resolution. All the men in this category had some history of overt passive homosexuality. Several women had developed such relations as well. The self-image of these women emphasized "helplessness," a sense of being a "pawn of fate" or a victim of society. The main drive was to find a protector, i.e., to be childishly submissive without guilt or fear. The function of the party for passive men was quite similar. One analyst commented about a male patient of this type: "[The party was] an outlet for [unconscious homosexual fantasies] without narcissistic thoughts. He takes orders from others but at the same time feels a part of an overwhelming destructive force. At the same time he satisfies his masochism."[214]

As we shall see, young radicals of Jewish background during the 1960s were not all that different, although cultural shifts in the larger society and changing patterns of child-rearing had produced subtle changes.

By the 1940s and 1950s many upper-middle-class progressive Jews had come to accept and propagate a secular, humanistic, liberal, and cosmopolitan view of the world. They had rejected traditional values for an emphasis on self-realization and self-expression. In terms of child-rearing, this meant paying lip service to an egalitarian family in which children were encouraged to express themselves and satisfy their impulses. Thus, not only was the father perceived as ineffective but every effort was made to ensure that children were not repressed or made to feel guilty. Maternal control remained *sub rosa* but was based on more subtle, sometimes unconsciously directed disciplinary measures.

Male children were thereby caught in a number of binds. One way to create distance from an infantilizing or engulfing mother is to adopt a negative identity, a self-consciously alienated stance toward family and social authority. However, a young man's rejection of that authority often conceals an underlying desire for clearly defined limitations on acceptable behavior. He seeks to gain control over an amorphous moral environment, both by exhausting the possibilities for sensation that the world offers and by restructuring the environment to produce a framework more conducive to self-fulfillment.

If prolonged, the resulting quest for sensation and affective experience denies the growing youth a glimpse of "ego integrity"—"the acceptance," in Erikson's words, "of one's one and only life cycle as something that had to be . . . as an experience which conveys some world order and spiritual sense . . . ."[215] Instead, he is left with an eviscerated sense of being hemmed in and cut off from life's immediacy. Like Don Juan's endless desire for new lovers, his thirst for new experiences reflects the emotional emptiness of any particular experience. Similarly, a life spent collecting experiences reflects a struggle for control over a threatening environment.

At the same time, the absence of benevolent paternal authority means that childhood fantasies of retribution from an all-powerful father are never tested against reality. Even as children test the limits of authority and find them receding before each probe, the fear of eventual retribution continues to mount. The gratifying sense of being a law unto oneself, unfettered by external powers, goes hand in hand with rising fears of punishment from fantasized omnipotent authority.

Lasch's remarks, quoted earlier, become particularly appropriate here. The results could be anticipated:

> . . . the divided perception of parental authority carries over into social action. On the one hand, authorities invite contempt because they allow so many violations of their own rules; on the other hand they threaten to exact a terrifying revenge at some unspecified moment in the future.[216]

The personality tendencies described in the last several pages parallel Jules Nydes's description of what he calls the "paranoid masochistic" character.[217] Nydes argues that such individuals tend to see both themselves and groups with which they identify as victims who are being persecuted. This sense of persecution derives partly from unconscious feelings of guilt. The paranoid masochistic person engages in aggression against others because he or she expects to be attacked. His aggression, which is accompanied by feelings of self-righteousness, is rarely satisfying. Indeed, he can often achieve gratification only when he is punished, and the punishment is interpreted as confirming his preconceived sense of persecution. Nydes contrasts this type with the "sadistic" authoritarian who identifies with the aggressor and takes out his hostilities against those who seem unable to fight back.

In Chapter 4, we describe power-oriented emotional dispositions similar to these as variants of an "inverse authoritarian" personality pattern. In our own discussion, however, we refrain from using Nydes's terminology. First, his language inadvertently seems to imply that all persons so characterized are pathological. More importantly, Nydes's work is based on a classical psychoanalytic model that leaves little room for partial ego autonomy and neglects the importance of pre-Oedipal object relations.

Nevertheless, the typology is suggestive. Theodore Reik, who was Nydes's teacher, suggested that a "paranoid masochistic" personality structure is modal among Jews.[218] He is partially supported by Lowenstein. Hartmann, Kris, and Lowenstein argue, however, that ego strength is the key element determining whether the "repression" of aggressive drives will lead to masochism or successful sublimation and high levels of creative potential.[219] Whiting and Child offer empirical support for this proposition from their analysis of a large number of primitive cultures. They find that, in general, paranoid suspicion varies according to the emphasis a given community places upon the repression of aggressive drives.[220] Some evidence for high levels of defensive projection among Jews does exist.[221] In a secondary analysis of a nationwide study, Greeley found the Jews scored lowest of all American ethnic groups in "trust in people."[222]

Of course this personality pattern was created and has been reinforced by the very real persecution to which Jews have historically been subject. However, it can contribute to marginality and a sense that the non-Jewish community is violently hostile, even when this hostility has greatly diminished, as is probably the case in the United States today.

Moreover, under normal circumstances, this pattern need not have political implications. Even in its personal neurotic form, it can result in considerable creativity. Take, for example, the case of "Jewish wit." Eighty percent of the stand-up comedians in the United States are of Jewish background. In a study of seventy-six Jewish comedians, David Janus found that their humor was a defense mechanism designed "to ward off the aggression and hostility of others." He believes that most of these comedians had overprotective, constricting mothers and were moved by a desire to break out of the Jewish world and gain acceptance: "Only a few will talk about their Jewishness with any sense of pride. . . . most of them will talk about their work for non-Jewish causes."[223]

Jewish comedians, Janus concludes, are overwhelmingly anxious people who turn most of their humor on themselves. Thus the humor serves as a "ritual exorcism for conflicts shared with Jewish audiences and it assures Gentile audiences that Jewish humor is not threatening."[224]

In sum, we view the extensive participation of Jews in radical movements in Christian societies as a function of several interrelated variables, including marginality and family structure. Their adoption of universalistic ideologies has been, from their perspective, quite rational in Christian societies.[225] (By the 1960s, of course, such commitments were being passed on from parents to children via direct political socialization.) The adoption of more radical chiliastic stances, involving strong identification with mass lower-class movements and a commitment to revolutionary action, is fostered by a family structure that tends to produce the personality tendencies outlined above. Where persons of this type have dealt successfully with problems of maturity, the results can be high levels of intellectual (or artistic) productivity and a strong commitment to universalistic egalitarian values. The aggressive needs of such individuals are directed toward ends which, in many cases, serve both themselves and the larger society.

When for some reason the maturation process has gone awry (as when there is an unusually weak father and/or overprotective and "seductive" mother), the neurosis of choice will be that described by Nydes. Adolescence, especially, will be characterized by a partial desublimation of aggressive drives and a high degree of defensive projection. Intensive and recurring efforts will be made to find external sources of strength in "powerful" male figures. At the same time, such individuals will become compulsively competitive as they attempt to demonstrate their masculinity to themselves. This competitiveness will be justified by fears of attack, which they will continually seek to provoke. Many of them, particularly during adolescence, will be caught in a bind from which there is no easy escape. Longing to merge with their mothers (to return to the lost "Garden of Eden," in Keniston's formulation), they will simultaneously fear the loss of ego boundaries. Thus, they will also engage in a desperate flight from their mothers.[226]

In times of relative social stability, this neurotic pattern may be highly personal. Where moderate outlets for radical activism are present, some of those characterized by such personality needs will tend to justify aggressive behavior on grounds that they are warding off attacks from an evil threatening "Establishment." They will find it increasingly easy to identify with a powerful militant working-class movement, or with militant blacks, as in the 1960s, because they will convince themselves that they view this group as weak and oppressed.

Thus, the sources of Jewish radicalism in the 1960s may be schematized in terms of the following diagram. We emphasize, once again, that the sociological and psychological dimensions are of equal importance. The same personality type, with another ethnic background and historical experience, might well adopt a very different political stance.

The importance of social, cultural, and political variables cannot be over-

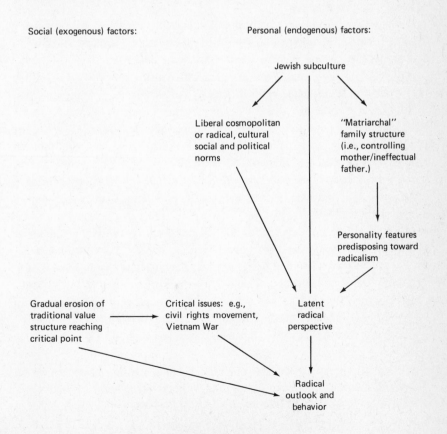

Social (exogenous) factors: Personal (endogenous) factors:

Jewish subculture

Liberal cosmopolitan or radical, cultural social and political norms

"Matriarchal" family structure (i.e., controlling mother/ineffectual father.)

Personality features predisposing toward radicalism

Gradual erosion of traditional value structure reaching critical point

Critical issues: e.g., civil rights movement, Vietnam War

Latent radical perspective

Radical outlook and behavior

emphasized. As Weinstein and Platt have stressed, the normal expectable sociopolitical environment is a powerful supporter of ego and superego controls. When these controls are weakened, individual self-control falters as well, and primitive fantasies are more likely to be acted out. Almost every modern sociopolitical revolution and accompanying social disorder have been characterized by tremendous increases in the incidence of violence, as well as various schemes for ending the family or introducing the "polymorphous perverse" sexuality of childhood as an adult norm. The particular content of some of these fantasies is partly determined by the changing content of the culture out of which the revolution springs, since some unconscious wishes can be influenced by that culture.[227]

These points are developed in greater detail in Chapter 4. At present, it suffices to say that social disorder most profoundly affects adolescents, who are in a particularly unstable developmental stage. Thus, during periods of heightened tension, even Jews who would be liberal or only moderately radical may find themselves carried along by the passions of the time, as these resonate with their own inner needs.

For the highly narcissistic radicals, of course, the "revolution" provided a temporary fantasy solution to their need to experience excitement and esteem. Thus a troubled young woman like Susan Stern could gravitate toward the Weathermen, in part because an association with "media stars" like Mark Rudd and Bernardine Dohrn made her feel like she was "someone." And, being part of the New Left, she felt that "wherever I went people loved me." At the same time, her relation to her image of "blond Christian America" was quite ambivalent. She wrote of painting on the wall of her house "an eight-foot-tall nude woman with flowing green blond hair and a burning American flag coming out of her cunt!" She had "painted what I wanted to be somewhere deep in my mind; tall and blond, nude and armed, consuming—or discharging—a burning America."[228]

A similar pattern emerges from the life and death of Ted Gold, a member of the Weather Underground who died when a bomb he was constructing exploded prematurely. Gold had been raised by liberal Jewish parents and sent to schools for the "academically talented" in New York, as well as to "radical" summer camps. By 1963 he was already, in his words, very "pro-Castro." In 1968, under the influence of Mark Rudd, he turned to revolutionary politics.[229]

As Sale wrote, in his very sympathetic short biography in *The Nation:*

. . . Gold, short, bespectacled, quiet, intellectual, controlled—must have found something enormously appealing in Rudd—tall, loose, attractive, outgoing, reckless. At Columbia (and after) they were continually talking about the need for courage, for "putting your body on the line," for shaking off "bourgeois hangups" about violence and death, for ceasing to be "wimps."[230]

Thus, by the time he joined the Weathermen, Gold had developed a fascination with violence and death:

. . . at the Weatherman "war council" in Flint, Mich. , . . . the greetings were four fingers slightly spread (symbolizing the fork which Charlie Manson's gang plunged into one of its victims. . . .

Violence . . . was the abiding theme. Gold made a speech in which he tried to show its immediacy.

A critic in the audience objected. . . . It sounds like a John Bircher's worst dream. There will have to be more repression then ever.

"Well," replied Gold, "if it will take fascism, we'll have to have fascism."[231]

We can infer from Sale's account that Gold was at least partly motivated by a need to exorcise and confront violence and, as such, to go down in history as a "man."

A friend who saw Gold two weeks before the explosion reports his having said, "I've been doing a lot of exciting underground things, and I know I'm not afraid to die." Another who knew Gold thinks it was more than just the absence of fear: "I think a desire for recognition was motivating him. He wanted to be in history—he wanted to be like Che, a tragic figure." And an adult at Columbia who knew Gold speculates: "I always felt that Ted, perhaps because of his size, or maybe his bookishness, had a kind of drive to get people to know who he was. . . ."[232]

On a deeper level, many Jewish radicals from "nice" families, who had always had doubts about their masculinity and their sexuality, may have felt that they could finally express both masculine aggression and sexuality freely because they were part of a powerful "revolutionary" group. More than that, they could recapture the polymorphous perversity of childhood. Their mothers would want them because, unlike their fathers, they were truly potent. At the same time, their masculine potency would protect them from being engulfed by their mothers. Finally, because time does not exist in the unconscious, they could imagine that their "Garden of Eden" would last forever.

The theme of seeking compensation for masculine inadequacy can be found in the writings of many Jewish radicals and some nonradicals. In Weimar Germany, Kurt Tucholsky leaves his dark-haired Jewish wife, developing an in-

tense and overwhelming attraction for a very blond German girl. He broods
about his relationship with his new love: "Sometimes I think: she would be a
thousand times happier with a blond cavalry officer, because he would be less
complicated and would perhaps better master life. . . . No, I am no victor in
a dance tournament."[233]

In America, many years later, Paul Jacobs, a radical who began his career
in the 1930s, muses on some of the fantasies which have directed his life in a
book called *Is Curly Jewish?*: "Curly is me, of course, although he exists only
in my imagination, where he is seventeen years old and six foot one, with lots
of wavy hair—unlike me, in my middle forties, five foot six and bald."[234]
Among major contemporary writers, these themes are exemplified in Norman
Mailer's celebration of what he perceived as the freedom of blacks from conventional restraints in his essay "The White Negro,"[235] and perhaps in his life
as well. Morris Dickstein makes this case in his very favorable discussion of
Mailer:

> Mailer is attracted by the life of action and longs to live in the heroic
> mold. He strains for an affinity with bullfighters, boxers, film directors,
> space explorers, romantic revolutionaries—all the street-fighters and
> drunken swaggerers of the world. Doomed by the accidents of talent
> and some inalterable wrinkle of character to be a writer instead, he
> places his work under the flag of adventure, sees it as an exploration of
> inner space, a struggle with death and dread. He repeatedly seizes op-
> portunities to prove himself in the active life, but his incursions into
> politics, filmmaking, and public speaking prove disastrous, redeemed
> only by the torrent of printed words which transforms them into retro-
> spective verbal triumphs. He revels in a protean variety of roles and
> occasions but is unable to bear "a last remaining speck of the one per-
> sonality he found absolutely unsupportable—the nice Jewish boy from
> Brooklyn. Something in his adenoids gave it away—he had the softness
> of a man early accustomed to mother-love."*

*This brings to mind the dreadful caricatures of Goldstein and Roth in *The Naked
and the Dead*. Mailer treats them throughout with a contempt (or self-contempt)
that borders on anti-Semitism. Even his hostile acknowledgment of this part of
his personality shows how far Mailer had traveled in self awareness.[236]

For some Jewish radicals, then, it is not only the oppression of third world
nations that attracts them as they move from cause to cause but, rather, the
imagined virility of these nations and their powerful leaders, with whom they
unconsciously desire to merge. As Abbie Hoffman described Fidel Castro: "Fidel sits on the side of a tank rumbling into Havana on New Year's day. . . .
The tank stops in the city square. Fidel lets the gun drop to the ground, slaps

his thigh and stands erect. He is like a mighty penis coming to life. . . ."[237]

And a Jewish ex-Weatherman reflects on his experiences and the experiences of those around him:

> . . . a lot of the Weatherman leadership was Jewish and had never been tough street kids, and I really believe that a tremendous amount of what they were doing was overcoming their own fears about their masculinity. . . . Most of them . . . had been intellectually aggressive, but all of a sudden they were trying to be tough street kids . . . I think there was a lot of self-hatred going on.[238]

Jews' self-doubt in this area tends, however, to inhibit their effectiveness as revolutionaries. Thus the "militant" activity of the Weathermen was largely play-acting, which could only have taken place in a society in which the "Establishment" acted under serious restrictions inhibiting its retaliatory powers. When Jewish radicals have engaged in contests with their less inhibited Christian counterparts in the aftermath of revolutions, they have invariably lost out. Kamenev and Zinoviev, after considerable vacillation both during and after the revolution, were easily shoved aside. And Trotsky, as Carmichael points out, exhibited a self-defeating passivity in his struggle with Stalin. Carmichael argues that Trotsky's verbal pyrotechnics misled observers on this issue.[239]

Most of the psychological elements that attracted young Jewish males to the radicalism of the 1960s can also be illustrated *in extremis* by the biographies of two young men who followed somewhat different political paths, Robert Starobin and Phil Ochs.

Bob Starobin was a New Left activist who tragically committed suicide in 1971 at age thirty-one. Linda Forcey, a friend, has written a sensitive and sympathetic biography, from which the following account is taken.[240]

Bob Starobin's father, Joseph, had been an active member of the American Communist party until 1954 and served as editor of the *Daily Worker*. He remained on the Left after leaving the party, although he was no longer very active. Bob, an only child, was born in 1939. His mother agrees that Bob was treated as a "prince" and wondered later if she and her husband overly protected him when he was a child. Because of his father's work in the party, mother and son were "very close" during Bob's early years. In Norma Starobin's words, "Bob had a love affair with me as most sons have with their mothers."[241] She regards Bob as having been a "normal" child, except for his severe temper tantrums, which started at age four and continued into adulthood.

The romance with his mother, punctuated with tantrums, continued into

Bob's adult life. They remained in close contact even after he left home. Forcey writes:

> Norma's letters to Bob . . . are highly charged statements of Norma's needs and expectations of Bob. She wrote him of her frustrations with Joe, her feelings of neglect, her lack of love. When Bob did not respond promptly or adequately she reacted angrily. She would write things like: "Not one word from you in three weeks. Shocking! Humiliating! And disturbing. What *is* the matter with you, your manners and concern."
>
> In return for his support, Norma offered her son all the monetary and psychic advice and comfort he needed, or wanted, or, all too often, did not want. At times Bob found her offerings difficult to accept. He often responded to her generosity with hostility. He said he wanted merely "an ordinary parental relationship" with her and Joe.[242]

Forcey describes a number of incidents during which Bob flared up at his mother, violently insulting her and swearing he would never speak to her or see her again. The occasions for his violent reactions were often trivial. Bob's mother sometimes thought that Bob was "psychotic" and worried about him.

Bob grew up in Greenwich Village and went to the usual progressive private schools and camps. As a child he refused to respond to physical attacks. On one occasion he let other children beat him without trying to fight back. In high school, however, he was quite authoritarian with younger children, dominating them with verbal rather than physical aggression. At the Little Red School House, a progressive private school, his teachers described him as "creative, capable, inquisitive, charming, but also demanding, overly protective of his own interests, short tempered, in need of a lot of affection."[243]

One of his radical Jewish classmates said of him, describing his fascination with violence in later years, "Starobin and his generation were typical Jews. They grew up in the world without action. And they longed for the one thing they were terrified of—violence."[244]

In the early 1960s, against the advice of the father, Bob embraced revolutionary politics. Friends described his behavior as rather "schizophrenic." He was generally quiet, reserved, and even shy. Then, when a crisis arose, he would suddenly become caustic and verbally violent, especially in a crowd.

Starobin was an activist throughout the 1960s, and played an important role in the Free Speech Movement at Berkeley while a graduate student. He continued as an activist even after he became a full-time teacher. His professional specialty was slavery, and, in the winter of 1970 he published a very successful book, *Industrial Slavery in the Old South,* with Oxford University Press. His work in this field tied in very closely with an increasing sense of identification with blacks, especially militant black groups.

In fact, Bob's admiration for the Black Panthers knew no bounds. In the summer of 1970 he waited six hours for Huey Newton to be released from prison and jotted down his reactions when Newton emerged. The occasion was for him, as he described it, an historic day:

Brothers screaming, shoving, swarming to touch Huey. . . .
Brothers everywhere. . . . What courage with hundreds of pigs around.
Huey says it is he who is weak, the people are strong.
Huey takes off his shirt. He has incredibly strong breast muscles. A
  Black girl hurtles over the car into Huey's arms.[245]

By that time, however, the Movement was winding down, and Starobin grew increasingly depressed. His girl friend at that time found these moods rather frightening:

Often, Kitsi recalls, . . . he would mutter political rhetoric about oppression, Vietnam, or Cambodia, or the hopelessness of the Black Panther cause, or whatever was the issue of the moment. He might repeat a political slogan over and over again. Kitsi never paid much attention to actual words. She always felt they were, at these times, only the top layer of whatever was obsessing him. She would say to him: "That's not what you're really talking about, Starobin." He would often agree and respond with another "what am I going to do?"[246]

In May 1969 he had delivered a paper on American slavery at a college conference. His black fellow panelists were very hostile and attacked him personally. In the fall of 1970 he attended a Black Panther convention which he felt had been "a farce." In early February 1971 Bob awoke after a restless night and shot himself.

Starobin was an extreme case, a young man tragically characterized by severe narcissistic deficits. As Meissner and Kernberg have pointed out, such people find it difficult to face the world once the excitement and adulation they have received by being the center of attention has disappeared.

All the themes we have discussed, however, are present here. There is a "love affair" with an active and intelligent mother; the desire to be close and yet escape her by adopting a negative identity; the fear of violence and the need to prove oneself a man; and the identification with black militants who seem strong and virile. Starobin probably would have faced personal difficulties at any time, but the events of the 1960s seem to have frozen him into a state of adolescent crisis. They provided him with the opportunity to act out his fantasies instead of facing his problems. And they temporarily gratified his narcissism. In fact, it appears that the waning of the Movement and his rejection by militant blacks precipitated his self-destruction. Having lived a fantasy for so long, he no longer had the strength to deal with prosaic everyday reality. The excitement of being part of the Movement provided gratification for his narcissistic needs, and its disappearance produced depression and despair.

Phil Ochs's life and death bears a certain resemblance to that of Bob Starobin, although the pathology was clearly more serious. Unfortunately, we know little about the dynamics of his early life, despite a book-length biography and a profile in *Esquire,* both quite sympathetic.[247] Ochs, a folk/protest singer of the 1960s, thrived on the excitement of mass rallies and the cheers of large numbers of people. His commitment to revolution and hostility to the Establishment were rather incongruously linked with admiration for the macho "gentile" heroes of western movies. As one friend noted: "The interesting thing about him was that he was sixty percent cultural conservative and forty percent political radical. He loved John Wayne, Audie Murphy, William Buckley and Che Guevera."[248]

As the Vietnam War ended and protest faded, Ochs's talent seemed to decline as well. He also grew increasingly paranoid. Convinced that the CIA was going to kill him, he carried about a number of weapons, including a hammer and sometimes a pitchfork. He hired bodyguards and bought an interest in a bar in New York's Soho, which he intended to make the center of the revolution. This activity led to very little, and, given the loss of the narcissistic gratification provided by large audiences, Ochs's pathology grew more severe. He created a whole new personality called "Lewt Train." He would call up his friends to tell them that he had killed Phil Ochs and was just using his body. Eventually Lewt Train became John Train, a persona with grandiose ideas about such exploits as invading Chile on horseback or taking Fidel Castro on a tour of America: "Ochs became a shifting combination of all the heroes he had ever admired: John Wayne, Audie Murphy, Yasir Arafat, Howard Hughes—men of power and action. . . . At times it almost seemed as if he were living a movie and watching it at the same time."[249] He became involved in drunken brawls again and again, threatening to kill people; always trying to establish his masculinity and create the revolution. It was to no avail. His hyperactivity was followed by a severe depression that ended in suicide. After he died, a large memorial concert was held for him. Thousands of the people in the Movement came. To them, Ochs was a tragic hero.

Phil Ochs's death was indeed a tragedy. We suspect, however, that the sources of his self-destruction were not that different from those of Bob Starobin. Once again we find a desire to prove one's masculinity, an ambivalence toward the larger Christian community, and an inability to deal with the world, once a temporary conjunction of social forces, which had enabled him to act out his fantasies, began to unravel.

In this chapter we have traced Jewish radicalism to the historically marginal position of Jews in Christian societies and to the family structure and personality patterns encouraged by their marginality. To these must be added parental political socialization, at least in America during the 1960s.[250]

There was another factor. As Max Weber pointed out in "Science as a Vocation" and elsewhere, liberal rationality weakened traditional religious faith and so left individuals naked in the world.[251] He suggested that the search for experience (the new irrationality) might be a response to that nakedness. In 1960s America, deracinated Jewish intellectuals epitomized such nakedness. However, they were not alone. Increasingly large numbers of middle-class professionals had come to share their perspective, for reasons we discussed in Chapter 1 and will return to in our concluding chapter. For this very reason the Jewish role in the decay of the American civic myth, while important, was not determinative. They may have hastened the decay; they did not cause it.

As Robert Haddad has argued in his study of Syrian Christians, whom he compares with Jews along the lines suggested in this volume:

> On the politically dominant community whose institutions are more or less formed and stable, the marginal community can have little effect. The latter's power to influence and shape is greatest at those junctures when the characteristic institutions of the dominant community are in the process of formation, radical modification or destruction by forces which the marginal community may or may not have helped generate, but which it is able to accelerate and focus.[252]

Indeed, it was partially the decay of the larger culture and the crisis of political authority in the United States in the 1960s that brought to the surface in many young Jews patterns of behavior which would not have emerged at another time. A variety of primitive fantasy "solutions" to the inevitable tensions we all face as human beings is available in our unconscious. These derive, in part, from the culture itself, in interaction with primitive drives and wishes. They are kept in check for most of us when we mature in an environment characterized by a self-confident authority structure. When public authority (including political authority) is weakened, such fantasies may be acted out.

Thus political revolutions with purely political causes can result in radical changes in social, cultural, and family life. Of course, the most primitive fantasies are never institutionalized, because they are incompatible with an organized social order. Many modern revolutions have produced calls for the end of the family and the glorification of free sexuality. Once the new revolutionary elite consolidates its power, however, these more "radical" elements are suppressed.[253]

In any event the special role of Jews in radical movements may belong to the past, not the future. Rejection of key segments of the American civic religion is now widespread. While Jews are probably still differentially active among the Left's intellectual cadres, they now consititute a much smaller proportion of it than in the past. Further, as we have pointed out, many Jews are now in the camp of the active supporters of the culture (and antagonists of the Left).

Some of the earliest opponents of the New Left were Jews, many of whom were ex-radicals. We suspect that many of them were radicals *manqué*. Having partly overcome their own hostility to the dominant culture, they were both angered and threatened by the ability of radical Jews to express such anger with impunity.

Since then the Jewish intellectual community as a whole has become somewhat more conservative, even as Jewish voters have begun to move to the right.[254] One finds an increasing number of Jewish names among writers for *The National Review, The American Spectator,* and other conservative and neoconservative journals, aside from those in *Commentary* and *The Public Interest*.

These people include many who at one time would have considered themselves moderately "progressive."[255] Though our studies were completed too early to test this, we suspect that many such people now feel a strong stake in the American system. Among the key factors in this shift were remnants of identification with the Jewish community and/or Israel. Many Jews have gradually come to feel that the existence of Israel depends upon both the strength and influence of the United States and its continued support of a Jewish state.[256] From their point of view, the weakening of America's institutions could have only negative consequences, as would an emphasis on the wickedness of "advanced capitalist states" and the virtues of third world nations, especially radical third world nations.

In addition, Jews in the United States are disproportionately represented in the newer educated professions. Their high levels of achievement have involved a successful campaign to replace advancement on the basis of family connections and traditional notions of character with "objective" examinations. Thus, attacks on such methods of recruitment to universities and the professions for purposes of affirmative action violate their sense of fairness.

They feel, too, that such measures are likely to injure the society and reduce opportunities for both themselves and their children.

Finally, the relatively favorable position of Jews in post–World War II America had partly depended upon the guilt that large numbers of middle-class white Protestants and Catholics felt about the Holocaust. Jews gradually discovered that, whatever assistance they may have offered minority groups in the past, a new generation of blacks or Hispanics felt neither guilt nor gratitude. Just as Jews had sought to overcome marginal status by identifying with larger movements, so did these groups. Thus, blacks and Hispanics were more likely to identify with "third world" peoples than with Israel, which many of them regarded as a white outpost of European imperialism. Further, leaders of both these minority groups were likely to support quota-like arrangements in professional employment.[257]

The conservative shift among Jews is essentially conditional, for nonderacinated American Jews find themselves in a bind. On one hand the thinking and activities of radicals and many liberals are increasingly seen by them as inimical to their interests and those of the larger society. On the other hand, a resurgence of traditional American values might well be accompanied by the renewed ascendancy of religious fundamentalism.[258] If that were to come, Jews might once again find themselves the victims of anti-Semitism, or, at least, part of a society in which being Jewish entailed serious costs.

Three further comments seem called for. First, while we have stressed the "subversive" role of Jews, it must not be forgotten that Jewish liberals and radicals have contributed significantly to the increasing sophistication of American culture, as well as to reforming its institutions in what we consider to be positive and humane ways. Second, we are not arguing that Jewish radicals are more hostile or more guided by unconscious hostility than other radicals or, for that matter, many conservatives and liberals. Everyone invests politics and other areas of social life with hostile motives. We are simply underlining the particular investment characteristic of Jewish radicals.[259]

Finally, we must again emphasize that the personality tendencies we have described are social in origin and, like Jewish radicalism itself, historically delimited. What evidence we have indicates that they are not modal among the newer generation of Israeli Jews, despite some important continuities, especially among those raised on a kibbutz.[260] Given the rapid changes that are now taking place in the child-rearing patterns of cosmopolitan Americans, we expect that the next generation of American youth of Jewish background may be quite different from those that preceded it.

4 The Authoritarian Left

THE STYLE AND RHETORIC of the American New Left was strongly influenced by young people of Jewish background. Their crucial role in the birth and growth of that movement was the outcome of historical, social, and psychological factors that have long facilitated the adoption of radical ideas among Jews. At the close of Chapter 3, we argued that the political ideology of many young Jewish radicals was congruent with a kind of inverted authoritarian personality syndrome that led them to oppose conventional social authorities. In this chapter we will broaden and systematize our argument to encompass authoritarian personality styles among both Jewish and non-Jewish radicals.

The classic authoritarian adopts conservative ideas to defend himself against his underlying conflicts and insecurity. But this process, we believe, can be turned inside out. The same set of personal conflicts can give rise to either a fervent espousal or rejection of the Establishment. The traditional authoritarian deflects his hidden hositilities onto outsiders and outgroups. The inverse authoritarian unleashes his anger directly against the powers that be while taking the side of the world's "victims" and "outcasts."

The anarchist thus may have much in common with the conventionalist, just as embarrassing similarities have been observed between the motivations and behavior of Stalinists and fascists. Of course, not all radicals are reactive rebels, just as not all conservatives are authoritarians. Careful evidence must be adduced to demonstrate that particular personality styles are linked to particular political ideologies. Unless this is done, psychology becomes a handmaiden of partisanship and even demagoguery.

The scholars who first formulated a theory of authoritarian personality were quintessential outsiders: leftist, internationalist, deracinated Jewish academics who were refugees from resurgent German nationalism, political reaction, and virulent anti-Semitism.[1] They created a psycho-social portrait of the authoritarian as insider—an insider by desperation who feared being pushed out, deprived of his middle-class status and forced into the proletariat, deprived of his proud Germanic heritage, and deprived of his parents' affection. The more these things slipped from his grasp, the tighter he clung to them, blaming "outsiders" for his precarious position. Thus he used foreigners, Jews, communists, and international bankers as psychologically interchangeable scapegoats.

These symbols of resentment coalesced into an image of the "Jewish menace"—an outsider taking over his country, a crafty financial manipulator cheating him of his economic status, and a political agitator undermining his hardwon social position. Thus, in Horkeheimer's famous phrase, anti-Semitism had nothing to do with Jews. Instead, it had to do with a search for outsiders against whom the authoritarian confirmed his own threatened status as insider.

When the theory of authoritarianism crossed the Atlantic, the emigrés from Hitler's Germany saw the same potential for evil lurking in American nativism—the same desperate clinging to insider status by those who feared change, the outside world, and themselves perhaps most of all. In Germany, writing from the perspective of neo-Marxist "critical theory," these theorists had counterposed a "revolutionary" personality—an ego strong enough to ward off irrational needs for dependence and domination against the predominant authoritarian cast of mind. Now, mindful of their new hosts' sensibilities, they termed the same syndrome a "democratic" personality, the psycho-political opponent of the anti-democratic authoritarian.

The experience of McCarthyism established this dichotomy firmly in the minds of the psychologically oriented intellectual community. The insiders, the conservatives who laid chauvinistic claim to representing the true America, were in fact the great enemies of American democracy. They must be opposed by the critical outsider, particularly the upper-middle-class intellectual who best approached the ideal of the psychological democrat.

The research of scholars like Herbert McCloskey seemed to establish scientifically that conservatives were psychologically deficient, i.e., lacking in the qualities that made for a democratic personality.[2] Studies using the F scale repeatedly showed conservatives to be more authoritarian than liberals.[3] The upper-middle-class liberal intellectual, by contrast, emerged as an exemplar of civil libertarianism, democratic commitment, and psychological health.

The left-wing outsiders could not gain political ascendance during this period, as the nation twice chose a paternalistic symbol of military strength over a liberal intellectual. But they believed they represented the cause of both justice and mental health. Thus the theory of authoritarianism added a psychological element to the Left's claim to represent mankind's future.

When the nation entered the 1960s, and the nativists' idealized image of America began to crumble under the stresses of civil rights and Vietnam, the outsiders pressed their claim to represent the future. Student protesters were seen as embodiments of the new man, the long-awaited democratic personality finally making its mark on social and political life. It seemed a contradiction in terms that this new force of progressivism and health could contain a latent authoritarian or anti-democratic potential. These traits had been consigned to the nativist, the right winger, the anti-Semitic crank.

Yet could there not be an inverse form of authoritarianism, an anti-democratic psychic potential that could lead avowedly libertarian forces of "progressive" politics into the same cul-de-sac of moral rigidity, intolerance, and coerciveness? Was it not possible that the "liberated generation" was bound to potentially dangerous unconscious personality dynamics no less than its forebears?

The idea of an authoritarian personality type was first developed by Erich Fromm, who discussed an "authoritarian-masochistic character" in a 1936 essay included in the Frankfurt Institute's *Studies on Authority and Family*.[4] He later elaborated his thoughts on psychological authoritarianism in his influential *Escape from Freedom*. As the prototype for later efforts to link Nazism, fascism, or anti-democratic politics with a specific personality syndrome, Fromm's work bears careful scrutiny.

The concept of authoritarian character was based on Freud's notion of an "anal" or sadomasochistic character structure.[5] Like Freud, Fromm saw character not as a set of behavior patterns but as the dominant underlying drives that motivate behavior. A man's character was not simply the sum of his actions, though character might be inferred partly from behavior. For example, the sadomasochistic character was seen as dominated by tensions arising from simultaneous aggressive and submissive desires. This tension arises from the demands of a rigid conscience that forces the individual to deny himself instinctual gratification. On one hand he[6] feels "bad" or "weak" for entertaining "evil" sexual fantasies or "selfish" desires for self-aggrandizement. On the other hand, his very self-denial creates a lingering potential for resentment and hostility toward others, especially those who get away with the activities he forbids himself. He desires to control others, even as he must control himself, and to the same end: to stamp out everywhere the weakness he feels and fears within. This motivational dynamic typically leads to obsessive orderliness, punctuality, stinginess, or obstinacy, all of which reflect attempts to rigidly control the outer and inner environment.

Fromm's primary concern, though, was with the political relevance of the sadomasochistic character, which he saw as a deep and abiding ambivalence toward authority. The individual's sadistic component is expressed as a craving for unrestricted power over others. Insofar as those in authority restrain him, he is literally "driven" to oppose them. To this extent, the sadomasochistic individual is a natural rebel against authority. Yet his lust for domination is really an attempt to cover up a deep-seated sense of his own weakness. His masochistic component is reflected in his feeling that he deserves to be dominated as punishment for his "bad" or unacceptable desires, including the desire for power. Rather than directly exercising power, he may reconcile these contradictory needs by losing himself in a greater power, thereby enjoying vicarious feelings of strength and dominance. For example, he may join a political or religious movement led by a charismatic figure. By submitting his will to that of the leader, he satisfies his need to submit. At the same time, his membership in an elect group preserves a feeling of superiority over nonmenbers.

Whether sadistic or masochistic strivings are most prominent at any given moment, inner ambivalence persists between the two. When social authorities show signs of weakness, the authoritarian's repressed aggressions may surface, leading him to reject and attack the "paper tiger" that no longer provides vicarious feelings of strength. So his relation to a given authority may shift from unquestioning obedience to righteous rebellion. The constant in his behavior is an alignment with power, wherever he perceives it, and a concomitant revulsion against weakness.

Most of the time, we would expect this type of person to be submissive toward in-group authorities like those of church and state, and to redirect his aggression against foreign gods, leaders, and peoples. It is primarily during a crisis of authority that submission gives way to rebellion and veneration of indigenous authority turns to hatred. Examples of such crises were the Protestant Reformation and, in our own century, the rise of fascism in the 1920s and '30s.

These historical examples were chosen by Fromm, who viewed this character type as historically long-lived and sociologically widespread. In his 1936 essay, he described it as typical of the great majority of mankind. In *Escape from Freedom,* he characterized it somewhat more narrowly, as typical of the European lower middle classes.[7] He argued that sadomasochistic needs helped account for the appeal of fascism to these strata. He then traced the spread of "authoritarian" personality traits to the changing socioeconomic condition of the middle class, and he charted the expression of these traits in new religious and political attachments.

Fromm argued that the rise of capitalism had brought not only increased possibilities of individual freedom and advancement but also feelings of personal powerlessness and individual insignificance. In addition, the masses felt tremendous envy and resentment toward the new moneyed elites. In the sphere of religion, pent-up hostility and envy were projected onto the despotic God of Lutheranism and Calvinism, whose demands for complete submission and admission of human wickedness prepared believers psychologically to subordinate their lives to ends determined by external authorities. Hostility and resentment also found their way into personal relations, in the form of suspiciousness and moral indignation. Finally, hostility was turned against the self, reappearing under the guise of conscience and duty and fueling an "inner worldly asceticism" that underlay both self-humiliation and self-righteousness. These traits were diffused throughout society, but were centered among the lower middle classes.

The Nazis eventually played on such needs to enhance their political power. Not only were the upper classes forced to share some of their wealth and prestige, but hostility could be legitimately focused onto Jews and political enemies. The little man could bask in a feeling of superiority over the rest of the world, as a member of the newly ascendant German nation and the Aryan race. At the same time, he could know his place once again, after prolonged social turmoil. His life was governed and regulated by powerful and resplendent forces—the nation, the party, the Führer. By serving these masters, he could vicariously partake of their power and glory. Thus the authoritarian character was the "human basis" of fascism, in the double sense that such an ideology fulfills needs for power and submission and is in turn furthered by them.

Fascism was not the inevitable political fulfillment of sadomasochistic personality needs. But such a polity seemed better able than democracies to offer personal fulfillment to such individuals. An important corollary was that, in many social and cultural contexts, the sadomasochistic character structure was not neurotic or pathological but normal, i.e., both socially adaptive and numerically predominant. In fact, Fromm specifically chose the term "authoritarian" to refer to clinically normal people with strong sadomasochistic drives, "because the sadomasochistic person is always characterized by his attitude toward authority. He admires authority and tends to submit to it, but at the same time he wants to be an authority himself and have others submit to him."[8]

Fromm's model of authoritarian character profoundly influenced later efforts to identify an anti-democratic or potentially fascistic personality type. Yet he differed significantly from those who followed his lead, by stressing that this character structure was both "normal" and subject to historical modification. Some aspects of this concept presaged later attempts to identify an authoritarianism of the Left. Fromm's most immediate and strongest influence, though, was on the landmark effort to transfer the study of authoritarian character from Nazi Germany to mid-century America.

When Fromm's colleagues Horkheimer and Adorno began their systematic study of authoritarianism, they were refugees, driven to America by the triumph of Nazism. Their work was guided by the anxious question, "Can it happen here?" As German Jews, they saw the strongest component of fascism as racism, specifically the anti-Semitism they had experienced.

The Authoritarian Personality was the product of Horkheimer and Adorno's collaboration with a group of more empirically oriented American social psychologists.[9] Their theory of an authoritarian type of person as a potential fascist stemmed from the Frankfurt Institute's earlier speculations, particularly Fromm's work. *The Authoritarian Personality* elaborated and systematized these theoretical insights and, most importantly, examined the relationship between antidemocratic ideas and authoritarian needs in individual human beings. To do so, they surveyed more than 2000 people, from college students to prison inmates, giving intensive clinical interviews to 150 of them. Their subjects filled out an extensive questionnaire dealing with their backgrounds, their attitudes toward social issues, and their personality tendencies. The smaller clinical study probed much more deeply into subjects' lives and family backgrounds by combining in-depth interviews with standardized personality tests.

The Authoritarian Personality's theoretical core lay in Adorno's contributions and in the overall guidance exercised by Horkheimer. Their main argument was that prejudice is not an isolated attitude but part of a broad tendency to divide one's world into "good" ingroups, of which one is or wishes to be a member, and "evil" outgroups, whose negative characteristics justify their segregation or elimination. Specific prejudices flow from this general ethnocentric disposition. Ethnocentrism, in turn, is an expression of authoritarian personality characteristics that are implanted during childhood.

The typical authoritarian's parents interpret the roles of parent and child in terms of dominance and submission. The household is controlled by a domineering father who is cold and punitive. His harsh discipline combines with emotional distance to reduce the child's self-esteem. If the child is punished, he must be "bad." At the same time, this creates underlying hostility against parental authority. The hostility cannot be directly and overtly expressed, since that would simply increase the child's guilt. After all, only bad children reject their parents. Eventually, feelings of worthlessness and aggression produce an overwhelming frustration. They must find an outlet that is psychologically safer than direct insurrection against one's parents.

This outlet is provided by the mechanism of prejudice. One's own per-ceived shortcomings are projected onto an outgroup. These very shortomings justify the redirection of hostility from parental authority and the societal au-thorites for which the parents served as prototypes toward the outgroup. The remainder of guilt-producing aggression is repressed, and ingroup authority is idealized. The outgroup is vilified as the repository of all those negative traits that one is afraid to see in either oneself or one's parents.

This thumbnail sketch of the theory, however, does not account for the enormous and lasting impact *The Authoritarian Personality* had in areas rang-ing far beyond the study of prejudice. This work proved most influential as a theory of political personality. In specifying the relations between personality functions and political behavior, it becomes relevant to our analysis of the New Left. Our discussion will carry us first inward, to the inner dynamic and child-hood genesis of authoritarianism, and then back outward, toward its impact on ideas and behavior. To Adorno and his colleagues, this path leads past the way-station of prejudices to the ultimate destination of fascism.

The linchpin of the authoritarian's personality is his intense ambivalence toward authority. Power relations are all-important to him, yet he can never be comfortable in the world of ever-shifting hierarchies of authority. Though he desires power and status, he also fears the responsibilities they bring. And while he chafes against external control, he welcomes the security of having decisions made for him. His personality is dominated by neither the wish to rule nor the wish to obey, but by the tension of trying to satisfy both desires at once. The authoritarian is a conflicted personality, a mind at odds with itself.

The authoritarian's primal personality conflict is between unusually fierce aggressive impulses and a rigid and punitive conscience that denies their expression. This intrapsychic clash of irresistible force with immovable object is the source of the many psychological mechanisms that make the authoritarian a special "type" of person. Equally important is his inability to understand rationally and deal with these competing needs. He is conscious of them pri-marily in his sense of being driven by forces beyond his understanding and control.

The authoritarian, then, is victimized by poor integration of his conscious rational faculties, his precocious conscience, and his hidden desires. His ego is continually threatened by the pressure of his desires for personal aggrandize-ment and the counter-pressure of his conscience's refusal to permit such "evil" impulses. Buffeted by forbidden desires and unable to temper them through rational comprehension, he relies on irrational defenses to preserve his sense of identity. On one hand, he represses his hostility and resentment of the societal authorities who deny him emotional gratification. He hides his inner rage be-hind a mask of submissiveness and obedience. Not trusting his own inner guides, he clings to socially approved external standards of morality and behavior. Opposed to introspection for fear of what he might see in himself, he finds the determinants of his destiny in mysterious external forces beyond his understanding or control. He perceives the world in terms of stereotypes, because recognition of life's uncertainties and complexities might undermine the oversimplified self-concept that protects him from anxiety.

This game of emotional hide-and-seek requires the strictest self-control in order to keep from admitting to consciousness the evil hidden within oneself. The authoritarian lives in fear that he will prove too weak to control his emotions, that his defenses will break down despite his constant vigilance. He attempts to cover this underlying fear of weakness with a veneer of toughness and an identification with powerful figures.

Were this the whole of the authoritarian syndrome, its effects might be confined to individual anxiety, passivity, and withdrawal. But repression is not sufficient to control such deep-seated conflicts. On the contrary, repression intensifies the inner struggle by bottling up powerful emotions outside the realm of consciousness, ensuring that pressure will continue to build. Relief requires that external outlets be found for internal but "ego-alien" conflict. The authoritarian carries out this externalization via the defense mechanisms of projection and displacement. As they emerge from his unconscious, he experiences threatening impulses as impinging upon him from "outside," hence as physically external, and attributes them to "outsiders"—racial or ethnic minorities, ideological opponents, and so on. By projecting his own undesirable characteristics onto outsiders, he rechannels aggression that cannot be directed against its original targets. The authoritarian thus displaces his hatred of authority onto those whose "evil" characteristics legitimize the negative emotions he dares not express against parents or superiors. In this way, the object of hostility serves as a lightning rod, protecting him from the consequences of his own inner storm of emotions.

The remaining traits of the syndrome follow from the authoritarian's "projectivity." Because he attributes to others what he fears and despises in himself, he is cynical about their motives and concerned that they not get away with the instinctual gratifications he is denied. He becomes preoccupied with secret plots and hostile conspiracies. Most importantly, his precocious conscience is now turned outward in the form of moral indignation, which justifies aggression against violators of approved norms. Adorno treats this as a key element in politicizing authoritarian personality needs:

> The individual who has been forced to give up basic pleasures and to live under a system of rigid restraints, and therefore feels put upon, is likely not only to seek an object upon which he can "take it out" but

also to be particularly annoyed at the idea that another person is "getting away with something." . . .

Once the individual has convinced himself that there are people who ought to be punished, he is provided with a channel through which his deepest aggressive impulses may be expressed, even while he thinks of himself as thoroughly moral. . . .[10]

Adorno is describing a man whose inner existence is externalized in both a psychological and sociological sense. He treats his deepest emotions as external to himself, displacing his innermost needs onto others. Ultimately he may attempt to eliminate psychic threats by exterminating other people.

How can such fearsome conflicts arise in a man that he relinquishes self-understanding and self-determination in a desperate effort to resolve them? Adorno and his psychoanalytically oriented colleagues believed that such pervasive personality trends must take root quite early in life. Their conception of the childhood genesis of authoritarianism was not guided by a prior systematic theory. It was developed in the course of interviews in which subjects were asked to describe their family backgrounds. On the basis of the interview material, clinical psychologist Else Frenkel-Brunswick sketched a portrait of the "authoritarian-producing" family setting as one segment of the overall study.[11]

This work was not entirely without theoretical predecessors. In particular, Frenkel-Brunswick's conclusions recall Erik Erikson's earlier speculations on the German family, in an essay on Hitler's psychological appeal.[12] In fact her later clinical studies become clearer when viewed through Erikson's theoretical framework.

Erikson discussed the role of a demanding and punitive father who deprives the child of a sense of self-worth, without serving as a prototype of the ideals toward which the child must strive for redemption. This father demands respect as his due without commanding respect through his actions. His harsh discipline creates ambivalence in the child, so that love and admiration are intermingled with hostility and fear. In essence, his paternal authority is based on power rather than respect.

In this image of the domineering but "flawed" father, Erikson located the source of "that severe German puberty which is such a strange mixture of open rebellion and 'secret sin', cynical delinquency and submissive obedience . . .,"[13] and whose ultimate political expression is fascism. The psychological appeal of Nazism lay in its "imagery of ideological adolescence," which provided outlets for pent-up hostility toward Jews and other "subhumans."

The central figure in this family drama, then, is the father, described by Frenkel-Brunswick as a "forbidding figure" who is "distant and stern, with a bad temper." His cold and remote domination of the family erects barriers between father and child that strip their relationship of warmth and caring. His disciplinary style is harsh and arbitrary, designed to force the child into submission. The essence of the father's strictness is not the amount of discipline exercised but its "quasi-persecutory" style. He alternates between "traumatic, overwhelming discipline" on some occasions and "neglect, including failure to give proper discipline" on others.

This emphasis on the "victimizing quality" of paternal discipline recalls Erikson's effort to distinguish the domineering "German father" from the stern but just Victorian patriarch, who could inspire both respect and affection:

> . . . the difference lies in the German father's essential lack of true inner authority—that authority which results from an integration of cultural ideal and educational method.[14]

Whether or not Erikson is right about Germany, this distinction helps account for the authoritarian's intense ambivalence toward paternal authority. A figure like the "German father" might inspire fear rather than awe and contempt rather than respect. Erikson argued that a child would sense the "emotional impotence" underlying the father's bluster and react with "pity and disgust."

The mother's role received somewhat less attention, since Frenkel-Brunswick considered the father as more psychologically salient. This issue was developed more systematically by Erikson, who viewed the mother-child relationship as a function of a strongly patriarchal family structure. He saw her status within the family as more that of a mature child than of an adult equal in stature to her husband. Her "proper place" is with the children, but her ultimate allegiance is to her husband. She thus becomes a go-between, at once the hated father's subordinate and the child's ally as its only buffer against paternal harshness. This ambiguous role creates a radical ambivalence in the child's view of its mother.

Frenkel-Brunswick posited a similarly ambivalent maternal relationship, in which "moralism and restrictiveness" are coupled with submissiveness and self-sacrifice. Though the mother might "devote" herself to her child, this is quite different from a genuinely warm relationship based on love rather than power.

The basic argument is that maternal affection is not shared fully but given and taken away on the mother's terms. Hence the child's ambivalence—an idealized image of the mother as saint and protectress coexists with a negative

view of her as "henpeckingly dominant," taking over "the threatening function of the family as a whole." But while both parents could be seen as dominating the child, the father remains the more dominant and influential figure,
the ultimate authority.

On the whole, Frenkel-Brunswick's clinical reconstruction of the authoritarian's family background is consistent with the theories of Fromm and Adorno.
They traced the genesis of this syndrome back to a "sadomasochistic" resolution of the Oedipal complex, in which the child never succeeds in coping with
aggressive feelings toward his parents. As Adorno described this process:

> . . . part of the preceding aggressiveness is turned into masochism,
> while another part is left over as sadism, which seeks an outlet in those
> with whom the subject does not identify himself: ultimately the out-
> group, (which) frequently becomes a substitute for the hated father. . . .
> Ambivalence is all-pervasive, being evidenced mainly by the simultane-
> ity of blind belief in authority and readiness to attack those who are
> acceptable as "victims." . . . Identification with the familial structure
> and ultimately with the whole ingroup becomes, to this kind of individ-
> ual, one of the main mechanisms by which they can impose authoritar-
> ian discipline upon themselves and avoid "breaking away"—a tempta-
> tion nourished continually by their underlying ambivalence.[15]

Research into family background and personality dynamics of the authoritarian thus came together in an overall developmental theory of the "potentially
fascist" personality, which was intended to alert Americans to the fascist potential in their midst. Adorno and his colleagues must have expected that this
theory would prove highly controversial. But they were caught unprepared by
the controversy that erupted over their research methods as well as their sub-
stantive arguments. In fact, the ensuing imbroglio has yet to abate, despite the
many hundreds of subsequent attempts to prove, disprove, or revise the arguments set forth nearly three decades ago. Today there is still widespread disagreement as to whether an authoritarian type of person exists or, given his
existence, how his personality traits are best classified and measured and how
they might influence his political ideas and behavior. Rarely has so much debate, discussion, and research produced so little progress in answering a presumably empirical or scientific question. As a result, one does well to heed
John Kirscht and Ronald Dillehay's warning against the deceptive simplicity
and intuitive appeal of the concept of authoritarian personality:

> We suffer from the apparent ease with which authoritarian behavior can
> be identified in real-life examples, especially in the pejorative use of the

concept to label what appears as an unyielding, paranoid reaction to the social world. . . . In fact, the concept has so many different aspects that investigators lack a common core of established meaning, and often assume connections between various dispositions that have never been examined satisfactorily.[16]

We have already discussed some of the technical inadequacies of *The Authoritarian Personality*. These inadequacies have had important implications for the development of the theory itself, and many scholars have tried to correct them and still preserve portions of the theory. Two related problems are particularly relevant to our own studies. First, considerable confusion persists over the "locus" of authoritarianism. Is it a syndrome of underlying, perhaps unconscious personality dynamics, or is it simply a set of conscious attitudes? Second, is the ideological expression of authoritarianism necessarily limited to right-wing politics? If we can conceive of a left-wing or even nonideological expression of authoritarianism, can its central characteristics be derived from the theory we have described or must it be substantially revised or even abandoned?

The Authoritarian Personality was guided by an overriding theoretical vision, whose validity was taken for granted. Horkheimer and Adorno viewed the empirical research not as a test of hypotheses about the emotional roots of political prejudice but as means to "concretize" their theory. They never doubted that the theory itself was correct. In light of this attitude, it is ironic that the widespread influence of their work stems mainly from the concise "scientific test" of authoritarianism it provided, in the form of the F scale. Since 1950, research on authoritarianism has usually meant research employing the F scale as a measure of "potential fascism."

The F scale was developed to measure attitudes that typically expressed an underlying authoritarian character structure. Yet there is a crucial gap between Fromm and Adorno's psychodynamic theories and the traits measured by this test. Quite simply, the F scale cannot test the relationship between psychodynamics and sociopolitical attitudes because the scale measures only the attitudes. It is simply assumed that these attitudes express deeper personality trends. *TAP* co-author Nevitt Sanford's account of the theory behind a single component of the F scale shows how many untested inferences lurk between theory and test:

Consider the item, "He is indeed contemptible who does not feel an undying love, gratitude, and respect for his parents." On the surface, this item expresses authoritarian aggression and authoritarian submission and, hence, might be classified as primarily a superego item. But the theory was that agreement with this extreme statement might well mask an underlying hostility toward the parents. In other words, we hypothesized that unconscious hostility toward the parents is a distinguishing feature of the highly ethnocentric person; our problem was to determine how this tendency might give itself away in an attitude scale. One answer was through signs of a reaction formation, this mechanism being a common one in the highly ethnocentric person. Thus, the present item had to do with an interplay of superego, ego, and id; an underlying unconscious, ego-alien tendency, coming mainly from the id, has led to anxiety of punishment (superego), which the ego seeks to ward off or reduce by transforming the forbidden tendency into its opposite. But this is not all. This is merely the authoritarian submission expressed in the item. "He is indeed contemptible" is an expression of authoritarian aggression. The ego must, so to speak, be doubly sure that punishment is avoided, and that the original id tendency finds some sort of gratification; hence it joins forces with the punitive agency and imputes the "badness" to other people, who may then be freely aggressed against in good conscience.[17]

Some part of this complex line of reasoning probably rings true to psychoanalytically inclined readers. Most social psychologists, on the other hand, would certainly question whether a single belief necessarily expresses such a labyrinth of hidden emotions. A certain skepticism, or at least agnosticism, is probably the most appropriate reaction. Clearly, Sanford and his co-workers simply inferred the alleged emotional substratum of such "authoritarian" attitudes from psychoanalytic theory.

Whatever the intended latent content of F scale items, their manifest content consists primarily in beliefs about human nature and one's proper relationship to other people. That is, the F scale measures certain aspects of social ideology which may or may not reflect deeper personality dispositions. The most that can be inferred from the correlation of "F" with other attitude scales is a unified social outlook, rather than the unity of personality and ideology found by Adorno and his colleagues.

All this has resulted in considerable confusion as to precisely what it is that the F scale measures. In trying to capture the psychodynamic complexity and latent emotional basis of fascist proclivities with a single paper-and-pencil test, the authors produced the opposite of what they intended. The F scale can create the impression that authoritarianism is nothing more than a set of beliefs, a cast of mind combining political conservatism with intolerance toward social deviance.

Some scholars have taken just this view, emptying the theory of its dynamic content by treating authoritarianism as a set of antidemocratic attitudes. For example, S. M. Lipset contends that authoritarianism is an outgrowth of lower-class cultural norms.[18] By this he means simply that, as surveys repeatedly show, lower-status people are less committed to democratic ideals, more attracted to extremist movements, and more imbued with social conservatism than are upper-status people in this country. This may be so, but such "authoritarianism" has little to do with the personality forces that Fromm and Adorno took to be the mark of authoritarian character. Such purely cognitive interpretations were encouraged by the social and cultural values that permeate *The Authoritarian Personality:* values that led the original researchers to equate underlying personality with social persona. Their assumption that the "natural" authoritarian was a lower-middle-class nativist was inadvertently revealed by Sanford in his response to growing criticism of their methods:

> The question, "Will the F scale differentiate groups of people who show authoritarian traits in their behavior from groups who do not show such traits?" is not one that has troubled the group very much. . . . For example, the project's secretary, a good observer to be sure, could tell with considerable accuracy from a subject's telephone conversation about an appointment whether she was dealing with a "high" or "low" (scorer), and if any doubt remained it was almost always dispelled by noting that subject's dress and manner when he or she appeared at the office.[19]

Use of the F scale has not only led to superficial readings of the concept of authoritarianism but also narrowed the concept to include only the ideological "right." The resemblance of conservative and "authoritarian" attitudes is so strong that some writers simply treat the two as parallel concepts. But if authoritarianism is nothing more than an extreme conservative ideology, why should it be considered an integral aspect of personality functioning? Edward Shils thus condemned the F scale as "political attitudes masquerading as personality dispositions . . . designed to disclose not authoritarian personality as such but rather the 'Right'—the nativist-fundamentalist Authoritarian."[20]

The test was intentionally "loaded" toward the political right because its creators, who were trying to identify potential fascists, saw fascism as a right-wing phenomenon. But if the potential for fascism lies not in conservative attitudes themselves but in the underlying personality trends they express, there should be some way of determining whether these trends might also be expressed in other attitudes.

If authoritarianism is to mean anything more than conservatism, or perhaps "pseudo-conservatism," we must rethink the basic questions that Fromm and Adorno failed to answer convincingly: who is an authoritarian, how do we identify his personality needs, and how may these needs affect his political behavior?

Despite the naiveté and ideological and perhaps cultural bias of much authoritarianism research, the original concept may yet guide us through the dark labyrinth leading from emotional to political conflict and from personality structure to social action. We believe that certain aspects of the theory of authoritarianism are indispensable to understanding the psycho-social distinctiveness of the New Left. But the threads of meaning must be carefully separated from the hidden assumptions and unquestioned dogma that lead only to blind alleys. In revising the theory, we shall attempt to establish a common core of meaning for the concept of authoritarianism. Our goal is to make the concept more scientifically meaningful and less open to abuse as a psychopolitical epithet. To this end we shall try to recover the theory's psychodynamic core while eliminating its ideological accretions.

Our aim is by no means taxonomic; we do not wish to "classify" student radicals as authoritarian. Instead, we hope to show that the psychological mechanisms explained by this concept help to illuminate certain ideas and activities prevalent among dissident youth as well as certain developments that influenced the direction of their movement. We shall provide, then, a speculative scenario of the interaction of psychological and situational factors that guided the political expression of their internal needs and desires. The writings and statements of New Leftists themselves will provide much of the evidence for this scenario. In later chapters we will test our theory with three studies of New Left activists in the United States and Germany.

> Authoritarianism of the sort we studied in the 1940's is a psychohistorical conception—it owed much of its content and structure to the period in which it was observed and formulated.[21]

With these words, Nevitt Sanford reminds us of the historical relativity not only of authoritarianism but of personality itself. He goes on to argue, "We could not hope fully to understand authoritarian leadership of the 1930's through studying Oliver Cromwell or Cotton Mather"; nor will authoritarians in today's postindustrial societies look much like "prefascist personalities in the highly industrialized society of the 1940's."[22]

On the surface, this seems a reasonable caveat for the study of personality and politics. Since personality is shaped by an ever-shifting matrix of social, economic, and cultural factors, it seems obvious that typical personality patterns will undergo considerable change over time. People change as their societies change, just as people in different societies differ from one another. Yet this may overstate the case for psychological relativism. After all, Fromm found Martin Luther to be "a typical representative of the 'authoritarian character.' "[23] He also argued that the psychological appeals of early Lutheranism and Calvinism were quite similar, in many respects, to those of Nazism.

There is no necessary contradiction between the viewpoints of Fromm and Sanford on this issue. The surface aspects of personality may change fairly rapidly on both the individual and aggregate levels. Attitudes, belief structures, the ways aggressive impulses are overtly expressed—all these may be rapidly affected by changing socioeconomic conditions and cultural mores. However significant such personality shifts may be for political behavior, they do not constitute changes in "human nature" as the term is generally understood.

Before asking whether some type of "authoritarian" personality trends might have surfaced within contemporary political movements, we must separate the enduring from the ephemeral characteristics of authoritarianism. It is hardly surprising, for instance, that 1960s radicals would reject F scale items designed to tap potential right-wing extremism. Nonetheless, the characterological core of authoritarianism may remain relatively constant, generating widely diverse political manifestations, including avowedly leftist perspectives.

Basically the theory seeks to explain feelings about authority, specifically the deep-seated emotional conflicts that produce conflicting wishes to submit and to tyrannize. Fromm and Adorno emphasized particular sociopolitical manifestations of this disposition—racial or religious prejudice and undemocratic "fascistic" political behavior. They described a syndrome of associated psychological traits and development fitted to these particular ideological and behavioral manifestations. But the psychodynamic nucleus of the theory is simply that a deep emotional ambivalence toward authority motivates behavior that expresses simultaneous aggressive and submissive desires.

Such ambivalence might exist in quite different developmental, dispositional, and situational contexts, and could find a variety of behavioral outlets other than racism or fascism. In fact, Fromm's initial work on the sadomasochistic character emphasized that psychological authoritarianism might be consistent with ostensibly anti-authority views and activities. He argued, in fact, that revolt against authority may stem from two fundamentally different psychological impulses, which he labeled "revolution" and "rebellion." The mark of a genuine psychological revolution is that "one revolts against a particular master, not because he desires another, but because he rejects all masters. This presupposes that his own ego will no longer permit masochistic dependence."[24] Strong enough to reject the perverse pleasure of irrational subordination, the psychological revolutionary obeys political authority only from his rational perception that it represents his true interests. This revolutionary personality is the normative ideal that later gave birth to theories of a democratic personality.

By contrast, psychological rebellion stems from the same ambivalent relationship to authority that otherwise results in unquestioning obedience. Both the obeisant servant and the rigid rebel are trapped between irrational love and equally irrational hatred of authority. The "positive-authoritarian" represses his hostility and allows himself only conscious feelings of love and loyalty toward his masters. He reaps the psychic reward of participating in power by serving as adjunct to the powerful. But the same personality constellation may instead result in rebellion against the powers-that-be:

> . . . the normally repressed hostility to authority bursts out as a hatred for authority just as fervent as the previous love and admiration. . . . Such people often respond to any authority they encounter with a defiance and rebelliousness just as automatic as the authoritarian type's reverence and servility. . . . While the positive-authoritarian character represses the negative side of his ambivalent feelings toward authority, the rebellious negative-authoritarian represses his love for it. His whole resistance is only superficial. In reality he has the same yearning for love and approval by the powerful. . . . He's always ready to capitulate. Anarchistic types often exemplify this rebellious character; when they turn into worshippers of power, little psychological change has taken place.[25]

This early passage avoids many pitfalls of later theories of authoritarianism. Fromm refuses to equate avowedly anti-authoritarian activity with psychological health. Instead he provides psychodynamic grounding for Marx's argument that the "infantile Left" could be as great an obstacle to human liberation as the authoritarian Right.

In *Escape from Freedom,* Fromm expanded upon his depiction of the negative-authoritarian, warning that his assertions of independence are dangerously misleading:

> It appears as if they are persons who oppose every authority on the basis of an extreme degree of independence. They look like persons who, on the basis of their inner strength and integrity, fight those forces that block their freedom and independence. However, the (negative-) au-

thoritarian character's fight against authority is essentially defiance. It is an attempt to assert himself and to overcome his own feeling of powerlessness by fighting authority, although the longing for submission remains present, whether consciously or unconsciously.[26]

Superficially, such people may appear to have transcended the underlying power needs and authority conflicts central to an authoritarian disposition. They might well consider themselves "liberated" from conventionalism and submissiveness. In reality, though, their overtly positive self-image and outward show of independence conceal emotional conflicts similar to those of Adorno's protofascist. The rebel's rigid opposition to authority is the Janus face of the traditional authoritarian's rigid obedience.

As with any mode of authoritarianism, a variety of political styles is consistent with rebellious impulses. The rebel's rejection of authority can give rise to a spectrum of behavior, ranging from unswerving hostility to a short-lived defiance that quickly crumbles when challenged. At one end of this spectrum is the rebel in whom "sadistic" or aggressive desires exercise the predominant influence on behavior. He may go through life opposing authority in any guise, making no distinction between legitimate and illegitimate authority. He is the embodiment of Genet's philosophical criminal, for whom authority per se is illegitimate. At the other end are those whose rebellion contains substantial "masochistic" or submissive elements. Their temporary opposition to authority is part of a quest for a new authority that can command their wholehearted loyalty. As Fromm described them:

> Such persons might fight against one set of authorities, especially if they are disappointed by its lack of power, and at the same time or later on submit to another set of authorities which through greater power or greater promises seem to fulfill their masochistic longings.[27]

All rebels, though, are driven to reject current authority, along with the traditions and conventions that create its aura of legitimacy. These "authoritarian revolutionaries" may appear in a fascist movement, but we can as easily conceive of them as avowed leftists, or in roles that resist ideological classifications. The concept transcends the restrictions Fromm and Adorno placed on its political import. Adorno, in fact, treats Fromm's rebel as one of several subsyndromes that deviate from the classic authoritarian pattern measured by the F scale. He describes this pattern as an inversion of the orthodox authoritarian syndrome, originating in the same harsh and loveless pattern of child-rearing, i.e., a cold and harsh family life dominated by a punitive father. What first differentiates positive from negative authoritarians is their differing response to paternal discipline:

> Instead of identification with parental authority, "insurrection" may take place . . . masochistic transference to authority may be kept down on the unconscious level while resistance takes place on the manifest level. This may lead to an irrational and blind hatred of *all* authority, with strong destructive connotations, accompanied by a secret readiness to "capitulate" and to join hands with the "hated" strong. . . . [The replacement of] dependency by negative transference. . . . when it is combined with an urge to take pseudorevolutionary actions against those whom the individual ultimately deems to be weak, is [the syndrome] of the "Rebel."[28]

In Adorno's model, hostility toward parental (and especially paternal) authority surfaces early and is generalized onto other representatives of societal authority, while submissive and dependent tendencies are repressed.

Adorno's rebel is characterized by "a penchant for 'tolerated excesses' " rather than rigid conformity. As a result of his total rejection of parental and social authority, he is "egotistical" rather than conscience-ridden. His need for nonconformity by definition allows him avenues of self-expression not available to the submissive authoritarian. In this sense he is less rigid than his conventionalist counterpart. Yet the same inner conflict pervades both submissive and rebellious modes of authoritarianism. It is a conflict over power, which is expressed as a preoccupation with potency, domination, and control. The authoritarian is thus distinguished by an

> overemphasis on the power motif in human relationships . . . a disposition to view all relations among people in terms of such categories as strong-weak, dominant-submissive, "hammer-anvil". And it is difficult to say with which of these roles [he] is more fully identified. It appears that he wants to get power . . . and at the same time is afraid to seize and wield it. It appears that he also admires power in others and is inclined to submit to it—and at the same time is afraid of the weakness thus implied. . . . [He] readily identifies himself with the "little people" . . . but he does so with little or no humility, and he seems to think of himself as strong or to believe that he can become so.[29]

In the traditional authoritarian, the need to submit predominates at the surface level. This desire is satisfied by obedience to conventional authority. In the rebel, the need for self-aggrandizement is paramount. A sense of individual identity is achieved through opposition to conventional authority. Latent submissive tendencies remain, however, pushing the rebel toward alliances with figures he perceives as more powerful than the traditional authorities he has rejected.

During the years following publication of *The Authoritarian Personality,* the "rebel" syndrome was generally ignored by scholars, buried by the controversy over the study's major findings and methods. More recently, a number of writers have dealt with the personality structures of avowedly anti-authoritarian individuals who are themselves reactively hostile to authority. Milton Rokeach, for example, argues that leftist and rightist radicals share a "dogmatic" approach to politics.[30] In his view, authoritarians of the Left and Right share ways of thinking about the social environment, rather than similar feelings about authority. Left authoritarianism is therefore a matter of cognitive style rather than emotional dynamics. Yet Rokeach falls back on Fromm's concept of politicized sadomasochistic ambivalence to explain the psychodynamic underpinnings of a dogmatic cognitive style.[31] Authoritarian emotional dynamics may indeed generate dogmatic adherence to political ideology or an "ideologized" view of the social and political world. But Rokeach fails to develop this notion of linkage between the cognitive and emotional realms.

Victor Wolfenstein's model of a "revolutionary personality" is a more direct effort to apply Fromm and Adorno's concepts toward understanding three revolutionary figures—Lenin, Trotsky, and Gandhi.[32]

The most important personality trait these revolutionaries seemed to share was an overriding concern with domination and submission, accompanied by feelings of victimization. Wolfenstein traces this concern to unusually strong Oedipal ambivalence, that is, an intense focusing of both love and hate on paternal authority. All three men partially identified with their fathers as models of masculine authority but rejected the traditional moral standards their fathers embodied. They were driven by the emotional conflict that this ambivalence engendered.

All three were able to deal with their internal crisis only by transferring their emotional involvement from the private to the public realm. In each case, the externalization of inner conflict was precipitated by contact with agents of a hostile political authority during late adolescence or young adulthood. The experience of being victimized by political authority, Wolfenstein argues, served a common paradigmatic psychic function. Internal conflicts could be displaced onto the representatives of external authority who forcibly imposed themselves on the youth's personal struggles. Their consequent rejection of authority represented an attempt to escape inner ambivalence by breaking completely with the father and the societal authority for which he served as prototype. These nascent revolutionaries could now deal with their own undesired aggressive impulses by projecting them onto external aggressors.

It is important to note that such "psychopolitical" rebellion can be precipitated by external political events. Once set in motion, though, the channeling of aggression onto the public realm helps resolve the strain of Oedipal ambivalence. As feelings of hatred are redirected outward onto one set of political objects, feelings of love can be expressed freely toward other objects. Ambivalence is resolved by compartmentalizing its components into pure love for the opponents of hostile authority and hatred of that authority and its representatives.

In Wolfenstein's model, the revolutionary is driven from within and without toward a Manichean view of the political world. His feelings of shared oppression provide the contact point for identification with a revolutionary brotherhood. A young middle-class student can thus consider himself the brother of oppressed peoples the world over, projecting his new-found feelings of solidarity onto peasants or proletarians. In his own mind, his love of "the people" brings him their love and acceptance in return. He becomes a self-chosen representative of the oppressed, a patron to the powerless. This identification helps him deny his own aggressiveness. He speaks and acts not for himself but for the worthy cause whose emissary he has become. He feels that "it is not I who am being abused by authority, who is in danger from it and hates it, but these poor oppressed people whom I have voluntarily undertaken to help."[33] By assuming the mantle of revolutionary agency, he gains self-aggrandizement through personal leadership and achieves a sense of self-denial through his subsumption into a brotherhood of equals.

The projection of positive feelings onto "the people" or "the oppressed" is matched by the negative emotions projected onto the oppressors—the enemies of the people. Hatred of authority is justified as a response to hatred by those who hold authority. Obviously there must be some basis in reality for the attribution of personal hostility and impersonal evil to political authorities. But only a minuscule proportion of the oppressed transmute their suffering into revolutionary opposition. Revolutionaries do not typically react to injustice by accepting or bemoaning their fate. They rise against the perceived oppressor, aided by an inner necessity that turns all hatred against encroaching authority and all love toward fellow victims. Political authority is thereafter seen as an actively malevolent force, as well as an object deserving of hatred.

One result of this projection is that sociopolitical authority appears to be overwhelmingly strong. It becomes a repository for the power of rejected paternal authority, as well as the "power drive" the revolutionary must exclude from his self-image. The commonly remarked asceticism of revolutionaries is in part an attempt to harden oneself as a reaction against the fear of such an overwhelming opponent. It is also, in part, an attempt to ward off guilt over transgressions against authority. Finally, asceticism serves as a means of avoiding temptation, as self-punishment for residual attraction to "bourgeois" self-gratification. The necessary self-control is attained by adherence to an ideology that serves as a system of authority and justification—in psychoanalytic terms, an external superego.

Whatever the biographical value of Wolfenstein's work, he points the way toward applying "authoritarian" psychodynamics to an understanding of revolutionary hostility against authority. His explanation retains the psychodynamic aspects of authoritarian theory while abandoning elements derived from the overt traits and behavior of 1930s European fascists and 1940s American nativists. Conventionalism and submissiveness, superstition and exaggerated sexual concerns are missing from or peripheral to this depiction. Instead, the psychodynamic core of the theory holds center stage. Strong Oedipal ambivalence is held to produce overriding concern with dominance and submission. This concern is politicized, partly through external political events, but also through the unconscious ego defensive mechanisms of externalization, displacement, and projection. Personality trends are expressed in revolutionary commitment in ways that suggest the impact of other ego defenses, such as splitting, denial, and rationalization.

This analysis of the internal sources of political behavior need not reduce the moral or intellectual stature of the individual. The revolutionary differs from other men in the particular constellation and interaction of these mechanisms, which are seen as universal in personality functioning. This analysis can in fact help explain what makes him special by depicting the forces most likely to fuel his political fervor. Whether these forces help make him an admirable or disreputable figure is a question that transcends the analysis itself.

For all this, Wolfenstein's model of revolutionary personality seems particularly unsuited to members or even the self-proclaimed revolutionaries of the New Left. Many personal characteristics he emphasizes, from rigid adherence to ideology to personal asceticism, are "Old Left" attributes widely rejected by radical youth in the 1960s.

To be sure, concerns for toughness, fitness for revolutionary struggle, and ideological "correctness" all surfaced within the New Left by the latter 1960s. These concerns were brought to the fore by the reappearance of Marxist groups originally relegated to the Movement's fringes. Their upsurge in popularity portended the growing irrelevance and coming demise of the New Left. The groups that seemed "left authoritarian" in their embrace of hardness, rigidity, and traditional ideologies ultimately prevailed by applying Leninist principles—superior organization, persistence, the formation of tightly knit cadres, the use of Machiavellian tactics. But their victory within the New Left soon proved Pyrrhic. This "new old left" finally captured the Movement's center by filling a growing vacuum. By the time a self-consciously Marxist-oriented vanguard emerged, there was no mass movement for it to lead.

The "true" New Leftists, it might be argued, reacted against both the politics and life style of the old-line "revolutionary" type. They rejected the authoritarian Left no less than the authoritarian Right, at least initially. The psychodynamics and political style of Wolfenstein's revolutionary type seem to have more in common with Adorno's traditional authoritarian conservative than with the self-consciously libertarian New Leftist. In the traditional authoritarian, crippling inner ambivalence is resolved by total submission to conventional authority, although hostile feelings are never completely subdued or displaced. In the revolutionary type, ambivalence is resolved by unrelieved hostility toward authority, while subsidiary submissive tendencies must be held in check by a variety of defense mechanisms. Both types control undesirable feelings toward authority by personal asceticism and submissiveness toward some greater power, whether that power is embodied in traditional institutions or revolutionary principles and leaders.

We need not conclude, though, that only two modes of authoritarianism exist, as mirror images at opposite ends of the ideological spectrum. By rejecting the equation of sadomasochistic ambivalence with right-wing politics, it becomes possible to envisage a variety of political styles that might reflect "inverse" authoritarian personality dynamics. Wolfenstein's model, which recalls Nydes's description of "sadistic" or overtly hostile aggressiveness, seems intuitively most applicable to the self-styled revolutionaries who appeared during the waning days of the student movement. On the other hand, some of the most overtly power-oriented among them had, in a single leap, traversed the distance from anti-political libertarian to "born-again" Marxist revolutionary in the manner of Fromm's power-worshipping anarchist.

Rupert Wilkinson's concept of the rigid anti-authoritarian may provide greater insight into the underlying inverse authoritarianism of the more typical New Leftist. Wilkinson describes this syndrome as one of reactive opposition to any and all authorities. This "rebel" resembles both Wolfenstein's revolutionary and the traditional authoritarian in his strong and deep-rooted ambivalence toward authority. His rebellious impulses are traced to his fear and consequent rejection of dependent feelings:

Rigid rebels can be hostile, abrasive, even autocratic, putting "principle" or self-assertion above compromise. They tend to have a plot com-

plex, investing powerful groups with sinister designs; this provides a rationale for rebellious expression, and . . . it may involve projection.
. . . Psychological rebels often want a cause to fight for. . . . But it
is not only a question of *needing* a cause, for a moral authority may
genuinely have instilled values which encourage rebellion. Thus, at an
early age some rigid rebels may have identified with religious, humane,
or reform-minded parents. . . .[34]

Wilkinson's concept of rigid anti-authoritarianism thus differs from similar ty-
pologies in its stress on the variety of developmental paths and behavioral styles
that may be associated with such a disposition. One corollary of anti-paternal
revolt, he notes, may be strong overt feelings of tenderness and even identification with female figures rather than an exaggerated "masculine" toughness.
Furthermore, various patterns of parental relations may contribute to such an
emotional state.

For example, both Adorno and Wolfenstein traced psycho-political rebellion to an insurrection against paternal authority. Wilkinson also considers a
family pattern more relevant to the parental relations often described by American student radicals of Jewish background:

One kind of rebel may be the sort of person who has felt shame and
irritation at a *weak* father, or frustration at generally submissive parents.
His parents may be so forebearing that he guiltily suppresses his irritation, while, like other rebels, still longing for a harder authority to strike
at and define himself against. At the same time, however, there is often
a special identification with an influential mother. . . . Some mothers
are possessive, demanding, and yet, in terms of real love, rejecting.
The effect on a child can be an intense conflict between dependence on
the mother and a wish to get away from her, to deny the weakness that
dependence signifies. Such feelings may lead to authoritarianism, especially if the father is absent, weak, or not particularly pleasant, so that
there is no benign male authority to emulate.[35]

This pattern provides an alternative interpretation of the "democratic" family
dynamic praised by Keniston and Flacks. Wilkinson makes this clear in a foot-
note added after the completion of his manuscript:

Since writing the above, I have read Keniston's analysis of eleven male
student radicals, which stresses an exceptional tie with a strong, humane
mother, ambivalence toward a father felt to be both strong and weak,
identification with humane parental values, and great emotional spontaneity. Keniston relates their values and activism to new historical fac-

tors, but I would add that both new and old rebels have sometimes shown a martyr complex, including a wish to be persecuted and to exaggerate persecution.[36]

Wilkinson's de-emphasis of Oedipal rebellion reflects the recent trend in depth psychology toward examining the role of pre-Oedipal object relations in later psycho-social development. Erikson, for one, has stressed the importance of a warm maternal relationship in the first years of life for the establishment of "primal trust" in the social environment.

Wilkinson's work also suggests a growing sophistication among those who apply psychoanalytic categories to psycho-political analysis. The relationship between private and public authority relations is far more complex than is suggested by the early Freudian model, which treats political authority as a surrogate father. The infantile and irrational components of political opposition and obedience are hardly exhausted by displaced revolts against the father.

More generally, Wilkinson's work points toward ways of relativizing the entire conceptual framework of the authoritarian personality. On the other hand his formulation of authoritarianism (like that of most of the writers we have discussed) suffers from the effort to develop a clinical terminology to deal with a particular political stance or set of attitudes. Such a procedure always leaves one open to the charge of creating clinical categories designed to "unmask" those particular groups whose politics one finds objectionable. Just as psychoanalysts are at their weakest when they attempt to apply clinical categories uncritically to political figures, political scientists and historians are at their weakest when they adapt clinical categories to political purposes. The social scientist who uses psychoanalysis to study political actors must respect the autonomy of both disciplines. This involves establishing connections between the social and personal realms, without violating the integrity of theories designed for each sphere. It means building bridges, not Procrustean beds. Of course, attempts to integrate psychoanalysis and history or politics may require some revisions in both spheres. In such cases, the changes should not simply be asserted. Their bases and the evidence for them must be clearly outlined.

These concerns underlay our effort to develop a revised theory of authoritarianism and to apply it to non-Jewish radicals in the United States and Germany. In doing so we shall rely primarily upon the clinical work of Anna Freud, Erik Erikson, Peter Blos, Otto Kernberg, and W. W. Meissner.

There is clearly a common core of agreement among the theorists we have discussed. All agree that the primary motivating force propelling the authoritarian is ambivalence toward power. That is, the authoritarian simultaneously fears and desires power as a paramount goal. He conceives power primarily in terms of strength or potency, control or influence over others, and enhancement of prestige or status. From his conflicted orientation toward the feeling of power, he develops a heightened sensitivity toward power relations. He comes to view the world primarily in terms of power "exchanges" and seeks to align himself with sources of strength and against those of weakness.

It is important to remember that these forces operate at the deepest levels of personality so that the individual is usually unaware of this inner dynamic. To the extent that this disposition remains largely unconscious, he may maintain a positive self-image—e.g., may see himself as moral or idealistic rather than "power-hungry," by displacing or projecting unacceptable power needs. Indeed, all our theorists would seem to agree that fairly high levels of defensive projection are characteristic of authoritarians.

At a deeper level, of course, authoritarians experience power as simultaneously desirable and aversive. The core of authoritarian disposition is the conflict between these contradictory feelings, while the conscious and unconscious attempts to resolve this conflict determine the distinctive complexion of the disposition for a particular individual. This implies that a wide variety of authoritarian styles exists, and that such people may exhibit considerable individuality. They are not simply textbook "types."

Concomitantly, this disposition would not necessarily influence the individual's political behavior. The form and direction of any political manifestation would depend upon factors external to his personality. For example, political expressions of authoritiarian disposition would presuppose an expectation that these needs can be fulfilled by political action. This expectation, in turn, is influenced by such varied factors as the political system and political culture, the changing social and political environment of the moment, and the immediate circumstances peculiar to particular individuals.

It seems plausible that many people could satisfy authoritarian needs through their personal relations, careers, religious beliefs, and so on. In fact, given the low salience of politics for most people most of the time, political manifestations of authoritarianism should occur most directly at times of social or political crisis. At such times politics touches peoples' lives directly, and the political realm is "moralized" so that political conflicts are viewed as moral struggles.

Once authoritarian needs are politicized, they may give rise to quite diverse political manifestations, depending on the individual's perceptions of his political environment. In secure dictatorial regimes, the need to identify with strength could easily manifest itself in obedience to traditional authorities, with residual resentment of authority channeled into hostility toward other nations or cultures. In times of crisis, especially when the regime's legitimacy is called into question, the same underlying disposition could have revolutionary political implications. When domestic authorities lose their aura of unquestioned superiority, in other words, the authoritarian may well turn the full force of his hostility against them. As Fromm argued, authoritarians often split their conscious feelings toward authority into total love for their own rulers and total hatred for the gods and governments of others. This emotional schism normally serves the powers-that-be as an internalized mechanism of social control. But "when [social] authority no longer succeeds in repressing the individual's negative feelings or transferring them onto other objects, his animosity may well turn against the authority itself."

Similar authoritarian needs among the German populace could have not only helped undermine the Weimar political order but also bolstered the ruling authorities of the Second and Third Reichs. More recently, and closer to home, inner conflicts that could be channeled into anti-communist agitation during the 1950s may have turned inward against the "Establishment" in the following decade.

What produces this personality structure? Here there is less consensus among the theorists. With the partial exception of Wilkinson, however, their emphasis is still upon Oedipal conflict and rebellion in patriarchal families. Recent developments in psychoanalytic theory bring such an analysis into question.

The most popular current psychological critiques of American society are not concerned with authoritarianism. Instead, they focus upon the "new narcissism" supposedly embodied by a "me generation" of burned-out idealists. In *Haven in a Heartless World,* Christopher Lasch argues that the authoritarian personality is not a problem today: "The narcissist, not the authoritarian, is the prevalent personality type."[37] But this view of the authoritarian's irrelevance is derived from the model developed by Adorno and his collaborators. Thus, the narcissist appears to be quite different. Such an individual craves adulation and excitement to overcome loneliness and pain, rather than merely lusting after power.

If we look more closely, however, we discover that the older models of the authoritarian personality have a good deal in common with the clinical picture of the narcissistic personality. The narcissist is not simply an authoritarian. Nevertheless, serious narcissistic problems lie at the core of the authoritarian personality. Today's emphasis on issues of narcissism may reflect current psychoanalytic concern over early relationships with one's parents (technically, pre-Oedipal object relations), as well as differences in the social expression of inner conflicts, rather than a fundamental shift in personality dynamics.[38]

In *The Paranoid Process,* W. W. Meissner discusses the similarity between traditional concepts of authoritarianism and his analysis of narcissism and the paranoid stance. His own theoretical construction is designed to deal more adequately with actual clinical material. Meissner sees both narcissism and defensive projection as normal parts of human existence which are necessary to the formation of any socially cohesive group. The difference between "normal" defensive projection and paranoia, then, is a matter of degree.[39]

Power relations are the central concern of paranoids, who tend to alternate between aggression and submissiveness. In situations where they feel they can dominate, they are ruthless in their self-assertion. When faced with a worthy antagonist, however, they retreat into submissiveness. They cannot conceive of situations that involve a combination of competition and cooperation. In their world one either dominates or is dominated. This perspective derives from their ambivalence about power. If they attempt to exercise power, they are so "bad" that they will be punished, i.e., totally destroyed. They cannot act without persuading themselves that they are invulnerable, facing an opponent too weak to retaliate.[40]

Their obsessive concern with issues of autonomy derives from the same ambivalence. They constantly assert their independence and seek situations in which they can feel that they are independent. Thus they can be oppositionists and may give the impression of psychological autonomy or ego strength. As Meissner notes, however, nothing could be further from the truth:

The paranoid is continually taken up in the struggle over personal autonomy, continually confronted with the threat of external control and subjection.

A mature and stable sense of autonomy can allow room for a relaxation of inner controls so as to permit a certain degree of spontaneity or even of regression for adaptive or creative purposes—regression in the service of the ego. It can also allow itself to be open to the suggestion or influence of others, or can even submit itself to their will. It is capable of recognizing and respecting the autonomy of others and allowing them their measure of self-determination and independence. It can do these things without a sense of shame or humiliation, without any loss of self-esteem or self-respect. The autonomous person can give in without giving up, without surrendering himself to another's control and prostrating himself in humiliating abjection.

The paranoid can do none of these things. His sense of autonomy is rigid and fragile and unstable. He cannot tolerate giving in to external control or authority. He is acutely sensitive to any such influence, whether external or internal. The subjective world of the parnoid is

marked by constant tension over the threat of giving in to external domination or to internal pressures—since both threaten the sense of autonomy. The relationship between this aspect of paranoid functioning and
the issues of power and control is central to the understanding of the
paranoid style. It also serves to clarify *the relation between the paranoid
style and the authoritarian attitude. Both are preoccupied with basic
issues of autonomy.* [Emphasis added.][41]

If the paranoid is ambivalent about his own autonomy, he also has difficulty
in deciding whether to identify with the victim or the aggressor; thus he can be
either a political rebel or an ardent supporter of the status quo. The choice
depends upon external circumstances. Indeed, some of Meissner's patients succeeded in identifying with both victim and aggressor at the same time. In any
event, both identifications serve similar sadomasochistic needs.[42]

When the decision is made to establish a negative identity—i.e., to place
oneself in opposition to the norms of the society—paranoids often construct
totalistic ideologies designed to protect them against pressures to conform:

> The negative identity develops as a form of protest and negation of a
> set of established rules, standards, and values which are formed by so-
> ciety and enforced by authority figures. The difficulty of maintaining a
> negative identity in the face of social organizations, regulations, and
> institutions which suppress the behaviors and norms congruent with the
> negative identity leads such individuals to frequently develop rigid ide-
> ologies as a means of sustaining the negative identity. The strong rebel-
> lion and opposition also involve significant elements of self-negation
> and self-denial, so that there is a determinant tendency to cling to total-
> istic ideologies resulting in considerable rigidity and negative conform-
> ity.[43]

Their capacity to do so is a function of their conflicts. Paranoids can be
quintessential intellectuals. They invest tremendous emotional energy into speculative systems, especially those that seek hidden meanings.[44] For this reason
paranoids may appear to possess considerable psychological insight into themselves. As Meissner points out, however, this can be misleading:

> One can easily be misled into thinking that the patient is demonstrating
> productive involvement with treatment, when in fact the concern with
> hidden meanings or hidden motives may be a reflection of an underlying
> paranoid process.[45]

The key to the paranoid's condition lies in a substratum of narcissistic deficits. Such people are haunted by deep feelings of unworthiness.[46] As Meissner puts it:

[They] are victims of an injured narcissism. They are all caught up in the inexorable process of struggling to salvage and preserve whatever remnants of narcissism are available to them. In fact, quite simply, the workings of the paranoid process . . . can be seen quite directly as a manifestation of this narcissistic conflict and torment.[47]

It is the continuous effort to overcome this torment that leads such individuals to exploit others and to demand both excitement and adulation. This also helps explain why they can either emphasize conformity, railing at those who deviate from conventional values, or rebel against a world which refuses to gratify their demands. Under appropriate circumstances, both stances can serve the need for constant reassurance.

Narcissists of this type alternate between periods of elation and depression because their sense of self-worth depends upon grandiose fantasies of being the protagonists of an epic drama which makes them the center of the world's attention. They are haunted and ultimately overpowered by a perennial concern of adolescence, which Dickens placed in the mind of David Copperfield: "Whether I shall turn out to be the hero of my own life. . . ."

The paranoid feels the basic concern for autonomy as an overwhelming burden: his heroism, his self-importance, must be recognized by the whole world to allay his dread that he plays only a minor role. Thus he vacillates between feelings of grandiosity and self-contempt and between

periods of driven investment in activities and relationships that bring about triumph, admiration, or immediate need gratification, alternating with periods of precipitate abandonment of tasks, relationships, and activities that fail to provide sustainment for their grandiosity—they withdraw from and devaluate aspects of social reality to protect themselves against failure.[48]

The struggle against "evil" social deviants can involve identification with a powerful leader and community. On the other hand, the struggle against an uncaring establishment can also make the paranoid feel "alive" by placing him at the center of a dramatic confrontation between good and evil. Political activity thus serves to intensify the experiences of everyday life by heightening the importance of one's actions and hence one's overall sense of self-importance. Otto Kernberg describes frenetic narcissists

> who alternate between periods in which they experience intense subjec-
> tive, emotional involvement with potential enemies whom they have to
> fight off, while obtaining in the process, a sense of aliveness, and other
> periods of painful experience of emptiness and lack of meaning of life,
> when the narcissistic features predominate and no immediate enemy is
> available.[49]

Kernberg and Meissner both trace these narcissistic pathologies to the child's early (pre-Oedipal) relationship with its mother. The problems may derive from either maternal rejection and coldness or a smothering overprotectiveness. In fact, these apparently antithetical maternal styles share a common underlying theme. In both cases the mother is using the child to fulfill her own narcissistic needs.[50]

The father, of course, also plays an important role. With respect to male children, Meissner argues,

> the relationship is one of distance and coldness and remoteness. These
> fathers generally reject their sons, in whom they see a reflection of the
> weak, inadequate and dependent aspect of themselves, with regard to
> which they feel shame and revulsion.[51]

Meissner accepts Nydes's distinction between sadistic and masochistic types but argues that both are responding to very similar needs. If we accept Meissner's approach, we can better understand why Fromm's rebel is more or less the inverse of Adorno's authoritarian.

The work of Meissner and Kernberg provides a psychodynamic model of authoritarianism that is ideologically neutral and built upon substantial clinical evidence. Meissner's paranoid can be either conservative or radical. Further, recognizing that injured narcissism underlies the authoritarian's ambivalence with regard to power enables us to explain a broader range of behavior than do traditional theories of authoritarianism.

It is important to remember that Meissner is describing a multi-dimensional continuum. At one end are individuals with a relatively cohesive sense of self and a strong capacity for intimacy. At the other end are individuals who are clinically "borderline personalities" or even schizophrenic. Most of us fall somewhere in between. In describing the "paranoid" type, Meissner's effort was to illuminate some of the mechanisms at work in reasonably "healthy people.'' However, the terminology he uses suggests otherwise, and we do not wish to create a misleading impression.

Further, we believe that "normality" is a balance of conscious and unconscious forces. Social and political upheavals can disturb this balance, especially for individuals facing some personal crisis, such as the loss of a loved one, retirement from work, or the tensions of adolescence. Whatever may be true of more traditional societies, adolescence in the west is associated for many with an increased use of projection and a search for enemies on the one hand and the solace of group memberships on the other.[52]

If the societal crisis is successfully resolved and the legitimacy of authorities restored, most young people will return to normal pursuits and may well achieve higher levels of personal integration. The result will be the same if the crisis results in important social changes. While the personalities of young people will respond to a changing balance of conscious and unconscious forces, the specifically authoritarian or paranoid elements that emerged will probably be attenuated.

For some young people, however, the experience can result in a freezing of adolescent patterns. This is most likely to occur if the public crisis in authority is not resolved—i.e., existing norms and standards are delegitimized, but no new societal standards are institutionalized.

Finally, while we think that Meissner's typology helps us understand why some people were drawn to the Movement (and our evidence supports this hypothesis), we certainly do not claim that it explains every case. When revolutionary or quasi-revolutionary movements become institutionalized, as the student movement had on many campuses by the late 1960s, they begin to serve as lightning rods for a wide variety of unconscious conflicts.

In both deed and doctrine, the New Left seemed somehow to embody images of both utopian idealism and Machiavellian cynicism, of principled libertarianism and unprincipled coercion. This duality allowed the student movement to function as a kind of political Rorschach test, leading some to proclaim as psycho-political liberation what others concemned as pathological "leftist fascism.'' Observers tended to become either enchanted or enraged by this strange admixture of populism and elitism, tolerance and moralism, asceticism and libertinism, and perhaps of drives toward both self-realization and self-destruction.

Some supporters of the New Left denied or minimized these dualities. They suggested instead that the fundamentally healthy and moral impulses of most radicals were unfairly linked with the destructive pathologies of a nihilistic fringe. It was argued, for example, that the Movement's composition changed markedly after the mid-'60s; that the healthy, idealistic vanguard was thereafter joined by "adventurists" and thrill-seekers who subverted the lofty goals and pristine tactics of the Movement's core.

There is indeed some evidence that a shift in demographic composition occurred, at least in the United States, especially after the watershed year of 1965. The upper-middle-class Jewish students from politically liberal, highly educated homes who dominated the early movement were increasingly joined by lower-middle-class Protestant and Catholic youths from politically conservative homes.

As Sale has pointed out, it is quite clear that the shift in the composition of the American Movement did result in changes in the Movement's style. For the moment, however, the issue is whether the change was from noncoercive idealism to coercion and eventually terrorism, or whether, whatever the demographic balance, the dualism we described above was present from the beginning.

There is an obvious difficulty with an account that suggests that the evolution to coercion and terrorism was a function simply of shifts in the social composition of the Movement. No such shift seems to have occurred in the European New Left, despite the similarly paradoxical mixture of high-mindedness and coerciveness that characterized the student movement in West Germany, France, and Italy. In 1969, the leftist social philosopher Jürgen Habermas called attention to the moral duality of the European Movement: "From the very beginning of the movement emancipatory forces have been connected with regressive ones. . . . the technocrats of protest as an end in itself have set off on the left a process of distintegration, which owes less to consistent strategy than to the ambivalence of the protest potential itself."[53]

That same year, Keniston made a similar observation about the American New Left, in contrasting

the "constructive and idealistic" young radicals I studied two years ago with the "nihilistic and violent" radicals who have purportedly replaced them today.

I believe there has been a change toward militancy, anger and dogmatism in the white student movement, but that it has been greatly exaggerated. . . .

Yet the mood, temper, and rhetoric of the student movement *has* drastically changed . . . [to a] more defiant, more angry, more politically revolutionary stance. . . . How do we account for this shift? Can we distinguish in any useful way between the "nihilistic" and "ideal-

istic'' activists? At this point, [the] clinician must remind himself of
. . . the essential ambivalence of human nature . . . the same person,
depending on circumstances, is invariably both an idealist and a nihilist.
. . . In short, if the distinction between nihilists and idealists among
today's student radicals holds water, it is with the essential qualification
that everyone is always a little of both.[54]

Keniston apparently considered this analysis to be a defense of the Movement's essentially idealistic tendencies. In the same way he asserted that "the move toward violent tactics" is "a reaction to the constant frustration that confronts the radical, who may end by covertly identifying himself with the very violence he is dedicated to oppose."[55] The controlling model thus remains that of the healthy radical, now driven to despair and violence by a sick and unyielding society.

This explanation seems overly facile, coming from a proponent of the essentially "healthy" and "protean" nature of the student movement. If these radicals were unusually adaptable and open to change, as Keniston claimed, why should political setbacks drive them so quickly to violence and nihilism? How could the nihilistic potential of a psychologically liberated generation be so easily activated? Just as importantly, the key concepts introduced to explain this shift—ambivalence, the link between idealism and nihilism, identification with the opposition—suggest a psychodynamic explanatory framework. Keniston, however, never developed this framework.

Like Habermas, Keniston employed the notion of "emotional ambivalence" to account for the paradoxes that were succinctly expressed in the 1968 SDS slogan, "armed love." But he implied that radicals' ambivalence was simply a matter of having potentially contradictory emotions toward violence and coercion, with external circumstances determining which emotion controlled their political behavior at a given time. In psychodynamic terms, though, ambivalence refers to a quite different and more volatile emotional state, a feeling of *simultaneous* attraction and repulsion toward an object or action. We would argue that many New Leftists, ambivalent toward power and violence in this sense, were at once fascinated and repelled by prospects of overt conflict and coercion. Moreover, this ambivalence was widespread from the Movement's origins but went unnoticed by those who sympathized with its initial goals and tactics.

The democratic Left's later concern over the Movement's destructive tendencies reflected partly the changing perceptions of observers and partly psychological and behavioral changes among participants. As Keniston himself pointed out, the same coercive tactics that were condemned in the late '60s had been widely condoned by supporters of the civil rights movement. Yet there was little tactical difference between "sitting in at a segregationist lunch counter (thereby preventing its owner from doing business) and occupying a Northern college administration building (thereby 'bringing the machine to a halt'). . . . In both cases individuals use their bodies to obstruct, disrupt, or prevent the orderly conduct of business as usual. . . ."[56]

It is easy to understand how northern white liberals could more easily sympathize with Kingman Brewster than with Bull Conner. The young activists began as the enemy of their enemies. As time went on, though, they increasingly "brought the war home," turning their crusade against their would-be liberal allies. The shift in "targets not tactics" was accompanied by a shift in rhetoric as young radicals became more self-consciously revolutionary. From its inception the Movement had refused to abide by the parliamentary rules of the game. But its support in the academic community began to abate in response more to unwelcome ideological justifications of coercive behavior than to the behavior itself. "Idealistic" coercion couched in liberal rhetoric could be tolerated more easily than "cynical" coercion justified in terms of pseudo-Leninist vanguard theories.

Keniston concluded that even the young terrorists who emerged after 1968 were frustrated idealists driven to violent tactics by harassment, defeat, and repression. Yet all political reformers face frustration. Some respond by redoubling their efforts, others concede defeat and withdraw from politics, and some are radicalized by their experiences. Moreover, the repression encountered by the New Left can hardly compare with that of many contemporary Russian dissidents, whose suffering seems to enhance rather than to undermine their sense of moral witness. In fact it is easier to understand the endorsement of violence by black activists, who had long experienced the repression that economically privileged young whites suddenly discovered. Yet even in their case, common experiences of frustration and repression cannot explain the very different political responses of a Martin Luther King and a Stokeley Carmichael. Different people simply respond to similar situations in different ways.

We cannot avoid the question of whether some frustrated idealists are drawn rather than driven to violent rhetoric or action. In counterpoint to Keniston, one might argue that the outbreak of terrorism during the movement's decline reflected a preexisting fascination with violence and destruction. This does not mean that the genuine moral impetus behind much student activism should be regarded as a mere way-station on the road to violent revolution. Only a few relatively militant radicals reached that destination, though many more were pulled in the same direction. Tom Hayden saw this as early as 1961, when the nascent Movement consisted of little more than an aspiring vanguard. He warned that "the student movement, which has rejected so many institutions and instruments of social change . . . has invented no substitute save a noble morality and in some cases a commitment to nonviolence that will dissipate soon if not secured in new social structures."[57]

To understand the Movement's rapid shift from idealism to Machiavellianism, one must begin with the "existential" moralism that was already present during its early liberal reformist phase. This was evident in SDS president Carl Oglesby's eulogy of the young white civil rights activists who helped forge the movement: "they wanted . . . to go South to get their hands and their heads—their lives—into the dangerous, the moral and therefore the authentic. The instinct from the beginning was to discover the streets!"[58]

From the first, then, the New Left combined nonviolent moral witness with an attraction to danger and excitement, abhorrence of power relations with an urge for confrontation with evil. That violence, coercion, and "power plays" would soon find their way into this movement is not the paradox it may seem.

We believe that the anarchic and experiential flavor of the early New Left expressed certain personality tendencies found among its predominantly upper-status Jewish component. These tendencies, described in Chapter 3, include strong proclivities toward impulse gratification and "self-expression" to compensate for narcissistic deficits incurred very early in life, particularly in maternal relations. Their frenetic experiments in self-assertion brought many of these young people into conflict with those social authorities that require the inhibition or repression of personal impulse. Even as they sought to undermine authority, however, they courted reprisals as propitiation for their transgressions. Their denigration of authority went hand in hand with furtive desires for punishment. In this way external authorities were invited to enact the prohibitions and limitations that they could not establish for themselves. Of course, this "masochistic" element in their activity was rarely recognized by young radicals. They viewed each Establishment reprisal as a new provocation that justified further retaliation, in a self-perpetuating and self-defeating cycle.

This syndrome can be characterized as a self-expansive or "protean" form of psycho-political rebellion. The protean rebel seeks out change, flux, and fluidity in his life style, while resisting all forms of psychological closure. His efforts find their purest political expression in some form of anarchism. He aims at the continual destruction of social institutions, insofar as they interfere with individual experimentation.[59] But such a permanent revolution cannot generate counter-institutions. It defines itself wholly in terms of opposition and negation. Protean rebellion is authoritarian because it is rooted in a deep ambivalence toward power that causes the rebel to oscillate between aggressive and submissive postures toward authority.

In its surface manifestations, the protean rebel is quite unlike the inverse authoritarian types described by Adorno, Fromm, and Wolfenstein. Their rigid rebel is simply the traditional authoritarian turned inside out. Instead of clinging to social convention and despising outsiders, he rejects all authority and takes on the negative identity of a social outlaw. Both stances are rooted in Oedipal ambivalence. The conservative authoritarian displaces forbidden hostility toward his parents, especially his father, onto outgroups. The rigid rebel acts out this hostility against social authorities that function, in part, as paternal surrogates. He seeks to attack and destroy a weakened Establishment, which he despises precisely for its weakness and lack of "toughness." His ultimate goal is to create a new political hierarchy that embodies the strength lacking in current institutions. The purest political expression of this syndrome is an authoritarian socialist regime.

Such rigid rebels were found most often among the non-Jewish youth who were increasingly radicalized during the late 1960s and early 1970s. As the Movement spread, and its non-Jewish component grew, the original anarchic style and themes became increasingly vested with the rigid rebellion characteristic of its newer recruits. Of course, there is nothing inborn about either syndrome. The Movement no doubt attracted rigid rebels from Jewish homes and protean rebels from Christian households, as well as many young people who fit neither pattern. We would simply argue that differences in cultural style, including child-rearing techniques, lead to different probabilities that each pattern will be found among Jewish and non-Jewish radicals.

In Chapters 5 through 9, we describe the results of research designed to test our propositions about the interaction of ethnicity and personality in the New Left. Before discussing this evidence, however, we shall present a more speculative scenario of how these two styles of psycho-political rebellion contributed to the rapid rise and fall of the New Left. We emphasize at the outset that these concepts are ideal types. Jews and non-Jews in the student movement may have adopted parts of both strategies as more primitive elements in their personalities were brought to the surface in crisis. However, our evidence indicates that most of them combined these elements in different proportions and in different ways.

Beyond this, we would not argue that the large Jewish presence in the early years of the American Movement was the sole determinant of either its content or style. As in all forms of social action, the same external forces were operating upon both Jewish and non-Jewish students. Part of the reason for their emphasis upon negating authority, rather than creating new institutions, lay in

the delegitimation of the Soviet Union and communist ideology which had occurred in the 1950s. In addition, as we suggested in Chapter 1, cultural changes
played an important role in determining both the style and content of the Movement. They were also partly responsible for the wide appeal of the themes
developed initially by students of Jewish background. Finally, the Movement
never succeeded in mobilizing the working class or any other possible source
of sustained mass support. We suspect that, had it been able to do so, revolutionary asceticism would have replaced experiential styles fairly quickly, as it
did for some in the 1970s. Anarchistic "acting out" and ascetic self-denial can
be two sides of the same coin. For example, Mao Tse-tung was an anarchist
at the beginning of his revolutionary career. He changed drastically once he
became the leader of a viable revolutionary movement.[60] And the Soviet communist movement was eventually able to draw upon the energies of large numbers of students whose leftism, in Lenin's terms, had been "infantile" during
most of the latter nineteenth century.

In Chapter 3 we argued that the strategy of the Jewish rebel was to project guilt
feelings onto an external authority and to accuse the authority of offenses that
render it unfit to judge the rebel. As Nydes puts it, "In anticipation of accusation by the authority figure he accuses the authority figure and tries to make
him feel guilty. Rather than submit to judgment, he indicts his judge."[61]

The overall dynamic of paranoid-masochistic aggression, then, proceeds as
follows. The individual identifies with a victim he perceives as persecuted. This
allows him to ward off guilt over aggressive impulses by projecting the impulses onto an authority figure. His stance toward authority is one of defensive,
hence justified, hostility, in response to an anticipated attack. The projection of
guilt allows him to feel self-righteous rage over real and imagined injuries to
himself or his objects of identification. Unlike Adorno's authoritarian, his motive for aggression is not to hurt a weaker enemy but to avoid being hurt by
counter-attacking against an assumed aggressor. Since this often leads him to
take on powerful authority figures, the effect is to provoke punishment. This
both gratifies his repressed masochistic longings and magnifies his self-
righteousness by confirming preconceived feelings of persecution. The goal is
a kind of apolitical anarchistic rebellion which reserves for the self the autonomy to experience a multiplicity of life styles and identities.

Unlike Wolfenstein's rigid revolutionary, this type of rebel does not shun
affective experience but yearns for it. Indeed, it is precisely experience and
sensation that he seeks, in contrast to the authoritarian closure against undesired
and feared parts of the self. Such an individual's revolutionary fervor would

not serve an idea or ideology, but an appetite for autonomous experience and a narcissistic impatience with boundaries that fence him off from the full range of experience to which he feels entitled.

The force of these themes within the early New Left has been noted by many commentators. For example, Nigel Young summarizes the early days of the Movement:

> . . . participation was everything; the feeling of solidarity did not end
> when each particular project came to an end; it moved on into other
> fields and other places. It represented a new synthesis, the beginnings
> of a visible alternative—an immanent counter-culture, that merged per-
> sonal expressiveness with political activism and personal commitment
> to social transformation. Rebellion, if it is to be permanent, can no
> longer risk its revolutionary ideals in the contamination of institutional-
> ized power.[62]

This interpretation of the early idealistic and morally infused student move-ment replaces Keniston's "post-modern" radical with the protean rebel as the archetypal New Leftist. His alleged openness to change and experimentation reappears as an endless quest for excitement and experience and an unwilling-ness to accept limitations on that quest. The overtly anti-authoritarian tenor of his dissent reflects an instinctive refusal to submit to any externally imposed authority—the political authority of the Establishment, the intellectual authority of ideology, or the personal authority of leaders. Moreover this anti-submissive impulse energizes social and political conflict. It generates personal confronta-tion with any authority requiring such submission.

Howard Zinn eulogized this "non-ideological" activism for "the experi-ence of participation, the feeling of freedom, and the expression of self" it provided.[63] SDS founder Todd Gitlin was equally succinct in defining the per-sonal meaning of his political activism: "To adopt a pattern of behavior and a life-style which does not conform to those of the majority means demonstrating externally the reconquest of one's individual autonomy."[64]

This is the politics of "the great refusal," as Marcuse termed it. It signifies a refusal to participate in repressive and authoritarian modern society and, by extension, a refusal to allow such a society to function. The dialectic of per-sonal withdrawal and revolt, of personalism and moralism, is nowhere better expressed than in Mario Savio's dramatic call to arms at Berkeley:

> There is a time when the operations of the machine become so odious,
> make you so sick at heart, that you can't take part, you can't even
> tacitly take part. And you've got to put your bodies upon the gears and

upon the wheels, upon the levers, upon all the apparatus, and you've got to make it stop. And you've got to indicate to the people who run it, to the people who own it, that unless you're free the machine will be prevented from working at all.[65]

The New Left was originally energized by the anti-political idealism of the politically virgin. But their idealism was quickly politicized by the demand that society provide an appropriate framework for personal transformation, i.e., for the retention of unlimited possibilities. As Tom Hayden and others argued, in rejecting the notion of a hierarchically ordered radical movement:

Power in America is abdicated by individuals to top-down organizational units, and it is in the recovery of this power that the movement becomes distinct from the rest of this country and a new kind of man emerges. . . . In the effort to open up this possibility for a new identity and a new movement, we are going to drift and experiment for some time to come.[66]

So power is to be withdrawn from hierarchical authority structures and recovered by the individual as personal autonomy. Autonomy, however, is not an end in itself but a means to an ill-defined end, the forging of new identities. For many young activists, this psychological transformation seemed more easily attainable than the sociopolitical changes it allegedly presupposed. Movement activity provided immediate feelings of individual autonomy and communal participation in opposition to a discredited authority, as well as the ability to drift and experiment with one's life rather than being channeled into an uptight gray-flanneled adult world. As a Berkeley activist recalled, "The FSM, with its open mass meetings, its guitars and songs, its beards, and its long-haired chicks, made the aloofness and reserve of the administrators, the turgid style of the pronouncements emanating from the University Information Office, the formality of the coat and tie world, seem lifeless and dull by comparison."[67]

A danger of this approach to life is ego diffusion, the attempt to override boundaries between self and other rather than to maintain them. The use of a political movement as a base for experiments in personal "liberation" suggests a desire to lose distance and boundaries, to personalize the world into an extension of self. As Erikson writes:

Some of our young people, combining emotional license with alternately violent and non-violent confrontation and with both intellectual and anti-intellectual protest, attempt to combine the gains of all revolutions in one improvised moratorium and often succeed only in endangering and even mocking them all.

Out of the combined revolutions of the oppressed and the repressed, of the proletarians, the unarmed, and the mental sufferers there seems to have now emerged a *Revolt of the Dependent*. That to be dependent means to be exploited is the ideological link between the developmental stage of youth, the economic state of the poor, and the political state of the underdeveloped. This could partially explain the astounding similarity of the logic used in confrontations both by privileged youth and by the underprivileged citizenry.[68]

The psychological strategy of this type of rebel was illustrated both at Berkeley and in the 1968 Columbia University strike. At Columbia, as earlier, it quickly became evident that police brutality provided a far more rapid means of radicalizing neutral students than did political education. Mark Rudd codified this insight by proposing to put university authorities "up against the wall" through militant confrontation, thus provoking a violent response that would unmask their underlying repressiveness. The same logic applied to the Establishment's "enforcers," the police themselves. Push the police hard enough, and they would hit back much harder, thereby exposing their violent and oppressive function in a repressive society. In psychodynamic terms, the policeman's violent response to provocation validates the attacker's sense of victimization and transforms his provocation into a legitimate preemptive counterattack.

To the extent that others share this perception of confrontation, the ranks of the Movement should swell. This was the pragmatic justification for "confrontationism." But the Machiavellian nature of this tactic—in each cracked head a new convert—went hand in hand with its existential appeal for radical leaders. The billy club seemed a necessary stimulus to revolutionary consciousness, a conveyer of personal authenticity. Carl Oglesby made this glowingly clear:

> . . . the policeman's riot club functions like a magic wand under whose hard caress the banal soul grows vivid and the nameless recover their authenticity—a bestower, this wand of the lost charisma of the modern self—I bleed, therefore I am.[69]

Rarely has the romanticization of violence extended so vividly to violence against oneself. Oglesby's paean to the truncheon is an almost paradigmatic statement of the paranoid-masochistic mentality. Rebellion against authority is justified so long as it is punished. Indeed the punishment itself justifies and legitimizes the rebellion by expiating the rebel's guilt and confirming his fear of and repressed hope for persecution.

Even at the time, many leftist commentators criticized the provocationist strategy as a form of "ego-tripping" (though "superego tripping" seems more appropriate) of dubious long-term effectiveness. The radical magazine *Win* called it "an unattractive form of goal displacement in which disruption (the means) becomes an end in itself." [70]

In general, though, "in-house" criticism at the time did not question the ethics of such confrontations, despite recognition of their problematic psychological origins as forms of "projective politics." Instead the issue was seen as primarily tactical—how to combat the police state without ultimately strengthening its hand. Despite often-expressed concern over the Establishment's manipulativeness, similar trends within the Movement tended to provoke the strategic criticism that such means would not produce the desired ends. Ethical questions about the relationship of means and ends faded under the impact of growing self-righteousness and Manichean moral dichotomies.

The decline of pacifism and principled morality were mediated by identification with surrogate victims, whose just causes were held to legitimize coercion, violence, and even terrorism. For example, Jean-Paul Sartre argued not only that Vietcong terror was justified but also that the NLF's historical role as a liberating force rendered it incapable of "illegitimate" violence. [71] Even the pacifist A. J. Muste, an inspirational figure to the early New Left, argued that "a distinction between the violence of liberation movements and imperialist violence" could allow pacifists to "support some who are engaged in violent action." [72] Many young activists soon proved willing to apply to their own rebellion what Camus once called "this casuistry of the blood," whereby "to justify himself . . . each relies on the other's crimes." [73]

As anti-militarism degenerated into anti-imperialism and anti-Americanism, young radicals began to view themselves as "the new niggers," and students per se as an oppressed class. In part this reflects their futile search for domestic agents of revolutionary change. In part it was also an extension of their identification with the victims of Establishment oppression. Students, too, could be victims, could enjoy the righteousness that comes from persecution. Instead of participating vicariously in the aggressiveness of third world revolutionaries, students could "move for their own liberation as well as others,' " as Rudd wrote. They could "fight back against the oppression of the blacks, Vietnamese and themselves." [74] When New Left intellectuals developed a theory of students as the "new working class," they appealed directly to this emotional nexus, arguing that "your own [battles] are more important personally and politically" [75] than the battle for others.

The "rigid" rebel, our second authoritarian type, need not follow such a tortuous path to untrammeled aggression. His power strategy is predominantly sadistic rather than masochistic, allowing him to release hostility directly and with minimal guilt. In response to a perceived injury or humiliation, he takes on the role of the aggressor against a weaker victim. His aggression is retaliatory and results in a vindictive sense of triumph.

This pattern of releasing hostility seems relevant to many youthful terrorists and sociopathic fringe groups, from West Germany's Red Army Faction to America's Symbionese Liberation Army. These young revolutionary "soldiers" were infused with the romance of cleansing violence against a paper-tiger Establishment, an authority powerful enough to inflict injury but too weak and disorganized to catch and hold a determined counter-attacker. For example, West Germany's Baader-Meinhof group considered themselves the agents of third world freedom fighters, a fifth column in "the hinterlands of imperialism" justified in acting "without scruples or misgivings."[76] As Gudrun Ensslin wrote in her journal following an act of "revolutionary" arson, "A burning department store with burning people should furnish the true Vietnam feeling."[77]

Identification with an aggressor is accompanied by the projection of guilt. This allows the rebel to express violent impulses against authority without feeling unpleasant pangs of conscience. Indignation against the established order thus substitutes for guilt feelings about one's own aggressive behavior. Rather than accepting and internalizing traditional social mores and feeling guilty over occasional transgressions, the rebel takes the initiative. He projects the prohibited impulses outward, attributing all aggression to his enemies. Clinical depression attests to the force of the infantile superego when turned against the self. The punitive fervor and vindictive hostility of the rigid rebel attest equally to its force when turned against others.

Inverse authoritarians of this type tend to establish negative identities during adolescence. As children they fail to internalize a benevolent ego ideal: a guiding set of standards derived largely from parental prototypes, whose attainment brings a sense of inner goodness. Instead, they are driven by a highly punitive superego, a perpetually guilty conscience that denies their capacity for goodness. With no positive guide for identity-formation, they embrace a sense of self grounded in the rejection of values and behavior that their parents deem acceptable. Ironically, the flight from an inner sense of "badness" draws such an individual toward the very goals and life styles that social authority deems wrong or evil.

The impetus toward a negative identity represented disappointment and animus toward parents perceived as cold, punitive and destructive. However, since

European and American non-Jewish families are predominantly patriarchal, the focus of animus is the father. The pattern differs for male and female children. The male child is torn by his desire to destroy and replace his father and his fear and guilt about such wishes. The female, on the other hand, is torn by her desire and fear of incorporating the power of her father. Given her perceptions of him, attempts at such incorporation are unconsciously perceived as very threatening. Her constant search is for a powerful object with which she can identify and incorporate safely.

Beyond depreciating paternal authority by flaunting his rebelliousness, the male adolescent may feel a need to avenge himself more directly against the father, to discharge anger over the father's combination of artibrary power and moral weakness. This dynamism can be expressed in the social and political arena by a tendency to "ideologize" the world, to treat people as concepts rather than as complex individuals. By perceiving the world in terms of ideological categories, one gains a sense of control over it. And control is a paramount issue for one who experiences life as a victim, as the object of control by powerful external forces, with the malevolent father as the prototype.

Moreover, an ideologized world is a dehumanized and emotionally detached world. Feelings of hatred can be externalized and displaced from the father— an individual human being toward whom mixed emotions are inevitable—onto a social and political system perceived as impersonal and totally hostile. The abstraction of personal animosity into ideological self-righteousness makes it easier to overcome residual guilt over the direct expression of hostility. An ideology can thereby function as a system of personal justification, an external counter to the superego's internal prohibitions. This process culminates in the adoption of a "revolutionary morality" that permits aggressive acts undertaken in the name of an abstraction like "the people." As an SDS national officer noted during his organization's shift toward revolutionary self-consciousness, "Instead of good and bad, we talk of revolutionary and nonrevolutionary."[78]

For all his overt aggressiveness, though, the "sadistic" rigid rebel is tormented by residual masochism stemming from his punitive superego. He continues to struggle with his inner sense of badness and the feeling that he should "surrender"—escape the constant tension by submitting to authority. He alleviates this need for masochistic surrender, in part, by giving himself up to a superior power—a good cause, a beloved leader, a hierarchical organization. But he also wards off this threat by emphasizing self-control in his personal life. As we noted, this is one source of revolutionary asceticism.

By punishing himself for his forbidden impulses, the rigid rebel gains a sense of ascendancy over merely human frailty, a transcendence he demands of both himself and the larger society. He must create a "new man" within himself by an act of self-will and self-control, just as the revolution must create the new man by the strict organization and control of social life.

In short, the rigid rebel recalls the classic picture of the radical as ideologue. His opposition to the "bourgeois establishment" could thus fulfill and legitimize needs for increased control of the internal and external environment. To paraphrase Erikson's comment on authoritarian idealism, such people could feel justified in being hard on others to the extent that they were hard on themselves.

Such rebels are characterized psychodynamically by rigid ego boundaries: For them, there seems to be a "bad" outside and a "good," pure inside, with the domains of self and not-self kept rigidly separate. We might expect them to find comfort not so much in people as in their ideas about people, which can substitute for the usual pleasure in human relationships. They could love human beings in the abstract, so long as they conform to some theoretical picture. Yet they might have little tolerance for human complexity, for human messiness, even for human neediness, either in themselves or in others.

One must not draw the line between these two types of "inverse" authoritarians too sharply. Both can claim to be identifying with the victim, whatever the real internal dynamics of their rage. Both can alternate between enjoying aggression for its own sake and desiring to be punished to justify preemptive aggression.

For example, Susan Stern, a young Jewish woman who joined the Weathermen, strongly desired to be punished in the aftermath of the "Days of Rage," as a way of proving that she was totally identified with "the oppressed":

> . . . not to go to jail would have made everything I had claimed about being a revolutionary meaningless. It's not that I wanted to go to jail: it's just that I wanted the judge to know I was just as contemptuous of him as the boys were, that women could hate just as much, could be just as disruptive and deaf to authority.[79]

On the other hand, she clearly took a great deal of pleasure in violence against an "Establishment" she perceived as weak:

> I was boiling, singing, dancing, erupting with the spontaneous surge of freedom, of having the streets. . . . "End the war in Vietnam," "Power to the people"; smash—a spectator who tried to stop a man from throwing a rock was jammed up against a wall and bashed with a fist and he fell like a sack of potatoes. More rocks. The sound of shattering glass everywhere. Destroy the capitalists' property or else take it for the people. We gobbled up the night in a singing roar, violent and wild, saying

clearly that we were on the side of the Vietnamese, on the side of freedom. . . .[80]

A similar movement between "sadistic" and "masochistic" poles is apparent in the attitudes and behavior of Gudrun Ensslin of the Baader-Meinhof group. We portrayed her vision of "a burning department store with burning people" as a fantasy that directly vented reactive aggression. But her moment of radicalization the previous year seemed to follow the pattern of defensive hostility occasioned by self-righteous identification with the victim. Consider her reactions to the shooting of a student by police, recounted by a traditional Marxist student leader who deplored her "actionism":

> She was making very emotional speeches. She was saying, more or less, "They'll kill us all—you know what kind of pigs we're up against . . . you can't argue with the people who made Auschwitz. They have weapons and we haven't. We must arm ourselves." . . . It was as if the event had brought some sort of revelation to Ensslin: "Now that I have experienced reality I cannot be a pacifist any longer." At times on the night after Benno Ohnesorg was shot she was crying so much we thought we'd have to lock her up. Later her view seemed to represent that of many of the "peaceful" antibomb faction—who were all for fighting it out on the Platz.[81]

The function of the "sadistic-masochistic" polarity is to differentiate modes of hostility that are experienced as quite different emotions, though they may result in rather similar behavior. They are useful as "ideal types" for social psychological analysis, rather than as clinical or therapeutic concepts. As such, they can help us identify distinct patterns of psycho-political opposition within that heterogeneous "movement of movements" that was the New Left. In particular individuals, though, these emotional processes may become so complex as to defy categorization, since internal psychodynamics are not bound by laws of logic and consistency.

For this reason, too, actual behavior is not always a good guide to underlying dynamics. Rigid rebels may behave in ways that suggest that they are protean types, although their underlying motivations may be quite different. It is usually forgotten that many Germans who later became Nazis who dedicated themselves to eliminating "bourgeois decadence" had spent a number of years as "bohemians" who acted out a variety of sexual and other fantasies. Many were, in fact, philo-Semites for a time, fascinated by the mysterious "sensuality" of Jews.[82] In the Movement, too, many non-Jews saw in Jews a freedom from the "hang-ups" which they felt resulted from their own "uptight" Protestant or Catholic backgrounds. Of course they also projected their own desires for the free expression of impulse upon blacks.

Let us now see whether our analysis can help bridge the gap between the seemingly very different political styles of the early and late New Left. We have argued that the potential for psycho-political rebellion was activated by external political developments, particularly the decline of the cold war and the advent of civil rights and Vietnam as major political issues. Of course, these events took place within the context of a society whose underlying civic culture was undergoing severe strain, mostly through its own internal dynamics, but partly through the influence of a cosmopolitan intellectual sector, in which Americans of Jewish background played a large role.

The challenge to external authority began during the early 1960s and escalated rapidly after 1964, when campus rebellions and inner city riots grew in number and intensity. Almost overnight, educational authority seemed to crumble as campus after campus was paralyzed by student strikes from 1966 to 1968, and long hair, rock music, and drugs became symbols of rebellion among college and then noncollege youth.

Whereas Jews and some upper-middle-class Protestants had dominated the first phases of the student rebellion, new cadres now flooded the movement. To these young people, domestic political authorities had become ideologically appropriate targets for rebellion. They had been stripped of their aura of "true inner authority," that self-confident strength of leadership that inspires confidence in followers and subordinates, not only because they became identified with racism and an unjust war but also because they lacked the power or will to punish those rebels who seemed to dominate college communities.

For latent authoritarian youths from conservative homes, pent-up aggression could now be expressed against an "Establishment" perceived as weak, for all its bluster. This aggression was legitimized by identification with selected oppressed groups, such as black militants and third world revolutionaries, who were perceived as strong and justly violent.

The new cadres of radical youth could thus satisfy several urges at once. They could act out forbidden impulses, symbolically destroy weakened authority, and identify with a power that would eventually establish a new authority structure in which they would be dominant.

Tom Wolfe captured the flavor of New Left identification with "black power" in his account of a party given by wealthy white liberals to raise funds for the Black Panther legal defense fund. He quotes one reaction to the guests of honor, who entered dressed in quasi-military regalia of black leather coats and berets: "These aren't civil rights *Negroes* wearing suits three sizes too big. . . . These are *real men*." [83]

Wolfe was satirizing the wealthy middle-aged "limousine leftists" to whom "radical chic" appealed rather than their children. But his critique of this group's response serves to remind us of the support that youthful white dissidents garnered among important sectors of the socioeconomic and political elites, such as liberal lawyers, journalists, and academics. This support, in combination with the tactical clumsiness of opposition forces, helped reassure young radicals that they held the moral and legal high ground.

The latter advantage was by no means insignificant. Early on, it became obvious to most upper-middle-class white radical students that they ran relatively little risk in "unmasking the establishment's repressiveness" with provocative and/or illegal activity. While radical blacks justifiably feared severe retribution in court or by police vigilante activity, white students learned to expect no greater punishment than a short jail term, often suspended or reversed on appeal, or at worst a beating. Such punishment was strong enough to justify expectations of Establishment oppression without posing serious threat to life and limb. As a result, civil disobedience and confrontation tactics served to strengthen their sense of righteousness, by confirming their self-image as brethren of other victims of oppression. As Jack Newfield wrote of the early civil rights movement:

> Students at Rutgers, Berkeley, Minnesota, Yale and Antioch rushed to the center of sit-in activity to get arrested. . . . [They were] beginning to realize a jail record could be a badge of honor. In those first few weeks, the sit-ins clearly liberated more white middle-class students in the North than it did Southern Negroes.[84]

But the experience of psychological liberation through political confrontation is probably best conveyed by the participants themselves. This experience is typified by the following account of a 1965 sit-in in a San Francisco hotel lobby, ostensibly to force the hiring of more blacks:

> One had to decide how much the cause meant to him: whether it was worth jail, a police record, maybe loss of a job and, perhaps most important, being recognized by the hostile majority as being on the other side. . . . The lobby was filled, and we each realized that *we were not alone*. One spent a lifetime keeping up one's guard for fear of being laughed at or looking foolish; but here we were, a thousand strong, and we knew that we all believed, that we had some core of our lives to share with one another. . . . It is only when the pull of involvement

wrenches you from the doubts and ambiguities and compromises that it is possible to have a sense of oneself, and to feel alive. A night in the Sheraton-Palace, a summer in Mississippi to know that there is a battle raging, and to know which side you are on. . . . So when the Press pointed out that 80% of the demonstrators were white students, and questioned whether they were agitating for jobs for Negroes or only using that as a pretext for something else, they were essentially right. We were concerned about those jobs, but there was much more at stake. . . . You were free of the whole sticky cobweb that kept you apart from each other and from the roots of your existence, and you knew you were alive and what your life was all about. It was the tactics of direct action . . . that made this possible. . . . The means the students used *were* the ends of the movement.[85]

There is no reason to doubt the genuine idealistic fervor of this expression of moral yearning and solidarity in dissent. In fact, this is precisely the point. Well before the widespread appearance of "adventurers" and terrorists in the New Left, consciously sincere radical activity could be motivated by an "impulsive" rebellion. Self-doubt and ambivalence were transcended by incorporation into a larger whole, a Movement stronger and greater than the individual. Direct action provided the opportunity to fight back against hostile authority, i.e., aggressive acts were justified as preemptive counter-attacks against expected persecution. The threat of mild punishment could relieve unconscious guilt feelings over rejecting authority; a night in jail confirmed one's fears of persecution, thereby justifying further counter-hostility.[86]

This dynamic strengthened the New Left's self-perception as a community of the oppressed. And feelings of oppression (and of community) served to justify stronger forms of retaliation. As the Movement became more insulated, it became increasingly violent as well. Gradually, the readiness to identify with oppressed groups merged with the conviction that the student Left itself was an oppressed minority, indeed the natural spokesman for other less articulate victims of oppression. Jerry Farber's image of "the student as nigger" added a popular phrase to the rhetoric of protest on American campuses.[87] Marcuse made an enormous impact on European student radicals with his call for "outlaws and outsiders" to "refuse to play the game" and to devote their lives to this "great refusal."[88] In West Germany in particular, the "great refusal" became the slogan of the students' self-proclaimed "extra-parliamentary opposition." Marcuse's image of negation henceforth became a catchword for counter-attack.

In this mode of psycho-political rebellion, social authority serves as a foil for experiments in self-definition and self-expansion. Unlike traditional authoritarians of right or left, the "pure" New Leftist does not remain trapped between conflicting aspects of self, necessitating rigid self-control. He is released from crippling ambivalence by his "principled" impulsivity. "When in doubt," Jerry Rubin counseled, "do it."[89]

The primary conflict, then, is between a self centered on narcissistic claims and a world that refutes those claims. Direct action was a sword that could cut this Gordian knot. As an early civil rights worker explained, confrontation liberates:

> . . . the trouble with trying to understand politics and society as they are taught in the university is that everything seems so complex. . . . It is only when one can confront it himself, only when it is reduced to its ultimate terms of what it means to the lives of individual men, that "society" can really be known and understood. . . . Whatever beauty, grace, love, or joy was shown in the course of the struggle . . . was made possible by . . . the unity of their ideals with what it was necessary for them to do in order to be men.[90]

Through political confrontation, the new man would emerge from the shell of the old. Personalism and self-expressive political style were the handmaidens of a voluntaristic approach to social change. One made the revolution by living the revolution: "Your politics is not your rhetoric or your positions on issues, it is the way you live your life."[91] If the Establishment could not be defeated in head-on conflict, it could be subverted by psychological "guerrilla warfare" and actively confronted by an "adversary culture" whose weapons were an expressive personal life style and egalitarian social relations. Slogans like "participatory democracy" were thus viewed not only as desirable goals but also as tools of social change. SDS vice-president Carl Davidson compared "PD" to a

> chronic and contagious disease; once caught it permeates one's whole life and the lives of those around us. Its effect is disruptive in a total sense, and within a manipulative bureaucratic system its articulation and expression amounts to sabotage.[92]

The flavor of the early New Left was thus more that of a secular Salvation Army than a goal-oriented political movement. Membership among the righteous was treated as a source of personal salvation; through active proselytizing the entire corrupt society might be similarly saved. But this vision of salvation demanded continual confrontation with social and political authorities. There were more defeats than victories when push came to shove, leading to rising frustration and disillusionment with the larger society's desire and capacity to

be saved. The inability to transform society rapidly and radically naturally placed
great strain on the challengers.

Their movement thus became increasingly susceptible to defection or withdrawal into the apolitical counter-culture. This resulted in considerable dilution
of its upper-status Jewish base. Experientially oriented radicals began to drop
out of the Movement as it lost its novelty and stopped promising personal
rebirth. Those who stayed transformed the politics of personal expression into
militant anarchism and situationism. By 1968 Howard Zinn could locate the
Movement's "anti-authoritarian" character in its willingness to "burn draft cards
in any society":

> . . . it is anarchistic . . . not just in wanting the ultimate abolition of
> the state, but in its immediate requirement that authority and coercion
> be banished in every sphere of existence, that the end must be repre-
> sented immediately in the means.[93]

This trend was highly influential in the European New Left as well. The
most important leaders of the student movement, like Rudi Dutschke in Germany and Daniel Cohn-Bendit in France, were self-conscious representatives
of an anarchistic tradition that counterposed itself to the traditional Marxist left.
Their equation of the personal and political aims of "the revolution" culminated in Cohn-Bendit's blunt statement of purpose:

> We do not make revolution for our children. . . . Sacrifice is counter-
> revolutionary and results from a form of Stalinist Judeo-Christian hu-
> manism; instead, we make revolution to get pleasure from life for our-
> selves, freely without any obstacles, once and for all.[94]

With rapidly increasing emphasis being placed on the vitalist and experiential aspects of psycho-political revolt, it is little wonder that the New Left
became a "carrier movement" for politicized avant-garde groups like the Yippies, the Dutch Provos, and the French enragés. The commitment of such
groups to irrationalism, spontaneous action, social disruption, and self-
gratification at once parodied and transmogrified radical style. As Jerry Rubin
exhorted, "When in doubt, burn. . . . To take what you need is an act of self-
love, self-liberation. When looting, a man to his own self is true."[95]

We believe that the precedence of style over content reflected the presence
of personality conflicts that could be alleviated temporarily by rebellion as an
"existential" act, whatever its form or focus. Because this rebellion was an
expression of submissive-aggressive ambivalence toward authority, many radi-

cals became trapped in an ideological posture that called for rejection of the "System," but not its actual destruction and replacement by an alternative set of social and political structures. Eventually, the dynamic of escalating protest forced them either to embrace all-out revolution by "any means necessary" or to withdraw from the field of battle.

In an essay on the cultural style of New Leftists, Irving Howe captured the essence of this dilemma and its consequences:

> [The "new leftist"] tends to think of style as the very substance of his revolt, and while he may, on one side of himself, engage in valuable activities in behalf of civil rights, student freedom, etc., he nevertheless tacitly accepts the "givenness" of society, has little hope or expectation of changing it, and thereby, in effect, settles for a mode of personal differentiation. Primarily that means the wish to shock, the wish to assault the sensibilities of a world he cannot overcome . . . so as perhaps to create an inner, private revolution that will accompany—or replace— the outer, public revolution. But [he] is frequently trapped in a symbiotic relationship with the very middle class he rejects, dependent upon it for his self-definition: quite as the professional anti-Communist of a few years ago was caught up with the Communist Party . . . the style of the "new leftist" tends to become a rigid anti-style, dependent for its survival on the enemy it is supposed to panic. . . . If he is to succeed in shocking them or even himself, he must keep raising the ante . . . is thereby caught up in the compulsiveness of his escalation . . . in effect, if not intent, it is a strategy of exclusion, leaving no place for anyone but the vanguard of the scarred.[96]

When faced with a choice between total commitment to violent revolution and abandonment of the political struggle, it is hardly surprising that most radicals chose the latter. On one hand, as Howe emphasizes, they needed an evil Establishment as a foil for their personal exercises in self-affirmation through political protest. On the other hand, the proposed negative identity of underground guerrilla was objectively far more dangerous than that of counterculture "outlaw." In short, many radicals were driven to a psychological impasse that paralleled their movement's political impasse. When political action ceased to fulfill their personality needs, they turned to privatized modes of self-expression, depleting the New Left of all but the most politicized, militant, and dogmatic elements—those for whom there could be no turning back.

A very few played the game to its conclusion in deadly earnest. In the United States the remnants of the Weathermen after the "Days of Rage" exemplified this alternative. For this tiny minority within the Movement, pragmatic political strategy gave way entirely to the psychological appeal of violent confrontation with authority. Direct armed confrontation could not hope to bring down the Establishment, but the liberated vanguard could draw revolutionary fervor from the crucible of battle.[97] Bernardine Dohrn stated this appeal with an almost touching ingenuousness, as part of a formal "declaration of war":

> Ever since SDS became revolutionary, we've been trying to show how it is possible to overcome the frustration and impotence that comes from trying to reform this system. Kids know that lines are drawn; revolution is touching all of our lives. Tens of thousands have learned that protest and marches don't do it. Revolutionary violence is the only way. . . . This is the way we celebrate the example of Eldridge Cleaver and H. Rap Brown and all black revolutionaries who first inspired us by their fight behind enemy lines for the liberation of their people. Never again will they have to fight alone.[98]

The psycho-political hallmarks of the Movement's militant last days are all here: the overt translation of personal needs into political strategies, the imitative affiliation with black militants, the Manichean imagery, the glorification of violence as liberating. It would be easy to forget that, as one member remarked to a sympathetic interviewer, "every Weatherman began as a moderate reformer who became disillusioned with the process of reform."[99]

For these white middle-class students, revolutionary violence gradually came to seem a logical extension of long and arduous effort to overcome their origins as "children of the oppressor." This goal led them to a negative identification with the world's outcasts and victims, whom they viewed as sources of both moral and physical strength. As agents of the oppressed, and the justly violent oppressed in particular, they could treat their own aggressive urges as morally legitimate. They could also eliminate lingering ambivalence toward social authority by provoking a wholly repressive response. Social repression retrospectively justified the provocation and reinforced their sense of victimization. Stuart Daniels has argued against those who treat the Weathermen's "later nihilistic tendencies as their *raison d'être*":

> The basic premise of the [New Left's] political position was that it was impossible for personal liberation to be attained in a repressive system. From this follows the involvement in civil rights work, the opposition to the Vietnam war, and finally the desire to abolish American imperialism. The Weathermen openly embraced [these ideas] and consequently their theory and activities reflect not only a desire for political revolution but an obsession with personal liberation. . . . The move to

bombings . . . merely confirmed a commitment to become deviants; to reject the totality of contemporary American existence/society. The guns merely gave a greater validity to their outlaw status . . . the intensely personal quality of their political activity . . . meant that they must choose a position that satisfied them from a human point of view. In order to be true to themselves and to continue as they began, the only logical choice was to become revolutionaries.[100]

As a few New Leftists moved toward self-destruction, many more turned toward more immediately rewarding and less dangerous modes of self-expression, such as mystical religions, nonpolitical communes, and the growing "human potential" movement. The remaining combatants were now increasingly joined by the type of ideologue who had shadowed the Movement since the beginning, despite repeated rebuffs. The New Left's protracted "identity crisis" finally permitted the resurgence of ideological leftists who had never doubted their political identities. Personalized rebellion ultimately helped fuel an upsurge of elements who scorned the "existential" New Leftist as a "Pepsi generation radical." They brought with them a proclivity toward a more familiar mode of authoritarian rebellion—that of the radical as rigid ideologue.

The combination of an ideological concern for mankind and an emotional aversion to human beings has guided—and misguided—revolutionaries all too often in our century. Its recurrence in the past decade is exemplified by a manifesto from a German SDS group, issued shortly after the murder of John F. Kennedy:

You are the ones who killed John Kennedy. . . . That a Kennedy is irreplaceable is an illusion that has been artfully created. The truth is that Kennedy acted in a world of interchangeable puppets. . . . The satisfied simulation of pain [in response to his death] is a symbol of collective imbecility; this revolting feeling of solidarity within a social system whose members are perfectly incapsulated in their own isolation exists only as a consequence of a forced collective psychosis. . . . People who do not understand what we are saying do not want to understand at all. They merely give truth to the strength of our statements. They show that they are passively accepting the coercion exercised by societal norms.[101]

It should come as no surprise that these radicals' potential for self-sacrifice might extend to a willingness to sacrifice others to a noble ideal. A Progressive Labor organizer's exhortation is all too typical of the rhetoric and the psychic reality associated with this disposition:

We will not be fully free until we smash this state completely . . . in that process, we're going to have to kill a lot of cops, a lot of judges, and we'll have to go up against their army.[102]

By the end, the Movement's impetus had created cadres of young people whose random aggression took on those sexual overtones classically associated with pathological sadism. Dotson Rader has described his own proclivities in this direction:

It was through the romantic marriage of sex and violence and politics and manhood and death that I came to understand how so much of what was apparently apolitical in American culture was indeed revolutionary: drugs, perverse sex, even Warhol's Hustler movies, on and on. . . .

Revolutionaries and bikeboys and other tough outsiders: the butch stance, the ruthlessness, the overstated masculinity, the power of their bodies, the independence and mobility evidenced by their lives, their position as outlaw, all consummated their appeal. . . . I could identify with revolutionaries liquidating a ruling class, or with a band of bikers terrorizing the straight countryside. I could identify with violence pitted against the established order.[103]

Rader also provides a concrete example of this syndrome's nihilistic overtones:

. . . in Easthampton . . . on codeine and grass, naked by a pool . . . Stephen asked, "Are you bored?" and I replied, "Dying of it." And Stephen . . . said, "Watch, this is for you" and grabbed a knife, and with its point cut the letter R into his thigh. . . . This I knew: they were better than me, for they were immediately open to violence. That I envied, their apparent lack of guilt over the natural pleasure they took in violence.[104]

Finally, as the Movement died, the torch was carried largely by small groups of conspirators, many of them persuaded that the whole world was engaged in a gigantic conspiracy to brainwash them. Ultimately they began to turn their rage on each other.[105]

During the late 1970s and early 1980s a number of ex-Weathermen surfaced and surrendered to authorities. By and large the charges against them were relatively minor, and they received only minimal punishment. Several turned their experiences into reasonably successful books, describing the paranoia of life underground, and, in a very few cases, analyzing their earlier motivations in terms not far removed from our own.[106]

A few retained their revolutionary commitment. In 1981, for example, David Gilbert, Katherine Boudin, and several others participated in an unsuccessful attempt to rob a Brink's armored car. Three persons were killed in the fracas. So much had the times changed, however, that not even those who had once "understood" why young people should be driven to violence in a society as corrupt as America offered any sympathy.[107]

In sum, the "sadistic" psycho-political rebellion of the New Left's final days was centered on an internal struggle which is mapped onto the world: the wish to submit is projected, and the pride that fights against that submission is conserved for the self. Such rebels are guided by an incorruptible inner vision—the repository of bruised narcissism—that cannot betray them, despite the failure of the *ad hoc* and imperfect movements that temporarily serve that vision. They are willing to follow rather grandiose goals with obsessive persistence, and to defend and rationalize these goals and programs in ways that could make them plausible for themselves and, at times, for others. It is not inconceivable that a few such people would follow their vision wherever it leads them, even to the barricades of revolution and terrorism.[108]

Part III

WHAT OUR STUDIES SHOWED

5 Studying the New Left: A New Approach

WE HAVE SKETCHED a portrait of the radical as inverse authoritarian, drawing on historical evidence as well as the theoretical insights of psychology, sociology, and political science. We have also postulated ethnic variations on this syndrome to explain the somewhat different appeals of radical ideology for Jews and Christians. In the following chapters we describe our efforts to test these hypotheses by studying contemporary radicals in the United States and West Germany.

Let us begin by describing our research procedures. The overall project consisted of four related studies. The first of these, a study of American college students, was the largest and most thorough. During the academic years 1971–73, we administered a survey questionnaire to over 1100 students at four large American universities. First, random samples of the student body were drawn from registration lists at Harvard University, the University of Michigan, and the University of Massachusetts at Amherst. To ensure that highly radical students were represented, we also took probability samples of a few campus activist groups. The response rate at these schools was just over 60 percent. Finally, we administered the same questionnaire to students in compulsory classes at Boston University.

Participation in the study was completely voluntary. Students selected for our sample were told that we were interested in understanding the sources of different political attitudes among college students.

We deleted from the sample sixty-seven subjects who identified their ethnogeographic background as Afro-American, Hispanic (Mexican, Cuban, and Puerto Rican), or Asian (Japanese and Chinese). Our analysis was thereby restricted to students of European extraction, who constituted the bulk of the white student movement. (The black movement was a quite different social phenomenon and lies beyond the scope of our study.) In addition, we conducted a separate statistical analysis of the Boston University sample, the only nonprobability subsample in the study. No significant differences in the distribution of the major variables separated this from the other campus samples.

The resulting overall sample of 1051 students is not an appropriate source for statistical inferences about the entire American student movement. It does, however, compare favorably with sampling techniques of the best-known studies in this field, such as those of Flacks and Block, Haan, and Smith. And it does allow us to draw inferences about the nature of student radicalism at several major universities including Michigan, the birthplace of SDS. Although these universities are certainly not representative of all postsecondary schools, they provide a mixture of public and private as well as elite and nonelite institutions. Finally, our major concern was to analyze the relationship between radicalism and a social psychological profile, rather than to estimate the distribution of this profile in the general student population.

Our subjects filled out a lengthy questionnaire that contained an unusual mixture of questions and tests. In addition to an extensive battery of questions about social backgrounds and political beliefs, it included a test of perceived family relations and two psychological tests, the Semantic Differential and Thematic Apperception Test, or TAT. All these instruments will be described in the next chapter. At the outset, though, a word about our social psychological tests is in order, since they were the most distinctive and unusual part of the survey.

We sought to avoid the problems that plagued previous psychological studies of student activism. Most of these studies relied on self-reports, asking subjects to describe themselves and accepting the resulting self-descriptions more or less at face value. By contrast, we decided to use projective tests or instruments that can be administered in a projective fashion. Such tests present a subject with an ambiguous stimulus and invite him to project his own feelings and needs into his response. For example, the TAT consists of a set of pictures about which subjects are asked to write fictional stories. Their stories are then analyzed by trained scorers, who seek out thematic material that gives insight into their underlying concerns—concerns they might not be willing or able to reveal on demand.

Long used by clinicians, such tests are being increasingly employed in survey research. They are much more difficult to interpret and validate than are simple self-reports.[1] We will discuss these issues at some length when describing the tests we relied upon. However, used carefully and in conjunction with other methods, they also offer many advantages:

1. They help narrow the distance between the researcher's predetermined view of his subject's inner reality and that inner reality as perceived and employed by the subject himself.

2. They enable the investigator to explore motivations of which the respondent is largely or wholly unaware and which the investigator is unlikely to intuit.
3. They provide an opportunity to study motivations that may be socially undesirable or ego-alien. Thus investigators are being equipped to surmount the barrier of social desirability.
4. They provide a wealth of data. Responses can be used to illustrate a variety of theoretical perspectives. They are not limited to the immediate focus of the investigator but may be reanalyzed by others in terms of different or unthought-of perspectives. Thus they provide a "bank" of information. As we shall see, this aspect proved particularly advantageous to our research.

The second and third points are probably the most important. As we argued in Chapter 2, students from middle-class cosmopolitan backgrounds tend to write self-reports that comport with their own ideal values. Moreover, these values are often shared by the researchers who administer the tests. When asked to write stories about ambiguous pictures, respondents are more likely to reveal proclivities that they conceal even from themselves.

A few of the college students we studied seemed aware that they might be revealing more of themselves than they wished to. They composed stories about animals or "gremlins" rather than human beings. Because we were concerned with the structure of relationships in the story, even these stories could be scored.

In an effort to probe more deeply and systematically into the radical psyche, we supplemented this survey with intensive clinical interviews of a small number of male students, equally divided into radical and nonradical, as well as Jewish and non-Jewish groups. Once again, participation was voluntary. Students who filled out our original questionnaire were asked to affix their name (or a pseudonym) and phone number to the questionnaire if they wished to participate. They were told they would be paid twenty-five dollars upon completing the interviews and the clinical tests.

After completing the questionnaire, these students were interviewed by a research team that included a clinical psychologist and a psychodynamically oriented psychiatrist. As part of the interview procedures, they received an additional set of clinical TATs, as well as a Rorschach (ink-blot) test. As abstract patterns, the Rorschach inkblots are even more ambiguous than TAT pictures. In addition, the scoring methods used to extract information from them are all but unknown to nonprofessionals. For these reasons, it becomes even more difficult for subjects to present ideal images of themselves. This clinical study is described in Chapter 7.

In a third study, conducted in 1974–75, we contacted one-time student activists and other radicals who had played important roles in the early to middle 1960s. We interviewed over 120 of these early New Leftists, who filled out a questionnaire incorporating most of the instruments used in our survey of students. We compared their responses with those of a group of nonradical business and professional people.

We chose to track down these early activists for three reasons. First, we wanted to determine whether, as Keniston and others had argued, the first generation of New Leftists had differed significantly from the radicals we studied during the early 1970s. Second, it could be argued that, by studying active radicals, we had not measured the psychological sources of student radicalism but, rather, the consequences of being a radical in a time of crisis. By 1974–75 the radical movement was moribund. We could then study ex-activists in a period of relative calm. Third, we wanted to test our hypotheses about the critical role played by radicals of Jewish background in the early stages of the movement. By the 1970s, the Movement had spread widely to other groups in the society, and we did not expect to find quite the same pattern of relatively high Jewish involvement that had characterized the early 1960s. Further, insofar as radicalism had become the "thing to do" on many campuses by the early 1970s, we expected that our theories would be more applicable to the early activists than to their successors.

Our findings are reported in Chapter 8, along with systematic comparisons between these early radicals and the radical students we interviewed during the Movement's latter days.

Finally, in November 1973, a translated version of our survey was administered to 230 male students at two West German universities. In many ways the West German student movement paralleled our own during its heyday. But when the American movement began its precipitous decline during the early 1970s, its German counterpart was able to entrench itself on many university campuses, creating a self-perpetuating radical culture. In addition, the German New Left offers a point of comparison particularly relevant to our research. It arose and flourished without the aid of the upper-status Jewish base that gave life and form to the American movement. It thus offers an important case study of contemporary student radicalism without Jews.

By studying these young radicals, we informally controlled for the effects that a Jewish background contributes to the social psychology of radicalism. We hypothesized that the West German radicals would closely resemble their American non-Jewish peers, while differing both from American Jewish radicals and from nonradicals in both countries. This would suggest that our theories can help to explain the inner dynamic of recent radical movements in both Europe and America. The results of this study, along with a discussion of the West German New Left in relation to our own, appear in Chapter 9.

Lichter had decided to study German students in 1973 for his doctoral dissertation. He had heard of Rothman's work and was excited by both the research instruments and the prospect of a comparative analysis. At that point, Rothman's hypotheses were primarily directed to the Jewish segment of the New Left. He had not developed a systematic model of non-Jewish radicalism, nor had he yet analyzed any of his data on American students. It was only two years later that we discovered the striking similarity of our initial findings and began to recognize their theoretical implications. It was then that our collaboration was initiated.

In Chapter 6, we will describe the instruments and findings from our survey of the American students. First, however, let us summarize the theoretical propositions that we sought to test. We expected to find that radicals differ systematically from nonradicals in their backgrounds, their upbringings, and their psychological orientations.

We predicted that Jews would be disproportionally represented among the ranks of the American radicals we studied. In particular, radical ideologies should appeal most strongly to "deracinated" Jews—people of Jewish background who no longer identify with their heritage. Moreover, a Jewish ethnic background should be the underlying link between all the other social characteristics commonly associated with the New Left.

Many studies of the student movement concluded that these young people had been psychologically liberated by their socially and culturally privileged family backgrounds. Specifically, their motives and values were seen as the products of upbringings by upper-middle-class professionals who held secular and liberal to radical outlooks and employed permissive or "democratic" child-raising techniques. We have argued, on the contrary, that this "revolt of the privileged," far from being a historically new phenomenon, really represented the continuation of a long tradition of upper-status Jewish radicalism. Therefore, we believed that these popular characterizations of the New Left applied primarily to its substantial Jewish component. Specifically, we hypothesized that it was primarily young Americans of Jewish background whose parents fit the descriptions of Keniston, Flacks, and others, while the social and political backgrounds of non-Jewish radicals were much more diverse.

Our analysis suggests that these differences in upbringing extended beyond social background to encompass everyday relations between parents and their children. Therefore, we predicted that radicals would perceive their parents quite differently from how nonradicals perceived theirs and that Jewish and non-Jewish radicals would also differ systematically from one another. We expected non-Jewish radicals to describe their families in terms recalling the traditional authoritarian type described by Erikson and Frenkel-Brunswick—i.e., as families dominated by a stern and punitive father who is seen as "flawed" or lacking "inner authority," and in which both parents are seen as harsh and uncaring.

Jewish radicals, by contrast, should describe the matriarchal families that gave rise to the stereotype of the "Portnoy syndrome." We emphasize that we expected this syndrome to hold true mainly for Jewish radicals, not for *all* Jews. We predicted that they would view their mothers as domineering and intrusive and their fathers as weak and distant. In addition, we thought that Jewish radicals would view their parents with ambivalent feelings, in contrast to the unalloyed hostility of their non-Jewish counterparts. Our predictions about the latter stemmed from Adorno's description of the inverse authoritarian, whose deep-seated hostility toward his parents is not redirected against outgroups, but bursts forth, in all its fury, against its original targets.

Finally, we sought to demonstrate that both groups of radicals were more likely than nonradicals to manifest a broad syndrome of inverse authoritarian personality traits. Within this syndrome of authoritarian rebellion, we also tried to identify two variants: the "rigid" rebellion of the non-Jewish radical and the "self-expansive" or protean rebellion of the Jewish radical.

In the psychological portion of this study, we seek to show that radicals are relatively likely to resemble the character type first described by Fromm as "the rebel." Such a person is motivated by a deep conflict over power and authority, which leads him simultaneously to desire and fear power. This conflict, generated by narcissistic deficits incurred early in life, prevents the rebel from dealing with other people in terms of genuine mutuality. Instead, he structures his life, and particularly his authority relations, around power exchanges. All social relations become a matter of winning or losing, dominating or submitting, commanding or obeying.

Although the rebel experiences life this way, he may find this outlook personally or ideologically unsatisfying. Therefore, he externalizes his conflict by projecting his own power orientation onto the outer world. Thus, society or the Establishment becomes his enemy, which he sees as an enemy of "humanity" that must be destroyed. He searches for powerful allies in this struggle and finds them in militant representatives of the oppressed, such as black or third world revolutionaries. A radical movement serves as a powerful ally in this struggle. It bestows the sense of heightened personal significance that comes from subsuming oneself into a community of believers.

In short, we hypothesized that radicals would be motivated by both a need for and fear of power, to the relative exclusion of concerns for intimate relationships based on mutuality. We also hypothesized that they would be relatively narcissistic and fixated on self-assertive or "phallic" psychosocial orientations. All these hypotheses were tested by analysis of the TAT material. In addition, we expected that radicals would differentially attribute power or potency to images of militancy, rebellion, and physical strength, while treating intellectuality as a sign of weakness. We tested these hypotheses by a rather unusual application of the Semantic Differential.

Finally, we expected to find systematic differences between Jewish and non-Jewish radicals. We hypothesized that the personality traits of non-Jews would be closer to those of the archetypal traditional authoritarian, including very low affiliative needs and a predominantly phallic orientation, to the virtual exclusion of a capacity for integration or mutuality. Among the Jewish radicals, we expected this pattern to be mitigated somewhat by the affiliative needs, low ego boundaries, and incorporative psycho-social orientation that characterize the self-expansive rebel.

Many of the differences between these two modes of rebellion, however, are too subtle to be captured by the relatively crude measurements of personality available to a survey questionnaire. It was for this reason that we carried out the clinical study, which offers a much better opportunity for systematic in-depth comparisons between Jewish and non-Jewish radicals.

We used both behavioral and attitudinal measures to identify New Leftists. On the whole, radical attitudes proved to be more clearly associated with other social and psychological characteristics than was activism. This is not surprising, in view of the high levels of political activism on American campuses during the early 1970s. Our primary measure of radicalism was the New Left Ideology scale developed at Columbia University during the late 1960s.[2] The authors were Richard Christie, a distinguished social psychologist, and two co-workers, Alice Gold and Lucy Friedman. Their instrument consists of a series of political statements with which subjects are asked to agree or disagree. Subjects rate each statement along a continuum from one to seven, where a rating of one indicates strong agreement and seven indicates strong disagreement. The scale is "balanced" to control for the tendencies of some people to agree with *any* statements on a test of this sort. That is, a "radical" response requires agreement with some statements and disagreement with others. A person's radicalism score is the sum total of his scores on all sixty statements in the test. Usually, though, researchers isolate particular subscales that are most closely related to the aspects of radicalism they wish to measure. We used statements from three of the five subscales: New Left Philosophy, Radical Tactics, and

Traditional Moralism. Typical items from each of these subscales are: "Real participatory democracy should be the basis of a new society" (NLP); "A mass revolutionary party should be created in this country" (RT); and "Police should not hesitate to use force to maintain order" (TM), respectively.

The test's authors reported that, during the 1968 Columbia University riots, the scale differentiated significantly between students who engaged in "confrontational" activities, on the one hand, and "nonconfrontational" activists and nonactivists, on the other. More recently, they have brought together a wide range of findings supporting their test's validity and reliability.[3] We also provided a measure of concurrent validation among our American student sample. New Left Ideology scores were highly correlated with their political self-descriptions, which ranged from "very conservative" to "revolutionary radical."

For our entire sample of students, the grand mean score on this short form of the New Left Ideology scale was 4.16. This means that for all students, across all items, the average score was almost precisely in the middle of the possible range from one to seven. On the other hand, there were students who offered either the most radical or least radical response to almost every statement listed: Individual averages ranged from a low of 1.66 to a high of 6.85.

For purposes of comparison, we classified as radicals those students scoring at least one standard deviation above the mean, which required an average score of 4.96 or higher. Students scoring below 3.25, one standard deviation below the mean, were called conservatives. The remainder, who scored between 3.24 and 4.95, were termed liberals. These designations are, of course, somewhat arbitrary. But they provide a convenient way of describing the traits of radicals in common-sense terms. Where appropriate, we will ignore these distinctions and simply calculate the overall relationship between radicalism and other variables.

We emphasize that radicalism was primarily defined in terms of attitudes. Although activism was certainly correlated with radical attitudes, we were primarily concerned with those young people who were rebelling against the "System." Many of our liberals and even some conservatives participated in antiwar demonstrations during the 1960s. They are nonetheless classified as liberals and conservatives, on the basis of their social and political beliefs.

We now proceed to the findings themselves, beginning with the social and ethnic origins of student radicalism.

6 Radical Youth: A Survey of Students

YOUNG PEOPLE of Jewish background provided a critical mass of radicals who helped transform the New Left from a relatively unimportant fringe group into a significant social and political force. When we analyzed the results of our own research, therefore, we began by asking whether Jews had remained at the cutting edge of radical politics during the early 1970s.

Our questionnaire asked subjects to identify each parent's religion and ethnic background. We classified students as Jewish if the ethnic background of both parents was Jewish, or if only one parent was of Jewish background but had raised the child as Jew or without religious training.

We found that students of Jewish background were indeed both more radical and more involved in protest activity than were students from non-Jewish families. On the New Left Ideology scale, the 410 Jewish students averaged 4.36, compared to 4.03 for the 649 non-Jews.[1] This difference is statistically highly significant (p < .001). As Table 1 shows, Jews were also very heavily represented among the most active protesters. They were three times as likely as non-Jews to have protested frequently and less than half as likely never to have engaged in protest. Almost one third (30 percent) of all Jewish students had participated in seven or more protests, compared to one in ten non-Jews. Conversely, only one in ten Jews had never protested, compared to one in four non-Jews. Finally, Jews were found almost twice as often among the most committed activists.

Overall, 13 percent of the Jewish students were frequent protest leaders or organizers, compared with 7 percent of the non-Jews. Clearly, students of Jewish background were differentially drawn to New Left politics and protests.

We asked next whether the high level of Jewish protest could be attributed to their radicalism, since radicals were more likely to protest than non-radicals. In other words, was Jewish protest simply a function of Jewish radicalism, or might their activism stem from other aspects of the Jewish experience?

Table 1. Number of Protests by Ethnicity[a] (%).

	Protests						
	None	1–2	3–4	5–6	7 or more	N	%
Jew	10	25	23	12	30	407	100
Non-Jew	26	32	20	11	11	645	100
N	210	303	224	122	193	1052	

$\chi^2 = 85.11$ D.F.$= 4$ P$<.001$

[a]Numbers represent the percentages of Jews and non-Jews at each level of protest activity.

To answer this question, we divided all students into conservative, liberal, and radical groups, according to the criteria described in Chapter 5. We then examined the rates of protest activity for Jews and non-Jews within each ideological category. The results are shown in Table 2. Radicalism and Jewishness independently increased the level of protest activity. Radicalism was strongly related to protest regardless of ethnicity, but the relationship was slightly stronger among Jews. In addition, the ethnic differences were sharpest at the highest level of protest. Two thirds of the Jewish radicals had engaged in seven or more protests; they were almost twice as likely to protest frequently as were non-Jewish radicals. Moreover, the differences between Jewish and non-Jewish nonradicals were even greater. Liberal and conservative Jews were each more than twice as likely as their non-Jewish counterparts to protest often. Equally revealing, half the conservative non-Jews never took part in a protest, as opposed to only one in four Jewish conservatives. Finally, only a single Jewish radical (out of 114) had *never* engaged in a protest, compared to almost one of every ten non-Jewish radicals.

Table 2. Number of Protests by Ideology, with Ethnicity Controlled (%).

JEWS					NON-JEWS				
	Radicalism					Radicalism			
Protests	Con	Lib	Rad	N	Protests	Con	Lib	Rad	N
0	25	12	1	41	0	50	24	9	169
1–2	34	31	6	100	1–2	34	33	19	202
3–4	16	28	16	95	3–4	8	24	19	129
5–6	13	13	10	50	5–6	4	11	18	72
7+	11	17	66	121	7+	4	8	35	72
N	44	249	114	407	N	124	422	98	644
%	100	100	100		%	100	100	100	

$\chi^2 = 117.18$ D.F.$= 8$ P$<.001$ $\chi^2 = 125.79$ D.F.$= 8$ P$<.001$

In summary, Jews were significantly more radical than non-Jews and far more prone to protest activity. They were three times as likely as non-Jews to engage in frequent protests and twice as likely to lead or organize protests. Moreover, their protest-proneness could not be attributed solely to their radical attitudes. At all points on the ideological spectrum, Jews were about twice as likely as non-Jews to protest frequently.

As a result, by every measure we employed, Jews made up a majority of the New Left on these campuses. Fifty-three percent of the radicals were of Jewish background, as were 63 percent of those who engaged in seven or more protests, 54 percent of those who led three or more protests, and 52 percent of those who formed three or more protest groups. So even in the waning days of the New Left, after radicalism and protest had ceased to be the province of a largely upper-middle-class Jewish avant garde, Jews remained the core of the committed.

Our findings demonstrate the importance of a Jewish ethnic heritage in predisposing young people toward radical politics and protest activity. But our dichotomy between Jewish and non-Jewish radicals may seem arbitrary. After all, Jews share an ethnic heritage, while "non-Jew" is a catchall term lumping together people of many different ethnic backgrounds and religious dominations. Even among Jews, considerable cultural, religious, and national differences may exist.

These religious distinctions moreover seem to ignore the radical Left's proclivity toward a secular or anti-religious outlook. Why focus on religious categories to explain radicalism, when those very categories are widely rejected by radicals? Finally, why focus on ethnic or religious distinctions at all, when this is only one of many aspects of the social backgrounds shared by many New Leftists? Myriad studies of the period showed that radicals' parents were indeed likely to be Jewish or nonreligious but also politically liberal, upper middle class, and permissive or nonauthoritarian in their child-rearing practices. Why should we concentrate on only one of this interlocking set of background factors that predisposed young people toward radicalism?

There is a single answer to all these objections. Quite simply, the dichotomy between Jews and non-Jews provided the most parsimonious means of accounting for the many other social and psychological aspects of New Left radicalism. The evidence for this conclusion comprises a considerable part of this chapter.* Let us begin our account by answering the questions we have just raised.

*In the discussion that follows, we will describe only the most important findings from a large body of data on our subjects' backgrounds and attitudes. A more complete presentation of this data can be found in Appendix A, Tables 21–27.

After examining our results, we concluded that there was little point in dividing the non-Jewish category into several ethnic or denominational components, because these subgroups differed only slightly in their adherence to radical ideas. Jews, by contrast, were substantially more radical than any of the non-Jewish religious or ethnic subgroups.

Our questionnaire asked students to identify the ethnic or national origins of both their parents. Since the results were essentially the same for both parents, we shall summarize only our findings for paternal background. Among non-Jewish students, almost two fifths had English or Scottish backgrounds, one fifth had Irish forebears, one sixth claimed German heritage, and about equal numbers—roughly one in ten—were of Italian or Polish ancestry. The remainder cited either East European or Canadian origins. The mean radicalism scores of these groups varied from a low of 3.88 for the Germans to a high of 4.21 for the Poles. Even the latter figure was only slightly above the overall sample mean of 4.17. So none of the non-Jewish ethnic groups scored more than slightly above average in radicalism, and they all scored well below the mean of 4.36 recorded by Jewish students.

Our findings regarding students' religious preferences and backgrounds were somewhat more complex. Once again, members of the various Christian religious groups differed but little from one another, and none were as radical as any of the Jewish groups. On the other hand, substantial political differences separated the theologically conservative and liberal Jewish groups. These patterns held true for both the students' own affiliations and those of their parents. The most striking findings, though, concerned the political views of students with nonreligious orientations and backgrounds. It is hardly surprising that atheists and agnostics were relatively radical. But we also found that this relationship was strongly mediated by ethnic background. This suggests that the association between secularism and radicalism was the product of a "deracinated" Jewish heritage, rather than a nonreligious upbringing in general.

Although we were primarily concerned with ethnic and religious background, the interplay of Judaism and secularism with radicalism was evident even from students' own religious identifications. About one fourth termed themselves Protestant, one fifth Catholic, and one third Jewish. Almost one in five called themselves nonreligious.

There was very little difference in the radicalism scores of the self-professed Christian groups. Catholics averaged 3.92, Protestants 3.87. Nor did the Protestant denominations differ substantially from one another.

All Catholic and Protestant groups, however, were less politically radical than any Jewish group. Among Jews, moreover, radicalism rose substantially as religious orthodoxy declined. Reform Jews were more radical than orthodox or conservative Jews, averaging 4.39, and Jews who specified no further affiliation were more radical still, averaging 4.61. In fact, unaffiliated Jews were even more radical than nonreligious students, whose average score was 4.50.

Nor is this the whole story. Even among nonreligious subjects, those of Jewish extraction were more radical than non-Jews. In fact, nonreligious ethnic Jews produced the highest group mean score, 4.74, while non-Jewish atheists and agnostics averaged only 4.40, about the same as reform Jews. Of course, irreligious non-Jews were still considerably more radical than any category of Christian believers.

The ideological difference between Jews and Christians was thus much greater than the differences among the various Christian groups. Among Jews, radicalism rose as religious orthodoxy declined. So the association between a secular outlook and a radical ideology could be explained, in part, by the Jewish ethnic origins of many nonbelievers.

These findings suggest that New Left radicalism was linked to the secular outlook of a particular segment of the American Jewish community. To examine this issue further, we asked students about their parents' religious affiliations. Once again, the patterns for both parents proved quite similar. The scores reported below were averaged from the two ratings.

As one would expect, students rated their parents as more religiously inclined than themselves. Less than one in twenty rated their parents as nonreligious. Slightly under 30 percent each came from Protestant and Catholic households, and 38 percent came from Jewish homes. Nonetheless, the relationship of religion to politics was quite similar to the results derived from the students' own preferences. Students from all Christian upbringings once again clustered together, with Catholics averaging 4.08 and Protestants 4.02.

Radicalism rose perceptibly among all students from Jewish homes. Those with orthodox, conservative, and reform Jewish backgrounds all averaged about the same, ranging only from 4.27 to 4.31. Another jump in radicalism occurred among students from nonaffiliated Jewish households. Students whose parents were Jewish but not affiliated with a particular group averaged 4.63 on the radicalism scale.

This suggests that children of deracinated Jewish parents became considerably more radical than Jews with religiously oriented parents. Indeed, the difference in radicalism between the children of "unattached" and religiously affiliated Jews was as great as the difference between affiliated Jews and Christians.

Even more striking were the different impacts of a nonreligious upbringing in ethnically Jewish and non-Jewish homes respectively. The children of irreligious but ethnically Jewish parents were the most radical of all, averaging

4.81. Yet non-Jewish students with irreligious parents averaged only 4.21, making them less radical than the children of orthodox Jews. Among non-Jews as well, the children of secular parents were more radical than the children of believers. But the difference was slight and not statistically significant. For a secular upbringing to have a major radicalizing impact, it had to be combined with a Jewish ethnic heritage.

This conclusion received further support from our findings on the importance of religion in the home. One would expect that children from religiously oriented homes would be less radical than those from households where religion was unimportant, whatever their parents' nominal affiliation. Once again, however, the association of secularism and radicalism proved to be mediated by Jewish ethnicity. At every level of parental piety, students from Jewish homes were more radical than those from non-Jewish homes. Further, the difference was greatest among the children of irreligious parents.

The mean difference in radicalism between Jews and non-Jews with "very religious" fathers was 0.24 (4.20 vs. 3.96); among students whose fathers were "not at all religious," the difference rose to 0.43 (4.64 among Jews vs. 4.21 among non-Jews). Thus, students from irreligious non-Jewish families were only about as radical as those from highly religious Jewish households. Once again, a secular background predicted only an average level of radicalism, unless it was combined with a Jewish ethnic heritage.

We have dwelt on students' religious backgrounds at some length, because the results corroborate several elements of our argument. First, it makes sense to use "Jewish" and "non-Jewish" as general categories to understand the religious and ethnic correlates of radicalism. The many distinctions among non-Jews were not very useful in explaining a propensity toward radical politics. Moreover, this ethnic dichotomy clarifies the influence of a secular orientation on radicalism. In contrast to previous researchers, we found that New Left radicalism was associated less with secularism per se than with the secularism of a segment of the American Jewish community.

Finally, this finding supports our argument that the Jewish role in the New Left was consistently understated by studies that failed to distinguish between ethnicity and religious affiliation. By focusing on religious preference, researchers found that radicals and protesters tended to come from nonreligious backgrounds. They thereby failed to document fully the relationship between Jewish *ethnicity* and radicalism. Our data suggest that the widely noted association between secularism and New Left radicalism reflected not an irreligious upbringing but rather a deracinated Jewish heritage.

We now turn to the relationship of radicalism to other elements of social background. Radical students, it was widely observed, tended to come from upper-middle-class families. Indeed, the New Left was sometimes called a "revolt of the privileged." But it was not simply economic privilege that allegedly predisposed them toward radicalism. Instead it was an upbringing by highly educated parents whose occupations were oriented toward intellectual activity and social service, rather than toward monetary rewards. In short, most radicals did not come from the homes of businessmen or corporate managers. Their fathers (and, to a lesser extent, their mothers) tended to be skilled professionals and intellectuals, whose advanced degrees reflected the needs of an emerging postindustrial society. Once again, however, this widely accepted social profile of the New Leftist applied primarily to the Movement's Jewish segment.

Consider, first, the proposition that highly educated parents were most likely to produce radical children. For our sample, this held true only within Jewish households. Radicalism actually dropped a bit as parental education rose from the high school to the college level. An upward shift in radicalism occurred only when a parent had some postgraduate education. Further, the mean radicalism score for non-Jewish students with highly educated fathers rose only slightly, from 4.01 to 4.07, far below the average scores of Jewish students at all levels of parental education. Among Jews, the radicalism score rose from 4.28 for subjects with high school or college-educated fathers to 4.48 for those whose fathers did postgraduate work. The trends were the same for mothers' education, although the differences were not quite as great. Finally, Jews accounted for half the households in which at least one parent had a postgraduate education.

Next, we compared radicalism scores according to father's occupation. The children of business executives were the least radical group, while those with upper-middle-class professional backgrounds were most radical. Within the professional sector, the children of teachers, professors, and educational administrators were significantly more radical than students from nonacademic households. This is precisely the pattern that most earlier researchers noted.

The picture changed markedly, however, when we controlled for Jewish ethnicity. Among non-Jews, students from professional households averaged only 4.06, well below the overall sample average, and not significantly higher than non-Jewish students from other occupational backgrounds. In sharp contrast, the children of Jewish professionals averaged 4.51, significantly higher than Jews in any other occupational category. In fact, children of non-Jewish professionals were less radical than Jews from any occupational group, except the children of business executives.

A very similar pattern appeared with regard to mother's occupation. Moreover, whereas Jews accounted for 40 percent of students whose fathers were professionals, they constituted a solid majority (56 percent) of those whose mothers worked in the educated professions, both academic and nonacademic. Richard Flacks was the first to note the preponderance of professional carrer women among the mothers of New Leftists.[2] Kenneth Keniston relied on Flacks's finding to speculate that New Left activists possessed "unusual capacity for . . . empathy and sympathy with the underdog, the oppressed, and the needy" because of their "identification with an active mother whose own work embodies nurturant concern for others."[3]

Our research suggests a simpler interpretation. New Left activists were disproportionately Jewish, and Jewish families contained a relatively high proportion of career-oriented mothers. So psychological speculation like Keniston's may represent a spurious causal inference, which reflects a failure to take account of ethnic differences.

In summary, the image of radical youth as the product of highly educated upper-middle-class professionals was valid mainly for Jewish students. The distinctiveness of Jewish radicals became even more evident when we examined students' political backgrounds.

Our questionnaire contained a number of items dealing with political orientations and conflicts within the family. One question simply asked subjects to identify each parent's political orientation. Eight categories were provided, including the conservative, moderate, and liberal wings of each major party, as well as "radical Democrat" and "socialist."[4] The parents of non-Jews clustered on the conservative end of the spectrum, the parents of Jews at the opposite end.

Over half the non-Jewish students identified their fathers as Republicans, including 15 percent who were termed conservative Republican. Only 15 percent called their fathers liberal Democrats. Among Jews, 40 percent saw their fathers as liberal Democrats, compared with only 2 percent as conservative Republicans. An additional 9 percent were "red-diaper babies"—the children of radical or socialist parents. Thus, about half the Jewish students were raised in a liberal or leftist political milieu, with one in ten claiming a heritage of political radicalism. By contrast, only 1 percent of the non-Jews rated their fathers as "radical" Democrats, and not a single non-Jewish subject came from a socialist background.

To determine whether radical students were following in their parents' political footsteps, we compared the radicalism scores of students who placed their parents in different political categories. We treated the eight categories as a continuum ranging from "conservative Republican" to "socialist."

The political preferences of parents and children were positively associated, regardless of ethnicity. The correlations were stronger, however, within Jewish families. In particular, "mother's party" accounted for three times as much variation among Jews as among non-Jews. For example, non-Jewish students were more than six times as likely as Jews to rate their mothers as conservative or moderate Republicans. Among these students, Jews averaged only 3.35 on the radicalism scale, compared to 3.72 for non-Jews. At the other end of the political spectrum, Jews were more than five times as likely as non-Jews to rate their mothers radical or socialist. Among this group, Jews averaged 5.41, compared to 4.80 for non-Jews. The results based on father's political preference were similar, although the differences were not quite as great.

In short, early political socialization accounted for only part of the difference in radicalism between Jewish and non-Jewish students. Students from Jewish backgrounds were far more likely to come from politically leftist families. But among students from conservative families Jews became more conservative than non-Jews. Among those from radical families Jews became more radical than non-Jews.

One reason for this difference may be that children in Jewish homes received more consistent political cues from their parents. To examine this possibility and to provide a somewhat more "objective" grounding for their parental ratings, we asked students what magazines they recalled seeing around the house regularly while growing up. Magazines with an ideological orientation were coded as conservative (e.g., *American Mercury, National Review, Reader's Digest*), moderate "left" (e.g., *Dissent, New Republic, Saturday Review*), and radical left (e.g., *Liberation, Masses and Mainstream, Monthly Review*). We then compared the numbers of such magazines found in the households of Jewish and non-Jewish radical students.

The results distinguished the two groups far more clearly than had their parental ratings. Among the Jewish radicals, 22 percent recalled seeing regularly at least one radical leftist publication, and 48 percent mentioned two or more moderate leftist magazines, while only 7 percent cited two or more conservative magazines. Among non-Jewish radicals, only 9 percent recalled any radical magazine, and 11 percent remembered two or more moderate left journals. About twice that number (20 percent) cited two or more conservative periodicals. In other words, the informational environments of the two groups were almost totally inverted. Jewish radicals were more than twice as likely as non-Jews to see radical publications, while non-Jewish radicals were three times as likely as Jews to see conservative journals.

These figures suggest that Jewish and non-Jewish radicals emerged out of quite different political milieus, the former decidedly radical, the latter more conservative. To probe these differences more deeply, we asked students to compare their own political views with those of each parent. We used a scale from one to seven, where a rating of one indicated that the parent was much more conservative than oneself and a rating of seven indicated that the parent was much more radical. Since the figures for father and for mother were almost exactly the same, we shall cite only the former.

Once again, we obtained opposite results for Jews and non-Jews. Among Jews, the more radical the child, the more radical he or she perceived the father. Among non-Jews, this pattern was reversed: the more radical the child, the more conservative the father.

To explicate this contrast, we divided the sample into three groups: those who rated their fathers as more conservative (about 40 percent of the sample), more radical (about one fourth of all students), and about the same as themselves (the remaining one third). Among non-Jews, students who rated their father about the same as themselves were the most conservative. Only those who saw themselves as more radical than their father approached the overall sample average in radicalism. The picture that emerged among Jewish students reversed this pattern. Once again, the most conservative students were those who viewed themselves in the father's political image. The most radical Jews, however, were not those who portrayed their father as relatively conservative, but those who saw him as even more radical than themselves. Thus Jewish radicals did not perceive themselves as ideologically closer to their parents than did non-Jews. In fact, both Jewish and non-Jewish radicals perceived themselves as more distant from their parents than did nonradicals. But non-Jewish radicals were moving away from a political milieu they perceived as conservative, while radical Jews were moving toward an ever-receding ideal of radicalism espoused by their parents.

Finally, we asked students about their parents' reactions to their political stance. They rated each parent's reaction along a scale from one to seven, where "one" indicated strong opposition, and "seven" strong support. Because findings for both parents were essentially the same, we present only the results for fathers' reactions.

Among non-Jews, radicalism was associated with paternal opposition. The more radical the child, the more negatively he or she perceived the father's reaction. This is not surprising, since radical non-Jewish subjects rated their parents as relatively conservative. By the same token, though, we might have expected Jewish radicalism to be associated with parental support. Instead, radicalism was highest among Jewish subjects reporting either paternal support or opposition, and lowest among those whose fathers were relatively neutral. The paternal support group averaged 4.43, the opposition group 4.54, and the neutrality group only 4.15.

Thus the picture is more complex than one of Jewish radicals enjoying the support of leftist parents and non-Jewish radicals rebelling against conservative parents. Radicalism among Jews seemed to reflect roughly equal portions of conflict and compliance with parental wishes. In fact, the most radical students among Jews and non-Jews alike were those whose parents opposed their political ideas. But many Jewish radicals could count on parental support, while almost all the non-Jews were at odds with their parents.

To explain these findings, we might hypothesize two patterns of family interaction linked to radicalism among non-Jewish and Jewish youth, respectively. As non-Jews became radical, they saw the political distance between themselves and their conservative parents increasing, producing a sense of estrangement. As Jews became radical, they perceived their parents as even more radical than themselves. So Jewish radicals enjoyed parental political support to a greater degree than did non-Jews, but even among Jews there was a mixture of parental support and estrangement. Their estrangement reflected not ideological rejection by conservative parents, but tactical disagreements with parents whom they perceived as quite radical. This hypothesis receives some support from the clinical study described in Chapter 7. Several young Jewish radicals told the interviewers that their parents were generally supportive but feared for their child's physical safety or future careers.

One thing seems clear. We need not stray far from home to explain the heavy concentration of Jews in the New Left. Their contribution to the radicalism of their time was rooted in the political heritage of one strand of American Judaism. It has often been observed that New Left radicals were attempting to carry out their parents' ideals, much to their parents' dismay. We suggest that this pattern existed primarily within the upper-middle-class, left-wing Jewish homes that many observers mistook for the prototypical "radicalizing" family setting. On the contrary, two cultures of radicalism were intermingled in the New Left. The Movement drew much of its strength from a tradition of radicalism held by upper-middle-class ethnic Jews, whose children set the style and tone of the early New Left. Their impact was gradually diluted, however, by infusions of non-Jewish young people in overt rebellion against the social and political conservatism of their middle- or working-class parents.

If there were truly two ethnically based "cultures" of radicalism within the New Left, they should be reflected in different patterns of child-rearing among the families of Jewish and non-Jewish radicals. We included in our survey the Parent-Child Questionnaire (PCQ), a test designed to uncover the relationships between young people and their parents.[5]

The PCQ consists of sixty adjectives or short descriptions, which subjects apply to each parent. Typical phrases are "considerate," "intrusive," "too easy-going,'' and "always giving advice." After each phrase, the subject rates a parent along a scale from one to eight, in which a score of one indicates that the parent is "not at all like" the description, and eight means "exactly like" the description.

The PCQ was developed by psychologists studying the relationship between parent-child relations and psychosomatic illnesses. Using this test, the investigators were able to distinguish among the family patterns of patients with asthma and hayfever, those with chronic upper respiratory infections, and a healthy comparison group. They also found that PCQ ratings were consistent with the ways patients described their parents in clinical interviews.

The PCQ has one serious limitation. It tells us how people recall their parents, not how the parents actually behaved toward their children. There is no easy way to get around this limitation. Even if we interviewed the parents themselves, they might be no more objective than their children about their behavior. Some subjectivity is thus built into our investigation. The important question is how this subjectivity affects the conclusions we draw from the test results. We shall return to this question after discussing the findings themselves. In any case, the PCQ probably minimizes the bias that enters into subjects' ratings, by presenting them with a large number of short descriptions and asking them to work as rapidly as possible. We chose it over other widely used questionnaires that ask people to describe their parental relations in full sentences, giving them a greater opportunity to think about how they "ought" to answer.

Another advantage of the PCQ is the breadth of information it supplies. In Chapter 2, we criticized the superficiality of surveys that asked students a single question about their family life such as, "Who made the decisions in your family while you were growing up?" By contrast, the PCQ provides sixty pieces of information about each parent. Moreover, one may glean additional insights by examining differences in the ways a child views his two parents.

On the other hand, all this information could become overwhelming or redundant. For example, if a young man rates his mother as particularly "considerate," "understanding," "cooperative," and "kind," have we really isolated four distinct opinions that he holds about her? Or might we conclude, more parsimoniously, that he views his mother as generally caring or benevolent? More generally, might the scores of PCQ ratings be condensed into a few underlying dimensions that account for much of the variation in people's views of their parents?

The statistical technique of factor analysis provides a convenient method of answering this question. It selects out groups of adjectives that account for the greatest variation in parental ratings. Consequently it enables us to focus on the most important dimensions of parent-child interaction.

Ratings of each parent were analyzed separately, with very similar results. In each case, over half the variation in parental descriptions was accounted for by four broad dimensions, or factors. The first dimension was one of general benevolence or caring. Parents rated high on this dimension were described as "considerate," "understanding," "dependable," "cooperative," "kind," and "warm." A second dimension, almost the obverse of the first, represented parental punitiveness. The most relevant descriptions were "sarcastic," "caustic," "angry," "bitter," "critical," "spiteful," and "ill-tempered." A third dimension was one of parental control or intrusiveness. For both parents, this dimension was formed from the adjectives "interfering," "controlling," "always giving advice," and "watchful." Subjects who applied these terms to their parents also rated their fathers as "strict" and "authoritarian," and their mothers as "overprotective." A fourth dimension represented parental weakness, drawing on the descriptions "gives in," "wants to be led," and "iron-willed." (Parents rated high on this dimension were described as *not* being iron-willed.) The final dimension seemed to represent a residual category of parental mildness not captured by the earlier "controlling" dimension. This last dimension draws on the adjectives "permissive" and "easy-going."

On the basis of their ethnic backgrounds and New Left Ideology scores, we divided all subjects into six groups: Jewish radicals, non-Jewish radicals, Jewish liberals, non-Jewish liberals, Jewish conservatives, and non-Jewish conservatives. Table 3 shows the average rating each group gave to their parents on the dimensions listed above. On each dimension, scores were standardized, with the average (mean) score set to fifty.

In their PCQ ratings, radicals differed from other students by describing their parents as relatively uncaring, punitive, and weak or ineffective. In addition, Jewish radicals viewed their mothers as particularly intrusive and their fathers as mild or undemanding. As a result, Jewish radicals were the only group to perceive their families as matriarchal. Finally, Jews in general viewed their parents as more caring, and their fathers as less demanding, than did non-Jews. After examining each dimension more closely, we will discuss the significance of the overall pattern of differences.

To begin with, radicals (especially non-Jewish radicals) rated both parents as least benevolent, while conservatives (especially Jewish conservatives) perceived their parents as most benevolent. In general, Jews viewed their parents more positively than did non-Jews. Among both groups, though, we found the same trend. As radicalism increased, so did negative evaluations of both par-

Table 3. Perceptions of Parents by Ethnicity and Ideology. [a]

PCQ DIMENSION	RADICALS		LIBERALS		CONSERVATIVES		Level of Significance [b]
	Jewish	Non-Jewish	Jewish	Non-Jewish	Jewish	Non-Jewish	
Caring							
Father	48.98	46.27	51.13	49.64	53.90	51.42	.001
Mother	48.06	46.71	51.51	49.33	54.04	52.01	.001
Punitive							
Father	38.34	43.90	35.08	35.09	34.72	34.47	.001
Mother	39.30	39.75	33.83	33.15	28.71	31.63	.001
Intrusive							
Father	49.07	51.35	49.41	49.25	54.24	51.79	.001
Mother	53.38	50.70	49.29	48.88	50.85	51.15	.001
Weak							
Father	51.58	50.96	50.29	49.83	46.94	48.97	.05
Mother	51.45	51.05	49.99	49.56	49.64	49.10	n.s.
Lenient							
Father	51.23	49.11	51.44	49.80	49.26	48.31	.10
Mother	49.70	48.60	51.13	49.74	53.90	51.42	n.s.
Patriarchal Family [c]	45.84	49.99	50.34	50.43	52.92	50.62	.01
N	110	99	248	412	44	121	

[a] Group mean scores. Except for "punitive," all scores are standardized factor scores, where $\bar{x}=50$, S.D.$=10$. "Punitive" scores are from the original PCQ Punitive scale, which was administered to 760 subjects.
[b] Statistical significance of difference between radicals' and nonradicals' mean scores.
[c] Paternal minus maternal intrusive rating.

ents. So our first major finding is that radicalism was linked to negative perceptions of one's parents as cold or uncaring.

A very similar pattern appeared on the "punitiveness" dimension. Among Jews and non-Jews alike, radicals viewed both parents as highly punitive, liberals rated them below average in punitiveness, and conservatives perceived their parents as least punitive. These differences were not affected by the fact that, within each ideological category, Jews again rated their parents somewhat more positively than did non-Jews.

Although radicals viewed their parents as rather aggressive, they did not picture them as figures of strength. On the contrary, radicals rated both their parents as weaker or less effective than other subjects rated theirs, perhaps indicating a rejection of what Erikson called the parents' "inner authority." Conservatives rated their parents as strongest or most effective, while liberals described their parents as moderately effective.

The intrusive dimension revealed a subtle interplay of ethnic and ideological differences. The relation between radicalism and parental control was curvilinear, with parents rated least intrusive by those in the middle of the political spectrum and most intrusive by those at either end. The only exception to this pattern were Jewish radicals, who rated their fathers as nonintrusive. Indeed, radical Jews rated their fathers *less* intrusive and their mothers *more* intrusive than did any other group. This is an important indication that Jewish and non-Jewish radicalism may have arisen out of different family settings. This difference between the radical groups did not reflect broader ethnic patterns of child-rearing. Among conservative students, Jews rated their fathers as considerably more intrusive, and their mothers slightly less intrusive, then did non-Jews. This was precisely the reverse of the ethnic differences found among radicals. In sum, Jewish radicals were drawn from households in which the mother was perceived as a domineering figure, while the father was relegated to the background. Non-Jewish radicals, by contrast, viewed both parents as relatively intrusive.

To highlight this key difference, we subtracted the "mother intrusive" from the "father intrusive" score for each subject to create an index of relative parental intrusiveness or control. Liberals and conservatives perceived their fathers as slightly more controlling, with the fathers of conservative Jews recording the most patriarchal scores. Non-Jewish radicals perceived both parents as about equally intrusive. Only Jewish radicals perceived their mothers as more intrusive than their fathers.

Although this evidence is not conclusive, it suggests that radical Jewish students did perceive their mothers as the dominant figure in the family. Using the "weakness" dimension would have yielded roughly the same results. A positive score indicates that the family was perceived as patriarchal, with the father the more controlling parent. A negative score indicates a matriarchal setting, with the mother seen as more controlling. The results are shown in the bottom row of Table 3.

Such a matriarchal family setting, consisting of a controlling mother and an ineffectual father, is a familiar stereotype of American Jewish family life. Among our subjects, though, this "Portnoy syndrome" applied only to the families of radical Jews. By contrast, conservative Jews reported the most patriarchal family backgrounds of all groups. Moreover, this is consistent with their paternal ratings on the other dimensions. Conservative Jews described their fathers as more caring, stronger, and more controlling than did any other group. By their own testimony, they are products of traditional patriarchal families, in which the father retained an authoritative stature.

Finally, the "mildness" dimension also differentiated family relations in terms of both radicalism and ethnicity. Maternal ratings produced only slight and insignificant differences among the groups. But Jews in general, and particularly radical and liberal Jews, perceived their fathers as relatively easygoing and lenient. Non-Jewish conservatives rated their fathers lowest on this dimension, followed by non-Jewish radicals. Since both these groups also rated their fathers as relatively intrusive, they appear to come from relatively patriarchal backgrounds, though not to the same degree as the Jewish conservatives.

On the whole, we found that radicalism in Jewish and non-Jewish families was associated with different patterns of child-rearing. The Jewish radical was more likely to come from a matriarchial family lacking in warmth or affection. Jewish radicals described both parents as relatively uncaring and ineffectual, with the father cold and distant and the mother intrusive rather than concerned or helpful.

The non-Jewish radical was even more rejecting of his or her parents, finding them lacking in warmth or benevolence. These radicals denied their parents' authoritativeness, viewing them as weak or ineffectual. But they described their fathers as relatively intrusive and demanding, a pattern characteristic of conservative families as well.

Before accepting these findings, we must return to the question we posed earlier: How meaningful are such ratings, based solely on our subjects' recollections? How can we know whether they accurately reflect their parent's actual characteristics? There is no certain answer to these questions, because neither child nor parent (nor, for that matter, an outside observer) is an objective judge.[6]

Even if we cannot objectively measure the actual behavior of parents, though, the child's perceptions can still provide valuable information about the subjective quality of family relations. For example, without making any assumptions about the accuracy of their parental descriptions, we can infer that radicals had negative and unsatisfying relationships with their parents. No doubt most parents would object to being called punitive or weak or uncaring. But the fact that radicals were especially likely to see their parents in those terms is important in itself. For one thing, this finding runs counter to the results of many earlier studies that attributed youthful dissent to "positive" styles of child-rearing and family interaction. One reason for this image, we have argued, was the nature of the questions asked. If a radical student is asked who made the decisions in his family, he may reply that he made his own decisions, because this conforms to his self-image as an independent thinker. The investigator may conclude that radicals come from "democratically" structured families, but an equally valid inference would be that radicals like to think they always make their own decisions. We cannot be sure whether the person became radical because of the upbringing he describes, or whether he views his upbringing that way because he is a radical.

Of course this objection can be turned against our own findings. It might be argued that radicals' current political perspectives led them to become critical of their parents, as symbols and carriers of discredited bourgeois authority. But several pieces of evidence argue against dismissing our results as the product of such "response bias." First, as we noted, our findings actually run counter to most previous studies. As a result of that research, most social psychologists rejected the notion that young radicals were rebelling against their parents. Second, this objection cannot account for several of our findings. For example, if radical adolescents were projecting their rejection of authority back onto their parents, we would expect them to perceive their fathers as highly intrusive. This dimension draws on several terms that should tap adolescent rebellion, including "strict" "controlling," "interfering," and the most overtly political description of all, "authoritarian." Yet it was not radicals but conservatives who rated their fathers highest on these traits. Similarly, radicals rated their fathers as "milder," that is, more lenient and easy-going, than did conservatives.

Perhaps most importantly, this objection cannot account for the differences between Jewish and non-Jewish radicals, which accorded with our own hypotheses. The two radical groups differed significantly on five of the nine dimensions.

Jewish radicals rated their fathers as significantly more caring, milder, and less intrusive, their mothers as more intrusive, and their families as less patriarchal than did non-Jewish radicals. Although both groups gave rather negative portrayals of their families, non-Jews described both parents as cold and harsh, with the family dominated by a traditional patriarchal father. Jews directed their resentment primarily against an intrusive mother, whom they saw as the more dominant parent. One cannot attribute radicals' parental descriptions to their ideological perspective without accounting for these ethnically based differences among the radicals themselves.

Ethnic differences in family relations may also help explain why previous studies produced a misleading portrait of a radical-producing child-rearing style. Jews in general rated both parents as more caring, and their fathers as less demanding, than did non-Jews. In addition, Jewish radicals viewed their fathers as relatively undemanding, their mothers as highly demanding, and their families as matriarchal. All these descriptions of Jewish family life were also elements of the "democratic," "permissive," maternally centered child-rearing style so often attributed to the households of radical youth.

Finally, while students of Jewish background made up a solid majority of the New Left, they remained a minority of the overall college population. As a result, many previous comparisons of radical and nonradical youth were also unintentionally comparing Jewish with non-Jewish family styles. By grouping our subjects according to both political ideology and ethnic background, we have uncovered instead two distinct cultures of radicalism in the households of Jewish and non-Jewish youth.

The American New Left was infused by a homogeneous subculture of upper-middle-class deracinated Jews who reported flawed relations with a mother perceived as domineering and punitive. Non-Jewish radicals were socially quite heterogeneous, often coming from lower status and politically conservative households. They described their parental relations in terms reminiscent of the so-called "authoritarian family."

Our findings recall Erik Erikson's impressionistic portrait of this family style. The popular stereotype suggests that authoritarian children are the products of patriarchal families. Erikson points out, however, that patriarchal English families produced democrats rather than fascists. What distinguished the "German father" was not only his harsh discipline but his lack of a sense of inner worth. Therefore he was unable to transmit the positive values of social authority to his children. In short, it is not patriarchy per se that yields rebellion or authoritarianism. Both patriarchal and matriarchal families can produce rebellion when the dominant parent is perceived as punitive or intrusive. Indeed, when both parents are perceived as benevolent, partriarchy is associated with a nonauthoritarian personality pattern.

These considerations lead to the central issues of our inquiry: Did radicals actually exhibit the inverted authoritarian personality syndrome that their flawed family backgrounds would lead us to expect? And did Jewish and non-Jewish radicals differ in ways congruent with the rigid and self-expansive modes of rebellion that we hypothesized? To answer these questions, we turn to the psychological core of our research.

PERCEPTIONS OF POWER

The first psychological test we employed was the Semantic Differential.[7] This is a test of the different shades of meaning that people ascribe to themselves and their world. It works in deceptively simple fashion. A person is asked to describe something—himself, an inanimate object, an emotion, etc.—by choosing between antonyms, such as soft vs. hard, rounded vs. angular, and high vs. low. As these examples indicate, many of the adjectives seem nonsensical, having nothing to do with the object under consideration. It is precisely this apparently nonsensical quality, however, that makes the test so interesting and useful.

A quarter century of research, conducted in many different languages and cultures, has shown that people's descriptions tend to cluster in meaningful ways, even if the meaning is not immediately obvious.[8] For example, if a person rates something as "strong," he is also likely to rate it as large rather than small, heavy rather than light, and thick rather than thin. A whole set of attributes, including strength, bulk, weight, and thickness, seem to form a single dimension of meaning, regardless of the object to which these attributes are applied. All these qualities seem to tap a general dimension of power or potency. The test's authors and users have isolated three such dimensions of meaningfulness that people apply to almost any aspect of the world around them. These are the evaluative (good vs. bad), activity (active vs. passive), and power (strong vs. weak) dimensions. Each is relatively independent of the others, so that a person who rates something as "good" will not necessarily rate it as "strong" or "active."

The test seems to show that people inhabit at least three dimensions of "semantic space." Without necessarily being aware of it, they judge a wide variety of objects in terms of goodness, power, and activity. Equally important, many descriptions that seem unrelated to these concepts are actually imbued with their meaning. The judgment of "light vs. heavy" seems to carry connotations of weakness vs. strength. So by asking someone to rate an object as light or heavy, thin or thick, etc., we gain insight into the strength or weakness he attributes to that object without his knowing that is our aim. It is this aspect of the Semantic Differential that gives it a projective quality.

We used this test to determine whether radicals differed from nonradicals in attributing power to certain social objects. We used pictures rather than words to represent the objects, in order to generate a more spontaneous response. Students were asked to rate each picture along a scale of one to seven where, for example, "1" equals light and "7" equals heavy. Although we were interested in the power dimension, we included antonyms from the other dimensions as well, in order to further confuse the issue. (In fact, several subjects thought they had "psyched out" the test by assuming that we "really" wanted to know whether they thought the objects pictured were good or bad.)

The first version of the questionnaire included pictures of a scowling young black male wearing sunglasses; a black professional man wearing glasses and a tie and sitting in front of a microscope; a white student protester in the midst of a crowd, his hand raised in a fist; and a white policeman in riot gear. In the second version, we added pictures of a student seated at his desk and a white

Rate according to the following scales:

Cold	1	2	3	4	5	6	7	Hot
Large	1	2	3	4	5	6	7	Small
Light	1	2	3	4	5	6	7	Heavy
Weak	1	2	3	4	5	6	7	Strong
Rough	1	2	3	4	5	6	7	Smooth
Dull	1	2	3	4	5	6	7	Sharp
Angular	1	2	3	4	5	6	7	Rounded
Thick	1	2	3	4	5	6	7	Thin
Treble	1	2	3	4	5	6	7	Bass

Semantic Differential picture.

female protester animatedly addressing a crowd. We also replaced the young black male with a leather-jacketed black militant. We chose these pictures to determine whether radicals attributed differential strength to militancy, protest, and "physical" power, and weakness to middle-class figures and sublimated "intellectual" power.

Many commentators on the Movement accepted the contention of radical students that they identified with blacks out of empathy for the weak and oppressed. Further, particularly after the mid-'60s, the New Left portrayed white radical youth themselves as weak and oppressed victims of the Establishment. Finally, they claimed to have transcended both "bourgeois" and "Old Left" hang-ups equating power with physical strength or brute force.

We argued, on the contrary, that many radicals identified with black and third world militants as a psychological means of incorporating their power. Similarly, identification with a radical movement might produce a feeling of surrogate power. The role of political outlaw could become a source of strength against a "paper-tiger" Establishment. If bourgeois identities were perceived as weak, militant opposition became an alternative source of power. Images such as a student at his desk or a black scientist might thus represent the eviscerated bourgeois intelligentsia against whom the militant outsider aligned himself. The sensation of power could be attained by rejecting such images of sublimation and docility. Psychologically as well as politically, for such radicals, power came through the barrel of a gun.

The results of the test are shown in Table 4. Radicals rated the black militant as more powerful than did nonradicals, while there was very little difference in their ratings of the black scientist.* Rather than seeing blacks as weak, radicals differentially perceived strength in black militancy, while viewing an intellectually oriented black as neither stronger nor weaker than did other students. Of course, each subject determined for himself why these figures were strong or weak. A radical might regard a black militant as physically strong but socially weak, because he is oppressed. If he rated the black militant as strong, however, we can assume that, whether consciously or not, he regarded the militant's power or strength as the more immediately salient characteristic. We should note that *all* groups rated the black militant as more powerful than the black scientist. The point is that radicals did so to a significantly greater degree.

The three pictures of white young people yielded similar patterns of results. Radicals rated both male and female protesters as stronger, and the nonprotesting students as weaker, than did nonradicals. As we hypothesized, radicals seemed to perceive participation in the student movement as a source of strength, while viewing a student engaged in intellectual endeavor as a feeble or impotent figure.

The picture of the white student protester is interesting in one other respect. It is the only picture on which conservatives differed from liberals almost as much as liberals differed from radicals. There was a linear relationship between

---

*The direction of the scores for our two versions of the black militant picture was the same, and both versions produced statistically significant results. Therefore we have combined them in the table.

Table 4. Semantic Differential Power Scores by Ethnicity and Ideology.[a]

POWER SCORE	RADICALS Jewish	RADICALS Non-Jewish	LIBERALS Jewish	LIBERALS Non-Jewish	CONSERVATIVES Jewish	CONSERVATIVES Non-Jewish	Level of Significance[b]
Black Militant							
Mean	16.80	16.38	15.77	14.98	15.00	14.50	.001
S.D.	(3.24)	(3.26)	(3.25)	(3.46)	(3.19)	(4.09)	
N	95	93	216	410	42	117	
Black Professional							
Mean	13.40	13.61	13.39	13.59	13.43	13.92	n.s.
S.D.	(3.12)	(3.02)	(2.76)	(2.91)	(2.38)	(3.21)	
N	94	92	217	410	42	115	
Policeman							
Mean	16.83	15.46	15.43	14.75	15.12	15.39	.001
S.D.	(3.31)	(3.35)	(3.35)	(3.17)	(3.30)	(2.85)	
N	95	93	218	414	41	114	
Male Protestor							
Mean	14.64	14.61	13.57	12.97	12.00	11.74	.001
S.D.	(3.86)	(3.39)	(3.38)	(3.56)	(4.09)	(3.90)	
N	95	94	215	411	43	115	
Female Protestor							
Mean	12.82	12.33	11.05	10.82	9.31	10.71	.001
S.D.	(4.08)	(3.89)	(3.80)	(3.31)	(4.61)	(3.59)	
N	49	70	117	202	22	75	
Student							
Mean	10.45	11.39	12.21	12.32	13.18	12.78	.001
S.D.	(2.82)	(3.08)	(3.10)	(2.43)	(2.40)	(2.94)	
N	49	70	119	198	22	76	

[a]Group mean comparisons.
[b]Statistical significance of difference between radicals' and nonradicals' mean scores.

political ideology and power attributed to the student protester. At any point in the ideological spectrum, the radicalism and potency scores rose together. On the other pictures, the main shift in power scores occurred between the liberal and radical groups. In general, then, it makes sense to compare radicals to all nonradicals. The psychological differences between conservatives and liberals were simply not as great as those between liberals and radicals.

Thus far we have treated radicals as a homogeneous group, without distinguishing between Jews and non-Jews. We did so because these ethnic subgroups did not differ significantly in their Semantic Differential power scores for the pictures we have analyzed. Regardless of their ethnicity, radicals attributed differential strength to black militancy and white student protest, and differential weakness to intellectual figures.

The picture of the riot policeman proved an exception to this pattern. As we expected, radicals viewed this image of physical force as much more powerful than did either liberals or conservatives. One might argue that radicals, because of their political experience, quite naturally view policemen as strong and powerful figures. Unlike conservatives, they have experienced policemen as physical or political opponents. The logic of this argument, however, suggests that active protesters should view policemen as stronger figures than do nonactivists. But when we controlled for protest activity, the differences between radicals and nonradicals' ratings remained unchanged.

Moreover, this argument cannot account for the striking difference between Jewish and non-Jewish radicals' power scores for this picture. Most of the difference between radicals and nonradicals was accounted for by the very high power scores of the Jewish radicals. This group's average score was significantly higher than that of non-Jewish radicals, who rated the policeman as only slightly more powerful than did conservatives. Indeed, the Jewish radicals' mean score of 16.83 represents the most power attributed to any picture by any of the six groups.

This was the first psychological finding to suggest that radicalism may have held different meanings for Jews and non-Jews. To explicate this initial difference, let us review the Semantic Differential findings in terms of our theory of inverse authoritarianism. The authoritarian views the world in terms of potency and power relations. He is drawn to high-potency figures representing the direct expression of power. The traditional conservative authoritarian aligns himself with socially approved authority figures and displaces his aggression onto outgroups. But the inverse authoritarian rejects social authority out of hand and aligns himself with militant opponents of the established order. These identifications give moral legitimacy to his desire to act out aggressive impulses by preaching or practicing "revolutionary" confrontation and violence. Thus he identifies potency with force and militancy, projecting fantasized power and vitality onto society's outcasts and outsiders. At the same time, he scorns his own bourgeois intellectual background as impotent, a projection of the weakness he fears in himself.

Adorno's rebel, who lashes out at all social mores and authorities with unalloyed fury and contempt, represents a total inversion of the authoritarian syndrome. Having found a moral cloak for his destructive impulses, he feels the same sense of malicious triumph that traditional authoritarians derive from subduing "degenerates" and other threats to social order.

Many variants of this syndrome differ noticeably from the outright sociopathy of Adorno's rebel. An important one concerns the ease with which hostile impulses can be transformed into aggressive behavior. For example,

Jews have come to place particularly strong constraints on direct expressions of aggression. As a result, radical Jews should be less ready to identify unqualifiedly with an aggressor who derives satisfaction from intimidating those weaker than himself, thereby calming his own projected fears of weakness. Instead they identify with the victim and justify aggressive behavior on grounds that they are warding off attacks from a threatening Establishment. In psychoanalytic terms, their hostility is not reactive but defensive. Their feelings of victimization justify "preemptive counterattacks" against potential aggressors.

This pattern could account for their perception of the policeman as a highly potent figure, a view not shared by their non-Jewish counterparts. For the Jewish radical, figures of social authority retain a particularly powerful and threatening character. A rigid rebel might convince himself that the Establishment was truly a paper tiger, a discredited regime ready to be toppled by revolutionary force. We suspect that Jewish radicals, by contrast, continued to attribute considerable strength to authority figures, whose power they both feared and envied.

Of course, this single piece of evidence cannot sustain such a chain of psychodynamic speculation. It does comport, though, with additional evidence gleaned from other projective tests. Thus far we have explored only the surface of psychic functioning—the tendency of radicals to attribute power to objects in their environment.

We have not yet shown that radicals have a strong need for power that predisposes them to identify with figures who represent strength and potency. We turn now to such questions of the inner motivation and psychodynamics of New Left radicalism.

PATTERNS OF MOTIVATION

In Chapter 2, we leveled a number of criticisms against the many studies that found radical students less authoritarian and more autonomous than conservative students. Questionnaires supposedly tapping these traits almost invariably translated approved political responses into psychological categories.

Our reservations about existing portrayals of radical youth led us to seek out psychological tests that might produce a deeper understanding of their motives and outlooks. We were seeking to uncover underlying motives and perceptions, especially the feelings and judgments radical youth might be unwilling or unable to reveal. Therefore we abandoned the direct approach in favor of projective psychological testing, the use of tests whose purposes cannot be detected by respondents. This type of test is particularly useful in eliciting information from intellectually sophisticated or "test-wise" subjects.

The most provocative findings were gleaned from the Thematic Apperception Test. Pictures were shown to our respondents with the instruction that they tell a story about the character(s) depicted. Our instructions were that they tell: "What is happening? Who are the people? What has led up to this situation? That is, what happened in the past? What is being thought? What is wanted? By whom? What will happen? What will be done?"

TAT protocols were handwritten in response to the above questions. It was suggested that five minutes be devoted to each story, or thirty minutes for the entire protocol. Six cards were used.[9] They tend to elicit the following themes:

1. The first card evokes themes of heterosexual conflict within the context of a relationship. Usually the woman is seen restraining the man from some impulsive, often aggressive reaction to an external challenge. His role is that of self-assertive bravado. She often represents good sense and restraint.
2. The second card typically yields themes of heterosexual seduction, often including mention of sex-appropriate or stereotyped roles during that process. Courtship and sexual desire are often mentioned in conjunction with the story.
3. The third card usually calls up stories of individual competition in the world of masculine contest, a man's solo confrontation with physical threat and victory or defeat.
4. The fourth card generates themes of intergenerational conflict, often in the context of a family business. Either cooperation or conflict and competition may be stressed.
5. The fifth card pulls for themes about the nature of sexual relationships, including feelings of guilt or shame, anger, rejection, or occasionally sexual violence. Sometimes a story about death or illness is offered to account for the woman's limpness and undress.
6. The last card generally evokes associations of either one's mother, particularly as intrusive, or a woman threatened by and afraid of an intruder.

Within these broad outlines, there is considerable room for imagination and creativity in a response. The test is intended to tap this creativity and, with it, the subject's fantasies and projections. It seeks to measure not perceptions, but *apperceptions,* the state of mind one brings to one's experience of the world.

Subjects write imaginative essays about each picture, creating plots and

Survey TAT, card 2.

Survey TAT, card 3.

developing characters, as a writer might create a short story. There are no correct answers, since each picture can be interpreted in a great variety of ways. Instead, the aim is to allow each storyteller to project his own underlying concerns and feelings onto his characters. By telling what the picture means to him, he also tells us what is on his mind, without being asked directly. The TAT thereby allows us access to the underlying fantasy life that helps shape our understanding and expectation of social reality. If dreams are the royal road to the unconscious, the TAT provides a poor man's path.

The story production can be analyzed in many ways. A thorough clinical analysis looks for salient themes and psychosexual levels represented, as well as specific transferences or categories of relationships and their qualities—i.e., what kind of tone pervades a story about lovers, about a man and a mother figure, etc. The clinician examines the structure of the story to determine, for example, whether the subject is providing a shallow or stereotyped response or speaking from a rich and well-elaborated internal sense of human relationships.

We present such detailed clinical analyses in Chapter 7. Initially, though, our interpretations were restricted to categories that could meet social scientific criteria of reliability and validity. When used in this manner, the TAT is not treated as a clinical test. The cards need not be administered by trained psychologists in a clinical setting. It is necessary only that they be shown to all subjects under the same conditions, and that the testers intrude as little as possible into the story-telling process. The stories are then analyzed by people who know nothing about the purpose of the study, according to scoring systems based on the actions and feelings depicted, rather than on the nature of the plot.

These methods were developed and tested by psychologists who wanted to use TAT material for the scientific study of social groups.[10] The scoring systems they created were intended to identify statistical differences between groups of people. They cannot be used with any confidence to probe the personalities of particular individuals.

Most of the scoring systems were derived from experimental settings. In this procedure, an experimental group is exposed to a stimulus, which is assumed to arouse an underlying concern or motive. For example, the power motive has been experimentally aroused by testing political candidates while they wait for election returns. Subjects are asked to write short stories about a series of pictures that have been selected to evoke the motive in question. These stories are then compared to stories written by a second group not exposed to the motive-arousing stimulus. The themes unique to the stories of the experimental group are used to devise the coding scheme. Finally, a scoring manual is compiled, so that trained scorers will come to the same conclusions about a particular theme.

In this way, researchers have discovered that people driven by a desire for power are likely to write stories in which one character seeks to control another, to impress others, or to build up prestige or reputation. By contrast, people motivated by a need for friendship are more likely to write about needing people, to express concerns for friends or relatives, and to inject feelings of love or loneliness into their stories.

Yet how can we really be sure that people express their innermost needs in these ways? How certain can we be, for example, that subjects exposed to the "power" stimulus were feeling only emotions of power? There is no simple resolution to this dilemma, since no incontestably valid measures of these motives exist, against which the TAT measures might be assessed. For example, TAT measures produce low correlations with nonprojective questionnaires asking people about their motivations. However, such questionnaires are themselves poor measures, since people may be unaware of their true motives or unwilling to admit to them. On the other hand, a quarter century of research has shown that people who write certain types of stories do tend to behave in ways that seem to reflect the concerns arising in their TATs. Though we lack demonstrably true or pefectly valid measures of these inner states, we can infer the test's accuracy by determining whether the TAT measures are related to the sort of behavior one would expect to be associated with a given motive. For instance, people who write power-oriented stories tend both to be argumentative, manipulative, and competitive in dealing with others and to accumulate "prestige" items. This technique is called "construct validity." It is widely used to assess measures of hypothetical constructs such as inner motives and psychodynamic categories. We shall discuss both the theoretical meaning of each TAT-measured motive and the evidence that the measure captures the underlying state it purports to represent.

Our subjects' TAT stories were scored for several key personality dimensions, including the need for power, hope for vs. fear of power, sublimation of power needs, need for affiliation or friendship, narcissistic pathologies, and modes of psychosexual development.[11]

Need for Power. Power motivation is scored when a character in a TAT story wants to control or influence others or is concerned about his reputation or prestige.[12] Examples of TAT expressions scored for "*n* Power" are: "He's fighting the champ—a chance to win a big purse"; "He wants to be President so he will go down in history"; and "He is a famous architect who wants to win a competition to establish who is the best architect in the world."

In day-to-day living, power motivation is related to activities that seem to reflect patterns of self-assertiveness and instrumental attitudes toward others. Such behavior includes participation in competitive and contact sports; impulsive aggressive activity, such as public arguments and the destruction of furniture and glassware to express anger; and sexual aggressiveness and unstable dating and marital relationships.[13]

These findings are reinforced by studies of small groups, which relate high *n* Power to competitive and aggressive modes of personal interaction. David Winter has summarized the results of these studies:

> *n* Power is related to having smooth relationships with those who make up one's inner circle or power base, but having a competitive or hostile stance toward those of higher status or power who are outside of the immediate group. . . . high *n* Power people attack established leaders of high status.[14]

Power-oriented people are also attracted to symbols of prestige. With social class controlled, *n* Power predicts ownership of color TVs, rifles and handguns, sports cars, and a large number of credit cards.[15]

The relationship between *n* Power and prestige possessions suggests that owning such items serves an expressive function. Because their owner possesses symbols of power and rank, he feels himself to be powerful. As McClelland emphasizes, "The *goal* of power *motivation* is to *feel powerful,* and influencing others is only one of many ways of feeling powerful."[16] Several other behavioral correlates of *n* Power may similarly produce a subjective experience of power. Positive correlations between *n* Power and alcoholic consumption exist across a wide range of social, economic, and national contexts. Fragmentary evidence suggests a similar relationship with respect to other mind-altering drugs.[17]

Among males, *n* Power is also related to vicarious participation in competitive sports (by reading about and watching sports events) and sexual activity (reading "men's" magazines).[18]

Finally, the experience of power is related to expansive risk-taking. Experimental studies show that high scorers in *n* Power take extreme risks in gambling situations and choose opponents well above or below their own level in contests of physical strength. *N* Power was also positively related to completion of an Outward Bound program, which stressed physical challenges and hardships to build a sense of personal mastery.[19]

In sum, a wide variety of studies have shown that people with high *n* Power scores behave in ways consistent with an underlying need to feel powerful.

Fear of Power. Power needs have also been divided into either the "hope for" or "fear of" power, according to whether the predominant orientation toward power is one of approach or avoidance.[20] The approach measure is not very useful because "hope" is consistently highly correlated with *n* Power itself. Fear of Power is much more interesting. It is scored when the subject reacts to power with doubt, conflict, irony, or feelings of deception, or when power is desired to benefit another party. In effect, it measures ambivalence, or what Winter and Stewart recently called an "aversive attraction" toward power:

> This aversive attraction involves an unusual sensitivity to power and awareness of power relationships in the world, coupled with a negative feeling about them. That is, an individual high in Fear of Power is interested in power in order to avoid the appearance of having power oneself . . . research evidence suggests that Fear of Power derives from the experience of powerlessness. . . . Power is experienced as both outside the self and inescapable.[21]

This motive resembles Meissner's concept of a "paranoid" stance, which we discussed in Chapter 4. High scorers in Fear of Power do seem to behave in ways indicative of paranoid tendencies, such as suspiciousness, mistrust, maladaptive anxiety, declining performance under stress, and a tenacious defense of personal autonomy. In a study of college women, Fear of Power was negatively related to self-discipline and positively related to lying. Other studies have linked Fear of Power to anxiety, stress, and high blood pressure. In an experiment in which subjects played a card game under competitive conditions, Fear was negatively associated with playing efficiency and overall skill.[22]

Concern for personal autonomy is perhaps the best documented correlate of Fear of Power. Among college students, Fear is associated with spending time alone and with avoiding academic structure. Students high in Fear prefer seminars to lectures, papers to exams, and essays to objective tests. They are also more likely to disregard academic deadlines. In a long-term study, Fear was positively related to dropping out of school, failing to return a follow-up questionnaire, and denying that peers had been influential in one's life.[23]

In sum, individuals strongly motivated by Fear of Power mistrust other people and institutional authority and are very concerned with protecting their own independence. These tendencies suggest that they may seek power in response to feelings of weakness and powerlessness in the manner of Meissner's "paranoid" style.[24]

Sublimated Power. McClelland and his associates have made two attempts to separate power motivation into overt or "personal" and sublimated or "socialized" components. This differentiation reflects the recognition that power strivings may be directed toward personal aggrandizement or sublimated into social goals. The difference is not simply between "good" and "evil" power-seeking. The rationalization of power drives into social purpose might produce a Marat or Savonarola. On the other hand, to invoke a psychoanalytic stereotype, a surgeon may be "merely" a sublimated sadist, but the sublimation is all-important.

The first effort to operationalize this dichotomy produced a straightforward division of power imagery into personalized power (p Power) and socialized power (s Power). For example, p Power was scored if a character sought power for his own good, and s Power was scored when power was sought for the good of another person, who did not solicit the power goal. Unfortunately, this intuitively plausible dichotomy proved of little use in predicting different sorts of behavior.[25]

In recent years, p and s Power have been supplanted by a quite different approach to measuring the sublimation or inhibition of power drives. In an analysis of folktales from many different cultures, McClelland and several colleagues isolated two independent clusters of words and concepts.[26] The first set of terms revolved around the theme of "impulsive power," including words involving hunting, war, acquisition, vigorous activity, and violent physical manipulation. The second set involved "activity inhibition," including terms associated with failure, fear, ineffectiveness, and negation. The purest single measure of activity inhibition proved to be the word "not." The researchers, who were studying alcoholic consumption, found that cultural approval of drinking was associated with "impulsive power" imagery in folktales, *except* when "activity inhibition" imagery was also emphasized. They argued that heavy drinking provides an immediate or impulsive way of feeling powerful, and that drinking might therefore provide an outlet for strong and unsublimated power drives. They tested this hypothesis on a sample of American males by coding subjects' TAT stories for n Power and activity inhibition, measuring inhibition by the frequency with which subjects used the word "not." They found that men scoring high in n Power and low in inhibition ("nots") were likely to drink heavily, while those high in n Power but also high in inhibition tended to be light drinkers.[27] Power, "nots," and n Affiliation scores could be used to predict behavioral patterns plausibility related to direct and sublimated manifestations of the power drive.[28]

Our subjects' TAT protocols were scored according to both systems of measuring power sublimation—i.e., p vs. s Power—as well as n Power minus "nots."

Need for Affiliation. This motive is defined as a concern to establish, maintain, or restore positive emotional relationships. To arouse n Affiliation, researchers asked an experimental group to rank themselves, friends, and classmates in terms of traits that they felt would make a person "likeable." Immediately thereafter, TATs were administered to the group. They scored significantly higher on n Affiliation than a control group.[29] Ensuing studies

Table 5. Thematic Apperception Test Motive Scores by Ethnicity and Ideology. [a]

MOTIVE	RADICALS		LIBERALS		CONSERVATIVES		Level of
	Jewish	Non-Jewish	Jewish	Non-Jewish	Jewish	Non-Jewish	Significance [b]
n Power	54.33	52.25	49.63	49.28	46.77	48.89	.001
Power-"nots"	53.73	51.88	49.92	49.34	47.19	48.84	.001
p Power	50.90	48.65	50.56	50.47	49.07	48.70	n.s.
s Power	51.27	51.20	49.29	49.79	48.11	49.82	.01
Fear of Power	53.68	52.73	49.68	49.01	47.52	49.35	.001
n Affiliation	50.77	48.24	50.51	49.11	53.67	51.15	n.s.
N	70	81	148	273	38	100	

[a] Group mean comparisons. Factor scores, where $\bar{x} = 50$, S.D. = 10.
[b] Statistical significance of difference between radicals' and nonradicals' mean scores.

have linked high n Affiliation with sensitivity to emotional facial expression, concern for peer relations, and sociable behavior such as telephoning, corresponding with, and visiting friends.[30] Recently researchers have focused on the relationship between n Affiliation and n Power. People who score high in both motives tend to avoid assertive behavior, seek strength in external sources, and view close personal ties as important. Those high in n Power but low in n Affiliation, by contrast, are self-assertive and reject close personal relationships.[31]

TAT Motive Scores. The group differences on the TAT motive scores are summarized in Table 5. Following the convention adopted by McClelland and Winter, the scores were standardized, with the overall mean set at 50. This permits easy comparisons of the distances separating the groups on the various motives. It also facilitates combined motive scores, such as unsublimated power (n Power minus "nots") and our measure of Fear of Power (Fear minus Hope).

The results suggest that New Left radicals had strong and unsublimated power needs, and were ambivalent toward power. Non-Jewish radicals were also low in affiliation needs. In short, radicals were significantly more likely than nonradicals to display the motivational pattern that writers since Fromm and Adorno have termed "authoritarian."

The linchpin of this disposition is a heightened need for power. Conservatives scored lowest on our measure of power motivation, followed by liberals. Then power scores rose sharply among the radical group. This abrupt rise meant that only radicals exceeded the average score for the entire sample.

The lowest power scores were recorded by Jewish conservatives, the highest by Jewish radicals. In fact, Jewish radicals scored significantly higher than non-Jewish radicals, despite the already high power scores of the latter. These differences suggest that, among these students, Jews may be more likely than non-Jews to translate power needs into radicalism.

These radicals' power needs were not only strong but also relatively unsublimated. When the need for power was combined with McClelland's measure of activity inhibition (Power-"nots"), the distance between radicals' and nonradicals' scores was not significantly altered. Similarly, radicals and nonradicals did not differ significantly in either p Power or s Power, the categories McClelland formerly used to measure sublimation of the power drive. In sum, then, we found no evidence of strong inhibitions that might sublimate or "socialize" the power needs of these radicals.

The final aspect of power motivation concerned ambivalence toward power, above and beyond the intensity of the power drive itself. Ambivalence was measured by subtracting "hope for" from "fear of" power, thereby controlling for differences in the level of power motivation. The results resembled our findings on the previous measures. Conservatives and liberals differed but little, while ambivalence surged among radicals.[32] Like the power need itself, ambivalence toward power was greatest among Jewish radicals.

We sought to determine whether this "power complex" among radicals was mitigated by a simultaneous concern for warm human relationships. In general, it was not. As a group, radicals scored significantly lower than other students on the need for affiliation.

This was the only personality variable on which Jews and non-Jews differed significantly, independently of ideological differences. Jewish conservatives, liberals, and radicals were all more "affiliative" than their non-Jewish counterparts. As a result, radical Jews scored above the overall sample average, but below the average for Jews alone. For non-Jewish radicals, there were no such complexities. They scored lower in affiliation needs than any other group in the study.

Our initial statement that radicals proved relatively authoritarian must be qualified somewhat, to take account of ethnic differences within the radical subgroup. Regardless of ethnic background, radicals did manifest strong and uninhibited power needs, as well as heightened ambivalence toward power. In addition, Jewish radicals were particularly concerned with power, while non-Jewish radicals showed a notable lack of concern for affiliation.

These findings run directly counter to the psychological portrait of New Leftists established by the vast body of research described in Chapter 2. Indeed the discrepancy is so great as to fairly cry out for some explanation. One possibility, raised by both Keniston and Flacks, is that the Movement had changed drastically by the early 1970s, when our study was conducted. In a 1971 article, Flacks and Milton Mankoff noted that recent Movement recruits were less likely than "veterans" to come from politically liberal and permissive upper-middle-class Jewish or nonreligious families.[33] They speculated that these sociological changes in the New Left's composition had diluted its psychological distinctiveness. Flacks's original argument, after all, was that young radicals' material and cultural advantages had liberated them from bourgeois concerns and values. As the New Left incorporated a broader constituency, such people were necessarily submerged into an increasingly heterogeneous mass movement. The special psychological character of the privileged vanguard was thus seen as a casuality of the Movement's growth.

All this sounds quite plausible, and our own data bear out Flacks and Mankoff's observations about the Movement's changing social base. But among the students we surveyed, this shift could not account for the association of radicalism with a power-oriented motivational syndrome. We found that radicals outscored liberals and conservatives in both n Power and Fear of Power, even with social background controlled. For example, radicals scored highest on both the need for and fear of power, even after controlling for fathers' occupation. Most striking of all, the highest scores were obtained by radicals from the homes of upper-middle-class professionals. They averaged 53.89 on n Power, compared to 51.13 for radicals from working-class backgrounds. On Fear of Power, the differences were even greater. The radical children of upper-middle-class professionals averaged 57.37, those from blue-collar homes only 47.82. These results are precisely the opposite of those we would expect, if Flacks's social psychological argument were correct in either its original or its revised form.

In fact, upper-status youth as a whole scored above average on both measures of power orientation, while lower-status youth scored below average. That is, the children of business executives and professionals exceeded the total sample mean of 50.00, while the children of white-collar, blue-collar, and lower-middle-class fathers all scored below the mean on both motives. These differences, however, were largely attributable to the large number of power-oriented radicals among the upper-middle-class groups. The conservative and liberal children of professionals actually scored below the mean on both the need for and fear of power. This is one more piece of evidence to contradict arguments that social advantage, psychological health, and political radicalism were interwoven in the "liberated generation."

The results for n Affiliation also failed to support Flacks's argument. On this measure, the radical children of upper-middle-class professionals averaged 50.16, not significantly higher than the average of 49.92 recorded by radicals from working-class families. The blue-collar group as a whole averaged 50.17, compared to 50.05 for all students from upper-middle-class homes.

These patterns recurred when we controlled for parental income, religion, and political ideology. In no instance did the high power/low affiliation motivation patterns of radicals prove an artifact of family background factors. Instead, radicals consistently scored high in the need for and fear of power and low in affiliation, across social background categories.

Apparently our psychological findings cannot be attributed to the New Left's changing recruitment patterns, in the manner suggested by Flacks. This conclusion received more direct empirical support from our study of leading figures in the early New Left, which is described in Chapter 7.

To some degree, though, the changing image of New Leftists' personality styles was probably rooted in reality. The transition from a largely upper-middle-class deracinated Jewish vanguard to a more broadly based mass movement was probably accompanied by shifts in the New Left's psychological make-up. But we disagree with previous researchers about the nature of this change. Flacks and Mankoff suggested that sociological heterogeneity brought a dilution of the founders' "liberating" characteristics. Keniston rejected the notion that more pathological "types" were recruited during the Movement's later years. Instead he argued that even the "nihilists" and "terrorists" of the early 1970s were essentially idealists who were frustrated by political events. Citing a similar argument made by Smith, Block, and Haan, he suggested that these frustrated idealists were "in a temporary and usually partial state of regression . . . [from their] long-range trajectory toward postconventional ethical thinking."[34]

We believe that the changing character of the New Left produced neither a dilution of nor temporary regression from a widespread "liberated" or "postconventional" dispostion. Instead, it represented a shift from one variant of inverse authoritarianism to another, corresponding to the Movement's changing ethnic and status composition. A complete outline of these differences requires a review of our remaining survey TAT and clinical findings. But a preliminary overview, based on the TAT data we have already presented, can be constructed from the recent work of David McClelland.

McClelland has developed a typology that may clarify the relationship of some of our TAT findings to authoritarian personality functions. In *Power: The Inner Experience,* he distinguished three "power strategies" among people who score high in *n* Power. McClelland argued, first, that a combination of high *n* Power, low *n* Affiliation and high Inhibition ("nots") leads the individual to a willingness to subject his own power drive to larger organizational structures. He called this pattern of motivation the "Imperial Pattern":

. . . he is ready to discipline himself, or even sacrifice himself for others in order to achieve collective power . . . he is readier to enforce a universalistic code of justice in which people are rewarded in terms of what they do for the system. . . . In a well functioning organization each person must be treated . . . fairly. The idea of universalistic justice within the system as a whole must be paramount.[35]

McClelland found that people showing the imperial pattern tend to join organizations and enjoy feeling a part of them. They also tend to keep their anger under control and, in general, to keep their feelings to themselves and avoid self-disclosure. McClelland views such people as "bureaucratic authoritarians" who can impel well-organized and efficient organizations toward a desired goal by combining institutional loyalty, the discipline of hard work, self-sacrifice for the group, and a passion for justice. A person with such a disciplined power drive is a potential "empire builder" in the sense that he is well suited to produce or strengthen organizational strategies of control. Hence the "imperial" label.

By contrast, a pattern of *low* inhibition levels, in conjunction with high power and low affiliative needs, seems to define a more impulsive power-oriented mentality. People with this motivational syndrome tend to reject institutional ties and to engage in overtly self-assertive or self-aggrandizing behavior. Men sharing this pattern tend to drink heavily, get into fights, and boast about their sex lives. McClelland regards this "conquistador" or "Don Juan" syndrome as a second authoritarian pattern. Such people seem willing to achieve heightened power goals by manipulating others, with little concern for their wishes or interests. They may be rebels against authority, but their rebellion, however it is rationalized, ultimately serves the cause of self-aggrandizement.

Finally, McClelland delineates a power orientation that bears less resemblance to authoritarian psychodynamics. This is the pattern of high power needs, low inhibition, but also high affiliation needs. McClelland calls this the "personal enclave" type. Such people view the self rather than others as the locus of their efforts to gain feelings of power. They seek to feel powerful by incorporating strength from external sources, through alliances with people, groups, or ideas they perceive as sources of power. Although they have the power motivation that might produce an assertive life style, their primary orientation is incorporative. They try to receive power through their association with others, rather than by gaining control over others. In short, they "try to build a kind of personal enclave that gives them a feeling of warmth, strength, and security"[36] and overcomes fears of inner weakness.

McClelland's studies revealed that enclave types tend to be religiously oriented, to value close personal ties, to have close relationships with their mothers, and to avoid overtly aggressive activities. We might also expect them to value associations with charismatic figures and with social movements that provide a sensation of group solidarity.

To summarize, McClelland has identified three power strategies, based on the interaction of high power needs with two other personality traits that might channel or mitigate an overt desire for power. The Don Juan type tries to satisfy his need to feel powerful in direct or unsublimated ways, with little concern for others. The imperial sublimates his power drive into highly rationalized or institutional channels. He justifies his power drives with reference to the goals of a larger structure. Thus the imperial incorporates himself into a broader entity that cloaks his goals with ideological justifications. The enclave type, by contrast, tries to incorporate the powerful external entity into himself. His strategy is essentially passive. By identifying with a powerful other, he vicariously participates in its potency.

While McClelland's types are not ours, they correspond to some motivational differences between Jewish and non-Jewish radicals, in ways that help illuminate ethnic variations in a syndrome of inverse authoritarianism. Our theory suggests that radical ideologies can provide a moral veneer for the expression of aggressive impulses. Thus the link between a conquistador mentality and radical politics is rather straightforward. We would expect that such people would be drawn to the New Left, regardless of their ethnic backgrounds. In the case of McClelland's other types, however, the link between personality and politics might well be mediated by ethnicity.

The rationalized power strategy of the imperial is reminiscent of the rigid, highly ideological Left authoritarian personified by the party-line adherents of state socialist regimes. In this country, this mentality was already familiar from the cadres of the Stalinist Left. It made a brief but vivid comeback during the latter days of the New Left as well. Such an ideologized power strategy became more popular, or at least more visible, as the Movement was augmented by non-Jewish young people in rebellion against traditional, patriarchal, politically conservative families. Among the students we studied, then, we expected imperials to be concentrated among non-Jewish radicals.

The power strategy associated with Jewish radicalism should more closely resemble the enclave syndrome. In contrast to the rigid authoritarian, the enclave type regards other people not as threats to his own potency but as surrogate sources of power. He reaches out toward others not to eliminate but to enfold them. Unlike the imperial or conquistador, this type of person truly needs other people. Like the other power-seeking types, however, he does not really grant them an existence independent of his own. Rather, he treats them

Table 6. TAT Motivation Patterns by Ideology and Ethnicity (%).

PATTERN	RADICALS		NONRADICALS	
	Jewish	Non-Jewish	Jewish	Non-Jewish
Conquistador	32	24	17	16
Imperial	18	24	13	18
Enclave	14	6	5	6
Other	36	46	65	60
%	100	100	100	100
N	71	83	186	374

p<.001

as extensions of his own self. In line with our model of the self-expansive rebel, these affiliative power-seekers should have been most prominent among the New Left's Jewish component.

To test these hypotheses, we divided our sample into four groups. The first three were high-power-oriented groups corresponding to McClelland's three authoritarian types. We classified as "conquistadors" those students scoring above the sample mean in n Power and below the mean in sublimation ("nots") and n Affiliation. The "imperials" were those who scored above average in power needs and sublimation and below average in affiliative needs. Each of these high power/low affiliation groups constituted slightly less than one fifth of the sample. The remaining high-power group, that of the personal enclave, consisted of students scoring above average in power and affiliative needs, and below average in sublimation. Only forty-nine students, or 7 percent of the sample, fell into this category. Overall, then, McClelland's three types accounted for just over two fifths of the total sample. The remaining students were grouped together as a residual "nonauthoritarian" category.[37]

After separating the sample into these categories, we examined the proportion of Jewish and non-Jewish radicals falling into each one. The results, shown in Table 6, conformed to our expectations. Non-Jewish radicals were disproportionately represented among the imperials, Jewish radicals among the personal enclave types, and both radical groups among the conquistadors. The probability of this distribution occurring by chance was less than one in a thousand. Each group of radicals comprised about one-tenth of the total sample. They accounted for over half again that proportion (16 percent) of the conquistadors, however, with Jews and non-Jews about equally overrepresented.

Non-Jewish radicals were also overrepresented among the imperials, accounting for 16 percent of this sublimated power group as well. Jewish radicals, on the other hand, formed only 10 percent of this group, matching their representation in the entire sample.

Finally, this pattern was reversed for the enclave power syndrome. Jewish radicals comprised over 20 percent of this group, double the expected proportion, while non-Jewish radicals were found only in proportion to their number.

In sum, the distribution of radicals was entirely consistent with our hypotheses. Neither radical group was ever underrepresented in any of the high-power categories. Both were overrepresented in two of the three categories, and found in precise proportion to their number in the third. By contrast, none of the four nonradical groups fell disproportionately into more than one of the high-power categories. The nonradical groups were clustered within the remaining non-power-oriented category, the only category in which radical students were underrepresented.

McClelland argues that the conquistador and imperial patterns represent two types of authoritarian motivational syndrome. By this admittedly crude definition, radical students comprised just over one quarter of the "authoritarian" segment, about two-and-one-half times their proportion in the total sample. Our own conception of authoritarianism draws on many more variables than these three motives. We were able to measure a number of additional traits, by drawing on scoring systems developed after our survey had been conducted. This illustrates the TAT's capacity as a data bank that can be reexamined for thematic content in ways not envisioned at the outset. We sent copies of the protocols to scorers trained in the new systems and added their findings to our data set. In this way we were able to examine two additional clusters of personality traits central to our model of the radical as inverse authoritarian: narcissistic pathologies and modes of psychosexual development.

NARCISSISM

Our theory posits that the sources of authoritarianism lie in injured narcissism. Initially, we were unable to test this hypothesis directly. Fortunately, in 1974 we discovered that Dr. Jennifer Cole, then a graduate student in clinical psychology, had developed a method of scoring TATs for narcissistic pathologies.[38] Unlike the previous content analysis systems, hers was derived clinically rather than experimentally, and as yet lacks evidence of construct validity. It is therefore quite speculative, and findings based upon it are only suggestive.

Cole and an associate scored two hundred randomly selected sets of TATs from our study. The scorers were not familiar with either the purposes of the study or the social and political characteristics of the subjects whose TATs they analyzed. They agreed on 90 percent of their assessments, indicating that the scoring system is very reliable.

The theory behind this analysis reflects a psychoanalytic perspective derived from the clinical study of male narcissism. Therefore we shall confine our discussion to the 117 male subjects whose TATs Cole examined. Much of this discussion is drawn from Cole's own unpublished work. We gratefully acknowledge her assistance and willingness to permit its publication in this form.

By narcissism we mean what Freud called secondary narcissism—the reservoir of self-esteem that enables the healthy individual to weather the strains and stresses of everyday life. In this sense, narcissism is not a term of opprobium or a synonym for egotism. It is a necessary component of the self-regard through which a stable identity is maintained.

Secondary narcissism is a transmutation of early infantile feelings of omnipotence. In the mature individual, a grandiose self-image gradually gives way to the satisfaction gleaned from living up to one's ideals and meeting the demands of conscience. The self-absorbed infant eventually learns to maintain his self-regard through accomplishment in the areas of love and work. This capacity to assess accurately one's own abilities and recognize the constraints imposed by external reality, and to adjust one's aspirations accordingly, best guarantees a sense of self-worth.

Secondary narcissism is thus an ever-fluctuating reservoir of self-esteem, which forms the basis of the individual's experience of himself and his world. Healthy narcissism is an adequate reservoir of positive self-feeling, which enables the individual to weather life's ups and downs. "Pathological" narcissism refers to the reliance on unhealthy mechanisms for regulating or enhancing self-esteem and maintaining a sense of identity. These mechanisms will be the object of our scrutiny.

One pathological method for raising self-esteem is an unrealistic distortion of self-perception that condenses a wishful or grandiose self-image with the actual self. Typical narcissistic defenses include denying the presence of undesirable qualities in oneself and projecting these threatening traits onto others. This devaluation of other people also protects one against envy.

In general, the narcissistic person uses others primarily to regulate his own self-esteem, rather than treating them as separate individuals with their own needs and identities. His unconscious fantasy is that others act as an extension of his own will. When they do not, he responds with rage and withdrawal. Pressure from others to abandon this outlook is experienced as a threat or attack. A typical counter-attack is the defense of externalization. One lays blame outside oneself and claims posession of the virtuous position, whatever that may be.

Cole attempted to measure these mechanisms by coding the TATs in terms of four categories:

1. *Heterogeneity of Theme.* Subjects were asked to integrate disparate fantasy elements triggered by the TAT card into a coherent story with an integrated theme. The presence of several distinct elements, complex motives, and impulses, if successfully knitted together, was considered homogeneous. Failure to choose any theme was scored positively, as indicating a failure to commit oneself. An example was the type of story in which the subject offered several possible situations, giving the reader several numbered endings to choose among. Simple "either-or" vacillation—e.g., "either he'll stay with her or leave and regret it"—was not scored for heterogeneity.

It was assumed that people who experience unusually strong pressure from fantasy and impulse, and are inclined to override reality demands in favor of their personal wishes and needs, would be reluctant to relinquish choice in favor of a single plot. This attitude toward the demands of external reality is typical of those who feel themselves to be "exceptions," and thus not subject to the limitations imposed on others. Adhering to task demands requires a certain sacrifice of potential gratification and a compromise between fantasy and reality. These are not tolerated very well by many narcissistic individuals.

2. *Self-Centered Orientation.* This category measures a subject's willingness to address the interpersonal issues triggered by the TAT card, rather than using the task as an opportunity to gratify exhibitionistic needs. Self-centered approaches include florid or dramatic content or language and an exclusive preoccupation with personally relevant issues.

This variable taps the tendency to transform a rather neutral task into an opportunity to gratify exhibitionistic needs. Through florid language or explicit self-reference, the individual calls attention to himself and away from the object relational possibilities offered to him.

3. *Narcissistic Attribution.* This category was scored positively when a subject attributed narcissistic—i.e., exploitative, manipulative, grandiose, cold, ruthless, haughty, hollow, or autoerotic—qualities to his characters or took this attitude towards the characters he created. For example, characters who rejected interpersonal attachments in favor of drug addiction or chronic alcoholism were scored positively. This variable was intended to reflect the narcissistic individual's projection of a negative self-image and consequent denigration of others as egotistical and Machiavellian.

4. *Low Boundaries.* A subject was expected to maintain adequate boundaries between himself and his characters and also among the identities, feelings, and thoughts of the characters in his stories. By contrast, the individual with pathologically low boundaries manifests a severe loss of distance from his projections and fantasies, a fluid dispersal of affect and fantasy through an ill-defined response, or violent emotional reactions to the characters whom he has created, as though they became real to him. For example, one subject termi-

Table 7. Narcissistic Pathologies by Ideology and Ethnicity, American Male Students.

NARCISSISM	RADICALS		NONRADICALS		Significance[a]
	Jewish	Non-Jewish	Jewish	Non-Jewish	
Heterogeneous					
X̄	1.19	1.13	1.01	1.02	.001
S.D.	(0.31)	(0.24)	(0.04)	(0.09)	
Self-Centered					
X̄	1.33	1.27	1.06	1.09	.001
S.D.	(0.37)	(0.27)	(0.16)	(0.17)	
Narcissistic Attribution					
X̄	1.20	1.14	1.00	1.03	.001
S.D.	(0.29)	(0.26)	(0.00)	(0.07)	
Low Boundaries					
X̄	1.22	1.10	1.03	1.07	.10
S.D.	(0.33)	(0.25)	(0.20)	(0.09)	
N	21	28	21	47	

[a] Statistical significance of mean difference between radicals and nonradicals.

nated a story because, he wrote, a character "so disgusts me that I cannot bring myself to continue." Of the four measures, low boundaries are the clearest indicator of pathology.

The results of this research were consistent across all four categories of narcissistic pathology, as shown in Table 7. On every measure, Jewish radicals produced the highest scores, followed by non-Jewish radicals. The nonradical groups finished a clear third, differing only slightly from one another. This pattern is entirely consistent with our theory, which links radicalism to narcissistic deficits, while treating Jewish radicals as the more conventionally "narcissistic."

The Jewish radicals, moreover, diverged from all other groups in their low ego boundaries. This recalls our portrait of the self-expansive rebel, who rejects any closure of self in favor of a ceaseless experimentation with new experiences, emotions, and identities. Such people may suffer a diminished ability to distinguish inner from outer reality. By merging themselves with "life," they gain an endless succession of new identities, at the cost of a single identity that stands apart from the continual flux of affect and experience. They experience the world as an extension of themselves, but they must struggle continually to distance themselves from their own fantasies and impulses. To explicate this self-expansive tendency that we found among Jewish radicals, we asked Cole to supplement her content analysis of the TATs with an in-depth clinical analysis.

Once the individual sets of TATs had been scored and the groups compared, Cole was informed of the purposes of our study. She then carried out a clinical study of the TAT protocols in an effort to more fully delineate the differences between Jewish and non-Jewish radicals. She found that the Jewish subjects typified the self-centered, gratification-oriented pattern ordinarily thought of as narcissistic, while non-Jews were "narcissistic" in a more technical sense.

The Jewish radicals tended to write stories concerned with impulse gratification. They often relied on flashy words in inflated, dramatic stories to get the reader's attention. Their characters, especially the men, were often given almost complete license to indulge their desires. This included a desire for dominance over the other people, who were treated as "need gratifiers," providing admiration and confirmation of one's uniqueness or grandiosity. In general, other people were treated as props in a scenario for the enhancement of the self. At the same time, recurrent anxiety appeared in regard to masculine adequacy and assertiveness. Their struggle to achieve distance and autonomy seemed to require other people, both men and women, to provide admiration, support, and confirmation of their identity. Cole concluded that the very pressure of needs continually demanding immediate satisfaction fueled an effort to retain an endless succession of possible identities, women, and causes. Their hunger for novelty and new audiences suggested an incorporative orientation. This was combined with a self-assertive grandiosity and exhibitionism that may represent a defense against fears of passivity and inadequacy. In sum, the Jewish male radical presented the classical willful, impulsive, exhibitionistic form of narcissistic personality who manifests a great deal of self-reference in his relations with others.

The non-Jewish radicals clustered around a quite different narcissistic pattern. Their stories suggested that they fantasized freedom from human desires and binding attachments, along with ideological strength and superiority or intellectual purity. They tended to project undesirable or ego-alien aspects of their self-image onto others, particularly those aspects relating to femininity, passivity, and submissiveness. Their characters were driven from without rather than from within. They almost always reacted to ideas or situational demands. People almost never acted in accordance with inner needs that could be felt, acknowledged, and accepted. Sexual appetites and longing for closeness were experienced as a humiliating bondage to human need and attachment. Women and submissive men ("fags") were scorned as weak, corrupt, degraded, contaminating, and defiling. The implication was that one must either avoid such people or be contaminated by them.

It can be argued that such characters represented disowned fragments of the self which were projected out onto other people. The unlucky recipients became the repository of all the scorn and fear the subject attached to the impulses he has disowned. For example, woman represents the driven, dominated, weak creature into which one will devolve if one does not exercise mastery over human attachments. Masculinity has little to do with women. A "real man" is one whom other men respect and fear.

The admiration of others seemed irrelevant to the non-Jewish radical. His struggle was largely an internal one centered on intellectual dominance and superiority, and on complete freedom from attachment. In his stories, personal relations were mainly a matter of differentiating oneself and establishing psychological distance. He pictured the world as a bad and dangerous place to be and controlled this danger by maintaining distance and vigilance and by avoiding feelings and human relatedness.

With this orientation, it is easy to see how ideological constructs might become the repository of narcissistic grandeur and perfection, representing the self purged of all compromise with reality. By imposing these constructs upon others, he establishes the moral superiority of the self over those who threaten his purity, and over that impure part of the self that is denied and projected.

This clinical portrait goes far beyond an interpretation of the statistical differences found between Jewish and non-Jewish radicals. Cole reports that 84 percent of the radicals' TAT protocols could be blindly sorted into the correct ethnic-religious group, relying only on her exposition of their differing character styles. Nonetheless, her clinical interpretation lays no claim to social scientific validity. By foregoing the rigor of scientific method in this fashion, however, we gain a depth and breadth of insight that flesh out the results of our formal thematic analysis.

Clinical analyses thus serve a valuable heuristic function when used to supplement social scientific research. They help guide interpretations of survey findings by placing them in a broader and more detailed psychological context, and revealing underlying patterns that link the survey findings in unexpected ways. These considerations led us to carry out the separate clinical study of students described in Chapter 7.[39]

PSYCHOSEXUAL DEVELOPMENT (PSD)

The TATs were scored for one remaining set of personality variables. This scoring system classifies fantasy material in terms of issues associated with the psychoanalytically derived stages of psychosexual development as described by

Freud and Erikson.[40] These stages describe emotional concerns associated with instinctual preoccupations and modes of relating to the environment. They reflect the following concerns: oral or receptive (preoccupation with getting, taking in, incorporating); anal or autonomous (preserving autonomy, holding on, maintaining); phallic or assertive (reaching out, intruding, expanding); and genital or integrative (relating, committing, connecting).

Psychoanalytic theory postulates a progression through these stages to explain emotional development during childhood. Abigail Stewart, a social psychologist, has applied this theory to the study of adolescents and adults as they renegotiate emotional issues first encountered as infants.[41] For example, issues of dependency and autonomy, first encountered in relation to parental figures, must be dealt with repeatedly as the individual's affective environment expands to include peers, teachers, bosses, and so forth. Each new relationship requires an emotional reorientation which is partially modeled after earlier experiences. More importantly, Stewart has tested the theory by examining the fantasy lives of people who seem to have different psychosexual orientations.

Stewart began by identifying people who behaved in ways that, according to psychoanalytic theory, reflect underlying concerns related to a particular psychosexual mode. She then examined TAT stories written by these individuals to see whether their fantasy processes differed as well. The differentiating TAT themes became the basis of a scoring manual intended to capture differing psychosexual orientations.[42] In a study of male college students, she isolated subjects who were high in one of the following areas of behavior and low in the other three:

Stage I. Oral. Eating breakfast regularly, having a substantial snack after dinner, smoking at least half an hour a day.

Stage II. Anal. Having a regular time of getting up and going to bed, and listing many bedtime rituals such as taking a shower, emptying the pockets of one's clothing, brushing one's teeth, urinating, opening the window, etc.

Stage III. Phallic. Having dated a lot in high school with different girls, and citing "reputation enhancement" and "sex" as the most important motives for dating.

Stage IV. Genital. Having a steady girlfriend to whom one is faithful, and reporting that on dates one studies and talks and makes love, as compared to doing other things. The criteria here were Freud's "love and work." (When asked what a healthy person should be able to accomplish in life, Freud's succinct answer was "to love and to work.")

After examining these young men's TAT stories, Stewart developed a coding system that differentiated among the fantasy patterns of the four groups. The coding system proved highly reliable in that two trained scorers usually agreed about coding the same material. Applying the scoring system to her full sample, she then found that it did differentiate among people who behaved in the ways cited above, to a degree highly unlikely to occur by chance.

In the TAT stories, four central issues emerged that were each treated in different ways, according to a person's predominant psychosexual orientation. The issue areas were one's relationship to authority, relationship to other people, feelings or affect, and orientation to action.

Behaviorally "oral" subjects fantasized that authority figures were benevolent and that other people provided immediate gratification. They expressed feelings of confusion, despair, loss, and abandonment. (Presumably these feelings arose in response to the environment's intractability toward their desires.) Their fantasized orientation to action was one of passivity and receptiveness.

Behaviorally "anal" subjects, by contrast, held fantasy views of authority as critical and reprimanding and of other people as hindrances to one's gratification. Their most salient affect was a concern about competence, including indecision over making choices that might reveal one's incompetence. Their primary orientation to action dealt with clearing up disorder, or bringing order into chaos.

Behaviorally "phallic" subjects expressed opposition toward and rebellion against authority figures. Their fantasized dealings with other people were characterized by exploitative interaction or withdrawal and flight. In general, other people were viewed egotistically, as lacking intrinsic interest but providing either opportunities or threats to achieving one's own ends. Characteristic feelings expressed in fantasy were those of anger, hostility, and resentment toward others. The predominant action-orientation, interestingly, was one of failure, often an unexpected failure that belied initial confidence.

Fantasies of behaviorally "genital" subjects revealed an image of authority figures as limited in power and unable or unwilling to provide support. In their fantasy lives, these subjects seemed removed from the issues of personal authority that precipitated fantasized submission or opposition at other stages. Their fantasized relationships with other people involved differentiation of clearly external others and interaction based on sharing and mutuality. In dealing with feelings, their stories showed evidence of affective complexity, as manifested in an acceptance of ambivalent or contradictory feelings toward an object. Finally, their main orientation to action was one of involvement with or commitment to work.

Stewart and several colleagues have undertaken long-term studies intended, in part, to establish further the validity of this scheme.[43] Their preliminary findings suggest that the scoring system does tap stages in a continuum of psychosexual development. In separate studies of young children, adolescents, and adults, the researchers have found that PSD (psychosexual development) scores generally rise with age, except during major life transitions, such as starting school, getting married, or being hired for one's first full-time job. Such events usually precipitate renewed preoccupations with unresolved issues from earlier developmental stages, and this was reflected in the subjects' TAT stories.

David McClelland has suggested that the power drive can be manifested in different ways, according to a person's psychosexual orientations.[44] In a study of males high in *n* Power, he found that those who were predominantly "oral" in PSD were most likely to read about sex and aggression, to share their innermost thoughts and feelings with others, to be intraceptive or psychologically minded, to have a pre-Oedipal maternal identification, and to report unpleasant dreams with themes of insecurity. Those at the anal stage reported more incidents of controlled anger, rejected institutional responsibility, considered work as boring and tedious, and spent the most time talking to the opposite sex at parties. Men at the phallic stage preferred a nonmonogamous style of relating to the opposite sex, and reported "playing the field" sexually. They most often admitted lying to family and friends, collected the most prestige possessions, drank most heavily, and reported strong dislike of child care. These findings represent the types of behavior that might be expected from power-oriented people who express their power needs in ways conforming to different psychosexual styles.

In sum, the evidence seems suggestive, if not yet conclusive, that Stewart's system does differentiate among people oriented toward different psychosexual modalities. As a result, we asked her to score our male subjects' TATs for PSD. (At the time, it was not clear that the system worked as well with females, although evidence is accumulating that it does.) We expected that the PSD findings would reveal additional differences between radicals and nonradicals, and we also hoped to find certain distinctions between Jewish and non-Jewish radicals.

Regardless of ethnicity, we expected radicals to score predominantly at the phallic-assertive stage, particularly in their oppositional stance toward authority figures. As Meissner points out, however, such a stance often reflects an underlying narcissistic deficit, which stems from poor parenting during pre-Oedipal development, primarily in the oral stage. We therefore predicted that the predominant concerns of our young radicals in the sphere of inner feelings would be oral-receptive rather than assertive. An oral-receptive affective orientation expresses lasting feelings of loss and abandonment, residues of emotional deprivation stemming from early parental rejection. Such a radical is not an angry young man so much as a sad and embittered young man who nurses his "narcissistic wounds."

Beyond this, the psychosexual adaptation of Jewish and non-Jewish radicals should diverge in ways suggested by their different parental perceptions. Our non-Jewish radicals perceived both parents negatively within a patriachal family setting. Therefore, we expected that their relatively high oral scores in the area of feelings would be augmented by high anal scores.

Among Jewish radicals, on the other hand, flawed parental relations centered on resentment against a cold and dominant mother. Psychodynamically, this type of childhood experience should result in continuing preoccupation with "oral" themes, i.e., receptive or incorporative modes of relating to one's internal and external environment, to draw in the affection and caring that were lacking in one's early life. In short, we expected that all radicals would score higher than nonradicals on the oral modality in the sphere of inner feelings. But we also expected Jewish radicals to outstrip even their non-Jewish counterparts. In addition, we expected the rigid rebellion associated with non-Jewish radicalism to show up in the anal-autonomous concerns. A rigid rebel should be characterized not only by phallic-assertive interpersonal relations but also by a need to maintain a sense of internal order while fending off impending emotional chaos.

The continuing inner salience of these receptive, autonomous, and assertive themes might well prevent radicals from dealing with themselves and others in an integrative fashion. Therefore we expected to find them less able than nonradicals to understand the limitations of authority, to establish personal relationships based on mutuality and sharing, to accept complex and ambivalent emotions, and to play and carry out work in a productive fashion.

When we compared radicals to nonradicals on the four PSD stages, the results confirmed most but not all of our expectations. These results are summarized in Table 8.

Jewish and non-Jewish radicals scored significantly higher than nonradicals in their phallic-assertive imagery and lower in genital-integrative imagery. On both stages, the most extreme scores were registered by the non-Jewish radicals. Our model of the male radical as psychosexually self-assertive and unintegrated thus applies best to non-Jews. Jewish radicals, as expected, scored highest in oral-incorporative imagery. Rather than asserting themselves against the world, they seemed to prefer drawing the world's gratification into them-

Table 8. Ideological and Ethnic Group Differences in Overall Stages of Psychosexual Development, American Male Students.[a]

PSD IMAGERY (%)	RADICALS		NONRADICALS		Significance[b]
	Jewish	Non-Jewish	Jewish	Non-Jewish	
Oral					
X̄	.276	.228	.197	.237	n.s.
S.D.	(.207)	(.177)	(.159)	(.183)	
Anal					
X̄	.256	.288	.291	.311	n.s.
S.D.	(.168)	(.161)	(.206)	(.184)	
Phallic					
X̄	.327	.370	.319	.288	.05
S.D.	(.221)	(.251)	(.196)	(.219)	
Genital					
X̄	.140	.113	.193	.164	.05
S.D.	(.168)	(.161)	(.187)	(.175)	
N	36	43	96	235	

[a] Scores are percent of total PSD imagery scoreable at each stage.
[b] Statistical significance of mean difference between radicals and nonradicals.

selves, after the fashion of McClelland's "enclave type." On the other hand, non-Jewish radicals confounded our expectations by failing to show particular concern for autonomy.

The PSD stage scores provide a general overview of how people deal with several important issues in life—their own feelings and their relationships to others, to authority, and to action. But these four issues may not be equally important to an individual's own psychosexual style, which distinguishes him from others. To provide a more fully differentiated portrait, we examined differences along each of these dimensions at every PSD level.

On the oral-receptive stage, we expected that both radical groups would score high on the feelings dimension, reflecting an early history of deprivation. Both groups did in fact outscore the nonradical groups on this dimension, although the differences were not statistically significant.

Jewish radicals scored highest of all groups on all four dimensions of orality. An incorporative orientation thus suffused their approach to several major life issues. They were most likely to view other people as sources of gratification, to characterize authority figures as benevolent, to picture people as passive recipients of events, and to express feelings of confusion and abandonment. Their generalized orality suggests that their radicalism may express that most deep-seated of utopian longings, the return to Eden. These young men seemed to be reacting against the loss of a world in which other people are sources of fulfillment, authority figures are trustworthy guides, and the outside environment meets the individual more than halfway. This is, of course, the world of early childhood. This paradisical state of inner and outer oneness provides a criterion of perfection against which the imperfections of later life are gauged. It is not surprising that those most dissatisfied with the social order should feel the loss of Eden most keenly. But the generalized "oral" tendency among Jewish radicals suggests that their yearning for a society that avoids the competition for scarce resources may express an orientation deeply rooted in their personality structures.

On the anal-autonomous stage, orientation toward action proved to be the key dimension in distinguishing between the two groups of radicals. Jewish radicals scored lowest of all groups, suggesting a desire to avoid strictures or closure in one's sphere of action. They seemed most willing to embrace disorder or chaos and to reject limitations on individual experience. Non-Jewish radicals, by contrast, produced the most imagery on this dimension, indicating their concern with eliminating disorder and establishing a clearly defined sphere of autonomous activity.

The phallic-assertive stage produced the most variegated portrait. Radicals differed significantly from nonradicals on all four dimensions. Regardless of ethnicity, radicals were most likely to structure authority relationships in terms of hostility and rebellion. This dimension concerns all fantasized authoritative objects, and hence treats a generalized orientation toward authority, not just attitudes toward political authority. So these radicals' predictable hostility toward political authority seemed to reflect a general tendency to see all authority relations as exploitative. Similarly, both radical groups scored high on the action dimension. This suggests a concern to assert oneself, while fearing that such attempts will end in failure. On the other hand, radicals scored lowest on the affect dimension. They were less likely to express feelings of anger than of loss and confusion. Finally, non-Jewish radicals exceeded all other groups in their phallic-assertive imagery regarding personal relations. In contrast to Jewish radicals, who pictured other people as willing sources of gratification, the non-Jews portrayed others primarily in Machiavellian terms, as either obstacles to one's designs or opportunities to be exploited. The Jewish radical's utopian world of benevolent relationships was replaced by a world in which people exist to be used.

The genital-integrative stage represents the psychoanalytic ideal of the mature individual's approach to life. It involves acceptance of emotional complexity, mutuality in dealing with others, commitment to productive work, and recognition of the limitations of authority. Unlike the preceding stages, which everyone encounters in childhood, these are ideals against which our efforts can be measured. The persistence throughout life of unresolved issues from the earlier psychosexual stages militates against the attainment of full genitality. So it is not surprising that our subjects produced less imagery at this stage than at any other. Even so, it is striking that radicals scored lower than nonradicals on three of the four genital-integrative dimensions.

No differences appeared on the authority dimension, although radicals might be expected to emphasize the limitations of authority. But their portrayal of authority figures was so charged with hostility and opposition as to preclude even ambivalence toward authority. Jewish and non-Jewish radicals both scored significantly lower than nonradicals on the dimensions of feelings and relations to others. Radicals were least likely to produce imagery involving acceptance of emotional ambivalence, a disposition toward sharing and mutuality, or a highly differentiated view of other people. In addition, non-Jewish radicals scored lowest on the action dimension, suggesting the absence of a strong commitment to productive work.

Overall, scores on the genital scale provided little support for Keniston's argument that New Leftists were unusually healthy because of their emotional complexity, empathy, and integration. On these measures of integrative psychosexual modalities, radicals scored lowest on precisely those dimensions that should reflect emotional complexity and interpersonal empathy. On none of the four life issues did they manifest a more integrative orientation than nonradicals.

In summary, the PSD findings enrich our model of inverse authoritarianism in its two ethnically rooted variants. In general, radicals' fantasy productions were oriented toward phallic-assertive modes of relating to their environment, and away from the genital-integrative modalities that should characterize "mature" individuals, according to psychoanalytic theory.

Among the non-Jewish radicals, the PSD material suggests an exploitative approach to human interaction, along with a lack of concern for mutuality or emotional complexity, and a desire to eliminate disorder. This pattern suggests a cold, rigid, and Machiavellian personality style. In combination with their generalized oppositional stance toward authority, these PSD findings fit the portrait of the radical as a rigid rebel resembling the traditional authoritarian.

The Jewish radicals shared this hostility toward authority and lack of acceptance of mutuality or ambivalence. The rigid rebellion that these findings suggest was, however, mitigated by a strongly incorporative orientation and a willingness to tolerate or even welcome disorder. To put it somewhat schematically, the non-Jewish radicals resembled the rigid rebel who wants to replace a weakened or discredited order with a stronger one, in order to preserve a sense of autonomy in the face of impending emotional chaos. The Jewish radicals looked more like the protean or self-expansive rebel who rejects all order, leaving him free to swim in a sea of apparently limitless possibilities and sources of gratification.

THE RADICAL SYNDROME

We have shown that radicalism among college students was related to a host of psychological traits measured by two projective tests. On the Semantic Differential, relative to other students, radicals perceived a black militant, a riot policeman, and protesting students of both sexes as figures of strength or potency. They rated a student in a classroom and, to a slight degree, a black scientist as relatively weak or impotent. On TAT measures of motivation, radicals scored relatively high on the need for power and the fear of (ambivalence toward) power. They scored low only on the need for affiliation or friendship. In their psychosexual orientations, male radicals appeared strongly "phallic" or self-assertive and lacking in "genital" or integrative capacities. Finally, male radicals scored high on all four measures of narcissistic pathology.

This pattern of results consistently supports our argument that radicals were characterized by a syndrome of inverse authoritarianism. Within this syndrome, we have also begun to isolate elements that distinguished Jewish from non-Jewish radicals. The Jewish radicals were more narcissistic, more oral-incorporative, and less phallic-assertive in their psychosexual orientations, more likely to transmute power needs into political radicalism, and more likely to view an image of a hostile Establishment as a powerful figure.

We have tentatively suggested some ways in which these differences suggest ethnically based variants of an inverse authoritarian disposition. Our argument is developed in more detail through the in-depth clinical findings. Before leaving the larger study, though, we must address some important issues concerning the relationship between personality and radical politics. Thus far we have presented our findings in the form of group comparisons. We showed, for example, that the most radical group of college students in our sample had higher need for power scores than did liberal and conservative students, and that this difference in power needs was probably too large to have occurred by chance alone. We chose this form of presentation for its clarity and simplicity, while leaving more technical statistical questions to our articles in scholarly journals.

These group comparisons, however, cannot address two important questions. First, are the personality traits measured by the Semantic Differential and

TAT each related to radicalism independently of one another? It could be, for example, that the radical group scored high on both n Power and Fear of Power because some radicals had high scores on both these measures, and others scored high only on n Power, while none scored high only on Fear of Power. If this were true, we would conclude that Fear of Power was not related to radicalism independently of its association with the need for power. In this hypothetical example, people who had a strong fear of power were radical only if they also had a strong need for power. Any association between radicalism and fear of power would therefore depend upon the association between fear of power and the need for power. By contrast, the need for power would be independently related to radicalism, because people high in need for power are high in radicalism, even when they are low in fear of power. Such a finding would not alter our conclusion that radicals scored high in both the need for and fear of power. But it would narrow our search for the independent predictors of radicalism. If fear of power never affects radicalism independently of the need for power, then "fear" cannot be a cause of radicalism, whereas the need for power might be. (We disregard, for the moment, the question of whether radicalism might have created these psychological traits, rather than vice versa.)

The issue is intimately related to a second question: How strong is the relationship between radicalism and the set of personality traits we have described? This really involves a cluster of questions about the influence of personality on political ideology. How strongly does each trait affect radicalism, independently of the effects of all other traits? And what is the cumulative effect on radicalism of all traits operating jointly? Is a person with all these traits more likely to be a radical than someone with only one or two such traits? How accurately can we predict that an inverse authoritarian will turn to radical politics? That is, by combining the independent effects of all these psychological test scores, how much of the variation in radicalism scores can we explain?

To answer these questions, we examined all psychological variables that were present on both versions of the questionnaire. Our next step was to ensure that the measures were not closely related to one another. This posed no problem for the Semantic Differential and TAT motive scores. None of these scores was related more than slightly to any other. The four narcissism measures, however, were all at least moderately related to one another. This meant that if a person scored high on one narcissistic trait, he was likely to score high on the others as well. So we simply added the four scores together to form a single index of narcissism.

The PSD scores posed a different problem. Individual stage scores were expressed as percentages of total PSD imagery. A subject's score on, say, the phallic-assertive stage represents the percentage of his psychosexual imagery that was considered "phallic." Since the total of all four scores must add up to 100 percent, we could determine a subject's score on any one stage simply by knowing his scores on the other three stages, and subtracting their sum from 100. Therefore the PSD stage scores were, by definition, related to one another. To meet this difficulty, we excluded all but the phallic-assertive scores, since this stage was most central to our model of radicals' psychosexual orientations.

These procedures left nine personality measures. For the Semantic Differential, we retained the power scores for the black militant, black scientist, white male protester, and policeman. From the TAT, we took the n Power, Fear of Power, and n Affiliation scores and, for males only, the phallic-assertive PSD score and the overall narcissism index.

Now let us return to the question of how these traits independently affected a person's radicalism score. We found that every trait was significantly related to radicalism, independently of the effects of all other traits. Of course, some were more strongly related to radicalism than others. Of those variables scored for both males and females, the need for power, fear of power, and potency ascribed to the white protester were the best predictors of radicalism, and were about equally important. They were followed in importance by the black radical potency score and the need for affiliation. The weakest contributions to explaining radicalism were made by the potency scores for the policeman and black scientist. In combination, these scores accounted for exactly one sixth (16.7 percent) of the variation in radicalism. This is a fairly impressive relationship, given the nature of our instruments. It means that one sixth of all the differences we found in students' political attitudes can be explained by seven measures of their fantasy lives and their perceptions of power.

Moreover, this is a minimal estimate of the relationship between personality and politics, since it excludes the PSD and narcissism measures. Among male subjects, the amount of phallic-assertive imagery added significantly to our ability to account for variation in radicalism scores. With this measure included, the eight personality variables explained almost one fifth (19 percent) of the variation in radicalism. Finally, we restricted our analysis to the 117 male students whose TATs received narcissism scores. For this group, the complete set of nine personality variables explained fully one third (33 percent) of the total variation in radicalism.

To a substantial degree, then, personality differences were linked to levels of political radicalism among these young people. Further, each personality trait independently predicted radicalism in the direction hypothesized by our model of the radical as inverse authoritarian. This consistent, independent, and cumulative impact suggests that the traits make up a syndrome of conceptually related but empirically independent characteristics, each of which increases a predisposition toward radical politics.

This is a very significant finding, but its importance should not be overstated. Our analysis did not show that all radicals were authoritarian. Indeed, we are not certain that an arbitrary cut-off point on any of these traits should be used to determine whether a person falls into an authoritarian or nonauthoritarian category. We prefer to view this syndrome as a continuum, along which a person is viewed as more or less authoritarian, according to his scores on a whole set of personality measures. The important point is that this broad and theoretically coherent personality syndrome was significantly related to a radical political perspective.

Finally, this mode of analysis lets us examine exhaustively the interplay between ethnicity and personality in explaining radicalism. On several psychological measures Jewish radicals outscored their non-Jewish peers. By examining the interaction of ethnic background with each psychological trait, we can determine which characteristics were more salient to Jewish than to non-Jewish radicals, as well as whether a Jewish background predicted radicalism over and above the effects of all personality traits.

We found that two variables predicted radicalism significantly better among Jews than among non-Jews, independent of the effects of all others. These variables were power needs and potency attributed to the policeman. Power motivation predicted radicalism regardless of a person's ethnicity, but its effects were significantly greater among Jews. This supports our speculation that Jews were most likely to transmute their power needs into political radicalism.

In Chapter 3, we cited historical reasons that might lead Jews to orient themselves toward both power and radical politics. Our first findings imply that the two orientations are sometimes linked, with the power needs feeding into a radical political perspective. By undermining the establishment, Jewish radicals may capture the experience of power and control denied him as a marginal man in a Christian society (as he perceives it).

The second variable with different meanings for Jewish and non-Jewish radicals was the perception of the riot policeman as a powerful or potent figure. The more potency a Jewish student attributed to the policeman, the more radical he was likely to be. Among non-Jews, the opposite occurred. The more radical the student, the *less* powerful he perceived the policeman to be. This striking difference suggests that a broad syndrome of inverse authoritarianism might be mediated by different ethnic styles. Jewish radicals may have understood their political struggle as one of strength against strength, using militancy to fend off threats from a strong and dangerous establishment. They assigned nearly identical power scores to the policeman and the black militant, scores higher than any other group assigned to any picture in the Semantic Differential test. Non-Jewish radicals were perhaps more likely to view their opposition as a paper tiger ready to turn tail when challenged. That is, they may have more closely resembled the classic authoritarian pattern of pitting perceived strength against weakness.

Our psychological inquiry has been directed toward the mental states of radical youth—the underlying traits, dispositions, and "cognitive space" measured by personality tests. Our test results point to a pattern of functioning that is associated with radical ideology. This provides an empirical basis for inferences about the psychodynamics of radicalism and the subjective "lifeworld" the radical inhabits. In addition, we have posited the existence of ethnic variations on this pattern, which is held together by overriding concerns for power and control.

If radicals are really more power-oriented than other people, this orientation ought to show up in their nonpolitical day-to-day activities. Specifically, their behavior should in some way express the concern for power that motivates them. Moreover, Jewish and non-Jewish radicals should express these concerns somewhat differently, in ways consistent with their developmental differences.

Our central argument is that radicalism itself can express authoritarian personality tendencies. We have also noted, however, that people with strong power needs tend to behave in particular ways in many other areas of life. We asked our subjects about several such aspects of their social behavior, including their drinking and driving habits and their physical and verbal aggression. Our analysis is confined to males, for whom such activities are most likely to function as outlets for aggression.

Our theory predicts that non-Jewish male radicals would behave in ways that break through the barriers of inhibition and directly express aggressive impulses. Jewish male radicals, by contrast, should express their aggression in sublimated forms, primarily through verbal bellicosity and contentiousness. They should be much more timid about directly expressing physical aggression.

On almost every measure of behavior, the results conformed to our expectations. Relative to other male students, the non-Jewish radicals tended to drive fast and recklessly, to drink liquor often and heavily, and to be involved in physical fights. By contrast, Jewish radicals were generally *less* likely than other students to engage in such activities, which may represent the physical "acting out" of aggressive impulses. On the other hand, Jewish radicals tended to be verbally aggressive. They were willing to "tell off" other people to a greater degree than either non-Jewish radicals or nonradicals.

We asked students three questions about their driving habits: what was the fastest speed you have ever driven, how many times have you been stopped for speeding, and how often were you driving a vehicle that was involved in an accident? The groups differed to a statistically significant degree on each of these measures. Non-Jewish radicals were most likely to have auto accidents and to be stopped repeatedly for speeding. They were also above average in high-speed driving. Jewish radicals had the lowest number of speeding tickets and drove the slowest of all groups.

Overall, 15 percent of the male subjects had been stopped for speeding two or more times. Among non-Jewish radicals, the proportion rose to more than one in four (26 percent), while only 10 percent of Jewish radicals fell into this category. One in six males (16 percent) were "accident-prone" drivers, with a history of two or more auto accidents. More than double that proportion (35 percent) of the non-Jewish radicals reported two or more accidents, as did 23 percent of the Jewish radicals. Finally, among all male drivers, the top speed driven averaged 97.5 miles per hour. The non-Jewish radicals averaged 101.6 m.p.h., while Jewish radicals averaged 93.4, lowest of all groups.

Reports about drinking habits are difficult to interpret, because people may be reluctant to admit that they drink heavily. Among college students during the early 1970s, there is an additional consideration. Radicals in particular might be reluctant to admit choosing such a "bourgeois" means of altering one's consciousness, given the greater peer approval of other drugs. Luckily, we were concerned less with actual consumption patterns than with differences in drinking habits between Jewish and non-Jewish radicals. A general unwillingness to admit to heavy drinking should not affect reported differences between these groups. We asked only about hard liquor in an effort to isolate serious drinkers, by controlling for collegiate and adolescent propensities toward beer and wine drinking.

It is widely recognized that alcohol can release one from inhibitions and that "drinking provides an immediate or impulsive way of feeling powerful."[45] McClelland and his associates have refined this insight by showing, under experimental conditions, the particular ways in which drinking increases males' fantasies of sex and aggression. McClelland has summarized their major findings: "Drinking alcohol in small amounts increased the frequency of *socialized* power thought, while in larger amounts it promoted thinking in terms of *personalized* power."[46] Thus heavy drinking, like reckless driving, may be a means of releasing relatively untrammeled power concerns.

We found that such a pattern characterized only non-Jewish radicals. We first asked students to estimate how often during the past year they had drunk hard liquor. Very few students admitted taking a drink more than once a week, but a third (34 percent) of the sample did report consuming hard liquor two to four times a month. As expected, 45 percent of the non-Jewish radicals, the highest proportion of any group, fell into this category of relatively frequent drinkers, compared to only 29 percent of their Jewish counterparts.

Even more telling were the differences in the *number* of drinks students were likely to consume on these occasions. We were less interested in alcoholic consumption per se than in the use of alcohol to loosen inhibitions. The vast majority of students (70 percent) reported that they generally have one to five drinks in a "typical situation" in which they drink hard liquor. Another two in ten (19 percent) said they generally had less than one drink or were nondrinkers. The remaining 11 percent admitted to being heavy drinkers, reporting that they generally had six or more drinks. Of these 3 percent selected the highest category, that of nine or more drinks.

The non-Jewish radicals clearly stood out as the bastion of two-fisted drinkers. One in ten generally had nine or more drinks, more than twice the proportion of any other group. Moreover, an additional 20 percent reported having six to eight drinks, compared to only 8 percent of the entire sample. Combining these categories, fully 30 percent of the non-Jewish radicals were heavy drinkers, almost three times the proportion of all male subjects. In striking contrast, only 2 percent of the Jewish radicals were heavy drinkers, less than one fifth the proportion of all males.

Finally, as a measure of overtly aggressive behavior, we asked subjects how often they had been in violent physical fights during high school. Three percent of all males reported fighting many times. The Jewish radicals were about average in this respect, with 4 percent, or one in twenty-five, involved in several fights. Among non-Jewish radicals, however, the proportion of frequent fighters rose to one in ten, by far the highest of all groups. This difference cannot be attributed to political factors since Jewish radicals were not particularly likely to get into fights. Rather, it seems to reflect the non-Jewish radicals' tendency to settle arguments with their fists, whatever the origin of the dispute.

Whereas many non-Jewish radicals were able to overcome any inhibitions against expressing aggressive impulses, Jewish radicals proved more prone to verbal forms of hostile behavior. We asked three questions designed to measure verbal aggression in situations of interpersonal stress: have you yelled at someone in traffic so that they could hear?; have you made hostile remarks to clerks or storekeepers because of poor service?; have you "told off" someone who tried to push ahead of you in a line? On all three measures, Jewish radicals were most likely to report doing so often, while non-Jewish radicals were indistinguishable from nonradicals. In all cases, the differences between the two groups were statistically significant.

About one eighth of the sample reported regularly yelling at others in traffic. The proportion of verbally hostile drivers among non-Jewish radicals was about the same, despite this group's aggressive driving habits. But almost one in five Jewish radicals (19 percent) regularly expressed their anger in this way. Similarly, about one tenth of all males frequently told off someone who tried to push ahead of them in line, as did 10 percent of the non-Jewish radicals. But over twice as many Jewish radicals, almost one in four (23 percent), frequently told off transgressors in such situations. Finally, only 6 percent of all males, and 4 percent of the non-Jewish radicals, regularly berated clerks or storekeepers. Once again, Jewish radicals were more than twice as likely to be verbally aggressive, with 13 percent complaining often about poor service. So Jewish radicals were likely to yell at other drivers rather than to hit the accelerator, and to vent their spleen rather than raise their fists at antagonists.

In sum, in their daily nonpolitical activities, radical young men behaved in self-assertive ways that often placed them in adversarial social contexts. The particular modes of self-assertion, though, divided along ethnic lines. Non-Jewish radicals were dangerously aggressive behind the wheel of a car, intemperate in their alcoholic consumption, and physically pugnacious. Jewish radicals, by contrast, expressed their aggression in verbal belligerence. They were the most contentious group in the sample.

These patterns of behavior are consistent with our expectation that Jews and non-Jews would express their aggressive impulses in quite different ways. The non-Jewish radicals behaved in a fashion reminiscent of Adorno's rebel, who "is characterized, above all, by a penchant for 'tolerated excesses' of all kinds, from heavy drinking . . . to proneness to acts of violence. . . ."[47] A very early typology, drafted by the Frankfurt Institute in 1939, described such people as attracted to "dangerous professions" such as "racing motorists [and] airplane aces."[48] Over thirty years after this typology was drafted to account for "pseudo-revolutionary" behavior, we found the same pattern of aggressive activities among American non-Jewish radicals. Given their upbringings in traditional authoritarian families and their power-oriented dispositions, these young men seemed to express in their everyday lives the rigid rebellion that, under the guise of independence from authority, "merely replaces . . . dependency by negative transference."[49]

Jewish radicals, although characterized by equally strong power motivation, seemed to deflect or sublimate their aggressive urges into verbal hostility. Their proclivities toward political organization and activism may have served a similar function. In both instances, aggressive impulses can be expressed in a less overt and more socially acceptable manner than the destructive behavior of the non-Jewish radicals. We suspect that the non-Jews were giving vent to more primitive impulses that Jewish radicals might advocate or fantasize but dare not carry out.

At the beginning of this chapter, we summarized a model of authoritarian rebellion and its variants. We hypothesized that radical students would be more likely to manifest inverse authoritarian traits than would nonradicals. Further, we predicted that Jewish radicals would best fit the pattern of self-expansive rebellion, while non-Jewish radicals would most closely resemble the rigid rebels long identified with the authoritarian Left.

In almost all instances, the evidence supported our hypotheses. Regardless of ethnic background, radicals appeared both relatively power-hungry and strongly conflicted over power relations. They were also relatively narcissistic, phallic-assertive in their psychosexual orientations, and lacking in concern for either close and reciprocal interpersonal relations or integrative modes of dealing with the world. All these findings conform to the theory of authoritarian psychodynamics described in Chapter 4. In addition, radicals tended to ascribe the most potency to images of militance and protest, while rating images representing intellectual power as relatively weak. This suggests that their authoritarian tendencies were expressed through reactive opposition to social authority and identification with its opponents, just the inverse of the traditional authoritarian's dependent posture toward authority and aggression against outgroups.

Apart from their common core of inverse authoritarian traits, Jewish and non-Jewish radicals differed markedly in their backgrounds and orientations. The non-Jews were quite diverse in their social backgrounds but tended to be brought up in traditional authoritarian families dominated by a cold and punitive father. Their TATs showed the least concern for warm personal relationships and the most self-assertive and least integrative psychosexual modalities. They alone seemed amenable to McClelland's "imperial" power strategy, in which a strong power drive is disciplined or sublimated to fit organizational or ideological imperatives. Finally, their behavior was characterized by a penchant for "tolerated excesses": heavy drinking, reckless driving, and physical fights. All these traits recall the rigid rebel as a single-minded power-seeker who vacillates between unremitting self-control and the unfettered acting out of aggressive impulses.

The Jewish radicals, by contrast, came from relatively homogeneous backgrounds corresponding to the popular image of the New Leftist as socially and culturally privileged. Their parents tended to be highly educated professionals who were nonreligious, politically leftist, and supportive of their child's political stance. They were often raised in matriarchal families and viewed their parents quite negatively, although not so negatively as non-Jews did. Their family dynamics seemed to be set in motion by intrusive and domineering mothers. They viewed their fathers as meek and distant figures incapable of challenging their mothers for dominance within the family circle. In their TATs, the Jewish radicals were both the most power-oriented group and the most ambivalent about power. Their psychosexual styles included strongly incorporative or "oral" orientations.

They alone favored McClelland's "enclave" power strategy, whereby power is attained by drawing strength from external sources. And they alone gave evidence of low ego boundaries. In all these traits, they resembled the self-expansive rebel whose sense of power and personal identity derive from a merger of self and environment. Finally, their behavior was verbally but not physically aggressive, allowing them greater room to retreat and fight another day, or perhaps to play new roles upon a different stage.

In sum, the Jewish and non-Jewish radicals shared a set of traits that allowed them to express their conflicted power orientations in political radicalism. Beyond that common core, however, they were very different people. Raised in sharply contrasting environments, they expressed quite different underlying concerns through overtly similiar political rhetoric and activity.

How should these findings affect our assessment of the New Left? Certain conclusions should *not* be drawn from our study. First, it does not prove our speculative scenario about the Movement's rise and decline. Social psychological data are an insufficient source of historical explanation. Similiarly, our findings support a psychoanalytically oriented theory about the relationship between personality and politics. But we cannot prove that our personality tests captured the character and movement of psychodynamic processes. There are no eyewitness accounts of such internal dispositions. What insights we gleaned came from psychological tests that provide only brief and perhaps distorted glimpses of the psyche.

In this task we were constrained by our adherence to social scientific methods. This approach can provide reliable and valid knowledge, but only at the cost of individual intuition or idiosyncratic insight. By the same token, our argument is a probabilistic one. We have not shown that all radicals were authoritarian or that all authoritarians were radicals. We have simply demonstrated an affinity between these two realms that would be highly unlikely to occur by chance. More formally, we have shown that a statistically and theoretically significant portion of the variation in political ideologies can be explained by social psychological factors, as our theory predicted. We cannot entirely rule out alternative explanations of our findings, although they do not seem to fit the data as well as our own interpretations.

What *can* we conclude with some confidence? We have demonstrated that the New Left contained two types of radicals whose backgrounds, upbringings, and personality patterns were much as we predicted. Among the students we surveyed, radicals were clearly distinguishable from nonradicals, as were Jewish from non-Jewish radicals, in their upbringings and personality styles. Moreover, these groups were distinctive in ways quite different from those suggested by theorists of a liberated generation. Our radicals appeared quite the opposite of the psychologically liberated or protean personalities alleged to be the vanguard of a new, more humane social order. Instead, the backgrounds, personalities, and behavior of these students consistently corresponded to our vision of the radical as an authoritarian rebel.

We should add some cautionary notes. We found very few right-wing students at the schools we sampled. Our "conservatives" were, for the most part, only moderately conservative. Our theoretical framework suggests that extreme rightists might exhibit many of the same personality characteristics as our radicals. However, our data do not permit a test of this possibility. Moreover, given the limitations of the F scale, we cannot be sure that Adorno et al. ever captured the personalities of right-wing radicals. Even if it did, it might well not apply today. In most European countries and the United States the dominant culture is far more tolerant of left-wing than of right-wing protest, a reversal of the situation prior to World War II. Thus, those drawn to the Right today may be quite different from those who participated in such movements during an earlier historical period.

Our findings and conclusions have also been constrained thus far by the use of a survey format. In general, the survey instruments were probably too crude to capture the most subtle dynamics of inverse authoritarianism and its variants.

It is possible, too, that survey responses might be unduly affected by the transient political milieu. Our later study of adult radicals was designed to minimize this possibility. In addition, our student study contained a clinical component designed to probe more deeply into these young peoples' personalities. We sought thereby to identify the deeper and subtler personality differences that distinguished Jewish radicals, non-Jewish radicals, and nonradicals.

7 Faces in the Crowd: Clinical Portraits

THE FINDINGS DESCRIBED in Chapter 6 were based on a standardized questionnaire given to a large number of students. But we were anxious to study some individuals in greater depth. Therefore we conducted intensive interviews and administered clinical personality tests to a small number of students. The tests we chose were the Rorschach (inkblot) test and a set of clinical TATs. All students in our survey were offered twenty-five dollars to participate in this phase of the study. Interested students affixed their name (or a pseudonym) and telephone number to the questionnaire.

The advantages of the clinical approach are obvious. Such tests and interviews provide us with a much richer portrait of our respondents and enable us to deal with them as individuals. The disadvantages are equally obvious. The procedure is both expensive and time-consuming. Thus, the in-depth part of our study was restricted to thirty-six males. About 55 percent of our original sample agreed to participate. We divided this group into four subgroups, based on their ethnicity and radicalism scores: radicals of Jewish background, nonradicals of Jewish background, non-Jewish radicals, and non-Jewish nonradicals. Hereafter we shall refer to the nonradical subjects as "moderates." Nine students were chosen randomly from each of these groups. All thirty-six successfully completed both the interviews and the personality tests.

The interviews were conducted by Rothman and Dr. Phillip Isenberg, M.D., a psychoanalyst who is Director of Resident Education at McLean Hospital in Belmont, Massachusetts. With the permission of the students involved, all interviews were taped, as were most responses to the clinical tests. The latter were administered by trained clinicians who knew nothing about either their subjects or the purposes of the study.

What follows is based upon an analysis of the material by Drs. Isenberg and Schnitzer. We should note that Dr. Schnitzer was quite favorably disposed toward the student Left. His ability to deal with his findings dispassionately is testimony to his professionalism.

Clinical TAT, card 12F. *Reprinted by permission of the publishers, from* Thematic Apperception Test *by Henry A. Murray, Cambridge, Mass.: Harvard University Press, copyright 1943 by the President and Fellows of Harvard College; copyright © 1971 by Henry A. Murray.* (Although card 12F was not used in our tests, it is the only card that may be reprinted.)

The Thematic Apperception Test has already been described in connection with our survey results. For the clinical version, we selected nine standard clinical TAT cards, along with a tenth created by Rothman for this study and designed to tap Oedipal fantasies.[1]

The Rorschach is probably even more widely known than the TAT. It consists of a series of ten cards on which inkblots appear. As each card is presented, the respondent is asked to describe what he sees. ("Tell me, please, what could this be? What might it be?") This first stage is called the "free association." In administering the Rorschach, clinicians make every effort to avoid influencing the response. After all the cards have been administered, however, the interviewer asks respondents to describe various responses in more detail ("the inquiry") and to explain the reasons for their descriptions.

As with all projective tests, the Rorschach is designed to provide insights into inner personality dynamics. In theory, the very ambiguity of the stimulus, along with the fact that the person interviewed does not tell a connected story, enables investigators to probe more deeply than they can with the TAT. On the other hand, because Rorschach responses may tap more primitive aspects of personality, the TAT is often more valuable for exploring the relationships among personality, ideology, and political action.

Psychologists have never agreed upon a formal scoring system for the clinically administered TAT. Most agree that certain kinds of themes are indicative of particular personality dynamics. Nevertheless, clinical interpretation of the Thematic Apperception Test is still an individual matter in which the experience and sensitivity of the clinician are all-important.

Rorschach, card IV. *Reprinted by permission of Hans Huber Publishers, copyright 1921 by Verlag Hans Huber Bern; renewed 1948.*

By contrast, several standardized scoring systems are used to interpret the Rorschach test. Some clinicians feel that such systems may be useful for exploring the formal structure of certain pathologies but not individual personality dynamics. They prefer to rely on their own experience to analyze the thematic content of Rorschach test responses. Most clinicians who use the Rorschach in this manner argue that the responses offered must be seen as a whole, because a given response to a particular card can mean very different things, depending upon other responses offered. Therefore, they are usually reluctant to offer examples of particular responses to support their interpretations.

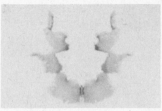

Rorschach, card VII. *Reprinted by permission of Hans Huber Publishers, copyright 1921 by Verlag Hans Huber Bern; renewed 1948.*

No matter how skilled the diagnostician, this procedure raises serious problems of reliability. Whatever precautions are taken, the possibility of bias can never be entirely eliminated. This is especially true when the investigator himself interprets the projective tests, or when they are administered and interpreted by staff members who are familiar with the nature of the investigation. This procedure was used in several well-known studies, including *The Authoritarian Personality,* Keniston's *The Uncommitted,* and Michael Maccoby's *The Gamesman.* Despite their popular success, the scientific value of these studies was severely compromised by the lack of blind-scoring procedures.

We took every possible precaution to ensure that those who administered and interpreted our results were unfamiliar with both our study and our hypotheses. When we could not, we attempted to check our interpretations by eliciting blind second opinions from other clinicians. These procedures are described below. In addition, in presenting our findings, we have included extensive quotations from the Rorschach and TAT material. Finally, the complete protocols have been placed on file with the Roper Public Opinion Center at the University of Connecticut. Thus interested readers have an opportunity to form their own judgments.

The case reports were analyzed by Dr. Robert Schnitzer, Director of Training in Clinical Psychology at McLean Hospital. The interviews were examined separately by Dr. Isenberg. Although they worked independently of our analysis of the survey materials, they were both aware of our main hypotheses and

of the identity of the respondents. As an additional check, therefore, six sets
of randomly selected protocols were interpreted blindly by Dr. Thea Goldstine,
then of the University of Michigan's Psychological Clinic. Her report on these
cases was substantially in agreement with that of Dr. Schnitzer.

The next stage involved an effort to determine whether meaningful group
comparisons could be developed. Working together, Drs. Isenberg and Schnitzer
agreed that a total of twenty-four themes could be found in the case reports.
Eight of these seemed to differentiate among the four groups. The reports were
then scored for the presence or absence of these eight themes. We shall first
describe and illustrate these themes and then discuss the thematic differences
that emerged among our groups.[2]

1. *The Wandering Fantasy:* Several protocols contained fantasies of wandering, which were often allied with the idea of exile or drifting. The major
protagonists in these fantasies were characterized by aimlessness and purposelessness. They perceived life as a voyage with no explicit goal or meaning.
Such stories were most commonly elicited by card 2 of the TAT. While such
fantasies may represent a number of themes, they express most clearly a profound sense of alienation.

The following story is typical. It was told by Clete,* a Jewish radical, in
response to card 2.

Being an indentured servant in a New England colony perhaps 300
years ago, is an extremely difficult task, as the man behind the plow
would be the first to tell us. He has been indentured for 37 years. . . .
Both he and all the people in the picture are from England. The older
woman is mistress of the farm here and the mother of the younger
woman. And it is unclear as to exactly why the man behind the plow
indentured himself, but there is talk of his mother having perhaps been
burned for witchcraft in England, and generally some vague talk . . .
people don't bring up such things. The past is left well enough alone.
The girl in the picture is the daughter of the mistress of the farm and is
holding a Bible and such things as were read 300 years ago, one of the
first copies of Milton's *Paradise Lost* to arrive in the colonies. Quite
naturally she has a good deal of affection for the servant who is only a
year or two her elder, and there is some talk on the farm that, perhaps
when he has served out his time, the two of them might be married.
. . . However, the man himself is not particularly fond of such a match.
He is quite fond of the girl, but he does not wish to remain in this
colony, does not wish to remain on the Atlantic seaboard. . . .
In the period of about two years after he has served his time, the

*The names assigned to the clinical subjects are pseudonymns.

man will most likely leave New England and go towards the Southwest, towards the areas which will later become the Spanish Colonies and Mexico. . . . Eventually he will reach California and become a merchant in one of the Spanish settlements on the Southern part of the coast, around what is now San Diego. There he will eke out [a living] until the wanderlust strikes him again and he takes ship. How much time do I have?

Interviewer: It's almost up.

Respondent: Takes ship on a ship which goes to the Western coast of [inaudible] . . . the East Indies where he's going. He'll die of malaria during the voyage.

2. *Negative Identity:* This theme was scored when the protagonist in a TAT story did something that he knew was wrong and would be condemned by his parents or by society. Stories describing the "hero" as misusing illicit drugs or committing a crime were a common way of expressing this theme. The respondent often fantasized that he had engaged in such criminal activities, to the horror or disappointment of the parent who was psychologically most important to him. Such imagery was often elicited by cards 7BF or 6BM of the TAT.

3. *Flight from the Mother:* Often allied with themes of negative identity and alienation was an expressed need to distance oneself psychologically from one's mother. Exile, wandering, or turning out to be "bad" were all ways of expressing this distance. Typically the subject would express this need for distance from his mother on card 6BM of the TAT.

Clete provided a good example of both negative identity and flight from a psychologically salient mother, in a story elicited by TAT card 6BM:

"Well, Ma, I had to do it." [Laughs]

Jeff is trying to console his aging mother for his ne'er-do-well life which has recently culminated in a senseless attack on a young couple which has netted the sum of $10.27, which, even in 1949, was not a particularly great sum, and which also resulted in the death of the young woman and injuring the young man.

Thus after having served in the armed forces during World War II, if not with distinction, certainly with honor, he was never able to find . . . his niche in civilian life, and . . . he's been tried for car theft, but he had a good defense. His mother's been aware of his somewhat illicit activities, partly involved in the drug rackets in New York City. He has come back to their home in Long Island almost to lean on her shoulder, 'cause he's scared for the beatings and murders he's committed. The old lady has tried her best to raise a good son, and has never been really able to quite understand. . . . And at this point what he really needs is not so much a helping hand as a slap in the face. At a time when he'd better get out of the state she is simply going to stand there watching Long Island Sound from the window [inaudible] the husband having died [inaudible]. But he'll wander the Eastern seaboard for several years before finally being picked up on an assault and battery charge. . . . He will get two to six for that.

4. *Masochistic Surrender:* Stories were scored for this theme when the protagonist surrendered to some powerful force or agent (or fate) to which he was allied or subjugated. Indeed, he was often either controlled by this force or fused with it. This theme also came out in responses to card 4 on the Rorschach, as in the case of Al, another radical Jewish respondent.

Free Association[3]

Subject: Um. . . . I see some kind of collision, and I have the feeling of two people sort of very tightly holding on to each other . . . um . . . just sort of enmeshed in each other

Inquiry

S: Okay. This one's not gonna be easy to say why I saw it as I did. But I'll. . . . This is the one with two bodies?

Interviewer: Uh huh.

S: I guess I just saw a variation in color and things coming together and colliding as two people just wrapping on to each other. Not easy to separate them from each other.

I: You mentioned a collision?

S: Yeah. I guess I meant something like maybe you should think of. Rolling around with each other holding on tight or just sort of tightly held to each other. Just sort of doing that. . . . I don't know how I'm going to fit this into the picture. Just sort of . . . kind of rushing together. You know. Just like a moment when they both need to do that and do that.

I: What made it seem like two people?

S: I don't know. Well it's . . . I mean [long pause] . . . I mean you could see these as legs for both of them. But mostly it was just the sense of something blending in the middle.

I: Did you see it as two legs?

S: No, not really. I saw it more just sort of like a kind of just energy. . . .

I: What kind of energy?

S: I wasn't sure. Just something rushing and maybe even a little panicking. They're not distinguished but just sort of holding on out of fear in some ways.

In his only other response to the card, Al saw it as representing "strong emotion." During the inquiry he once again spoke of attempts to fuse together out of panic or frenzy.

5. *Mother as Salient:* Material from the interviews and projective tests was used to determine which parent was perceived as having greater importance and/or meaning. This decision was necessarily based upon an appraisal of the overall pattern of fantasy produced for the Rorschach and TAT, as well as from the interviews.

6. *Father as Flawed:* This was scored when a paternal figure was described as having a defect, flaw, or significant personal blemish. This response frequently included a judgment about the father's moral corruptibility or weakness when confronted with functions one could reasonably expect him to carry out successfully.

This theme was elicited by a number of TAT cards, as well as card 4 of the Rorschach, where a masculine authority figure is seen as powerful but also as somewhat ridiculous. Two examples should suffice. The first is a story told about card 7BM of the TAT by Bill, a young ex-Catholic activist who had just dropped out of college:

> These two men are business partners. The older is a much better businessman; he is deceptive, cunning, and has no principles. At one time he brought the younger man into his business because he thought the younger man was really sharp and could really make it in the business world. . . . the young man has moved up rather quickly in the business seeing the older man as a protector. [However] the older man now sees that the young man is too soft and will never make it. [At this point Bill's tone of voice became cold, hard, and sarcastic.] He has just told the young man that he is fired. The old man, who is very cold himself, can't stand softness and he sees that in the younger man. A short time ago he had just begun to let the young man know about the underhanded and semi-illegal things that his business was involved in. The young man couldn't deal with this and was upset. That's why the

older man is getting rid of the younger man. He refused to go along with him on an underhanded deal.

The older man will eventually be caught because his adventures will be more and more illegal as he tries to save his business and make it grow, but he will die of a heart attack before he ends up in court.

Cliff, another young non-Jewish activist, described the inkblot on card 4 of the Roschach as follows:

Free Association

What I see here is this dog in the cartoons, is his name Clint?—a giant dog with a bad disposition. At this moment he's stomping on a cat which is his favorite pastime.

Inquiry

Interviewer: Where did you see the dog?

S: This comic is about a big dog that has a bunch of freaky kids around that talk to him. He has these monstrous feet. He's drawn from below. He walks around on his back feet and he likes to terrorize. So this looks like he's stomping on a cat. He has a little head just like this and these feet are perfect for him.

7. *Machismo:* Machismo was scored when the respondent emphasized exaggerated, exhibitionist, body-oriented, "hypermasculine" posturing behavior by the male hero of his story. Such stories were usually, but not exclusively, elicited by TAT card 17BM. Typical responses involved a self-preoccupied emphasis on showing off muscular prowess. A story by Arnold, a young Jewish radical, illustrates the theme succinctly:

This guy looks—this looks like a really macho guy. And very kind of muscular and exercising all his masculinity by climbing these ropes and he's looking on the audience, to the arena saying . . . "Dig it! I'm a man. And look at my muscles. Look at how I'm climbing up, climbing up this rope. Look at me. Hot shit!"

8. *Treating People as Concepts:* Subjects scored for this theme tended to stereotype and overgeneralize when discussing people and their behavior, in both their interviews and TAT stories. Often there was a glib and overinclusive quality to their statements. They tended to relate stories or assert their opinions in a dogmatic way, without attention to the varied and complex possibilities in

the situation being described. A number of subjects tended to "intellectualize" interpersonal relations.

Some of our respondents were somewhat aware of such tendencies in themselves. One moderate non-Jewish respondent, whose remarks during his interview were almost entirely abstract, admitted that he had no close personal relationships. He considered himself a "brain." He felt that this fact made him unfit for normal social intercourse and unacceptable to most people.

Another moderate student turned card 2 into a completely abstract discussion of males and females as "types." He conveyed no sense of possible subtlety or individuality in the relationships among the people in the picture:

> I guess it's a community picture of a few people, say somewhere on the American frontier—don't know where or what year. . . . The most dominant fact seems to be sexism. . . . As always it means that no one can do what they want—neither the male nor the female because there's not much else for them. The females are thinking about the male and what it would be like to be with him, and the competition of the other female. The male is mainly thinking about getting the job done so he can have some supper and rest. Probably nothing but the same thing will happen for many many days in the future.

The group differences on these eight themes are summarized in Table 9. None of these personality variables differentiated Jews from non-Jews to a statistically significant degree. Nor did Jewish and non-Jewish moderates differ significantly from one another. By contrast, we did find a coherent set of signifi-

Table 9. Group Differences on Case Report Themes, Clinical Subjects.

| | RADICALS | | NONRADICALS | | |
THEME	Jewish	Non-Jewish	Jewish	Non-Jewish	Significance
Negative Identity	8	5	1	2	.01 [a]
Masochistic Surrender	9	6	4	2	.01 [a]
People as Concepts	5	7	1	1	.01 [a]
Wandering	8	0	0	1	.005 [b]
Machismo	9	4	6	4	.025 [b]
Flight from Mother	9	0	2	2	.005 [b]
Mother Salient	8	3	2	3	.025 [b]
Father Flawed	3	8	3	3	.025 [b]
N	9	9	9	9	

Statistical significance as determined by Fischer's exact test:
[a]Radicals vs. nonradicals.
[b]Jewish radicals vs. non-Jewish radicals.

cant differences between radicals and moderates. Moreover, Jewish and non-Jewish radicals differed from one another in important respects.

Radicals were significantly more likely than moderates to manifest tendencies toward a negative identity, masochistic surrender, and treating people as concepts. In addition, Jewish radicals alone were differentiated by themes of wandering or alienation, machismo, flight from mother figures, and treatment of the mother as the more salient parent. Non-Jewish radicals perceived their fathers as more salient but also as flawed.

To interpret these differences, we began with the set of traits that distinguished our radical subjects, regardless of their ethnicity. A radical orientation was associated with dispositions toward a negative identity, masochistic surrender, and treating people as concepts. This set of traits can be thought of as a cohesive psychological structure, if we consider the need for a negative identity as the basic disposition. This implies a force driving the individual away from some threatening inner figure and toward an alienated state or self-imposed "bad" identity. This impetus is opposed by a desire for masochistic surrender, a wish to give oneself up to a powerful object, to "participate" in its power by becoming part of it. The tension between these competing forces gains expression in the social and political arena via the tendency to treat people as concepts. This tendency could displace an essentially unconscious psychological dynamic onto a public, institutional, or group-oriented level of experience. Each of these psychological structures, then, in interaction with the others, can create a psychological predisposition to adopt a radical stance, when conditions permit. A public social crisis can convert this latent radical perspective into a fully developed radical political ideology.

This scenario seems most relevant to the psychodynamics of the Jewish radical. This group demonstrated much more conformity on these traits than did non-Jewish radicals. For the Jewish radical, the adoption of a negative identity was apparently designed to create distance from a threatening mother, who was viewed as seductive, controlling, engulfing, or unusually demanding. The emotions generated by the flight from the mother may be expressed by the wandering fantasy, which was so prevalent in the TAT stories of the Jewish radicals.

Many of our Jewish radicals found themselves unable to develop a commitment to a life plan. Yet they were fearful of their mother's criticism because of this lack of direction. Their emphasis upon "machismo" was part of a frantic search for an imitative affiliation with powerful males, as a source of strength in the flight from the mother. They needed such an ally because they did not perceive their fathers as providing such strength.

Despite the tensions these radicals felt in their maternal relationships, they described their mothers as politically liberal and relatively sympathetic to their political activity. Ironically, this maternal acceptance or support tended to undermine the defensive usefulness of the son's activism, at times driving him more deeply into rebellion than he might otherwise wish.

The psychodynamics of non-Jewish radicals did not come into such clear focus, probably because of their greater social heterogeneity. We might expect that psychological similarities would be outweighed by differences between radicals with such disparate backgrounds as Bill, who came from a lower-middle-class Catholic background, and Jim, whose parents were liberal professionals and relatively high-status Protestants. Nonetheless, some common features did emerge. Generally, the non-Jewish radicals were less involved in their fantasy life with their parents. The father, who was usually the more salient parent, was perceived as powerful and punitive, if also flawed. The parents of the non-Jewish radicals were generally less overtly ideological and more conservative than those of the Jewish radicals (although two of the nine Christian radicals were clearly living out their parents' radical values). Seven of nine scored positively for treating people as concepts, indicating the high degree to which this group displaced their inner conflicts onto social and political issues.

The only variable that significantly differentiated the non-Jewish radicals from all other subjects was their image of the father as flawed. We infer from this that non-Jewish radicals were in conflict with their father's authority, which they tended to depreciate or flout through rebelliousness. Their disappointment with and hatred of a "flawed" father led to the desire to avenge themselves, i.e., to discharge anger at the father's combination of arbitrary power and weakness. A number of non-Jewish radicals shared the pattern of desiring to punish society for the weaknesses it shared with their devalued fathers.

These interpretations depend upon the assumption that the clinical material actually reveals deep personality structures. We recognize that this assumption is open to question. Did we in fact uncover the hidden psychodynamics of a radical ideological "superstructure?" Or did we merely redefine the inevitable characteristics of one type of radical stance? That is, did we simply translate into psychological categories these young people's criticisms of the prevailing establishment, feelings of alienation and powerlessness, and desires to transform social, political, and personal relationships? Did the flight from mother, the negative identity, and the wandering fantasy represent a self-dramatization of their real position in the world, which revolved around deep-rooted conflict with the status quo? Finally, large numbers of college youth were radicalized during the anti-Vietnam protest. Did we simply tap their ephemeral reactions to political realities of the 1960s, enhanced by their vulnerability to the draft and their concern for the oppressed?

The preponderance of evidence weighs against these alternative interpretations. First, the clinicians' independent interpretations clearly complemented and explicated the findings of our survey material. Second, clinically administered TATs and Rorschachs give every evidence of tapping underlying character structures rather than their surface manifestations. Most importantly, though, we should not have found such striking differences between Jewish and non-Jewish radicals if their responses were merely reactions to the radical's "real world" situation. The ethnic differences we uncovered thus militate against attributing our findings to a common radical perspective. They also comport with ethnic differences in the survey data, particularly with the very different parental images of Jewish and non-Jewish radicals. Finally, our notion of ethnically delimited variations on a radical personality style also received additional support from an independent analysis of the Rorschach protocols. We turn now to that analysis.

Shortly after the Rorschachs were administered, they were scored in terms of widely used formal categories developed by Bruno Klopfer and others.[4] The scorers were Dr. David Harder and Ms. Debbie Greenwald, clinical psychologists at the University of Rochester Medical School. Neither of them knew anything about either our study or the subjects whose protocols they scored.

The formal Rorschach scores lay unused for almost two years. Then, at a conference where preliminary clinical findings were presented, our interpretations were challenged by Dr. David Gutmann, chairman of the Division of Psychiatry at Northwestern University Medical School. We agreed to check the matter by having Dr. Gutmann interpret the Rorschach scores. While he inevitably knew the purposes of the study, any bias on his part would be greatly reduced by the constraints of the scores themselves. Further, interpretation of the categories developed by Klopfer et al. has been more or less standardized. Thus the analysis would be open to evaluation by other clinicians.

As a final check, we performed a multivariate statistical analysis, which showed that the Rorschach scores significantly differentiated among Jewish radicals, non-Jewish radicals, and moderates along lines consistent with our theory.[5] The differences we found are described below, along with Dr. Gutmann's interpretations of their clinical import.[6] We shall discuss in turn the scores dealing with cognition, affect or emotion, and pathology.

Cognition. The first set of Rorschach variables that differentiated among the groups concerned intellectual energy, creativity, competence, independence, and the ability to perceive reality with accuracy. Overall, they measure what is commonly thought of as ego strength. The first of these is "R" or

Response Total. R scores are based on the number of scorable responses. It indicates intellectual productivity, as well as the degree of energy available to make responses. Low response rates can indicate a depressed, constricted, or suspicious stance; an overly high total may indicate mania or overcompliance.

The W score refers to "wholes," the use of the whole blot in constructing a response. A high W score usually indicates intellectual energy and the ability to integrate experience. If not backed up by such inner resources as a rich capacity for fantasy life, however, it may reflect flashy pretentiousness and intellectual exhibitionism.

The M score registers the tendency to see human figures in movement. It refers to the contours of fantasy production. It can measure the capacity for inner control, the ability to delay gratification by using compensatory fantasy, and the potential for intellectual and emotional autonomy.

The F+ score is based on the number of stimulus forms that are accurately perceived. It refers to the capacity for reality testing and abstract thinking. Like the M score, it can also indicate a capacity to delay gratification, because it seems to demonstrate an ability to abstract from the total experience of the card (i.e., from its shades, colors, and contrasts) some formal quality of the stimulus—that is, its outline.

The O score refers to the proportion of Rorschach "originals" produced by a subject. It registers his capacity to offer novel interpretations, particularly to those areas of the card which generally stimulate only banal responses. As such, it can be a measure of creativity or arbitrariness, depending on the quality of the F+ score.

The P or "popular" responses measure both conventionality and judgment. They reflect the respondent's capacity to interpret correctly the most commonly perceived forms on the cards. Respondents who cannot see these forms usually have a severe problem in dealing with the pragmatic aspects of their world, while respondents who *refuse* to see them are usually "protesting too much"— they are *insisting* on their unconventionality. Intelligent and creative respondents usually produce a mixture of originals and populars, and they usually elaborate the popular forms in interesting and novel ways.

The S response refers to the use of the white space rather than the inked surface of the blot. In effect, respondents who attend to the white space are turning the figure into ground, and ground into figure. This tendency in perception is linked to negativism and stubbornness in behavior but also to creativity and originality: the original thinker must avoid being overly coerced by the obvious, prepotent features of his world.

The Dd score captures the tendency to deal with little noticed, not clearly defined areas of the card. It can reflect boldness and originality, expressed in impatience with conventional restraints, or it can refer to psychopathy—a cavalier disregard of obvious realities.

The Jewish radicals scored uniformly low across the board on the intellectual and ego strength indicators. Their relatively high W scores and paucity of M responses suggest intellectual pretentiousness and ambition that goes beyond personal resources. Otherwise, theirs was not an impressive performance. They did assert their individuality by avoiding the popular responses, but their negativism was not compensated by creativity or intellectual vigor. They were notably low on original responses, on M responses, and (less importantly) on white space responses.

The non-Jewish radicals presented a different picture. Across the board, they showed a mixture of intellectual power and reserve. They did not give a plethora of responses, but those that they did produce were often marked by originality, reasonable form, boldness of integration, and subjective richness. In contrast to their Jewish compatriots, disciplined vigor seemed a keynote of the non-Jewish radicals' intellectual functioning.

Affect. We turn now to the scores related to emotion and impulse. The CF score refers to responses in which the subject attends mainly to the color component of the card and gives it priority over form. The stimulating color elements dominate his attention at the expense of more formal "intellectual" elements. Accordingly, the CF score refers to infantile and narcissistic predilections. cF responses point in the same direction. They are scored when the subject responds to a "textural" element of the card, e.g., "looks like fur." They refer to pregenital wishes for tactile and immediate comfort. Often found in deeply narcissistic individuals, they reflect a wish to see the world in terms of personal comfort and security.

Like the CF and cF responses, the C'F score indicates a hypersensitivity to the "emotional" and affective aspects of the environment, as opposed to its more formal, "intellectual" features. But C'F responses point to a different, heavier mood tone than the CF and cF responses. They are scored when the dark tones of the card dominate the respondent's perception and take precedence over form. He does not seek out the comfort and excitement offered by the card. Instead he dwells on the more negatively toned elements: the dark oppressive tones. This response tendency betokens not comfort seeking, but comfort avoidance. Depressive and frightened individuals use or overuse this determinant—all those who lack basic trust in the "goodness" of the environment and who look for reasons to inhibit their spontaneous response to the world. It is also used by masochistically self-dramatizing individuals—those who wish to make a point of their misery and pain.

The M/C score refers to the balance between the introversive (movement

Table 10. Group Mean Rorschach Scores for Clinical Subjects.

RORSCHACH CATEGORIES	RADICALS		NONRADICALS	
	Jewish	Non-Jewish	Jewish	Non-Jewish
Cognition				
Responses (R)	34.38	30.44	32.00	34.00
Wholes (W)	38.00	40.22	36.44	36.00
Movement (M)	8.50	18.56	19.22	11.62
Forms (F+)	60.75	68.11	70.67	59.38
Originals (O)	19.38	25.00	28.00	18.63
Populars (P)	10.88	13.11	15.11	12.50
Space (S)	4.38	5.89	6.22	7.63
Unusual Detail (Dd)	12.88	10.56	8.67	12.25
Affect				
Color Form (cF)	3.00	0.44	1.78	0.88
Form Shade (C'F)	5.38	1.78	2.67	8.63
Extroversion (M/C)	.544	.420	.445	.572
Texture (CF)	8.63	5.67	7.44	7.25
Pathology				
Confabulation (CONF)	10.25	17.00	4.44	4.38
Fabulation (FAB)	9.63	16.78	12.44	16.25
Contamination (CONT)	0.88	1.22	1.22	0.00
Misperceived Movement (M−)	1.25	3.22	2.00	2.63
Autism (AUT)	1.25	2.33	0.89	0.00
Peculiar Verbalization (PEC)	4.38	7.56	2.33	2.13
N	8	9	8	9

responses) and the extroversive (color responses) elements of personality. This ratio indicates whether the subject is prone to respond to his inner promptings or to the pressures, coercions, and excitements coming from his immediate surroundings.

The non-Jewish radicals exhibited the highest level of introversion and the lowest tolerance of emotion among the groups. In contrast, Jewish radicals achieved the highest overall scores with respect to emotional stability.

A clear pattern is emerging: the non-Jewish radicals stressed intellect, mental organization, inner control. Their emphasis on cognitive control was matched by their need to master their emotions, their appetites, their need for others, and their spontaneity. They recall the classic picture of the radical as ideologue. We might expect them to find comfort not so much in people as in the "big picture" (note their high rank on the W score), in their *ideas about* people, which can substitute for the usual pleasure in human relationships. They could love human beings in the abstract, so long as they conform to some theoretical picture. But they might have little tolerance for human complexity, for human messiness, even for human need, either in themselves or in others. Their potential for idealistic self-sacrifice might extend to a willingness to sacrifice others to a noble ideal.

The Jewish radicals moved in the other direction. They did not shun affective experience. Rather, they seemed to yearn for it, seeking experience and sensation, whether pleasurable or painful. (Note their high scores on both cF and C'F.) They moved toward people not as *objects* but as providers of and occasions for excitement. They had no long-standing interest in other individuals per se and might lose interest in others once their novelty—their capacity to provide new forms of experience—has worn off. We would speculate that their "revolutionary" fervor did not serve an *idea;* rather it served their appetite for experience, as well as their impatience with boundaries that fenced them off from the full range of experience to which they felt entitled.

Pathology. Finally, we consider scores that betoken loss of distance, disturbed cognitive functioning, and mild to severe psychopathology.

The Fab (Fabulation) score is relatively innocuous. It is scored when the respondent elaborates his response in a mildly personalized fashion, by bringing in embellishments that are not directly suggested by the stimulus itself. Fab represents some loss of distance, but also the work of a lively imagination.

The PEC (peculiar verbalization) score is more ominous. It refers to odd, tortured phraseology. PEC reflects some loss of the inner sense of lexical consensus on which clear communication is based. This breakdown may reflect either transient anxiety or some psychotic process.

The Conf (confabulation) score is less ambiguous. The elaborations on which it is based point to more than lively fancy. Conf represents a true loss of distance. The subject experiences, rather vividly, some drama "out there" in the card itself. His later associations take off from earlier associations and lose their grounding in the features of the card itself. The Conf tendency is most pronounced in manic and paranoid states.

The M− score must always be taken seriously. M− is scored when human movement is seen in the card, but the human form itself is misperceived. This indicates that action potentials that are denied in the self are being experienced, inappropriately, in others. This often signifies paranoid tendencies.

The AUT and CONT (Autism and Contamination) scores both refer to thought disorder. For example, in contaminations, two images seen in the same area of the blot are formed into one inclusive *concept* solely because of their spatial contiguity. In other words, as is common with schizophrenics, the abstract and the concrete are confounded: physical proximity betokens logical closeness or lexical equivalence. Accordingly, when these signs appear, a psychotic or borderline process must be considered.

The non-Jewish radicals were clearly the most pathological of our groups. Approximately 28 percent of their responses indicated notable and scorable evidence of psychopathology and even severe thought disorder. Given their obsessive intellectual control, avoidance of affect, rigid boundaries, and at least superficial concern for accuracy, the high scores of the non-Jewish radical respondents indicated a paranoid pattern. Their pathology appeared to be a side effect of high and rigid ego boundaries. For such people, there is always a "bad" outside and a "good," pure inside. The goodness of the self and the badness of the other are both overvalued, but the domains of self and not-self are kept rigidly separate.

The Jewish radicals did not significantly exceed the nonradicals in the number of their pathological responses. Nonetheless, it is worth noting that their pathologies of choice were very different from those of the non-Jewish radicals. They seemed to represent the converse state of ego diffusion: the attempt to override boundaries between inner and outer, or self and other, rather than to maintain them. In their case, confabulation points to intellectual pretentiousness, as well as to their wish to lose distance and boundaries and to personalize the world into an extension of self. On the whole, the non-Jewish radicals seemed deployed along the obsessional-paranoid continuum, whereas the Jewish radicals presented a collage of neurotic and borderline styles, ranging from hysteria to character disorder and hypomania. There were one or two classically paranoid individuals among them, but these were far outweighed by the representatives of more diffuse pathological styles. In this respect, the Jewish radicals differed but little, in style or degree, from the moderate students.

The formal Rorschach scores, then, appear to support and enrich our previous analysis. The non-Jewish radicals seem to have utilized the movement as an opportunity to lessen the tensions produced by a painful ambivalence toward power and authority. For them, opposition to the bourgeois establishment could fulfill and legitimize their needs for increased control of the internal and external environment. To paraphrase Erik Erikson's comment on authoritarian idealism, they could feel justified in being hard on others to the extent that they were hard on themselves.

On the other hand, the Jewish radicals we interviewed apparently desired continual expansion of self, rather than closure against undesired and feared aspects of self. Their radicalism seemed experiential rather than ideological, the product of diffuse alienation rather than a closed Weltanschauung.

In sum, the non-Jewish radicals appeared to be involved in an internal struggle that they mapped onto the world. Their wish to submit was projected outward, and the pride that fights against that submission was conserved for the self. With the Jewish radicals, the struggle was less internalized. Their primary conflict was not between conflicting aspects of themselves but between a self that was centered on narcissistic claims and a world that refutes those claims.

Our research was guided by a search for personality patterns that transcended the boundaries of individual psyches. Yet each of the thirty-six students we interviewed was in many ways unique. It is partly for this reason that we decided to describe several of our respondents in greater detail. There is another reason too. One great danger of research into personality and politics is its tendency to give the impression that the individuals studied are the only ones who respond to reality partly on the basis of unconscious or irrational motives. Our analysis may seem to suggest that radical students were the only ones adopting ideological stances as a way of dealing with personal problems. Our point is rather that all patterns of adjustment to the world involve some integration of essentially primitive elements. By showing how these operate in political moderates as well as radicals, we hope to counter a bias that pervades many psychoanalytically oriented studies of social movements.

In the following detailed studies of three Jewish radicals, two non-Jewish radicals, and two moderates, we have attempted to choose relatively typical representatives of our various groups. We have tried to illustrate the various ways in which all world-views are related to patterns of adaptation (or non-adaptation). We have been careful to select some radicals who, by any standards, are reasonably healthy, as well as nonradicals who suffer from reasonably severe disabilities. The names given to our respondents are fictitious. The people themselves, and their styles of personality and politics, are very real.

THREE JEWISH RADICALS

CARL: Going Underground

Carl eased himself into the chair for his interview. He was neatly dressed in shorts and sandals, and though he had a full beard, his hair was cut short. He was willing to be interviewed because he could use the money, but he didn't think that either the tests or the interviews would prove anything.

During the tests he tried to appear cooperative but kept his head turned well away from the microphone. As the tests progressed, he became more and more anxious. He also yawned frequently. At their conclusion, he told the interviewer that he was glad they were over, that they had been tedious, and that he didn't like having to "look for things that aren't there."

The interviews were another matter. Although he never became animated, Carl was interested and anxious to talk about himself and his life.

Carl was twenty-three years old. He had graduated the previous June from an eastern university and had been unemployed for several months. He really didn't know what he wanted to do with his life. He liked movies and photography but had no deep interest in any career. In the meantime he had gone "underground" and joined a revolutionary organization. He was quite proud of this action because the organization contained working-class people, unlike the SDS, with which he had been affiliated during his college days. On the other hand, he was somewhat frightened of some of the men in the group, whom he found quite violent. Indeed, their presence made him feel very ambivalent about the group. Nonetheless, he felt that violence was sometimes necessary, and revolution was unavoidable.

Carl's conversion to a revolutionary stance was rather gradual. He went to the 1968 Democratic national convention a "semi-radical," was disgusted by what happened there, and became involved with SDS. He was also strongly influenced by his political science professors. The key experience, however, was his junior year of college abroad. He felt rather disorganized the whole time he was in Europe and gradually found himself moving toward a revolutionary Marxist stance. When he came back to the United States, he participated in a number of demonstrations and became affiliated with several radical organizations. However, he never did anything really violent.

While talking about his political views, Carl's language was peppered with radical slogans: "The cops are the military arm of the capitalist state"; "Sexism and racism stem from capitalism"; and so forth. He portrayed the future as an anarchist socialist society in which the family ("the most oppressive structure in the modern world") was eliminated and men and women were equal. Children would be "free" and cared for in special centers.

Carl was aware that he was an angry person who, in the past, had not asserted himself as much as he wished. Now, he said, "I don't take any shit from anyone for anything any more" but admitted to handling his aggression by refusing to get involved and avoiding situations where *individual* aggression (as opposed to being part of a demonstration) would be necessary. He still found it almost impossible to speak before radical groups. Although the members of his group called each other "comrade," he admitted that he felt no deep attachment to anyone. He expressed a desire to spend his life traveling and seeing people.

Carl was not sure why he became a radical. His parents had been radicals in their younger days and were still quite liberal. They had no objections to Carl's present political stance beyond prudential ones. Both held fairly high-level positions in the Department of Health, Education & Welfare, where his mother earned more than his father.

He thought that his Jewishness might have something to do with his radicalism. He no longer identified as a Jew, for his upbringing had been completely secular. On the other hand, he noted that Jews did tend to be intellectuals, and "intellectuals are drawn to radicalism." He had read Keniston's *Young Radicals* and agreed that youthful dissidents were carrying out the ideals of their parents.

His discussion of his parents and his childhood was peculiarly flat. The family was one in which very little warmth was expressed. He described his parents as neither hostile nor emotionally close. His mother was the controlling person in the family and obviously the most salient person in his life. He had very little to do with his father, "who always gives in; never puts up a fight." On the other hand, his mother always seemed to criticize him and his two younger brothers. He could never seem to please her, no matter what he did. He no longer felt very close to her and had sort of drifted away. He was once close to the political science teacher who helped convert him to radicalism, but he had also turned out to be a "weakling" when the crunch came.

Carl was born with a serious physical defect. He was blind in one eye and had a serious operation when he was eight years old. He remembered feeling shy and anxious about this as a child and always felt like an "outcast." His childhood left a residue of self-disgust, and he had few good relationships with his peers. Nor did he ever have a close relationship with a woman. He had met a girl in Europe, but their relationship ended when he returned to the United States. He had also been somewhat interested in a girl in this country, but nothing came of that relationship either. At the moment he really had no one. He seemed to feel defensive about his failure to establish heterosexual bonds, and told the interviewer that professional revolutionary activity was incompatible with the kind of close relationships that women demanded.

Carl's Rorschach and TAT responses were almost a caricature of an obsessional character structure. There was evidence of great anxiety and even more of depression, as well as a tendency to regress to very primitive levels of psychological functioning. Carl was uncertain about his own mental processes and afraid of his thoughts and feelings. His personal relations appeared to be distant and impoverished. He found it difficult to see individuals as full human beings or to separate them from his fantasies.

The tests did not indicate any great capacity to generate direct hostility, but they did reveal a good deal of covert negativism and a feeling of being fated to suffer. Part of this had to do with Carl's inability to deal with his own aggressive impulses.

The tests also indicated Carl's yearning to surrender himself to something larger than himself, which would control him. At the same time, his self-image was rather grandiose, and part of him felt able to control things by thinking about them. He used a good deal of defensive projection and revealed a tendency to read extra meaning into things.

Hardly any benign figures with whom he could identify appeared in his TAT stories. Women were seen as damaging and having excessive expectations. Overall, a sense emerged that Carl regarded his fate as residing not in his own hands but rather in some force outside himself, which directly controlled his life. Yet he was still somewhat involved in attempts to preserve his autonomy. The TAT stories confirmed his view of himself as an outcast with the need to establish a negative identity.

On the Rorschach, Carl segregated things that most respondents see as wholes. He stayed with small details and described the edges of the inkblots, offering simple descriptions of the outlines without organizing his percepts into a meaningful pattern. He clung to the trivial, the neutral, the repetitive, and the familiar, thus reducing emotional stimuli to proportions he could manage and minimizing their impact upon him. The TAT stories mirrored this pattern. Almost all his characters were emotionally fragmented, distant, and uninvolved. He described people who were not bothered, scared, stunned, traumatized, or shocked by anything. In his stories, activity was reduced to a minimum, and movement was suspended. It was almost as if the world itself were paralyzed.

Card 1 of the TAT provides a good example of some of these themes. Carl responded in part:

> I don't know, perhaps he was bawled out by his teacher or mother or something. Something to do with his violin playing, I presume. I should say, you know, he did something wrong and got bawled out for it. He is very discouraged, as I said before. He is looking at the instrument. It looks like he is thinking he never wants to play it again. He looks pretty young to be playing that kind of instrument, also. He will probably go through something like this a number of times, I would think, as far as being very discouraged about playing. He has probably got a lot of pressure on him, also, to play, and he probably doesn't want to be there in the first place. Whether he will enjoy playing or quit playing in the end I can't say.

On card 2, the wandering theme so common to our radical Jewish respondents was very evident, but, again, Carl's overall approach to the TAT also came through:

> The girl with the books is on the left of the picture. She seems to be just wandering around and somehow came into the scene, where she looks very out of place. I don't know if she was wandering. She also doesn't look very happy. She was walking around this field, this situation with the horse, perhaps the family is doing some planting. She doesn't appear to be thinking about the situation she is in. Her mind appears to be somewhere else. She is just staring out into space and not looking at the other two figures. She will continue walking on and sort of wandering in a half dazed state. She does not appear to be focussed; her eyes don't seem to be focussed on anything. She looks very sad, like she just received some bad news that something bad had happened that was surprising. She looks very much removed from the rest of the picture.
>
> I think she will continue wandering on, go home, and be depressed, at least for a day or two, because she looks as if she is really in a bad state.

The feeling of sadness and martyrdom that suffused both these stories appeared even more sharply on card 6BM. Notice also how emotionally flat the persons in the story are:

> There are two figures in the picture, one a young man and, I would say, his mother. Perhaps they are at a funeral. They both have very concerned looks on their faces and look somewhat disappointed. Let's say that his father, or her husband, died. It probably happened only a couple of days ago. This is still somewhat of a shock, but not an instantaneous shock. What they are doing is probably looking at the body just before it is going to be buried. Maybe they are thinking about him and his life and how their lives related to him. I guess after they leave the room, the body will be buried and they will complete the funeral. They will go back to their lives, whatever that might be.

On card 12M, Carl's passivity and sense of being controlled by larger forces were indicated quite clearly, along with his desire for masochistic surrender:

> This is some kind of horror movie. The guy lying down with his eyes closed is being hypnotized by the older gentleman. The older guy

has a movie showing a number of people being hypnotized by this guy. He is trying some kind of experiment on these people, not only to hypnotize them, but to get them to be under his direction at all times. . . . He is thinking that things are going well, and the other guy's unconscious so he can't really think. He'll succeed in his kind of hypnotism of this guy and he's got some wild schemes to create some kind of monsters or robots whatever. . . . They'll put him into some kind of power position on an international scale, and I think he'll fail.

Carl's response to card 10 illustrates his sense of drift and accompanying desperation and depression. These themes seemed closely tied to an inability to relate to his family:

I get the feeling it's a couple who live in an isolated area. They appear pretty elderly, in maybe their fifties or sixties. I think they heard some bad news, perhaps about their son, who had an auto accident and died. I think they loved him a great deal . . . I guess they cared a great deal for their son and even though their lives weren't connected on a day-to-day basis, they still really cared about and wanted to be connected in his life as part of their lives. And now they're old, and they're wondering. . . . Doesn't appear to be too much more to get really excited about and live for. . . . They'll continue living [and] I guess become even more isolated because they've lost touch with their son.

Carl's sexuality focused primarily on oral or incorporative themes. His tendency to regress to primitive modes of thought was quite evident from his response to card 13f. He stated that the man and woman in the picture have just had sexual intercourse, and continued:

The woman is an alcoholic. He appears about to leave but he is taking his time leaving. He is not rushed. There is nothing sudden or unexpected. Even though they slept together, they don't feel very close emotionally. They are not even looking at each other. So he has got all this emotional situation, which is very heavy for him. She is feeling quite removed, too, and discouraged because she has been through this whole situation before with a number of men and it is nothing new. It is ending the same way as it always has in the past.

He will go back to his job. I don't think it will affect him that much—just an aberration from his normal life. But she will continue to drink. She is quite well off. I get the feeling that they are very lonely and they will commit suicide in a couple of years.

I must be in a bad mood today for some reason. I have the same kind of theme in all these stories.

Two more examples will suffice. In both, the central characters were detached from existence and frightened or depressed. The theme of purposelessness also emerged, as did that of being subject to forces to which one must submit.

On card 17BM Carl described the man's mental state as follows:

> I guess he is in the middle of his performance, and he is concentrating on it because . . . that is his profession and he is skilled at it, but he is not totally involved in it. It is not an all-encompassing thing, you know. In five or 10 minutes, when he is finished, he will be thinking about something else. . . . He appears to be staring out at the crowd. I guess anyone in this kind of profession travels a lot, and he is very removed from most of the people in the act. I guess he will keep on traveling and doing this for a couple more years.

And card 18BM evoked the following story:

> He is threatened with being beaten up and he would like to resist, but he is outnumbered. . . . He has no chance and the man behind him is just holding him to make sure he doesn't get away. . . . He wants to resist but he knows he can't. He is just really hoping it will come out o.k., because his fate doesn't appear to be in his hands.

Carl didn't think his fate was in his own hands either. He always felt himself to be an outcast, a wanderer who could not even understand what his mother wanted. He defended himself against her by continuing to drift. Yet he longed to be overcome by someone or something that would end his loneliness and depression and restore that "Garden of Eden of faint memory."

CLETE: NOBODY KNOWS MY NAME

Clete was a sophomore at a prestigious university at the time of his interview. He was one of two radicals who never told us his real name. Given his suspiciousness, it is hard to know why he was willing to participate in the study at all. He came to both the testing sessions and the interviews rather sloppily dressed in blue jeans and a torn shirt, though he was always neatly groomed.

When the Rorschach was administered, he spoke only the minimal amount required, in a voice so quiet that it was difficult to hear him at all. For most of the test situation he seemed anxious, depressed, and sullen.

When the tester assured him that the results were confidential and noted that she didn't know his name, he responded, "Nobody knows my name." "Nobody?" the interviewer asked. "Nobody," he repeated decisively, "Nobody!"

Clete was very unhappy with the university he was attending. He felt that it lacked opportunity or meaning for him. He had come to learn how to learn, he said, but there were too many scientists there, and the whole institution was basically quite irrelevant. He had no particular plans and didn't know where he was going.

He had been a member of SDS but dropped out because he saw no chance for revolution until the advent of a real depression. He felt closest to the Progressive Labor group, because it took a "real" revolutionary stance. Clete agreed with PL that the economic structure of the society must be fundamentally changed in order to create a decent world.

Clete's parents were upper-middle-class professionals. His father was a lawyer and a professor at a major law school. Both parents were fairly radical, and he himself "had been pretty radical from the time he had become politically conscious." During the interview Clete denied that he felt any religious identity. His parents were secular humanists who did not think of themselves as being Jewish. He specifically denied that his Jewish background was of any importance and said he lacked any sense of affiliation with his family or with the larger ethnic community into which he had been born.

His first major political activity was to lead a strike at the very liberal "elite" independent school to which his parents sent him, because they considered the schools on Manhattan's Upper West Side to be "so bad." His parents supported him in his strike effort, although they expressed some concern about both his personal safety and his future career.

Clete described his mother as a temperamental woman who was difficult to please. His father was more passive and offered little discipline while Clete was growing up, except on those few occasions when he lost his temper. Clete claimed to be proud of both parents, describing them admiringly as "very smart."

Clete clearly wished to keep the interviewer at a distance and to offer as little information as possible on the projective tests. Nonetheless, a fairly clear picture emerged of key aspects of his personality. There was, for example, strong evidence of his difficulties in interpersonal relationships, including an inability to understand the motivations of others or to empathize with them.

His Rorschach and TAT responses showed considerable impulsivity, difficulty in controlling hostile feelings, and a chilling blandness with regard to aggression. Additional themes included a preoccupation with masculinity and "macho" behavior. It also became clear that Clete had internalized high performance expectations with which he was very uncomfortable. Partly as a result, he felt that his fate was sealed.

More particularly, Clete's TAT stories indicated that he felt cut off from both his own emotional life and that of others. He tried to deal with this by rationalizing, but underneath a self-assured front lay a feeling of rootlessness. He was thus something of an orphan in the world. His stories revealed themes of wandering, barrenness, and a longing to recapture a "lost" infantile union which was deeply regressive and tied to self-destructive impulses.

Neither of Clete's parents really existed for him as models. He saw his mother as emotionally inaccessible and absorbed in her own preoccupations, as someone who never recognized her son's needs, much less attempted to meet them. He pictured her as blind to the rage he directed against her, which was reflected in his fantasies of criminal activity.

Clete succeeded in externalizing his inner-affective state, projecting both his anger and emptiness out onto the social world. People became mere symbols of these affects, and his scornful and intolerant descriptions of them reflected sadistic feelings which were ultimately turned against himself. The lives of those in his TAT stories almost invariably ended badly, revealing a great deal of depression on their author's part. On the surface, Clete's radicalism seemed to fulfill his wish for power and control over others. Underneath this wish, however, one sensed a suspicion of people's motives, which he perceived as always uncertain. Thus his desire for control was a protective device. Clete tried to act out hostility against people in the world who did not support him. Given his basic personality, though, it seemed unlikely that he would ever become an active revolutionary.

Clete's story for TAT card 1 provided an excellent example of many of these themes. It captured his peculiar combination of desires for both omnipotence and self-destruction:

> Young Joe is preparing to write a piece for the solo violin. . . . He must keep up with the various aspects of life which everyone else has to keep up with, and right now Joe is thinking about chucking this particular work, wishing that he could. Perhaps he will take up the violin and play it for a while and forget about writing the music. He will not compose anything for five or six years and after that time he will compose a work which will receive mixed reviews and will not be

acclaimed as a masterpiece although he is seen as a promising young worker.

He will, at about the age of fifteen or sixteen, feel some disgust with his work and feel pretty defiant and will give up the violin and decide to end his days as a construction worker, achieving the rank of foreman on a high rise in midtown Manhattan on the still uncompleted thirty-second floor of which he will fall, at the age of twenty-eight, to his death.

Earlier in this chapter we quoted Clete's story for card 2, which had the same "bad ending," combining a wandering theme with a sense of loss, even to the title of the book (*Paradise Lost*) that the young girl in the story was carrying. Clete's response to card 6BM, also cited earlier, offered examples of both a "negative identity" and wandering imagery, but added a clear sense of his sadism, his bland indifference to people, and his hostility toward his mother. These same themes were repeated again and again in his stories. For example, the story he created for card 7BF dealt with a young drug addict and his unsuspecting mother:

Teenage drug addiction is rather [inaudible] sort of thing, and young Oscar here from the small town of Terre Haute, Indiana, seems to be about to let himself get caught up in it. . . . He's done his first skin popping in the year 1967 and was first introduced to it at a baseball game. . . . He's not mainlining, just popping under the skin, but Oscar has now come down from his blissful dream and is confronting his mother who has seen the marks on his arms and asked him what it was. Oscar rolled down the sleeves of his shirt and his mother naturally has no idea about what he was doing. His mother does not suspect any evil on the part of her son and so she accepts whatever answer he gives. Oscar will search out a man who gives him smack and dabble with that again, not understanding that it could lead to dependency. Eventually, he will begin to realize that perhaps it could be a harmful thing. However, he also realizes that there is a great deal of money to be made in it. He will waylay a man one night in the Ghetto area of Gary, Indiana, and find himself a connection with someone rolling in dope.

His story to card 8BM ended with: "His wife will eventually leave him and go back east, and Marvin will lead a solitary life in the woods." In card 17BM the protagonist of the story pursued and married a prostitute, but "she doesn't respond. For many years of his life he will be alone." And card 18BM ended in a crescendo of violence:

He'll strike out at this man and he has him in the sights of his high-powered rifle, and he'll shoot him in the head with a bullet. Arnie will gun down the man who let the contract out on him. He hopes no one hears the shots. However, he will be betrayed by another informer, and this other guy will collect. They will have flowers sent to Arnie's funeral.

ARNOLD: THE WAY BACK HOME

One more Jewish radical is worth at least a brief discussion because of both his experiences and his partial self-awareness.

Arnold was an open homosexual and a member of "Gay Jewish Liberation." His Rorschach was full of themes dealing with masochistic surrender, and his TAT combined the themes of flight from his mother, wandering, and negative identity. Card 5 elicited the following story:

It's a woman out in Great Neck or Scarsdale, and they've got some money, but she's really worried about her son because she knows he's been looking funny recently and looks like he might be taking junk. So here it is late at night and she's peering into the living room. She's really sort of scared and she wants to see if her son is taking junk. After all her son is bright, he has been doing well in school and should wind up going to Columbia or something like that or Brandeis. But what's really gonna happen is her son is taking junk and he's gonna leave home and hitch to New York and hitch to San Francisco and I don't know what's gonna become of him but his mother is gonna be very freaked out.

Arnold was raised by lower-middle-class parents in Brooklyn. For most of his life, his relationship with them was extraordinarily hostile. More recently, however, he was able to establish what he saw as a good relationship with his mother. She was not happy about his homosexuality, but she had learned to accept it.

When Arnold was growing up, his neighborhood was changing as blacks began to move in:

I grew up in —— which was Jewish and was becoming black and Spanish, and my mother was terrified of violence. I was terrified of violence—scared shitless of violence and I never knew how to deal with it.

Despite their lack of money, his parents scraped together sufficient funds to send him to Columbia University. He wanted to go for a number of reasons, one of which was to escape his Jewish environment:

> I suppose there was a thing in my head about not wanting to be with the same kind of people I went to high school with, and there would be some new kind of people there who were not, I suppose, petty bourgeois and who could be cultured.
> Well, I think . . . I was trying to get away from the Jewishness of —— and into a cultured world. I probably saw that as not Jewish.

Columbia, however, was a disappointment. Most of his friends turned out to be Jewish. He was intimidated by the Christians there and hated them at the same time.

> Well, you know, I came from a lower middle class family and at Columbia there were all these very good looking blond boys from prep school, with tweed jackets, who had the ability to make contact with women.

It seemed to him that all the Jewish girls were looking for "WASP" males. He "compensated by becoming an aggressive intellectual," and then a radical intellectual. He admitted that his hatred of the WASPs led first to his fantasies about a possible mass revolutionary movement at Columbia and then to his participation. He also described the "energy coming from the black community" as contributing to his radicalization. Finally, he recognized that his actions (and those of others like him) had something to do with his Jewishness but still did not quite understand the mechanisms involved:

> Of course you know I compensated for it in a typically Jewish way, I think, by being super brilliant and intellectually aggressive. I was miserably unhappy and a lot of the way moved to pour out the tremendous hatred of society by becoming a revolutionary.
> . . . this dream of a mass movement at Columbia that would actually move enough people to disrupt that class [i.e., the WASPs] was, like, something that had been in my mind for a long time.
> . . . my activity in the civil rights movement was maybe less in terms of a genuine love, say, for black people at that time than with some kind of identification with the white people who were disaffected from white society.

He was very convinced that the student rebellion could not have occurred at Columbia if there had not been so many Jews there (though he exaggerated their number):

> Let me put it this way—it's clear that Columbia couldn't have happened if Columbia men were traditional WASPs. It only happened because it became 80 percent Jewish and the Jews were susceptible to energy coming from the black community and the war in Vietnam.

Although he denied his Jewishness at the time, Arnold now felt that it played a key role in his own radicalization, as well as that of most other Jewish radicals at Columbia:

> [Of course] we did not move self-consciously as Jews—did not say we were Jews—because we didn't know that, we weren't able to do that. We were still having to rebel against a lot of repressed aspects of being Jews. I don't know, but I suppose at this point a lot of the movement on the east coast is still Jewish, but mostly doesn't want to see that some of the reason for what it is, is because it is Jewish. It denies [these] feelings, but I think it has [them].

After graduating from Columbia, Arnold went to a midwestern university to work toward a master's degree. There he became involved with the Weathermen and participated in the Chicago "Days of Rage." He was arrested and placed on probation. As to the Weathermen, he was convinced that

> a lot of the Weathermen leadership was Jewish and had never been tough street kids, and I really believe that a tremendous amount of what they were doing was overcoming their own fears about their masculinity, by taking on . . . male standards. Most of them . . . had been intellectually aggressive, but all of a sudden they were trying to be tough street kids. . . . I think there was a lot of self-hatred going on. . . .

The "Days of Rage" marked a turning point in Arnold's life. He had been heterosexual, but found sex increasingly painful. Somehow the experience of violence convinced him that his desire to be "hyper-macho" was a front, and that he really wanted to be soft. In any event, soon thereafter he turned to both heavy drug use and homosexuality.

Despite Arnold's feeling that this change of sexual identity solved his emotional problems, both his Rorschach and TAT responses indicated high levels of pathology. The themes expressed were very similar to those of Carl, Clete, and several other Jewish radicals, though perhaps somewhat more intense.

At the time of the interview, Arnold was working sporadically and participating in radical politics. However, he was careful to emphasize that he didn't necessarily trust most "goyish" revolutionary movements. The "goyim" still had it in for the Jews, he claimed, and the "straights" still had it in for people like himself. He was convinced (and this was the only time in the interview that he showed any anger) that in the end the straights would "have to be taken care of," if a peaceful world were to emerge.

TWO NON-JEWISH RADICALS

The non-Jewish radicals we interviewed and tested presented a marked contrast to radicals of Jewish background. The wandering theme and flight from the mother were largely absent, as was the emphasis on machismo. Rather the dominant themes, even among our more healthy subjects, revolved around conflict with a punitive but flawed father whose "weapons" the son desired to obtain for himself.

BILL: The Revolution Will Never Come

Bill had been a junior at a prestigious university until he dropped out (temporarily) to devote his full time to politics. He had since been elected to a minor political office in the community where the university was located.

The initial impression of both the interviewer and the testers was of a warm, engaging, busily involved young man. Bill was neatly dressed in a studiously casual work-shirt-and-jeans style and sported a well-groomed mustache. He seemed very young and very well scrubbed. Both the testing and the interviews fascinated him, and he took an obvious pleasure in producing and describing his responses to the tests. During the testing he took off on a number of wild tangents, in an obvious attempt to impress the interviewers and to assure himself that he occupied center stage—although the tangents were not fully under his control.

The same pattern occurred in the interviews. Again and again Bill worked himself into a frenzy of excitement as he described his life. He would then grin sheepishly and tell the interviewer that he really enjoyed his own rhetoric, which he called his "crazy thing." In our last interview he expressed a certain fear of having gone too far, asking what it was that most people saw on the Rorschach and expressing the hope that he could get some "professional" feedback.

Both the interviews and the tests revealed a heavily conflicted young man with a great deal of dependency and depression, which he dealt with by denial, hyper-activity, and projection. Both clinicians who independently examined his protocol classified him as a borderline personality.

Bill talked first and at length about his current political involvement. He found politics very exciting and had thoughts of becoming a "pro" at it. At the same time he was not sure that "the game was worth the candle," for the great majority of Americans were not radical, and he saw little hope for a revolution in his lifetime. He had no immediate plans to run for office again. Instead, he really wanted to spend some years traveling but thought he would probably finish college and go to law school.

Bill had been born into a Catholic family and grew up in a rather affluent neighborhood. This had always been a source of humiliation to him, because his father was only a skilled blue-collar worker. From the time he was very young, he felt that his father was a "nothing" compared to the professional people who constituted the bulk of the neighborhood population. He expressed considerable anger at his father for this reason, and was quite aware of his feelings. He was also angry at his father for being very "authoritarian" and abusing both him and his mother. His father had been ashamed of him because he was poor in sports and had a speech impediment. Indeed, his father had tried to shame him out of his difficulty by insulting him. On the other hand, Bill expressed some sympathy toward his mother, who (he said) hated his father as much as he did, although she never did stand up to him.

His overt rebellion against his father started quite early. He could remember arguing with his father about religion (Bill broke with the Church in early adolescence) and about black people. He described his father as a racist, and father and son had locked horns often over this issue. Bill admitted, though, that he provoked these arguments not so much out of his outrage at injustice as from a desire to demonstrate his independence.

Early in adolescence Bill became interested in politics. His first hero was President Kennedy, but as the decade wore on he became increasingly radicalized and moved from one group to another. By the time he entered high school, he was a convinced socialist and "revolutionary." Although he supported "reformist" actions such as the grape boycott and the McCarthy president, campaign, he felt much more radical than most others involved in those groups.

Once in college his radicalism escalated still further. He became involved in a rent strike and organized students on campus to disrupt the ROTC and to press for "student power." He considered himself an anarchist, joined SDS, and eventually became a Weatherman. He was "busted" by the police several times and was involved in some violent activity, which both excited and frightened him.

Since being elected to office, he found that he could speak well. He felt that his voice gave him the power to obstruct meetings and to convince people to think the way he did. He described his tactics, especially the disruptive ones, with considerable glee.

His radical political activity took up most of his time. He was never very close to any woman but claimed to be very active sexually. He felt friendly toward some girls but found it hard to get romantically involved with them. Sometimes he feared that he was really a homosexual (he confided hesitantly), but he had no active homosexual experiences. On the other hand, he experimented widely with drugs. During his college career he had tried psilocybin, marijuana, LSD, and cocaine. He admitted that he took such drugs because he got lonely and depressed about the world. And his loneliness and depression were related to his political views. In his own eyes, he was a victim of the structure of the society, a society that needed a revolution. But the revolution would never come, he felt, at least not in his lifetime.

Card 1 of the TAT conveyed a sense of Bill's perceptions of his parents and his own future.

He has just come home from school and is staring at the violin because he is supposed to practice now. Yet the violin represents the fact that his parents don't care for him. . . . He will eventually start practicing and go through a few hours. Then he will go up to his room and start to cry. His parents think they love the boy a great deal, but they do not perceive what the boy is going through in terms of what he feels about them and the violin.

As he grows up he will continue to practice and play the violin and be quite good and will continue to grow further and further away from his parents. He will be very independent of them from an early age on. He won't become a violinist, but he will play very well. He will resent his parents, but they will be so busy they will never realize this. . . . He will be a very independent person in terms of not trusting and not wanting to be at all dependent on other people, and he will have to overcome that and what his parents have done to him if he is to be a happy person. I do not know if he will succeed or not in that.

The same theme can be found in TAT picture 2. Bill clearly saw his parents as totally unsupportive in his early years. He remained torn between a desire to rebel against them and a longing for them.

On the TAT as well as in his interviews, Bill's father played a central role.

Earlier we quoted his response to card 7BM, in which his father was seen as deeply flawed. In card 8BM his rage toward his father was even more clearly revealed, as was his desire to seize his father's "weapon" and to win his mother. In his story, a son and father are hunting, and the father is showing the son how to use a gun to shoot deer:

> They go off in the woods together and the father kept repeating the instructions. The deer came; the father shot it once and was going to shoot it again, but the son used his supernatural powers and made the gun backfire, getting the father in the gut.
>
> Here we are a couple of hours after the accident. The father will die, and the boy won't be charged with anything because it was an accident; and he and his mother will live alone together.

Bill's response to card 17BM gives a clear picture of his exhibitionism and, even more importantly, of his underlying depression and fatalism:

> He's a middle-aged acrobat who is practicing. He has been a mediocre acrobat for 20 years and knows that he does not have much time left. He is looking at some younger acrobats practicing and realizes that they are doing things that he was never able to do and will never be able to do. He is just sorry he is so old and will have to find something else to do and doesn't know what to do. The question is whether he will quit the circus before he is told he has to. He is sensitive enough to know this. He knows this is his last season. He never got married, so he will be lost with nothing to do. He never made much money. He has no other skills, so he will become an alcoholic and work as a janitor and live out the rest of his life alone.

Throughout his description of his life and on his psychological tests, there was no evidence that Bill saw people as capable of working together or having a positive regard for each other, although he longed for these things. He had no sense that life could be gratifying and really did not expect either satisfaction or success. He used activity as a way of avoiding depression but viewed the world as a place where people were out to do him in. He saw most relationships in terms of domination and submission, and he constantly needed to devalue authority.

His negative identity was designed to punish his parents, and he ridiculed society and felt ridiculed by it, even though the result was just what he feared— a sense of humiliation and of being abandoned.

Bill relied heavily upon hypomanic activity, as well as projection and denial, to deal with underlying depression and dependency. He saw his parents as the source for all the bad things that happened to him in his lifetime, and he projected his own problems with his family onto political ideas and conflicts. Thus he attempted to deal with his inner impulses by projecting their causes onto the outside world. He saw people in general, and himself in particular, as having been dehumanized by impersonal forces. He denied and caricatured his father's authority and projected his relationship with his father onto all authority figures. Nevertheless, he identified with his father and wanted to turn his father's (fantasized) power against him, so as to control the father with his own weapons.

Finally, Bill had a strong sadistic streak. To be sure, he identified with the underdogs and worked hard to correct the evils that he thought society inflicted upon them. At the same time, he had nothing but contempt for those he was supposedly serving. Indeed, the contemplation of their "suffering" gratified his sadistic impulses.

CLIFF: A VERY MEANINGFUL EXPERIENCE

Cliff was a 27-year-old graduate student in history at a large university. He was a slim young man of about average height and long, flowing hair. During his tests he was friendly and cooperative, although occasionally a little anxious. The pattern was the same during the interviews. He was always lucid, fairly dramatic, and quite intense. He had a strong sense of his own intellectual superiority, which was only partly concealed by a deferential pose.

Cliff came from an Irish-Catholic family. His grandfather had immigrated to America and found a job as a railroad worker. His father taught English in a military academy. He described his father as an authoritarian, but with a sentimental side that had revealed itself only occasionally. His father was far more liberal than his fellow teachers at the academy, something Cliff had not realized until he developed some political awareness. He saw his mother as a long-suffering, rather depressed woman. In general he felt that his parents had lived reasonably successful but dull lives.

Cliff, the youngest of four children, was the only radical in the family. He saw his life as rather uneventful during his early school years, though he felt that his parents had pushed him so hard that he had sometimes cheated to obtain good grades. In school he related reasonably well to boys of his own age. He regarded himself as physically unattractive to girls, however, and was uncomfortable with them. Later, in college, he was surprised to find that some

women did regard him as attractive. He was flattered by their admiration but
had not established close relations with anyone in particular.

Cliff first became involved in activist politics as a senior in college. Until
then he had simply been a hard-working student. He had good (though not
close) relations with a number of people, from which he derived considerable
satisfaction. Then he participated in a sit-in over such student demands as open
enrollment and representation on faculty committees.

The sit-in, he said, was a mild affair compared with the one at Columbia.
The students took ashtrays with them and were careful not to trash the offices.
But the president of the college was a "reactionary," and Cliff developed an
enormous hostility to him. In any event, he was ultimately forced to leave the
college. He spent the next year organizing, supported by various radical groups
and the American Civil Liberties Union, and then moved to a state university.
There, having been radicalized by his recent experiences, he became a leader
of the local SDS chapter and saw the student movement grow by leaps and
bounds.

Cliff got into trouble again after an altercation with Dow Chemical Company recruiters, along with numerous other conflicts. He finally left school after
what he called the "orgasm" that followed the Cambodian incursion. After
another year spent in radical activities that he did not specify, he decided to
come east and enter graduate school. Since then he had remained somewhat
involved in organizing and politics, but far less than in the past, in part because
the Movement "sort of died away."

To Cliff, politics was a matter of power. Political issues were basically
economic at their source, and the economic power of capitalism could only be
overturned by force. Present society was both sick and hypocritical.

In his view the "New Left" represented a distinct advance over the Old,
which had been too rigid and disciplined. Further, the Old Left had failed to
be concerned with such issues as sexism and racism and, most importantly,
personal growth. For all these reasons it had become "regressive."

Joining the New Left had "put it all together" for him. He enjoyed talking
before large crowds and swaying them. He claimed to have radicalized 1,000
students on a campus of 6,000, and the issues he raised had gotten to the state
legislature. Looking back, he felt that the activism of that period was the high
point of his life. He admitted to very ambivalent attitudes about authority.
Whenever he saw a policeman, he became enraged. He emphasized, however,
that this was not the reason he became a radical. He was responding to real
conditions rather than psychological needs.

He was not sure now that he wanted to complete his Ph.D. This would be
"capitulating" to the system. He was getting older, however, and decisions
were being forced upon him.

Cliff clearly enjoyed the expression of aggression, and his attitude toward it was quite romantic. Indeed, a kind of romantic glow suffused his fantasy life in general. Responses to two of the TAT cards illustrate this nicely.

He told the following story to card 17BM:

> This is Douglas Fairbanks, Jr., who had an incredible body and played the Thief of Bagdad. He was very good. This is definitely the guy. At one point he jumps off the porch and is escaping his would-be captors. He had stolen a lot of things. I do not know where it was, but I think he is trying to get away with something to eat or he was caught stealing. Anyway he jumps off the balcony and sails through the air on this rope and jumps on the other end. It could also be Jimmy Cliff going down the side of the precipice when the Jamaican narcotic agents are after him. . . . It is a small man who is able to use his smallness because he is compact. And he is successful whether he is a thief, a circus performer, or a drug dealer. In this case he is going to successfully lose his captors or successfully make it from one trapeze to another, and he is going on to thrill the world of Bagdad or Jamaica with his further exploits.

Card 18BM evoked the following story:

> This is Brendan Behan, apprehended by the law; the nameless and faceless law has apprehended him again. He's brilliant, physically unattractive, yet incredibly attractive as a person. Right now the immediate future for him is the drunk tank. In fact, that's the whole future for Brendan Behan. But he has something to say on his way to it which is important. He is about to make some comments on the background of the police officers arresting him . . . and on the cowardliness of those who called the cops on him. He had begun to write one afternoon and became pissed off at the way he was writing, so he headed for his favorite bar. He has been drinking for four hours. He is not an unhappy man. He is going to be dead pretty soon but he's not unhappy.

On the other hand, Cliff found the world of books and intellectual activity rather unappealing. Hence his ambivalence with regard to the possibilities of an academic life. For example, card 13MF:

> This man is a student and he cannot bear to face the books that are on his desk. His wife is sleeping, and life is a struggle for him because she is always indolent and lolling around in bed when he has got to face those books that are sitting there opposite him. While his wife is asleep, doing nothing, leaving him with responsibilities for the more distant

future, he struggles his way through graduate school. . . . But he has this incredible frustration about these books and the need to build up his will to meet them. He will sit down there pretty soon and begin to examine them.

Ultimately his fifth book is not well received, so he eventually accommodates himself to life at a medium-rate university. . . . And he eventually begins to like to read . . . it is not as painful for him anymore.

Cliff, then, was a romantic. He wanted to do bold things—to break away from routine. He was the soldier of fortune, the con man, the hero. Though the 1960s focused these aspirations on student rebellion, in another epoch he might have chosen a number of other causes.

Why was he this kind of person? It is impossible to say with any certainty. We could detect ambivalence and hostility toward his father, along with unresolved Oedipal feelings. These feelings came through clearly in two of the TAT cards. For example, he told the following story to card 8BM:

The boy is on the operating table. . . . What lies in his future is death, not by the bullet wound, which was severe, but the inability of the surgeon who is going to operate on him. You see the surgeon as grotesque versus the adolescent boy. . . . And what is causing the trouble is just his inefficiency, the inefficiency of being a poor medical practitioner. He might have been hurt in the war by the bullet wound, but they are going to kill him on the operating room table. The doctor is just a bit drunk.

And card 7BF was a straight seduction scene:

This is the attempted seduction of a too-young boy in a drawing room by a woman of thirty-five. He is simply too young, and she will try to seduce him, even though he's thirteen. Right now he is extremely uncomfortable. He was sent over there by his mother to pick up some clothing, but the woman has kept him around and has asked him if he wanted anything to drink. She is lustful. He is just incredibly uncomfortable.

And so Cliff was at loose ends, awaiting renewed opportunities for high adventure and aggressive action; for new occasions when he could defy authority and remake the world, with all the excitement that entails—a world in which

Douglas Fairbanks lives forever, meeting and overcoming challenge after challenge.

TWO MODERATES

As we emphasized earlier, a danger inherent in the psychological study of politics (especially when dealing with adolescents) is the tendency to give the impression that only those people under investigation are driven by unconscious or irrational motives. This was not true of our respondents. A number of our nonradicals had obvious and severe emotional problems and were just as activated by needs of which they were unaware as were the radicals. We have included a detailed description of two nonradical subjects, one of whom was a fairly rigid conformist.

RALPH: The Importance of Being Normal

Ralph was a twenty-one-year-old senior at a prestigious university. He was interviewed three times, and on each occasion he arrived exactly on time. He was casually and neatly dressed in blue jeans, with longish hair that was neatly combed. During the last interview he seemed particularly nervous and admitted that he felt that way because he was going to take the projective tests. He said that he had agreed to the whole procedure because he hoped to use the situation to improve himself, but now he was not so sure. During the administration of the projective tests he said little aside from his formal responses and tried to seem very businesslike. However, his hands trembled whenever he used them to point something out on the Rorschach cards. He left as soon as he completed the tests.

Ralph planned to go to medical school and was in a "pre-med" program. He said he enjoyed all his subjects, including organic chemistry, which had a campus-wide reputation of being "extremely tough."

His own portrait was that of a rather privileged, conventionally liberal young man of upper-class Protestant background, although somewhat snobbish. He had attended private schools almost all his life and was a member of a very exclusive club at his university.

He regarded himself as a liberal democrat (with a small d), defending the importance of free speech, equality for women and blacks, and reforms designed to improve the society so that everyone could live harmoniously with everyone else. His picture of the nation's future was optimistic and reassuring. Politics was not very important to him, but he felt that the political system could handle current problems and saw little need to change it. As to his own future, he was confident that medicine was a good solid profession and that he would be successful at it.

Ralph felt that he related fairly well to his parents but said relatively little about them. Although he noted that he was an only child, and that his parents had married when his father was forty and his mother thirty-eight, he regarded these facts as trivial in terms of his own development. He portrayed his father as rather uninteresting, but quickly added that he and his father were close and had spent a good deal of time together when he was young. He mentioned only one issue from his early adolescence. When he was about thirteen, his father gave him a lecture on the "facts of life." Ralph described it as embarrassing, stilted, and uninformative. He seemed very conflicted about sex, although he claimed to have slept with a number of women. In fact, his discussion of his sexual activity led almost immediately to discussions of guilt feelings he "used to have" about masturbation and his occasional use of drugs (LSD, mescaline, and marijuana). He had tried them at a time when he was very bored with school. His guilt about that activity seemed particularly strong, however, and he still felt ashamed.

Ralph had always done well but not brilliantly in school. He was sometimes depressed, he said, but mostly felt satisfaction about the place he was finding for himself in society. In general his social, academic, and family life seemed rather well organized, but there was little overt evidence of great interest or enthusiasm for anything in particular.

Ralph reported several dreams, which had occurred between interviews, and which could not be fully analyzed, given the nature of the interview situation. Together with his responses to the projective tests, however, they gave some indication of his inner life. In one of the dreams, he related:

> I was walking down a country road and came upon a barn where there were knives hanging from the ceiling. I was afraid that they might all come down and hurt me, so I knocked them down with a pole to be safe. Then my parents were somehow with me and another man, who was evil. I followed him outside and he magically destroyed the engine of my car and left it a smoking hole. I threw an axe at him, but it just grazed him and he smiled at me rather patiently.

This dream, which was probably a response to the interview and testing situation, revealed a good deal of anxiety, with feelings of guilt and shame as major preoccupations. In general, Ralph felt an insurmountable heaviness and oppression in relation to external requirements, which he saw as mainly imposed by his mother. His TAT stories, for example, frequently dealt with moral transgressions that forever tarnish a person who had previously been an exemplar of upright behavior. The stories also described people who felt defeated and resigned to defeat as a result of guilt. Thus it seemed clear that most of Ralph's aggression was turned inward, with the exception of some anger directed against his mother. His father posed too great a threat for Ralph to permit his hostility to surface.

In some ways Ralph portrayed classical Oedipal fixations. Since his father was seen as a very powerful and potentially castrating male, his own feelings of helplessness were defensively exaggerated. His strong need to conform, then, was designed to protect himself from unconscious sources of guilt, fear, and shame. The ability to conform enabled him to keep these in check, for the most part, and his work and relationships with others indicated a reasonably high level of ego strength.

Ralph's response to card 1 of the TAT illustrated some of these themes, especially his depression and his anger at his mother, whom he saw as forcing him to renounce play:

This is a young boy who spent much of the afternoon playing outside with his friends. He had a very good afternoon, having a lot of fun, probably playing some sort of game, like hide-and-seek or tag, in which he was very good. . . . He is also taking violin lessons, which he doesn't want to take, but which his mother is making him take, and he is right at the point where he is having the most fun and everything was working well, when his mother came to the back door and said that he had to come in and play the violin. At this point, he said he couldn't come in because he was playing, and she said that he *had* to come in, and they had a little spat. She just happened to yell louder than he did, so he had to go in. When he got into the house, they were still arguing. He was sort of complaining and whining because he knew eventually he'd have to do it no matter what he said. His mother was so upset she almost threw the violin at him, so he went and sat down at first and was very uncooperative. He just sort of made bad noises and strange things because he didn't really want to play and just wanted to irritate his mother. Eventually, he realized he had to play, so he did a little bit of practice the way you are supposed to, and his mother left the room. He played a little longer, and finally put down the violin—not in a rage, but in a very dejected mood because he was forced to do this, and he sat there and looked at what he was doing, and he left the violin. . . .

Later this afternoon he will go through his exercises and finish them
and then his mother will come in and say he's been a good boy, and
he'll say he was sorry, and then he'll go out and play, and the whole
thing will be over.

Ralph's Oedipal disappointment, along with his turn to intellectual pursuits
in an attempt to sublimate and discipline his feelings, came out fairly clearly
in his response to card 2, despite the reversal of sex roles. He told the following story:

There are three characters in this, and the woman on the right is
obviously pregnant. What probably happened is that the girl who is in
the foreground . . . was a very good friend in childhood with the man
in the picture and, as time went on, sort of fell in love with him . . .
he just took her for granted and it never got to be anything physical.
She was just very much in love with him, whereas he was still a friend,
and they just went around together all the time, but he didn't really love
her in that sense at all and didn't even realize that she loved him. . . .
They grew up and he met this other woman and fell in love with her,
and they got married, and now she is pregnant. . . . The first woman
has books in her hands and is dressed in a sort of chaste—I mean,
almost Spartan manner—and she has resigned herself to studying and
being kind of intellectual and only going out on dates and that sort of
thing. She has sort of spurned men in general because of this one rejection, and she is looking off into the distance, feeling sort of sorry. . . .
This has been her one big love affair and it's flopped and she either just
will grow into an old spinster gracefully or if she sees something like
this happen again she might take the big step and go into a convent or
something and completely shut herself off from the possibility of anything like this happening again.

The issue, however, had not been completely settled. Ralph was forced to
defend himself against an inner rage that constantly threatened to burst out. He
seemed capable of doing this under most circumstances, but this very need to
control his rage drove him even further into a conformist posture. In this way
he was very similar to some of the traditional authoritarians described by Adorno
and Wilkinson. He was a "failed rebel" whose life was only half lived.

Ralph was continually anxious about the possibility of his rebellious urges
breaking through and interpreted this as a fear that he would not be able to
meet the expectations of those in authority. Yet there were compensations. His
fantasy life was less threatening than that of many young non-Jewish radicals.
His fantasies were full of themes that involved being misled or punished by

older men. The fantasies of the radical students, on the other hand, almost invariably ended in self-destruction. Ralph's life was dominated by anxiety. Many of our radical subjects, on the other hand, were always fighting potentially severe depressions.

Ralph's fears about his own aggression and its consequences were illustrated nicely by the story he told to card 6BM:

This is a mother and her son, and what has happened is that her son has just done a terrible thing. He was working at a job which he didn't enjoy at all, was very unhappy about it, and the night before, after he left work, he was just very bored, feeling very dull, and got into trouble. He's a pretty intelligent guy, a nice guy, very popular, sweet sort of fellow, but he just was thoroughly disgusted when he left work, and he went to a bar and started drinking. He had a few drinks and was talking to a couple of fellows, and one drink led to another. Actually, they got quite drunk, and the subject of politics came up. The guy who was sitting next to him had completely opposite views to his and they began to argue. The bartender broke them up and told them to go outside and not come back. They couldn't buy any more drinks then, so they went outside and got into a fight. This man here had a physical fight, and this guy hurt the other man quite badly, because he hit him and knocked him down, and the other guy hit his head on the curb when he fell. He's in the hospital, and they don't know whether he'll live or die.

This man was picked up by the police shortly after, of course, and was arrested for drinking, public disorder, drunkenness and assault and, you know, along with the things that he did. He has always been a very upstanding man, a very nice guy, had never done anything wrong before, and he is dressed very conservatively. His hair is neatly combed; he looks like a normal guy, but he has to come back and tell his mother this. The police are standing a few feet off, but you can't quite see them. She is quite upset at this point, and he has told her, but she hasn't quite realized the full impact of the story. . . . He is just completely consumed by shame; he knows what a terrible thing he has done, what a complete waste he's made of everything he's done to this point. . . . In the future, he will go on trial and a lot of friends will come and testify for him, but the other guy will not die—he will recover—so they will let him off because the judge realizes that he will get a suspended sentence and that things just got too much for him, that it was an exceptional incident, and he is really not a hard core criminal at all. The incident will be wiped out and there will be no repercussions with his mother or anyone. It will be just a sort of blot on his life that's there,

but he doesn't have to worry anymore, so things will turn out all right
in the end.

Other TAT stories involved larceny, grave-robbing, and other crimes but
were structurally similar to the story recounted above. Themes of heterosexual
situations leading to problems and violence popped up frequently in the stories,
although somehow things rarely ended in complete disaster. There were also
numerous stories of old men who dupe, exploit, or blackmail younger men.

The meaning of the dream reported earlier, which occurred after Ralph's
first interview, now begins to make sense, especially in the light of two other
recurrent dreams he reported. In the first, he and a friend were driving in a car.
They arrived at an intersection, at which a man was trying to fix a stoplight.
They decided to make a U-turn to avoid the stoplight. Although they waved at
the man (or at friends on the sidelines), they were not recognized. In the second
dream Ralph was driving down a strange street when he suddenly came upon
a field of tall grass. There were huge birds in the fields, owls the size of cows,
and they moved very slowly. In the dream, Ralph saw the birds and noted that
they were owls, but the scene did not strike him as very strange.

These dreams had a common theme expressed by "not coming up to a
stoplight" or "not having the things move very much." Everything was under
control, except in the one case when the interviewer seemed to be probing too
deeply. Then Ralph's rage came to the surface, and he struck out at the interviewer to defend himself against what might be revealed.

Ralph, in short, was conventional because he had to be. Rather than explore
his own violent urges, he preferred to stick to the rules, because only then
could he hope to control himself. But the control adds up to a very constricted
if "normal" personality.

DON: INTIMACY AND IDENTITY

Don was a senior history major at a prestigous university. His father was a
wealthy New York stockbroker of German-Jewish extraction, and the family
never really lacked for the good things of life. He was sent to "progressive"
private schools as a child, where his "creativity" was always appreciated. His
Jewishness didn't seem a particular problem to him. He accepted it without
being strongly committed.

He was not exactly glib in his interview, but he exhibited considerable
facility in discussing any topic that emerged. He was always in control of both
himself and, to a certain extent, the interviewer. He spoke well, seemed gen-

erally aware of his feelings, and was quite convincing in the way he presented himself. His speech reflected his well-educated cosmopolitan intellectual outlook, but he also seemed very sincere in his feelings about social and political events. His performance when being tested was rather similar. He seemed a bit more agitated than he had during the interviews, moving about and shifting in his seat, but he kept his attention on the tests and obviously enjoyed talking and being listened to. After the tests had been completed, he asked questions about them, in an obvious effort to get some feedback as to what they told the interviewer about him.

Don's discussion of his family was rather ordinary. He was not terribly close to his father, though they had a "loving" relationship. He felt that his parents were quite satisfied with each other and had grown closer as the years passed. He especially admired his mother's ability to change and find new meanings in life as her children grew older. She was clearly very important to him, and he felt that she had profoundly influenced his life.

As the interview proceeded, Don admitted that he was rather cynical about having been admitted to the university he was attending. He really didn't have that much respect for himself. His confidence was largely a pose, he said, and he would have felt better had he worked harder for his achievements. He described himself as rather anxious and then discussed at length his current relationship with a young woman, with whom he had been living for about a year. He described their relationship as a warm and good one with no real difficulties. The problem was that he didn't know where to go with it. He had given some thought to marriage, but part of him felt that he wasn't ready to spend the rest of his life with this person. He didn't want to be tied down.

For one thing, he hadn't really "found himself." He had not made a solid career choice and wanted to take a year off after graduation as a ski instructor at Aspen. He was seeking this "moratorium," he said, because he felt he was being propelled faster than he wanted to go. He was at least partially aware of inhibitions that were preventing him from doing everything that he really wanted to do.

The psychological tests confirmed the creativity and intelligence of this young man. They also confirmed his partial "disengagement" from life. He clearly had not settled upon an identity and enjoyed taking on a variety of roles ("playing tricks"), provided he did not push things too far. For example, although his questionnaire and his interview marked him as a young person of moderate to liberal views, he came to his interview dressed in clothes that were clearly designed to impress the interviewer with his nonconformity, i.e., a plaid shirt, coveralls, boots and a "Mao style" jacket.

The "trickster" element was apparent in his stories as well. In a number of them he seemed merely to be playing a role. Nevertheless, he was clearly preoccupied with the problem of developing an appropriate identity and a concomitant life style. He was afraid to commit himself, both for fear of having to prove that he really was what he seemed to be, and from a reluctance to give up "alternative identities." His TAT stories suggested anxiety over closeness with women, whom he tended to view as castrating. They also suggested that talking and intellectualizing often served as a way of avoiding taking on what he conceived as a masculine role. Many of these anxieties seemed to have an Oedipal source. He was unable, even in fantasy, to allow himself to really enjoy intimacy with his family.

His response to card 1 demonstrated his creativity, his ability to express his feelings, and his general enjoyment of life.

It's a boy thinking about what he could be doing. He just got this violin as a present. The wrapping paper is beneath it, and he is staring at the violin and thinking about many things—that there are tiny people inside it and this is a Trojan violin; and he is thinking about space ships and either making this into a space ship or would rather be building something than playing the violin. He is a very curious boy and is wondering about what to do with the violin. If he learns to play it and never forgets his first thoughts, he will always be trying to express his feelings through the use of it. He goes through life with an enjoyable pastime and continues to enjoy the violin.

His description of card 2 revolved around another theme: the romance (in fantasy) of living close by his mother after his father dies. However, he could only enjoy the fantasy in a rather unemotional way.

This is a family—mother, daughter, and son—who have gotten to a place which is in a remote part of the country, but they have managed to arrange their lives, buildings and grounds to make it as they like. . . . He [the son] is very satisfied with his life, doing exactly what he wants. Mother seems to be looking out over the farm and thinking about her life. She is also satisfied with what she is doing. Her husband died several years ago, and she continues to work and enjoy life as a person. She was never dependent on her husband for life or enjoyment. She is looking very pleased with herself. . . . They seem happy enough to manage whatever goes on. They will be smiling with self-satisfaction, none of them looking at each other, indicating that they are a team, but they are individuals, too.

His Oedipal fantasies also emerged clearly in card 7BF:

> This is the grocery boy coming to deliver to this young lady. She has gotten him to sit with her on this chair . . . the lady is dressed in a low-cut bathrobe with the nightgown underneath it, giving him a strange smile. He seems unhappy, unsure what to do. This lady is known as the local "weirdo." She is opening a desk drawer and showing him strange little objects, little skeletons, just toys, but most peculiar. There are marbles, ashtrays, and other things. The boy is completely freaked and runs out without asking for a tip. He never forgets this woman and for years after wonders what would have happened if he had stayed around.

Almost as if he felt he had gone too far in revealing his own fantasies to himself, many of Don's later responses reverted to themes of play, and magic and magicians. Life can be fun, he seemed to be saying, if one doesn't take anything too seriously.

Card 12M showed him to be a magical, merry prankster who enjoyed life with his frivolous jokes.

> The magician is waving his hand over the boy's head, and it is not raising the boy into the air, but raising the magician's knee and heel into the air. He is now standing like a cane. Next thing, the boy waves his hand in the air and the man's other leg slowly comes to the same position so the man appears to be kneeling in air. The boy waves his hand some more and the man spins around; still he's trying to be the magician and control what's going on. The magician asks the boy how he did it and the boy says it's all done with strings. The lights come on and the magician turns out to be a cardboard man and the boy is a ventriloquist who had a partner pulling strings in the rafters. After this, the boy is famous as the grand magical merry prankster.

He repeated essentially the same theme in card 17BM, where he saw the man on the rope as

> the great circus rope dancer. He climbs up to the top of the rope and he is upside down, waltzes down the rope and then he takes out a big scissors and cuts the rope down below, and the audience is amazed. Now, how is he going to get down? He clicks his fingers and the upper part of the rope folds down and over and he slides down. It turns out that he had the rope attached to two points by nearly invisible wire, and

he comes down and the audience applauds and he laughs and he goes off to the dressing room to prepare for another show.

So Don did have problems with intimacy and with defining himself, as well as with his sexual identity. All these issues seemed related to unresolved Oedipal problems. On the other hand, he displayed great ego strength. He could develop warm relationships with other people, and he could both work and play effectively.

We noted earlier that projective tests, especially when given to adolescents, tend to overstress primitive elements and psychological problems. Don's problems were not particularly serious for a young person; indeed, his adjustment seemed good. He was, in short, a reasonably successful and fairly well-integrated college student. Whether he took his moratorium or not, he should be able to cope better than most with normal life problems in a world which, after all, is not a rose garden.

Viewed from a psychoanalytic perspective, human existence is a combination of comic, dramatic, ironic, and tragic elements.[7] No human being is ever free of internal conflicts; nor is any human behavior entirely "rational." To be healthy is merely to cope reasonably effectively: to be able to love, work and play. Our respondents varied widely in their ability to deal with life's problems. But all of us, under the clinician's eye, would exhibit a good deal of primitiveness in our personality makeup.

With this caveat in mind, let us summarize some of our clinical findings, while adding a few additional details on some other young people who were part of our study.

Of the four groups of students we interviewed, the non-Jewish moderates were perhaps the most diverse. The personality of one resembled that of the Jewish radicals. This young man had secretly disengaged himself from his mother, whom he experienced as quite overbearing. While accepting her ambitions, he turned them to his own uses, which were more idiocentric and rather more selfish. As with most of our Jewish radicals, however, he was still engaged in a flight from his mother. Another non-Jewish moderate, by contrast, resembled a number of the non-Jewish radicals in feeling pulled toward a life of political dedication. However, his personality was so rarefied as to preclude involvement in contemporary events. He saw himself as superior to all social conventions. In fact he was simply too asocial to join a real movement of any kind.

Two other moderate non-Jews were too closely tied to conservative fathers to break ranks with their values. Others were too anxious about being liked by other people to join a struggling radical movement. A triumphant radicalism, however, would find them among its cadres on the basis of these same mechanisms.

These young men were followers of convention—almost any convention. All four of these non-Jewish moderates, however, had attained reasonable levels of adjustment. At least two others were too emotionally disturbed to be able to focus on the outside world. Their energies were totally invested in coping with internal demands.

The Jewish nonradicals were a more homogeneous group. They were universally more liberal than their non-Jewish counterparts. Indeed, four of them considered themselves as "left liberals." All four experienced competitive rivalries with their fathers, which somewhat inhibited the full development of their masculinity, and they idealized and deprecated their fathers at the same time. None of them could quite bring himself to step outside the bounds of liberal thought and action. To be radical (i.e., to rebel against their essentially liberal fathers) was seen as taking unfair advantage, and as a kind of patricidal acting out of impulse. These four cases were the clearest ones involving classical Oedipal conflicts in our entire sample.

Perhaps more importantly, all our Jewish nonradical subjects seemed to have difficulty breaking with their mothers and would feel guilty about abandoning them even psychologically. They felt strong needs to maintain family traditions, one of which was to be helpful, caring, and responsible toward one's mother (as well as, by extension, toward other members of the family).

One Jewish moderate was quite conflicted over this issue. He perceived his mother as overbearing and overprotective and had a strong wish to adopt a negative identity as a means of flight. The pull of family ties prevailed, however.

Finally, at least two Jewish moderates were fairly disturbed individuals. Both were quite depressed and had difficulty with their impulses. Arthur was an impulsive, promiscuous personality with many perverse tendencies. David was quite the opposite; he scrupulously defended himself against his impulses by adopting obsessive rituals. Neither would search out radical orientations, partly because Arthur had resolved his problems through sports, and David through religion.

Radicalism during the 1960s thus had quite different meanings for the Jews and non-Jews we studied. Within the Jewish group, the psychological correlates of radicalism were clearly defined. Among the non-Jews the meaning varied somewhat, depending on ability, talent, and psychological assets or liabilities. Some of the non-Jewish radicals we studied had fairly good ego strength and organizing capacity. This was certainly true of Cliff, despite his sadism, as well as of another young man, Walter, who had taken positions of leadership.

On the other hand, a few of the non-Jewish radicals had little capacity to cope with reality. Chuck, our most radical non-Jewish respondent, spent much of his young life on drugs in an attempt to cope with his own defective self-image. He was essentially an unfeeling, mechanical person, whose massive aggressive needs were channeled into an image of himself as a misfit. When we interviewed him, he was about to drop out of school. It seemed likely that he would someday slip into antisocial behavior that goes beyond the bounds that can be justified by any ideology.

Many of the radical non-Jews seemed to be in overt rebellion against their fathers, while adopting most of the same personality configurations. This was not universally true, however. Nick, for example, felt that he was following in his father's footsteps. His basic rebellion seemed to be against his mother's conservatism, and he identified with an aggrandized image of his father. Like a number of our non-Jewish radicals, he wanted a political career and planned to go to law school. Unlike most of the others, though, Nick remained closely involved with his family.

Cliff, too, was not exactly a rebel. Rather, he seemed to be carrying his father's liberalism one step further and adopted as his own one element (the sentimental side) in his father's personality. Nevertheless, in his romantic way, he seemed every bit as authoritarian as his father was.

The most radical Jewish respondents resembled each other closely, particularly in their global anti-authority orientation. There was, however, a second, rather less radical Jewish group. They were less enamored than the first with the rhetoric of revolution and had been followers rather than active leaders in the Movement. Most were looking forward to becoming part of an "Establishment" but insisted that they join on their terms. Most seemed to sense that their radicalism would not provide a permanent framework for their lives, and at least one was already in psychotherapy.

For example, Steve was the son of a judge and planned to to go law school. He expected that his parents' authority and position would entitle him to special treatment. Steve's radicalism served him as a kind of "moratorium" before he settled down to a more conventional liberal position.

Nevertheless, with one or two exceptions, the Jewish radicals did share a sense of exile and other features that are likely to inhibit personal development, whether they are swept along on a new wave of radicalism or opt for a more conventional life style, accepting the "System." Indeed, many of them felt "fated" to take a road that would ultimately prove self-destructive.

Do these themes really reflect the underlying personality dynamics of these radicals or have we but measured the personal consequences of their increasing despair at the possibility of meaningful change? Alternatively, by this time the student movement might have recruited many people who did not share the characteristics of the New Left's first generation. Conceivably our results might reflect both factors.

Although there are no easy answers to these questions, we think our own conclusions best explain our findings. Let us take first the objection that our tests measured the impact of events upon personality rather than vice versa. This interpretation might explain the high power scores of radicals, and possibly their ambivalence toward power. It can not explain their propensity toward narcissistic pathologies, their lack of affiliative concerns, or their Semantic Differential potency scores. Nor can it explain their family relations, which, according to psychoanalytic theory, should result in just the personality patterns we found. Further, the hypothesis that events shaped radicals' personalities cannot explain why our two radical groups differed along certain key dimensions. Why should the same events have yielded different psychological results for Jews and non-Jews?

In an effort to test the argument that involvement in the radical movement (and consequent despair) explained the scores received by respondents, we compared those who had been active for only a short time with those who were long-time participants. We found no statistically reliable differences between the two groups.

Finally, our clinical findings replicated our survey findings almost precisely. It is difficult to believe that the Rorschach responses of these young people merely mirrored their relatively limited involvement in radical politics. After all, most were full-time students, not professional political organizers.

The objection that our results captured the personality dynamics of latecomers to the movement rather than of the more idealistic early cadres is less easily met by our data. Some of our evidence, though, does bear on this question. For example, a number of our subjects were graduate students who had been involved in radical activity since the late 1960s. We found no personality differences between them and their younger radical colleagues. Further, the major change in the movement's demographic composition was the shift away from Jewish predominance. There is little reason to suspect that the young Jewish radicals we studied in the early 1970s were very different from those who became involved earlier. Nevertheless, as a more powerful test, we decided to trace the radicals who had been active during the Movement's early stages and administer the same questionnaire to them. The results of that research form the subject matter of our next chapter.

Finally, although their frustration over the Movement's lack of success does not necessarily explain the personalities or activity of these young people, one cannot ignore the role of the external environment in directing personality and behavioral tendencies. For example, these youths might have dealt with their problems in very different ways if they had matured several years earlier.

In his study of working-class adult males in New Haven during the 1950s, Robert Lane discovered that poor relations with parents, especially fathers, did not lead to political rebellion.[8] Lane's work was completed during a period when the cultural and political authority of the system had not come under challenge. What would Bill have been like under such circumstances? He might never have rebelled against his father without the supports provided by the culture of the 1960s. Even if he had, the rebellion probably would not have taken a political direction. It is also quite unlikely that he would have become involved in a drug culture.

Cliff, too, might have taken another direction. The military could have provided an outlet for his romanticism, as part of an anti-communist crusade, or he might have followed in his father's footsteps. As for Arnold, had he grown up in his hometown of New York during the 1950s, he might simply have entered therapy in an attempt to deal with the ambivalence of his sexual orientation. If not, he most probably would have kept his homosexuality a secret as best he could.

Would Ralph have needed to maintain such rigid defenses in a calmer political period? We doubt it. We suspect that the very disorder he found about him was one of the dynamic elements in this rigidity. Don might still have been involved in a search for identity. On the other hand, the cultural milieu of an earlier period might have structured it for him more easily.

Of course, all this is highly speculative. We have no way of knowing what these young people would have been like at another time. We are persuaded that their internal balance would have been different, but we do not know in what ways, and we certainly cannot be sure that they would have been happier.

8 Radical Adults: The Adversary Culture

WE UNDERTOOK OUR STUDIES during the last days of the student movement, when many young radicals seriously debated the efficacy of guerrilla warfare as a political alternative. Many of these militant dissenters were still in grammar school when Newfield's "prophetic minority" emerged out of the ruins of the Old Left to call for a new radicalism dedicated to existential and humanist ideals. It is possible that the first generation of New Leftists, the generation of the *Port Huron Statement,* the freedom rides, and the Berkeley uprising, was quite different from the radical youth of the highly polarized and ideologized early 1970s. We also wished to determine the extent to which Americans of Jewish background constituted the leading edge of the New Left during its early days.

To confront these questions directly, we decided to interview individuals who had been prominent New Left activists and intellectuals during the early and middle 1960s. We constructed a list of names from such sources as Sale's history of SDS,[1] Black's *Radical Lawyers,*[2] and radical journals like *Liberation, Dissent, The Nation,* and the *New York Review of Books.* In addition, we reviewed articles on the New Left that appeared in the New York *Times* from 1964 to 1968. Individuals who were cited in three or more articles as New Left spokesmen or identified as long-time Movement organizers, writers, and so on, were added to the listing. The total list numbered 290 names. Owing to financial limitations, we could interview only people living in the metropolitan areas of Boston, New York, Washington, D.C., Chicago, and San Francisco. Within these geographic boundaries, 165 subjects could be located, 57 percent of the original list. Of this group 121 agreed to be interviewed, a response rate of 73 percent. Interviewers administered a questionnaire containing many of the instruments from our research on college students, including the New Left Ideology scale, Parent-Child Questionnaire, and TAT. Insofar as we could determine, those we contacted were demographically representative of our overall list, including the proportion who were of Jewish background.

The interviews were conducted over a period of several months during 1974 and 1975. At that time, the average age of the group was forty-one. Most were in their twenties or early thirties at the onset of their involvement with New Left causes. At that time many were graduate students or young professionals just beginning careers as academics, lawyers, and journalists. A few were older leftists long identified with radical politics.

As a result of their social and political involvement, many went on to become household names. Among them were leading figures in SDS, the Resistance, the Yippies, civil rights and antiwar organizing groups, and the alternative or "underground" press. Many have remained in the public eye as radical scholars at universities and policy institutes, advocates for public interest groups, and writers and journalists. Several became identified with feminist issues or the woman's movement, although the group was predominantly male. Of the 121 early New Leftists interviewed, only 18, or 15 percent, were women.

The group had retained its leftist perspective. Almost 90 percent called themselves "radical," including 35 percent who specified that they were "revolutionary radicals." These self-descriptions translated into genuinely radical views across a broad spectrum of social and political attitudes. On the New Left Ideology scale, their mean score was 5.25, compared to only 2.96 for the nonradicals.

These early New Leftists thus form the cutting edge of what Lionel Trilling termed an adversary culture, whose values and perspectives are antithetical to the traditions and orientations of Middle America.[3] Their outlook was widely held to be rooted in a fundamentally new mode of consciousness, which was hailed by radical critics like Charles Reich and Theodore Roszak as a revolutionary cultural breakthrough.[4] Conservative intellectuals, by contrast, derided them as examples of an emerging new class, whose hostility toward traditional values and social institutions threatened the very fabric of capitalist democracy.[5]

Our strategy was to compare these radicals with people of roughly the same age and social status who represented the perspective of "Main Street." We could then determine whether these two groups really constituted two distinct cultures: the social psychological "lifeworlds" of traditional Middle America on one hand and an adversary culture on the other. Equally important, we could find out whether these two groups differed in the same ways that distinguished radical college students from nonradicals.

As a comparison group of nonradicals or "traditionals," we selected a sample of business and professional people active in community affairs in a small northeastern city. Their names were randomly selected from membership lists of nonpolitical civic service organizations such as the Kiwanis and Rotary Clubs,

Chamber of Commerce, and so forth. Out of the 110 subjects contacted, 106 (96 percent) consented to interviews. This group was slightly older than the radical adults, averaging forty-seven years of age. It also contained a somewhat higher proportion of women—29 percent.

Our choice of a community to study was dictated by funding limitations. We cannot claim that it is representative of the American heartland. In addition, we found few extreme conservatives in our local sample. On the other hand, few if any had even flirted with radicalism during the 1960s. Most were relatively moderate in their politics. They were, however, the type of Middle Americans whom New Left writers had described as having all the negative personal and social characteristics against which the Left was rebelling.

We informed all subjects that we were engaged in a study of social change. We described our questionnaire in much the same terms as we had to our student subjects. Since this was a more sophisticated group, however, we hired interviewers who were more experienced in administering questionnaires. For our New York interviews we obtained the cooperation of the Bureau of Applied Social Research at Columbia University. In other parts of the country, colleagues and friends recommended experienced interviewers. None of the interviewers were told anything about the purposes of the study.

The social background characteristics that differentiated these two groups were almost identical to those that distinguished radical students from their more conservative schoolmates. The early New Leftists' families were financially well off, with highly educated parents who were often employed as professionals. Their parents were also predominantly nonreligious and politically liberal or leftist. In addition, their families were politically aware. As children, they recalled participating frequently in political discussions.

The most striking characteristic of this group, though, was its cohesive ethnic background. Using the same criteria employed in our study of students, 75 percent of these early New Leftists were classified as ethnic Jews, compared with only 10 percent of the "traditionals."

The political attitudes of our adult radicals differed hardly at all according to ethnicity. The Jews averaged 5.24 and non-Jews 5.26 on the New Left Ideology scale, a similarity echoed by their self-descriptions: 88 percent of the Jewish subjects and 90 percent of the non-Jews termed themselves radical, and the remainder liberal. Among the nonradical sample, by contrast, 27 percent called themselves liberal, 40 percent middle of the road, and 33 percent conservative.

Their common political stance aside, the two radical groups diverged on

almost every social characteristic we measured. Among the nonradicals, we
found no systematic differences between Jews and non-Jews. Further, the small
number of Jewish nonradicals prevented any meaningful evaluation of the causal
role of Jewish ethnicity.

On a purely descriptive level, however, we uncovered a pattern of systematic differences in the social backgrounds of the Jewish radicals, non-Jewish
radicals, and nonradicals. The social profile generally attributed to the entire
New Left instead applied primarily to its sizable Jewish component. On all
variables, the social and attitudinal differences were greatest between the Jewish radicals and the traditionals. The non-Jewish radical group usually fell
somewhere between the other two, and was by far the most socially heterogeneous. The complete data are tabulated in Appendix B, Tables 28–30.

Most radicals were either hostile or indifferent to religion, as one would
expect, while most nonradicals called themselves moderately religious. But a
surprising one in five non-Jewish radicals called themselves "deeply religious," twice the proportion found among the nonradicals. By contrast, fully
half the Jewish radicals expressed hostility toward religion, and only one person expressed deep religious convictions. The differences were apparently rooted
in childhood upbringings. The trends were similar for both parents, but the
groups were most clearly differentiated by their mothers' attitudes. One in seven
Jewish radicals described their mothers as hostile to religion, compared with
only 1 percent of their non-Jewish counterparts, and none of the nonradicals.
Similarly, over half the Jewish radicals regarded their mothers as indifferent
toward religion, compared with two fifths of the non-Jewish radicals and only
one in twelve nonradicals. At the other end of the scale, less than one in twenty
Jewish radicals described their mothers as deeply religious, compared with a
third of the non-Jewish radicals and almost half (45 percent) of the nonradicals.

To summarize, these early New Leftists grew up in far less religiously
oriented homes than did the nonradicals. But among the radicals, Jews were
much more likely than non-Jews to come from irreligious backgrounds. Two
thirds of the Jewish radicals described their mothers as hostile or indifferent
toward religion, compared with fewer than half the non-Jews. And a surprisingly large minority of non-Jewish radicals had deeply religious mothers, compared with a handful of the Jewish radicals.

These differences in home environments were reflected in radicals' current
religious feelings. Jewish radicals were overwhelmingly irreligious. Non-Jews
were somewhat less so, with a substantial minority maintaining deep religious
convictions. In fact, non-Jewish radicals were twice as likely as nonradicals
(21 percent vs. 10 percent) to call themselves deeply religious. In our student
study, we found that a secular family background was associated with radical-

ism only among Jewish subjects, suggesting that deracination, rather than secularism per se, was the key variable. Although the differences were less dramatic among early New Leftists, the results point in the same direction.

The three groups came from equally diverse political environments. Among the nonradicals, about half came from Republican households, two fifths from Democratic households, and only 1 percent from socialist homes. The remainder said their parents lacked any political affiliation. Non-Jewish radicals' parents were more likely to be Democrats, but not socialists. About half came from Democratic family backgrounds, slightly fewer than two fifths from Republican backgrounds, and none from socialist homes.

In sharp contrast to both, the Jewish radicals were actually more likely to come from socialist than from Republican families. About one in ten had socialist parents, another two thirds came from Democratic families, and fewer than one tenth were raised in Republican households. Thus the "Old Left" heritage of the radical group was limited entirely to its Jewish component. This is precisely what we found among radical students during the early 1970s. Among early as well as later New Leftists, many Jews were following in the footsteps of liberal or radical parents, while many non-Jews had drawn away from politically conservative parents.

This conclusion was reinforced by our subjects' depictions of their parents' ideological leanings. The nonradicals characterized their parents as predominantly conservative or moderate, while radicals were far more likely to grow up in liberal or leftist households. This leftward tendency was clearly strongest among the Jewish radicals. The non-Jews were drawn from the entire political spectrum.

Among the nonradicals, almost half rated their mothers as conservative, and another third as moderate. Just under one in ten placed their mothers on the extreme right, and about the same number viewed their mothers as politically liberal. Only a tiny minority (2 percent) placed their mothers on the radical left.

If the nonradicals were drawn from predominantly conservative backgrounds, the Jewish radicals were equally good representatives of a left-wing heritage. Three quarters called their mothers either liberal or radical, and one in six placed their mothers on the radical left. By contrast, only one in ten placed their mothers on the right side of the political spectrum.

Finally, the non-Jewish radicals were equally likely to place their mothers on the far left and far right, with 11 percent choosing each category. Another one in five termed their mothers conservative, and 30 percent selected the liberal category.

The ratings of fathers' ideology produced similar results, with one revealing exception. All three groups rated their fathers as somewhat more conservative than their mothers, but the difference was especially great among non-Jewish radicals. Over one quarter (27 percent) called their fathers extreme right-wingers, compared with one tenth of the Jewish radicals and the nonradicals alike.

On the whole, then, early New Leftists rated their parents as more liberal or leftist than did nonradical adults. But this apparently obvious finding conceals far more information than it reveals. Among the radicals, Jews were almost twice as likely to place their parents on the left as on the right, while non-Jews were three times as likely to come from conservative families. Thus, Jewish radicals were drawn primarily from liberal or radical families, non-Jewish radicals from families at both ends of the spectrum, and nonradicals from moderate or conservative households.

The three groups differed in the intensity as well as the direction of their early political experiences. Jewish radicals engaged in the most frequent political discussions with their parents, most nonradicals reported discussing politics only occasionally, and non-Jewish radicals were again a heterogeneous group. About a third of each radical group reported having frequent political discussions with their fathers, more than double the proportion of nonradicals. But non-Jewish radicals were also the group most likely *never* to have engaged their fathers in political discussion. One in four non-Jewish radicals could recall *no* politically oriented talks with their fathers, compared with one in five nonradicals, and one in seven Jewish radicals.

The two radical groups were more sharply differentiated with regard to their mothers. Jewish radicals were twice as likely as non-Jews (30 percent vs. 15 percent) to talk to their mothers frequently about politics. Among nonradicals, this figure dropped to 12 percent. Jewish radicals were thus the only group who discussed politics with their mothers as often as they did with their fathers. At the other end of the scale, non-Jewish radicals were again the group most likely to report no political discussion. Almost one in three (30 percent) never talked politics with their mothers, compared with one in four nonradicals.

What stands out from our data is the tendency of Jewish radicals to come from relatively politicized and leftist family backgrounds. Their families were distinguished by the presence of a politically liberal or radical mother who frequently discussed politics with her child. This pattern corresponds to the image of New Leftists conveyed by most studies of 1960s radicals. Once again, though, this image applied primarily to radicals with Jewish ethnic backgrounds.

More broadly, Jewish radicals and nonradicals came from quite different but equally homogeneous ideological milieus, while non-Jewish radicals were more heterogeneous. The nonradicals came from families that were religiously oriented, politically moderate, and moderately political. The Jewish radicals were raised in predominantly nonreligious or antireligious homes in which both parents were politically liberal or radical and likely to transmit these political views to their children. Finally, the non-Jewish radicals could not be neatly categorized. Sizable subgroups recalled nonreligious, leftist, and politically engaged home lives. On the other hand, substantial proportions reported religious, apolitical upbringings by highly conservative parents.

These differing ideological milieus correspond to differences in socioeconomic status. Because many writers and academics were included in the radical sample, one would expect them to come from relatively well-educated families. Indeed they did, relative to the nonradicals. The latter group reported that over half their fathers and two thirds of their mothers had no more than a high school education. Only 12 percent of their fathers and 1 percent of their mothers undertook graduate study.

Parents of radicals were much more likely to have pursued advanced degrees. As usual, though, the trend was considerably stronger among Jewish radicals. One in three Jewish radicals reported that their fathers undertook graduate studies, compared with one in five non-Jews. On the other hand, a substantial proportion of non-Jewish radicals' parents were high school dropouts. Thirty-six percent of their fathers failed to finish high school, twice the proportion among Jewish radicals (17 percent), and even higher than the 32 percent dropout rate among nonradicals' fathers. The proportional differences were essentially the same for their mothers.

Thus Jewish radicals were the group most likely to come from highly educated families and least likely to have relatively uneducated parents. Non-Jewish radicals, too, were more likely than nonradicals to come from highly educated families. But they were also the group most likely to have poorly educated parents. The percentage of Jewish radicals' fathers who entered graduate school was twice as great as the percentage who dropped out of high school. Among non-Jewish radicals, these proportions were reversed.

These differences in education were mirrored by those of economic status. Nonradicals tended to describe their family's economic level as average while they were growing up, whereas radicals in general were more likely to see their parents as well off. But while Jewish radicals were clustered at these two levels, two in five non-Jewish radicals rated their families as financially troubled.

Taken together, the data on parental education and finances suggest that Jewish radicals were drawn primarily from intellectually and economically privileged backgrounds, while non-Jewish radicals were drawn more heavily from the bottom of the status hierarchy. Both differed from the successful "middle Americans" we sampled, whose parents were more likely to be of average financial means, and to have some college education.

All three groups were about equally likely to report that their fathers were businessmen. But only 22 percent of the nonradicals had fathers who were professionals, compared with 30 percent of the non-Jewish radicals and 42 percent of the Jewish radicals. The nonradicals were most likely to come from working-class backgrounds, with almost one in three (31 percent) citing that category, as opposed to about one in five radicals (21 percent of the non-Jews and 18 percent of the Jews). The Jewish radicals were least likely to come from white-collar families, with fewer than one in ten citing that category, compared with one in five non-Jewish radicals and one in six nonradicals.

The status differences were even more apparent from mothers' occupations. Nonradicals' mothers were most likely to be housewives. Only one in five worked outside the home, less than half the proportion of radicals' mothers. Moreover, the mothers of Jewish radicals were sharply distinguished from the other two groups. Very few subjects had mothers who were either businesswomen or blue-collar workers. Therefore we separated working mothers into an upper-status group of businesswomen and professionals and a lower-status group of white- and blue-collar workers. Among both nonradicals and non-Jewish radicals, about three fifths of the working mothers fell into the lower-status category. In sharp contrast, four fifths of the Jewish radicals' working mothers were upper-status career women. Most of these were professionals; only a few were businesswomen.

The occupational data confirm our impression of the radical Jews' socioeconomic distinctiveness. They were most likely to come from well-off, highly educated, upper-middle-class households, with both parents pursuing careers in the professions. Radical non-Jews were much more likely to come from lower-status, poorly educated, financially troubled homes, in which the mother worked to bring in needed income rather than to pursue her own career aspirations. In addition, however, a sizable subgroup mirrored the upper-status origins of their Jewish counterparts.

To summarize, the social background usually associated with the early New Left proved most characteristic of Jewish radicals, who constituted a substantial majority of the original New Left leadership. The non-Jewish minority proved far more hetergeneous, often resembling the nonradicals. These differences replicated our findings among college students in the waning days of the student movement. Among both early and late New Leftists, a secular, politically liberal or leftist high-status background was associated with radicalism only among

Americans of Jewish background. It appears that the social and cultural homogeneity of the adversary culture mainly reflects the milieu of the deracinated American Jew.

We turn now from social background to childhood development, focusing on relations with parents and peers. To gain a sense of the stability of family life, we asked our subjects whether they had lived with both parents while growing up. Radicals were significantly less likely to have been raised by both parents. Only 8 percent of the nonradicals were raised by a single parent, a proportion that was doubled (16 percent) among Jewish radicals and trebled (24 percent) among non-Jewish radicals. In most cases, this situation resulted from divorce rather than from the death of a parent.

We also inquired about their families' geographic stability. Radicals were less firmly rooted in their communities. Eighteen percent of the Jews and a third of the non-Jews reported that they moved around a lot during childhood, compared with 12 percent of the nonradicals.

Male radicals tended to be problem children, getting into fights and creating disciplinary problems in school. Forty percent of the male Jewish radicals and 35 percent of their non-Jewish fellows reported having disciplinary difficulties, compared with only 10 percent of the nonradicals. Of course, the difficulties cited by radicals were sometimes linked to their political opinions or activities. Therefore our interviewers asked whether the problems mentioned had any reference to a political or ideological aspects. Even after deleting all politically inspired problems, radicals were still about two-and-one-half times as likely as nonradicals to report disciplinary problems (23 percent vs. 9 percent). Over half these difficulties concerned behavioral problems such as vandalism and other petty crimes. The other problems included truancy, academic trouble, and so on.

Radical males also tended to get involved in physical fights during childhood. Well over 40 percent of both radical groups reported fighting more than once or twice, compared with 30 percent of the nonradicals. The difference between groups was much greater for those involved in frequent fights (five or more). Only 4 percent of the nonradicals fell into this category, compared with 10 percent of the Jewish radicals and almost one in four (23 percent) non-Jewish radicals. This finding is quite similar to our results for college students.

Additional evidence of early aggressive tendencies was provided by asking what physical sports one engaged in as a youth. Non-Jewish radicals were significantly more likely than other groups to take part in dangerous contact sports such as tackle football, boxing, and ice hockey. One in five non-Jewish radicals played two or more such sports, compared with only one in twenty subjects among both the Jewish radicals and the traditionals.

We have seen that radicals, particularly the non-Jews, enjoyed less stable family lives than nonradicals and directed more aggressive and anti-social tendencies toward peers and school authorities. The most crucial element of radicals' early interpersonal relations, however, concerns the internal dynamics of their families.

Our evidence was gleaned from the Parent-Child Questionnaire. Most of the variation in parental images could be reduced to a few broad clusters, which were very similar to those that emerged from the student PCQ ratings.

The college students seemed to judge their parents in terms of five broad criteria: benevolence or caring; punitiveness; weakness; lenience or permissiveness; and intrusiveness. The adults produced almost precisely the same set of judgments, including clusters of adjectives representing all but the first (caring) dimension in their paternal ratings and all but the last (intrusion) in their maternal descriptions.[6]

One new PCQ dimension did emerge for both parents. It seemed to represent emotional distance, and was formed primarily from the adjectives "distant," "aloof," and "often apart." This single dimension accounted for almost half the total variation (44 percent) in all maternal PCQ ratings, and over one fourth the variation in paternal ratings.

We analyzed six dimensions: punitiveness; weakness; strictness; distance; intrusiveness (fathers only); and caring (mothers only). The ways in which the three groups depicted their parents on these dimensions are shown in Table 11.

The evaluative dimension, the most important in terms of variance explained, also proved most useful in differentiating among all three groups. Non-Jewish radicals held the most negative perceptions of their fathers but also the most positive maternal images. Jewish radicals held the most negative maternal perceptions and also somewhat negative paternal images. Only the nonradical group held relatively positive views of both parents.

Any inference that radical subjects might have been rebelling against traditional authoritarian families was belied by their perceptions of parental discipline. Both radical groups perceived their parents as relatively permissive, and Jewish radicals scored highest on both scales. These results suggest that the radicals' negative parental images did not simply represent an ideological rejection of one's parents as figures of authority. One would expect such rejection to extend to the "strictness" dimension, which included the judgment that a parent was "authoritarian." Nor was their parents' permissiveness part of a principled democratic style of child-rearing. Rather, the lack of strictness was

Table 11. Perceptions of Parents by Ethnicity and Ideology Among Adults.[a]

PCQ DIMENSIONS	Jewish Radicals	Non-Jewish Radicals	Traditionals	Level of Significance
Punitive				
Father	51.73	53.69	46.42	.001
Mother	52.31	46.82	49.10	.01
Weak				
Father	50.84	48.07	50.08	n.s.
Mother	49.21	51.01	49.66	n.s.
Strict				
Father	47.24	49.75	52.33	.001
Mother	45.50	46.80	53.61	.050
Distant				
Father	51.70	52.97	47.55	.001
Mother	50.68	50.54	49.24	n.s.
Intrusive				
Father	52.70	49.20	47.80	.01
Mother	X	X	X	X
Caring				
Father	X	X	X	X
Mother	47.30	50.17	53.34	.001
N[b]	78/79	33/34	102/107	

[a] Group mean factor scores. Standard scores, where $X = -50$, S.D. $= 10$.
[b] Father/Mother.

linked to a broader pattern of emotional distance. Both radical groups found their parents to be distant or aloof, although the differences were statistically significant only for their paternal perceptions. In addition, radicals, especially Jewish radicals, rated their mothers low on the "caring" dimension, indicating a relative absence of warmth and understanding. Finally, Jewish radicals saw their fathers as intrusive or interfering, their permissive disciplinary style notwithstanding.

These data suggest not only that the radical and nonradical groups held quite different images of their parents but also that Jewish and non-Jewish radicalism reflected very different family styles. Nonradicals described their parents positively, as strict but caring, benevolent, and emotionally involved with their children. Jewish radicals seemed dissatisfied primarily with their maternal relationships, picturing their mothers as permissive but cold and punitive. They viewed their fathers somewhat less negatively, as permissive but also somewhat punitive and aloof. Non-Jewish radicals, by contrast, held strongly negative images of their fathers and somewhat positive views of their mothers. They rated their fathers as relatively punitive, aloof, and intrusive, and their mothers as benevolent and permissive.

In sum, the nonradicals held positive images of both parents, while each radical group reacted negatively toward a single parent. Radical Jews reported flawed relations with their mothers, radical non-Jews with their fathers. In general, this pattern also accorded with our findings among college students. There, too, radicals depicted their parents as punitive, cold, and uncaring. There, too, Jewish radicals seemed most troubled by a domineering mother, non-Jews by a punitive father. The main difference between the two studies concerned non-Jewish radicals' attitudes toward their mothers. Among early New Leftists, this group described their mothers as benevolent and rather passive. The non-Jewish student radicals viewed their mothers as uncaring, punitive, and somewhat strict and intrusive. In other respects, the results were quite compatible.

Unfortunately, our factor analysis for this sample did not produce an intrusiveness dimension for perception of mothers. Therefore we lacked the test of patriarchal vs. matriarchal family structure that we employed among students. Nevertheless both our clinical findings and the emotional reactions of respondents to their parents suggest that the families of Jewish radicals were essentially matriarchal. And once again, our findings do not support the notion that patriarchy produces authoritarian traits. Rather, the key factor is the overall warmth and benevolence of the family setting, at least as the children perceived it.

The findings for adult radicals may also shed light on the "permissiveness" ascribed to the families of radical youth in the 1960s. These early New Leftists did rate both parents as relatively permissive. But they placed the permissive disciplinary style in a context of emotional neglect rather than warmth and concern. In short, the parents of many radicals may have been more permissive with their children because they cared less about them.

So far we have documented a family resemblance between the first generation of New Left leaders and the last wave of the student movement in the early 1970s. In their ethnic and social backgrounds, as well as in their family relations, these early New Leftists look rather like elder siblings of the radical students who followed them a decade later. In their TAT-measured personality traits, the older and younger radicals appear almost identical twins: the adult radicals differ from the nonradical comparison group along precisely the same lines that distinguished radicals in our student sample.

The adults' TATs were scored along the same dimensions as the students', including *n* Power, Fear of Power, p (personal) and s (social) Power, action inhibition ("nots"), *n* Affiliation, psychosexual development, and narcissistic pathologies. In addition, they were coded for two themes that were not scored for students: intimacy and achievement motivation.

Intimacy. This recently developed system grew out of concern over the meaning of the *n* Affiliation measure. Although high *n* Affiliation scorers maintained closer contacts with their friends, other indicators were rather ambiguous. For example, they were sometimes rated by others as relatively approval seeking, self-assertive, and egotistical. Some researchers concluded that the *n* Affiliation system was tapping both the desire for close human relations and the fear of rejection.

A University of Minnesota psychologist, Dan McAdams, suggested that the fault lay in a scoring system that emphasized the act of establishing, maintaining, and restoring relationships.[7] Thus high scorers included individuals whose fear of rejection often led them to act in a manner that was designed to gain affection but was sometimes self-defeating. To overcome this difficulty, McAdams developed a scoring system for TATs designed to tap the capacity for intimacy, defined as relationships characterized by openness, caring, and reciprocity.[8] The coding scheme is closely related to Harry Stack Sullivan's "collaborative relationship" and Martin Buber's "I-thou" encounter. People scoring high on Intimacy prefer egalitarian, nonmanipulative relationships characterized by reciprocal and noninstrumental dialogue, openness, and concern for the well-being of others. In stories scored high for Intimacy, protagonists indicate caring and concern for the welfare of others, and good interpersonal relationships are perceived as convivial and enjoyable in themselves.

McAdams followed standard experimental procedures to arouse Intimacy motivation and to develop a scoring system that measures it. He has also conducted a number of studies to test whether he is, in fact, tapping a need for intimacy. He found that persons scoring high on Intimacy were more likely than low scorers to be characterized by others as "natural," "warm," and "loving," and less likely to be perceived as "dominant," or "self-centered." Other evidence includes the manner in which high scorers structure their roles in psychodramas.[9]

We learned of his work as this book was nearing completion. Lack of time and funds precluded rescoring the 710 student protocols for intimacy needs. In lieu of this, we asked McAdams to rescore the adult TATs. As usual, he was told nothing about either their identities or the purposes of the study.

N Achievement. In addition, adult TATs were coded for achievement imagery, the first TAT motivational category developed by McClelland. *N*

Achievement is scored when a character shows concern over performing well in relation to a standard of excellence, as opposed to situations in which activity is routinized or structured by external rewards. Many studies have shown that high levels of achievement imagery predict moderate risk-taking and entrepreneurial or managerial success, even in noncapitalist societies. N Achievement does seem to measure an orientation toward efficiency and successful performance. Finally, in McClelland's best-known work, *The Achieving Society,* he showed that achievement imagery in children's readers was related to national rates of economic growth.[10] On the basis of this and other evidence, he argued that achievement motivation is central to a character structure suited to promoting industrial development. In fact, drawing on Max Weber's celebrated formulation, he suggested that it is a key intervening variable linking the "Protestant" work ethic with the spirit of modern capitalism.

Without endorsing this psychohistorical speculation, it seems clear that n Achievement should be less in evidence among representatives of an adversary culture that rejects precisely this perspective. We differ from some researchers in hypothesizing that the rejection of achievement concerns represents not a higher stage of consciousness but rather the predominance of personality themes focused on issues of power and control. To assess this hypothesis, let us examine the TAT findings.

The motivation scores are shown in Table 12. Jewish and non-Jewish radicals alike significantly exceeded the nonradicals in both their need for and fear of power. Jewish radicals scored highest on both these measures, but the difference between the two radical groups was dwarfed by their mutual distance from the nonradicals. In addition, we found no evidence that the radicals' power orientations were relatively sublimated or inhibited. The three groups produced almost exactly the same amount of s (social) Power imagery, and the radicals were a bit higher on p (personal) Power, but the differences were not statistically significant. Moreover, McClelland's current measure of sublimated power (n Power minus "nots") increased the distance between radicals and nonradicals beyond the difference produced by n Power alone. If anything, then, radicals appeared less capable of sublimating their power needs than did nonradicals.

Nor was this power orientation softened by a concern to maintain positive interpersonal relations. Radicals scored relatively low on n Affiliation and Intimacy alike, with the lowest scores produced by the non-Jewish radicals. The group differences in Intimacy ratings were markedly greater than for n Affiliation. Thus radicals' low n Affiliation scores cannot be interpreted as an immunity to fears of rejection, since they scored even lower on a "purer" measure of the capacity for warmth and intimacy. Finally, both radical groups, as expected, scored significantly below nonradicals in their achievement needs.

Table 12. TAT Motivation Scores for Adult Social Activists.[a]

MOTIVE	Jewish Radicals	Non-Jewish Radicals	Traditionals	Significance[b]
n Power				
X̄	6.31	5.67	3.64	.001
S.D.	(4.21)	(3.21)	(2.90)	
p Power				
X̄	1.65	1.78	1.39	n.s.
S.D.	(1.35)	(1.44)	(1.36)	
s Power				
X̄	1.37	1.44	1.36	n.s.
S.D.	(1.20)	(1.34)	(1.18)	
Power-"nots"				
X̄	4.26	3.78	1.19	.001
S.D.	(3.83)	(3.39)	(5.11)	
Fear Power				
X̄	2.78	2.50	0.95	.001
S.D.	(3.79)	(3.28)	(1.55)	
n Affiliation				
X̄	1.50	1.11	2.17	.05
S.D.	(1.71)	(1.71)	(2.17)	
Intimacy				
X̄	1.68	0.56	3.00	.001
S.D.	(1.89)	(0.71)	(2.27)	
n Achievement				
X̄	5.07	5.06	7.08	.01
S.D.	(3.34)	(3.02)	(3.99)	
N	54	18	88	

[a] Group mean comparisons.
[b] Statistical significance of difference of means test.

In short, on the TAT measures of motivation, all our findings among 1970s students were reproduced among adults. Radicals once again manifested strong, unsublimated power needs. They were highly ambivalent toward power and relatively unconcerned with close personal relations. In addition, they showed little concern for achievement, i.e., living up to a self-determined standard of excellence. Moreover, Jewish radicals once again outscored their non-Jewish peers on *n* Power and Fear of Power, while the non-Jews again produced the lowest *n* Affiliation scores, a finding accentuated by their even lower Intimacy scores.

The replication of findings was equally complete on Stewart's measures of

Table 13. Stages of Psychosexual Development, Adult Male
Social Activists. [a]

PSD IMAGERY (%)	Jewish Radicals	Non-Jewish Radicals	Traditionals	Significance[b]
Oral				
$\bar{X}$	.265	.205	.234	n.s.
S.D.	(.270)	(.200)	(.257)	
Anal				
$\bar{X}$	.219	.212	.218	n.s.
S.D.	(.217)	(.191)	(.220)	
Phallic				
$\bar{X}$	.213	.339	.125	.01
S.D.	(.225)	(.355)	(.191)	
Genital				
$\bar{X}$	.261	.178	.390	.01
S.D.	(.226)	(.200)	(.279)	
N	47	14	62	

[a] Group mean comparisons.
[b] Statistical significance of difference of means tests.

psychosexual development, as Table 13 reveals. Jewish and non-Jewish male
radicals both scored significantly above nonradicals in phallic assertive imagery
and below them in genital-integrative imagery. Non-Jewish radicals again best
fit a "rebellious" psychosexual pattern. They scored highest of the three groups
in phallic themes and lowest in genital themes. The Jewish radicals, also like
their youthful counterparts, scored highest of all groups in oral-incorporative
themes.

In most respects, then, PSD findings from the student and adult studies
were identical. There was one point of divergence, however, that raises an
interesting theoretical issue. According to psychoanalytic theory, adolescents
should be strongly concerned with phallic-assertive themes while mature adults
should transcend some of these concerns and move on to issues of personal
integration. In our research, the expected differences between young people
and adults were primarily confined to nonradical subjects. The college students
produced less imagery at the genital-integrative level than at any other, regardless of their ideology or ethnicity (although radicals, of course, scored even
lower than nonradicals). All the adult groups produced greater proportions of
integrative imagery than any of the student groups. But the difference between
young people and adults was greater by far among nonradicals. Nonradical
adults produced 21 percent more integrative imagery than did nonradical students, compared with differences of 12 percent among Jewish radicals and only

6 percent among non-Jewish radicals. For the nonradical adults, there was a concomitant lessening of concerns for personal autonomy and assertiveness characteristic of adolescents and young adults. By contrast, the non-Jewish radical adults scored almost as heavily at the phallic stage as their student counterparts. Among non-Jewish radicals, adults were considerably lower in phallic imagery than students, but the drop-off was not nearly so great as among nonradicals.

We emphasize that such comparisons are quite speculative. We are comparing the scores of two different samples, consisting of young people and adults. To compare the effects of aging on the psychosexual development of radicals and nonradicals, one would have to test the same people at different points in their life-cycles. But the results do raise an interesting possibility.

While people normally pass from a self-assertive adolescent stage to integrative issues associated with adulthood, radicals may remain disproportionately fixated at a phallic-assertive level of development, continuing to be concerned with adolescent themes of self-assertion and rebellion.

The results for narcissistic pathology, shown in Table 14, did not converge quite so closely with our findings among students. Radicals again scored significantly higher than nonradicals on three measures: thematic heterogeneity; self-centered orientation; and narcissistic attribution. The three adult groups produced virtually the same scores on the measure of low boundaries. Cole and

Table 14. Narcissistic Pathologies among Adult Male Social Activists.[a]

NARCISSISM	Jewish Radicals	Non-Jewish Radicals	Traditionals	Significance[b]
Heterogeneous				
X̄	1.19	1.54	1.04	.001
S.D.	(0.53)	(0.90)	(0.25)	
Self-Centered				
X̄	1.63	1.92	1.04	.001
S.D.	(0.85)	(1.21)	(0.29)	
Narcissistic Attribution				
X̄	1.66	2.04	1.07	.001
S.D.	(1.16)	(1.68)	(0.39)	
Low Boundaries				
X̄	1.14	1.12	1.14	n.s.
S.D.	(0.47)	(0.59)	(0.65)	
N	54	18	88	

[a] Group mean comparisons.
[b] Statistical significance of difference of means test.

others have argued that adolescents are particularly susceptible to disturbances in ego boundaries, since psychic issues at that stage of life center upon identity formation. This may account for our failure to replicate among adults the differences between radical and nonradical students on this variable.

In one important respect, though, the narcissism scores from the two studies parallel the psychosexual development scores. The adults' narcissism scores were uniformly lower than those of the students. The drop was far greater, however, among nonradicals. This pattern is consistent with our speculation that radicals tend to become frozen at certain developmental levels, even as nonradicals continue the process of maturation.

In addition, the highest scores on the other three measures of narcissism were produced by non-Jewish radicals. Among the students, the Jewish radicals scored highest on all four variables. This was the only instance in the two studies in which the TAT measures produced somewhat different patterns among adults and students. It is difficult to know how to interpret this difference, if indeed it should be interpreted at all. One might speculate that the Jewish radicals proved slightly more open to maturation processes than their non-Jewish counterparts. Thus the Jews, in addition to being somewhat less narcissistic, were also slightly less assertive and more integrative in their psychosexual orientations, more affiliative, and more inhibited in expressing their relatively strong power drives.

On the other hand, all these differences were very small and could be attributed to random fluctuations in the test scores stemming from sampling error. Moreover, the small size of the adult radical sample, particularly its non-Jewish segment, militates against broad generalizations. Given the limitations of sampling, uncontrollable variations in test administration, and the relative crudeness and instability of the TAT in tapping underlying personality traits, it is not surprising that *all* differences between Jewish and non-Jewish radicals weren't perfectly replicated in separate samples of college students and middle-aged adults. It is more noteworthy that such thoroughgoing replication was achieved, despite all these limitations.

By far the most important finding was the degree to which radicals systematically differed from nonradicals on the TAT measures, reproducing the pattern of psychological differences we first observed among college students. Indeed the association between personality and politics proved considerably stronger within the adult sample. Following the statistical procedures described in Chapter 6, we found that the TAT variables accounted for 37 percent of the variation in their New Left Ideology scores. With the phallic-assertive PSD scores added to the analysis for male subjects, the proportion of ideological variance explained rose to 44 percent.

Finally, we examined the drinking and driving habits of male radicals. We recall that non-Jewish radical students expressed their power needs in everyday life through heavy alcoholic intake and a heavy foot on the accelerator. We expected the same patterns to hold true for the adult radicals.

This time, we found no systematic difference in drinking habits. Non-Jewish radicals did drink hard liquor most often. Almost half reported that they took a drink at least twice a week, compared with two in five traditionals and only one in four Jewish radicals. These differences, however, were not statistically significant. Moreover, the traditionals were most likely to drink heavily, with one half (56 percent) reporting an average intake of three or more drinks, compared with 36 percent of the non-Jewish radicals and 25 percent of the Jewish radicals. In any case, the results were inconclusive, although we found once again that Jews drank less heavily.

The driving records were more in line with our expectations. Non-Jewish male radicals significantly exceeded the other groups in the speeds they drove, the speeding tickets they received, and the number of accidents they had. Jewish radicals, by contrast, scored lowest on all these measures of reckless or dangerous driving habits. During the three years preceding their interviews, non-Jewish radicals admitted receiving an average of almost five speeding tickets apiece, about twice as many as the other two groups. Their average top speed driven was 98 m.p.h., significantly higher than the 94 m.p.h. averaged by nonradicals and 90 m.p.h. by Jewish radicals. During the same period, they were involved in an average of 1.5 accidents apiece, compared with about 1.1 for the other two groups. This is precisely the pattern we observed among college students.

Thus non-Jewish adult radicals tended to drive aggressively and take risks on the road. This aggressive behavior distinguished them sharply from their Jewish peers, who were significantly less likely to use automobiles as instruments of self-assertion.

Once again, although the evidence is only suggestive, these behavioral differences generally accord with our theory. Non-Jewish radicals seemed most likely to lack impulse control and to express aggression directly. Jewish radicals, on the other hand, were more timid physically. Their participation in the Movement may have provided a means of gaining strength by uniting with a powerful force.

In both surveys, we were able to distinguish among Jewish radicals, non-Jewish radicals, and nonradicals in terms of their reported social and family backgrounds. The secular, politically oriented, and leftist upper-middle-class upbringings popularly associated with New Left activism proved characteristic only of the Jewish radical group.

The three groups were also distinguishable in their parental relations. Both radical groups held strongly negative parental perceptions. Jewish radicals viewed their mothers as distant and punitive, while non-Jewish radicals saw their fathers as punitive and intrusive. Nonradicals portrayed both parents as relatively strict but benevolent.

Finally, TAT imagery distinguished radicals from nonradicals in terms of radicals' strong power needs, fear of power, and narcissism, and nonradicals' concerns for affiliation, intimacy, and achievement. In addition, male radicals had strongly assertive or "phallic" psychosexual orientations, while nonradicals demonstrated greater "genital" or integrative orientations. These findings point to a syndrome of psychopolitical rebellion among adult radicals that matched the pattern we found among students.

The psychological data replicate many, but not all, of the differences we found between Jewish and non-Jewish student radicals. Among both students and adults, Jewish radicals outstripped their non-Jewish counterparts in both the need for and fear of power. The non-Jews were again the least affiliative group, a finding now strengthened by their low Intimacy scores. On the narcissism measures we failed to find the expected differences in ego boundaries, but the PSD scores replicated precisely the patterns of our student study. In their psychosexual orientations, radical Jews were again the most incorporative.

The self-assertive, nonintegrative syndrome of the traditional authoritarian was again most characteristic of radical non-Jews. These findings suggest that non-Jewish radicals again best approximated the pure inverse authoritarianism of Adorno and Fromm's rigid rebel.

The behavioral evidence reinforces this impression. Radicals lacked geographic roots in their youth and tended to come from broken families. Both conditions, however, occurred most frequently among the non-Jews. Among males, both groups of radicals had disciplinary problems as children, but the non-Jews were far more likely to get into physical fights and to engage in combative contact sports. In later life, non-Jews were far more likely to drink heavily and drive aggressively.

Our data offer little support for the view that early and late New Leftists differed in their underlying motivations or personality orientations. On the contrary, they suggest that radicals and nonradicals of both generations differed along many of the same dimensions. Radicals in both studies conformed to our model of inverse authoritarianism. On every measure that produced statistically significant differences, radicals scored in the predicted direction. Conversely, on none of these measures did radicals differ in the direction predicted by models of the New Leftist as psychologically liberated.

It is possible, of course, that our adult New Left sample consisted of "burnt out" radicals whose personalities reflected their frustration over years of failure to achieve changes in American society. However, several factors argue against this explanation. Most of the radicals we interviewed had achieved some success in their professional careers, generally in government, universities, or the media. None had gone underground or had experienced lengthy prison terms. There was little in their personal lives that could realistically have accounted for the particular pattern of responses we found. Nor would this explanation account for our supporting data among students, including both survey and clinical findings, which were equally consistent with our hypotheses. Of course, one can never be sure. We sought out our adult respondents in a period of relative social peace, partly to eliminate the possibility that our earlier student results had captured temporary traits produced by social crises.

At the least, then, the data suggest that the adversary culture does inhabit a lifeworld quite different from that of Middle America. The radicals' egocentric and self-assertive orientations contrast sharply with the psychological liberation once claimed for the New Left. Instead it may be that traits like narcissism and a heightened power drive are necessary to sustain a commitment to radical social change. This would militate against the facile conjunction of "progressive" politics with psychological health. In its place we are left with an old conundrum. Those best suited to lead a revolution are ill-equipped to fulfill its promise.

9 Radicalism Without Jews: The West German Student Movement

UNLIKE THEIR AMERICAN PEERS, continental European students draw on long traditions of ideological engagement and organized political activity. European universities during the nineteenth and the early twentieth century were hotbeds of radical activity, and students figured significantly in many of the revolutions that occurred. Marx himself pointed to the role of students in the German upheaval of 1848.

Radical parties of the Left were the first to take systematic advantage of youthful enthusiasm and to establish youth auxiliaries, although right-wing movements such as the German *Burschenchaften* and the French *Camelots du Roi* also attracted many young people.

In Germany, a socialist youth movement was initiated as early as 1904. Both the French and the English Socialist parties set up youth affiliates somewhat later. In all three countries, youth groups were more militant than the parent party and were supported by the Left within the party. In consequence, the parent organization often found itself at odds with its youth groups. In France, the youth section of the Communist party was heavily Trotskyite during most of the 1920s. In Germany, socialist youth groups frequently clashed with the Social Democratic party because of what they considered to be its timidity.

Where more than one major party of the Left existed, youth was generally drawn to the more radical. In both France and Germany, the socialist youth groups were eclipsed by the communists. Liberal and conservative parties in Europe attempted to create their own youth groups, but without much success. In fact, the only parties which could compete with the Left were Catholic political parties, such as the German Center party, or parties of the radical right, such as the National Socialists. Youth forces and counterforces varied substantially from country to country, and they were related in each case to the nation's culture and its political and social structure.

In France, the authoritarianism of family life encouraged youthful rebellion. Further, the very fragmentation of French society and politics not only offered the university student an opportunity to choose among many ideologies, but also provided the rationale for the bohemian nihilism that became the hallmark of Paris's Left Bank. For the most part, it was left-wing causes that inspired the majority of student activists. Socialist and, later, Communist parties not only were associated in the minds of these students with freedom from all the "bourgeois" restraints but also allowed the activists to identify with the working class.

In Germany, youthful militancy was channeled more easily into the radical Right. The sons of peasants, white-collar workers, and army officers embraced National Socialism with the most fervor and the most genuine idealism. The Social Democrats and Communists did manage to maintain considerable support among the younger population throughout the 1920s, but in the last years of the decade they lost out to the National Socialists.

The French and German experiences differed in other ways. In Germany, a number of nationally organized and ostensibly nonpolitical youth movements had developed at the turn of the century. These groups stressed direct contact with nature through long hikes and traditional dancing, and encouraged a cult of male companionship. In general, the youth who joined these movements were reacting against the centralization and mechanization of bourgeois society. They longed for a nonrepressive society at the same time that they desired to submerge themselves in a group. They also longed for the restoration of a traditional German society, as they understood it, and emphasized the purity of the German *Volk*.

While the organized youth movements were never extended to the university level, their precepts were not without support there. Infatuation with the idea of the German *Volk* and the romantic glorification of German society were vital aspects of life within the dueling fraternities that were so important at the university. Here again there were many splits, but the general movement of university students was to the Right—and to the anti-Semitic Right at that. By the late 1920s, the National Socialist party had captured the leadership of rightist groups at many institutions.

There were those among German youth, including many who had been members of the earlier youth groups, who resisted the Nazi regime. Yet while it lasted, the Nazi movement was notoriously successful in drawing upon youthful energies to create its own version of a new and better world to replace the "decadent," bureaucratic, bourgeois culture that had preceded it.

In England the pattern was quite different. Young people, and especially middle-class students, did flock to the Labour party, especially in the 1930s, but the whole tradition of English life worked against a massive commitment of the types which characterized both France and Germany.

In the years following World War II, student political activity in Europe virtually disappeared. When the nature of the Soviet regime became known, the Communist party seemed less attractive, and this was associated with a general decline in ideological fervor. Furthermore, in every European country full employment was the norm, and the economic success of mixed economies vitiated criticisms of the status quo.

The situation differed, of course, from country to country. English students had never developed a reputation for real political activism; thus the decline there was only relative. In Germany, the decline in political activity by students was so pronounced that they became known as the "skeptical generation." Their concern with postwar reconstruction and their reaction against any ideological commitments were in striking contrast with student activism during the Weimar period. In France, student activism continued during the late 1940s and declined in the 1950s, only to reemerge with the later phases of the Algerian War.

During these years of political torpor on campus, however, forces were at work that would provide the setting for renewed—and occasionally explosive—student activism. The size of student populations was growing rapidly throughout Europe. The demand for higher education was outpacing the resources that governments were willing or able to expend in order to meet it. In France and Germany especially, the ratio of students to faculty was mounting, and overcrowding of university facilities was becoming a critical problem. Moreover, the erosion of traditional patterns of authority in the society and the greater independence of young people were beginning to have implications for the structure of authority within the university. And, as the Soviet Union moved toward a policy of coexistence and new generations entered universities, ideological disillusionment became a matter of history rather than a personal experience. Finally, the growth of mass communications, particularly television, created the possibility of mobilizing students to an extent not conceivable in previous decades.

What crystallized all of these factors into a sudden wave of student activism in the late 1960s was the emergence of a radical student movement in the United States. The traumas associated with the racial crisis, American policy in Vietnam, the military draft, and, indeed, the relationship of the United States (and Western Europe) to the developing nations of the world had caused widespread repercussions on European campuses. The civil rights movement provided a new set of tactics for American students, tactics that were further refined as student opposition to the Vietnam War grew. By way of television, the civil rights and Vietnam demonstrations became part of a common European experience, and young activists capitalized on this experience by traveling from one country to another to foster a rebellious mood among European students.

Developments in the United States influenced Europe in an even more profound manner. To Europeans, as indeed to the rest of the world, the United States had come to symbolize Western political and economic institutions. The impact of the American model was especially great among European youth. Impressed by American power and economic dynamism during the 1950s, many accepted the United States as the embodiment of their own hopes and aspirations. They self-consciously absorbed American ideas and fashions, both by direct contacts with tourists and indirectly through the television programs and movies that blanketed Western Europe. American cultural styles thus permeated the consciousness of European youth during the postwar period, in part through the influence of the mass media.[1]

During the 1960s, ironically, these imported images of America helped turn emulation to disgust. Television graphically portrayed first, America's denial of equal rights to its own black citizens, and second, its involvement in an increasingly unpopular war. Anthony Smith recently wrote of this phenomenon:

> In the last fifteen years, as a result of the spread of television almost everywhere, America has become the most abundantly observed society in history. No single society has ever revealed itself so completely to its friends and enemies, or employed self-revelation as a principal means of social change. It has meant . . . that the rest of the world has been invited to judge America according to what American standards are imagined to be rather than according to the standards of the judge. America is condemned for the violence of its policemen even though the speaker lives in Paris or Santiago. America is condemned for its internal tensions, though the speaker lives in Brixton or Beirut. . . . The images which American television presents to the world arrive prepacked in hostile judgements. For most of the world America is now a preoccupation rather than a reality.[2]

For many students, awareness that the United States had failed to solve a racial problem that seemed to be getting worse, along with disillusionment with American foreign policy, served to discredit the whole structure of their own societies.

The way was opened, then, for the revival of utopian radicalism—for fresh assaults upon society and upon the structure of the universities themselves, considered now as pawns of the larger, corrupt community.

American influence on the European New Left was felt first in West Germany, which in many ways became the prototype for continental student radicals. There is a double irony in this. Many of the "American" ideas that strongly influenced first German and then other European radical youth were, in fact, the work of Nazi-period German refugees like T. W. Adorno and Herbert Marcuse. The social criticism they published in the United States was translated and recrossed the Atlantic, to inspire the radical youth of their original homeland. Indeed, Marcuse's work became far more influential among German radicals than it ever was within the less ideological American Movement.

Of greater import than this crisscrossing of ideas, however, was the changing relationship of America and Western Europe, especially the changing image of America held by European youth. After World War II, America became more than Europe's protector against Soviet expansionism. Particularly within Germany, the United States was accepted as the very model of a liberal democracy, the ultimate referent in the Germans' effort to establish a domestic parliamentary political system. To this extent, the Allies' victory was ideological as well as military. Despite residues of authoritarian social attitudes, most Germans accepted the superiority of democracy over fascism, at least insofar as democracy's leading representative offered strong and concrete economic and military support. The postwar German Federal Republic was created on the American model and flourished under American tutelage.

Then, in the 1960s, the American patina of moral and political superiority was tainted by news reports and television images graphically depicting unexpected struggles in the American south and then in Southeast Asia. Young German radicals quickly mirrored the American preoccupation with race and Vietnam, rather than focusing on indigenous issues. Anti-Americanism soon became a leitmotif of West German student protest. Even the rejection of their own national heritage was mediated by revulsion against its creator and champion. America was the light that failed, the benevolent father unmasked as racist murderer, and the German Federal Republic was its favored—and corrupted—son. By the late 1960s, when America's most extreme radicals were calling themselves revolutionary outlaws, they had willing counterparts in West Germany—all of them outlaws against America.

America's unwitting role in fostering a European New Left can easily be overstated. We emphasize it here because we believe it has been neglected in previous analyses. The first major precipitating event was purely internal, a schism within the German Left. At its 1959 party conference, the Social Democratic party formally renounced the Marxist principles that formed its historic credo. Henceforth, the SPD would function as a democratic leftist alternative, along the lines of the pragmatic noncommunist European socialist parties.

To a new generation of party leaders, this decision seemed a necessary step, if the SPD was ever to become a democratically elected governing party. Predictably, though, it outraged the party's youth affiliate, the *Sozialistische Deutsche Studenten* (hence "SDS," though unrelated to the American SDS).

Major European parties have long maintained strong campus groups as spawning grounds for the adult organization. Student affiliates regularly uphold their parent party's ideals with moralistic fervor and chafe at the political compromises that inevitably seem to undermine those ideals. But this break with the past struck deep emotional chords within the members of the SDS. It meant giving up an ideological and spiritual heritage and becoming an ordinary political assemblage, bound together by narrow self-interest rather than a common dream of revolution. Once the Marxist anchor was cut away, the party would be at the mercy of prevailing political currents, like any other party. This the students could not brook, and in 1961 the SDS formally split with the parent party. (The SPD continued to have difficulty with its young idealists. Their new student group, the *Sozialistischen Demokratische Hochschulbund*, soon moved so far to the left that it in turn was expelled. And for the past decade, the SPD has been buffeted by the leftist demands of their current youth group, the Young Socialists or JUSOs.)

Even before the formal break, the SDS had been casting about for ideological alternatives to their increasingly liberal and non-Marxist parent group. They took their new models from among the growing ranks of radical American intellectuals who challenged the American model of the "good society." A number of their books were translated and widely distributed among German intellectuals during this period. C. Wright Mills's *The Power Elite* (which so influenced Tom Hayden), Vince Packard's *The Hidden Persuaders,* and John Kenneth Galbraith's *The Affluent Society* all appeared in German translations by 1960. They were soon joined by Michael Harrington's *The Other America.*

By mid-decade, anthologies of black power writings and revisionist analyses of the cold war had found a German audience. America's aims in rebuilding a democratic Germany were now pictured as those of restoring German capitalism to help integrate an imperialistic international system. Horkheimer and Adorno's return to Frankfurt, along with Marcuse's lecture tours, focused attention on their critique of bourgeois democracy as latent fascism, and of America as a "one-dimensional" society that precluded human liberation.

The German Left was far more responsive than the American Left to these critiques of American democracy. The latter was suspicious of "ideas" per se as the enemies of self-expressive action. German radicals, schooled in a more ideological tradition, welcomed the new conceptual tools that justified their own shift from theory to "praxis." Moreover, the influence of the new radical literature far outstripped its readership. Many protesters, of course, had never heard of American radicals like Mills or Baran and Sweezy, and were familiar with Marcuse only by reputation. But the most active and committed radicals, such as SDS leaders Rudi Dutschke and Bernd Rabehl, developed their ideas through close reading of this literature. They popularized the criticism of bourgeois democracy as a proto-fascist practitioner of social and psychological "manipulation" and "repressive tolerance." They argued for a "great refusal" against this anti-human system, and its replacement by an anti-authoritarian participatory democracy. Under a new socioeconomic system, they argued, all men could achieve a "new sensibility" transcending bourgeois repression and mutual exploitation. The task at hand, however, was to destroy the present system.

These were the concepts and catchwords that rallied protesters to the cause of an "extra-parliamentary opposition." As Kurt Shell writes, radicalization began with the "counterculture" of critical academics

who were being "received" by initially small groups of students and scholars and who provided intellectual tools and articulate conceptual language to the latent dissidence which had largely lacked—since the end of the war—the weapons with which to attack the liberal system. These small groups were able to exploit a basic somewhat unreflected commitment to democracy among larger masses of students, once the American scene exploded with domestic and external violence; using the armory of critical concepts (e.g. "manipulation") developed in America on the basis of American phenomena and transmitted within the German university environment.[3]

The new radicalism first gained widespread influence at Germany's "Berkeley," the Free University of Berlin. It would prove far more important in shaping a national student movement than Berkeley itself had been. The Free University was created in 1947 in response to student demonstrations against communist domination of the city's famed Humboldt University. The students, the city's residents, and the Western occupying powers stood together in their resolve to create a new university to symbolize West Berlin's status as an outpost of freedom and democracy in the struggle against totalitarian communism. The Free University, then, was very much a product of the cold war. It was to serve as an emblem of

the self-confidence of a whole people who profoundly believed that they were "on the right side" and showed their pride in this. West Berlin was the showplace of the German Federal Republic; furthermore, it was the showpiece of the virtues of Western democracy, and its university had been designed to be the same.[4]

To fulfill this purpose, the new university had to differ radically from the traditionally rigid and hierarchical German university. Its charter directed that students, represented by a formally recognized association, play an active role in making decisions and setting educational policies. The Free University thus became the vanguard of educational reform in the German Federal Republic. Although student power dissipated under the pressures of growth and bureaucratization, they retained a unique capacity for involvement and influence in university life. And Berlin remained the model for a new, more democratic university.

Throughout the university's first decade, Berlin students also retained their political solidarity with the faculty and the general populace. Students joined other Berliners in demonstrations against the East German regime. They led the protests against Soviet military action in East Berlin in 1953, and again in Hungary in 1956. They took to the streets in frustration and outrage over the Berlin Wall's sudden appearance in 1961.

Even before this last great shock of the cold war, though, West German students in Berlin and elsewhere were becoming less concerned with Soviet expansionism than with Western colonialism and imperialism. At the time, such matters concerned only a tiny minority. As in the United States, however, the relaxing of cold war tensions made it possible once again to direct social criticism toward "free world" states. And within West Germany, the SPD's repudiation of Marxism left the SDS as the sole repository of radical socialism. Instead of acting as an affiliate of a parent party in the traditional European manner, the SDS was free to form its own policies.

The Free University's SDS chapter was particularly strong, for several reasons. The university's special character attracted students who refused to abide by the authoritarian power structures of other European universities. Students, especially politically involved students, had a far greater voice in Berlin than elsewhere. In addition, many students were refugees from East Berlin or other parts of East Germany. Although they shared a common hatred of Soviet domination, many retained a strong commitment to some form of socialism. Finally, West Berlin's peculiar status in a divided Germany provided a special inducement for young radicals. Only in Berlin were college students exempt from the draft for the duration of their studies.

Student radicalism was not confined to Berlin. Strong SDS chapters also existed at Frankfurt—home of the Frankfurt School of radical sociology—at Munich, and at a few other universities. But it was in Berlin that the first significant protests occurred, and a radical movement was born.

The first stirrings came in 1964, when more than a thousand students protested against the official visit of Congolese Prime Minister Moise Tshombe. The demonstration was quite mild compared with those soon to come. At one point, though, the protesters broke through police cordons, to the amazement of policemen. It was the first time demonstrators had challenged police authority since the founding of the Federal Republic. Participants and commentators agreed on the symbolic importance of this event:

> This was an act of de-socialization, the impact of which was extraordinarily great. . . . The principle of authority had been ostensibly challenged; the consensual nature of power relations in that isolated outpost of Western democracy had been severely shaken.[5]

The action provoked a strongly negative public response. The students were denounced in the press, and the major political parties and unions registered their official disapproval. The radicals, on the other hand, were taken aback by their unexpected political isolation. They responded with criticisms of public opinion as a "manipulated consensus" within an authoritarian social system. In the words of one SDS report, "the ruling classes" prevent reform "far less through the use of open terrorist repression than through a subtle instrumentation of integration and manipulation."[6]

This critique left SDS with a major tactical problem. How could radical change be fomented in a society lulled to sleep by manipulation, repressive tolerance, and "consumption terror"? One tack was to withdraw into study groups or bohemian communes that at last preserved one's own freedom from societal "manipulation." Occasionally, the liberated few would emerge to engage in some intentionally outrageous activity that revealed the absurdity of bourgeois conventions and institutions. Some groups disrupted classes and meetings; others confined themselves to provocative manifestos. A Berlin SDS-affiliate, Kommune I (commune number one), gained the greatest notoriety through its 1967 attempt to enliven Vice-President Hubert Humphrey's state visit with smoke bombs and pie-throwing. It is hard to say whether the public was more outraged by this planned mock-riot or by the commune's highly publicized sexual libertarianism. Even the name of their leader, Fritz Teufel ("devil" in German), seemed calculated to provoke polite society. Kommune I succeeded to the degree that Teufel was arrested and SDS was forced publicly to disassociate itself from the alleged bomb-throwing anarchists.

Another radical alternative was to concentrate recruitment efforts on the universities, where young people were not yet fully integrated into the "System." Particularly in Berlin, the SDS was able to capitalize on discontent with the university administration. They rode on a wave of dissent reminiscent of the "Free Speech" controversy that had recently awakened the protest potential at Berkeley. In 1965, students struck over the administration's refusal to allow a leftist writer to speak on campus. This was the first student strike in the history of the German university system. The next year witnessed another first, when students staged a sit-in to protest departmental restrictions on their political activities. Also during this period, the first anti-Vietnam War demonstrations took place, and Berlin's America House was pelted with rocks and eggs.

Just as at Berkeley, criticism of the university quickly opened out into criticisms of society at large. SDS militants sought to convince the mass of protesters that the university's actions reflected its repressive function within an authoritarian society.

The SDS, like its American namesake, was not a politically homogeneous organization. Various chapters and affiliates operated relatively independently, and a broad spectrum of leftist positions found varying degrees of representation. Moreover, as the strongest national Marxist student group, SDS served as a rallying point for independent Trotskyite, Maoist, and other quasi-Marxist sects. Outside observers generally distinguished two major ideological factions, the "traditional" revolutionary Marxists and the anarcho-communist "anti-intellectual" or "anti-authoritarian" wing. The former group concerned itself primarily with theoretical analyses of "late capitalism" and argued that Marxist education was a necessary prelude to revolutionary activity. But it was the "anti-authoritarians," with their emphasis on provocation, confrontation, and self-expressive political protest, who would take the lead in radicalizing a much broader stratum of students.

This faction was led by a refugee from the East named Rudi Dutschke, editor of *Der Anschlag* ("Attack"), who espoused a confrontationist strategy well before it became a popular tactic of American SDS. He called for immediate revolution, set off by the spontaneous, self-liberating acts of individuals. Dutschke advocated violent street confrontations as a means of overcoming the "acute feelings of powerlessness . . . of those who are integrated into capitalist society." Provocative actions would provide a psychological release from repression while "[unmasking] both the latent and manifest violence of the system, the terrorism of its institutions, the brutality of the police."[7] Dutschke's voluntarism and libertarianism, his emphasis on psychological rather than economic alienation, and his identification with militant oppressed groups place him squarely in the New Left mainstream. Indeed, he would soon personify the New Left to many millions of Germans and other Europeans.

The core of the German student movement was notably less ambivalent about violent revolution than was the American New Left. Germany's strong

Marxist tradition, and the SPD's "betrayal" of that tradition, undoubtedly played a role in this.

Despite SDS's continual agitation and moderate success in Berlin, however, the flow of radicalism remained a trickle until 1967. Only about 2 percent of West Germany's students demonstrated or signed petitions against the Grand Coalition. Carefully planned national conferences on Vietnam and the "critical state of democracy" failed to draw more than one to two thousand participants. For all intents and purposes, student radicalism was confined to West Berlin.

One June night in 1967, this situation changed dramatically. Berlin radicals had planned a demonstration against a visit by the Shah of Iran. Protesters, counter-protesters, police, and television crews converged in a pitched battle. During the melee, a policeman shot and killed a student bystander named Benno Ohnesorg. The Ohnesorg shooting became Germany's emotional equivalent of Kent State. There was one key difference, however. The Kent State shootings marked the culmination and final upsurge of an exhausted movement. Ohnesorg's death, on the contrary, crystallized latent opposition to the system. It marked the beginning of a nationwide student movement, polarizing the populace in a manner similar to the 1968 Democratic Convention in this country. Twenty thousand Berlin students marched behind Ohnesorg's coffin, which was transported to Hanover for the funeral. In Hanover, a far more significant event occurred. Twenty thousand more students attended the funeral, and at a mass meeting they formally organized an "extra-parliamentary opposition" (APO). From its inception, the APO was dominated by left-wing elements. The strongest of these elements by far was the SDS, and the controlling SDS faction was the anarcho-syndicalist group led by Dutschke. The West German New Left now entered its "anti-authoritarian" phase, the most vital and controversial period of its existence.

European students quickly became familiar with the pronouncements of "Dutschkism," in large part a practical application of Marcuse's teachings. In the Dutschke-Marcuse vision, the subtly repressive, modern industrial Leviathan flourishes by buying off the workers, draining third world resources, and permitting domestic dissent only until protest threatens the system. This limited toleration of political dissent is "repressive," since it purposely fosters the illusion that human liberation is possible within the existing order. This false consciousness, in tandem with material comfort, stifles any widespread revolutionary impulse. Only a tiny vanguard of psychologically liberated individuals within the universities are capable of resisting integration into the system. They must engage in "creative agitation," disrupting the mechanisms of social conditioning, and giving others a glimpse of the personal autonomy that defines itself through active opposition toward social institutions.

This doctrine justified direct action and confrontation on both personal and political grounds. First, social disruption would open people's eyes to social repression and to the state's brutal response to truly serious opposition. Second, the protesters achieved their own psychological liberation through activity that negated and transcended the system's "de-humanizing apparatuses." So a revolutionary vanguard was necessary, but one quite different from what Lenin had envisaged. Its role was not to adopt a correct line and maintain party discipline but to create revolutionary consciousness, above all, within its own ranks.

The West German New Left's claim to leadership thus rested in part on a "psycho-political" argument: its leadership of the masses was based upon the students' superior revolutionary consciousness, their transcendence of one-dimensional bourgeois mentality. Indeed, a primary goal of the revolution was to spread this "new sensibility" throughout society, to replace the "performance principle" of capitalism with a "new reality principle" based on real human needs. It would not take a revolution to create the "new man" of Marxist-Leninist theory, for he had already appeared among the children of the advanced middle class. Now they sought a revolution to remake society in their own image. Thus Dutschke argued:

> . . . the fundamental prerequisite of democracy lies in the existence of conscious and creative men—new men characterized by radically new needs and interests, by an antiauthoritarian character structure.
>
> A conscious democratic autonomy must be created among the masses and the individuals that compose them. . . . it can develop only through the permanent conflict with dogmatic-authoritarian forces and essentially depends upon the acquisition of consciousness by the masses.[8]

Not surprisingly, this doctrine of a permanent revolution by a moral and psychological elect was used to justify all sorts of provocative activity. Dutschke himself was loath to condemn any act that might further the advancement of a revolutionary mentality. Even political murder was unacceptable only because the leaders of modern bureaucratic society were no longer "individual" enough to personify evil:

> There are no longer individuals to be hated. . . . In advanced industrial societies everybody at the top is interchangeable. Therefore terroristic violence against persons is no longer necessary.[9]

This remarkable statement epitomized the coldly abstract nature of Dutschke's social criticism. For all his celebration of the individual, there is very little recognition of individuality, particularly in his speeches and tracts. People and social institutions alike are reduced to abstractions and general categories. This almost fetishistic attention to theoretical abstractions, to the detriment of concrete social analysis, was characteristic of the German New Left as a whole. The concrete issues that generated the most enthusiasm were "foreign imports"—repression in Iran and South Africa, colonialism in Angola and, above all, American imperialism in Vietnam. As we noted earlier, youthful opposition to "bourgeois democracy" was largely a rejection of American moral and political hegemony. The radicals' disdain for the Federal Republic paled before the fervor of their new-found anti-Americanism. Hence the peculiarly detached quality of their domestic protest. German authorities were excoriated for being "agents of U.S. imperialism." The real enemy lay elsewhere, across the Atlantic. Mehnert recalls asking Dutschke

> why the SDS had jumped on problems that were far away from West Berlin and the Federal Republic, instead of fighting for issues closer to home. He explained that this was due to his . . . friends' disgust over the contradiction between America's claim as "guarantor of Berlin's freedom" and its role as the enemy of freedom in the Third World.[10]

The fervent identification with third world revolutionaries gave the radicals a sense of morality in opposition, which replaced the discredited moral authority of Bonn and Washington. Their apparent internationalism was really a militant ersatz nationalism, an attempt to fill the emotional void created by the rejection of their own past. They regained the exhilaration of striding alongside the forces of right and justice, of riding the wave of the future. Dutschke's often-quoted statement that "the struggle of the Vietcong . . . is our struggle" thus carried deep emotional resonances. The students were waging guerrilla warfare against their own heritage. An emotional alliance with the third world served the same needs some American radicals fulfilled by attaching themselves to the Black Panthers. They gained the strength of righteous militance and totalistic opposition, and they found a cause to justify their anger against a light that had failed.

Militant protest peaked with the 1968 Easter riots. On April 11, a would-be assassin shot and seriously wounded Dutschke, setting off riots in university towns throughout West Germany. The intense suspicion and hostility that had built up between the radicals and much of the populace boiled over into street fighting that left two dead, hundreds injured, and over a thousand arrested.

The rioting crystallized public opposition to student protest. Polls taken shortly thereafter found two thirds of the populace (and almost nine out of ten

West Berliners) opposed to the protesters. The major political parties and unions denounced the militants, and the conservative press announced that Dutschke had reaped a harvest of violence that SDS itself had sown. In addition, the radical movement lost an undeniably dynamic leader; after a lengthy recuperation, Dutschke went to England to resume his studies. His departure from the political scene, along with the virtually unanimous condemnation of the general public, left the student movement in disarray.

The united "anti-authoritarian" opposition quickly fragmented into a host of proto-Marxist or anarchist sects. The SDS itself went into rapid decline, ending with its dissolution in 1970. Out of its ashes arose a neo-Stalinist group calling itself Spartakus, after the leader of a Roman slave revolt, whose name had previously been appropriated by German Leftists shortly after World War I. Although the contemporary Spartacists never attained the influence of their namesakes, they built up a campus following that rose to several thousand members by the mid-1970s.[11] Groups like Spartakus, the Marxist-Leninist German Communist party (DKP), and similar local organizations represented a reawakening of Old Left sentiment on West German campuses. They failed to gain the sympathies of large numbers of students, as the SDS had. Nonetheless, they entrenched themselves on many campuses by taking advantage of academic reforms designed to democratize the university. These reforms, passed by the German parliament in response to student unrest, gave students a major voice in governing campus affairs. Thus by packing meetings, intimidating opposition, and so forth, disciplined radical groups were sometimes able to prescribe Marxist curricula and force the hiring and promotion of "progressive" instructors.

Elizabeth Noelle-Neumann, director of the Allensbach Public Opnion Institute, summarized this situation:

> The [West German] student revolution started from the Berkeley campus. In the seventies, though, American and German developments split off from each other. In the Federal Republic, the attitude climate and the shift of political energy toward the left have been conserved. The complete transformation of the university structure since the mid-sixties into a *Gruppenuniversität* has created sites where the active, left-oriented students find fertile ground for their activities.[12]

The smallest of these groups of students, though the most publicized, were direct descendants of the SDS's provocationist or "actionist" core. On campus, they included "Spontis," anarchistic advocates of spontaneous, direct action, and "Chaoten," who attempted to create chaotic turmoil by disrupting classes and examinations, physically threatening and attacking professors and students whose politics they found objectionable, and so forth. Among the latter are Maoist groups like the Communist party of Germany, or KPD. (The simultaneous presence of *three* competing "German Communist Parties"—the Maoist KPD, Stalinist DKP, and Leninist KPD-AO—bespeaks the pervasive factionalism that turned the campus Left into a "red kaleidoscope.")

But the most notorious actionists no longer functioned on campus but underground. They were the tiny terrorist groups that sprang up in the late '60s, periodically emerging from underground networks to engage in spectacular hijackings, kidnappings, and political murders. By late 1977, the Federal Criminal Bureau estimated that a hard core of 1,200 "ultras" was operating within a wider network of about 6,000 sympathizers who provide funding, safehouses, and other assistance.[13] A government report issued at the same time tallied up the toll of a decade of terrorism: 27 dead and 92 injured, in addition to over a hundred unsuccessful murder attempts.[14]

The first terrorist group is still the most widely known. Calling itself the Red Army Faction (RAF), it is best known as the Baader-Meinhof gang, after the names of two principals. The conjoining of these names, Andreas Baader and Ulrike Meinhof, lovers and political outlaws, epitomizes the union of intellectual radicalism and apolitical thuggery in the terrorist underground.

Meinhof was a child of the progressive upper middle class. She was born into a religiously oriented academic family; both parents were art historians. Orphaned at fourteen, she was influenced by her foster mother, a deeply religious professor of education who helped found a pacifist political party. Meinhof participated in "ban the bomb" marches in 1958 and 1959, and two years later married the editor of an influential "radical chic" magazine, *Konkret,* which combined sex with left-wing politics in a manner somewhat akin to *Evergreen.* The SPD-CDU alliance and the Ohnesorg shooting pulled her into the extra-parliamentary left. Then, in 1968, her private life and political hopes simultaneously disintegrated. A bitter separation and divorce cut her off from the *Konkret* circle of wealthy radical intellectuals; the student movement went into decline with the Dutschke shooting and the failure of the Paris uprising; the Soviet attack on Czechoslovakia destroyed any remaining illusions about the USSR as a socialist alternative.

Against this background, she attended the trial of Baader and Gudrun Ensslin, who had set fire to a Frankfurt department store to dramatize their disgust for the "consumption terror" of bourgeois society. Ensslin was a pastor's daughter, with a social and educational background similar to Meinhof's own. Baader was something else again—a dark, handsome "man of action" without intellectual interests or moral scruples, who relished the excitement of playing

Bonnie and Clyde. His personality combined the egotism and magnetism of the sociopath. His flair for action, unfettered by doubt, proved irresistible to a few conflicted and guilt-ridden radical intellectuals who, as one of them later wrote, longed "to plunge into anesthetizing actionism."[15]

Meinhof was an early convert to the appeal of both Baader and actionism. In May 1970, she engineered Baader's escape from jail in a dramatic shoot-out with police. Her only alternative now was to go underground and start a new life as a revolutionary guerrilla. From her own perspective, though, she had cut the Gordian knot of indecision, frustration, and despair that had immobilized her. It was not only Andreas Baader who plunged to freedom that spring day.

For alienated quasi-intellectuals like Meinhof, terrorism represented a final opportunity to reject the seductive material advantages and the spurious moral standards of an evil system. Her new role of revolutionary outlaw combined self-denial with self-assertion. By turning her back on wealth and social privilege, she demonstrated her revolutionary credentials. At the same time, she freed herself from social repression and manipulation; she created in herself a "new man sensibility" that transcended bourgeois standards of good and evil. Within the system, no qualitative personal or political change seemed possible. Now everything was possible, every act justified. For Meinhof, revolution was "a catchword that broke down taboos" and "blocked the path from bad conscience to resignation."[16] Her new RAF compatriot Bernward Vesper expanded upon this point. The revolutionary needn't fear a bad conscience, he wrote, because any act of resistance was justified against a "morally illegal" society.[17] Baader, who was not concerned with matters of conscience, put it most directly: "A criminal act is in itself already a political act."[18]

Over the next few years, this promise of revolutionary freedom attracted hundreds of young people to the ranks of the political outlaws. Most were in their twenties, the products of an academic or otherwise intellectual milieu. In 1975, for example, a small group took hostages at the German embassy in Sweden, demanding the release of twenty-six jailed comrades. Of these "commandos," two were students, a third the son of a millionaire businessman, the fourth a writer's son. The list of those whose freedom they demanded included nine students and only two workers.

The young outlaws of the RAF and similar groups embarked on a series of spectacular actions, capped by the 1972 bombings of U.S. Army installations in five German cities, leaving four dead. Soon thereafter, Baader, Meinhof, and three other RAF leaders were captured. For the next few years, their compatriots sought to force their freedom, or at least wreak vengeance on their captors. In November 1974, the Chief Justice of West Berlin was murdered.

Four months later, the leader of the Berlin Christian Democratic party was kidnapped, and an attack on the German embassy in Sweden caused a number of deaths and left several more wounded. In 1977 the Federal Republic's chief prosecutor and the chairman of the important Dresden Bank were murdered in separate incidents. The banker was the godfather of one of his assailants. Then a leading spokesman of German industry was kidnapped and later murdered, after the government refused to release already imprisoned terrorists. Most dramatic of all was the skyjacking of a Lufthansa jet by a team of Germans and Palestinians, in a final effort to free the imprisoned RAF leaders. The skyjackers were killed or captured by West German commandos, though not before they murdered the plane's pilot. When word of the failure reached Baader, he and two other RAF members committed suicide, choosing martyrdom over life imprisonment. Thousands of youths in European cities protested their alleged murder by prison guards, but a team of distinguished doctors from outside Germany verified the finding of suicide.

After that violent denouement, no major acts of political violence took place in West Germany for a number of years. However, terrorists still gleaned considerable sympathy from the intellectual community. To a far greater degree than the Weathermen, the RAF and their allies were able to "swim like a fish among the people," at least among a certain segment of the people—radical teachers, students, journalists, lawyers, and even clerics. Their willingness to aid those who commit acts of political violence stems from a deep-rooted revulsion toward the social system. At the height of terrorism in 1977, a Frankfurt student expressed his sense of community with the RAF and against the Establishment: "Who are the terrorists? Perhaps the United States and the business tycoons. This country is no more than a colony of American imperialism."[19] And the University of Giessen's student newspaper published an unsigned letter claiming to speak for many students who felt "furtive joy" at the murder of the chief federal prosecutor.

Studies of university students completed as late as 1978 revealed widespread sympathy for radical rejection of the federal republic as well as support for violence to achieve political ends.[20] One third of all students polled, and over half the political activists, called force a "legitimate means" to carry out political goals. One fifth of the activists, and 8 percent overall, specifically endorsed the use of violence against people. Of students calling themselves "far left," almost half (46 percent) proclaimed themselves willing to use political violence against other people.

So it is little wonder that the terrorist fringe found fertile ground on campuses. Their ideas were widely shared there, even when their activities were rejected on tactical grounds. A Bonn radical coolly dissociated herself from the

RAF in this fashion: "The militant anarchists aren't all wrong when they say we're becoming a police state. Only, [their] nihilism speeds up the coming of the police state. . . . [Besides,] their German is atrocious."[21]

It would be a mistake, then, to focus too narrowly on the tiny minority of "ultras"—the Baaders and Meinhofs of the movement. Baader seems to have been a relatively typical sociopath, who briefly managed to justify his aggressive impulses in terms of a nihilistic political credo. Meinhof, though more complex, was almost a caricature of a certain psychoanalytic stereotype. She personified the morally rigid pacifist turned avenging angel, whose initial aversion to violence served to conceal strong aggressive impulses. Once these impulses were freed they acquired the same moral patina that was once attached to pacifism. Then the rigid denial of violence was transformed into a fascination with violence. In her prerevolutionary youth, she once wept hysterically—"almost had a small nervous breakdown"—when a companion unexpectedly fired a shotgun. After her conversion, she calmly affirmed the morality of killing policemen: "Of course one can shoot."[22]

The West German student movement resembled the American in many facets of its social concerns and internal dynamics. Indeed, we have shown how German radicals often followed the ideological and tactical leads of their American compatriots. In its social composition, however, the German New Left differed from the American in one major respect. It was a radical movement almost totally devoid of Jewish participants. The reason for this is all too obvious. The enormous influence of the Jewish community on Germany's radical heritage was abruptly ended by the Holocaust. The few Jews who were not murdered or exiled during the Nazi period today constitute a tiny and mostly elderly minority in the German Federal Republic. In short, there were almost no Jewish German New Leftists because there are so few Jewish young people in West Germany.

The German student movement thus provides a striking counterpoint to the American situation, where Jews provided a critical mass for the new radicalism of the 1960s. As a result, West Germany represents a case study of the social psychology of student radicalism without a Jewish constituency. By studying German college students, we sought to test the value of our model of inverse authoritarianism in predicting radicalism across ethnic as well as national boundaries. This model should apply as readily to German as to American radicals. On the other hand, where American radicals of Jewish background differed from non-Jewish radicals, we would expect German radicals to resemble the latter. In the American surveys, ethnic differences appeared primarily in the social backgrounds and perceived family relations of radicals. We expected German radicals to mirror the social diversity and rebellion against parental conservation and "authoritarian" child-rearing that characterized non-Jewish American radicals, in contrast to the socially privileged, maternally centered family backgrounds that typified Jewish radicals. Unfortunately we lacked the resources to duplicate the clinical study of American students or to examine many of the personality themes that hinted at ethnic variants on our model of radical personality.

In 1973, a translated and slightly revised version of the American student survey questionnaire was administered to 220 male students drawn in equal number from the universities of Konstanz and Tübingen.[23] In addition to demographic information, this questionnaire contained self-reports on social and political attitudes and behavior; two projective psychological tests, the Thematic Apperception Test (TAT) and Semantic Differential; and our test of family interaction, the Parent-Child Questionnaire (PCQ). The German version contained additional sociopolitical attitude measures which we used to establish the validity of our primary measure of ideology, the New Left Ideology scale.

Unfortunately, a random sample could not be obtained for the German study. Subjects responded to public announcements of a study of political socialization, for which participants were paid. They gathered at an appointed time and place and completed the questionnaire under the supervision of test administrators. Although the lack of a random sample prevents us from generalizing our findings, our primary concern was to identify psychopolitical "types," even if their general distribution cannot be accurately estimated.[24]

The problem of measuring radical ideology took on added dimensions in this study. Our measure of radicalism, the New Left Ideology scale, was developed at Columbia University and was phrased in terms of the issues and catchwords of the American New Left. Despite some overlap, the American and West German student movements arose out of different political milieus, emphasized somewhat different sets of issues, and addressed them with different ideological vocabularies. To ensure that we tapped genuine ideological divisions among German students, we supplemented the New Left Ideology scale with two indigenous measures of social and political attitudes. The first was a scale designed to measure attitudes toward socialism. We asked subjects whether they supported or opposed the abolition of private ownership of banks and industries, worker control in factory decisions, a free economy and private enterprise, and the stability of current social and economic relations. The "socialistic" response, of course, was to support the first two positions and oppose the latter two. Factor analysis revealed that each of these items in fact contributed to a general dimension of capitalist vs. socialist sentiments. The second was a conservatism scale that had been developed and tested by German social scientists at Konstanz University.[25] Students were asked to assess eighteen statements dealing with the nature and proper aims of man, society, and government. These statements were derived from ideas that have characterized conservative thinkers in Germany and elsewhere. In fact, the test was based upon a well-known counterpart developed in this country by the political scientist Herbert McCloskey. Representative items include: "Every man needs something that he can fully and completely believe in"; "Under current conditions, freedom must first be understood to mean freedom from social and political control"; and "The striving for personal property is an inalterable part of human nature" (our translations).

We soon discovered that it was prudent to provide these "back-up" scales. Factor analyses disclosed that the New Left Ideology scale contained several dimensions for our German subjects. We decided to use only one of these, which accounted for the greatest proportion of the variation in their attitudes. This dimension was also the easiest to interpret substantively. It consisted of statements dealing with the need for truly revolutionary change and the legitimacy of violent or highly coercive political tactics. People scoring high on this "radical tactics" dimension tended to agree with statements such as "A mass revolutionary party should be created in this country," and "Disruption is preferable to dialogue for changing our society." They tended to disagree with statements such as "Although our society has to be changed, violence is *not* a justifiable means," and "There is no justification for shouting down political speakers, regardless of their viewpoints."

We used this "radical tactics" dimension of the New Left Ideology scale as our main measure of radical attitudes. This measure correlated .44 with the Socialism scale and −.38 with the Conservatism scale, with both correlations highly significant statistically (p < .001). The moderate size of these correlations indicates that German students' attitudes toward radical tactics, socialism, and conservatism were definitely related to one another but represented somewhat different dimensions of political ideology. Therefore our confidence in the relationship between personality and radicalism would be bolstered if we obtained similar results using all three scales.

In addition, we were interested in the social and psychological milieus of the radical and revolutionary activists who figured so prominently in campus politics. West German universities had remained much more politicized than their American counterparts, with many political groups competing for campus influence. Therefore we asked students to name politically oriented groups in which they were currently active. Based on these reports, we were able to divide campus activists into four ideological groupings: the revolutionary left (18 students); the nonrevolutionary left (35 students); moderates (17 students); and conservatives (9 students). These categories were defined as follows:

1. *Revolutionary* activists participated in Marxist-oriented groups advocating the violent overthrow of the social and political order. These groups included the "Spartacists" of the *Marxistische Studentenbund,* the German Communist party or KPD, and smaller local revolutionary groups.

2. *Leftist* activists belonged to social democratic organizations that accepted parliamentary democracy as a legitimate context for social change. They included the Social Democratic party (SPD) and its Marxist-oriented youth wing, the Young Socialists or JUSOs, the *Sozialistische Hochschulbund,* and politically active conscientious objector groups.

3. *Moderate* activists belonged to groups that were neither avowedly "left-" nor "right-wing." They included the Free Democrats (FDP) and its youth organization, the German Young Democrats, as well as avowedly nonpartisan groups such as Amnesty International and environmental protection organizations.

4. *Conservative* activists participated in groups representing the right wing of the political spectrum, such as the Christian Democratic party (CDU) and its student affiliate, Junge Union, the religiously oriented Ring of Christian Democratic Students, and a politically active army veterans' organization.

The preponderance of left-wing activists and the paucity of rightists reflect the ideological tenor of the campuses we surveyed. Students belonging to both moderate and nonrevolutionary leftist groups (e.g., the JUSOs and environmental protection groups) were assigned to the latter category. There were no such overlapping memberships among either radical or conservative activists, perhaps reflecting a heightened insularity on either end of the political spectrum.

We turn now to our findings for both ideological radicals and the core group of committed radical activists identified above.

In our studies of American New Leftists, we found that non-Jewish radicals came from quite diverse social backgrounds, with a good many rebelling against the conservative values of their parents. To see whether this was true of West German male radicals as well, we first divided our subjects into radical, moderate, and conservative groups on the basis of their New Left Ideology scores. In addition, we will turn to the activist subsample to determine whether a particular social background might be associated with radical activism, if not radical ideology.

The results paralleled our findings for non-Jewish American students. The German radicals were no more likely than nonradicals to come from homes that were either Protestant or Catholic, rich or poor, well or poorly educated. The few differences that did arise belied any expectation that these radicals came from a socially or economically privileged sector of the populace. Radicals' fathers were actually less well educated than the fathers of nonradicals. Fifty-seven percent had no more than a grammar school education, compared with 43 percent for the entire sample, and only 23 percent had acquired a college degree, compared with 33 percent for the sample as a whole. It is not surprising that radicals were slightly less likely to come from the homes of upper-middle-class professionals than were other subjects (21 percent vs. 27 percent). In fact, we found no significant association between radicalism and parental occupation or any other measure of social or economic status. The sons of businessmen and managers, blue- and white-collar workers, farmers and shop-owners were all about equally likely to acquire radical ideas or join leftist groups.

The only aspect of a student's social background that was related to radical ideas or activities was his parents' political affiliation. The German questionnaire was not as extensive as the original American version, and we did not inquire about parents' political attitudes. We simply asked subjects which of the three major parties their fathers identified with most closely—the Social Democrats (SPD), Free Democrats (FDP), or Christian Democrats (CFU). The SPD and CDU are much more clearly parties of the political Left and Right, respectively, than are the Democrats and Republicans in this country. An affiliation with one or the other is thus more often a meaningful clue to ideological leanings. The FDP introduces a complicating factor. It contains both left and right wings, and has at times allied itself with both of the other parties. It is probably fair to say that the FDP represents an intermediate political grouping of both "left liberal" reformers who shrink from the residual socialist leanings of the SPD, and right liberals who uphold various laissez-faire or libertarian doctrines, or who resist the religious cast of the predominantly Catholic CDU. With some distortion, then, one could identify the SPD as the uneasy inheritor of a socialist tradition, the FDP as the representative of various strands of European liberalism, and the CDU as a traditional conservative party.

Whatever the precise ideological implications of these party affiliations, radicals did tend to view their fathers as disproportionately oriented toward the SPD. Half the radicals placed their fathers there, compared with 35 percent of the entire sample. By contrast, only one third of the radicals classified their fathers with the relatively conservative CDU, compared with 44 percent of all subjects. The differences among activists were very similar. Forty-seven percent of the revolutionaries and 55 percent of the other leftists placed their fathers with the SPD, compared with 35 percent of the moderates and none of the conservatives, all of whom came from CDU-oriented households.

These differences, although statistically significant, were not as substantial as one might expect. They produced a correlation between radical attitudes and father's party preference of only .09.[26] Even after excluding students from FDP households, to maximize distinction between left- and right-wing family backgrounds, the correlation rose to only .19.[27] Moreover, only a minority of either ideological radicals or revolutionary activists came from SPD-oriented households, despite the statistical association of radicalism with an SPD orientation. This anomaly stems from the fact that fewer than one third of the entire sample characterized their fathers as SPD-oriented. Despite their tendency to gravitate toward radical ideas and activities, they were outweighed by the children of CDU or FDP partisans. This disparity reflects West German political realities. The SPD had only once received a majority of the vote in a national election and never surpassed even the 40 percent level until the 1960s. Moreover, the children of working-class parents, a bulwark of the SPD, are greatly underrepresented in German universities.

Thus our sample contained a large proportion of radicals who came from families that were rather conservative in their political orientations.

To determine whether these students were actively rebelling against their parents, we asked how their own political views compared with those of their father, how their fathers reacted to their political views, and what kind of politically oriented reading matter they recalled seeing around the house while growing up. Their responses produced substantial evidence of rebellion against fathers perceived as conservative and as antagonistic toward their sons' political aspirations.

When our subjects compared their own political views with those of their fathers, the results provided a graphic illustration of the leftist political culture that pervades many German universities. Students placed themselves on a scale from one to seven, where "one" indicated the political Right and "seven" the Left. Fewer than one in twenty placed themselves to the right of their father, and just under one in four viewed themselves as having about the same orientation as their father. The remaining three quarters saw themselves as politically left of their fathers. Almost half (47 percent) placed themselves far to their fathers' left by selecting six or seven on the seven-point scale. Radicals displayed only a slightly greater leftward shift than did nonradicals, although the movement was so general as to leave little opportunity for any group to move farther leftward than any other.

Some differentiation did arise among the activists. Almost half (47 percent) of the nonrevolutionary activists placed themselves far to the left of their fathers, about the same proportion as among the entire sample. Among the revolutionaries, however, the figure rose to more than three fifths (61 percent). The remaining two fifths of the revolutionaries termed themselves as similar to or only slightly left of their fathers, compared with well over half the other groups. Of all seventy-nine young activists, only two placed themselves to the right of their fathers.

Radicals and nonradicals were much more divergent in describing their fathers' responses to their own political views, with radicals encountering significantly greater antagonism and hostility. About two thirds of the sample reported paternal support or neutrality toward their politics. Thus only one third perceived any generational conflict over their politics. Radicals, by contrast, were almost evenly divided, with 48 percent reporting paternal opposition and 52 percent paternal support or neutrality. Among those who backed up their political doctrines with action, the differences were much greater. Just one in four nonrevolutionary activists, leftists and rightists alike, could look to their fathers for support. Among revolutionaries, only one in ten enjoyed paternal support. Over two thirds of the revolutionaries counted their fathers as hostile, compared with two fifths of the other leftist activists and only one quarter of the moderates and conservatives.

Such ratings are, of course, purely subjective. They describe a student's impressions of his father, rather than his father's actual political position. As such, they describe the son's experience of political conflict or continuity with his father, something that is important in its own right. These West German radical students experienced this relationship in terms of distance and estrangement, if not outright rebellion.

To provide a more objective measure of this experience, we asked about the publications students recalled seeing in their homes during childhood. We coded periodicals with conservative or right-wing perspectives (e.g., *National und Soldatenzeitung, Christ und Welt*), on one hand, and those with liberal or left-wing perspectives (e.g., *Konkret, Simplizissimus*), on the other. If radical students were predisposed toward current perspectives by growing up in left-leaning, politically aware households, we would expect that their parents, on average, read more left-oriented and fewer right-oriented periodicals than did parents of nonradical students. Allowing for the exigencies of memory, this should show up in our subjects' recollections. Our findings, however, point in the opposite direction. First, radicals recalled seeing almost exactly the same number of conservative publications as did nonradicals. Second, and more telling, radicals recalled seeing significantly *fewer* liberal or leftist publications than did nonradicals. This was true of both ideological radicals and members of revolutionary groups.

It seems unlikely that radicals would differentially forget or repress memories of leftist publications. If anything, most evidence on selective recall suggests that they would best remember the publications most similar to their current views. The apparent paucity of such periodicals in their households weighs strongly against the possibility that they were predisposed toward a radical outlook at an early age.

This completes our portrait of the social and political backgrounds of West German radicals. We again caution readers that our sample was not random. This means that our results do not necessarily provide an accurate portrait of radicalism among male college students at Konstanz and Tübingen, much less for the entire German student movement. Nonetheless, our findings proved quite suggestive for understanding the social origins of student radicalism.

The German radicals' backgrounds were strikingly similar to those of non-Jewish American radicals. In their social backgrounds, they were virtually indistinguishable from nonradicals. They were no more likely than other students to come from households headed by wealthy, highly educated professionals. In their political backgrounds, they tended to be drawn from families on either the left or right end of the political spectrum, rather than on the middle.

Even radicals raised in Social Democratic households, however, seemed to be in rebellion against parents they perceived as conservative and hostile. Moreover, they were somewhat less likely than other students to discuss politics with their parents or to recall seeing left-wing publications around the house.

In sum, German radicals gave little indication of continuing family traditions of leftist ideology or behavior. Instead, they seemed to be actively rebelling against parents who were either genuinely conservative or insufficiently radical to satisfy their more fervent children. We certainly found no indication of the political continuity that characterized the families of many American Jewish radicals. Like non-Jewish radicals across the Atlantic, these young rebels felt politically and emotionally disinherited.

We turn now to the social psychology of student radicalism in West Germany. We expected that German male radical students would resemble non-

Jewish American radicals in their family relations and psychological orientations. Specifically, we predicted that these radical subjects would fit our model of the rigid rebel. This type of radical is raised in a traditional patriarchal family whose child-rearing patterns involve harsh, inconsistent discipline and a lack of emotional warmth. The child develops a desire to rebel against and destroy his parents, especially his father, while repressing desires to submit. He begins to perceive the world in terms of power relationships, envying the strong and fearing the weakness he senses in both his father and himself. His experiences create an instinctive mistrust of authority, which generates in turn a need to relieve the tension of continual opposition. The need to feel powerful becomes a primary motivating force, coexisting with a contradictory wish to submit to a greater force.

Participating in a movement for radical change means release from this painful ambivalence. A feeling of power can be attained by incorporating oneself into a movement greater than the individual, a movement whose militant oppositional stance is perceived as strength. Pent-up aggression can be expressed against a weak establishment and legitimized by identification with selected oppressed groups, who are perceived as strong and justifiably violent, rather than weak and downtrodden. Let us see whether this model accurately predicts the family relations and personality traits of these German radicals.

The authoritarian family is dominated by a father who is uncaring and distant, as well as a harsh and punitive disciplinarian. The mother is subservient toward her husband, but henpeckingly domineering toward her children. She too can be cold, harsh, and ill-tempered toward the child, perhaps out of resentment over the demands of the self-sacrificial feminine role in this family. Such a family constellation results in the child's negative identification with parental authority. Rather than functioning as positive role models who are integrated into the child's ego ideal, the parents are seen as unredeemably villainous. This early experience paves the way for adolescent insurrection against social authority.

To see whether German radicals actually perceived their parents in these ways, we included a translated version of the Parent-Child Questionnaire in our survey. For the data analysis, the fifty-six PCQ adjectives were divided into the scales designated by its authors. These scales measure the degree to which a parent is portrayed as benevolent, protective, punitive, abandoning, and controlling. In terms of these scales, an authoritarian family would be one in which the father is highly controlling, both parents are punitive and abandoning, and neither parent is benevolent or protective. These are, in fact, roughly the results

Table 15. PCQ Perceptions of Parents Scores by Political Activism, German Male Students.

PCQ SCALE	Revolution-aries	Leftists	Moderates	Conserva-tives	Significance Level[a]
Father					
Benevolent					
Mean	3.36	3.75	3.99	4.25	.01
S.D.	(1.06)	(1.10)	(0.94)	(1.06)	
Protective					
Mean	4.42	4.81	5.32	5.18	.05
S.D.	(0.84)	(1.19)	(0.92)	(1.44)	
Abandoning					
Mean	5.40	4.81	4.85	4.19	n.s.
S.D.	(1.09)	(1.62)	(1.31)	(1.10)	
Punitive					
Mean	6.27	5.31	4.67	4.31	.01
S.D.	(0.83)	(1.64)	(1.44)	(1.99)	
Controlling					
Mean	6.32	5.29	5.27	5.50	.01
S.D.	(0.94)	(1.34)	(1.65)	(1.61)	
Mother					
Benevolent					
Mean	4.03	4.32	4.52	4.92	.05
S.D.	(1.04)	(1.05)	(0.99)	(0.66)	
Protective					
Mean	6.11	6.50	7.04	6.57	.05
S.D.	(1.14)	(1.29)	(0.86)	(1.22)	
Abandoning					
Mean	3.58	3.96	3.65	3.40	n.s.
S.D.	(1.18)	(1.22)	(1.24)	(0.78)	
Punitive					
Mean	4.86	4.78	3.83	3.46	.10
S.D.	(1.53)	(1.55)	(1.33)	(0.83)	
Controlling					
Mean	5.53	5.24	4.85	4.86	.10
S.D.	(1.94)	(1.61)	(1.53)	(1.41)	
N	17	35	17	9	

[a] Statistical significance of t-tests comparing revolutionaries and leftists with moderates and conservatives.

we obtained for non-Jewish American radicals. Almost precisely the same pattern characterized the German radicals, all of whom were non-Jewish.

This pattern can be observed most clearly by comparing the average scores produced by the four activist groups, shown in Table 15. Revolutionary activists rated both their parents highest on the punitive and controlling scales and lowest on the benevolent and protective scales. They also rated their fathers highest on the abandoning scale. So the revolutionaries portrayed their families as most "authoritarian" on nine out of the ten PCQ dimensions. The sole exception was the maternal abandonment scale, on which the nonrevolutionary leftists scored highest. Moreover, the nonrevolutionary leftists also rated their parents as more authoritarian than did moderates and conservatives on every dimension save that of paternal abandonment.

A linear pattern thus emerges. On almost every dimension, revolutionaries rated their families as most authoritarian, followed by other leftists, while activists not on the left perceived their parents as least authoritarian. The differences between leftist and nonleftist activists approached statistically significant magnitudes on all measures except those of paternal control and maternal abandonment. And revolutionaries alone rated their fathers as significantly more controlling than did all other activists.

When we turn to the correlations between radicalism and familial authoritarianism, we find a very similar pattern. Radical ideology was significantly correlated with all measures of authoritarianism except parental control. This is shown in the left-hand column of Table 16. To provide a means for comparing these relationships with our findings among activists, we assigned the number "one" to conservatives, "two" to moderates, "three" to leftists, and "four" to revolutionaries. We then used these rankings to correlate the degree of radical activism with activists' perceptions of their parents.[28] This procedure produced correlations roughly comparable to the association between ideology and

Table 16. Correlations of Radical Ideology and Activism with Perceptions of Parents.[a]

PCQ SCALE	New Left Ideology	Activism
Father		
Benevolent	−.17**	−.26**
Protective	−.11†	−.25*
Punitive	.15*	.40**
Abandoning	.19**	.22*
Controlling	.05	.19*
Mother		
Benevolent	−.24**	−.25*
Protective	−.20**	−.20*
Punitive	.14*	.29**
Abandoning	.10†	.06
Controlling	.06	.15†
N	220	78

†p<.10
*p<.05
**p<.01

[a] For New Left ideology, correlations are Pearson's r; for activism, Spearman's rho.

parental ratings. The results are shown in the right-hand column of Table 16. On almost all the PCQ measures, familial authoritarianism was more strongly associated with radical activism than with radical ideology. Even parental control, which was virtually unrelated to radical ideology, was significantly correlated with radical activism.

Thus in terms of both ideology and activism, West German male radicals perceived both their parents as relatively punitive, abandoning, and lacking in benevolence and protection. In addition, radical activists perceived both parents as relatively controlling. Most of the correlations were rather low but statistically significant, and most were strongest among activists.

These results are quite reminiscent of our findings among American non-Jewish radicals, both students and adults. Any given parental characteristic was only slightly related to radicalism, but to a degree unlikely to occur by chance alone. Most importantly, virtually the same pattern recurs in all three studies. All variables except parental control were significantly related to radicalism in the directions we predicted, i.e., the direction of the traditional authoritarian family. This reinforces our suspicion that it is not the amount of discipline but its harshness and, perhaps, its inconsistent application that make for parents' authoritarian style. One can easily see how a child might develop problems in dealing with authority if his parents are uncaring, distant, and punitive. The degree of discipline thus may be less relevant to familial authoritarianism and consequent adolescent rebellion than the spirit in which it is meted out. On the other hand, West German revolutionary activists did view their fathers as highly controlling. So the evidence is mixed on this point.

To summarize, radicalism was associated with a broad pattern of unsatisfying relations between parent and child, with radicals most likely to portray their parents in terms of the authoritarian family. In addition, this portrait seemed especially relevant to radical activists. The correlations were generally stronger among the activists, and only among activists was radicalism significantly associated with parental strictness or control. In general, the more radical the student, the more authoritarian he perceived his parents. Finally, revolutionary activists stood apart from all others, including other leftists, in viewing both parents as harsh, controlling, uncaring villains.

Again, the issue is not one of patriarchy. The fathers of nonradical subjects were no less dominant than the fathers of radicals. Nonetheless, the nonradicals tended to perceive both their parents as benevolent and concerned.

The family relations described by these German radicals could easily create conflicts over authority that would predispose young people toward authoritar-

Table 17. TAT Motivation Scores by Political Activism, German Male Students.

MOTIVE	Revolu-tionary	Leftist	Moderate	Conserva-tive	Significance Level[a]
n Power	50.00	52.02	47.77	43.91	.05
Fear of Power	52.04	51.45	47.60	44.76	.05
N	17	34	17	9	

[a]Significance of t-tests comparing revolutionaries and leftists with moderates and conservatives.

ian personality traits. But did they in fact develop such traits? As in the American study, we addressed this question with projective and quasi-projective psychological tests, analyzing students' TAT themes and Semantic Differential power scores. We asked our German subjects to write stories about the same TAT pictures that we gave to American students. Owing to financial limitations, however, we could score their protocols for only two themes, the need for and the fear of power. We selected these two measures because they tap the deep-seated ambivalence toward power that forms the core of an authoritarian disposition.

The results for activists are shown in Table 17. The nonrevolutionary leftists had the highest need for power scores, followed by the revolutionaries. For the fear of power, this order was reversed, with revolutionaries scoring highest, followed by the other leftists.

Moderates scored well below both groups of leftists, and conservatives scored lowest of all. The differences between leftist and nonleftist activists were statistically significant for both measures.

We then examined the relationship between power imagery and radical ideology among the entire sample. As Table 18 reveals, students who endorsed radical tactics also scored highest on both the need for and fear of power. To

Table 18. Correlations of Radical Ideology and Activism with TAT Motivation Scores, German Male Students.

	IDEOLOGY			
MOTIVE	New Left Ideology	Socialism	Anti-Conservatism	Activism
Need for Power	10†	.15*	.14*	.22*
Fear of Power	.13*	.14*	.13*	.22*
N	220	214	220	78

†p<.10
*p<.05

ensure that this pattern was not restricted to a relatively narrow dimension of radicalism, we also measured the association of power imagery with attitudes toward socialism and conservatism, using the measures we described earlier. Students who strongly endorsed socialism and strongly rejected conservative attitudes also scored highest in both the need for and fear of power. In fact, both personality traits were more closely associated with these broad measures of political ideology than with our New Left Ideology scale. This probably reflects the greater salience of broad ideological issues for the German New Left, as well as the technical difficulties of adapting an American attitude scale to the West German political context.

The most important finding is that radicals had significantly greater power needs and conflicts than nonradicals, regardless of how we measured radical ideology—as support for socialism, rejection of conservatism, or endorsement of violent or revolutionary tactics.

Thus both ideological and activist radicals proved most prone to a simultaneous desire for and fear of power. Their combination of high n Power and high Fear of Power scores suggest the presence of strong power needs that may be projected onto political opponents. These radicals might indeed experience their power needs as defensive reactions to Establishment oppression. Our data cannot tell us whether their political opponents behave coercively, as radicals alleged. But the data may help us understand the intensity with which radicals reject sociopolitical authority as illegitimate, whatever the validity of their rejection.

We predicted further that radicals' power conflicts would lead them to identify potency with militancy and brute force, while rejecting intellectual power as eviscerated or impotent. To test these predictions, we used several of the Semantic Differential pictures developed for the American student study, which were again scored for perceived potency. The pictures included the white male and female protesters, the policeman, and the white male student seated at his desk.

Because most of the people pictured were obviously Americans, they might have had a different emotional resonance for German students. We could only rely upon our judgment that pictures of young protesters, a policeman, and a student would be readily identifiable as such to European audiences.

For the most part, the results bear out our assessment. Among activists, as Table 19 shows, the revolutionaries stood apart from all other groups by attributing power to the four pictures in a manner conforming to our model. Revolutionaries rated the male and female protester and (to a lesser degree) the policeman as significantly stronger than did other activists, and the studious young man as significantly weaker.[29] Their highest potency rating, as well as

Table 19. Semantic Differential Power Scores by Political Activism, German Male Students.

	Revolution-aries	Leftists	Moderates	Conserva-tives	Significance Level[a]
Radical Male					
Mean	5.76	4.53	4.76	4.78	
S.D.	(0.75)	(1.62)	(1.72)	(1.64)	.001
Radical Female					
Mean	5.29	4.51	4.63	4.11	
S.D.	(1.31)	(1.69)	(1.54)	(1.69)	.05
Nonradical Student					
Mean	4.06	4.22	4.35	4.77	
S.D.	(1.19)	(1.21)	(1.41)	(1.30)	.05
Policeman					
Mean	5.00	4.69	3.82	4.56	.10
S.D.	(1.54)	(1.67)	(1.67)	(1.74)	
Number of Subjects	17	35	17	9	

[a] Significance of t-tests comparing revolutionaries with all other activists.

their greatest divergence from other groups, was elicited by the picture of a male protester. It seems reasonable to infer that these radicals perceived New Left militancy as a source of strength, while attributing weakness to more scholarly pursuits of college students.

The same results were obtained for radical ideology, with one exception, as Table 20 shows. The picture of a policeman failed to produce a significant correlation between radical ideology and perceived potency, although the correlation with radical activism was significant. This was the only instance in which the tests failed to support our model. Interestingly, even this result replicated our findings for American students. In the American student study, only Jewish radicals perceived the policeman as relatively powerful. The lack of any comparable association with radical ideology among non-Jews in America and Germany alike again suggests that this measure taps an ethnically limited aspect of radical personality style.

Otherwise, our Semantic Differential findings followed much the same pattern as the TAT results. Support for radical tactics was only slightly associated with perceptions of protesters as powerful figures, although the correlations approached statistical significance. The endorsement of socialism and rejection

Table 20. Correlations of Radical Ideology and Activism with Semantic Differential Power Scores, German Male Students.

	New Left Ideology	Socialism	Anti-Conservatism	Activism
Semantic Differential				
Radical Male	.10†	.21**	.14*	.17†
Radical Female	.10†	.16*	.15*	.19*
Nonradical Student	−.25**	−.16*	−.17**	−.16†
Policeman	.00	.07	.00	.17†
Number of Subjects	220	214	220	79

†p<.10
*p<.05
**p<.01

of conservatism, however, produced somewhat higher correlations. Finally, all these measures of radical ideology were significantly associated with perceptions of the studious young man as relatively weak or impotent.

Scholars and journalists have rarely found it difficult to interpret German political life in terms of such social psychological concepts as the "German family" or the "Nazi personality." To provide empirical confirmation of such concepts is a much more arduous task.

On our projective psychological instruments, radical activists and adherents of radical ideology did exhibit the pattern of traits predicted by our model of intense authoritarianism. The lack of strong correlations prohibits any facile equation of radical ideology or behavior with psychological authoritarianism. Yet the consistency of the results suggests that, for this sample, radicalism was not unrelated to authoritarian rebellion, particularly among activists. Despite the lack of a random sample and the use of rather novel psychological tests intended for American subjects, the results replicated almost every finding from our American studies. The German radicals closely resembled their American non-Jewish counterparts in both their social diversity and psychological homogeneity. They exhibited the same political and personal rejection of their parents, and the same power complex, which they apparently resolved by adopting the negative identity of social outlaw.

These findings suggest that our social psychological model of authoritarian rebellion may be useful in understanding the internal dynamics of the West German New Left. Even a few authoritarians within the activist core of an unstructured protest movement can have an effect on the course of the movement far out of proportion to their number. So the model may indeed help us to illuminate the dynamics of the German student movement, as well as the behavior of some participants.

The German New Left paralleled the American in its progression from early "existential" idealism through increasing militance in both goals and tactics, ending in violence and ideological isolation. Our data suggest that, for some of these radicals, a Marcusian "great refusal" may have given ideological expression to the identification of strength with opposition and militancy. The need to subsume their individuality into a strong oppositional movement would have facilitated the transformation of functionally specific political groups into the *Lebensbunde*—all-embracing radical communities—of the 1970s. The concomitant increase in militancy, whatever its immediate political causes, may have functioned as a reaction against an underlying desire to "give in" to authority. Total opposition, as well as total submission, releases one from ambivalence.

On one level, the German New Left's increasing militancy stemmed from political frustration and moral outrage. But these factors do not explain why frustration and outrage led some students to disavow rational strategies of social change and to embrace "actionism"—the use of confrontation—not to change society but to draw revolutionary fervor from the crucible of battle. Thus our theory can help us understand how their moral righteousness was gradually transformed into terrorism.

This approach does not, however, answer all the questions one should like to have answered. Perhaps most importantly the German Left was characterized by an ideological seriousness and willingness to engage in violent action against persons that went far beyond the actions of the American or even the French Left, though not the Italian. Our studies do not tell us why this should be so. We suspect that our instruments failed to capture significant differences between national groups, and that a full understanding of such differences would also require an in-depth discussion of the continuing differences between German and American culture.

Part IV

CONCLUSION

10 The Student Left in Perspective

IT IS DIFFICULT to recapture the emotional fervor of the 1960s today. To many of the young people—and some not so young—who made up the New Left almost anything seemed possible. A new world was on the verge of being born.

To be sure, many cultural themes developed by the New Left had a long European pedigree in one form or another. Bohemianism, the free expression of sexuality, a desire to end the family, and so forth can be found as far back as a number of Christian heresies.[1] Such themes have also been rallying cries of some radicals in almost every modern revolution since 1789. They occur especially in conjunction with attacks from both the Left and the Right on the "dessicated rationality" of bourgeois society. And certainly the rather vague Marxism of the early New Left and the more explicit Marxism of the late 1960s were not unfamiliar.

The New Left, however, was almost unique in the dizzying array of challenges it presented to the political and social system. The anti-Establishment temper encompassed rejection of "politics as usual," of political and economic institutions, of social tradition and sexual mores, and even of western culture itself.

It was not new for students to issue radical critiques of the existing social order. What was new was the multi-faceted and eclectic nature of this student movement. From its inception, it was less a new "Left" than a revolt of the disenchanted and the dissaffiliated, a quasi-political expression of middle-class psychological alienation. In 1966 Jack Newfield tried to summarize this mélange of competing and coexisting themes:

> What is explicitly *new* about the New Left is its ecumenical mixture of political traditions that were once murderous rivals in Russia, Spain, France, and the United States. It contains within it, and often within individuals, elements of anarchism, socialism, pacifism, existentialism,

humanism, transcendentalism, bohemianism, Populism, mysticism, and black nationalism.[2]

Even at the time, this listing seemed somewhat arbitrary. The "isms" could have been extended almost indefinitely, to include, for example, tendencies toward communitarianism, decentralism, syndicalism, and so forth. If there was a single "ism" that encompassed the others, it was the Movement's radical pluralism—the desire to see a hundred flowers bloom in the "spiritually barren" soil of modern life. This pluralism accounts in part for the New Left's ability to function as a political inkblot test for outside observers, eliciting the strong emotions and diverse interpretations that spring from confusion and uncertainty. The young radicals challenged society in such a vague and generalized fashion that conservatives could not fail to be affronted or reformers heartened by the unexpected growth of the new social and political force. Michael Harrington thus greeted the early reformist New Left as "the prophetic minority of our times" who would generate a "united and effective [radicalism], a mass movement in the very center of society."[3] Zbigniew Brzezinski dismissed the Movement as a "death rattle" of the historically obsolete, a doomed revolt of neo-Luddites against modern "technotronic" society.[4] By the late '60s, Herbert Marcuse would entrust the mantle of revolutionary agency to dissident youth as harbingers of the new "sensual society" he had foreseen in *Eros and Civilization*.[5] And at the other end of the political spectrum, President Pompidou decried the May 1968 Paris revolt as signaling the collapse of "our civilization itself."[6]

Whatever else it was, the New Left became the cutting edge of what Max Weber termed the "disenchantment of the world."[7] The new radicals rebelled against all facets of what they saw as the faceless and soulless structure of "corporate liberalism." But they rejected with equal fervor the Marxist-Leninist alternative that had so animated their predecessors of the thirties. The liberal and communist "Establishments" initially served as twin foils for the new radicals' groping efforts at self-definition. All too soon, they revealed themselves instead to be the Movement's Scylla and Charybdis. The young activists who tried to steer between them were either pulled back into the reformist mainstream or carried down the cul-de-sac of ideological sectarianism.

The "schizophrenic" quality of the Movement was not unrelated to the character of its participants. Our data on student and adult radicals actually point to two types of psycho-political rebellion. The protean rebels who dominated the early stages of the American student movement were predominantly Jewish, although this group also included some Protestant respondents from liberal cosmopolitan backgrounds. The evidence suggests that these young people were attempting to deal with narcissistic injuries by further undermining an already weakened cultural superego and ego. They fantasized that, by so doing, they could bring an end to western scientific rationality and hence to time itself. Thus they would achieve a feeling of immortality in a world in which they could safely swim in a sea of experience. The popularity of writers like Norman O. Brown and Charles Reich testifies to these fantasies, as do the popularity of various eastern religions and the development of the drug culture. Had these young people actually come into power, they might well have attempted to establish a repressive regime that would have sought to crush all those who stood in the way of their unlimited freedom. The fate of many communes established during the 1960s supports this speculation.[8]

The second type of radical, the rigid rebel, was rather different. In general, as our studies demonstrate, such people were raised in lower-middle-class, socially conservative environments. Psychodynamically, they resemble more closely the traditional authoritarian described by Adorno et al. or Erikson.[9] Such individuals conceive themselves as rebels against weak and corrupt authorities. The erosion of the authority of social institutions provides them with a mechanism to vent their rage at "authoritarian" fathers. Their parents had directed their own aggression against "communists" or blacks. Now the children vented hostility against the "Establishment" or capitalism. The ideology was different, but it served similar psychological needs. Such individuals seem to have become more significant in the American student movement in the late 1960s and early 1970s. They had turned to the Left because the political culture of the 1960s permitted them to "act out" under the moral patina of radicalism.

A number of German and American intellectuals refused to recognize the parallels between the New Left and the extreme Right because a part of them resonated with the radicals. In Germany, it was only after the mindless terrorism of the Baader-Meinhof group became too obvious to deny that its methods were rejected. Even then, some intellectuals tended to regard such terrorism as merely the corruption of a once noble ideal.[10]

To be sure, most student radicals were not authoritarians, or, at least, their authoritarianism was not captured by our instruments. All we can say is that we found a larger number of authoritarians among the student radicals than we did in our comparison groups. We believe that these young people exercised an influence far beyond their numbers, but our study does not enable us to explain why many young people, who did not differ from conservatives or liberals in any way that we could measure, chose a different political path.

Further, the majority of students who became involved in the civil rights or antiwar movements were not radicals. They were simply protesting against what they considered an unjust war and other elements of social injustice. Once a movement becomes established, all sorts of people are drawn into it for a host of reasons, including social norms among their peers. At that point, individual psychological explanations of behavior become less and less relevant, as do social class or other sociological explanations.[11]

That many nonradical young people invested their views with considerable emotional energy is not surprising. Everyone's social and political views derive some of their emotional charge from nonrational sources. In times of crisis the most rational individuals can invest their opponents with all sorts of "evil" impulses. Given a reasonable balance of such unconscious forces and a reasonably autonomous ego, such individuals retain the ability to learn and to modify their views, provided they have access to a variety of sources of information. Nevertheless, the widespread appeal of some elements of the counter-culture indicates that many young people resonated with the themes espoused by the most radical protesters for reasons that went beyond the crises of the period.[12]

The American New Left's flirtation with violence and terrorism was narrowly based and transient. Even the relatively widespread violence of May 1970 was the work of only a tiny minority of antiwar dissenters. Further, the Cambodia-Kent State protests were the final eruption of widespread campus dissent—not an overture to the seventies but a coda of the sixties. Such bizarre aberrations as the SLA, although products of "a decade of defiance," hardly helped to expand the base of radical dissent.

Thus, despite sporadic outbreaks of violence by remnants of the Weather Underground which surfaced as late as the early 1980s, the Movement's energies after 1972 were channeled almost entirely into electoral politics. With Nixon's reelection that fall, the era of mass protest came to an abrupt end. The Left seemed in disarray. One-time activists now took refuge in cultural or "spiritual" radicalism. Rennie Davis became a disciple of Jai Guru Dev, the adolescent "perfect master" from India. Jerry Rubin immersed himself in the human potential movement and later became a Wall Street broker. Others redirected their energies into the arena of sexual politics, working for female or gay liberation. The seventies also brought new causes that eventually attracted Movement veterans, such as protests against building nuclear reactors. In 1976 David Dellinger could assert that the struggles of the sixties had merely shifted to new fronts, where the overall battle with the Establishment continues to rage:

> With a powerful shove from feminists and gays, and a tug from new
> therapies and ancient spiritual movements, the new radical is struggling
> to unite the personal, political, spiritual and the material. The move-

ment is healthier and more revolutionary than it was in the late 60's
. . . new centres of power and direct resistance are . . . undermining
outworn beliefs on which the existing institutions rely: competition, inequality of wealth and power, male supremacy, white dominance, the
superiority of representative to participatory democracy, violence.[13]

To some extent this smacks of putting the best face on a bad situation. But
Dellinger did put his finger on the most enduring legacy of the New Left—the
creation of a new political agenda and the establishment of an "adversary culture" that retains its influence on American life. No more than 10 to 15 percent
of the college population ever classified themselves as part of the radical Left.
Of course, this figure represents several hundred thousand, perhaps even a million, young people. Moreover, their activism and commitment brought them
influence far out of proportion to their numbers. Despite an inability to institutionalize their protest, they managed to push the bulk of moderate students
toward a less sanguine view of American politics and institutions. If the New
Left failed to radicalize the campuses, it succeeded in shifting the entire political spectrum to the left. In Lipset's words, "the calm of the 1970s [witnessed]
a dramatic generational shift to the left within the families of those who are
able to send their children to college."[14]

Campus-based protest was most successful not in winning recruits to the
Movement but in defining the terms of political debate, so that single-issue
protest quickly broadened into a generalized attack on the social system. America did not just have a race problem, it was a racist society. The Vietnam War
was not just a bad or immoral policy, it was the outcome of American imperialism. In 1973 Daniel Yankelovich summarized several years of polling data
concerning antiwar attitudes:

The small core of political radicals, though never more than 10–15 percent of the college population, took the lead in interpreting the war in
terms that were harshly critical of the United States, its motives, its
institutions, and its moral impulses. Because they were so disturbed by
the war, the great mass of college students accepted the radical critique
and . . . joined with the New Left in its attack on the universities and
other institutions that were interpreted as being part of the web of im-
morality and misuse of power that students associated with the war.[15]

The erosion of support for American institutions had solidified into widespread hostility toward authority and suspicion of traditional values. Lipset made
this point by comparing national student surveys taken in 1971, just after the
Cambodia-Kent State protests, and in 1973, after quiet had returned to the

campuses and late '60s activists had graduated.[16] He found evidence that political alienation actually increased in the intervening years. By 1973 half the students sampled agreed that "the Establishment unfairly controls our lives; we can never be free until we are rid of it," up 4 percent from 1971. Almost two thirds (63 percent) believed America was "a democracy in name only and that special interests run things," an increase of 7 percent. The evidence was not always consistent. For example, the proportion who found America to be "a 'sick' society" dropped from 45 to 35 percent. But substantial numbers of the educated young obviously continued to view their society with a jaundiced eye. In 1975 the Gallup organization found similar sentiments on American campuses; the pollsters also discovered that the longer a student had been in college, the greater was his "disillusionment with American institutions." Polls conducted in the late 1970s indicated that while the bitterness had declined, the disillusion by and large remained.[17]

Political alienation need not always be associated with political activity. The absence of overt protest has not meant a return to '50s quietism. Elite campuses have become bastions of left-liberal and radical social criticism, particularly with regard to "life style" issues such as environmentalism, support for "radical" third world regimes, sexual freedom, and radical feminism. There has been some leveling off on these issues and perhaps a slight retreat on a few of them. There is no evidence, however, of a return to the period before "the revolution."

The institutionalization of more radical attitudes on college campuses was facilitated by an influx of radical academics into social science and humanities departments all over the country. Many "Movement intellectuals" of the early sixties, like Richard Flacks and Al Haber, finished school and became faculty members by the decade's end. Disciplines like economics and political science today contain radical caucuses, of which the Union of Radical Political Economists (founded by Haber, among others) was a prototype. More generally, college teachers in the social sciences and humanities are the most politically liberal occupational group in America today, and leftist sentiments are especially prominent in these fields. Moreover, the faculty at prestigious schools and those who publish widely are most likely to hold leftist attitudes.[18]

Despite the conservative turn of public opinion in the 1970s and early 1980s, then, a predominantly liberal or progressive professoriate continues to nourish critical and reformist tendencies among college youth. Even if young people are less persuaded by "progressive" arguments than they were a decade ago, they are far more skeptical about the traditional values of their society.

Similar attitudes have developed beyond the campus. The New Left's anti-institutional outlook and anti-bourgeois value scheme has fed into the "new liberalism" increasingly held by the upper middle class. Indeed, the "radical" values and orientations expressed by SNCC and SDS workers in the early sixties have become the conventional wisdom of college-educated urban professionals, especially those under thirty-five. Drawing on survey data collected over the past three decades, Everett Ladd has argued that these groups have become "a reformist intelligentsia" which rejects "traditional bourgeois values . . . and traditional cultural norms and life styles, together with older codes of behavior."[19]

This represents a nearly complete inversion of the political cleavage that predominated until the 1960s, which pitted a conservative business-oriented middle class against a reformist working class. The new radicalism brought the concerns of a growing leftist intelligentsia to the center of political discourse. The bread-and-butter issues that had historically divided the working and middle classes were now supplemented by sociocultural "life style" issues that pitted blue-collar and lower-middle-class groups against the college-educated professional and managerial "knowledge elites." Surveys conducted by the National Opinion Research Center during the 1970s and early 1980s show that today people with college degrees or so-called "new class" occupations such as journalism are far more likely than other groups to say that they reject bourgeois values like work, thrift, and material success, and favor "self-fulfillment over economic security and providing for one's family." They are also much more likely to favor legalized abortion and marijuana usage and to express more liberal opinions on homosexuality and premarital or extramarital sex. To a significantly greater extent than other groups in the population, they favor increased public spending on environmental protection, urban problems, and the educational system, and they are less likely to support government spending for crime prevention and military defense. Finally, these groups are certainly less committed to the traditional values of the society than they were in the 1950s, and they are no longer convinced of America's unique goodness.[20]

These attitudes are centered among people who have been most exposed to the ideas and activities of the New Left—those who were graduated from northeastern and west coast colleges after the early 1960s. It can hardly be argued that the New Left is solely or even primarily responsible for the rise of new forms of liberalism in American political and social life. After all, the factors that contributed to the formation and growth of new forms of liberalism also contributed to the formation and growth of the New Left itself. The student movement, then, helped to forge the new political agenda that has replaced bread-and-butter liberalism for many on the Left. As Yankelovich concluded, "the enduring heritage of the 1960s is the new social values that grew on the nation's campuses during that same fateful period and now have grown stronger and more powerful.''[21] Whatever their other successes and failures, the youthful radicals of that decade propelled a new set of values from the fringes to the very midst of contemporary social conflict.

This development was slowed by the 1980 election of a conservative Republican as president, but it was by no means halted. The Right has been able to reverse some of the changes institutionalized during the 1960s. There is little evidence that it has produced a fundamental change in underlying attitudes.[22]

As many studies have documented, the great mass of American voters was always quite hostile to the liberal cosmopolitan stance adopted by the Democratic party in the late 1960s. The overwhelming rejection of George McGovern in 1972 testified eloquently to that fact. Carter's defeat in 1980 stemmed partly from his inability to project an image of competence and partly from Reagan's ability to avoid being identified as an extremist. On the other hand, the defeat of several prominent liberal senators was, to a considerable extent, the function of more effective mobilization by conservative political forces. Such groups made basically conservative voters aware of the cosmopolitan liberalism of those who had been representing them.

It is true that many one-time radicals have moved closer to the political center, and that those who remain on the Left are currently in disarray. But the entire political spectrum has shifted well to the left in recent years. Today's liberals have absorbed many of the "radical" ideas that infused the New Left two decades ago. Moreover, social attitudes considered marginal if not deviant little more than a decade ago are now accepted as natural by substantial segments of the middle class.[23] While working-class people remain somewhat more conservative about such matters, the evidence indicates that they are far more accepting of the new morality than they once were and far less supportive of the "sacredness" of American institutions.[24]

German developments followed an even more radical course. By the late 1970s, journalists, government officials, and scholars agreed that perhaps a fifth of all West German students had become entrenched in a self-perpetuating radical subculture.[25] The politicizing of the academy, especially within disciplines like sociology and political science, remains a severe problem, which is exacerbated by the political apathy of most nonradical students. Flora Lewis, European correspondent for the New York *Times,* described the campus scene in 1977:

> . . . the wave of student revulsion in 1968 . . . never really receded in West Germany.

Professors have the right to co-opt faculty recruits, with life-time tenure, so the far left has been able to reinforce and expand its hold where it was established in those days of open conflict.

Clearly, the militant leftists are a small minority. . . . The silent majority is studious, nonpolitical, indifferent to agitated appeals, and it is precisely because of their refusal to be involved that the minority has captured much of the leadership.[26]

In addition to the revolutionary groups, a number of leftist organizations offer ex-protesters the opportunity to continue working for radical change within the system. The SHB provided a campus base for left-wing socialists, and the JUSOs became a continual irritant to the Social Democrats, with their popular front policies and radical reform programs. As we pointed out in Chapter 8, a few radicals even began the "long march through the institutions," seeking out civil service jobs that would allow them to undermine the regime from within.

Perhaps most disturbing for the future is the prevailing climate of opinion in the universities, where the political system is widely ridiculed, communism is widely endorsed, and the use of political violence is justified. These findings were reported by the Allensbach Public Opinion Institute, based on a 1978 poll of 500 students at thirty-three universities.[27] The pollsters found that two thirds of all students, and five sixths of the activists, thought communism to be a "good idea," though most rejected the way it is practiced by existing communist states. Fewer than a quarter opposed the entry of communists into West European governments. Lest this be taken as a purely civil libertarian view, students were asked about coalitions in their own self-governing bodies. As many rejected coalitions with the conservative Ring of Christian Democratic Students as with communist groups. Among activists, 60 percent opposed coalitions with the RCDS; only 27 percent disdained the communists.

The appeal of communism seems linked to widespread rejection of the Federal Republic's parliamentary democracy. This has not receded since the sixties. Over half the students agreed that "free and equal discussion is no longer carried on in [West Germany], and true opposition is no longer tolerated," up 5 percent from 1967 when the same question was asked at the height of student unrest. Two thirds agree that the political party system is undemocratic, again up slightly from 1967. And four fifths view the university as authoritarian, the same percentage as a decade ago, despite the vast reforms that have taken place. Two other findings are particularly ominous for the democratic potential of the studentry. In 1967, fewer than half agreed that "the Constitution is being increasingly undermined and falsified in a reactionary and authoritarian direction.'' In 1978 over 60 percent endorsed that view. And fully two thirds agreed that ''the government and parliament no longer represent the people's interest,'' compared with 47 percent in 1967.[28]

Increasing alienation from the parliamentary system has been accomplished by increasing politicization on campus. Since 1967, the proportion involved in campus religious groups has dropped from 9 to 2 percent while participation in political parties, their youth organizations, and student political organizations has risen from 13 to 31 percent.

Normally, one might applaud political concern and involvement by students. But this presupposes a commitment to democratic processes that is lacking on West German campuses. As we pointed out in chapter nine, a rather large number of German students say they are willing to use violence against people to achieve their political ends.

It is hard to imagine that so many West German students are willing to kill other people on ideological grounds, despite their questionnaire responses. Yet we should beware of underestimating the continuity of certain themes that run through Dutschke's ''anti-authoritarianism,'' the RAF's unvarnished terror, and the student opposition today. These young radicals have shared a common revulsion toward bourgeois society and an identification with its opponents, a self-righteousness that breeds intolerance, and a preference for action and spontaneity as a political style.

After a period of relative quiescence during the late 1970s, terrorist activity began to rise once again in Germany during the early 1980s, directed primarily against American military personnel, even as young people in West Berlin battled the police for a variety of causes, including a lack of what they considered adequate housing. Nuclear energy and the issue of nuclear weapons in Germany have attracted a far larger constituency, which threatens to rend the German Social Democratic party.

In West Germany, then, the polarization of the sixties has receded only slightly. The student opposition still inspires fear and suspicion among the populace. Their misgivings have been institutionalized in controversial laws that restrict radical lawyers' access to their clients and prevent one-time radicals from holding government jobs. For all its hard-won economic might and international influence, the Federal Republic struggles still to protect herself against her own children.

Explanations of the sea change that occurred in America and then Europe in the 1960s abound. Few today would accept the analyses of the student movement and its consequences proffered by Keniston, Flacks, Charles Reich, and others. However, scholars such as Inglehart still speak of the emergence of a post-bourgeois or post-materialist generation, an analysis that commands a certain amount of support. Marxists and neo-Marxists, on the other hand, continue to offer analyses that relate current developments to the alienation produced by advanced capitalist society.

Such theories seem to miss the point. In light of recent events in China, Cuba, Vietnam, and elsewhere, the old Marxist categories (even in new bottles) and liberal humanists' explanations fail to persuade. They seem no more convincing than the analyses of those conservatives and neo-conservatives who blame the events of the past two decades merely on the betrayal of a new class or the influence of bad ideas.

Without an overall theory we are left with explanations in terms of particular events or with historical analyses that trace the ideas of the New Left back to their many antecedents. On reflection, however, it is clear that the Vietnam War or the race issue might well have produced quite different reactions in another epoch. Further, one can find antecedents for almost any revolutionary movement that has ever developed. The number of social and political themes that can be created by human beings is not infinite, and in modern pluralistic societies most of them are expressed by one marginal group or another. The problem is to determine why at one period, rather than another, a particular combination of these ideas moves from the margins of society to the center of political controversy. It is clear that something more profound than a particular set of events was involved in the changes in America and Europe that began in the 1960s.

Daniel Bell, in *The Cultural Contradictions of Capitalism,* has explicated some of the shifts in American culture that paved the way for the upheavals of that decade.[29] Bell argues that liberal capitalism in the United States and elsewhere was based partly on a religious sensibility that emphasized individualism only within the frame of cultural parameters that stressed self-discipline, hard work, and sexual restraint. Anthony Wallace captures these cultural assumptions in his perceptive discussion of the development of a small American industrial community in the nineteenth century:

It was in Rockdale, and in dozens of other industrial communities like Rockdale, that an American world view developed which pervades the present—or did so until recently—with a sense of superior Christian virtue, a sense of global mission, a sense of responsibility and capability for bringing enlightenment to a dark and superstitious world, for overthrowing ancient and new tyrannies, and for making backward infidels into Christian men of enterprise.[30]

The religious values that underlay the culture of communities like Rockdale began to erode during the late nineteenth century, partly as the result of rationalizing tendencies inherent in liberal capitalism itself.[31] As they did, religious justifications for the limitations imposed by the culture were replaced by a belief in material progress as an end in itself. Hard work and self-restraint in a liberal capitalist system would lead to secular progress and ever better tomorrows for all. By the 1940s, however, as Leo Lowenthal discovered, the "idols of production" had been partially replaced by the "idols of consumption."[32] By the late 1950s, segments of an affluent middle class were adding to the consumption of material goods, the consumption of experience ("self-realization") as a desired end. Lacking a religious base, the requirements of work and self-discipline had been further undermined by affluence. The beats of the 1950s were certainly an expression of this, but there were many others, as the popularity of the writings of Erich Fromm and Abraham Maslow attests.[33]

This shift in cultural values was accompanied and encouraged by the growth of a stratum of service personnel, itself a product of economic and social as well as ideological developments in American society.[34] Many of these people were highly educated professionals working either in the public sector or in areas associated with the creation, dissemination, and transmission of knowledge.

The growth in size of this stratum is indicated in data provided by Bell. In 1889–90, 382 doctorates were granted in the United States. The total number of such degree recipients as of 1967 was close to 400,000. In 1940 only 5 million Americans had completed four or more years of college. By the mid-1960s, the figure had jumped to some 12 million.[35] These are quantum jumps, even allowing for population increases.

These "Metro Americans," as Erich Goldman called them, tended to be rather skeptical of traditional values, of the economics of liberal capitalism, and of American foreign policy.[36] They provided the readership for new, sophisticated critical journals such as the *New York Review of Books,* and, on another level, of such magazines as *Playboy,* whose combination of liberal politics and promotion of sexual "liberation" developed wide appeal among college-educated professionals.[37]

Richard Flacks and Kenneth Keniston both stressed that the children of this stratum of the population provided the initial cadres and sympathizers of the student movement. Indeed, both authors discovered that the values and attitudes of the first generation of student militants did not differ all that much from those of their parents.[38]

Academics and other intellectuals constituted an important segment of the new stratum. By the mid-1960s, a half million academics were teaching at

American universities.[39] Moreover, the graduates of these universities were providing audiences for books and essays written by urban intellectuals who lacked university attachments. Most studies indicate that, while the academic profession has been somewhat more liberal than the population as a whole since the turn of the century, the gap grew markedly during the 1950s and 1960s. Thus, in 1944, college faculties voted only 3 percent more Democratic than the general public; in 1952 they voted 12 percent more Democratic; and in 1972 they gave George McGovern 18 percent more votes than did the general public.[40]

Voting statistics tell only part of the story. Academics, especially in the social sciences, were gradually replacing the Protestant milieu of elite universities with a particular kind of secular humanism. They tended to be critical of nativist American institutions and to emphasize the inequalities which, they argued, were concealed by national rhetoric. They also stressed the negative effects of an impersonal capitalist society whose heritage still emphasized authoritarian repressiveness. It was from the academic community that the children of the new middle class learned of the advantages of a democratic, egalitarian society, characterized by the free (and thus healthy) expression of emotion. They also learned that society itself was responsible for social problems that once had been blamed on the individual, and that society should take the responsibility for solving those problems. The lessons were reenforced by large numbers of books and articles purporting to demonstrate these propositions. We have already argued that the social science that produced such studies was not without flaws. Nonetheless, by the early 1960s the propositions produced by it had become the conventional wisdom in the academy, and, in a watereddown version, among those who had been educated in the academy.

If the universities were having renewed impact upon the ideas and behavior of segments of the middle class, their influence was magnified by the postwar revolution in communications and transportation. In earlier times the bohemianism of New York and other major cities had had little impact on small towns or even the ethnic enclaves of metropolitan areas. This was changing rapidly. Key elements of change included the widespread availability of automobiles, jet aircraft, and television. The last, especially, meant that what happened in New York and other urban pacesetters became the common property of the nation within a relatively short time. Simultaneously, America for the first time developed a network of national news media. Those who staffed the television networks and the national print media, like *Time* magazine and the New York *Times,* were increasingly college-educated liberal cosmopolitans. As T. H. White and David Halberstam have pointed out, they gradually came to share the views of liberal intellectuals, not least because they lived in New York or Washington, D.C.[41] By the late 1950s, they were becoming a force to reckon with. By providing intellectuals with a larger audience, they helped to extend the intellectual community's influence to ever broader segments of the populace.

Jewish intellectuals and media personnel played an important role in this process. The growing appeal of writers of Jewish background to a large number of non-Jewish "Metro Americans" in the 1950s provided the first evidence that the disenchantment with the world characteristic of a large number of deracinated Jews was now shared by many other people.

The general movement of the academy and the media to the left in the late 1960s and 1970s, then, was not merely a function of the crises of the 1960s. Rather, it was an acceleration of previous trends, which had been partly obscured by the cold war atmosphere of the 1950s.

As a result of these trends, liberal capitalism today is characterized by a series of inner contradictions. The unconscious restraints that underlie the rationality of action in liberal capitalist societies are eroded by both affluence and rationality. Rationality undermines the religious foundations of restraint, and affluence undermines the need to discipline one's behavior in the marketplace. Rational self-interest, restrained by unconscious assumptions about the legitimate parameters of behavior, is replaced by the pursuit of any sensation or experience that gives satisfaction without directly harming others. Marriage and child-rearing become experiences in self-realization rather than duties and obligations. Children are not disciplined because parents want to allow them to "realize themselves" and because it is too much trouble.[42] Such shifts in behavioral norms are encouraged by an ever-growing knowledge stratum in the academy and the media, whose expansion and influence was itself a function of the affluence and complexity of advanced capitalist societies.

The result can be, eventually, lessened ego capacity and a loss of meaning in life. Life is inescapably a source of continuing narcissistic injury for all of us. The values provided by religions and civic myths traditionally provide meaning and a sense of purpose that enable reasonably healthy people to cope with existential anxiety. When these erode, the ability to maintain a balance between instinctual drives and the demands of reality may be compromised.[43] It should come as no surprise then, as our TAT results suggest, that an erosion of this psychic balance occurred first during the 1960s among the very cosmopolitan segments of society on whom traditional restraints exerted the least influence.

Further evidence for this hypothesis comes from a study in which we are currently engaged. Preliminary findings indicate that people employed in the knowledge sectors of society are more likely to be "post-materialists" than are those employed in more traditional sectors of the economy. However, they are also more likely to manifest a greater need for power and a higher level of narcissism, as well as a lower need for achievement. These relationships are not strong, but they are statistically significant.[44]

These findings strengthen our argument that political conflicts associated with the civil rights movement and the Vietnam War were responsible for bringing to a head changes that had been slowly developing over previous decades. These conflicts merely added fuel to the fire. Weinstein and Platt pointed out that the strength of the ego requires a "normal expectable environment" in which cultural authorities and norms are relatively authoritative. As political and cultural authority declined in the 1960s, so did the authority of the family and ego strength. Such is always the case in revolutionary (or pseudo-revolutionary) eras. At such times, people seize the opportunity to act upon fantasies that they normally keep under control. All such fantasies contain universal elements, but their content is also partly determined by the cultural norms of the society in which the individual lives.[45]

In the 1970s, the traditional patterns of cultural and social authority were further weakened by new perceptions of scarcity. Contemporary liberal capitalism has justified itself partly by the promise of affluence. With this promise gone, or at least compromised, an important prop to its legitimacy has been seriously undermined. And erosion of support for traditional institutions continues, despite some signs of leveling off.[46] Rejection of traditional cultural norms regarding appropriate behavior, whether this involves joining quasi-religious or secular cults, crime, stealing books from libraries, random violence, or the increasing incidence of sadomasochistic behavior, continues at a high rate.[47] Further, disaffection from traditional cultural patterns and institutions is spreading from its middle-class nucleus to wider segments of the middle and working classes.[48] In short, there is good reason to believe that the personality tendencies we have described are becoming characteristic of a larger segment of the population.

For the moment, this group has not been effectively mobilized behind an ideology with widespread appeal. However, its members are available as cadres for a leadership that develops such an ideology. We therefore suspect that the politics of most western societies will, in the near future, be characterized by increasingly intense, and perhaps violent, quasi-ideological conflict. The recent outbreak of battles between police and "disaffected" youth across continental Europe may be a harbinger of future struggles.[49]

If the decay of societal values has reduced ego control, the effects of such decay are now apparent in the changing patterns of family dynamics. Serial monogamy is on the increase, and there is some evidence of its negative effects upon capacities for ego autonomy.[50] Child-rearing patterns in both "alternative" and "mainstream" families seem to be contributing to the same end.[51]

In the society at large, progressive cosmopolitan segments of the middle class continue to attack traditional values, including traditional family patterns, notions of achievement, ritualistic supports for the system, and religious values.[52] In the meantime, an ever-smaller segment of the population, which remains loyal to such nativist values, feels increasingly threatened and hostile. Recent political trends indicate that some of these people are quite ready, should the opportunity arise, to engage in punitive countermeasures.

There are countervailing forces. A few liberal cosmopolitans and neo-conservatives are suggesting that the pendulum has swung too far; that some traditional American values may be worth preserving and that young people need both freedom and a structure of authority. However, one cannot restore a nonrational set of values by rationalist appeals to the utility of doing so. Indeed, the ultimate result of Reagan's domestic and foreign policy initiatives may well be to heighten the mutual antagonism of nativist and cosmopolitan sectors of society, as the latter mobilize to meet the challenge of a "counter-Reformation," thus leading to renewed radicalization on both sides.[53] Reagan is equally unlikely to succeed in his efforts to reestablish American leadership in Europe. In the period immediately following World War II, the acceptance of such leadership was based upon a widespread image of American goodness and power. Aside from other factors—and whatever the objective merits or weaknesses of Reagan's views—attempts to emphasize American strength at this point in history are perceived by many as the irrational and rather desperate posturings of a weakened bully.

Under such circumstances, the future of the imperfect pluralist democracy that has characterized the United States for the past several hundred years does not seem very bright. This pattern of democratic authority has depended heavily upon an inherently unstable psychic development, which may have produced its own erosion. Some intellectuals welcome this erosion as a harbinger of a possibly better tomorrow. We agree that many traditional values now under attack have become quite dysfunctional. It does seem clear that economic growth on this planet can not continue indefinitely. Further, our technology has led us into a world in which, for the first time, the species does have the power to self-destruct. Conceivably, the developments we have been discussing are but the first stages in a readjustment that will lead to a more adaptive pattern of human integration.

We remain skeptical. Modern man appeared on this planet perhaps 40,000 years ago. For most of recorded history, human beings have lived under au-

thority systems imposed from the outside, either by the community as a whole or by the few who held power. Democracies (or "polyarchies") in the modern world have by and large been limited to Europe and countries settled by Europeans. They have not been notably stable even in those areas during their relatively brief span of existence. It seems to us that, despite the real difficulties also facing authoritarian regimes such as the Soviet Union, the burden of proof lies heavily with the optimists among us.

Appendix A

Relationships Between Radicalism and Social Background, for American College Students.

Table 21. Mean Radicalism scores by Religious Preference for Subjects and Their Parents.[a]

		Subject	Mother	Father
Catholic	X̄	3.92	4.11	4.06
	S.D.	0.84	0.89	0.89
	N	227	302	284
Conservative	X̄	3.78	3.96	3.98
Protestant	S.D.	0.90	0.92	0.93
	N	101	143	132
Liberal	X̄	4.06	4.08	4.15
Protestant	S.D.	0.94	0.95	0.95
	N	84	75	78
Other	X̄	3.91	3.97	4.02
Protestant	S.D.	0.89	0.93	0.91
	N	60	100	103
Orthodox	X̄	4.12	4.29	4.33
Jew	S.D.	1.00	1.00	1.02
	N	25	95	112
Conservative	X̄	4.09	4.25	4.29
Jew	S.D.	0.85	0.89	0.89
	N	136	155	149
Reform	X̄	4.39	4.37	4.19
Jew	S.D.	0.96	0.93	0.91
	N	132	86	77
Jewish, No	X̄	4.61	4.68	4.58
Denomination	S.D.	0.95	1.05	1.07
	N	48	40	49
Jewish,	X̄	4.74	5.01	4.60
Nonreligious	S.D.	1.03	1.21	1.11
	N	55	11	10

Table 21. Continued

		Subject	Mother	Father
Non-Jewish,	X̄	4.40	4.10	4.27
Nonreligious	S.D.	0.87	0.55	0.94
	N	143	17	33
Other	X̄	3.99	3.67	3.94
	S.D.	1.00	0.89	1.24
	N	30	16	20
	F = 9.49	F = 4.30	F = 3.03	
	D.F. = 10	D.F. = 10	D.F. = 10	
	p < .001	p < .001	p < .001	

[a] Parental scores were reported by subjects, not their parents.

Table 22. Radicalism by Father's Piety, with Ethnicity Controlled. Breakdown and ANOVA.

	Radicalism		
Father's Piety	X̄	S.D.	N
Very Pious			
Jewish	4.10	0.71	95
Non-Jewish	3.94	0.94	204
Moderately Pious			
Jewish	4.26	0.95	148
Non-Jewish	4.01	0.86	202
Not Very Pious			
Jewish	4.50	1.03	144
Non-Jewish	4.12	0.87	179

ANOVA

Variable	F	D.F.	Sig.
Piety	6.25	2	.002
Ethnicity	26.65	1	.001
Piety × Ethnicity	2.16	2	.06

Table 23. Radicalism by Father's Education, with Ethnicity Controlled. Breakdown and ANOVA.

		Radicalism	
Father's Education	X̄	S.D.	N
High School or Less			
Jewish	4.32	0.93	82
Non-Jewish	4.01	0.94	193
College, Undergraduate			
Jewish	4.25	1.01	160
Non-Jewish	4.01	0.89	253
Postgraduate			
Jewish	4.48	0.92	88
Non-Jewish	4.07	0.76	66

ANOVA

Variable	F	D.F.	Sig.
Education	2.96	2	.05
Ethnicity	24.78	1	.001

Table 24. Radicalism by Father's Occupational Status, with Ethnicity Controlled. Breakdown and ANOVA.

		Radicalism	
Father's Occupation	X̄	S.D.	N
Blue Collar			
Jewish	4.29	0.89	15
Non-Jewish	3.97	0.99	73
White Collar			
Jewish	4.13	0.88	69
Non-Jewish	4.02	0.96	129
Self-Employed			
Jewish	4.38	0.99	88
Non-Jewish	3.94	0.82	84
Business Executive			
Jewish	4.01	0.77	31
Non-Jewish	3.67	1.10	31
Professional			
Jewish	4.51	0.99	184
Non-Jewish	4.06	0.84	280

ANOVA

Variable	F	D.F.	Sig.
Occupation	3.69	4	.001
Ethnicity	29.42	1	.001

Table 25. Radicalism by Father's Political Preference, with Ethnicity Controlled. Breakdown and Summary Statistics.

	Conservative Republican	Moderate Republican	Liberal Republican	Conservative Democrat	Moderate Democrat	Liberal Democrat	Radical Democrat	Socialist
JEWS								
X̄	3.59	3.78	3.72	4.10	4.28	4.48	4.74	5.06
S.D.	0.37	0.78	0.78	0.99	1.01	0.91	1.06	0.78
N	3	17	7	18	48	72	11	6

eta = .32 r = .32

	Conservative Republican	Moderate Republican	Liberal Republican	Conservative Democrat	Moderate Democrat	Liberal Democrat	Radical Democrat	Socialist
NON-JEWS								
X̄	3.97	3.80	3.59	4.12	4.06	4.55	4.61	—
S.D.	1.10	0.91	0.84	1.03	0.93	0.96	0.85	—
N	44	94	21	29	63	44	5	0

eta = .28 r = .22

Table 26. Radicalism by Mother's Political Preference, with Ethnicity Controlled. Breakdown and Summary Statistics.

	Conservative Republican	Moderate Republican	Liberal Republican	Conservative Democrat	Moderate Democrat	Liberal Democrat	Radical Democrat	Socialist
JEWS								
X̄	3.63	3.29	3.82	4.13	4.04	4.54	5.37	5.46
S.D.	0.72	0.65	0.35	1.14	0.87	0.83	1.03	0.51
N	3	14	5	17	56	77	9	7

eta = .50 r = .46

	Conservative Republican	Moderate Republican	Liberal Republican	Conservative Democrat	Moderate Democrat	Liberal Democrat	Radical Democrat	Socialist
NON-JEWS								
X̄	3.68	3.74	3.96	3.94	4.15	4.48	4.80	—
S.D.	1.13	0.93	1.00	1.06	0.91	1.05	0.82	—
N	29	78	30	38	66	54	3	0

eta = .32 r = .27

Table 27. Radicalism by Father's Reaction to Subject's Politics, with Ethnicity Controlled.

REACTION	RADICALISM		
	Mean	S.D.	N
Opposition			
Jewish	4.54	0.97	126
Non-Jewish	4.26	0.84	168
Neutrality			
Jewish	4.15	0.88	126
Non-Jewish	3.89	0.79	263
Support			
Jewish	4.43	1.00	131
Non-Jewish	3.94	1.07	154

	Jews	Non-Jews
$r =$	$-.04$	$-.13^*$
$eta =$	$.17^*$	$.18^*$

$^*p < .01$

Appendix B

Social Attitudes and Backgrounds of Radical and Traditional Adults

Note. For Tables 28–30, all chi-squares are calculated from raw cell frequencies, with subjects divided into traditional, Jewish radical, and non-Jewish radical categories.

Trad. = Traditional   Rad. = Radical
JR = Jewish Radical   NJR = Non-Jewish Radical
*P < .05   **P < .01   ***P < .001

Table 28. Attitude Toward Religion (%).

	SELF				FATHER				MOTHER			
	Trad.	Rad.	JR	NJR	Trad.	Rad.	JR	NJR	Trad.	Rad.	JR	NJR
Deeply Religious	10	7	1	21	33	9	4	19	45	12	4	32
Moderately Religious	70	6	7	3	44	32	34	26	43	28	29	24
Indifferent	14	39	43	32	21	46	48	42	13	49	53	41
Hostile	6	48	49	44	1	13	14	13	0	11	14	3
N	107	121	87	34	99	112	81	31	101	119	85	34
χ^2	128.33***				42.75***				72.84***			

Table 29. Parents' Political Orientations (%).

	FATHER				MOTHER			
		PARTY PREFERENCE						
	Trad.	Rad.	JR	NJR	Trad.	Rad.	JR	NJR
Republican	49	16	11	32	51	17	7	41
Democrat	44	58	61	50	38	67	75	48
Socialist	2	9	12	0	1	6	8	0
None, Independent	5	17	16	18	10	10	10	10
χ^2		37.93***				46.19***		
		IDEOLOGY						
	Trad.	Rad.	JR	NJR	Trad.	Rad.	JR	NJR
Extreme Right	10	15	11	27	9	5	3	11
Conservative	50	10	5	23	47	10	7	19
Moderate	26	18	20	13	34	20	17	30
Liberal	14	43	49	27	8	50	57	30
Radical Left	0	14	16	10	2	15	17	11
χ^2		73.60***				82.45***		
		POLITICAL DISCUSSION						
	Trad.	Rad.	JR	NJR	Trad.	Rad.	JR	NJR
Never	19	17	14	25	25	22	19	30
Seldom	31	22	21	22	36	28	30	24
Occasionally	36	29	33	19	27	24	21	30
Frequently	14	32	31	34	12	26	30	15
χ^2		13.72*				11.30		
N	103	116	84	32	105	117	84	33

Table 30. Parents' Socioeconomic Status (%).

	FATHER				MOTHER			
			EDUCATION					
	Trad.	Rad.	JR	NJR	Trad.	Rad.	JR	NJR
<H.S.	32	24	17	36	20	18	14	24
H.S. Grad.	31	16	19	9	46	25	27	21
College B.A.	10	15	14	18	21	31	29	35
	15	18	17	15	12	11	12	9
Postgrad.	12	27	33	21	1	16	18	12
χ^2		27.45***				26.16***		
			OCCUPATION					
	Trad.	Rad.	JR	NJR	Trad.	Rad.	JR	NJR
Business	30	30	30	27				
Prof.-Tech.	17	19	22	12	8	28	33	15
Prof.-People	5	19	20	18				
White Collar	17	12	9	21	13	11	8	21
Blue Collar	31	19	18	21				
Housewife	NA	NA	NA	NA	79	61	59	65
χ^2		17.44*				22.26**		

	FAMILY FINANCIAL CONDITION			
	Trad.	Rad.	JR	NJR
Troubled	23	29	24	41
Average	55	38	40	29
Well Off	22	33	36	29
χ^2		11.44*		
N	107	121	87	34

Notes

CHAPTER 1: RISE AND FALL OF THE NEW LEFT

1. Aristotle, *Rhetoric*, in Richard McKeon, ed., *The Basic Works of Aristotle* (New York: Random House, 1941), p. 1404.

2. Samuel Eliot Morison, *Three Centuries of Harvard* (Cambridge: Harvard University Press, 1936), p. 185.

3. Louis Hartz, *The Liberal Tradition in America* (New York: Harcourt Brace, 1955).

4. Robert Bellah, "Civil Religion in America," in William C. McLoughlin and Robert Bellah, eds., *Religion in America* (Boston: Beacon Press, 1968), pp. 3–20.

5. See such articles and books as S. M. Lipset, "Why No Socialism in the United States," in Seweryn Bialer and Sophia Sluzar, eds., *Sources of Contemporary Radicalism* (Boulder, Colo.: Westview Press, 1977), pp. 31–149 and *passim;* J. Rogers Hollingsworth, ed., *Nation and State Building in America* (Boston: Little, Brown, 1971); William Nisbet Chambers and Walter Dean Burnham, *The American Party Systems,* 2nd ed. (New York: Oxford University Press, 1975); and Anthony F. C. Wallace, *Rockdale* (New York: Knopf, 1978). While many other factors played important roles in nineteenth- and early twentieth-century American history, it seems quite clear that, in a comparative perspective, the particular pattern of European settlement was a key variable. Nor is the American south an exception. The self-proclaimed aristocracy of the southern planter class was a pseudo-aristocracy. As several commentators have pointed out, the basic ideology of the south was liberal-capitalist. See Hartz, *Liberal Tradition.* Indeed, as Hartz argues, America's liberal ideology was at least partially responsible for her difficulty in resolving the issue of race as compared, say, to Brazil. See Louis Hartz, *The Founding of New Societies* (New York: Harcourt, Brace & World, 1964), pp. 53–63.

6. Murray Kempton, *Part of Our Time* (New York: Simon and Schuster, 1955), pp. 320–21.

7. Arthur Liebman, *Jews and the Left* (New York: John Wiley and Sons, 1979), pp. 365–74. Joseph de Martini found that at the University of Illinois during the 1930s, members of the (radical) American Student Union "were predominantly Jewish." Letter to S. M. Lipset, February 8, 1971.

8. Stanley Kunitz, "The Careful Young Men," *The Nation* 184 (Mar. 9, 1957): 200.

9. For discussions of all of these themes as developed by a host of social commentators, see Douglas T. Miller and Marion Nowak, *The Fifties* (New York: Doubleday, 1977), and Morris Dickstein, *Gates of Eden: American Culture in the Sixties* (New York: Basic Books, 1977).

10. Daniel Bell, *The Coming of Post-Industrial Society* (New York: Basic Books, 1973), and S. M. Lipset, ed., *The Third Century: America as a Post-Industrial Society* (Stanford: Hoover Institution Press, 1979). See also the discussion and references in Chapter 10 of this book.

11. See Everett Carll Ladd, Jr., and S. M. Lipset, *The Divided Academy* (New York: McGraw-Hill, 1975); David Halberstam, *The Powers That Be* (New York: Knopf, 1979); Lipset, *Third Century;* and the discussion and references in Chapter 10. The Ladd and Lipset and Lipset books cited above contain references to a number of surveys of the attitudes of these groups.

12. Bell, *Coming of Post-Industrial Society.*

13. Stanley Rothman, "The Mass Media in Post-Industrial America," in Lipset, *Third Century,* pp. 345–88.

14. For a discussion and supporting citations see Chapter 9.

15. Allen Ginsberg, *"Howl" and Other Poems* (San Francisco: City Lights Books, 1956).

16. Jack Newfield, *A Prophetic Minority* (New York: Signet, 1966), p. 33.

17. Ibid.

18. Ibid., p. 26.

19. S. M. Lipset, *Rebellion in the University,* 2nd ed. (Chicago: University of Chicago Press, 1976).

20. Daniel Yankelovich, *The Changing Values on Campus* (New York: Washington Square Press, 1972), and *The New Morality: A Profile of American Youth in the '70s* (New York: McGraw-Hill, 1974).

21. Cited in Newfield, *Prophetic Minority,* p. 47.

22. Quoted in Elizabeth Sutherland, ed., *Letters from Mississippi* (New York: McGraw-Hill, 1965), pp. 17, 47–48.

23. Bruce Payne, "The Quiet War," in Mitchell Cohen and Dennis Hale, eds., *The New Student Left* (Boston: Beacon Press, 1966), p. 88.

24. Bruce Payne, "SNCC: An Overview Two Years Later," in Cohen and Hale, *New Student Left,* p. 82.

25. Todd Gitlin, "The Battlefields and the War," in Cohen and Hale, *New Student Left,* pp. 125–26.

26. Payne, "Quiet War," p. 87.

27. Thomas Kahn, "The Political Significance of the Freedom Rides," in Cohen and Hale, *New Student Left,* pp. 59, 63.

28. Paul Jacobs and Saul Landau, *The New Radicals* (New York: Vintage Books, 1966), p. 18.

29. Newfield, *Prophetic Minority,* p. 73.

30. Ibid., p. 141.

31. Ibid., pp. 73–74.

32. Jacobs and Landau, *New Radicals,* pp. 20–21.

33. Ibid., pp. 17, 20, 24–25.

34. Payne, "Quiet War," p. 91.

35. Robert Haber, "From Protest to Radicalism: An Appraisal of the Student Movement," in Cohen and Hale, *New Student Left,* p. 38.

36. Cited by Kirkpatrick Sale, *SDS* (New York: Vintage Books, 1973), p. 276.

37. Mario Savio, "An End to History," in S. M. Lipset and Sheldon Wolin, eds., *The Berkeley Student Revolt* (New York: Anchor Books, 1965), p. 216.

38. For a more sympathetic account than that of Lipset and Wolin, see Hal Draper, *Berkeley: The New Student Revolt* (New York: Grove Press, 1965).

39. Jack Weinberg, "The Free Speech Movement and Civil Rights," in Lipset and Wolin, *Berkeley Student Revolt,* p. 221.

40. Robert Somers, "The Mainsprings of the Rebellion," in Lipset and Wolin, *Berkeley Student Revolt,* p. 549.

41. Weinberg, "Free Speech Movement and Civil Rights," p. 224.

42. Somers, "Mainsprings of Rebellion," pp. 540ff.

43. Savio, "Introduction," in Draper, *Berkeley,* pp. 1, 6.

44. Sale, *SDS,* p. 7.

45. Ibid., p. 53.

46. These and the following quotations are from the excerpts reprinted in Jacobs and Landau, *New Radicals,* pp. 150–71.

47. Andrew Kopkind, *New Republic,* June 19, 1965, p. 18.

48. Sale, *SDS,* pp. 89–90.

49. Interview with Newfield, quoted in Sale, *SDS,* p. 90.

50. Letter from W. H. Ferry, A. J. Muste, and I. F. Stone, published in *Guardian,* June 27, 1964.

51. Tom Hayden, "The Politics of 'The Movement,' " in Irving Howe, ed., *The Radical Papers* (New York: Doubleday, 1966), p. 362.

52. Harrington, in Andrew Kopkind, ed., *Thoughts of the Young Radicals* (New York: New Republic, 1966), p. 71.

53. Richard Rothstein, "Evolution of the ERAP Organizers," in Priscilla Long, ed., *The New Left* (New York: F. Porter Sargent, 1969), p. 274.

54. Sale, *SDS,* p. 137.

55. Crowd estimates from this period are notoriously unreliable. Unless otherwise noted, the figures given here represent uneasy compromises from among Movement, press, and police estimates.

56. Staughton Lynd, "Coalition Politics or Nonviolent Revolution?" *Liberation,* June–July, 1965, p. 21.

57. William Price, *Guardian,* Apr. 24, 1965.

58. Steven Kelman, *Push Comes to Shove* (Boston: Houghton Mifflin, 1970), p. 118.

59. Julian Foster and Durward Long, eds., *Protest! Student Activism in America* (New York: Morrow, 1970), pp. 59ff., 89ff., 365.

60. Carl Oglesby, "Decade Ready for a Dustbin," in Mitchell Goodman, ed., *The Movement Toward a New America* (Philadelphia: Pilgrim Press, 1970).

61. Karen Wald, *New Left Notes,* Nov. 6, 1967.

62. Frank Bardacke, in Goodman, *Movement Toward a New America,* p. 478.

63. Quoted in Nigel Young, *An Infantile Disorder? The Crisis and Decline of the New Left* (Boulder, Colo.: Westview Press, 1977), p. 221.

64. Sale, *SDS,* p. 427.

65. Klaus Mehnert, *Twilight of the Young* (New York: Holt, Rinehart & Winston, 1977), p. 34. This is a somewhat revised translation of *Jugend im Zeitbruch* (Stuttgart: Deutsche Vertags-Anstalt, 1976). References from the English edition will be designated *Twilight;* those from the German edition, *Zeitbruch.*

66. Young, *Infantile Disorder,* p. 313.

67. Quoted by Sale, *SDS,* p. 281.

68. Ibid., p. 206.

69. Vern Visick, "The Rank Protest of 1966–67: A Short History and Analysis" (mimeographed paper, Divinity School, University of Chicago, Oct. 25, 1967).

70. Richard Flacks, "The Liberated Generation: An Exploration of the Roots of Student Protest," *Journal of Social Issues* 23 (July 1967): 66.

71. *New Left Notes,* Dec. 23, 1966.

72. New York *Times,* May 7, 1967.

73. *New Left Notes,* May 22, 1967.

74. Cited in Sale, *SDS,* p. 419.

75. Ibid., p. 381.

76. Quoted in Meryl Levine and John Naisbitt, *Right On* (New York: Bantam, 1970), p. 70.

77. Linda Rennie Forcey, "Personality in Politics: The Commitment of a Suicide" (Ph. D. diss., State University of New York at Binghamton, 1978), p. 93.

78. Sale, *SDS,* p. 445.

79. Yankelovich, *Changing Values on Campus.*

80. Cited in Lipset, *Rebellion,* p. 49.

81. R. Vaughan, "Confrontation and Disruption," *Life,* Oct. 18, 1968, pp. 76–81; Ernest Dunbar, "Vanguard of the Campus Revolt," *Look,* Oct. 1, 1968, pp. 23–29.

82. Mark Rudd, "University in Revolt," in Jerry Avorn, *Up Against the Ivy Wall* (New York: Atheneum, 1968).

83. Sale, *SDS.*

84. Bill Ayers and Jim Mellen, "Hot Town: Summer in the City," *New Left Notes,* Apr. 4, 1969.

85. Mike James, quoted in "Extent of Subversion in the 'New Left,' " hearings before the Subcommittee To Investigate the Administration of the Internal Security Act and Other Internal Security Laws of the Committee on the Judiciary, U.S. Senate, part 4, 1970, p. 606.

86. See the discussion in Chapter 4, pp. 192–201.

87. Susan Stern, *With the Weathermen* (Garden City, N.Y.: Doubleday, 1974), p. 96.

88. Ibid.

89. Lorraine Rosal, *New Left Notes,* Aug. 23, 1969.

90. Stern, *With the Weathermen,* p. 96.

91. Hearings before the Subcommittee To Investigate . . . Internal Security Laws, U.S. Senate, part 4, 1970.

92. Stern, *With the Weathermen,* p. 148.

93. Stuart Daniels, "The Weathermen," *Government and Opposition* 9, no. 4 (Autumn 1974): 441.

94. Accounts of Dohrn's exact words vary. The version quoted here is from Sale, *SDS,* p. 628. Cf. Paul Walton, "The Case of the Weathermen," in Ian Taylor and Laurie Taylor, eds., *Politics and Deviance* (Harmondsworth: Penguin, 1973), p. 167.

95. Martin Walker, *Guardian,* Oct. 27, 1970.

96. Tom Hayden, "The Trial," *Ramparts,* Sept. 1970, p. 42.

97. Sale, *SDS,* p. 653.

98. *May 1970: The Campus Aftermath of Cambodia and Kent State,* Report by the Carnegie Commission on Higher Education, 1971. See also Sale, *SDS,* p. 637.

99. Roger Lewis, *Outlaws of America* (Harmondsworth: Penguin, 1972), p. 175.

100. Daniels, "Weathermen," p. 442.

101. Karl Fleming, profiled in *Newsweek,* Oct. 12, 1970.

102. William Harris, quoted in Vin McLellan and Paul Avery, *The Voices of Guns* (New York: Putnam and Sons, 1977), pp. 19–20.

103. Ibid., p. 146.

104. Mehnert, *Twilight,* p. 57.

105. Dotson Rader, *Blood Dues* (New York: Knopf, 1973), p. 7.

CHAPTER 2: INTELLECTUALS AND THE STUDENT MOVEMENT

1. Phillip G. Altbach and David H. Kelly, *American Students* (Lexington, Mass.: D. C. Heath, 1972).

2. Kenneth Keniston, *Young Radicals* (New York: Harcourt Brace Jovanovich, 1968) and *Youth and Dissent* (New York: Harcourt Brace Jovanovich, 1971); Richard Flacks, "The Liberated Generation: An Exploration of the Roots of Student Protest," *Journal of Social Issues* 23 (July 1967): 52–75. For German analyses, see Jürgen Habermas, *Protestbewegung und Hochschulreform* (Frankfurt: Suhrkamp, 1969); and Erwin Scheuch, "Soziologische Aspekte der Unruhe unter den Studenten," *Aus Politik und Zietgeschichte,* Beil. zu *Das Parlament,* Sept. 4, 1968.

3. The OPI was created by Paul Heist and George Younge. For use of the scale in Germany, see Rudolf Wildenmann and Max Kaase, *Die unruhige Generation* (Mannheim: University of Mannheim, 1969).

4. Keniston, *Youth and Dissent,* p. 311.

5. Ibid., p. 314.

6. Herbert Marcuse, *Eros and Civilization* (Boston: Beacon Press, 1966), pp. xi–xxv.

7. Charles Reich, *The Greening of America* (New York: Random House, 1970), pp. 241–42.

8. Ibid., pp. 271–72.

9. Endorsement on the rear cover of paperback edition of Reich, *Greening of America.*

10. Joseph Adelson, "Inventing the Young," *Commentary* 51 (May 1971): 43–48. One well-known radical Harvard professor described Keniston's subjects as the most manipulative he had ever met (Personal communication, 1972).

11. For a summary of the relevant literature, see David L. Westby, *The Clouded Vision* (Cranbury, N.J.: Associated University Presses, 1976).

12. Herman Kahn and Anthony J. Wiener, *The Year 2000* (New York: Macmillan, 1967).

13. David Gutmann, "The Subjective Politics of Power: The Dilemma of Post-Superego Man," *Social Research* 40 (Winter 1973): 570–616.

14. Edward Shils, "Plenitude and Scarcity," *Encounter* 32 (May 1969): 37–58.

15. Lewis Feuer, *The Conflict of Generations* (New York: Basic Books, 1969).

16. Irving Howe, ed., *Beyond the New Left* (New York: McCall, 1970), pp. 19–32, 40–54.

17. Oscar Glantz, "New Left Radicalism and Punitive Moralism," *Polity* 7 (Spring 1975): 281–304.

18. Henry A. Alker, "A Quasi-Paranoid Feature of Students' Extreme Attitudes Against Colonialism," *Behavioral Science* 16 (1971): 218–27.

19. Larry Kerpelman, *Activists vs. Non-Activists: A Psychological Study of American College Students* (New York: Behavioral Publications, 1972).

20. Westby, *Clouded Vision*, pp. 80–81.

21. See Stanley Rothman, "Mainstream Political Science and Its Discontents," in Vernon Van Dyke, ed., *Teaching Political Science* (Atlantic Highlands, N.J.: Humanities Press, 1977), pp. 1–33.

22. Kenneth Keniston, *Radicals and Militants* (Lexington, Mass.: D. C. Heath, 1973), p. xii.

23. Flacks, "Liberated Generation"; S. M. Lipset, *Rebellion in the University* (Chicago: University of Chicago Press, 1971); Alice R. Gold, Lucy Norman Friedman, and Richard Christie, *Fists and Flowers* (New York: Academic Press, 1976); and Stanley Rothman, Anne Bedlington, Robert Schnitzer, and Phillip Isenberg, "Ethnic Variations in Student Radicalism," in Seweryn Bialer and Sophia Sluzar, eds. *Sources of Contemporary Radicalism* (Boulder, Colo.: Westview Press, 1977), pp. 151–212.

24. Everett Carll Ladd, Jr., and S. M. Lipset, *The Divided Academy* (New York: McGraw-Hill, 1975). Some 66 percent of clinical psychologists and 79 percent of social psychologists approved of the emergence of radical student activism (Ladd and Lipset, *Divided Academy*, p. 365). The 50 percent participation figure is based on our reanalysis of the Carnegie data.

25. Ronald Inglehart, "The Silent Revolution in Europe: Intergenerational Change in Post-Industrial Societies," *American Political Science Review* 65 (Dec. 1971): 991–1017.

26. See, for example, scales used to measure support for "Democratic Principles," collected in John P. Robinson, Jerrold G. Rusk, and Kendra B. Head, *Measures of Political Attitudes* (Ann Arbor: Institute for Social Research, University of Michigan, 1968), pp. 163–86.

27. As in Henry C. Finney, "Political Libertarianism at Berkeley: An Application of Perspectives from the New Student Left," *Journal of Social Issues* 27 (1971): 35–62.

28. Wildenmann and Kaase, *Die unruhige Generation*, p. 11.

29. For a detailed recent study that comes to conclusions rather similar to ours, see John L. Sullivan, James Pierson, and George C. Marcus, "An Alternate Conceptualization of Political Tolerance: Illusory Increases, 1950s–1970s," *American Political Science Review* 73 (Sept. 1979): 781–94.

30. See the quotation from the *Harvard Crimson* in Arnold Beichman, *Nine Lies About America* (New York: Library Press, 1972), p. 81.

31. These remarks are based on Rothman's interviews of Harvard students just after the event. Many of the same students also justified the disruption of psychologist Richard Herrnstein's classes at Harvard.

32. This is typical of the questions used by Haan, Block, and Smith in their "Child Rearing Practices Report." Their articles include: Norma Haan, M. B. Smith, and Jeanne

Block, "Moral Reasoning of Young Adults: Political-Social Behavior, Family Background, and Personality Correlates," *Journal of Personality and Social Psychology* 10 (1968): 183–201; M. Brewster Smith, Norma Haan, and Jeanne Block, "Social Psychological Aspects of Student Radicalism," *Youth and Society* 1 (Mar. 1970): 261–80; Jeanne H. Block, Norma Haan, and M. Brewster Smith, "Socialization Correlates of Student Activism," *Journal of Social Issues* 25 (1969): 143–77; and Jeanne H. Block, "Generational Continuity and Discontinuity in the Understanding of Societal Rejection," *Journal of Personality and Social Psychology* 27 (1972): 333–45.

33. Klaus Allerbeck, "Soziale Bedingungen der studentischen Radikalismus" (Ph.D. diss., University of Mannheim, 1969).

34. Block, Haan, and Smith, "Socialization Correlates," pp. 164–65.

35. Herbert Hendin, *The Age of Sensation* (New York: W. W. Norton, 1975). See also Urie Bronfenbrenner, *Two Worlds of Childhood* (New York: Russell Sage Foundation, 1970), and Christopher Lasch, *Haven in a Heartless World* (New York: Basic Books, 1977).

36. S. M. Lipset, *Rebellion in the University,* 2nd ed. (Chicago: University of Chicago Press, 1976), p. 103. Unfortunately, we have been unable to obtain a copy of the author's tapes and codebook and thus could not complete a reanalysis of the data.

37. James L. Wood, *The Sources of American Student Activism* (Lexington, Mass.: Lexington Books, 1974), pp. 117–22.

38. Flacks, "Liberated Generation," pp. 52–75. See also Lillian E. Troll, Bernice L. Neugarten, and Ruth J. Kraines, "Similarities in Values and other Personality Characteristics in College Students and Their Parents," *Merrill-Palmer Quarterly of Behavior and Development* 15 (1969): 323–36.

39. The example is taken from the codebook used in the study.

40. For the OPI items, see Form F of the OPI (1968).

41. For studies relying on the OPI which come to these conclusions, see Westby, *Clouded Vision;* Charles Hampden-Turner, *Radical Man* (New York: Anchor Books, 1971); and Richard C. Braungart, "Youth Movements," in Joseph Adelson, ed., *Handbook of Adolescent Psychology* (New York: Wiley Interscience, 1979).

42. See W. W. Meissner, John E. Mack, and Elvin Semrad, "Classical Psychoanalysis," in Alfred Freedman et al., *Comprehensive Textbook of Psychiatry,* 2nd ed., 2 vols. (Baltimore: Williams & Wilkins, 1975) 2:535.

43. Of course, all of these writers disagree violently with each other. For further discussion, see pp. 70–72.

44. It should be noted that the OPI manual conservatively limits its relevant psychological domain to "certain attitudes, values, and interests relevant to academic activity and the functioning of late adolescents in educational contexts" (Paul McReynolds, "Review of OPI," in Oscar K. Buros, ed., *Personality Tests and Reviews* vol. II [Highland Park, N.J.: Gryphon Press, 1975], p. 498).

45. See Kathleen Mock and Paul Heist, "Potential Activists: The Characteristics and Backgrounds of a Capable and Challenging Minority" (unpublished paper, Center for Research and Development in Higher Education, Berkeley, Ca., 1969), and Joseph Katz, "The Activist Revolution of 1964," in Joseph Katz et al., *No Time for Youth* (San Francisco: Jossey-Bass, 1968). See also the reviews of the OPI by Norman Wallen and Richard Coan in Buros, *Personality Tests and Reviews,* pp. 1139 and 496–97, respectively.

46. Buros, *Personality Tests and Reviews,* p. 1139. We are omitting the technical

details of our statistical critique of these scales and others that we shall discuss, as well as our critiques, in some cases, of the samples used. For such details see S. Rothman and S. Robert Lichter, "The Case of the Student Left," *Social Research* 45 (1978): 535–609. For an even more comprehensive analysis, see S. Robert Lichter, "Psychopolitical Models of Student Radicalism" (Ph.D. diss., Harvard University, 1977).

47. Sylvan Kaiser, "Superior Intelligence: Its Contribution to Neurogenesis," *Journal of the American Psychoanalytic Association* 17 (1969): 452–73; *Chronicle of Higher Education,* May 23, 1977, p. 4.

48. T. W. Adorno, Else Frenkel-Brunswick, Daniel Levinson, and R. Nevitt Sanford, *The Authoritarian Personality* (New York: Harper and Row, 1950).

49. Martin Jay, *The Dialectical Imagination* (Boston: Little, Brown, 1973), p. 227.

50. Theodor W. Adorno, "Scientific Experiences of a European Scholar in America," in Donald Fleming and Bernard Bailyn, eds., *The Intellectual Migration* (Cambridge, Mass.: Belknap Press, 1969), p. 363.

51. Herbert Hyman and Paul Sheatsley, " 'The Authoritarian Personality': A Methodological Critique," in Richard Christie and Marie Jahoda, eds., *Studies in the Scope and Method of the Authoritarian Personality* (Glencoe, Ill.: Free Press, 1954), p. 119.

52. Edward Shils, "Authoritarianism: Right and Left," ibid., p. 158.

53. John Kirscht and Ronald Dillehay, *Dimensions of Authoritarianism* (Lexington, Ky.: University of Kentucky Press, 1967), p. 56.

54. Adorno et al., *Authoritarian Personality,* pp. 226, 255.

55. Herbert McCloskey, "Conservatism and Personality," *American Political Science Review* 52 (1958): 27–45.

56. Bernhard Cloetta, *Fragebogen zur Erfassung von Machiavellianismus und Konservatismus* (Konstanz: University of Konstanz, 1972), p. 85.

57. Milton Rokeach, *The Open and Closed Mind* (New York: Basic Books, 1960).

58. Flacks, "Liberated Generation," p. 63.

59. Ibid., p. 71. Tau$_c$ (Tau corrected for ties). Probabilities are based on two-tailed tests.

60. Charles Osgood, George Suci, and Percy Tannenbaum, *The Measurement of Meaning* (Urbana: University of Illinois Press, 1957). For a detailed discussion, see Chapter 3.

61. The levels of statistical significance are .50 and .31.

62. See note 36.

63. Kenneth Keniston, *The Uncommitted* (New York: Harcourt, Brace & World, 1965).

64. See Keniston, *Youth and Dissent,* pp. 143–72. The key essay was "The Sources of Student Dissent," *Journal of Social Issues* 23 (July 1967): 108–37. In *The Uncommitted,* Keniston, drawing upon events at Berkeley, did raise the possibility of his alienated students turning against the society. As noted, however, he carefully distinguished the alienated of the early 1960s and the radicals he studied in his later work.

65. Keniston, *Young Radicals,* pp. 309–10.

66. W. W. Meissner, *The Paranoid Process* (New York: Jason Aronson, 1978), pp. 283–320.

67. Brent Rutherford, "Psychopathology, Decision-Making, and Political Involvement," *Journal of Conflict Resolution* 10 (1966): 387–407.

68. Quoted in Simon Wolin and Robert M. Slusser, *The Soviet Secret Police* (New York: Praeger, 1957), pp. 68, 70.

69. Melita Maschmann, *Account Rendered,* trans. Geoffrey Strachan (New York: Abelard-Schuman, 1965), p. 10.

70. Keniston, *Young Radicals,* p. 53.

71. Ibid., p. 56.

72. Ibid., pp. 61–62.

73. Ibid., p. 57.

74. Ibid., p. 59.

75. Ibid., p. 52.

76. In one instance, Keniston describes an unusual amount of intense aggression in a subject's early memories. One memory concerned the youth's hitting a deeply envied younger brother. He recalled his father telling the younger brother to retaliate by sneaking up behind him and striking him with a club or knife. This unusually sadistic image of the father occurred in conjunction with feelings of longing for paternal affection. Keniston suggests that such aggression paved the way for later inhibitions of violence in the political arena. But the association of murderous rage with longings for intimacy and rivalry for a father's love is a constellation frequently related to a paranoid orientation in males. The father seems to have represented evil and danger to this subject, rather than order and fairness. One might well expect that such an image would lead to superego problems. The example is taken from Jennifer Cole, "Narcissistic Character Traits in Left Activists" (Ph.D. diss., University of Michigan, 1979).

77. Abraham Maslow, *Motivation and Personality* (New York: Harper and Row, 1954).

78. Quoted in Donald W. Keim, "To Make All Things New: The Counterculture Vision of Man and Politics," in J. Roland Pennock and John W. Chapman, eds., *Human Nature and Politics* (New York: New York University Press, 1977), p. 207.

79. Inglehart, "Silent Revolution in Europe"; Ronald Inglehart, *The Silent Revolution: Changing Values and Political Styles Among Western Publics* (Princeton: Princeton University Press, 1977).

80. Inglehart, "Silent Revolution in Europe," p. 994.

81. Inglehart, *Silent Revolution.*

82. Inglehart, "Silent Revolution in Europe," p. 1007.

83. In his book, Inglehart writes less about personality than about ideology and values. Nevertheless, he still tends to conflate these concepts.

84. Marcuse, *Eros and Civilization.*

85. Michael Maccoby, *The Gamesman* (New York: Simon & Schuster, 1976), pp. 210–33.

86. Marcuse, *Eros and Civilization.*

87. See Lasch, *Haven in a Heartless World,* and his *The Culture of Narcissism* (New York: W. W. Norton, 1978).

88. Whether one ascribes narcissism or self-development to recent trends may largely depend upon one's perspective. The evidence itself is ambiguous. For example, in Japan a series of studies has documented the decline of "traditional" values. Increasing numbers of Japanese youth chose a life that "suits one's own taste" rather than a "pure and just life." Other studies reveal a sharp drop in responses to the statement "Never think of yourself, give everything in service to society." In this country, a recent Harris survey conducted for *Playboy* magazine reveals that the most innovative upper-status males, i.e., those most attuned to social change, environmental protection, participatory democracy, etc., also believe more strongly than "traditionals" in adorning one's body

with jewelry, using cocaine and hallucinogens, and engaging in practices such as transcendental meditation. Such males are also more likely to believe it is important to choose physically attractive women as marriage partners. Are such people relatively "self-realized" or "narcissistic" or both? The question is not merely rhetorical. Indeed, it cuts to the core of the problems of social scientific interpretation with which we are concerned.

For the Japanese evidence see Nathan Glazer, "Social and Cultural Factors in Japanese Economic Growth," in Hugh Patrick and Henry Rosovsky, eds., *Asia's New Giant* (Washington, D.C.: Brookings Institution, 1976), pp. 856–57. For the *Playboy* study see *The Playboy Report on American Men* (New York: Playboy, 1979).

89. James Fishkin, Kenneth Keniston, and Catherine MacKinnon, "Moral Reasoning and Political Ideology," *Journal of Personality and Social Psychology* 27 (1973): 110.

90. See, for example, Lawrence Kohlberg, "The Development of Children's Orientations Toward a Moral Order: I. Sequence in the Development of Moral Thought," *Vita Humana* 6 (1963): 11–33; "Stages and Sequence: The Cognitive Developmental Approach to Socialization," in D. A. Goslin, ed., *Handbook of Socialization Theory* (Chicago: Rand McNally, 1969), pp. 347–480; "Stages of Moral Development as a Basis for Moral Education," in C. M. Beck et al., eds., *Moral Education: Interdisciplinary Approaches* (Toronto: University of Toronto Press, 1971), pp. 23–92; and most recently *The Philosophy of Moral Development,* vol. I (San Francisco: Harper and Row, 1981).

91. For a critical review of Kohlberg's work, see William Kurtines and Esther Blank Greif, "The Development of Moral Thought: Review and Evaluation of Kohlberg's Approach," *Psychological Bulletin* 81 (Aug. 1974): 453–70; and Robert T. Hall and John U. Davis, *Moral Education in Theory and Practice* (Buffalo: Prometheus Press, 1975).

92. Fishkin, Keniston, and MacKinnon, "Moral Reasoning and Political Ideology," p. 117.

93. At one point, Kohlberg apparently suggests that a positive correlation between level of moral development and political liberalism is evidence of the test's construct validity. See C. B. Holstein, "Irreversible Stepwise Sequence in the Development of Moral Judgment: A Longitudinal Study of Males and Females," *Child Development* 47 (1976): 51–61. Professor Holstein cites one of Kohlberg's scoring manuals.

94. See the example summarized by William J. Bennett and Edwin J. Delattre, "Moral Education in the Schools," *Public Interest,* no. 50, Winter 1978, pp. 81–98. It is quite clear that in this case Kohlberg simply passed off as a Stage 6 solution one that more closely resembled Stage 3, by his own criteria, because it was the solution he preferred.

95. See note 33 for references.

96. Haan, Smith, and Black, "Moral Reasoning of Young Adults," p. 198.

97. Keniston, *Radicals and Militants,* p. 86.

98. Haan, Smith, and Block, "Moral Reasoning of Young Adults," pp. 199–201.

99. See Rothman and Lichter, "Case of the Student Left," and Lichter, "Psychopolitical Models."

100. Fishkin, Keniston, and MacKinnon, "Moral Reasoning and Political Ideology."

101. The authors' conclusions are broadly consistent with their published group means, but the probability statistics they cite repeatedly in support of these conclusions are inappropriate, given their use of nonrandom contact samples.

102. Milton Mankoff and Richard Flacks, "The Changing Social Base of the American Student Movement," *Annals of the American Academy of Political and Social Sciences* 395 (May 1971): 54–67.

103. Haan, Smith, and Block, "Moral Reasoning of Young Adults," pp. 200–201.

104. Lawrence Kohlberg and R. B. Kramer, "Continuities and Discontinuities in Childhood and Adult Moral Development," *Human Development* 12 (1969): 93–120; see esp. pp. 103, 105–12.

105. "Adolescent Moral Development," in Adelson, *Handbook of Adolescent Psychology*.

106. Richard E. Nisbett and Timothy Decamp Wilson, "Telling More Than We Can Know: Verbal Reports on Mental Processes," *Psychology Review* 84 (May 1977): 233, 231, 248.

107. See Leon J. Kamin, *The Science and Politics of IQ* (New York: Halsted Press, 1974); Victor D. Sanua, "Differences in Personality Adjustment Among Different Generations of Jews and Non-Jews," in Martin K. Opler, ed., *Culture and Mental Health* (New York: Macmillan, 1959), pp. 443–66.

108. Sale, *SDS*, p. 82.

109. Richard Blum, "Epilogue: Students and Drugs," in R. Blum et al., *Students and Drugs: Drugs II* (San Francisco: Jossey-Bass, 1969), p. 377.

CHAPTER 3: RADICAL JEWS

1. See the references in Chapter 2.

2. Frederick Solomon and Jacob R. Fishman, "Youth and Peace: A Psychosocial Study of Student Peace Demonstrators in Washington, D.C.," *Journal of Social Issues* 20 (Oct. 1964): 54–73.

3. See Kirkpatrick Sale, *SDS* (New York: Vintage, 1973), and Arthur Liebman, *Jews and the Left* (New York: John Wiley and Sons, 1979).

4. Quoted in Liebman, ibid., p. 549.

5. Ibid.

6. Ibid., p. 68. See also Philip Meyer and Michael Maidenberg, "The Berkeley Rebels Five Years Later: Has Age Mellowed the Pioneer Radicals?" (mimeographed, Feb. 1970).

7. See Richard Flacks, "The Liberated Generation: An Exploration of the Roots of Student Protest," *Journal of Social Issues* 23 (July 1967): 52–75. Flack's published estimate is lower than ours, but see p. 82.

8. Richard Braungart, "Status Politics and Student Politics," *Youth and Society* 3 (Dec. 1971): 195–208. Again, Braungart's published estimate is lower than ours, for reasons we shall discuss shortly.

9. We wish to thank Professor Adelson for providing us with data from his study.

10. Alexander W. Astin, "Personal and Environmental Determinants of Student Activism," *Measurement and Evaluation in Guidance* 1 (Fall 1968): 149–62.

11. David R. Schweitzer and James Elden, "New Left as Right: Convergent Themes of Political Discontent," *Journal of Social Issues* 27 (1971): 141–66, and personal correspondence.

12. Robert S. Berns, Daphne Bugental, and Geraldine Berns, "Research on Student Activism," *American Journal of Psychiatry* 128 (1972): 1499–1504; Thomas Piazza, "Jewish Identity and the Counterculture," in Robert N. Bellah and Charles Y. Glock, *The New Religious Consciousness* (Berkeley: University of California Press, 1976), pp. 245–64.

13. The Harris poll is cited in S. M. Lipset, *Rebellion in the University* (Boston: Little, Brown, 1972), p. 86.

14. For the percentages before the sample was adjusted, see Mrs. Erwin Angres, "Values and Socialization Practices of Jewish and Non-Jewish College Students" (typescript, n.d.).

15. We wish to thank Professor Richard Braungart for making the necessary data available to us. Our own study indicates that an even larger role was played by young people of Jewish background during the early years of the New Left (see Chapter 8).

16. Roger M. Kahn and William J. Bowers, "The Social Context of the Rank and File Student Activist: A Test of Four Hypotheses," *Sociology of Education* 43 (Winter 1970): 38–55.

17. Everett Carll Ladd, Jr., and S. M. Lipset, *The Divided Academy* (New York: McGraw-Hill, 1975), pp. 149–68.

18. New York *Times,* May 19, 1968, p. 1.

19. Sale, *SDS,* p. 204ff.; Milton Mankoff and Richard Flacks, "The Changing Social Base of the Student Movement," in Philip G. Altbach and Robert S. Laufer, *The New Pilgrims* (New York: David McKay, 1972), pp. 46–62.

20. Sale, *SDS,* p. 204.

21. Dotson Rader, *Blood Dues* (New York: Knopf, 1973), pp. 7ff, 112ff. See also Dotson Rader, "The Day the Movement Died," *Esquire* 78 (Nov. 1972): 130ff.

22. Annie Gottleib, review of *Charlie Simpson's Apocalypse,* by Joe Esterhas, *New York Times Book Review,* Jan. 27, 1974, pp. 4–5.

23. For a selection of the general literature see, among other sources, Robert S. Wistrich, *Revolutionary Jews from Marx to Trotsky* (London: George G. Harrap, 1976); George Lichtheim, "Socialism and the Jews," *Dissent* 15 (1968): 315–42; Werner Sombart, *Der proletarische Sozialismus,* vol. 2, *Marxismus* (Jena: Gustave Fischer, 1924); Adolf Kober, "Jews in the Revolution of 1848 in Germany," *Jewish Social Studies* 10 (Apr. 1948): 135–64; and Werner Cohn, "Jewish Political Attitudes—Their Background," *Judaism* 8 (Fall 1959): 312–22.

24. Robert Michels, *Political Parties* (New York: Collier Books, 1962), pp. 246–47.

25. Rudolf Schay, *Juden in der deutschen Politik* (Berlin: Welt-Verlag, 1929).

26. Wistrich, *Revolutionary Jews;* Donald Niewyk, *Socialist Anti-Semite and Jew* (Baton Rouge: Louisiana State University Press, 1971); and J. P. Nettl, *Rosa Luxemburg* (London: Oxford University Press, 1966).

27. Quoted in Niewyk, ibid., p. 17.

28. Istvan Deak, *Weimar Germany's Left-Wing Intellectuals* (Berkeley: University of California Press, 1968), p. 24.

29. Ibid., pp. 28–29.

30. Harold Poor, *Kurt Tucholsky and the Ordeal of Germany, 1914–1935* (New

York: Charles Scribner's Sons, 1968), and Walter Laqueur, "The Tucholsky Complaint," *Encounter*, Dec. 1969, pp. 76–80. As Laqueur points out, both the style and themes of Tucholsky and the people around paralleled those of the 1960s American New Left, to a certain extent at least.

31. There are a number of studies of the Frankfurt School and its members. These include Martin Jay, *The Dialectical Imagination* (Boston: Little, Brown, 1973); Susan Buck-Morse, *The Origins of Negative Dialectics* (New York: Free Press, 1977); and Zoltan Tarr, *The Frankfurt School* (New York: John Wiley and Sons, 1977).

32. New York: Rinehart, 1941.

33. Some of Fromm's other books include *The Sane Society* (New York: Rinehart, 1955); *Zen Buddhism and Psychoanalysis* (New York: Harper & Brothers, 1960); *Beyond the Chains of Illusion* (New York: Simon and Schuster, 1962); and *The Anatomy of Human Destructiveness* (New York: Holt, Rinehart & Winston, 1973); and, as editor, *Socialist Humanism: An International Perspective* (Garden City, N.Y.: Doubleday, 1965).

34. See, for example, Peter G. J. Pulzer, *The Rise of Political Anti-Semitism in Germany and Austria* (New York: John Wiley and Sons, 1964); Egon Schwarz, "Melting Pot or Witch's Cauldron: Jews and Anti-Semitism in Vienna at the Turn of the Century," in David Bronson, ed., *Germans and Jews from 1860–1933: The Problematic Symbiosis* (Heidelberg: Cave Winter Universität-Atsverlag, 1979), pp. 262–87; Ilsa Barea, *Vienna* (New York: Knopf, 1966); Robert Wistrich, "Dilemmas of Assimilation in Fin-de-siécle Vienna," *Wiener Library Bulletin* n. s. 32, no. 49–50 (1979): 15–28; A. Barkai, "The Austrian Social Democrats and the Jews," *Wiener Library Bulletin* 24 (1970): 32–40.

35. Schwarz, "Melting Pot or Witch's Cauldron," p. 273.

36. Wistrich, *Revolutionary Jews;* Barkai, "Austrian Social Democrats."

37. F. Fejtö, as quoted in Paul Lendvai, *Anti-Semitism in Eastern Europe* (London: MacDonald, 1972), p. 370.

38. Wistrich, *Revolutionary Jews;* "The Jewish Background of Victor and Friedrich Adler," *Leo Baeck Institute Yearbook* (London) 10 (1965): 266–76.

39. Walter P. Simon, "The Political Parties of Austria" (Ph.D. diss., Columbia University, 1957), pp. 251–80.

40. See Lendvai, *Anti-Semitism*, and William O. McCagg, "Jews in Revolutions: The Hungarian Experience," *Journal of Social History* 6 (Fall 1972): 78–105.

41. See McCagg, "Jews in Revolutions," and Lendvai, *Anti-Semitism*.

42. R. V. Burks, *The Dynamics of Communism in Eastern Europe* (Princeton: Princeton University Press, 1961), p. 163.

43. Ibid., p. 166.

44. For a discussion see ibid., pp. 305–17.

45. Burks, *Dynamics of Communism*, p. 160.

46. Ibid., p. 160. See also Lendvai, *Anti-Semitism;* Celia S. Heller, *On The Edge of Destruction: Jews of Poland Between the Two World Wars* (New York: Columbia University Press, 1977), pp. 254ff.; and Jan B. de Wyndenthal, *The Communists of Poland: An Historical Outline* (Stanford: Hoover Institution Press, 1978), pp. 26–27.

47. Burks, *Dynamics of Communism*, p. 160.

48. Ibid., and Lendvai, *Anti-Semitism*.

49. A. H. Halsey and M. A. Trow, *The British Academics* (Cambridge: Harvard University Press, 1971), pp. 413–19.

50. Institute of Jewish Affairs, "Arab Propaganda Around the World: A Survey," *Background Paper,* no. 17, Dec. 1969; Francois Fejtö, *The French Communist Party and the Crisis of International Communism* (Cambridge: MIT Press, 1967); and Annie Kriegel, *Communisme au Mirror Français* (Paris: Éditions Gallimard, 1974), pp. 177–96 and 218–25.

Most studies of the French Jewish community skirt this issue, although Paula Hyman does note the prominent role of Jews in more "advanced" literary circles in late nineteenth-century France. See Paula Wolf, *From Dreyfus to Vichy* (New York: Columbia University Press, 1979), pp. 17–23.

51. P. Kruijt, *De Onkerheilkheid in Nederland* (Groningen: P. Noordhoff, N.V., 1933), pp. 265–67.

52. Hugh Thomas, *Cuba; or, The Pursuit of Freedom* (London: Eyre and Spottiswoode, 1971), pp. 577, 597, 1101. For their role in support of the left-wing terrorist group in Argentina see the New York *Times,* June 10, 1981.

53. Albert Memmi, *Portrait of a Jew* (New York: Viking Press, 1971), pp. 276–77.

54. Liebman, *Jews and the Left.*

55. The literature on the subject is immense. On the whole Liebman, ibid., provides a good summary. See also Irving Howe, *World of Our Fathers* (New York: Simon and Schuster, 1976); Zvi Gitelman, *Jewish Nationality and Soviet Politics* (Princeton: Princeton University Press, 1972); Lionel Kochan, ed., *The Jews in Russia since 1917* (London: Oxford University Press, 1970); Nora Levin, *While Messiah Tarried* (New York: Schocken Books, 1977); Ezra Mendelsohn, *Class Struggle in the Pale* (Cambridge: Cambridge University Press, 1970); and Henry J. Tobias, *The Jewish Bund in Russia* (Stanford: Stanford University Press, 1972).

56. Quoted in Erich Goldhagen, "The Ethnic Consciousness of Early Russian Jewish Socialists," *Judaism* 23 (Fall 1974): 483.

57. Robert I. Brym, *The Jewish Intelligentsia and Russian Marxism* (London: Macmillan, 1978), p. 3.

58. Leonard Schapiro, "The Role of Jews in the Russian Revolutionary Movement," *Slavonic and East European Review* 490 (Dec. 1961): 160.

59. Ibid.

60. Quoted in Wistrich, *Revolutionary Jews,* p. 189.

61. Ibid., pp. 177–88.

62. Goldhagen, "Ethnic Consciousness," p. 486.

63. Howe, *World of Our Fathers,* p. 23.

64. See Levin, *While Messiah Tarried.*

65. H. Lumer, ed., *Lenin on the Jewish Question* (New York: International Publishers, 1974), p. 107.

66. Adam B. Ulam, *The Bolsheviks* (New York: Macmillan, 1965), p. 190.

67. Gitelman, *Jewish Nationality.*

68. Schapiro, "The Role of Jews," p. 165.

69. For a discussion of Trotsky's attitudes toward his own Jewishness, and the effects this may have had upon later failures in his battles with Stalin, see Joel Carmichael, *Trotsky* (London: Hodder and Stoughton, 1975). See also Joseph Nedava, *Trotsky and the Jews* (Philadelphia: Jewish Publication Society of America, 1971).

70. Lendvai, *Anti-Semitism,* p. 53; Stanley Rothman, *European Society and Politics* (Indianapolis: Bobbs Merrill, 1970), p. 220.

71. See Khrushchev's remarks as quoted in Kochan, *The Jews in Russia,* pp. 36–37.

72. Liebman, *Jews and the Left;* Howe, *World of Our Fathers.*

73. Thomas Sowell, ed., *American Ethnic Groups* (Washington, D.C.: Urban Institute, 1978), pp. 111–12.

74. L. Glen Seretan, *Daniel DeLeon: The Odyssey of An American Marxist* (Cambridge: Harvard University Press, 1979), p. 78.

75. Howe, *World of Our Fathers,* p. 253.

76. Sowell, *American Ethnic Groups,* pp. 112–15; D. J. Bogue, *The Population of the United States* (Glencoe, Ill.: Free Press, 1959), p. 706.

77. Quoted in Ladd and Lipset, *Divided Academy,* p. 153.

78. Ibid., p. 152.

79. This was a study of various American elites conducted jointly by Harvard University and the Washington *Post* and reprinted by the *Post* in 1976.

80. E. J. Epstein, *News from Nowhere* (New York: Random House, 1973), pp. 222–23.

81. Muriel Cantor, *The Hollywood TV Producer* (New York: Basic Books, 1971).

82. Office of Communications, United Church of Christ, "Critics and Criticism in the Mass Media," a survey conducted by Louis Harris and Associates (mimeographed, n.d.).

83. S. R. Lichter, "Media Support for Israel: A Survey of Leading Journalists," in William C. Adams, ed., *Television Coverage of the Middle East* (Norwood, N.J.: Ablex, 1981), pp. 40–52.

84. Ladd and Lipset, *Divided Academy.* In a Carnegie-Foundation-supported study, Ladd and Lipset drew a sample of 100,000 academics from 303 schools. Slightly over 60 percent of those contacted filled out the questionnaires. The publication figures for Jewish scholars in the social sciences are based on a reanalysis of their data. Heavy publishers are defined as those who had published twenty or more articles.

85. See Martin Meyer, *The Lawyers* (New York: Dell, 1966), pp. 27, 28, 100, 101. The figure on the proportion of Jews at elite law schools is derived from reanalysis of the Ladd and Lipset data.

86. Dennis Wrong, *Skeptical Sociology* (New York: Columbia University Press, 1976), p. 142.

87. Nathan Glazer and Daniel Patrick Moynihan, *Beyond the Melting Polt,* 2nd ed. (Cambridge: MIT Press, 1970), pp. 147–51.

88. Thomas Dye, *Who's Running America* (Englewood Cliffs, N.J.: Prentice-Hall, 1966), p. 183.

89. Werner Cohn, "Sources of American Jewish Liberalism: A Study of the Political Alignments of American Jews" (Ph.D. diss., New School, 1956), p. 134.

90. Lawrence H. Fuchs, *The Political Behavior of American Jews* (Glencoe, Ill.: Free Press, 1956), p. 130. As Fuchs points out, given the nature of migration from the Soviet Union such persons were clearly of Jewish background.

91. This summary is based on Liebman, *Jews and the Left;* Howe, *World of Our Fathers;* Stephen D. Isaacs, *Jews and American Politics* (New York: Doubleday, 1974);

Fuchs, *Political Behavior;* Cohn, "Sources of American Jewish Liberalism"; and other sources.

92. Howe, *World of Our Fathers,* p. 93.

93. Liebman, *Jews and the Left;* Fuchs, *Political Behavior;* and Harvey Klehr, *Communist Cadre* (Stanford: Hoover Institution Press, 1978), pp. 37–46. See also Nathan Glazer, *The Social Bases of American Communism* (New York: Harcourt, Brace & World, 1961).

94. New York: Knopf, 1978.

95. Fuchs, *Political Behavior;* Liebman, *Jews and the Left.* Jews also provided the basic support for both the Liberal and American Labor parties. See William Spinrad, "New York's Third Party Voters," *Public Opinion* 21 (Winter 1977–78): 549–51.

96. Cohn, "Sources of American Jewish Liberalism," pp. 120–22.

97. Everett C. Ladd, "Jewish Life in the United States: Social and Political Values" (mimeographed, 1978), pp. 31–32. (This essay will appear in Joseph Gitler, ed., *Jewish Life in America: Perspectives from the Social Sciences* [New York: New York University Press, forthcoming]. The pages cited are from the original manuscript.)

98. Howe, *World of Our Fathers.* For a recent discussion of one segment of New York's radical Jewish intelligentsia during the 1940s and 1950s, see William Barrett, *The Truants: Adventures Among the Intellectuals* (Garden City, N.Y.: Anchor, Doubleday, 1982).

99. Cited in Ladd and Lipset, *Divided Academy,* p. 158.

100. See note 5, Chapter 1.

101. Linda Rennie Forcey, "Personality in Politics: The Commitment of a Suicide" (Ph.D. diss., State University of New York at Binghamton, 1976); Liebman, *Jews and the Left;* Howard Bruce Franklin, *Back Where You Came From: A Life in the Death of the Empire* (New York: Harper's Magazine Press, 1975); Jonah Raskin, *Out of the Whale: Growing Up in the American Left* (New York: Links Press, 1974).

102. These findings are based on reanalysis of the Ladd-Lipset data. Ladd and Lipset developed a "liberalism" scale and divided their respondents into five categories, ranging from "most conservative" to "most liberal" based on their responses to scale items.

103. Ladd and Lipset, *Divided Academy.*

104. Ibid.

105. Ibid.

106. See the list of names published in the Spring 1969 *P.S.* (the newsletter of the American Political Science Association), p. 48.

107. This estimate is based on personal attendance of meetings of the group and analysis of the signatures on various newsletters.

108. Our estimate of the membership of the Union of Radical Political Economists is based on the composition of the editorial board of the *Review of Radical Political Economics* in its early years. We would conservatively estimate that eight of the fifteen names that appeared as members in vol. 2 of the journal were Jewish.

109. See a discussion of some of these historians in Robert James Maddox, *The New Left and the Origins of the Cold War* (Princeton: Princeton University Press, 1973).

110. See the list of authors in Beatrice and Ronald Gross, eds., *Radical School Reform* (New York: Simon and Schuster, 1969), and the discussion of some of the radicals by Diane Ravitch, *The Revisionists Revised* (New York: Basic Books, 1978).

111. Like many other Jewish radicals, Horowitz has become somewhat more conservative during the past several years.

112. Victor Navasky, "Notes on a Cult; or How To Join the Intellectual Establishment," *New York Times Magazine,* Mar. 27, 1966, pp. 28ff. It is widely accepted that Jason Epstein (Barbara Epstein's husband) and a senior editor and vice-president of Random House, has played a key role in determining policy at the *Review*. For further discussion see Suzannah Lessard, " 'Moral Myopia,' the New York Review and the New York Intellectuals," *Washington Monthly,* Nov. 1973, pp. 15–29, and Richard Kostelanetz, *The End of Intelligent Writing: Literary Politics in America* (New York: Sheed and Ward, 1973). See also Philip Nobile, "A Review of the New York Review of Books," *Esquire* 77 (Apr. 1972): 103ff.; and Dennis H. Wrong, "The Case of the 'New York Review,' " *Commentary* 50 (Nov. 1970): 49–63. As late as 1974, about 40 percent of the readership of the *NYRB* was probably Jewish. See Charles Kadushin and Herman Kane, "Change Readers and Other Intellectuals: A Comparison," *Change* 6 (Sept. 1974), pp. 23ff.

In his study of American elite intellectuals Kadushin found that 50 percent were of Jewish background. (*The American Intellectual Elite* [Boston: Little, Brown, 1974]). He found little ideological difference between elite Jewish and non-Jewish intellectuals, although Jews were clearly more active politically and dominated the relatively small group of those he defined as radicals. The lack of clearer differentiation may have been partly a function of the time at which Kadushin conducted his survey, as well as the kinds of questions he asked. Specifically, a large number of the questions concerned the Vietnam War. Other studies indicate that, very early on, Jews in general and Jewish intellectuals in particular were among those most violently opposed to that war. By the time of Kadushin's study, opposition had become much more widespread. See John E. Mueller, "Trends in Popular Support for the Wars in Korea and Vietnam," *American Political Science Review* 65 (June 1971): 358–75; and David Armor et al., "Professors' Attitudes Toward the Vietnam War," *Public Opinion Quarterly* 31 (Summer 1967): 159–75.

113. Tom Wolfe, "Radical Chic: That Party at Lenny's," *New York,* June 8, 1970, pp. 27–56.

114. Norman Podhoretz, *Breaking Ranks* (New York: Harper and Row, 1979); Merle Miller, "Why Jason and Norman Aren't Talking," *New York Times Magazine,* Mar. 26, 1972, pp. 34ff. For a rather negative picture of some of the "neo-conservatives," see Peter Steinfels, *The Neo-Conservatives: The Men Who Are Changing America's Future* (New York: Simon and Schuster, 1979).

115. We have discussed some of these changes in Chapter 1. For a more detailed analysis, see the citations in notes 23 and 26 of that chapter.

116. Charles A. Madison, *Jewish Publishing in America* (New York: Sanhedrin Press, 1976), pp. 284–85.

117. Ibid., pp. 249ff.

118. See Stephen Birmingham, "Does a Zionist Conspiracy Control the Media?" *More,* July–Aug. 1976, pp. 12–17. Birmingham's answer quite correctly is no. But his article does indicate both that Jews play a major role in the media and that their role is predominantly a liberal or "progressive" one.

119. The data is from the joint Washington *Post*–Harvard study. We wish to thank Professor Verba for providing a breakdown of his respondents' religious backgrounds.

120. J. W. Johnstone et al., *The News People* (Bloomington: University of Illinois Press, 1976). These findings are based on our reanalysis of Professor Johnstone's data, which we wish to thank him for providing.

121. *Time,* July 29, 1966, p. 57, and David Armstrong, *A Trumpet to Arms: Alternative Media in America* (Los Angeles: J. P. Tarcher, 1981). Jewish students also seemed to have played key roles on student newspapers at major liberal universities, at least until the early 1970s. See the New York *Times,* Oct. 8, 1970, p. 47c.

122. Ben Stein, *The View from Sunset Boulevard* (New York: Basic Books, 1979); Michael Robinson, "Prime Time Chic," *Public Opinion* 2 (Mar.–May 1979): 42–48.

123. Stein, *View from Sunset Boulevard,* p. 28.

124. See S. M. Lipset and William Schneider, *The Confidence Gap: What Americans Think of Their Institutions* (New York: Macmillan, 1982).

125. Linda Lichter, "Occupational Portrayals in Television Entertainment: A Content Analysis of Businessmen, Doctors and Law Enforcement Personnel" (Ph.D. diss., Columbia University, 1982).

126. Marie Winn, "What Became of Childhood Innocence?" *New York Times Magazine,* Jan. 25, 1981, p. 44.

127. Ibid., and Tony Hiss and Jeff Lewis, "The 'Mad' Generation," *New York Times Magazine,* July 31, 1977, pp. 14ff.

128. For the Institute for Policy Studies, see Gary T. Grayson and Susan Lukowski, *Washington IV* (Washington, D.C.: Potomac Books, 1975); *New America* 16 (Mar. 1979): 1f; and Rael Jean Isaac, "The Institute for Policy Studies: Empire on the Left," *Midstream* 26, no. 6 (June–July 1980): 7–18. Our list of early Nader group members was derived from varous biographies of Nader. On radical (and progressive) judges and lawyers, see the New York *Times,* Mar. 10, 1973, p. 33; Peter Vanderwicken, "The Angry Young Lawyers," *Fortune* 84 (Sept. 1971): 74ff., and Jonathan Black, ed., *Radical Lawyers* (New York: Avon Books, 1971).

129. The "progressive" activities of these foundations are discussed in *New America* 16 (Mar. 1979), as well as various studies of progressive and environmental groups published by the Heritage Foundation. See also Carl Gershman, "New Left: New Face," in *Freedom at Issue,* Mar.–Apr. 1979, pp. 3–5, and Anthony Smith, *The Shadow in the Cave* (Urbana: University of Illinois Press, 1973), pp. 232–33. Some of these sources are quite hostile to the activities in which these foundations are engaged, but we have no reason to doubt the accuracy of their listings.

130. Ladd, "Jewish Life in the United States." It should be stressed again that such progressivism is primarily confined to "deracinated" Jews. Those Jews who identify strongly with their ethnic and religious background do not differ substantially from their non-Jewish counterparts. For example, on students, see Piazza, "Jewish Identity and the Counterculture." Our own studies confirm his findings.

131. New York *Times,* Jan. 18, 1975, p. 38.

132. For the activities of the Science for the People group, and Wald, Lewontin, and Gould, the last two of whom are, according to Tom Bethell, self-proclaimed Marxists, see, among a number of other sources: Tom Bethell, "Burning Darwin To Save Marx," *Harper's,* Dec. 1978, pp. 31ff.; Michael Ruse, "Charles Darwin and the 'Beagle,' " *Wilson Quarterly,* Winter 1982, pp. 174–75. Sociobiology Study Group of Science for the People, "Sociobiology—Another Biological Determinism," in Arthus L.

Caplan, ed., *The Sociobiology Debate* (New York: Harper and Row, 1978), pp. 280–303; *Christian Science Monitor,* July 9, 1976.

133. Harvey Wasserman, a veteran of 1960s radicalism, was one of the founders of Clamshell Alliance. Richard Pollack is the associate editor of *Critical Mass Journal,* and Bruce Rosenthal is one of its important spokespersons. On these figures and others, see *Christian Science Monitor,* May 24, 1977; *Daily Hampshire Gazette,* May 2, 1977; *Christian Science Monitor,* May 2, 1977; New York *Times,* June 24, 1978, p. 6; New York *Times,* Apr. 30, 1977, p. 8; and New York *Times,* July 12, 1980, p. 1. On the Sierra Club, see *Public Interest,* Winter 1979, p. 121; *Harper's,* Feb. 1978, p. 10; and New York *Times,* Jan. 14, 1979, p. 29. On the Gay Power movement in San Francisco, see Herbert Gold "A Walk on San Francisco's Gay Side," *New York Times Magazine,* Nov. 6, 1977, pp. 67ff.

134. This is true despite the prominence of many non-Jews, such as Kate Millett, in the early days of the movement. For example, in Vivian Gornick and Barbara K. Moran, eds., *Women in Sexist Society* (New York: Basic Books, 1971) at least eleven of the twenty-seven articles whose authors are identified were written by Jews.

135. Carolyn Stoloff, "Who Joins Women's Liberation," *Psychiatry* 36 (Aug. 1973): 325–40.

136. Review of "Jews and American Politics," *New York Times Book Review,* Nov. 10, 1974.

137. Glazer and Moynihan, *Beyond the Melting Pot,* p. 1.

138. Michels, *Political Parties,* pp. 247–48.

139. Fromm, *Beyond the Chains of Illusion,* p. 5.

140. Isaac Deutscher, *The Non-Jewish Jew and Other Essays* (New York: Hill and Wang, 1970), p. 27.

141. Jerry Rubin, *We Are Everywhere* (New York: Harper and Row, 1973), pp. 74–75.

142. Fuchs, *Political Behavior,* pp. 190–91.

143. Charles Liebman, *The Ambivalent American Jew* (Philadelphia: Jewish Publication Society of America, 1973).

144. Sigmund Freud, "Some Character Types Met With in Psychoanalytic Work," in *Collected Papers of Sigmund Freud,* 5 vols. (London: Hogarth Press, 1949–50) 4: 321.

145. Theodore Reik, *Jewish Wit* (New York: Gamut Press, 1962), p. 231.

146. Liebman, *Jews and the Left.*

147. Ibid., pp. 6–24.

148. Ibid., p. 590.

149. Ibid., p. 83.

150. Ibid., p. 94.

151. Ibid., p. 86.

152. Brym, *Jewish Intelligentsia.*

153. Liebman, *Jews on the Left,* p. 89.

154. Ibid., p. 93. See also pp. 77, 451–52, and *passim.*

155. See Chapter 5.

156. See Glazer and Moynihan, *Beyond the Melting Pot,* p. ixff.

157. Our own data (Chapter 6) confirm those of Ladd and Lipset and others. Inci-

dentally, whatever may have been true in the past, we found American Jews of German backgrounds to be only slightly less radical than those whose ancestors came from Eastern Europe.

158. The hypothesis is related to the "status inconsistency" argument developed by some sociologists to explain the radicalism of middle-class Jews. However, as Liebman notes, it is certainly not always the most well-to-do Jews who are the most radical (Liebman, *Jews and the Left*, pp. 17–20). Further, marginality is a more general concept and permits more effective comparative analyses. Incidentally, *pace* Liebman, while the richest Jews are not necessarily the most radical, radical Jews generally came from middle-class backgrounds, at least initially.

159. Liebman, *Ambivalent American Jew*.

160. Raphiel Patai, *The Jewish Mind* (New York: Charles Scribner's Sons, 1977), p. 230.

161. *Syrian Christians in Muslim Society* (Princeton: Princeton University Press, 1970), pp. 5–6, and *passim*. The senior author of this volume benefited greatly from discussion of these issues with Professor Haddad, whose work on marginality has not received the attention it so richly deserves.

Obviously, adopting a secularist nationalist stance is not a universalist solution in the same sense that Marxism is. The point is that, for Christian Arabs, it redefined the social universe so as to minimize the differences between the marginal and dominant groups by establishing an identification that included both. At the same time it served to weaken the values of the superordinate group. As with Jews, the strategy has not always been successful. Incidentally, we are not suggesting that the strategy is a conscious one. Obviously, those arguing for the new identification usually do so because they consciously believe in its superior qualities.

162. Burks, *Dynamics of Communism*.

163. Ulf Hammelstrand, "Tribalism, National Rank Equilibrium and Social Structure," *Journal of Peace Research,* no. 2, 1967, pp. 81–103.

164. Jay, *Dialectical Imagination*.

165. Paul Hollander, *Political Pilgrims* (New York: Oxford University Press, 1981). It cannot be stressed too often that the basic animosity is toward the dominant culture. Political radicalism is primarily a mechanism for undermining the culture. In a sense, to use Marxist terminology, it is "epiphenomenal."

166. New York: William Morrow, 1967, pp. 163–70.

167. The Jewish reaction here parallels that of many less developed countries in their own search for identity. Thus African or Arab socialism is touted as a uniquely humane version of advanced thought. Similarly, as Levinson has pointed out, the commitment of Chinese intellectuals to a "more advanced" form of Marxism was related to their being able to use it to reestablish the superiority of their own nation. See Joseph Levinson, *Modern China and Its Confucian Past* (New York: Anchor Books, 1964).

168. Leonard Fine, "The Dilemmas of Jewish Identity on the College Campus," *Judaism* 17 (Winter 1968):10–21.

169. New York: Random House, 1969, pp. 232–33.

170. Ibid., p. 145.

171. Ibid., p. 235.

172. Reik, *Jewish Wit*, p. 119.

173. Cuddihy's book was published by Basic Books in 1974. Horowitz's review appears in *Contemporary Sociology* 5 (Mar. 1976):111.

174. Rubin, *We Are Everywhere*, p. 71.

175. Roger Kahn, *The Battle for Morningside Heights* (New York: William Morrow, 1970).

176. Paul Cowan, *The Making of an Un-American* (New York: Dell, 1970).

177. Anthony Scaduto, "Won't You Listen to the Lambs, Bob Dylan," *New York Times Magazine*, Nov. 28, 1971, pp. 34ff. For a full-scale biography see Anthony Scaduto, *Bob Dylan* (New York: Grosset and Dunlap, 1971).

178. New York: Basic Books, 1977. See the review by Marion Magid in *Commentary*, Feb. 1978, pp. 78–82.

179. John Berendt, "Phil Ochs Ain't Marchin' Anymore," *Esquire* 4 (Oct. 1976): 110ff.

180. See our discussion of Keniston in Chapter 2.

181. See Lloyd D. Easton and Kurt H. Guddat, eds. and trans., *Writings of the Young Marx on Philosophy and Society* (New York: Doubleday/Anchor Book, 1967), pp. 244–45ff.

182. See Rothman, *European Society and Politics,* pp. 33, 211.

183. See W. H. Chaloner and W. O. Henderson, "Marx/Engels and Racism," *Encounter,* July 1975, pp. 18–23; Saul K. Padover, *Karl Marx: An Intimate Biography* (New York: McGraw-Hill, 1978), p. 327.

184. Ibid. See also Jerrold Seigal, *Marx's Fate* (Princeton, N.J.: Princeton University Press, 1978). Perhaps the best recent discussion of Marx's attitude toward Jews and Judaism is Julius Carlebach, *Karl Marx and the Radical Critique of Judaism* (London: Routledge and Kegan Paul, 1978). His book contains a very complete bibliography. Carlebach tends to discount the argument that Marx's attitude toward Jews was motivated in part by self-hatred.

185. Quoted in Wistrich, *Revolutionary Jews*, p. 56.

186. Ibid.

187. See Wistrich, *Revolutionary Jews,* and Reik, *Jewish Wit*. Arthur Liebman, *Jews and the Left*, pp. 15–16, dismisses the argument that Jewish self-hatred may be related to Jewish radicalism, because not all Jewish radicals have shared this syndrome. His facts are correct, but his logic is faulty. Such arguments, after all, are probabilistic; i.e., the two patterns can be causally related even if the relationship does not manifest itself in every case.

188. Poor, *Kurt Tucholsky,* pp. 92, 217–21.

189. Ibid., pp. 221–22.

190. Rubin, *We Are Everywhere*, pp. 75–76. Yet he cannot escape a certain ambivalence here:

> I personally feel very torn about being born Jewish. I know it made me feel like a minority or outsider in Amerika from my birth and helped me become a revolutionary. I am shocked at Julius Hoffman and Richard Schultz 'cause they try to be so Amerikan. Don't they know they're still "Jewish" no matter how much "power" or "security" in Amerika they have?

Ibid., p. 75.

191. Schwarz, "Melting Pot or Witch's Cauldron," pp. 277–79.

192. Stanley Rothman and Phillip Isenberg, "Freud and Jewish Marginality," *Encounter*, Dec. 1974, pp. 46–54. We should note that we ourselves are persuaded of the validity of substantial portions of psychoanalytic theory. Nor do we believe that Freud's desire to undermine the dominant culture provides more than a small part of the explanation of the emergence of psychoanalysis in late nineteenth-century Europe.

193. Deutscher, *Non-Jewish Jew*, p. 24.

194. Rothman, *European Society and Politics*, pp. 346–47.

195. Frederich Nietzsche, *The Birth of Tragedy and the Genealogy of Morals*, trans. Francis Golfing (New York: Doubleday, 1956), p. 168.

196. Rudolph Lowenstein, *Christians and Jews: A Psychoanalytic Study* (New York: W. W. Norton, 1951), p. 134.

197. Mark Zborowski, "Cultural Components in Responses to Pain," in Peter Rose, ed., *The Study of Society* (New York: Random House, 1967), pp. 152–64; Bernard Tursky and Richard A. Sternbach, "Ethnic Differences Among Housewives in Psycho-Physical Skin Responses to Electric Shock" and "Further Physiological Correlates of Ethnic Differences in Responses to Shock," in *Psychophysiology* 1, no. 3 (1965): 241–46 and 1, no. 4 (1965): 67–74.

198. Michael Argyle, *Religious Behavior* (London: Routledge King and Paul, 1958), pp. 97–99; Lowenstein, *Christians and Jews*, pp. 125–28; and N. Goldberg, "Jews in the Police Records of Los Angeles, 1933–1947," *YIVO Annual of Jewish Social Science* 5 (1950): 266–92.

199. James Bieri, Robin Lobeck, and Harold Plotnick, "Psychosocial Factors in Differential Social Mobility," *Journal of Social Psychology* 58 (1962): 183–200.

200. Charles R. Snyder, "Culture and Jewish Sobriety: The Ingroup-Outgroup Factor," in Marshall Sklar, ed., *The Jews* (Glencoe, Ill.: Free Press, 1958), pp. 560–64. One scholar who does accept the Kantian explanation is Nathan Glazer. See "Why Jews Stay Sober," *Commentary*, Feb. 1952, pp. 181–85.

201. David McClelland, William Davis, Rudolf Kalin, and Eric Wanner, *The Drinking Man* (New York: Free Press, 1972).

202. Heinz Hartman, Ernst Kris, and Rudolph M. Lowenstein, "Notes on the Theory of Aggression," *Psychological Issues* 55, monograph 14 (1964): 74.

203. Ruth Landes and Mark Zborowski, "Hypotheses Concerning the Eastern European Jewish Family," in *Psychiatry* 13 (1950): 452.

204. Herbert Krugman, "The Interplay of Social and Psychological Factors in Political Deviance" (Ph.D. diss., Columbia University, 1952), p. 164.

205. Grete L. Bibring, "On the 'Passing of the Oedipus Complex' in a Matriarchal Family Setting," in Rudolf Lowenstein, ed., *Drives, Affects, Behavior* (New York: International Universities Press, 1953), pp. 278–84. Bibring does not specifically mention Jews in this essay. However, the "relatively large group" on which she based her analysis was probably disproportionately Jewish, given the characteristics of psychoanalytic clientele in the late 1930s and 1940s.

206. Landes and Zborowski, "Hypotheses Concerning the Eastern European Jewish Family," p. 453.

207. Bibring, "On the 'Passing of the Oedipus Complex.' " We are not arguing that the Oedipal phase of development is a central issue in all cultures at all times. However, it seems to us that it has been of considerable significance in nineteenth- and twentieth-century Europe.

208. Martha Wolfenstein, "Two Types of Jewish Mother," in Margaret Mead and Martha Wolfenstein, eds., *Childhood in Contemporary Society* (Chicago: University of Chicago Press, 1955), pp. 424–42.

209. Otto F. Kernberg, *Borderline Conditions and Pathological Narcissism* (New York: Jason Aronson, 1975), pp. 235ff., and W. W. Meissner, *The Paranoid Process* (New York: Jason Aronson, 1978), pp. 700–714, *passim*.

210. Alfred Kazin, *Starting Out in the Thirties* (Boston: Little, Brown, 1962); and Milton Himmelfarb, "Negroes, Jews and Muzhiks," *Commentary,* Oct. 1966, pp. 83–86.

211. Christopher Lasch, *Haven in a Heartless World* (New York: Basic Books, 1977), pp. 188–89. Lasch's volume contains much that is extremely perceptive, and we have drawn upon it from time to time. Overall, however, it is seriously flawed, for reasons described in Stanley Rothman, "Lasch on Narcissism," *Political Psychology* 2 (Spring 1980):75–79.

212. See Chapters 5 through 9 of this book.

213. Krugman, "Interplay of Social and Psychological Factors," pp. 99–100.

214. Ibid., p. 130.

215. Erik Erikson, *Childhood and Society,* 2nd ed. (New York: W. W. Norton, 1963), p. 268.

216. Lasch, *Haven,* p. 189.

217. Jules Nydes, "The Paranoid-Masochistic Character," *Psychoanalytic Review,* Summer 1963, pp. 215–51.

218. Reik, *Jewish Wit*.

219. Hartmann, Kris, and Lowenstein, "Notes on the Theory of Aggression," p. 74.

220. J. W. M. Whiting and Irvin L. Child, *Child Training and Personality: A Cross-Cultural Study* (New Haven: Yale University Press, 1953).

221. Defensive projection is a process whereby individuals attribute painful impulses or ideas that arise from internal conflicts onto the external world. Thus their wish to injure others becomes the wish of others to injure them. A certain amount of defensive projection (i.e., healthy suspiciousness) is adaptive. However, a high degree of projection, as in paranoia, is pathological.

222. "Political Attitudes Among White Ethnics" (paper presented at a meeting of the American Political Science Association, Sept. 1971) (mimeographed), table 12.

223. As reported in *Time,* Oct. 2, 1978, p. 76.

224. Ibid.

225. Historically, Christianity has been quite intolerant of other faiths. In a sense, the only hope diaspora Jews had for full citizenship lay in the undermining of Christian culture. As we have seen, however, the forces unleashed as a result of that undermining can be at least as hostile to the real and ideal interests of both identifying and deracinated Jews as was the old regime.

226. Kenneth Keniston, *The Uncommitted* (New York: Harcourt, Brace & World, 1965). There is increasing evidence of the importance of the father in encouraging the child's psychic separation from the mother and hence the development of a sense of self. See Ernest L. Abelin, "The Role of the Father and the Origins of Core Gender Identity" (revised version of a paper presented at a meeting of the New York Society of Freudian Psychologists, Apr. 24, 1977) (mimeographed).
Aside from the evidence already presented, additional data are consistent with our

arguments about parental roles in diaspora Jewish families and their consequences for males. For example, the comparative work of both Strodtbeck and Giordano supports our discussion of the salient role of the mother in Jewish familes. Further, Slavin found that, while favorable attitudes toward female equality varied inversely with score on "threatening female imagery" in responses to TAT pictures, one group of respondents deviated from the norm. This group, which was 60 percent Jewish, scored high on measures of both "threatening female imagery" and female equality. They also scored quite low on a measure of "castration anxiety." In short, the commitment to equality on the part of these young males seemed to be based on their fear of women and their desire to deny the reality of sexual differences. See Fred I. Strodtbeck, "Family Interaction, Values and Achievement," in David McClelland, ed., *Talent and Society* (New York: Van Nostrand, 1958), pp. 135–91; Joseph Giordano, *Ethnicity and Mental Health: Research and Recommendations* (New York: Institute of Human Relations, 1973); and Mal Slavin, "The Myth of Feminine Evil: A Psychoanalytic Exploration" (Ph.D. diss., Harvard University, 1972).

227. Fred Weinstein and Gerald M. Platt, *The Wish To Be Free: Society, Psyche, and Value Change* (Berkely: University of California Press, 1969).

228. Susan Stern, *With the Weathermen* (Garden City, N.Y.: Doubleday, 1974), p. 243.

229. J. Kirk Sale, "Ted Gold: Education for Violence," *The Nation,* Apr. 13, 1970, pp. 423–29.

230. Ibid., p. 426.

231. Ibid., p. 428.

232. Ibid., *passim.*

233. Quoted in Poor, *Kurt Tucholsky,*, p. 60.

234. Paul Jacobs, *Is Curly Jewish?* (New York: Atheneum, 1965), pp. 3–4.

235. Norman Mailer, "The White Negro," *Dissent,* Summer 1957, pp. 276–93.

236. Morris Dickstein, *Gates of Eden: American Culture in the Sixties* (New York: Basic Books, 1977), p. 144. We would not agree that Mailer's portrayal of Goldstein and Roth, or any of his later writing, demonstrates an increase in real self-awareness. The ability of intellectuals to discuss their psychological problems, often at great length, is frequently merely a more complicated defense against dealing with the real issues. Narcissists, as both Kernberg, *Borderline Conditions,* and Meissner, *Paranoid Process,* note, are quite prone to this.

237. Abbie Hoffman, *Revolution for the Hell of It* (New York: Dial Press, 1968), p. 13.

238. This quote is from a discussion with "Arnold" (a pseudonym), one of the students who was interviewed for our study. The interview is on tape.

239. Joel Carmichael, *Trotsky,* and his article "Trotsky's Agony," *Encounter,* May 1972 and June 1972, pp. 31–41; 28–36.

240. Forcey, "Personality in Politics."

241. Ibid., pp. 57–58.

242. Ibid., p. 59.

243. Ibid., p. 72.

244. Ibid., pp. 80–81.

245. Ibid., p. 137.

246. Ibid., p. 183.

247. Berendt, "Phil Ochs Ain't Marchin' "; Marc Eliot, *Death of a Rebel* (New York: Anchor Press/Doubleday, 1979).

248. Berendt, "Phil Ochs Ain't Marchin'," p. 132.

249. Ibid., p. 136.

250. There is evidence that Marx shared some of the background and personality characteristics we have ascribed to Jewish radicals in general. Jerrold Seigal, *Marx's Fate,* notes the excessive concern of Marx's mother with his health (p. 49). He suggests that "there is reason to believe that Henriette Marx's mothering was rather intrusive and manipulative." He points out that Marx's most characteristic behavior in his later life consisted in doing just those things (such as ignoring health considerations) that his mother had warned him against (p. 50). And his relations with her were hardly cordial. By contrast, Marx's realtions with his father were always warm (p. 50).

Further, Marx's notable aggressive behavior was almost entirely verbal. Despite one probably apocryphal story, told by Engels, of his having faced down some soldiers, there is no evidence of physical courage. In 1848, when the attempt by Marx and Engels to establish a newspaper in Germany failed, Engels joined the revolutionaries, while Marx returned to Paris. (David McClellan, *Karl Marx: His Life and Thought* [New York: Harper and Row, 1973], p. 223.)

251. H. H. Gerth and C. Wright Mills, eds., *From Max Weber* (London: Kegan Paul, Trench, Trubner, 1947), pp. 129–58.

252. Haddad, *Syrian Christians,* p. 3.

253. Weinstein and Platt, *Wish To Be Free.* For the paranoia that can accompany revolution see also, Melvin J. Lasky, *Utopia and Revolution* (Chicago: University of Chicago Press, 1976).

254. Milton Himmelfarb, "Are Jews Becoming Republicans?" *Commentary* 72 (Aug. 1981): 27–31.

255. We use the term "progressive" in this book as a synonym for "liberal cosmopolitan." The person we have in mind is one who is naturally drawn to new ideas critical of the existing culture, because they are new and critical, without necessarily being tied to a given ideological position.

256. It seems clear that some Jews, including Martin Peretz and Dick Russell, ended their financial support of *Ramparts* for what they considered to be its pro-Arab stand. See Warren Hinckle, *If You Have a Lemon, Make Lemonade* (New York: G. Putnam's Sons, 1973), p. 337.

257. See the remarks of Leonard Fine at Smith College, as reported in the *Daily Hampshire Gazette,* Oct. 10, 1980.

258. See the series of articles in the New York *Times,* Aug. 17, 18, 19, 1980, on evangelicalism and politics in the recent presidential election.

259. For a discussion see Meissner, *Paranoid Process,* esp. pp. 796–818.

Obviously the variables we have listed can not completely explain why some Jews have become radicals and others have not. Additional variables may be involved. For example, student political activism in the 1960s was largely a middle-class phenomenon. Poor Jews were too busy surviving economically to contemplate such activity. And for Jews and non-Jews alike, "accidents" (i.e., uniquely individual experiences) may lead in other directions. Further, both political attitudes and personality conflict may be blunted or redirected as individuals react to new information. Some Jewish progressives withdrew from the Communist party in the face of the overwhelming evidence of Stalin's crimes. Many others did not. Why some individuals can accept information of this kind while others rationalize it away is difficult to know. The particular individual's age, degree of ego autonomy and capacity for reflection are obviously key variables here.

260. See Bruno Bettelheim, *Children of the Dream* (New York: Avon, 1969).

CHAPTER 4: THE AUTHORITARIAN LEFT

1. For an intellectual and social history of this group, see Martin Jay, *The Dialectical Imagination* (Boston: Little, Brown, 1973).

2. Herbert McClosky, "Conservatism and Personality," *American Political Science Review* 52 (1958): 27–45.

3. See the discussion of "authoritarianism and political beliefs" in John Kirscht and Ronald Dillehay, *Dimensions of Authoritarianism* (Lexington, Ky.: University of Kentucky Press, 1967), esp. pp. 57–69; cf. Alan Elms, *Personality and Politics* (New York: Harcourt Brace Jovanovich, 1976), pp. 30–34; William Stone, *The Psychology of Politics* (New York: Free Press, 1974), pp. 153–55.

4. Erich Fromm, "Sozialpsychologischer Teil," in Institut für Sozialforschung, *Studien über Autorität und Familie* (Paris: Alean, 1936), pp. 77–135.

5. Sigmund Freud, "Character and Anal Eroticism" (1907), in *Collected Papers of Sigmund Freud,* 5 vols. (London: Hogarth Press, 1949–50) 2: 45–50; see also "Three Essays on Sexuality" (1905) in vol. 7 of *The Standard Edition of the Complete Psychological Works of Sigmund Freud,* 24 vols. (London: Hogarth Press, 1953).

6. Fromm and Adorno et al. concentrated on male authoritarianism. Therefore, except when otherwise indicated, our discussion of this concept is limited to its workings among males.

7. Fromm, *Escape from Freedom* (New York: Farrar and Rinehart, 1941).

8. Ibid., p. 186.

9. T. W. Adorno, in Adorno, Else Frenkel-Brunswick, Daniel Levinson, and R. Nevitt Sanford, *The Authoritarian Personality* (New York: Harper and Row, 1950), p. 976. Hereafter cited as *TAP.*

10. Adorno, *TAP,* pp. 232–33.

11. Else Frenkel-Brunswick, "Parents and Childhood as Seen Through the Interviews," *TAP,* pp. 337–89.

12. Erik Erikson, "Hitler's Imagery and German Youth," *Psychiatry* 5 (1942), reprinted in *Childhood and Society* (New York: W. W. Norton, 1950), from which the material cited below is taken.

13. Ibid., p. 332.

14. Ibid.

15. Adorno, *TAP,* pp. 759–62.

16. Kirscht and Dillehay, *Dimensions of Authoritarianism,* p. 130.

17. R. Nevitt Sanford, "Authoritarian Personality in Contemporary Perspective," in Jean Knutson, ed., *Handbook of Political Psychology* (San Francisco: Jossey-Bass, 1973), p. 150.

18. S. M. Lipset, "Democracy and Working Class Authoritarianism," *American*

Sociological Review 24 (1959): 482–501; cf. Kirscht and Dillehay, *Dimensions of Authoritarianism,* pp. 35–41.

19. R. Nevitt Sanford, "The Approach of the Authoritarian Personality," in J. L. McCary, ed., *Psychology of Personality* (New York: Logos, 1956), p. 332.

20. Edward Shils, "Authoritarianism: Right and Left," in Richard Christie and Marie Jahoda, eds., *Studies in the Scope and Methods of "The Authoritarian Personality"* (Glencoe, Ill.: Free Press, 1954), p. 158.

21. Sanford, "Authoritarian Personality in Contemporary Perspective," p. 163.

22. Ibid., p. 164.

23. Fromm, *Escape from Freedom,* p. 84.

24. Fromm, "Sozialpsychologischer Teil," p. 131 (our translation).

25. Ibid.

26. Fromm, *Escape from Freedom,* pp. 191–92.

27. Ibid.

28. Adorno, *TAP,* pp. 762–63.

29. Ibid., pp. 237–38.

30. Milton Rokeach, *The Open and Closed Mind* (New York: Basic Books, 1960).

31. Ibid., pp. 69–70.

32. E. Victor Wolfenstein, *The Revolutionary Personality* (Princeton: Princeton University Press, 1967). See esp. pp. 165–73.

33. Ibid., p. 170.

34. Rupert Wilkinson, *The Broken Rebel* (New York: Harper and Row, 1972), p. 120.

35. Ibid., pp. 55–60.

36. Ibid., p. 122.

37. Christopher Lasch, *Haven in a Heartless World* (New York: Basic Books, 1977), p. 156.

38. See Otto Kernberg, *Borderline Conditions and Pathological Narcissism* (New York: Jason Aronson, 1975), pp. 223–24.

39. W. W. Meissner, *The Paranoid Process* (New York: Jason Aronson, 1978), ch. 28 and *passim.*

40. Ibid., p. 31.

41. Ibid., p. 108.

42. Ibid., pp. 667–69, and *passim.* Similarly, the paranoid can be rigidly ascetic, or emphasize the acting out of all impulses. Indeed, some of Dr. Meissner's more seriously ill patients did both at different times. Of course, such patterns are quite characteristic of even "normal" adolescents, as Anna Freud pointed out in *The Ego and the Mechanisms of Defense* (New York: International Universities Press, 1967). She also described the paradoxical gratifications of "identifying with the victim," and cited examples that are still relevant to understanding the "altruism" of some young (and old) radicals. There is, for instance, the public benefactor who "with the utmost aggressiveness and energy demands money from one set of people in order to give it to another" (p. 130). Such an act is simultaneously altruistic and egoistic, for genuine benefits accrue to the solicitor as well as the recipient of funds. "As in the process of identification with the aggressor, passivity is transformed into activity, narcissistic mortification is compensated for by the sense of power associated with the role of benefac-

tor, while the passive experience of frustration finds compensation in the active confer-
ring of happiness on others'' (p. 134).

The most extreme version of altruism stemming from identification with the victim
is also illuminating. It is the case of ''the assassin who, in the name of the oppressed,
murders the oppressor. The object against which the liberated aggression is directed is
invariably the representative of the authority which imposed renunciation of instinct on
the subject . . .'' (p. 130).

43. Meissner, *Paranoid Process*, p. 21.

44. Such energies can be used for quite creative ends as well, especially among
persons who are only mildly paranoid and have strong egos.

45. Meissner, *Paranoid Process*, p. 524.

46. The need to perceive oneself as persecuted is essentially a defense against such
feelings.

47. Meissner, *Paranoid Process*, p. 617.

48. Kernberg, *Borderline Conditions*, p. 328.

49. Ibid., p. 19.

50. Meissner, *Paranoid Process*, pp. 701–71.

51. Ibid., p. 717.

52. On adolescence see Peter Bos, *The Adolescent Passage* (New York: Interna-
tional Universities Press, 1979), pp. 1–36; Peter Blos, *On Adolescence* (New York:
Free Press, 1962), p. 130; Anna Freud, *Ego and Mechanisms of Defense*, pp. 137–38;
Peter Blos, ''When and How Does Adolescence End: Structural Criteria for Adolescent
Closure,'' in Sherman Feinstein and Peter Giovacchini, eds., *Adolescent Psychiatry*
(New York: Jason Aronson, 1977) 5: 11–12; Meissner, *Paranoid Process*, p. 650–51;
Erikson, ''Reflections on the Dissent of Contemporary Youth,'' *International Journal
of Psycho-Analysis* 51 (1970): 12.

53. Jürgen Habermas, *Toward a Rational Society* (Boston: Beacon Press, 1970),
pp. 45–46.

54. Kenneth Keniston, *Youth and Dissent* (New York: Harcourt Brace Jovanovich,
1971), pp. 271–73.

55. Ibid., p. 269.

56. Ibid., p. 271.

57. Tom Hayden, ''A Letter to the New (Young) Left,'' in Mitchell Cohen and
Dennis Hale, eds., *The New Student Left* (Boston: Beacon Press, 1967), p. 7. There is
some evidence that Tom Hayden was himself swept up by revolutionary rhetoric in the
late 1960s. See Peter Collier, ''I Remember Fonda,'' *New West*, Sept. 24, 1979, pp.
19–24.

58. Carl Oglesby, ''Introduction,'' in C. Oglesby, ed., *The New Left Reader* (New
York: Grove Press, 1969), p. 18.

59. The term ''protean man'' was first used by Robert Lifton, although the meaning
he gives to the term is somewhat different from ours. It was later used by Keniston to
describe his young radicals. Again, however, he uses the term rather differently than
we do, although some of the characteristics both he and Lifton see as typified by protean
types are shared by the Jewish radicals we studied. See Lifton, *History and Human
Survival* (New York: Vintage Books, 1971), pp. 311–31, and Keniston, *Young Radicals*, pp. 257–90. These protean rebels, if they attained power, would not necessarily

be less authoritarian than the rigid rebels whom we describe below. The behavior of Rakosi and others like him in Eastern Europe strongly suggests otherwise.

60. Theodore H. White, *In Search of History: A Personal Adventure* (New York: Harper and Row, 1978), p. 194.

61. Jules Nydes, "The Paranoid-Masochistic Character," *Psychoanalytic Review*, Summer 1963, p. 220.

62. Nigel Young, *An Infantile Disorder? The Crisis and Decline of the New Left* (Boulder, Colo.: Westview Press, 1977), p. 46.

63. Cited ibid., p. 45.

64. Ibid., p. 46.

65. Mario Savio, quoted in Hal Draper, *Berkeley: The New Student Revolt* (New York: Grove Press, 1965), p. 98.

66. Cited in Paul Jacobs and Saul Landau, *The New Radicals* (New York: Vintage Books, 1966), pp. 272–73.

67. Ibid., p. 213.

68. Erikson, Reflections on Dissent," p. 13.

69. Carl Oglesby, "Decade Ready for a Dustbin," in Mitchell Goodman, ed., *The Movement Toward a New America* (Philadelphia: Pilgrim Press, 1970), p. 740.

70. David Osher, "Roar Lion Roar," *Win*, June 15, 1969; cited in Young, *Infantile Disorder*, p. 459.

71. Cited in Young, *Infantile Disorder*, p. 233.

72. Ibid., p. 172.

73. Ibid., p. 233.

74. Cited in Oglesby, *New Left Reader*, p. 296.

75. Cited in Young, *Infantile Disorder*, p. 108.

76. Andreas Baader, 1973 Bundeskriminalamt records, cited by Klaus Mehnert, *Jugend im Zeitbruch* (Stuttgart: Deutsche Verlags-Anstalt, 1976), p. 158.

77. Cited in Klaus Mehnert, *Twilight of the Young* (New York: Holt, Rinehart & Winston, 1977), p. 116.

78. Nick Egleson, quoted in Young, *Infantile Disorder*, p. 258.

79. Susan Stern, *With the Weathermen* (Garden City, N.Y.: Doubleday, 1974), p. 318.

80. Ibid., p. 24.

81. Jillian Becker, *Hitler's Children* (New York: J. C. Lippincott, 1977), p. 72.

82. See Hannah Arendt, *The Origins of Totalitarianism* (New York: Harcourt Brace, 1951).

83. Tom Wolfe, *Radical Chic and Mau-Mauing the Flak-Catchers* (New York: Bantam Books, 1973), p. 7.

84. Jack Newfield, *A Prophetic Minority* (New York: Signet, 1966), pp. 40–41.

85. Gerald Rosenfield, "Generational Revolt and the Free Speech Movement," *Liberation*, Dec. 1965–Jan. 1966, cited in Jacobs and Landau, *New Radicals*, pp. 213–14.

86. The pattern was obviously accentuated by the movement itself. The role of crowds in permitting more primitive conflicts to become reactivated has been widely commented upon by psychoanalysts and others. In the age of television some of the same effects can be achieved through the mass media. See Phylis Greenacre, "Crowds

and Crisis: Psychoanalytic Considerations,'' in *The Psychoanalytic Study of the Child* (New York: Quadrangle Books, 1973) 27: 136–55.

87. Gerry Farber, *The Student as Nigger* (Hollywood, Ca.: Contact, 1969).

88. Herbert Marcuse, *One-Dimensional Man* (Boston: Beacon Press, 1964), pp. 257–58.

89. Jerry Rubin, *Do It!* (New York: Simon and Schuster, 1970).

90. Jerald Rosenfield, cited in Jacobs and Landau, *New Radicals,* p. 216.

91. Todd Gitlin, cited in Young, *Infantile Disorder,* p. 46.

92. Carl Davidson, cited in Young, *Infantile Disorder,* p. 48.

93. Howard Zinn, in Priscilla Long, ed., *The New Left* (Boston: Porter Sargent, 1969), pp. 56–59.

94. Daniel Cohn-Bendit, *Obsolete Communism: The Left-Wing Alternative* (New York: McGraw-Hill, 1970), p. 130.

95. Rubin, *Do It!,* p. 127.

96. Irving Howe, "New Styles in 'Leftism,' " in Jacobs and Landau, *New Radicals,* pp. 289–90.

97. See Stuart Daniels, "The Weathermen," *Government and Opposition* 9, no. 4 (Autumn 1974): 430–59.

98. Bernadine Dohrn, cited in Harold Jacobs, ed., *The Weatherman* (New York: Ramparts, 1970), pp. 509–10.

99. Martin Walker, *Guardian,* Oct. 28, 1970; cited in Daniels, "Weathermen," p. 445.

100. Daniels, "Weathermen," pp. 455, 446. Recently a few early activists have blamed some of the New Left's shift to "bizarre" behavior on the media. Because they were part of the Establishment, and thus hostile to the young radicals, Todd Gitlin argues, reporters emphasized such activity to discredit the movement. The heady effect of the publicity received encouraged many students to act in ways that would bring them more attention. See Todd Gitlin, *The Whole World Is Watching* (Berkeley: University of California Press, 1980). While it may contain an element of truth, the argument as a whole simply does not hold up. Elite media personnel, and especially television personnel, tended to be at least mildly progressive and, thus, rather sympathetic to the student movement. See Stanley Rothman, "The Mass Media in Post-Industrial America," in S. M. Lipset, *The Third Century: America as a Post-Industrial Society* (Stanford: Hoover Institution Press, 1979). One additional piece of evidence is especially suggestive. In 1970, T. J. Madden attempted to test the hypothesis that conservative editors tended to emphasize the role of such fringe groups and "bizarre" activities. He administered a questionnaire to personnel at the Philadelphia *Inquirer*. To his surprise, he discovered that the more liberal the reporter or editor, the more likely he was to play up these groups and activities.

Madden's findings are consistent with our perspective. During the middle and late 1960s, liberal media personnel resonated with the young radicals and saw these "bizarre" activities as further evidence of the corruption and decay of traditional institutions. They gave such activities more play because primitive elements in their own personalities were supportive of them. In retrospect, and in calmer times, they have "forgotten" such commitments. We are not, of course, suggesting conscious deception. Rather, with the reemergence of superego and ego control, they no longer can recall their feelings during the period, especially feelings which are quite repressed under normal circumstances. (See T. J. Madden, "Editor Authoritarianism and Its Effect on News Display," *Journalism Quarterly* 48 (Winter 1971): 887–96.)

101. From a Dec. 1963 Manifesto of Subversive Aktion, a Munich group, cited in Gianni Statera, *Death of a Utopia: The Development and Decline of Student Movements in Europe* (New York: Oxford University Press, 1975), pp. 63–64.

102. Cited in Newfield, *Prophetic Minority,* p. 119.

103. Dotson Rader, *Blood Dues* (New York: Knopf, 1973), pp. 7–8.

104. Ibid., p. 165.

105. See the New York *Times* articles on the U.S. Labor Party, Oct. 7 and 8, 1979.

106. For example, Jane Alpert, *Growing Up Underground* (New York: William Morrow, 1981).

107. See Sheldon Wolin, "Separating Terrorism from Radicalism," New York *Times,* Nov. 3, 1981, and Lucinda Franks, "The Seeds of Terror," *New York Times Magazine,* Nov. 22, 1981, pp. 34ff.

108. We emphasize again that the majority of those active in the civil rights and antiwar movements were not of this type. Most were simply protesting against perceived social and political injustice. Their occasional tendencies to act out fairly primitive impulses, and to ascribe base motives to their opponents, were a function of the passions induced by social upheaval. Our theory is designed to explain the behavior of ideological radicals only, and not all of these were authoritarians.

When a social movement becomes sufficiently widespread, individuals are attracted to it for all sorts of reasons, including accidents of time and place. Thus many young people who were radicalized during the 1960s, and who sometimes behaved in bizarre ways, were simply caught up in the Zeitgeist of the period.

CHAPTER 5: STUDYING THE NEW LEFT

1. See, for example, the criticisms raised in Oscar K. Buros, ed., *Personality Tests and Reviews* vol. II (Highland Park, N.J.: Gryphon Press, 1975).

2. Alice Gold, Lucy Friedman, and Richard Christie, "The Anatomy of Revolutionists," *Journal of Applied Social Psychology* 1 (1979): 26–43.

3. Alice R. Gold, Lucy Norman Friedman, and Richard Christie, *Fists and Flowers* (New York: Academic Press, 1976).

CHAPTER 6: RADICAL YOUTH

1. There are several reasons for the large proportion of Jews in the sample. First, although they constitute only 3 percent of the American populace, they are very disproportionately represented among the college population, especially in elite schools. For example, students of Jewish background accounted for almost one third of the student body at Harvard and nearly half the student body at Boston University. Second, the radical groups we sampled, such as the "People's Party" at the University of Michigan, had large proportions of Jewish members. Finally, by removing all non-Caucasians from the study, we automatically increased the proportion of Jews in the remaining sample. As a result, our data base certainly overestimates the proportion of radicals who were

Jewish in the American student movement during the early 1970s. On the other hand, we did not choose the campuses we sampled to be representative of all postsecondary institutions.

The evidence cited in Chapter 3, as well as our own study of early New Leftists, suggests that ethnic Jews constituted a majority of the New Left in its formative years. At the very least, we have demonstrated that young people of Jewish background provided a critical mass for this radical movement. Therefore, our main concern is to delineate the similarities and differences in the backgrounds and orientations of Jewish and non-Jewish radicals, rather than to estimate the proportion of Jews within the New Left during its last years as a mass movement. This goal is not affected by the proportion of Jewish students in the sample. Finally, the number of Jewish subjects does not affect the relationship between Jewishness and radicalism, i.e., the tendency for ethnic Jews to become radical out of proportion to their number.

2. Richard Flacks, "The Liberated Generation: An Exploration of the Roots of Student Protest," *Journal of Social Issues* 23 (July 1967): 52–75.

3. Kenneth Keniston, *Youth and Dissent* (New York: Harcourt Brace Jovanovich, 1971), p. 154.

4. This part of the study posed a special problem. Children's ratings of their parents' values are notoriously subjective. Clinicians and social scientists alike have learned to mistrust retrospective reconstructions of family life. We shall deal with this difficulty at length when we discuss our subjects' perceptions of their parents' personal qualities. For now, we note that the problem varies in magnitude according to both the inferences one wishes to draw and the evidence available for cross-checking. For example, while some subjects might distort their parents' political views, there is no reason to believe that such distortion would vary systematically according to ethnicity. For our purposes, then, the problem of valid recall demands circumspection in drawing inferences but need not halt our investigation altogether.

5. Martin Jacobs, "The Addictive Personality: Predictions of Success in a Smoking Withdrawal Program," *Psychosomatic Medicine* 34 (1972): 30–38; M. Jacobs, "The Use of Projective Techniques in Research Design: The Family Interaction Test," *International Psychiatry Clinics* 3 (1966): 237–64; M. Jacobs, Luleen S. Anderson, Howard D. Eisman, James J. Muller, and Sidney Friedman, "Interaction of Psychologic and Biologic Predisposing Factors in Allergic Disorders," *Psychosomatic Medicine* 29 (1967): 572–85.

6. Richard Neimi, "A Methodological Study of Political Socialization in the Family" (Ph.D. diss., University of Michigan, 1967), p. 58.

7. Charles Osgood, George Suci, and Percy Tannenbaum, *The Measurement of Meaning* (Urbana: University of Illinois Press, 1957).

8. C. Osgood and James Snider, eds., *Semantic Differential Technique* (Chicago: University of Chicago Press, 1969); Fred Kerlinger, *Foundations of Behavioral Research* (New York: Holt, Rinehart & Winston, 1973).

9. The questionnaires filled out by approximately half the sample contained only the first five pictures listed below. The sixth, showing a women peering into a room, was added during the course of the survey for its value in tapping defensive projection. Before analyzing the data, we multiplied by 1.2 the TAT scores of subjects who responded to the original set of five pictures.

10. The most prominent of these psychologists is David McClelland, who initiated

the use of standardized TAT scoring systems with his pioneering work on the achievement motive. In the early 1950s, he developed a system for inferring a person's need for achievement from his or her TAT stories. Since that time, hundreds of studies have been conducted to test whether the system in fact measures an inner motivation toward achievement. Most scholars now agree that it does, although many do not accept McClelland's attempts to extrapolate his findings to the study of whole societies. For example, other things being equal, subjects who scored high on the need for achievement while in college were more likely to become successful entrepreneurs than were subjects who scored low on the measure.

For discussions of various studies of the achievement motive and entrepreneurial success see David McClelland and David Winter, *Motivating Economic Achievement* (New York: Free Press, 1969). See also David Winter, David McClelland, and Abigail Stewart, *Competence in College* (San Francisco: Jossey-Bass, 1981). There is some evidence that high need-for-achievement scores also predict academic success.

For a good, if somewhat dated, overview to this approach to studying motivation see John Atkinson, ed., *Motives in Fantasy, Action, and Society* (New York: Van Nostrand, 1958).

11. Constraints of time and funding prevented us from scoring the TATs of all 1,051 subjects. We were able to score 710 sets of TATs randomly selected from our total sample, after excluding unusable tests. Sets of TATs were excluded if any story contained less than twenty-five words, or if a subject simply described the picture rather than writing stories designed to answer the questions given in the instructions.

12. See the scoring manual in David Winter, *The Power Motive* (New York: Free Press, 1973), pp. 247–345.

13. Ibid. See esp. ch. 7, pp. 96–142.

14. Ibid., pp. 117–18.

15. Ibid., ch. 7.

16. David McClelland, *Power: The Inner Experience* (New York: Halsted Press, 1975), p. 17.

17. David McClelland, William Davis, Rudolf Kalin, and Eric Wanner, *The Drinking Man* (New York: Free Press, 1972).

18. Winter, *Power Motive*.

19. Ibid.

20. Ibid., pp. 76–86, 261–63.

21. David Winter and Abigail Stewart, "The Power Motive," in Harvey London and John Exner, eds., *Dimensions of Personality* (New York: John Wiley and Sons, 1978), pp. 421–22.

22. Winter, *Power Motive*, pp. 143–63.

23. Ibid., pp. 148–51; A. Stewart, "Longitudinal Prediction from Personality to Life Outcomes Among College-Educated Women,: (Ph.D. diss., Harvard University, 1975).

24. In their 1978 article "The Power Motive," Winter and Stewart suggest that high Fear of Power scorers feel that power-oriented behavior is legitimate only if it tends to equalize "resource inequality," or to aid the powerless. They cite evidence from studies showing that Fear of Power is associated with lending expensive possessions and the choice of teaching as a profession, and that Fear scores were raised by showing subjects a film about the church's duty to help the poor. Several objections can

be raised against this interpretation. First, none of these findings necessarily implies that the high Fear scorer is willing to give up his *own* power to others. Rather, he acts as their patron or benefactor, thereby consolidating his own authoritative position relative to the one who receives his help. Indeed, the choice of teaching as a profession could reflect an unwillingness to engage in direct competition with peers and a desire to interact with subordinates. Of course, Fear is scored when power is desired for social ends. But as Anna Freud pointed out, the psychodymanics of social "altruism" may involve aggression and egoism rather than sympathy and selflessness (see note 42, Chapter 4, as well as our discussion of social power in this chapter.)

In any event, the preponderance of the evidence on high Fear scores dovetails with Meissner's description of the paranoid process (W. W. Meissner, *The Paranoid Process* [New York: Jason Aronson, 1978]). Elsewhere in Winter and Stewart's article they cite experimental sutdies linking Fear of Power to paranoia among male schizophrenics (p. 423). In conjunction with the evidence we have cited, this seems to support our portrayal of the high Fear scorer as someone who desires absolute power to protect himself against his perceived sense of weakness. He can act on his power drive only when he can persuade himself that his opponent is weak or that he is seeking power not for himself but for others. As Winter wrote in explaining "why male paranoia should be thought to involve specifically the avoidance aspect of the power motive (i.e., Fear of Power), the paranoid has a desire for power . . . he fears the effect of his own desire for power, and fears the power of other people . . . there is an additional fear of losing power. Thus while power is attractive, it is also aversive . . ." (Winter, *Power Motive,* p. 144). Indeed, Winter has come to agree that high Fear, in conjunction with high *n* Power, strongly suggests a motivational constellation similar to that of authoritarianism (Winter, personal communication, 1980).

25. McClelland et al., *Drinking Man,* pp. 351–56.

26. Ibid., pp. 73–98.

27. Ibid., pp. 123–41, 162–97.

28. McClelland, *Power: The Inner Experience,* pp. 263–313.

29. J. Atkinson, R. W. Heyns, and J. Veroff, "The Effect of Experimental Arousal of the Affiliation Motive on Thematic Apperception," *Journal of Abnormal and Social Psychology* 49 (1954): 405–10.

30. J. Atkinson and E. L. Walker, "The Affiliation Motive and Perceptual Sensitivity to Faces," *Journal of Abnormal and Social Psychology* 53 (1956): 38–41; J. B. Lansing and R. W. Heyns, "Need for Affiliation and Four Types of Communication," *Journal of Abnormal and Social Psychology* 58 (1959): 365–72; Byron Groesbeck, "Toward Description of Personality in Terms of Configuration of Motives," in Atkinson, *Motives in Fantasy.*

31. McClelland, *Power: The Inner Experience,* ch. 8.

32. Some recent work has raised questions as to whether *n* Affiliation is a sufficiently pure measure of the desire for close human relationships. In response, psychologist Dan McAdams, a former student of McClelland, has developed a new scoring system designed to measure the capacity for intimacy. His system was developed too late to be applied to our student subjects. We did, however, apply it to our adult subjects in the research described in Chapter 8.

33. Milton Mankoff and Richard Flacks, "The Changing Social Base of the Amer-

ican Student Movement,'' *Annals of the American Academy of Political and Social Sciences* 395 (May 1971): 54–67.

34. Kenneth Keniston, *Radicals and Militants* (Lexington, Mass.: D. C. Heath, 1973), p. 273.

35. D. McClelland, ''Modes of Experiencing Power'' (unpublished manuscript, 1975), pp. 8, 18. This manuscript was an early draft of *Power: The Inner Experience*. There, a comprehensive treatment of the ''imperial'' type appears in ch. 8.

36. McClelland, *Power,* p. 281.

37. There is another reason for caution in interpreting these tabulations. Percentage breakdowns are easily presented and readily understandable. But they are necessarily somewhat arbitrary, lumping together everyone who scores above or below a certain level, as if one passed or failed a psychological test of authoritarianism. This is why we usually compare group mean scores on a test, to provide a better sense of the distances separating each group. But even this method, also chosen for clarity and ease of presentation, divides students into three political groups, based on somewhat arbitrary cut-off points on the spectrum of their political ideology scores. A still better method would be to examine the continuous relationship between personality and political ideology. Then we could determine whether, as radicalism rises, a trait like the need for power declines, or rises slightly, or rises with equal rapidity. We present precisely such an analysis later in this chapter, to determine the strength of the relationship between personality trends and radical politics. We caution the reader that all these strategies of presenting information are simply different ways of looking at the same scores. Each strategy highlights certain aspects of our findings, while leaving other aspects in the shadows.

38. Jennifer Cole, ''Narcissistic Character Traits in Left Activists'' (Ph.D. diss., University of Michigan, 1979).

39. Cole did not discover similarly high narcissism scores among our radical female subjects. Indeed, while the results were not statistically significant, radical women scored slightly lower than nonradical women on the narcissism scale. Cole suggests that women joined the New Left to satisfy affiliative rather than narcissistic needs. However, the evidence of our other instruments lends little support to this hypothesis. On all other instruments for which females were scored, they exhibited an authoritarian pattern quite similar to that of our male subjects. Therefore, we suspect that the problem may lie in the scoring system itself. As we have pointed out, the system was derived from psychoanalytic theories on male narcissism. We think it likely that the categories developed on this basis did not adequately tap female narcissism.

40. Sigmund Freud, ''Three Essays on the Theory of Sexuality,'' in *The Standard Edition of the Complete Psychological Works of Sigmund Freud,* 24 vols. (London: Hogarth Press, 1953) 7: 125–243; Erik Erikson, *Childhood and Society* (New York: W. W. Norton, 1950), pp. 48–97.

41. Abigail Stewart, ''Measuring Affective Development in Adults'' (unpublished paper, Radcliffe Data Resource and Research Center, Cambridge, Mass., 1979).

42. Abigail Stewart, ''Scoring Manual For Stages of Psychological Adaptation to the Environment'' (Boston University, 1977).

43. Abigail Stewart, ''Psychological Adaption to Life Changes in Children and Adults'' (Paper presented to the annual meeting of the Eastern Psychological Association, Philadelphia, 1979).

44. McClelland, *Power: The Inner Experience,* pp. 30–76.

45. McClelland et al., *Drinking Man,* p. 84.

46. McClelland, *Power: The Inner Experience,* p. 257.

47. Adorno et al., *Authoritarian Personality,* p. 763.

48. Ibid.

49. Ibid.

CHAPTER 7: FACES IN THE CROWD

1. The card designed by Rothman is now being used at McLean Hospital.

2. To test the reliability of this thematic analysis, we asked Drs. Carolyn Malthus and Sharon Burr, staff psychologists at McLean Hospital, to independently score all protocols for four of these themes: negative identity, people as concepts, father flawed, and flight from mother. Their scoring was totally blind, i.e., they knew nothing about either the study or the subjects whose protocols they examined. Dr. Malthus's and Dr. Burr's scores were in agreement over 80 percent of the time.

A more extensive discussion of the entire thematic analysis is presented in Phillip Isenberg, Robert Schnitzer, and Stanley Rothman, "Psychological Variables in Student Activism: The Radical Triad and Some Religious Differences," *Journal of Youth and Adolescence* 6 (Mar. 1977): 7–24.

3. When Rorschachs are administered, respondents are permitted to offer as many interpretations of the inkblot as they desire. Since we were dealing with a particularly intelligent and articulate group of young people, we limited the number of responses to four. We are presenting the free association and the inquiry together, but readers should remember that inquiries were made only after the student had responded to all ten cards. Of course we are not presenting the complete response. Some of the Rorschach protocols ran to thirty typed pages.

4. Bruno Klopfer et al., *Developments in the Rorschach Technique,* vol. I (New York: Harcourt, Brace & World, 1954); Roy Schaefer, *Psychoanalytic Interpretation in Rorschach Testing* (New York: Grune and Stratton, 1954); and Martin Mayman, "Reality Contract, Defense Effectiveness, and Psychopathology in Rorschach Form Level Scores," in Klopfer et al., *Developments in the Rorschach Technique* III (New York: Harcourt Brace Jovanovich, 1970).

5. For a more technical discussion of the statistics and the interpretation, see David Gutmann, Stanley Rothman, and S. Robert Lichter, "Two Kinds of Radicals: A Discriminant Analysis of a Projective Test," *Journal of Personality Assessment* 43 (1979): 12–22. Unfortunately, during the interim period two sets of TAT and Rorschach protocols, those of one radical and one nonradical Jew, were misplaced. The patterns derived from the remaining thirty-four protocols were so clear-cut, however, that two additional sets probably would not have affected our overall results.

6. Dr. Gutmann pointed out to us that our results might best be explained by narcissistic deficits derived from poor parenting during the pre-Oedipal stage. Our original interpretation had emphasized Oedipal power conflicts. (See Stanley Rothman, Anne Bedlington, Robert Schnitzer, and Phillip Isenberg, "Ethnic Variations in Student Radicalism," in Seweryn Bialer and Sophia Sluzar, eds., *Sources of Contemporary Radicalism* [Boulder, Colo.: Westview Press, 1977].) The results of Gutmann's analysis,

our own analysis of our survey data, and our discovery of W. W. Meissner's study (*The Paranoid Process* [New York: Jason Aronson, 1978]) combined to persuade us that he was essentially correct. On the other hand, our data (including Gutmann's own interpretations of Rorschach tests) indicate that Gutmann's earlier work on narcissism among radical youth was incomplete, in that it emphasized personality dimensions that mainly applied to Jewish radicals. (See his "The Premature Gerontocracy: Themes of Aging and Death in the Youth Culture," *Social Research* 39 [Aug. 1972]: 416–48.) We suspect that his preliminary conclusions were derived from the fact that most young radicals whom he saw in psychotherapy were of Jewish background.

7. Roy Schaefer, "The Psychoanalytic Vision of Reality," in *International Journal of Psycho-Analysis* 51 (1970): 279–97.

8. Robert Lane, *Political Ideology* (New York: Free Press, 1962).

CHAPTER 8: RADICAL ADULTS

1. Kirkpatrick Sale, *SDS* (New York: Vintage, 1973).

2. Jonathan Black, *Radical Lawyers* (New York: Avon, 1971).

3. Lionel Trilling, *Beyond Culture* (New York: Viking, 1965).

4. Charles Reich, *The Greening of America* (New York: Random House, 1970); Theodore Roszak, *The Making of a Counter-Culture* (New York: Doubleday, 1969).

5. See, e.g., B. Bruce-Briggs, ed., *The New Class?* (New Brunswick, N.J.: Transaction Books, 1979). Our list of radical adults was initially chosen by a graduate student, following the procedures we outlined. Later, we asked another student to duplicate these procedures. No names were included in our final sample unless they appeared on both lists. Our coders agreed on 97 percent of the cases. They differed on only eight persons.

6. Even these differences were largely due to quirks in the statistical procedures used to generate the dimensions. The adjectives that cluster around the concept of "caring" (i.e., "understanding," "kind," "warm," "considerate," "dependable," and "cooperative") were important to the paternal ratings as well but were subsumed under the "punitive" dimension. That is, a person who rated his father high in spitefulness, cruelty, selfishness, etc., was also likely to rate him low in kindness, warmth, and all the other aspects of benevolence listed above. So for the adult sample, the paternal "punitiveness" dimension actually constituted a more general "high punitiveness–low benevolence" polarity. The same phenomenon prevented a maternal "intrusiveness" dimension from emerging, as it did in our study of college students. The adjectives that measured maternal intrusiveness among the students, including "interfering," "controlling," and "intrusive," were here subsumed into the broader dimension of maternal punitiveness. In fact, the punitive dimensions for both parents were so broad, each drawing on about twenty different adjectives, that they might be thought of as representing general evaluative or "good versus bad" judgments.

7. Dan McAdams, "Themes of Intimacy in Behavior and Thought," *Journal of Personality and Social Psychology* 40, no. 3 (1981): 573–87.

8. Dan McAdams, "A Thematic Coding System for the Intimacy Motive," *Journal of Research in Personality* 14 (1980): 413–32.

9. Dan McAdams, "Studies in Intimacy Motivation," in Abigail Stewart, ed., *Motivation and Society* (New York: Jossey-Bass, 1981).

10. David McClelland, *The Achieving Society* (New York: Van Nostrand, 1961).

CHAPTER 9: RADICALISM WITHOUT JEWS

1. See, e.g., William Read, *America's Mass Media Merchants* (Baltimore: Johns Hopkins University Press, 1976); Jeremy Turnstall, *The Media Are American* (New York: Columbia University Press, 1977).

2. Anthony Smith, *The Politics of Information* (London: Macmillan, 1978), p. 20.

3. Kurt Shell, "The American Impact on the German New Left," in A. N. J. den Hollander, ed., *Contagious Conflict* (Leiden: E. J. Brill, 1973), p. 35.

4. Gianni Statera, *Death of a Utopia: The Development and Decline of Student Movements in Europe* (New York: Oxford University Press, 1975), p. 52.

5. Ibid., p. 62.

6. Cited in René Ahlberg, "Die politische Konzeption des Sozialistischen Deutschen Studenten," *Aus Politik und Zeitgeschichte,* May 15, 1968, p. 10.

7. Rudi Dutschke, "Die Widersprüche des Spätkapitalismus, die antiautoritären Studenten und ihr Verhältnis zur dritten Welt," in Uwe Bergmann et al., *Rebellion der Studenten; oder, Die neue Opposition* (Hamburg: Fischer, 1968), pp. 75–76.

8. "Rudi Dutschke in Prag: Liberalisierung oder Demokratisierung," interview in *Konkret,* no. 5, May 1968; cf. Reimut Reiche, "Verteidigung der 'neuen Sensibilität,' " in Klaus Dörner, ed., *Die Linke Antwortet Jürgen Habermas* (Frankfurt: Europaische Verlag, 1969), pp. 91–103.

9. Interview in *Spiegel,* July 10, 1967, p. 33.

10. Klaus Mehnert, *Jugend im Zeitbruch* (Stuttgart: Deutsche Verlags-Anstalt, 1976), pp. 154–55.

11. Ibid., p. 457. This estimate includes the MSB's "sister organization" in West Berlin, the Arbeitsgemeinschaft von Demokraten und Sozialisten, or ADS.

12. Elisabeth Noelle-Neumann, "Wie demokratisch sind unsere Studenten?" *Frankfurter Allgemeine Zeitung,* Oct. 2, 1978, p. 5 (our translation). That is, a university system governed according to the principle of group parity (*Gruppenprinzip*), with students, staff, and faculty all involved in decisions on educational policy.

13. New York *Times,* Sept. 28, 1977.

14. New York *Times,* Oct. 30, 1977.

15. Jan Carl Raspé, in Christl Bookhagen et al., *Versuch der Revolutionisierung des bürgerlichen Individuums* (Berlin: Kommune 2, 1969), p. 48.

16. Renate Riemick, "Wahres über Ulrike," in Ulrike Meinhof, *Dokumente einer Rebellion* (Hamburg: Konkret, 1972), p. 105.

17. Bernward Vesper, in Andreas Baader et al., "Vor einer solchen Justiz verteidigen wir uns nicht" (pamphlet, Frankfurt, 1968), p. 21, cited in Klaus Mehnert, *Jugend in Zeitbruch* (Stuttgart: Deutsche Verlags-Anstalt, 1976), p. 163.

18. Quoted in *Spiegel,* Apr. 8, 1972, p. 22.

19. Boston *Globe,* Sept. 25, 1977.

20. Noelle-Neumann, "Wie demokratisch sind unsesere Studenten." For more detailed discussion, see Chapter 10.

21. New York *Times,* Sept. 22, 1977.

22. Quoted in Jillian Becker, *Hitler's Children* (New York: J. C. Lippincott, 1977), p. 150.

23. The questionnaire was actually administered to 300 students, including 80 females. We found, however, that very few of the females were either ideological radicals or political activists of any stripe. To retain them in the data analysis would confound ideological with gender-related familial and personality differences. For this reason, and because funds for both computer time and personality test scoring were in very short supply, females were dropped from the analysis.

24. Within this limited exploratory context, it appears unlikely that the results were artifacts of the sampling procedure. First, institutional statistics show that the sample was representative of the university population in terms of age, sex, religion, and major subject. (It was slightly skewed toward the lower socioeconomic levels, probably an effect of payment for participation.) A high degree of variation in political ideology was obtained, and political activists were well represented, as is described below. Second, we can compare our results to those obtained from our two American studies. However "volunteer effects" might distort the German sample, they would almost certainly not recreate the same associations between personality and politics that appeared within independently obtained probability samples of American students.

25. Bernhard Cloetta, *Fragebogen zur Erfassung von Machiavellianismus und Konservatismus* (Konstanz: University of Konstanz, 1972).

26. We used a gamma statistic to measure these correlations.

27. Even these figures may overstate any differences in the childhood political milieus of radicals and nonradicals. When we asked whether one's father had ever been affiliated with a different political party, no additional radicals cited the SPD, but 5 percent of the nonradicals did. Only two students, neither of them radical, responded that their fathers had preferred the Communist party. The differences shrank even further when we asked students to assign their fathers to the left or right wing of his preferred party. We sought to isolate the SPD's left wing, which represented the only radical segment of the German electorate during the postwar period, aside from tiny splinter groups. Radicals were only slightly overrepresented among students claiming this leftist heritage. Fourteen percent assigned their fathers to the left wing of the SPD, compared to 9 percent of all subjects, a statistically insignificant difference. This question also elicited an unexpected finding at the opposite end of the spectrum. Radicals were actually more likely than nonradicals to place their fathers on the right wing of the CDU, a political stance roughly analogous to that of conservative Republicans in the United States. In fact, about twice as many radicals placed their fathers on the right end of the spectrum (the CDU's right wing) as on the left end (the SPD's left wing): 28 percent versus 14 percent.

28. The statistic was Spearman's rho, a nonparametric ordinal measure of association.

29. Note that the significance test used for the Semantic Differential comparisons compares revolutionaries with all other activists, whereas the test used for the PCQ and TAT comparisons groups revolutionaries with other leftists. Nonrevolutionary leftists produced potency scores virtually identical to those of nonleftists. Indeed, on all measures of personality and family relations except for n Power, revolutionary activists appear more "authoritarian" than other leftists, as one would expect. On the PCQ and

TAT measures, however, the nonrevolutionary leftists also conform to our model to a greater degree than moderates and conservatives.

CHAPTER 10: THE STUDENT LEFT IN PERSPECTIVE

1. For example, "The Brethren of the Free Spirit" spread widely over France, Germany, Switzerland, and Austria during the thirteenth and fourteenth centuries. The Brethren advocated common ownership of all property, denounced the family, and advocated completely free sexuality. For a brief discussion of these and other sects of the period see Igor R. Shafarevich, *The Socialist Phenomenon* (New York: Harper and Row, 1980), pp. 18–46.

2. Jack Newfield, *A Prophetic Minority,* (New York: Signet, 1966), p. 16.

3. Ibid., p. 14.

4. Zbigniew Brzezinski, *Between Two Ages* (New York: Viking Press, 1971).

5. Herbert Marcuse, *An Essay in Liberation* (Boston: Beacon Press, 1966).

6. *Journal Officiel, Assemblée Nationale,* May 14, 1968, p. 1772.

7. Max Weber, "Science as a Vocation," in Hans Gerth and C. Wright Mills, eds., *From Max Weber* (New York: Oxford University Press, 1946), p. 155.

8. Benjamin Zablocki, *Alienation and Charisma* (New York: Free Press, 1980).

9. See the discussion and references in Chapter 4.

10. See the review of Werner Fassbinder's movie, *Terrible Toy,* in New York *Times,* Sept. 9, 1980.

11. Gerald M. Platt, "Thoughts on a Theory of Collective Action: Language, Affect and Ideology in Revolution," in Mel Albin, ed., *New Directions in Psychohistory* (Lexington, Mass.: Lexington Books, 1980), pp. 69–94.

Of course, the possibility of being drafted to fight in a war whose justice was questionable motivated large numbers of young people whom the New Left was able to mobilize. The prosperity of the 1960s was also a factor. Young people in colleges and universities were convinced that they would be able to live their definition of the good life, no matter what. (See Steven Kelman, *Push Comes to Shove* [Boston: Houghton Mifflin, 1970]). It is no accident that the decline of the student movement coincided with the end of the draft and the slowing down of economic growth. When only the committed radicals remained, the movement had a good many generals but very few troops.

12. Many of those who opposed the New Left were also motivated by nonrational impulses. Our clinical case studies suggest that some opposition to change and disorder was a defensive reaction against the fears of the individuals involved that they would not be able to control their own impulses.

13. Op-ed page, New York *Times,* Oct. 9, 1976.

14. S. M. Lipset, introduction to *Rebellion in the University,* 2nd ed. (Chicago: University of Chicago Press, 1976), p. xii.

15. Daniel Yankelovich, *The New Morality: A Profile of American Youth in the '70s* (New York: McGraw-Hill, 1974), p. 8.

16. Lipset, *Rebellion,* p. xxxix.

17. Cited Ibid.

18. Everett Carll Ladd, Jr., and S. M. Lipset, *The Divided Academy* (New York: McGraw-Hill, 1975). Some scholars, relying on the data for this and later studies,

maintain that college teachers are not really very liberal. This is certainly true if one examines the profession as a whole. Engineers and faculties in business schools and schools of agriculture tend to be relatively conservative in their views. However, these are not the teachers who influence student perceptions on the nature of the American social and political system.

19. Everett C. Ladd, "Pursuing the New Class: Social Theory and Survey Data," in B. Bruce-Briggs, ed., *The New Class?* (New Brunswick, N.J.: Transaction Books, 1979), pp. 103–4.

20. Ibid. See also *Public Opinion* Oct.–Nov. 1981, pp. 30–33, and S. Robert Lichter and S. Rothman, "Media and Business Elites," ibid., pp. 42ff.

21. *Public Opinion* Oct.–Nov. 1981. See also S. M. Lipset and Earl Raab, "The Election and the Evangelicals," *Commentary*, (Mar. 1981), pp. 25–31.

22. See the articles on changing American values by Everett Ladd in *Public Opinion* (July–Aug. 1978), pp. 48–53, and (Sept.–Oct. 1978), pp. 14–20.

23. Yankelovich, *New Morality*, and Everett C. Ladd, "Jewish Life in the United States: Social and Political Values" (mimeographed, 1978). In this essay Ladd traces the development of a number of political attitudes since 1952. He notes that while Jews have become slightly more liberal, non-Jews are beginning to catch up.

24. Yankelovich, *New Morality*, p. 9.

25. New York *Times*, Nov. 11, 1977, and Dec. 12, 1977; Thomas Nipperday, "The German University in Crisis," in Paul Seabury, ed., *Universities in the Western World* (New York: Free Press, 1975), p. 125; and Guenter Lewy, "The Persisting Heritage of the 1960's in West German Higher Education," *Minverva* 18 (Spring 1980): 1–28.

26. New York *Times*, Nov. 13, 1977.

27. Elisabeth Noelle-Neumann, "Wie demokratische sind unsere Studenten?" *Frankfurter Allqemeine Zeitung*, Oct. 2, 1978; "University Student Attitudes in Germany," *Newsletter of the International Council on the Future of the University* (New York), Aug. 1979, p. 1.

28. A small group of right-wing terrorists has emerged in recent years. Unlike middle-class left-wing terrorists, these young people seem to come primarily from working-class or lower-middle-class backgrounds.

29. New York: Basic Books, 1976. See also Stanley Rothman and S. Robert Lichter, "Alienation and Authoritarianism in Advanced Capitalism," *Society* 19 (May 1982): 18–24.

30. Anthony F. C. Wallace, *Rockdale* (New York: Knopf, 1978), p. 474.

31. See Daniel Bell, *Cultural Contradictions of Capitalism* (New York: Basic Books, 1976). In some ways Bell's argument parallels that of Max Weber and Joseph Schumpeter. See the latter's *Capitalism, Socialism and Democracy*, 3rd ed. (New York: Harper, 1950).

32. "Biographies in Popular Magazines," in P. F. Lazarsfeld and F. Stanton, eds., *Radio Research: 1942–1943* (New York: Duell, Sloan and Pearce, 1944).

33. See the discussion in Chapter 2, pp. 69–72.

34. Bell, *Cultural Contradictions;* Daniel Bell, *The Coming of Post-Industrial Society* (New York: Basic Books, 1973).

35. Bell, *Coming of Post-Industrial Society*, p. 214.

36. Eric Goldman, *The Tragedy of Lyndon Johnson* (New York: Knopf, 1969).

37. *The Playboy Report on American Men* (New York: Playboy, 1979).

38. See the discussion in Chapter 2, pp. 61–69.

39. Stanley Rothman, "Intellectuals and the American Political System," in S. M. Lipset, ed., *Emerging Coalitions in American Politics* (San Francisco: Institute for Contemporary Studies, 1978), pp. 325–52.

40. Ibid.

41. Theodore H. White, "America's Two Cultures," *Columbia Journalism Review*, Winter, 1969–70, pp. 8–13; David Halberstam, *The Powers That Be* (New York: Knopf, 1979). See also Stanley Rothman, "The Mass Media in Post-Industrial America," in S. M. Lipset, *The Third Century: America as a Post-Industrial Society* (Stanford: Hoover Institution Press, 1979), pp. 345–88.

42. Christopher Lasch, *Haven in a Heartless World* (New York: Basic Books, 1977) and Lasch, *The Culture of Narcissism* (New York: W. W. Norton, 1978); Herbert Hendin, *The Age of Sensation* (New York: W. W. Norton, 1975); Urie Bronfenbrenner, *Two Worlds of Childhood* (New York: Russell Sage Foundation, 1970); Alice Rossi, "A Biosocial Perspective on Parenting," *Daedalus* 106 (Summer 1977): 1–31.

43. Fred Weinstein and Gerald M. Platt, *The Wish To Be Free: Society, Psyche, and Value Change* (Berkeley: University of California Press, 1969).

44. Stanley Rothman and S. Robert Lichter, "A Changing American Character?" (Mimeographed).

45. Weinstein and Platt, *Wish To Be Free*.

46. *Public Opinion*, Jan.–Feb. 1979, and Apr.–May 1980.

47. Edward A. Wynne, "What Are the Courts Doing to Our Children?" *Public Interest*, Summer 1981, pp. 3–18; Mary Douglas and Aaron Wildavsky, "Risk and Culture" (unpublished draft manuscript, 1980).

48. Yankelovich, *New Morality*.

49. New York *Times*, Aug. 2, 1981.

50. M. C. Hetherington, M. Cox, and R. Cox, "The Development of Children in Mother-Headed Families," in D. Reiss and H. Hoffman, eds., *The American Family: Dying or Developing?* (New York: Plenum Press, 1979), pp. 117–44; George Masnick and M. J. Bane, *The Nation's Families: 1969–1990* (Boston: Auburn House, 1980); Henry B. Biller, "The Father and Personality Development: Paternal Deprivation and Sex-Role Development," in Michael E. Lamb, ed., *The Role of the Father in Child Development* (New York: John Wiley and Sons, 1976). See also the report of later research in *Time*, January 4, 1982, p. 81.

51. B. T. Eiduson, "Emergent Families of the 1970's: Values, Practices, and Impact on Children," in Reiss and Hoffman, eds., *The American Family*.

52. Mary Ann Glendon, "Marriage and the State: The Withering Away of Marriage," *Virginia Law Review* 62, no. 3 (Apr. 1976); Herve Verenne, "Symbolizing American Culture in Schools," *Character*, Apr. 1981, pp. 1–8.

53. Recently Yankelovich has suggested that many cosmopolitans, somewhat disappointed with a "self-realization" life style, are returning to slightly more traditonal modes of behavior. His data are open to quite another interpretation. Such individuals are now available for mobilization by new secular or religious ideologies that promise to provide larger frameworks of meaning for their lives. Reagan's domestic or foreign policy could provide the occasion for just such mobilization. See Daniel Yankelovich, *Searching for Self-Fulfillment in a World Turned Upside Down* (New York: Random House, 1981).

Index

ABC television, 97
Abolitionism, 4, 9
Academic Press, 106
Achievement motive, 341–43, 446–47. *See also* Motivation patterns
Achieving Society, The (McClelland), 342
Activism: attitudes vs., as index of radicalism, 211; level of, in youth survey, 213–15; typology of, in German study, 370
Adelson, Joseph, 51, 81
Adler, Max, 88
Adler, Victor, 87–88, 123–24
Adolescence, 134–36, 177
Adorno, Theodor W., 85–87; on authoritarian personality, 59–60, 87, 151–54, 156, 157, 159–61, 163–65, 168, 169, 172, 176, 182, 183, 210, 235, 272, 348, 389
Affect, Rorschach scores on, 290–92
Affiliation (TAT score), 244–45, 448
Affirmative action, Jewish opposition to, 144–45
Affluent Society, The (Galbraith), 355
Age of Sensation, The (Hendin), 69
Aggression: ethnicity and expression of, 269–72; and Jewish personality patterns, 125–34, 136–43, 183
Albright College, 36
Alcoholism, 126–27, 269–72, 347
Alexander II (czar of Russia), 91
Alfred A. Knopf (publisher), 106
Alker, Henry, 52
Allensbach Public Opinion Institute, 363, 395
Alperowitz, Gar, 104
America House (Berlin), 359
American Council of Education survey, 81
American Mercury, 221
American Political Science Association, 104
American Spectator, The, 144
American Student Union, 5, 101
American Youth Conference, 5
Amherst. *See* Massachusetts, University of, at Amherst
Anal-autonomous psychosexual orientation, 258–63

Anal character structure. *See* Sadomasochistic character structure
Anarchism, 181, 183, 359
Anschlag, Der (periodical), 359
"Anti-authoritarianism" in German New Left, 359–61, 363, 396
Antidraft movement, 22, 25, 27–30, 32, 34, 196
"Anti-imperialism," 22, 28
Antioch College, 193
Anti-Semitism, 84, 88, 90, 91, 98, 100–102, 110, 115, 116, 120, 122, 145–47, 151; Stalin's, 89, 94
Antiwar movement, 22, 25–31, 34, 391; and European activism, 352–54, 359, 360, 362; New Left's withdrawal from, 30
APO (German extra-parliamentary opposition), 360
Arafat, Yasir, 142
Argyle, Michael, 126
Aristotle, 3
Armies of the Night (Mailer), 29
Atheneum Publishers, 106
Attitudes vs. activism as index of radicalism, 211
Austerlitz, Friedrich, 88
Austria, Jews in, 87–88, 119
Authoritarian personality, 59–61, 146–77, 181–201; Fromm on, 148–51, 156, 157, 159–63, 165, 168, 172, 176, 182, 210; Meissner's "paranoid" and, 173–77; narcissism and, 172–77; original theory of, outlined, 151–57; "rebellion" vs. "revolution" and, 161–65; revised theory of, summarized, 160, 170–72, 181–82; technical shortcomings of original study, 59–61, 157–60; Wilkinson's "anti-authoritarian" and, 168–70; Wolfenstein's "revolutionary personality" and, 165–68. *See also* Inverse authoritarian personality
Authoritarian Personality, The (Adorno et al.), 59–61, 87, 151–65, 279
"Autonomy" scales, 57–59
Avery, Paul, 44
Axelrod, Pavel, 92